CW00642408

Crime, Justice, and Discret
in England, 1740–1820

Crime, Justice, and Discretion in England
1740–1820

PETER KING

OXFORD
UNIVERSITY PRESS

OXFORD
UNIVERSITY PRESS

Great Clarendon Street, Oxford OX2 6DP

Oxford University Press is a department of the University of Oxford.
It furthers the University's objective of excellence in research, scholarship,
and education by publishing worldwide in

Oxford New York

Auckland Bangkok Buenos Aires Cape Town Chennai
Dar es Salaam Delhi Hong Kong Istanbul Karachi Kolkata
Kuala Lumpur Madrid Melbourne Mexico City Mumbai Nairobi
São Paulo Shanghai Taipei Tokyo Toronto

Oxford is a registered trade mark of Oxford University Press
in the UK and in certain other countries

Published in the United States
by Oxford University Press Inc., New York

British Library Cataloguing in Publication Data

Data available

Library of Congress Cataloging in Publication Data
King, Peter.
Crime, justice, and discretion in England, 1740–1820 / Peter King.
Includes bibliographical references.
1. Crime—England—History—18th century. 2. Criminal justice, Administration
of—England—History—18th century. 3. Crime—England—History—19th century.
4. Criminal justice, Administration of—England—History—19th century. I. Title.
HV6949.E5 k56 2000   364.942'09033—dc21   00-024775
ISBN 0-19-822910-0 (hbk.)
ISBN 0-19-925907-0 (pbk.)

1 3 5 7 9 10 8 6 4 2

Typeset by Kolam Information Services Pvt. Ltd, Pondicherry, India
Printed in Great Britain
on acid-free paper by
Biddles Ltd.,
Guildford and King's Lynn

For my mother
CHRISTINE LETTICE KING
1918–1961

Acknowledgements

This book is the product of a long project and during it I have received help of many kinds. On the archival side, particular thanks must go to the Essex Record Offices, to their kind and helpful staff and to their excellent catalogues. I am also indebted to the staff of the Public Record Office, and of the Bedfordshire, Berkshire, Bristol, Cambridgeshire, Devon, Gloucestershire, Northamptonshire, Shropshire, and Wiltshire Record Offices. Text and subject came closest to colliding, perhaps, when I found myself being locked in with the records in a cell at Colchester Castle (once the house of correction but by that time the Colchester Record Office) while the sole archivist took a break. Financially I am indebted to the ESRC for the research studentship during which I first became interested in this subject, to the Ellen McArthur Fund at Cambridge, to the Research Fellowship provided by Liverpool University, to the University College Northampton Research Committee, and to the ESRC 'Crime and Social Order' initiative whose funding of a very different project on the rise of juvenile delinquency 1780–1840, while it meant putting this book on hold for a while, enabled me to refine the age-related database on which many of the tables and figures in Chapters 6 and 8 are based. Thanks are due to the late Joan Noel and particularly to Cris Gostlow, my research assistant on the ESRC project, for their work on those graphs and tables and for their patience in the face of my constant demands for last-minute changes and adjustments. I shall also always be grateful for the many hours of counting and collating that Gwen Holmes put in at an earlier stage to establish the figures on which a number of the tables elsewhere in the book are based. Many thanks for their forbearance and sense of humour must also go to Pat Ellis, Anne Gilkes, Emma Austin, Joy Knight, Denise Kelsey, Penny Hubbard, Charlotte Spokes, and Michelle Webster, who have been involved at various stages in word processing the manuscript; to Steve Varty for his work on Map 5.1; and to all at the UCN Research Centre for providing me with a friendly and supportive place in which to write.

I have been grateful for the broadly co-operative and constructive ethos that those working on the history of crime have usually maintained over the years, which has meant that at various times I have benefited from verbal comments, written responses, and/or helpful references from many scholars, including John Styles, James Cockburn, James Linell, David Sugarman, Martin Wiener, Douglas Hay, Deirdre Palk, Barry Godfrey, Clive Emsley, Roger Ekirch, Tim Hitchcock, Heather Shore, Thomas Sokoll, Simon Renton, Loraine Gelsthorpe, Thomas Green, Vic Gatrell, John Langbein, Ruth Paley, John

Rule, Jim Sharpe, Bob Shoemaker, John Walter, and David Philips. I owe a particularly large debt to Randall McGowen, John Beattie, Joanna Innes, and Paul Griffiths, who also read the whole of the final manuscript and offered very useful comments upon it. I am also grateful to all those who, at various conferences and seminars (and especially at the long eighteenth-century seminar at the Institute of Historical Research) offered comments on papers based on various chapters, as well as to colleagues at UCN—staff, research students, postgraduates, and undergraduates—who have provided all kinds of feedback over the years. Errors and misjudgements remain my own.

My greatest debts, however, are to my parents, Gwen and Trevor Holmes, who have supported me so lovingly (as well as contributing through their labours) during the writing of this book; to Lee Hodgson-King for her patience far beyond the call of duty, for her love and support through good times and bad—during what must at times have seemed like a never-ending journey; to Joshy for being such fun and so full of wonder; to the various Christian communities and churches I have been involved with during these years, and to the many people (whether they would acknowledge her/him or not) who have, by being themselves, touched me with God's love during the long journey of this book.

Peter King

Contents

List of Figures and Maps

List of Tables

List of Abbreviations

Che.C.	*Chelmsford Chronicle*
E.R.O.	Essex Record Office
I.J.	*Ipswich Journal*
P.R.O.	Public Record Office
V.C.H. Essex	*Victoria County History, Essex*
O.B.S.P.	*Old Bailey Sessions Papers*

Introduction

This book focuses on one central and particularly contested aspect of the law—property crime and the ways it was dealt with, defined, and perceived. Using both a detailed study of the Essex court records and more diverse sources drawn from all over England, it attempts to construct a social history of the process by which those accused of property crime were handled both formally and informally by the institutions, groups, and individuals responsible for the administration of the criminal law, as well as analysing those who found themselves on the receiving end of the law. It focuses on the final period of what has recently been called ' "Old Regime" criminal justice', on the last three-quarters of a century before both the repeal of the bloody code and the introduction of professional police forces.[1] This was, it could be argued, the golden age of discretionary justice in England. The whole criminal justice system was shot through with discretion—about this at least almost all historians of crime agree (as did contemporaries, whether they advocated criminal law reform or opposed it). The criminal justice system relied on the participation of a wide range of social groups at almost every stage in the prosecution process and gave them extensive discretionary powers. Although the formal criminal law and the legal handbooks sometimes appeared rigid and inflexible, in reality the administration of the eighteenth-century criminal justice system created several interconnected spheres of contested judicial space in each of which deeply discretionary choices were made. Those accused of property offences in the eighteenth century found themselves propelled on an often bewildering journey along a route which can best be compared to a corridor of connected rooms or stage sets.[2] From each room one door led on towards eventual criminalization, conviction, and punishment, but every room also had other exits. Each had doors indicating legally acceptable ways in which the accused could get away from the arms of the law, while some rooms also had illegal tunnels through which the accused might sometimes be smuggled to safety. Each room was also populated by a different and socially diverse group of men and women, whose assumptions, actions, and interactions, both with each other and with the accused,

---

[1] M. Wiener, *Reconstructing the Criminal. Culture, Law and Policy in England 1830–1914* (Cambridge, 1990) p. 57.
[2] S. Box, *Deviance, Reality and Society* (2nd edn., London, 1981), p. 158.

determined whether or not he or she was shown to an exit or thrust on up the corridor.

This study is founded on a detailed analysis of the methods used to deal with offenders at each stage, in each room, and the ways that criminal law procedures and practices changed over time (influenced by such factors as changing perceptions of the prevalence of crime). However, whenever possible another set of issues has also been addressed. At every decisive point on the accused's journey, an attempt has been made to analyse the circumstances in which decisions were made, the social status of the key decision-makers, the depth of discretionary choices available to them, and the extent to which those choices were shaped by formal legal rulings, by the need to negotiate with other groups that also played decision-making roles, by the informal pressures that the accused and his or her friends (or enemies) could bring to bear, or by the underlying discursive frameworks which influenced the ways that different social groups used their discretionary powers.

By addressing these issues, this study aims to build on, and critically assess, a number of the core themes found in the very considerable body of work on the history of crime and criminal justice in eighteenth-century England that has been published since the early 1970s.[3] That work has followed a number of directions. Some of it has focused on very particular concerns, such as the changing nature of the trial or the 'reform' of prison regimes. However, a handful of much broader themes has informed and become central to the historiography of crime and criminal justice in this period. A desire to understand the experiences, actions, and attitudes of the poor has been one of those themes, inspiring both detailed studies of individual offences and several attempts to link changes in recorded property crime to short-term changes in levels of poverty and deprivation.[4] Equally the different forms of power the state has exercised through the criminal justice system—through changing policing and penal policies, for example—have become core areas of investi-

---

[3] An excellent critical review of this work is J. Innes and J. Styles, 'The Crime Wave. Recent Writing on Crime and Criminal Justice in Eighteenth-Century England', in A. Wilson (ed.), *Rethinking Social History. English Society 1570–1920 and its Interpretation* (Manchester, 1993), pp. 201–65. For the most recent overview of general works, P. King, 'Locating Histories of Crime. A Bibliographical Study', in *British Journal of Criminology*, 39 (1999), 161–74. The field's best introductory texts are J. Sharpe, *Crime in Early Modern England 1550–1750* (2nd edn., London, 1999); C. Emsley, *Crime and Society in England 1750–1900* (2nd edn., London, 1996). References to these works in this volume refer to the first editions unless otherwise indicated.

[4] For key works on the history of the trial, see Chapter 7. Outstanding works on particular offences and on crime levels and poverty include D. Hay, P. Linebaugh, J. Rule, E. P. Thompson, and C. Winslow, *Albion's Fatal Tree. Crime and Society in Eighteenth-Century England* (Harmondsworth, 1975); E. P. Thompson, *Whigs and Hunters. The Origin of the Black Act* (Harmondsworth, 1975); J. Styles, 'Our Traitorous Money Makers. The Yorkshire Coiners and the Law, 1760–83', in J. Brewer and J. Styles (eds.), *An Ungovernable People. The English and their Law in the Seventeenth and Eighteenth Centuries* (London, 1980), pp. 11–20; D. Hay, 'War, Dearth and Theft in the Eighteenth Century. The Record of the English Courts', *Past and Present*, 95 (1982), 117–60; J. Beattie, *Crime and the Courts in England 1660–1800* (Oxford, 1986), pp. 141–266.

gation. The development of an increasingly subtle and detailed picture of how the administration of the criminal justice system worked[5] has not, however, always led to greater agreement among historians about who controlled the law, about how important a role it played in relationships between different social groups, or about the extent to which the law—as both ideology and practice—underpinned and legitimized the rule of the eighteenth-century élite. Thus, while this volume will both reassess the relationship between poverty and property crime, and offer a detailed analysis of the changing forms through which the state administered the criminal law in relation to property offenders, it also attempts to contribute substantially to the extended (if sometimes diffuse) debate that has arisen about the role of the criminal law in eighteenth-century social relations.[6] Historians of eighteenth-century society have tended to give the law, and in particular the criminal law and the criminal justice system, a more central role in their analyses of the nature of power and authority than those who have written about other centuries. 'The Law', Edward Thompson argued, was 'elevated during this century to a role more prominent than at any other period of our history', and recent textbooks on the social history of the eighteenth century have reflected this by including extensive discussions of this issue as well as of crime itself.[7] In no small part this

[5] The core work here is Beattie, *Crime*, although many articles and longer works have also provided very valuable detailed studies; see, for example, D. Hay, 'Crime, Authority and the Criminal Law. Staffordshire 1750–1800' (Ph.D., Warwick, 1975); S. Pole, 'Crime, Society and Law-Enforcement in Hanoverian Somerset' (Ph.D. Cambridge, 1983); G. Morgan and P. Rushton, *Rogues, Thieves and the Rule of Law. The Problem of Law Enforcement in North-East England 1718–1800* (London, 1998); P. Linebaugh, *The London Hanged. Crime and Civil Society in the Eighteenth Century* (London, 1991). Important monographs on specific aspects include M. Ignatieff, *A Just Measure of Pain. The Penitentiary in the Industrial Revolution* (London, 1978); J. Cockburn and T. Green (eds.), *Twelve Good Men and True. The Criminal Trial Jury in England 1200–1800* (Princetown, 1988); R. Ekirch, *Bound for America. The Transportation of British Convicts to the Colonies 1718–1775* (Oxford, 1987); V. Gatrell, *The Hanging Tree. Execution and the English People 1770–1868* (Oxford, 1994). For the major pre-1970 research see the first four volumes of L. Radzinowicz, *A History of English Criminal Law and its Administration from 1750* (London, 5 vols., 1948–86, vol. 5 with R. Hood).

[6] D. Hay, 'Property, Authority and the Criminal Law', in Hay *et al.* (eds.), *Albion's Fatal Tree*, pp. 17–63; Brewer and Styles (eds.), *An Ungovernable People*, pp. 11–20; J. Langbein, 'Albion's Fatal Flaws', *Past and Present*, 98 (1983), 96–120; P. King, 'Decision-Makers and Decision-Making in the English Criminal Law 1750–1800', *Historical Journal*, 27 (1984), pp. 27–54; P. Linebaugh, '(Marxist) Social History and (Conservative) Legal History. A Reply to Professor Langbein', *New York University Law Review*, 60 (1985), 212–43; T. Green, *Verdict According to Conscience. Perspectives on the English Trial Jury 1200–1800* (Chicago, 1985); J. Sharpe, 'The People and the Law', in B. Reay (ed.), *Popular Culture in Seventeenth-Century England* (London, 1985), pp. 262–5; R. McGowen, '"He Beareth not the Sword in Vain". Religion and the Criminal Law in Eighteenth-Century England', *Eighteenth-Century Studies*, 21 (1987), 210; C. Herrup, *The Common Peace. Participation and the Criminal Law in Seventeenth-Century England* (Cambridge, 1987); D. Hay and F. Snyder, 'Using the Criminal Law, 1750–1850. Policing, Private Prosecution and the State' and D. Hay, 'Prosecution and Power. Malicious Prosecution in the English Courts 1750–1850', both in D. Hay and F. Snyder (eds.), *Policing and Prosecution in Britain 1750–1850* (Oxford, 1989); Innes and Styles, 'Crime Wave'; I. Gilmour, *Riot, Risings and Revolution. Governance and Violence in Eighteenth-Century England* (London, 1992), pp. 147–83; Gatrell, *The Hanging Tree*.

[7] E. P. Thompson, *Customs in Common* (London, 1991), p. 34; J. Rule, *Albion's People. English Society 1714–1815* (London, 1992) pp. 226–49; F. O'Gorman, *The Long Eighteenth Century. British Political and Social History 1688–1832* (London, 1997), pp. 286–94; D. Hay and N. Rogers, *Eighteenth-Century English Society. Shuttles and Swords* (London, 1997), esp. pp. 97–113.

is due to the influence of Douglas Hay's seminal article 'Property, Authority and the Criminal Law', which argued cogently that 'the criminal law was critically important in maintaining bonds of obedience and deference, in legitimising the status quo, in constantly recreating the structure of authority' as well as suggesting that 'the criminal law, more than any other social institution, made it possible to govern eighteenth-century England without a police force, and without a large army'.[8]

These ideas have not gone unchallenged. Exactly how central the criminal justice system was and which social groups used it and gained most from it— both as a practical tool and as a system of ideas—has become a matter of extensive debate, as has the nature of the legislative process in relation to criminal justice issues.[9] A number of important questions have yet to be subjected to detailed scrutiny, however. It remains unclear, for example, precisely which social groups, social interactions, and discursive formations were decisive in shaping many important arenas within the judicial process. More specifically the absence of detailed work on certain parts of the criminal justice system makes it difficult to assess how useful the selective application of the power to show mercy was to different social groups; how effective the theatre of the law was in reinforcing or legitimizing the rule of the élite; and how deeply sentencing and pardoning decisions were shaped by the power of élite influence and by the authorities' desire for exemplary punishment on the one hand, and by broader notions about the kinds of people who deserved lighter punishment and about the harshness of the bloody code, on the other.

By exploring stage by stage the ways the criminal justice system dealt with property offenders and by analysing more precisely who used the law, for what purposes, in what contexts and with what effects, this study aims both to reassess the role of the law in this period and to underline its importance as an arena of struggle, negotiation, and accommodation in which eighteenth-century social relations were forged, and in which its reciprocities and fissures were reflected. The law wore many faces in the eighteenth century. In theory at least, it criminalized a vast range of offences from swearing to sodomy, from

[8] Hay, 'Property', pp. 25 and 56.

[9] For the general debate, see works in note 6. On the debate about the proliferation of capital statutes, see Hay, 'Property' pp. 18–23; Langbein, 'Albion's Fatal Flaws', pp. 115–19; Innes and Styles 'The Crime Wave', pp. 240–50. R. McGowen, 'Making the "Bloody Code"? Forgery Legislation in Eighteenth-Century England', in N. Landau (ed.), *Law, Crime and English Society 1660–1840* (Cambridge, forthcoming). On Parliament's role in creating social legislation including criminal law bills, see J. Innes, 'Parliament and the Shaping of Eighteenth-Century English Social Policy', *Transactions of the Royal Historical Society*, 40 (1990), 63–92; J. Hoppit, 'Patterns of Parliamentary Legislation 1660–1800', *Historical Journal*, 39 (1996) 109–31; studies contextualizing particular criminal justice bills include J. Beattie, 'London Crime and the Making of the "Bloody Code" 1689–1718', in L. Davidson, T. Hitchcock, T. Keirn, and R. Shoemaker (eds.), *Stilling the Grumbling Hive. The Response to Social and Economic Problems in England 1689–1750* (Stroud, 1992), pp. 49–76; N. Rogers, 'Confronting the Crime Wave. The Debate over Social Reform and Regulation 1749–1753', in the same volume, pp. 77–98; R. McGowen, 'From Pillory to Gallows. The Punishment of Forgery in the Age of the Financial Revolution', *Past and Present* (forthcoming).

false weights to forging wills, from idleness to infanticide; but to study all types of offence and the myriad ways they were dealt with by the judicial system would require a series of volumes. In this book, therefore, both the few non-property crimes that were defined as felonies and the vast range of non-property offences that were dealt with by summary court hearings or misdemeanour indictments have been largely set aside, although further work on these areas would undoubtedly provide important insights into the role of the law in eighteenth-century society.[10]

1. Sources, Definitions of Property Crime, and Court Jurisdictions

In reconstructing the series of often brief but interconnected dramas that each individual accused of property appropriation was forced to play a part in until he or she gained access to an appropriate exit, the historian meets a myriad of problems. As we move through the play from the initial victim/accused negotiations, through committal and trial proceedings to sentencing, pardoning, and punishment, the later acts are relatively well documented, but even here complex evidential difficulties remain. Fragments of certain speeches survive—most frequently the formal charge in the indictment read out at the beginning of the public trial, more sporadically the much more useful depositions taken down from witnesses during pretrial proceedings. Occasionally a selective script of sorts is available, for the public trial proceedings at least, in the shape of printed trial accounts or judges' notes. In general, however, the highly varied and often voluminous legal records created by the courts and the printed and personal sources also available have to be carefully combed and analysed in order to reconstruct even a very partial picture of who was present at each stage, what evidence was presented, what negotiations took place, and what decisions were made, in what circumstances and for which reasons. Since legal requirements about formal record-keeping only gradually emerged as the accused got nearer to conviction and sentence, the earlier informal stages of the judicial process are far more difficult to reconstruct, although it was there that the vast majority of the accused made their exit. Many offenders, for example, escaped prosecution by compounding—paying the victim off in exchange for the charge being dropped. However, compounding a felony was illegal and the parties to such agreements deliberately left no record of their negotiations, which means that the number of accused who escaped through this particular tunnel is impossible to calculate.

---

[10] Misdemeanour and summary justice are still relatively understudied for the eighteenth century but see, for example, R. Shoemaker, '*Prosecution and Punishment. Petty Crime and the Law in London and Rural Middlesex 1660–1725*' (Cambridge, 1991); J. Innes, 'Prisons for the Poor. English Bridewells 1550–1800', in F. Snyder and D. Hay (eds.), *Labour, Law and Crime. An Historical Perspective* (London, 1987); P. King, 'The Summary Courts and Social Relations in England 1740–1820' (forthcoming) and D. Hay, 'Patronage, Paternalism and Welfare. Masters, Workers and Magistrates in Eighteenth-Century England', *International Labor and Working Class History*, 53 (1998), 27–48.

In following one specific but very broad subgroup of offenders—those accused of property appropriation—through these various stages, this study focuses on a form of lawbreaking that was central to contemporary discussions about the criminal law and its effectiveness. Along with crimes of extreme violence, such as murder or rape, crimes against property were the chief types of offence that came to mind when contemporaries spoke about 'crime'. The main yardstick with which the eighteenth-century public measured changes in the prevalence of crime, for example, was the length of the assize calendar, which was frequently noted and commented on in newspapers, pamphlets, and judges' speeches. Since nearly 90 per cent of those awaiting trial at the assizes were property offenders, this effectively meant that property appropriation was the key element of lawbreaking on which contemporaries focused their attention.[11]

For the purposes of this volume, property offences have been defined as lawbreaking acts involving the appropriation of goods, money, or services, whether by direct theft or by indirect forms of appropriation such as fraud, forgery, receiving, or extortion. Thus, the very small minority of indictments that involved damage to property without any transfer of ownership, such as arson or animal-maiming, are excluded. All definitions of crime are, of course, social constructions changing over time and between societies, social groups, and individuals. Thefts of tools and personal or household items were, for example, undoubtedly regarded as 'crimes' by a much higher proportion of the population than would have applied that term to smuggling, wrecking, coining, poaching, or gleaning.[12] In focusing on property crime, this volume is not therefore studying a discrete and universally understood set of actions. Nor is a simple definition of crime as lawbreaking activity necessarily a solution to the problem of delineating the boundaries of such a study. For example, the most commonly indicted form of property appropriation in mid-eighteenth-century Essex was the use of false weights and measures. However, the numerous prosecutions generated by Essex's surveyors of weights and measures were treated with roughly the same indifference by eighteenth-century commentators as minor traffic offences are today and their inclusion in any

---

[11] I.J., 16 Aug. 1760; Che.C., 10 Mar. 1776, 8 Aug. 1794, 1 Aug. 1800; M. Madan, *Thoughts on Executive Justice* (London, 1785), p. 87. In the Essex assizes felony files only 10.4 per cent of the accused in four sample years (1776, 1786, 1790, 1795) were not charged with property appropriation. P.R.O., Assi 35/ 216, 226, 230, 235. Although the law made a rather arbitrary distinction between two types of lawbreaking—misdemeanours and felonies—only the latter were usually regarded as 'crimes'. T. Williams, *Every Man his Own Lawyer* (London, 1812), p. 420.

[12] See, for example, three essays in Hay *et al.*, *Albion's Fatal Tree*; C. Winslow, 'Sussex Smugglers', pp. 119–66; J. Rule, 'Wrecking and Coastal Plunder', pp. 167–88; D. Hay, 'Poaching and the Game Laws on Cannock Chase', pp. 189–254; P. Munsche, *Gentlemen and Poachers. The English Game Laws 1671–1831* (Cambridge, 1981); N. Freedman, 'Plebs or Predators? Deer-Stealing in Whichwood Forest, Oxford-shire in the Eighteenth and Nineteenth Centuries', *Social History*, 21 (1996) 1–21; P. King, 'Gleaners, Farmers and the Failure of Legal Sanctions in England 1750–1850', *Past and Present*, 125 (1989), 116–50; C. Hill, *Liberty against the Law* (London, 1997) pp. 47–144; Styles, 'Our Traitorous Money Makers'.

discussion of property crime rates would tend to confuse rather than clarify the issues.[13]

It is often very difficult to define precisely what constituted an illegal act of appropriation in the eighteenth century. Contemporary writers, like many recent historians, not infrequently compared the number of indictments with 'real' levels of crime (i.e. with the vastly greater number of lawbreaking acts, prosecuted or unprosecuted, committed over a given time period) in order to make sense of changing levels of property crime indictments.[14] However, contemporary discussions of the amount of property crime that remained unprosecuted were based on very rough commonsense notions of what constituted a theft and the borderlines remained ill-defined and highly problematic. The same act was often subject to very different interpretations according to the context in which it occurred. The act of taking grain from another's field could, for example, be a summarily triable offence if the corn was still standing unharvested, an indictable larceny if it had been cut and gathered but not yet carted away, or a legal act of gleaning if carting had been completed. Since the harvest was an uneven process it was often impossible to establish in which of these contexts grain had been taken, which perhaps explains why eighteenth-century farmers so often complained about the frequency with which gleaners stole from the sheaves.[15]

The boundary between legality and illegality also changed over time. Many new statutes involving, for example, different forms of forgery or offences committed by bank or post office employees were passed during this period in an attempt to protect new forms of property or commercial transactions. Moreover, historians continue to debate the extent to which the eighteenth and early nineteenth centuries witnessed the legal redefinition as theft both of rural customary rights such as wood-gathering and of many of the perquisites generated by industrial processes.[16]

Given these interpretational problems and the further possibility that some property crime accusations were essentially malicious actions arising from personal animosities rather than actual acts of theft, the boundaries of any

---

[13] In Essex, 1748–52, more than fifty individuals per year were indicted for false weights or balances. E.R.O. Q/SPb 14; F. G. Emmison, *Guide to the Essex Record Office* (2nd edn., Chelmsford, 1969), p. 7.

[14] Hay, 'War'; Beattie, *Crime*, pp. 10–12 and 199–264.

[15] King, 'Gleaners'.

[16] Radzinowicz, *History*, I, pp. 637–52; B. Bushaway, 'From Custom to Crime. Wood-Gathering in Eighteenth and Early Nineteenth-Century England. A Focus for Conflict in Hampshire, Wiltshire and the South', in J. Rule, (ed.), *Outside the Law. Studies in Crime and Order 1650–1850*, Exeter Papers in Economic History, 15 (Exeter, 1983); J. Rule, 'Social Crime in the Rural South in the Eighteenth and Early Nineteenth Centuries', *Southern History*, 1 (1979), 137; Hay *et al.* (eds.), *Albion's Fatal Tree*, p. 13; Thompson, *Customs*, pp. 97–184; Innes and Styles, 'Crime Wave', pp. 217–18; A. Wood, 'Social Conflict and Change in the Mining Communities of North-West Derbyshire c.1600–1700', *International Review of Social History*, 38 (1993) 31–58; Linebaugh, *The London Hanged*; J. Styles, 'Embezzlement, Industry and the Law in England, 1500–1800', in M. Berg (ed.), *Industry in Town and Country before the Industrial Revolution* (Cambridge, 1983); King, 'Gleaners'.

study of property appropriation are inevitably blurred.[17] Indeed, it has usually been the sources themselves, rather than theoretical definitions of what constituted a 'crime' or an act of illegal appropriation, that have largely determined historians' lines of enquiry. Lacking any systematic source material about informal sanctioning processes or any equivalent of modern victim surveys or self-report studies, historians of eighteenth-century crime have inevitably focused on the records of the three main types of court that dealt with criminal charges—the summary or petty sessions courts, the quarter sessions, and the assizes. Since the overwhelming majority of formal hearings about property appropriation took place in these courts, they also provide the main basis for this study but it is important that the extensive overlaps between the jurisdictions of these courts and those of other types of tribunal be understood.

The boundaries between the civil and the criminal law were extremely blurred in the eighteenth century. Those who considered themselves to be victims of acts of appropriation often had to decide not only whether or not to prosecute, but also whether to become plaintiffs in a civil suit or prosecutors in a criminal one. Victims of indirect forms of appropriation, such as fraud, forgery, or uttering, were very frequently faced with the latter decision. In the 1780s, for example, the Essex farmer John Lambert, having paid too much for a horse after being given false information about its age, ignored the civil remedies available and indicted the horse dealer for fraud—a transportable offence. A huge variety of more direct appropriations were subject to similar borderline interpretations. Offences or dubious actions committed by those who hired horses or other goods and failed to abide by the terms of hiring; who borrowed tools and failed to return them; who mistook others' property for their own; who appropriated goods they believed had been abandoned; or who refused to return articles left temporarily in their custody are just some of the more obvious examples.[18]

Moreover the propertied not infrequently used expensive civil law proceedings to impoverish or imprison poorer adversaries who were often unable to pay damages or costs, and therefore found themselves imprisoned as debtors and under the discretionary power of the plaintiff. Farmers occasionally tried to punish gleaners in this way. Gentlemen and game-preserving associations punished some poachers very severely using a similar process. At the summary level in particular it was often almost impossible to decide whether a hearing was a civil or a criminal one—a theme I have dealt with in detail elsewhere.[19]

[17] D. Hay, 'Prosecution and Power', pp. 343–95.

[18] Sharpe, *Crime in Early Modern England*, p. 6; E.R.O., Q/SBb 330/9 for the unsuccessful prosecution; Williams, *Every Man*, pp. 245, 469, and 518; for civil cases involving horse frauds, see *Che.C.*, 11 Jan. 1791, 12 Aug. 1791; Hay, 'Prosecution and Power', p. 374; E.R.O., P/COR 2–20.

[19] King, 'Gleaners', pp. 128–30; Hay, 'Poaching', pp. 233–5; *Che.C.*, 15 Aug. 1783; Munsche, *Gentlemen*, pp. 23–4, 56, 89–92; King, 'Summary Courts'.

Although the authors of legal handbooks often produced neat boundaries defining the point at which acts of appropriation ceased to be subject only to civil remedies and became indictable as felonies, in reality the borders were ill-defined and often unguarded. The traffic across them was two-way. Interpersonal disputes occasionally reached such a pitch that one side would indict the other for a property offence even though no act of appropriation had taken place—perhaps as a means of gaining the advantage in a parallel civil suit. Equally, acts of appropriation that could have been treated as felonies were sometimes resolved as interpersonal disputes in various civil tribunals.

Although the vast majority of the property appropriation cases that reached a court with criminal jurisdiction were heard by magistrates in the local summary courts or tried at the quarter sessions or assizes, there were also other courts with limited powers to try subgroups of property offenders. In the sixteenth century the manorial courts were probably the most important. In many parts of Essex these courts were still dealing with wood thefts and other minor forms of property appropriation in 1600 but here, as elsewhere, the manorial courts had almost entirely ceased to perform such functions by 1750.[20] The English forest courts continued to punish wood, turf, and game appropriation in the eighteenth century, using a variety of minor sanctions, and the Court of Attachments in the Essex royal forest of Waltham was no exception. The confiscation of guns was the penalty most often recorded in game-related cases, but the court's jurisdiction was limited to a small part of south-west Essex and by the 1760s it appears to have been punishing only one or two offenders per year. The forest officers could, of course, mobilize other sanctions. In 1739 the underkeepers prosecuted two notorious deer-stealers, 'Lord' Rogers and Nepus Fuller, at the Essex assizes. Rogers was convicted under the Black Act and hanged but when Fuller was acquitted, the keepers' only sanction was to confiscate the guns he had left hidden on Widow Rogers' land. When internal squabbles among the local élite closed the Court of Attachments for over a decade in the 1770s and early 1780s its final decline was accelerated. By the turn of the century the regulation of forest offences was increasingly dependent on the local magistrates and on very occasional prosecutions in the major courts as the forest officers' own powers were rapidly evaporating.[21]

---

[20] Sharpe, *Crime in Early Modern England*, pp. 25–6, 83; S. Webb and B. Webb, *English Local Government from the Revolution to the Municipal Corporations Act. The Manor and the Borough* (1908), pp. 64–118; K. C. Newton and M. McIntosh, 'Leet Jurisdiction in Essex Manor Courts during the Elizabethan Period', *Essex Archaeology and History. The Transactions of the Essex Archaeology Society*, 3rd ser., 13 (1981), 3–15.

[21] E. P. Thompson, *Whigs*, pp. 38–9; Epping Forest Commission, *The Rolls of the Court of Attachments of the Royal Forest of Waltham in the County of Essex* (London, 4 vols, 1873), especially vol. 2, p. 116; W. R. Fisher, *The Forest of Essex. Its History, Law, Administration and Ancient Customs* (London, 1887), esp. p. 103; *The Genuine Proceedings at the Assizes on the Home Circuit Held in March 1739* (London, 1739), pp. 8–10; E.R.O., Epping Petty Sessions Books, 20 Dec. 1782, 11 Aug. 1786; P.R.O., Assi 35/220 and 238; *Che.C.*, 11 July 1783; Thompson, *Customs*, p. 103. Thefts from mines might be punished by local mining courts—

Since the King's Bench seldom dealt with original cases involving property offenders and was relatively rarely used as a review court for summary convictions, it seems to have played a very minor role in relation to disputes involving property appropriation.[22] The importance of the military courts can, however, be easily underestimated. The army's courts martial dealt with many cases of theft by soldiers, thefts of civilian property being particularly harshly dealt with. In places such as Colchester, where a large and troublesome garrison was stationed for long periods during the French wars, the number of cases involved could be considerable.[23] The London-based Admiralty Court's jurisdiction over felonies committed at sea was much less important, but other localized courts dealing with appropriations around the coastline were sometimes significant. When a powerful group of Essex oyster-dredgers attacked what they regarded as the illegal pilfering of the local oyster-beds in the 1780s, they used both prosecutions in the major courts and hearings at the Colchester Court of Conservancy or 'Admiralty' Court as it was known locally.[24]

The range of formal courts which might be involved in at least a few property appropriation cases was therefore broad and the boundaries between them were often ill-defined. Moreover, while it is rarely possible to reconstruct the informal sanctioning systems used by family and kin, by neighbours, by parish authorities, by friendly societies, or by the many other social networks that arose from everyday social and economic relations, these cannot and should not be ignored. Those who broke the norms of trust and reciprocity so central to economic survival and social peace by appropriating their neighbour's property could be punished in a myriad of ways without reference to the formal courts organized by the local or central state. A society such as this may perhaps best be seen, to quote Ignatieff, as 'a densely woven fabric of permissions, prohibitions, obligations and rules, sustained and enforced at a thousand points'. When it came to resolving disputes over property appropriation in the eighteenth century, some of those points were located within the formal courts and particularly within the summary courts, the quarter sessions, and the assizes. However, popular justice was meted out in various arenas and

A. Wood, 'Custom, Identity and Resistance. English Free Miners and their Law 1550–1800', in P. Griffiths, A. Fox, and S. Hindle (eds.), *The Experience of Authority in Early Modern England* (London, 1996), p. 258; see also H. Arthurs, *Without the Law. Administrative Justice and Legal Pluralism in Nineteenth-Century England* (Toronto, 1985), pp. 21–5.

[22] Beattie, *Crime*, pp. 18–19; Sharpe, *Crime in Early Modern England*, p. 22; W. Blackstone, *Commentaries on the Laws of England* (Oxford, 4 vols., 1765–9), p. 256. It is hoped that Douglas Hay's forthcoming study of Staffordshire King's Bench cases will throw much needed light on this subject.

[23] G. Steppler, 'British Military Law, Discipline, and the Conduct of Regimental Courts Martial in the Later Eighteenth Century', *English Historical Review*, 102 (1987), pp. 867–77; A. Gilbert, 'Military and Civilian Justice in Eighteenth-Century England. An Assessment', *Journal of British Studies*, 17 (1978), 41–65.

[24] P. King, 'Prosecution Associations and their Impact in Eighteenth-Century Essex', in Hay and Snyder (eds.), *Policing*, pp. 196–8.

the evidence generated by the three main types of court must be interpreted with this in mind.[25]

In particular it is necessary to be very clear about the size of the so-called 'dark figure' of unrecorded crime, which in the context of eighteenth-century studies is usually equated with unindicted crime.[26] Any precise calculation of the size of the dark figure is, of course, impossible, not only because no systematic record was kept of unprosecuted crime, but also because the definition of what constituted a property crime was and is so problematic. Even if we ignore borderline property appropriation disputes as well as petty industrial pilfering, poaching, hedgebreaking, and other summarily triable offences, and define 'real' property crime in a fairly restricted way as those acts of appropriation which most contemporaries would have regarded as indictable, it is clear that only a very small proportion of indictable property offenders were ever brought to the quarter sessions or assizes. Colquhoun, for example, estimated that a maximum of one offender in ten was indicted in late eighteenth-century London and in his more pessimistic moments he seems to have thought that one in a hundred might be a more accurate estimate.[27]

Many Essex parishes came up with similar guesses in 1836 in reply to the Constabulary Commission's questions on the proportion of offenders that had been apprehended. 'Not one in twenty' was one response from West Ham and similar pessimism can be found in rural Essex. Some country parishes replied simply 'none', whilst reporting that petty thefts and sheep stealing were wide-spread. Wormingford and Messing thought one-tenth was a maximum figure, while the Stisted estimate of not more than one in fifty echoed a similar observation from Buckinghamshire that 'a fiftieth part only' of felonies were reported. The Commission's questions were subject to various interpretations, and responses differed accordingly with some respondents taking a more optimistic line, but overall after forty years of growing financial encourage-ments to prosecutors and various rural policing experiments, contemporaries' perceptions of the extent of unprosecuted crime seem to have been broadly similar to those of Colquhoun in the late 1790s.[28] The tiny proportions of Essex horse and cattle theft advertisements, and of Northumberland animal thefts recorded under the Border Compensation Laws, that resulted in prosecutions also suggest a very large dark figure. In the one instance where almost every

[25] M. Ignatieff, 'Total Institutions and Working Classes. A Review Essay', *History Workshop Journal*, 15 (1983), 167–73; M. Ignatieff, 'State, Civil Society and Total Institutions. A Critique of Recent Social Histories of Punishment', in D. Sugarman (ed.), *Legality, Ideology and the State* (London, 1983), pp. 202–6; Chapter 2 for further discussion.

[26] Beattie, *Crime*, pp. 199–235; Hay, 'War'; Sharpe, *Crime in Early Modern England*, pp. 42–8.

[27] P. Colquhoun, *A Treatise on the Police of the Metropolis* (London, 2nd edn., 1796), p. vii; (5th edn., 1797), p. 206; Emsley, *Crime*, p. 21.

[28] P.R.O., H.O. 73/5, 6 and 9; *PP*, 1839, XIX, pp. 38–9; R. Storch, 'Policing Rural Southern England before the Police. Opinion and Practice, 1830–1856', in Hay and Snyder (eds.), *Policing*, pp. 222–3 and pp. 265–6, which provides evidence that when systematic enquiry was made in one parish the number proved to be very large.

offence was recorded—the forgery of Bank of England notes—a ratio of one in a hundred appears rather optimistic, despite the fact that the bank invested large amounts of money in the prosecution of offenders.[29]

Even if the ratio for most indictable property crimes averaged out at around one in ten, this would have meant that indictment levels were ten times as sensitive to changes in the proportion of victims who chose to prosecute than they were to changes in the absolute level of offences being committed. An increase of 5 per cent in the former would, all else being equal, result in a 50 per cent rise in indictment levels. A 5 per cent increase in offences would have only one-tenth of that effect. The section of this study that deals with changing levels of recorded property crime and with the backgrounds of those formally accused before the major courts (Chapters 5 and 6) has therefore been placed after that which analyses the pretrial stages of the offender's journey towards criminalization and punishment (Chapters 2 to 4). If relatively small changes in the attitudes, actions, and interactions of the prosecutors, law-enforcement agencies, and magistrates who controlled the pretrial process could affect indictment rates so easily, the significance of changing levels of recorded crime cannot be assessed until these decision-making patterns have been analysed.

Part 1 therefore deals in three chapters with the process of coming to trial. Chapter 2 looks at victims and their reactions, at detection, and at pretrial options and negotiations. This is then complemented by an assessment of the various individuals, groups, and institutions, both official and unofficial, that might offer assistance to the victim during these processes—constables, thief-takers, local social networks, prosecution associations, etc. (Chapter 3). The final stage of the accused's pretrial journey—committal proceedings and magistrates' summary hearings—is then analysed in Chapter 4. Part 2 begins by using this knowledge of pretrial processes as the basis for an alternative reading of property crime indictment patterns, which questions whether fluctuations in recorded crime should be mainly related to broader social and economic changes rather than to less obvious shifts in the attitudes and interactions of the various gatekeepers who controlled pretrial processes.[30] The accused themselves are then analysed in Chapter 6, which uses a life-cycle perspective and a gendered analysis to offer fresh insights on the vulnerability of different subgroups of the population to formal prosecution in the courts. Part 3 completes the accused's journey through the courts by looking at jury trials, courtroom interactions, and verdicts (Chapter 7); at judges' sentencing procedures, and the impact of age and gender on them (Chapter 8); at pardoning policies (Chapter 9); and at the rituals that surrounded the death sentence and the gallows (Chapter 10). A concluding chapter then draws

---

[29] *P.P.*, 1839, XIX, p. 5; Gatrell, 'Decline', pp. 267–8; Morgan and Rushton, *Rogues, Thieves*, pp. 49–50.

[30] A rather similar analogy is used in Herrup, *The Common Peace*, pp. 65–6.

together evidence from Chapters 1 to 10 in order to address broader issues about the role of the law in eighteenth-century social relations.

Since many of the detailed findings in this study are based on the Essex court records, a very brief description of the economic and social history of that county between 1740 and 1820 is included here, although much fuller accounts can be found elsewhere.[31] Essex contained no large areas of sparsely populated uplands or heaths and only one woodland region of any size—Epping and Waltham forest. Variations in population densities were not therefore as stark as they were in some counties, although the influence of London in the south-west and of the cloth manufacturing towns in the north produced two major areas with substantially higher population densities. From around 135,000 in 1723 the county's population rose to 227,500 in 1801, matching the national rate of increase almost exactly. Underlying this overall expansion three diverse movements were occurring in Essex. The cloth-manufacturing industry of northern Essex declined rapidly producing increased unemployment, slowing down population growth, and forcing towns such as Braintree, Halstead, and Colchester to develop as marketing centres serving the growing needs of the surrounding agricultural communities. The population of south-west Essex, by contrast, expanded rapidly as rich Londoners found it an increasingly attractive place to set up residence and as market gardening and other industries expanded. Meanwhile the county's agricultural and coastal regions experienced a more measured and geographically varied expansion in trade, productive capacity, and population.

The years between 1750 and 1815 were a period of improvement and growing profitability in Essex agriculture and the trade (and varied consumer demands) created by the agricultural sector, along with improvements in road and water transport, brought growing prosperity to the larger market towns. Arable farming increasingly predominated in the later eighteenth century, although nearer London dairy farming also expanded. Most of Essex had been enclosed long before 1700 but the ownership of land was not as concentrated as it was in some counties. The Essex gentry was a remarkably fluid group and, since vast estates were usually accumulated in areas away from London, the county had relatively few great landowners. Essex agriculture reached a high peak of improvement and profitability between 1770 and 1815 and even the rapid decline of the area's main industry could not prevent Arthur Young from describing Essex in 1784 as 'one of the finest and richest counties' in England.

---

[31] For further discussion—P. King, 'Crime, Law and Society in Essex 1740–1820' (Ph.D. Cambridge, 1984), pp. 7–26; *V.C.H. Essex*, 2; A. Brown, *Essex at Work 1700–1815* (Chelmsford, 1969); K. Burley, 'The Economic Development of Essex in the Later Seventeenth and Early Eighteenth Centuries' (Ph.D. London, 1975); C. Shrimpton, 'Landed Society and the Farming Community of Essex in the Late Eighteenth and Early Nineteenth Centuries' (Ph.D. Cambridge, 1965); A. Brown, *Prosperity and Poverty. Rural Essex 1700–1815* (Chelmsford, 1996); P. Sharpe, *Adapting to Capitalism. Working Women in the English Economy 1700–1850* (London, 1996). For silk, straw plait, and lace see pp. 38–70. A. Young, *General View of the Agriculture of the County of Essex* (2 vols., London, 1807), vol. 2, 395.

However, these gains were not spread evenly across the population. Between the 1780s and the 1820s the process of social differentiation seems to have gathered pace in Essex. The high grain prices of the French wars benefited the farmers and prompted many of them to adopt a more genteel lifestyle, but the bread-dependent family budgets of the labouring poor were badly affected and real wages remained static or declined. Not surprisingly, therefore, the severe dearth of 1800–1 witnessed an unprecedented rise in threatening letters and incendiarism, while rising unemployment and economic dislocation after 1815 brought a fresh wave of machine breaking and arson.[32]

During most of the period covered by this study, however, this polarization process was only just beginning to become evident. The gentry élite remained confident despite its relative fluidity. The well-established, increasingly prosperous yeomanry were developing their own sources of authority through parish vestries and other bodies, and it was not until the 1790s or beyond that the propertied began to feel that the relative social stability of the eighteenth century was beginning to be eroded.

[32] Shrimpton, 'Landed Society', p. 4; P. Muskett, *Riotous Assemblies. Popular Disturbances in East Anglia 1740–1822* (Ely, 1984); Brown, *Essex at Work*, p. 162; A. Charlesworth (ed.), *An Atlas of Rural Protest in Britain 1548–1900* (London, 1983) p. 69; E. Hobsbawm and G. Rudé, *Captain Swing* (London, 1969); P. Hills and L. Swash, *Horrid Lights. Nineteenth-Century Incendiarism in Essex* (Essex, 1994); A. Brown, *Meagre Harvest. The Essex Farm Workers' Struggle Against Poverty, 1750–1914* (Chelmsford, 1990), pp. 2–8. T. Richardson, 'Agricultural Labourers' Wages and the Cost of Living in Essex 1790–1840. A Contribution to the Standard of Living Debate', in B. Holderness and M. Turner (eds.), *Land, Labour and Agriculture* (London, 1991), pp. 78–89.

Part 1

Pretrial Processes

2

Victims, Informal Negotiations, and Prosecution Options

In the unfolding drama of most property crime prosecutions the central role was played by the victim. As the foreign observer Cottu noted in 1820, 'The right of prosecution . . . is placed entirely in the hands of the offended party, who becomes . . . the sole arbiter of the fate of the offender, and can . . . either prosecute him with the utmost rigour of the law, or soften a part of its severity against him, by modifying the form of the indictment, or even pardon him altogether, by omitting to prefer any complaint against him.' Between 1740 and 1820 officials only took responsibility for prosecutions involving property appropriation in very exceptional circumstances, such as major coining or forgery cases.¹ It was the victim who provided the momentum, the driving force that moved a dispute towards a trial in the major courts. If the victim refused to react, the judicial system remained inert and ineffective. If the victim chose to take on the expensive, time-consuming, and often complex task of organizing the detection, arrest, and possible committal of the offender, he (or occasionally she) found that an array of discretionary powers fell into his hands. Despite the technical legal restraints designed to limit his discretion, in practice the victim had immense freedom of manoeuvre. If he decided to call the process to a halt by making a settlement or applying informal sanctions, it was rarely possible to prevent him. Even after the committal proceedings, at which the magistrates decided whether or not to imprison the accused await- ing trial, prosecutors remained highly influential. Some undermined the trial process completely by failing to appear, while many influenced the verdict and final sentence by the type of charge they brought, by the way they brought it, and by petitioning the trial authorities for a particular outcome. The first chapter of this section on pretrial processes therefore focuses on the victims and their decisions—their initial reactions, their detection methods, their negotiations with suspects, and finally the choices they made between the committal proceedings and the trial. Chapters 3 and 4 then explore the assistance available to victims and the role of committal proceedings and of the summary courts.

---

¹ M. Cottu, 'The Administration of the Criminal Code in England and the Spirit of the English Government', *The Pamphleteer*, 16 (1820), 23; Emsley, *Crime*, p. 138; Hay, 'Crime, Authority', p. 339.

1. Victims' initial reactions and detection methods

It is impossible to study pretrial processes from the court records alone since these, by definition, cover only those cases in which informal solutions were not chosen by the victim. Lacking the systematic victim surveys of the late twentieth century, the historian must, therefore, fall back on contemporary diaries and other personal writings in order to consider such basic questions as: how frequently were eighteenth-century households subjected to acts of illegal appropriation? Were all social groups vulnerable to theft and how did victims react? Essex diarists offer occasional insights. The Bocking clothier John Savill records unsolved burglaries on both his own and his neighbours' households; while the Maldon miller John Crosier lists at least five local crimes among his sporadic diary entries. Diaries from other counties are much more systematic and illuminating. Nicholas Blundell's Journal, the meticulous day-to-day re-cord of a Lancashire gentleman between 1702 and 1728, records fifteen occa-sions when he was the victim of property appropriation and includes a spectrum of informal reactions but only two public prosecutions. Diaries are not victim surveys.[2] Diarists often did not bother to record minor losses or may never have discovered them. Major incidents, or occasions when the diarist did decide to prosecute, are more likely to be recorded than minor ones in which either the offender was never apprehended or informal methods were used. Moreover, in some cases later editors may have excluded brief entries indicating that the diarist had been the victim of minor pilfering. However, by using diarists who kept reasonably systematic day-to-day records, it may be possible to make minimum estimates of how frequently certain social groups were victims of property appropriation.

The eight diarists used here include two farmers, a farmer's wife, a shop-keeper, a clothier turned banker, two clergymen, and a gentleman.[3] Their diaries cover 132 years and record thirty-five potentially indictable property crimes, four attempted felonies (mainly burglaries), and four summarily triable

[2] Brown, *Essex People*, pp. 12–13, 38–40, 49; J. Bagley (ed.), *The Great Diurnal of Nicholas Blundell of Little Crosby, Lancashire* (Record Society of Lancashire and Cheshire, 3 vols., 1968–72). For a parallel use of diaries (and a related source—account books) to study civil disputes, see C. Muldrew, 'The Culture of Reconciliation. Community and the Settlement of Economic Disputes in Early Modern England', *Historical Journal*, 39 (1996), 915–42. On victim surveys, F. Heidensohn, *Crime and Society* (London, 1989), pp. 165–70.

[3] W. Branch-Johnson (ed.), '*Memorandoms for' the Diary between 1798 and 1810 of John Carrington Farmer, Chief Constable, Tax Assessor, Surveyor of Highways and Overseer of the Poor of Bramfield in Hertfordshire* (London, 1973); 'Diary of William Ford of Branscombe, Devon 1789–91', Devon Record Office Z19/36/4; B. Cozens-Hardy, *Mary Hardy's Diary* (Norfolk Record Society, 1968)—a Norfolk farming and brewing family 1774–1809; D. Vaisey, *The Diary of Thomas Turner 1754–65* (Oxford, 1985)—a Sussex shopkeeper; J. Fiske (ed.), *The Oakes Diaries, Business, Politics and the Family in Bury St Edmunds 1778–1827. Volume 1. Introduction. James Oakes' Diaries 1778–1800* (Suffolk Records Society, 1990)—a yarnmaster and banker; J. Beresford (ed.), *The Diary of a Country Parson. The Reverend James Woodforde*, 5 vols. (Oxford, 1924–31), only his years at Weston Longville, Norfolk 1776–1802 used here; F. Stokes (ed.), *The Bletcheley Diary of the Rev. William Cole 1765–67* (London, 1931); Bagley, *The Great Diurnal*, excluding the years when Blundell was abroad.

property offences committed against the household of the diarist, as well as numerous occasions when neighbours suffered similar appropriations or when the diarists caught potential thieves in suspicious circumstances. Despite the problems of defining precisely what constitutes a felony, these households therefore experienced, on average, a minimum of three property appropriations per decade. If the original manuscripts, rather than later edited versions, had always been consulted, this figure might be substantially higher.[4] However, while theft was a fairly frequent experience, the role of prosecutor was not. The diaries only record three major court prosecutions arising from these eight households, two of them being Blundell's. In addition, one other diarist had the satisfaction of seeing the offender convicted for a similar offence against a neighbour, and on three occasions the accused was examined before a magistrate but not committed for trial. By casting the net more widely to include appropriations against thirteen other households recorded in autobiographies, letters, and more sporadic diaries, a total of nearly sixty property offences have been identified, but only two of these twenty-one households appear to have resorted to formal prosecution.[5]

Unfortunately diary keepers are not a typical sample of victims. Only the better-off and literate had the time, materials, and motivation to keep thorough records of this type. Could less wealthy groups expect to experience the same substantial levels of property appropriation as these eight diarists? Poorer households may have been less vulnerable. They had less items worth stealing and, equally important, they did not employ servants. At least a sixth of the offences recorded in the diaries were committed by this group. Nicholas Blundell's particularly high vulnerability, for example, was partly due to the

[4] Branch-Johnson, *Memorandoms*, pp. 133–4, 143; Devon Record Office, Z19/36/4, 1 September 1790; Cozens-Hardy, *Mary Hardy's Diary*, pp. 20, 42, 51, 53, 84. (The edited version contains fewer entries for the final fifteen years of Mary's life. All the appropriations recorded are in the first twenty years of the diary. Later ones may have been edited out.) Vaisey, *Diary of Thomas Turner*, p. 13; Fiske, *The Oakes Diaries*, 1, pp. 260, 275, 302, 321, 386–8, 390; Beresford, *Diary of a Country Parson*, 2, pp. 61–2, 225–6; 3, p. 59; 5, pp. 105–7, 142, 296, 305, 327, 373, 396; Stokes, *Bletchley Diary*, pp. 11, 258; Bagley, *The Great Diurnal*, 1, pp. 46, 96, 103, 133–4, 174, 178, 181–3, 242, 253; 2, pp. 21–3, 27, 91, 112–14; 3, p. 95, 131, 133, 138, 154, 218. Only Ford and Blundell's diaries are unedited. Occasions when the diarists were given 'bad money' excluded.

[5] J. Ayers (ed.), *Paupers and Pig Killers. The Diary of William Holland, a Somerset Parson 1799–1818* (Gloucester, 1984), p. 45; W. Hutton, *The Life of William Hutton* (London, 1816), p. 38, 73, 88; C. Thomas-Stanford (ed.), *The Private Memorandums of William Roe of Withdean, Sussex, 1775–1809* (Brighton, 1928), p. 4; W. Matthews (ed.), *The Diary of Dudley Ryder 1715–16* (London, 1939); G. Eustace, 'The Tomkins Diary', *Sussex Archaeological Collections*, 71 (1930), 41; D. Gibson (ed.), *A Parson in the Vale of the White Horse. George Woodward's Letters from East Hendred 1753–1761* (Gloucester, 1983) p. 70; F. J. Manning (ed.), *The Williamson Letters 1748–1765* (Bedfordshire Historical Record Society, 1953), pp. 76–7; the Day Books of John Clifton of Oundle, joiner—Northamptonshire Record Office ZA 8731–8747, 18 July 1778 (my thanks to Nick Hemmings for this reference); M. Saxby, *Memoirs of a Female Vagrant by Herself* (London, 1806), p. 4; Brown, *Essex People*, p. 49; C. Moritz, *Journeys of a German in England. A Walking Tour of England in 1782* (London, 1983), p. 121; L. G. Mitchell (ed.), *The Purefoy Letters 1735–53* (London, 1973), pp. 137–41; A. Kussmaul (ed.), *The Autobiography of Joseph Mayett of Quainton 1783–1839* (Buckinghamshire Record Society, 1986), pp. 32–5, 64, 78.

fact that he kept twelve resident servants, who had privileged access to a rich array of household goods. However, the poor's possessions were at risk for the opposite reason. They had no servants to guard their property in their absence and they were often away from home working for others. Working people's autobiographies suggest other specific vulnerabilities. Labourers and artisans travelling in search of work were particularly soft targets. The apprentice William Hutton, for example, after running away from his master and appropriating some of his money in the process, became a victim himself when his bundle containing a new suit of clothes, a bible, food, and money was stolen from a barn. When Mary Saxby ran away from home 'some women of the town' got her drunk and stole her clothes. Joseph Mayett, a farm labourer, was extensively defrauded by those who held power over him in the army, while his parents had part of their poor relief payments stolen by intermediaries.[6] However, while diaries and personal records suggest that each status group had its own set of vulnerabilities, these records also indicate that they had much in common. The majority of the thefts recorded in the eight diaries involved food, drink, fuel, fowls, or handtools—items owned by rich and poor alike although not in equal quantities.

Once a property appropriation had occurred how did most victims react? The first decision they made was whether or not to attempt to detect, pursue, and apprehend the offender. Many entries suggest that the diarist quietly accepted the loss and made no significant response to the theft. Given the expense, inconvenience, and uncertainty involved in detecting the offender, let alone in prosecuting him, this course must have seemed extremely attractive. If small amounts of food, fuel, or other immediately consumable goods had been taken, there was little hope of regaining the stolen items and therefore little incentive to trace the offender. Even if the stolen property was reasonably valuable many victims were discouraged by their low expectations of success and by the lack of any obvious line of enquiry to pursue. The potential prosecutor was most likely to commit himself to finding the offender if he could focus his activities on a particular suspect during the first upsurge of anger that usually accompanied the discovery of a theft.[7] This identification of an initial target might occur if the offender was seen committing the crime or carrying the stolen goods, if a suspicious character had been spotted in the area, or if a servant, lodger, or customer known to have had access to the stolen goods was understood to have been in the vicinity at the time of the theft and could be searched after a warrant had been obtained from a magistrate.

---

[6] Bagley, *The Great Diurnal*, 1, p. 43. E.R.O. Q/SBb 198/4; *Che.C.*, 17 Aug. 1787; Hutton, *The Life*, pp. 34–8; Saxby, *Memoirs*, p. 4; Kussmaul, *The Autobiography*, pp. 32–5, 78.

[7] In 1723–4, for example, Blundell recorded that his henhouse, his pigeon house, and his cellar had been raided, but gave no indication he had tried to detect the offenders. Bagley, *The Great Diurnal*, 3, pp. 95, 131, 135–8. W. Blizzard, *Desultory Reflections on Police* (1785), Letter 5 analyses a victim's immediate irrational anger.

Table 2.1. Detection Methods, Essex Quarter Sessions Depositions (Larceny Only), 1748–1800

A. *Some Indication of Detection Method*	No.	%
1. Seen in act of theft	49	26.4
2. Seen in area	25	13.4
3. Accused had access to stolen goods as: employee, lodger, or customer	16	8.6
4. Seen carrying stolen goods or suspicious bag	12	6.4
5. Buyer stopped thief, or buyer-information leads to arrest	26	14.0
6. Stopped on general suspicion by watch, constable, or official	6	3.2
7. Watch deliberately set, resulting in capture	11	5.9
8. Vagrants etc. searched, stolen goods found	11	5.9
9. Traced through footprints or trail	4	2.2
10. Suspicion led to marking goods and detection	4	2.2
11. Stolen goods advertised in newspaper	2	1.1
12. Evidence of accomplices	13	7.0
13. Evidence of fellow workmates	3	1.6
14. Attempted restitution failed	1	0.5
15. Accused overheard planning theft	2	1.1
16. Seen openly gleaning	1	0.5
Total	186	100.0
B. *Inadequate information*	No.	
1. 'Suspected'	22	
2. Goods found in accused's possession	23	
3. 'Confessed' on evidence of circumstances that induced a confession	24	
Total	69	

Source: E.R.O. Q/SBb Years = 1748–9, 1754–65, 1771–4, 1783–6, 1792–4, 1800

Between 1740 and 1800 just over half the Essex quarter sessions depositions in which methods of apprehension are described indicate that detection was initiated in one of these circumstances (Table 2.1). However, a much smaller proportion of victims as a whole had evidence of this quality on which to act. The quarter sessions depositions do not cover a random sample of detective methods. They only record successful detection operations and the 25 per cent that contain no description of the apprehension of the accused may include a larger proportion of cases in which the offender was not initially recognized.

Despite these difficulties, the depositions do indicate the main forms of activity undertaken. Circulating information to local retailers, neighbours, and law enforcement officers was usually the victim's second line of action. Vagrants and travellers with suspicious-looking bags were frequently stopped and searched. If any valuables were found on them they were likely to be held until ownership was established. Local traders and pawnbrokers were often required to 'stop' anyone attempting to exchange particular stolen articles for cash, and about one-seventh of Essex quarter sessions offenders were detected through information supplied by buyers (Table 2.1). If the price was too low or the circumstances dubious some traders 'stopped' suspected thieves without any specific instructions from the victim. In 1774 Thomas Pepper travelled halfway across Essex to dispose of a hundredweight of stolen hops, but the prospective buyer had them advertised and the theft was uncovered.[8]

Essex offenders were occasionally detected by tracing footmarks or trails of feathers or hay (Table 2.1), but victims who had suffered depredations over an extended period sometimes resorted to more subtle techniques. When property was difficult to mark other materials were mixed with it—coloured beans were added to coal heaps and specially knotted string was hidden in trusses of hay. The thief, who was usually an employee, could not then claim that the goods were his own. Valuables and large animals were marked as a matter of course and some major thefts were detected because the offender had failed to eradicate these marks or had aroused suspicion by doing so.[9] Other victims used the more expensive alternative of organizing some form of surveillance. In 1799 a Wanstead farmer upset by low grain yields 'set a watch to discover whether any person should come in the course of the night' and the nocturnal appropriations of a local labourer were discovered. However, only about one indictment in twelve arose from victims' deliberate attempts to trap repeated offenders in these ways and many watchers must have sat up all night to no purpose, as Elizabeth Swift did at Blundell's instigation in 1727.[10]

Since a very small proportion of these quarter sessions offenders were detected as a result of the independent activities of constables, watchmen, and thieftakers, the victim was clearly the main instigator of detection activity at this level. The absence of assize depositions makes it more difficult to discuss the role of policing networks and private individuals in more serious cases and, as Chapter 3 will show, the victim might receive extensive help from these sources when a major felony had been committed. However, even when the crime was a capital one the victim remained the key player without whose involvement little could be achieved by other groups. How did he or she react once an offender had been identified and apprehended?

2. Victim/accused negotiations and the use of informal sanctions

As the diaries make clear, when the victim and the accused came face to face, formal prosecution was the exception; negotiation and informal sanction the norm. The major courts had no monopoly over punitive sanctions in the eighteenth century. Indeed, they usually had to content themselves with processing a few scraps and particularly tough morsels which those involved

---

[8] E.R.O. Q/SBb 271/10. 316/44 and 350/54. *The Whole Proceedings of the King's Commission of Oyer and Terminer, and Gaol Delivery held for the County of Essex . . . March 1774* (Chelmsford, 1774) p. 9.

[9] *Che.C.*, 19 Apr. 1765 for a shopkeeper detecting his servant by putting marked coins in the till. Fiske, *The Oakes Diaries* p. 321; shopkeepers often marked even the smallest items—E.R.O. Q/SBb 323/66. *I.J.* 8 Jan. 1763.

[10] E.R.O. Q/SBb 378/81; Bagley, *The Great Diurnal*, 3, p. 218.

in informal sanctioning processes threw their way or spat out as indigestible, and as therefore requiring the tougher teeth of the criminal law. Parliament found it difficult to change this situation. Although the laws against compounding were intended to limit severely the negotiations between victim and accused, they do not appear to have been very successful. Colquhoun expressed the thoughts of many contemporary writers in commenting: 'Notwithstanding the severity of the law, the composition of felonies . . . is carried on to a much greater height than it is almost possible to believe.' Nor did the involvement of the magistrates put an end to the victim's discretionary powers either before or after the committal proceedings. Victims quite frequently needed a Justice of the Peace's (JP's) help early in their investigations in order to obtain a search or arrest warrant, but the magistracy did not necessarily use these powers to insist that a prosecution should ensue if the stolen goods were found and the offender apprehended. Blundell records three situations in which the granting of a warrant led to the detection of the offender, two of which were resolved informally without further reference to a magistrate.[11]

What were the alternatives to prosecution available to the victim? The possibilities and permutations were almost endless but, apart from those negotiated at committal hearings, which will be discussed in Chapter 4, they can be analysed under four headings: settlements involving the transfer of material resources to the victim; the imposition of informal physical, social, or economic sanctions by the victim; the mobilization of communal sanctions against the accused; and the informal use of other state institutions, such as the army or the civil courts, to punish the offender.

Uppermost in most victims' minds once the crime had been discovered was the desire to get their goods back as quickly as possible. This issue often determined the victim's attitude to the prosecution option. When Peggy Barnes was apprehended by a Walthamstow shoemaker for shoplifting in 1774 she badly mismanaged the ensuing negotiations. Initially he was satisfied with the return of his shoes and allowed her to go on her way, but he later realized that she had not returned the buckles and when he overtook her again she was immediately taken into custody.[12] Restitution was a particularly important issue when the victim had strong emotional links with the property lost, as was often the case in horse thefts, or when the theft involved a high proportion of the victim's wealth. In 1772 the *Chelmsford Chronicle* reported that an Essex man had 'sent the crier offering a reward of twenty guineas' to anybody who would return his stolen savings, assuring them he would take no advantage of the law. Once he had recaptured his property, the victim's

[11] Colquhoun, *Police*, pp. 231–2; Blackstone, *Commentaries*, 4, pp. 132–3; Bagley, *The Great Diurnal*, 1, p. 242, 2, p. 112–14. For a different emphasis, Langbein, 'Albion's Fatal Flaws', p. 103; E. Crittall (ed.), *The Justicing Notebook of William Hunt 1744–1749* (Devizes, 1982), p. 17 on victims' strategic use of warrants.
[12] E.R.O. Q/SBb 277/32; they probably came to a second arrangement since Barnes was never indicted.

willingness to pursue or apprehend the offender tended to evaporate. William Limbury of Berkhamstead twice fought pitched battles with thieves in 1800 and 1801 to regain his stolen geese, but he made no attempt to arrest the offenders. Even if the offender was apprehended, restitution was often enough to prevent any further action by the victim. Robert Case, for example, avoided both prosecution and dismissal in 1801 by confessing that he had stolen from a fellow servant's box and then returning all the cash immediately.[13]

Victims often extracted payments or services from the accused in exchange for non-prosecution. A Surrey servant who had stolen substantial amounts of her master's goods 'agreed to make the matter up' for five pounds ten shillings, which was to be paid at one shilling per week. Blundell's pilfering servant Richard Ainsworth, having failed to placate his master by returning the stolen goods, then offered to help rebuild a house if Blundell would drop the indictment. The Buckinghamshire gentleman Henry Purefoy offered to take a guinea from a former servant, giving in exchange his assurance that 'no further prosecution shall be had against her by reason of taking the strong beer, provided she is secret and says nothing of it to anybody'.[14] Purefoy's desire for secrecy was understandable. The offence of compounding in which, to quote Blackstone, 'the party robbed not only knows the felon, but also takes his goods again, or other amends, upon agreement not to prosecute' was punishable with imprisonment. However, it was very rarely brought to trial in felony cases in the eighteenth century and Essex prosecutors not infrequently told the examining magistrate quite openly that they were only proceeding with the prosecution because the accused had refused to restore the stolen goods or 'make satisfaction for the same'.[15] Fear of being themselves accused of breaking the law may, however, have been one reason why so many victims opted for a different set of options, imposing informal sanctions on the accused rather than extracting material resources from him or her.

The simplest informal sanction available to the victim was a lecture or warning. When Parson Woodforde caught Paul Bowden lopping his trees he merely 'gave him a lecture and told him to take care for the future'. This option was rarely used unless the accused appeared suitably contrite. The offender's best starting-point in such negotiations was therefore an apology. Sarah Pearce, for example, was prosecuted in 1792 because when 'she was desired to ask pardon' she replied, 'there is your property. I shall not do anything of the kind.' Physical punishment was another option, particularly in cases involving servants or young boys. Victims often referred young

    [13] *Che.C.*, 11 Sept 1772; Branch-Johnson, *Memorandoms*, pp. 52, 64; Beresford, *Diary of a Country Parson*, 5, p. 327.
    [14] *The Proceedings at the Assizes of Peace, Oyer and Terminer for the County of Surrey . . . July 1740 to which is added the Genuine Proceedings at the Assizes for the County of Essex* (London, 1740), p. 10; Bagley, *The Great Diurnal*, 1, pp. 174–82; Mitchell, *The Purefoy Letters*, pp. 137–41.
    [15] Blackstone, *Commentaries*, 4, p. 133; Emsley, *Crime*, p. 140; E.R.O. Q/SPb 15 Apr 1771.

offenders to other authority figures. William Holland, after discovering his neighbour's 17-year-old son pilfering his plum trees, simply 'told the father of it' while other boys were corrected by their schoolmasters. As late as the 1830s physical punishment was the preferred option of a West Ham farmer who suffered massive depredations on his crops but, as attitudes to violence began to change, victims may have increasingly risked being prosecuted or bound over for assault, as several Essex farmers were when they used physical sanctions against gleaners.[16]

The most effective informal sanction in cases involving employees was dismissal. Employers such as William Hardy sometimes confined the punishment to withdrawal of privileges or status, but more frequently the accused lost his or her employment. William Hutton decided 'an instant separation was requisite' when he found a female servant had stolen his books. Blundell got rid of at least three servants for petty theft between 1705 and 1714, although on one occasion he relented temporarily 'upon her great submission'. Servants and apprentices often dismissed themselves by running away after a theft, as Purefoy's servant did in 1736, but as Purefoy's correspondence shows, the employer's main constraint in these situations, apart from the personal affection that sometimes grew up between families and their servants, was the difficulty they had in replacing them.[17]

When the offender was not an employee but was a local resident other sanctions could be utilized. In 1790 William Ford 'turned off Peter Board and gave him . . . notice to quit Woodhead House in consequence of his having received hares', and eviction was also widely used by landlords and their agents in cases involving poaching, woodstealing, and other property offences. Woodforde reacted to the discovery that a neighbour had lopped limbs off his trees by threatening to take him before a magistrate and by forbidding him or his family 'from coming into my yard after water'. The sanction was probably short-lived. Three days later his neighbour promised that 'he never would do so again nor let any of his family' and Woodforde forgave him on that condition.[18] However, the loss of access to the local water supply was not an inconsiderable punishment and victims could sometimes find a number of similar ways to make everyday life more difficult for those who had broken their trust.

[16] Beresford, *Diary of a Country Parson*, 3, p. 59; *O.B.S.P.* (Feb. 1792) p. 136. For a boy suspected of theft ordered 'to be corrected at school' P.R.O. H.O. 42/2/99. Ayres, *Paupers and Pig Killers*, p. 45; Emsley, *Crime*, p. 40; *P.P.* 1839, XIX, p. 40; King, 'Gleaners', pp. 135–6. On changing attitudes, P. King 'Punishing Assault. The Transformation of Attitudes in the English Courts' *Journal of Interdisciplinary History*, 27 (1996), 43–74.

[17] Cozens-Hardy, *Mary Hardy's Diary*, p. 20; Hutton, *The Life*, p. 88; Bagley, *The Great Diurnal*, 1, p. 96, 242, 2, p. 112–14; Mitchell, *The Purefoy Letters*, pp. 136–52.

[18] Devon Record Office, Z19/36/4, 20 Dec. 1790; P. Horn, *The Rural World. Social Change in the English Countryside 1780–1850* (London, 1980), pp. 260–2; Hay, 'Poaching', p. 232; Beresford, *Diary of a Country Parson*, 5, pp. 105–6.

If the community took the victim's side a much wider range of sanctions became available. In a world where neighbourliness was an important buffer against acute distress, and where mutual aid and reciprocity were vital, even the poorer sections of the community had many ways of punishing an offender by withdrawing the right to borrow money, food, tools, or means of transport. Integrity and trust were the foundations of the system of neighbourhood exchange which protected many rural families from the vicissitudes of the market. Although the mutuality of this world went largely unrecorded and has not therefore received much attention from historians, exclusion from it could be extremely painful and potentially disastrous.[19] The community also had more direct ways of expressing its anger. The impounding or mutilation of animals were two widespread forms of retaliation in certain kinds of local disputes and in most communities a range of social sanctions also existed. Joking, gossip, and the ostracization of the accused took various forms such as his exclusion from privileged and much-coveted places around the alehouse fire. Pilferers also risked losing their membership of the local box club, which meant exclusion from important times of conviviality and ceremony as well as the loss of material benefits such as sickness insurance. Many friendly society regulations specifically laid down that thieves would be removed. Nonconformist congregations also used expulsion or the loss of certain privileges to discipline those involved in dishonest appropriations, as Joseph Mayett's sister-in-law found out to her cost. The role of local churches in informal sanctioning processes remains obscure but clerical admonitions were certainly one of the lesser sanctions resorted to. In 1800 the Reverend William Holland was asked to speak to a young woman caught stealing potatoes. Unfortunately he had no hard sanctions to apply and his diary records that she was 'a wench so ignorant, so savage and so stupid, what I said could have but little influence'.[20]

The farmers and traders who ran many local vestries and who were the main local employers had much greater leverage. Farmers could refuse to employ reputed thieves or exclude them from access to cheap grain supplies. Shopkeepers and publicans might refuse credit or demand the repayment of debts. Essex artisans were boycotted by potential customers if they were known to receive stolen goods. Vestries sometimes sat in direct judgement on offenders. In 1782 a Wimbledon man was examined by the vestry on a

[19] J. Walter, 'The Social Economy of Dearth in Early Modern England', in J. Walter and R. Schofield (eds.), *Famine, Disease and the Social Order in Early Modern Society* (Cambridge, 1989), p. 111; M. Reed, 'Gnawing it out. A New Look at Economic Relations in Nineteenth-Century Rural England', *Rural History*, 1 (1990), 83–94.

[20] Stokes, *The Bletchley Diary*, p. 83 on impounding; R. Suggett, 'Some Aspects of Village Life in Eighteenth-Century Glamorgan' (B.Litt. Oxford, 1976), pp. 99–106; J. McMullan, 'Crime, Law and Order in Early Modern England', *British Journal of Criminology*, 27 (1987), p. 256; M. Reed, 'The Peasantry of Nineteenth-Century England. A Neglected Class?', *History Workshop Journal*, 18 (1984) 66; Northamptonshire Record Office, regulations of Walgrave Friendly Society; J. Priest, *General View of the Agriculture of Buckinghamshire* (London, 1813), p. 348. Kussmaul, *The Autobiography*, pp. 78–9; Ayres, *Paupers and Pig Killers*, p. 25.

charge of receiving stolen coals but 'it being the first misdemeanour...laid to his charge and upon his promise of future amendment his offence was remitted'. Vestries frequently manipulated other policy decisions in order to punish offenders. In 1806, for example, the Wormingford vestry used the settlement laws to have Margaret Laysell removed from the parish after its largest farmer accused her of appropriating his grain. A decade earlier Hannah Smith was dismissed from Great Yeldham Industrial School 'for having taken and sold Mr Poole's ploughiron'. In many Essex parishes it was vestry policy to punish those who had committed thefts by refusing to give them the customary annual handout from charitable foundations. In 1788 Halstead's landholders even tried to use access to gleaning rights as a sanction announcing that 'any poor person being detected within one year of stealing wood, underwood, faggots, bushes, turnips, coleseed...shall not be permitted to glean'. Only the pauper's right of appeal to a magistrate prevented most vestries from also using the withdrawal of poor relief to punish errant members of the labouring poor.[21]

Almost all these sanctions were applicable only if the accused was an inhabitant of the locality. If he was not the parish authorities might use the vagrancy or settlement laws to have him punished or removed, but the only other major informal sanction available was some form of communal violence. Joint action sometimes punished rural residents but the tradition of crowd action against thieves was strongest in London and the larger towns where it was much less likely that the victim and the immediate witnesses would know the offender. Throughout the eighteenth century urban crowds quite frequently punished criminals informally by ducking them in a pond or attacking them with dirt and stones, the main targets usually being young pickpockets. Although these punishments may have been preferable to commitment to gaol awaiting trial, they were no easy option for the accused. In 1785 a 16-year-old pickpocket died after a severe set of duckings in a pond off the Tottenham Court Road, and a year earlier another pickpocket had a heart attack after being taken from pump to pump for a succession of such punishments. 'The rage of the Street', as Defoe called it, paralleled in a more immediate form the pardoning procedures of the authorities. The crowd often held such offenders under water until they were almost drowned before finally releasing them, just as many capital convicts were reprieved only a short while before they were due to be hanged.[22]

[21] *Che.C.*, 15 Feb. 1788 for a threatened boycott of receiving blacksmiths. F. Cowe (ed.), *Wimbledon Vestry Minutes 1736, 1743–88* (Surrey Record Society, 1964), p. 72; Branch-Johnson, *Memorandoms*, p. 52; Walter, 'The Social Economy', pp. 100–5; King, 'Gleaners', p. 144; E.R.O., D/P 275/28/2; 152/25/2 and 18/8/3; *Che.C.*, 25 July 1788. Kussmaul, *The Autobiography*, p. 72.
[22] King, 'Gleaners', pp. 132–4. R. Shoemaker, 'The London "Mob" in the Early Eighteenth Century', *Journal of British Studies*, 26 (1987), 287–9; *I.J.*, 20 Dec. 1760, 11 June 1763; Beattie, *Crime*, p. 180; F. McLynn, *Crime and Punishment in Eighteenth-Century England* (London, 1989), p. 7; *The Times*, 11 Apr. 1785 and 24 May 1785.

If these different types of informal sanction or negotiated settlement were deemed inappropriate by the victim or the local community, they might still avoid indicting the offender by mobilizing other state institutions or legal structures. The recruitment of the accused into the armed forces was one important alternative. This was often done at the committal stage, but it was also an option used by victims without the formal involvement of a magistrate. James Oakes having proved the boy Pentuney guilty of several petty thefts 'immediately sent for his mother and his Uncle' and decided to 'send him to sea'. The Williamson letters record that after his servants had captured a highwayman in 1761 the victim resolved not to carry him before a justice. In the presence of a large crowd the accused, an 18-year-old apprentice, had knelt and begged for mercy, pleading necessity and the recent death of his father. When he found this story to be correct the victim allowed his servants to walk him to Westminster and have him 'put aboard a man of war'.[23] If the offender was already in the armed forces another cheap option was available—the military courts. The Colchester Association for the Prosecution of Felons was well aware of this. When a member informed the association in 1801 that he had 'detected a soldier with part of his property upon him and...wished to know whether he should give him up to the military law or prosecute him at the expense of the association' the committee quickly agreed to the military option.[24] In addition, as we have already seen, a variety of property appropriation cases could be taken to the civil, forest, or local admiralty courts rather than to the magistrates. Moreover, as Chapter 4 shows, many of those who did decide to take the accused before a magistrate were happy to resolve the case at that level and thus avoid having to prosecute in the major courts.

Although the immense range of discretionary powers available to victims in the early stages of the pretrial process were rarely limited by formal legal rulings, their decisions were not taken alone. Victims were subjected to a wide variety of pressures from other groups or individuals. Unfortunately, the diaries rarely record these interactions but at least four broad groups can be identified—the victim's family and friends; the accused, his family, and supporters; local community leaders and inhabitants; and the crowd present at the time of the crime. Some victims made wide consultations before making their decisions. In 1708 Blundell discussed Richard Ainsworth's prosecution on seven different occasions. Three times the accused asked for pardon. Once Blundell agreed to meet him and a mediator, a local blacksmith, for negotiations. Blundell also discussed the case with his lawyer and with some of the committing magistrates, but just before the assizes he had to consult other local gentry because he was still undecided 'whether it were better to try him or

---

[23] Fiske, *The Oakes Diaries*, p. 321; Manning, *The Williamson Letters*, pp. 76–7 (my thanks to John Styles for this reference).

[24] Colchester Borough Association Minute Book 1783–1809 (privately held by Jackson and Powis, Colchester); Steppler, 'British', pp. 867–77; *Che.C.*, 8 Mar. 1793.

compound with him'. The accused often used intermediaries to negotiate with the victim. In 1761 the Essex blacksmith John Coney sent a local weaver to beg the victim to forgive him. If the accused was young the parents were usually the main mediators. Poor parents might have to accept their son's enlistment but less drastic outcomes could also be negotiated. John Jubb's master agreed not to prosecute him when the apprentice's father 'made him satisfaction to the full value'.[25]

Women not infrequently took conciliatory roles in these negotiations. Having raided Woodforde's trees, his neighbour initially sent his wife to confess the fact and ask him not to be 'angry at it'. When the Essex offender William Page sent his wife to return the stolen goods and plead for mercy she wisely chose to negotiate with the woman of the household, for women also played a conciliatory role within victims' families. Enraged by a female servant who had stolen his beef, Blundell was ready to throw her out immediately, but his wife begged him to pardon her and he eventually did so. A year earlier Blundell had been presented with a petition by several local inhabitants including a clergyman and a painter asking him to drop another prosecution. Unfortunately he is virtually the only diarist who records the names of those involved in pretrial negotiations, but other records indicate that overseers, employers, constables, and vestrymen, as well as the clergy, acted as arbitrators or petitioners for pardon. Since the trial was a test of the victim's character as well as of the accused, the opinions of local interest groups were important and victims were often encouraged to settle matters informally by pressure from neighbours, parish officers, and local notables. Vestries concerned at the financial consequences and the accused's employers, who may not have wanted to lose their services, were particularly likely to favour informal resolutions. Finally, the victim sometimes had to deal directly with the crowd. In 1785 a London newspaper reported that having detected a coachman in stealing a lady's watch 'the populace were anxious to have the fellow prosecuted'. However, the victim, delighted at recovering her valuables, 'not only suffered him to go unpunished' but was also about to 'give him a gratuity for his dishonesty' before 'the mob' prevented her.[26]

Pretrial negotiations clearly took place in a wide variety of circumstances. In particular, when the victim first caught up with the accused he often had little physical assistance and was, therefore, in a weak bargaining position. The outcome of negotiations at this point largely depended on the physical forces ranged on either side. In 1799 an Essex victim was assaulted when he refused

---

[25] Bagley, *The Great Diurnal*, 1, pp. 174–82; E.R.O. Q/SBb 225/4; *Che.C.*, 26 Nov. 1784 for a prosecution avoided 'through the entreaties of friends'; Anon., *The Last Dying Speech of John Jubbs Executed at Chelmsford April 1714* (Norwich, 1714).

[26] Beresford, *Diary of a Country Parson*, 5, pp. 105–6; E.R.O. Q/SBb 379/82–3; Bagley, *The Great Diurnal*, 2, p. 21 and 112–4; K. Wrightson, 'Two Concepts of Order. Justices, Constables and Jurymen in Seventeenth-Century England', in Brewer and Styles, *An Ungovernable People*, pp. 31–2; Storch, 'Policing', p. 225; Branch-Johnson, *Memorandoms*, pp. 132, 144; *The Times*, 13 Sept. 1785.

the thief's offer to pay him 'anything he desired' for a stolen goose. When a Mersea Island farmer caught four fishermen stealing his poultry in 1762 he 'offered to forgive the offence on their paying him a fair market price' but when they refused he unwisely tried to arrest them on his own and was killed in the ensuing fight.[27] If the accused was either a settled member of the community or was successfully captured and returned to the victim's parish, negotiations became less hazardous and more controlled. What were the main factors that influenced the victim's decision about whether or not to prosecute at this point?

There can be little doubt about the major reason why so few victims chose to prosecute. As *The Times* observed, 'nine-tenths of the breaches against the laws escape detection from the trouble and charges consequent on prosecution'. At every stage of the process the victim had to sacrifice time, energy, and cash. The committal proceedings had to be attended by the victim and the witnesses, as well as by the accused, and the nearest active JP might be many miles away. Travelling to the trial was usually expensive, particularly in Essex where the most densely populated areas were a considerable distance from the assize and quarter sessions town of Chelmsford. During the sessions the exact time of the trial was unpredictable and several frustrating days were often spent waiting to be called. The victim had to pay expenses for both the witnesses and himself during this time. He was also expected to bear part of the administrative costs of the judicial system by paying various fees to its officials. John Beattie has estimated that most Surrey prosecutors faced expenses of between £1 and £3 and this accords well with the Essex evidence, although total costs could be considerably higher. As Chapter 3 indicates, an increasing number of prosecutors began to receive help with these expenses after 1750 but many continued to shoulder almost all the burden themselves; even when costs were paid by the court they were never overgenerous and rarely included the cost of apprehending and committing the accused.[28]

Faced with these disincentives the potential prosecutor had to be strongly motivated, but a number of other circumstances might undermine his resolve. Many were pessimistic about the likely outcome if they brought the case to trial. In Essex only about half the accused were convicted and many cases were lost on obscure points or poorly written indictments. Even if a conviction was obtained, the sanction applied might be light. In 1708 Blundell spent over £3 in prosecuting Richard Ainsworth but, although he was convicted, he was immediately released after being burnt in the hand. Even if the victim was sure

---

[27] E.R.O. Q/SBb 377/80. For similar assaults on victims, E.R.O. P/LWR 6 27 Aug. 1789 and Q/ SBb 196/15, 197/17; *I.J.*, 28 Aug. 1762.
[28] *The Times*, 5 Dec. 1785; Colquhoun, *Police*, p. 227; for the difficulties of long waiting periods, *P.P.* 1816, V, p. 211; Beattie, *Crime*, pp. 41–8. A sample of nine detailed bills submitted to the Essex quarter sessions (Q/SBb 201/25, 205/27–30, 269/38–40, 340/27) reveals three between £1 and £2, three between £2 and £3, three between £3 and £4. Some contemporaries believed £5 to £10 was more realistic, Ekirch, *Bound for America*, p. 29.

that the offender was guilty he might be very reluctant to prosecute unless the evidence was watertight, as James Oakes was in 1789, despite the fact that he was 'clear beyond all doubt' about the identity of the culprit.[29]

The other major disincentive to prosecution was fear—fear of the accused's response or fear of community disapproval. Even after he was arrested the accused could put pressure on the victim by threatening reprisals either by himself, if he were acquitted, or by his associates. In 1761 an Essex horse thief told his prosecutor that 'if he should live to come out of gaol again, he would do for him', and similar threats are recorded in other Essex cases. Witnesses also suffered problems. The northern Essex labourer Robert Challace, who was the key witness in the case against William Babin, was set on by both Babin's servant and his mother, who tried to stab him with a pitchfork. Property was equally at risk. In 1761 the *Ipswich Journal* reported that a mare had been killed and further reprisals threatened in order to intimidate those involved in detecting a local felon. Fear of counter-prosecution could also be an important weapon. Many of the middling sort regularly broke the turnpike, game, or swearing laws. If the accused was a local resident he might know enough about the victim to threaten a counter-prosecution which could result in a substantial fine or the loss of a valuable horse. In 1800, for example, the Essex gleaners struck back at a local farmer by having him fined for swearing profane oaths—a particularly useful form of prosecution because the size of the fine rose with the social status of the swearer. Victims might also be vulnerable to the threat of civil proceedings. To avoid counter-measures several Essex victims had to place advertisements in the *Chelmsford Chronicle* apologizing for wrongfully charging their neighbours with felony.[30]

Fear of community disapproval was another strong motive for the non-prosecution of the offender. It was hardly surprising that when the future assize judge Dudley Ryder had his pocket picked by a prostitute whom he had already paid for services rendered, he showed no inclination to prosecute. Victims who brought such cases were frequently humiliated by the eighteenth-century courts. Fanny Davis, a notorious Essex thief, avoided a highway robbery charge because the victim 'did not like to prosecute a poor weak woman lest he should meet with the contempt of the crowd and the laugh of the lawyers'.[31] Prosecutors might also be afraid of communal reactions if they obtained a capital conviction and the offender was hanged. The parliamentary reports of the early nineteenth century, with their highly selective use of testimony, probably overstressed this point, but some prosecutors were sub-

[29] Bagley, *The Great Diurnal*, pp. 182–3; Fiske, *The Oakes Diaries*, p. 260.
[30] E.R.O. Q/SBb 226/10, 322/58, 196/12–14, 197/17; *I.J.*, 6 June 1761. Hay, 'Prosecution', p. 357; King, 'Gleaners', p. 124; R. Burn, *The Justice of the Peace and Parish Officer* (London, 13th edn., 4 vols., 1776), 4, p. 267. *Che.C.*, 5 Oct. 1792 and 18 Dec. 1772.
[31] Matthews, *Diary of Dudley Ryder*; Anon., *An Authentic Account of the Celebrated Miss Fanny Davis* (1786), p. 36; *O.B.S.P.* (Dec. 1792), p. 121.

jected to communal sanctions in these circumstances and others undoubtedly had grave misgivings about the use of the death sentence against property offenders. Unless the prosecutor was a rich manufacturer or landowner subtle pressures could be applied by social and business contacts. Shopkeepers were particularly vulnerable. After reporting a shoplifting prosecution brought by a Colchester trader in 1790, *The Times* noted that many similar charges could be laid 'but the tradesmen are afraid of offending their best customers and quietly put up with the loss'.[32]

In rural areas the heaviest pressure against the formal prosecution of offenders came from the local ratepayers. As Sir Michael Foster noted, victims 'frequently choose rather to continue a pilfering fellow among them than to take the burden of wife and children'. In 1808 hedgebreakers with large families were said to 'carry on the trade with impunity as the farmers are not fond of providing entirely for a family of young children'. The logic of many farmers was roughly, as follows, 'I know (he) is a thief, he has robbed me. He robs us all in turn . . . However he has a large family. They cost us nothing now out of the rates but if we put him in prison . . . that would cost us a pretty deal.'[33]

Given these pressures, it is not surprising that so few diarists were willing to prosecute property offenders. However, the victim was not completely without assistance (Chapter 3) and there were a number of forces that pushed him or her towards prosecution. A simple desire to see the offender severely punished or to remove him from the community so that he could do no further harm obviously formed the basic motivation in many cases. In others the desire to retrieve the stolen goods may have encouraged the victim to involve officials who then made it difficult for him to back out once the offender was apprehended. The nature of the crime was very important. Small-scale pilfering might be tolerated for decades, but robbery or burglary with violence were much more likely to mobilize victims and communities into detecting and prosecuting the offender. Prosecution was also more likely in periods of particular anxiety about crime. When the Essex newspapers printed a wave of reports about crime in the Colchester area in 1765, victims seem to have temporarily lost their usual reluctance and initiated prosecutions on very flimsy evidence.[34] Victims who were members of particular interest groups, such as the oyster dredgers of eastern Essex, had a much higher propensity to

[32] R. McGowen, 'The Image of Justice and Reform of the Criminal Law in Early Nineteenth-Century England', *Buffalo Law Review*, 32 (1983), 112; Gatrell, *The Hanging Tree*, p. 102; *I.J.*, 27 Aug. 1763; D. Hay, 'Manufacturers and the Criminal Law in the Later Eighteenth Century. Crime and "Police" in South Staffordshire', in *Police and Policing. Past and Present Society Colloquium* (July 1983), 1–70; *The Times*, 29 Nov. 1790.

[33] Ekirch, *Bound for America*, p. 41; T. Batchelor, *General View of the Agriculture of Bedfordshire* (London, 1808), p. 609; *P.P.*, 1843, XII, p. 75.

[34] P. King, 'Newspaper Reporting, Prosecution Practice and Perceptions of Urban Crime. The Colchester Crime Wave of 1765', *Continuity and Change*, 2 (1987), 423–54.

prosccute if that group had decided to clamp down on a specific form of appropriation, and prosecution associations sometimes formed the nucleus of such attacks (Chapter 3).

In most theft cases the victim's decision was intimately tied up with the character, attitude, and previous behaviour of the accused. Strangers or vagrants were often more difficult to apprehend, but once captured they were more likely to be prosecuted. Woodforde kept a close eye on the activities of strangers and of the ten property appropriations recorded in his diary, the only one that ended in prosecution was committed by two 'idle fellows' previously unknown in the parish. If the accused was a local resident he was much less likely to be prosecuted if influential opinion within the community regarded him as a first offender with a previous good character. Pleas that this was the accused's first offence were something of a tradition in negotiations with the victim. In 1800 William Page's wife pleaded to a northern Essex alehousekeeper that 'she did not believe her husband had ever wronged any person before' and another Essex offender even begged forgiveness on the grounds that he had only stolen coal from the victim on one previous occasion. Offenders who could not make such claims were in a very weak bargaining position. Blundell's eventual decision to prosecute Richard Ainsworth, despite the latter's frequent entreaties, was almost certainly linked to the fact that Ainsworth had stolen from him before and been let off without formal prosecution.[35]

The diaries of men like Oakes, Woodforde, and Holland suggest that young offenders were also much more likely to be punished informally by verbal or physical chastisement; by dismissal from service; or by recruitment into the armed forces. As Hanway observed, 'in the case of young offenders . . . before they are brought to a magistrate, who it is imagined will order a commitment to Bridewell . . . every other expedient has first been tried which the authority of a parent or master can extend to'. If, like the 18-year-old apprentice whom Williamson refused to prosecute, a young offender could also claim poverty and the need to support a dependent family, he had every chance of avoiding indictment. The confessions of many older offenders contained hopeful references to the size of the offender's family, which was usually linked to a plea that 'it was his great poverty that drove him to it', and even if their own poor rates would not be affected, victims sometimes took a more lenient view if such claims proved to be genuine. Wealthier accused fell back on different tactics. After noting that a shoplifter 'of considerable fortune' had bought off her prosecutor, Holland recorded his disgust that 'money should be able to screen a person from justice'. Compounding was a lucrative and less damaging option for the victim, and many types of property offender would have found

[35] Beresford, *Diary of a Country Parson*, 2, pp. 61–2, 213; E.R.O. Q/SBb 379/82, 225/1, 378/81, 225/4; Bagley, *The Great Diurnal*, 1, pp. 96, 174.

it easier to negotiate an informal settlement if they had cash immediately available. Those with strong contacts in the intersecting circles of the local gentry, magistracy, and clergy might also have found it easier to avoid prosecution, as Henry Purefoy's hunting companions did in 1751, but the diaries also include cases in which respectable connections failed to save the offender from formal prosecution.[36]

The importance of the accused's character and connections can be more fully analysed from the records created at the trial and pardoning stages of the judicial process but one further aspect of the character of the accused was important in a subgroup of cases. Sometimes the accused was the potential prosecutor's enemy before the alleged crime was ever committed. It is impossible to calculate how many property crime accusations were brought to further personal conflicts rather than in a genuine attempt to bring an offender to justice, but the weak control that the law exercised over prosecutorial decisions left considerable scope for indictments designed to damage, terrorize, or fleece the accused. Unfortunately such prosecutions are difficult to identify in the formal court records, while diarists are unlikely to present their activities as malicious even if they were. However, from the fragmentary evidence available, it appears that the majority of these prosecutions did not revolve around property crime accusations but around cases involving assault or trespass. The Essex records also include allegations of malicious prosecution in cases involving seditious words and sodomy, while indictments and summary prosecutions against farmers and carriers for turnpike offences were fairly common. In the latter cases, as in summary prosecutions for game offences, the informant gained a substantial part of the proceeds if the accused was found guilty, and for this reason, as much as from malice, the Essex poor were not slow to accuse farmers and others of such offences.[37]

The apparently straightforward nature of the vast majority of theft indictments and depositions makes it difficult to calculate how frequently major court prosecutions were malicious. Accusations of indirect appropriation, which formed about 5 per cent of Essex indictments, may have been more prone to abuse. Innocent tradesmen could easily lay themselves open to charges of receiving, uttering counterfeit coin, or fraud but the court records rarely contain any positive evidence of malicious motives behind these prosecutions. Petitions for pardon not infrequently argued that the prosecutor had such motives but this may often have been a last desperate defence rather than an accurate reflection of the victim's attitudes. Malicious prosecutions in

---

[36] Fiske, *The Oakes Diaries*, p. 321; Beresford, *Diary of a Country Parson*, 5, p. 327; Ayres, *Paupers and Pig Killers*, p. 45 and p. 29; E.R.O. Q/SBb. 232/24; Manning, *The Williamson Letters*, pp. 76–7; J. Hanway, *The Defects of the Police* (London, 1775), p. 59; *London Chronicle*, 15 July 1762; Mitchell, *The Purefoy Letters*, pp. 160–5; Bagley, *The Great Diurnal*, 2, p. 21–3.

[37] Hay, 'Prosecution and Power'; Beattie, *Crime*, p. 38; King, 'Gleaners', pp. 135–6; *Che.C.*, 12 Mar. 1790; E.R.O. P/LWR 8, 27 Jan. 1790; P.R.O. S.P. 36/91/219; E.R.O. Q/SR 760.

property crime cases occasionally came to light through the Essex newspapers. The Colchester farmer John Ward, for example, was set up beautifully in 1786. Having been assaulted and had their gleaning sacks threatened the previous year, the gleaners hid a money box at the bottom of a bag of gleanings and then charged Ward with larceny when he removed it because they had gleaned without his permission. The farmer then found himself committed for trial, and the complex legal manoeuvrings he undertook to extricate himself from confinement cost him dearly. In the same year the *Chelmsford Chronicle* attacked the 'savage' farmer who had prosecuted an innocent sheep drover after several flocks became intermingled on the road to Smithfield. Other employees and servants may well have suffered similar problems and at least one other malicious prosecution came to light through the *Chelmsford Chronicle* in the late eighteenth century, but malice, revenge, and avarice almost certainly tainted only a small minority of Essex property crime indictments during this period.[38]

Faced by a wide spectrum of options, most victims were swayed in their decisions by several countervailing forces. The strongest currents—fear of financial loss, of revenge, or of communal disapproval—favoured informal resolution, but the victim was more likely to swim against those currents if the offence involved violence to persons or property, if anxieties about crime were already high, or if the community felt it was time to prevent the offender from doing further harm. Whether he was choosing between informal sanctions or between different types of formal indictment, the victim's perception of the character and background of the accused was crucial. Vagrants, 'idle fellows', and old offenders might arouse his anger. Pleas of youth or poverty might appeal to his humanity. Generous offers of compensation or the potential dependence of a family on the rates touched him more directly in his pocket. However, the impact of each of these forces also varied according to the wealth and social status of the victim. If so few victims chose to prosecute, did the small subgroup who propelled the accused into the formal judicial system come only from the wealthier social groups? Although no systematic information is available about victims in general, the recognizances taken at the committal hearing do give the occupation of the potential prosecutor and a more quantitative approach is therefore possible at this stage.

3. The Prosecutors

Who prosecuted crime in eighteenth-century England? In Essex the social status of prosecutors can be most systematically analysed by using the recognizances recorded in the quarter sessions minute books. Even these did not

---

[38] Hay, 'Prosecution and Power', p. 368; E.R.O. Q/SBb 330/9; P. R.O. H.O. 47/6; *Che.C.*, 6 Oct. 1786, 16 Mar. 1787, 17 July 1789; King, 'Gleaners', p. 124; *Che.C.*, 29 Dec. 1786, 6 and 13 Apr. 1770.

Table 2.2. Occupational Status of Prosecutors, Essex Quarter Sessions, 1760–1800, and Social Structure of the Essex Population

Occupation	(A) % in the total Essex Population	(B) % of Prosecutors for Felony	% of Prosecutors for Assault
1. Gentry	3	5.5	3.0
2. Professionals	2	1.8	0.8
3. Farmers, Yeomen, etc.	11.5	34.8	22.0
4. Tradesmen and Artisans	31.5	33.0	41.5
5. Maritime occupations	6.5	3.4	3.4
6. Husbandmen }	39.5	3.7	3.4
7. Labourers }		17.8	25.8
8. Paupers	6	—	—
Total numbers	40,000 Households	707 cases	238 cases

Notes:
A. Based on Brown *Essex at Work 1700–1815*, p. 108—occupational groupings of household heads in Essex 1723 and 1800. Group 4 includes artisans (20%), processing industries—brewing, milling etc. (3%), innkeeping, shopkeeping, and other commercial occupations (6.5%), and transport workers (2%). Group 7 includes farmworkers (36%) and non-agricultural labourers (3.5%).
B. Brown does not include singlewomen or servants. For the purposes of comparison singlewomen, military men, officials, and servants have been excluded from column B (i.e. about 8% of felony prosecutions and a slightly higher percentage of assaults). Wives were listed under the occupations of their husbands.
   Group 1 includes esquires; Group 2 clerics, surgeons, and schoolmasters; Group 3 farmers and yeomen; Group 4 includes all others given specific occupations from alehousekeeper to woolcomber. Within Group 4 innholders and victuallers represented 8.8% of both felony and assault prosecutors (alehousekeepers and publicans included); major food processors (bakers, butchers, millers, maltsters, brewers) 5.8 and 4.2%; blacksmiths and farriers 2.8 and 2.9; shopkeepers, grocers, and merchants 2.5% in both cases; building workers 3.7 and 5.9%. Group 6 includes husbandmen and gardeners.

Source: Essex Record Office Sessions Books. Q/Smg 19–28. 'Recognizances to appeared and prosecute'. Prosecutors whose occupations were not given were excluded (less than 10%).

include all prosecutors. Clerical procedures were not always watertight and some recognizances did not record the victim's occupation, while a few property crime victims brought 'voluntary bills' direct to the court and thus avoided being bound by recognizance.[39] However, if the diverse occupations in the recognizances are put into broad categories a clear pattern emerges (Table 2.2). Over one-third of the prosecutors bringing felony cases to the Essex quarter sessions, 1760–1800, were farmers or yeoman, exactly a third were tradesmen or artisans, and between one-fifth and one-sixth were

[39] Emsley, *Crime*, p. 144; Cottu, 'The Administration', p. 59. The core archives are the Sessions Minute Books. E.R.O. Q/SMg—these describe victims and witnesses separately after 1760 and enable prosecutors acting on behalf of others to be identified. For the reliability of the recognizances—J. Cockburn, 'Trial by the Book? Fact and Theory in the Criminal Process, 1558–1625', in J. Baker (ed.), *Legal Records and the Historian* (London, 1978), pp. 60–3; Hay 'Crime, Authority', p. 611.

labourers. Since the label 'husbandmen' appears, in Essex at least, to have been mainly given to servants in husbandry or others of similar status, the overall proportion of labouring men was nearly 22 per cent.[40] In assault cases two-fifths of prosecutors were tradesmen or artisans, over a quarter were labourers, and just over one-fifth were farmers. The gentry, maritime occupations, and professionals made up the remaining 10 per cent. (Table 2.2)

There are a number of problems with this kind of tabulation. The gentry's involvement might be underestimated because they may have been more likely to bring indictments without first being bound by recognizances. By adding information from indictments, which mention gentry status but never give the occupations of other victims, it can be calculated that at least 6.6 per cent of quarter sessions victims, 1782–98, were labelled as gentry and that 9.6 per cent of victims whose occupations are known were so described. However, the title of gentleman was becoming debased in this period. As Bailey's *Dictionary* pointed out in 1782, 'everyone will not make a gentleman that is vulgarly called so nowadays'. Tanners, vintners, potters, and theatre managers all felt free to use the title openly and these percentages therefore overestimate the proportion of prosecutors that came from the leisured landed élite. Victims tended to maximize the status description they gave themselves in these circumstances. James Wright of Rochford, for example, was described as an esquire in the court records but appears in the freeholder's books as a malster.[41]

The category of tradesmen and artisans in Table 2.2 is also highly problematic. The majority of these prosecutors were in trades that required considerable capital, such as innkeeping, shopkeeping, or food processing, but many others followed occupations like bricklayer or looker that required virtually no investment. The variable relationship between occupational description and wealth or status causes many problems here. The recognizances took no account of the fundamental status divisions that existed in many trades. Those labelled as carpenter or blacksmith, for example, would include apprentices, semi-skilled workers with few hopes of ever becoming masters, and wealthy master artisans employing several workers. About one-fifth of the late eighteenth-century Essex poor were journeymen artisans working for wages that were little higher than a labourer's,[42] but in Table 2.2 they have

---

[40] For men described as husbandmen in indictments who are clearly servants in husbandry or labourers in the more detailed depositions, E.R.O. Q/SBb 242/21 or 268/39. Literacy levels amongst husbandmen were much closer to those of servants than they were to those of farmers, King, 'Crime, Law', p. 189.

[41] N. Bailey, *An Universal Etymological English Dictionary* (London, 1782); P. Corfield, 'Class by Name and Number in Eighteenth-Century Britain', *History*, 72 (1987), 43; E.R.O. Q/SMg 24, Q/RJ 1/8.

[42] In both of the rural Essex communities where information is available (Ashdon and Ardleigh) 19 per cent of male household heads registered as in need of assistance in the harvest crises of 1795–1801 were artisans. E.R.O. D/P 18/18/2; T. Sokoll, *Household and Family among the Poor. The Case of Two Essex Communities in the Late Eighteenth and Early Nineteenth Centuries* (Bochum, 1993); P. King, 'Pauper Inventories

been included by default among the middling sort under the umbrella label of tradesmen and artisans. Some artisans would have been worse off than the labourers. Of Essex prosecutors 1 per cent were weavers—a deeply impoverished occupation in Essex by the later eighteenth century. Quite a high proportion of artisan prosecutors followed occupations of intermediate status such as carpenter, cordwainer, bricklayer, or wheelwright, in which the majority of workers owned little capital; 13 per cent of the Ashdon poor relieved in 1801 were from these four trades which contributed nearly 5 per cent of felony prosecutors. Even the more highly capitalized ironworking trades, which accounted for a further 3 per cent of prosecutors, included victims who were journeymen or apprentices. In 1767, for example, the quarter sessions was asked to defray the prosecution expenses of James Merriday because he was 'a journeyman blacksmith'.[43] If literacy is any guide to whether or not artisan prosecutors were masters rather than journeymen, Merriday was not alone. Over a third of artisan prosecutors could not sign their names. Since widows and single women, a particularly lowly paid and economically vulnerable group, were also excluded from Table 2.2, it appears that at least a quarter of Essex quarter sessions prosecutors were members of the labouring poor.[44]

Quarter sessions depositions provide deeper if less systematic insights into the status of both victim and accused. A random sample of all the surviving quarter sessions' informations of 1761 and 1762, for example, reveals the following alleged incidents: a woolcomber whose coal was stolen by a weaver's wife; a blacksmith taking coal from a miller; a labourer accusing a 'travelling woman' of removing money from his pockets while she was embracing him in a field; a labourer charging a workmate with stealing his waistcoat and other clothing; two labourers and a widow who took, cooked, and ate a farmer's fowls; a workhouse resident whose clothing had been taken by a fellow inmate; a tailor whose coal had been appropriated by a labourer; and a farmer who committed one of his employees to trial for stealing his oats. By using all the surviving depositions for twenty-six sample years between 1748 and 1800 the occupational breakdown of prosecutors found in the recognizances is confirmed and a more thorough, if still very approximate, picture of victim/ accused relationships can be developed (Table 2.3). In most of the quarter sessions prosecutions brought by farmers, tradesmen, or artisans the accused was a labourer or servant, although a sizeable minority were directed against

---

and the Material Lives of the Poor in the Eighteenth and Nineteenth Centuries', in T. Hitchcock, P. King, and P. Sharpe (eds.), *Chronicling Poverty. The Voices and Strategies of the English Poor 1640–1840* (London, 1997), p. 168.

[43] E.R.O. D/P 18/18/2; Q/SBb 248/7; Beattie, *Crime*, pp. 194–5.

[44] Literacy figures based on marks or signatures in the deposition sample used for Table 2.3. For literacy rates by occupation see King, 'Crime, Law', p. 189. Single women and widows constituted 4.5 per cent of felony and 10.3 per cent of assault prosecutors 1760–99.

Table 2.3. Victim/Accused Relationships Essex Quarter Sessions 1748–1800

Victim	Accused Gent	Prof.	Farmer	Tr. and art	Marit.	Hubs.	Lab. & se.	Total	% of victims
Gentry	—	—	—	4	—	—	7	11	7.1
Professionals	—	—	—	—	—	1	1	2	1.3
Farmers	—	—	—	5	—	6	49	60	38.7
Tradesmen and artisans	—	—	—	17	—	—	32	49	31.6
Maritime occupations	—	—	—	1	2	—	—	3	1.9
Husbandmen	—	—	—	—	—	—	4	4	2.6
Labourers and servants	—	—	—	3	1	1	21	26	16.8
Total	—	—	—	30	3	8	114	155	
% of all accused	—	—	—	19.3	1.9	5.2	73.5	99.9	

Notes: E.R.O/ Q/SBb 180–380 (1748–1800). All surviving depositions for a sample of twenty-six years, 1748–9, 1754–65, 1771–4, 1783–6, 1792–4, 1800. Excluding cases where the occupations of either the accused or the victim is unknown. Single females with no occupation excluded. Wives included if the occupation of the husband is given. Indictments and recognizances were used where possible to fill in gaps. Fraud and misdemeanour excluded.

other artisans or commercial men. Labourers occasionally indicted artisans but most of their prosecutions were directed against men of roughly similar status.

How different was the picture at the assizes? Since cases involving the theft of expensive animals or large amounts of money and valuables were always heard at the assizes, the wealthier and more socially prestigious sections of the population may have prosecuted there rather more often than at the quarter sessions. Unfortunately neither the recognizances nor the depositions of the Essex assizes have survived, but the limited evidence available does not suggest that the occupational structure of assizes prosecutors would have been drastically different from that found at the quarter sessions. The assize agenda books gave the victim the title of 'esquire' in less than one case in twenty-five and, even allowing for unsystematic recording and the need to use a wider definition of gentry status, it is unlikely that members of the patrician élite were responsible for a substantial proportion of assizes prosecutions. Rich and poor alike suffered from break-ins, robberies, pickpocketing, and the theft of valuables or savings, and until the late 1780s all Essex prosecutors who valued the stolen goods at more than 1 shilling (the equivalent of one-tenth of a labourer's average weekly wage) had to prosecute at the assizes. The sixteen prosecutors whose occupations are identified in the 1774 Essex assize 'proceedings' included four farmers, three shopkeepers, two victuallers, two artisans, an apprentice, a labouring man, a 'poor servant', a prostitute and a gentleman hop grower. Between 1782 and 1798 the forty-six recognizances transferred to the assizes after originally being registered at the quarter sessions followed a similar pattern: 6 per cent of these prosecutors were labelled gentlemen, 46 per cent were farmers, 28 per cent were tradesmen or artisans, 17 per cent were husbandmen or labourers.[45]

How do the Essex quarter sessions prosecutors compare with those of other counties such as Staffordshire, Somerset, Surrey, Berkshire, or Bedfordshire? Although historians have not always grouped occupations in the same way, a common pattern is discernible. In most counties the usual figure for the gentry was between 5 and 7 per cent, and only in Staffordshire do gentry and professionals appear to have constituted more than 10 per cent of felony prosecutors. Unskilled labourers and husbandmen provided between 18 and 22 per cent of prosecutors with known occupations in the three predominantly rural counties, but a slightly lower proportion in counties with large industrial and urban sectors, possibly because it is less easy to identify unskilled workers within the complex web of urban artisan trades. The middling strata dominated the prosecution process in every county, representing between two-thirds and three-quarters of prosecutors. However, the key occupations within this group varied greatly. In rural counties like Somerset and Essex farmers were nearly as important as tradesmen and artisans. In Surrey, where urban prosecutions dominated, only one prosecutor in twelve was a farmer, while two-thirds were tradesmen or artisans—merchants, shopkeepers, and victuallers being especially prominent.[46]

When the occupational status of quarter sessions prosecutors is compared with figures on the Essex population as a whole (Table 2.2) farmers emerge as by far the most active group. Only one-eighth of the population were farmers but they initiated 35 per cent of felony prosecutions. The gentry and clergy played a relatively minor role, forming only a slightly higher proportion of prosecutors than they did of the population as a whole. The involvement of tradesmen and artisans was roughly proportionate to their numbers in the population and labourers, although they appear in considerable numbers, were not as active overall as the other main groups. It is not difficult to explain the relative dominance of the middling sort among prosecutors for theft. They were more likely to have the resources available to mount a prosecution and they exposed their property to additional risks by employing servants. Farmers, traders, and master artisans were not only vulnerable to the theft of personal and household goods but might also lose goods or tools either stored,

[45] *The Whole Proceedings . . . Essex . . . March 1774*; P. R.O. Assi/31/12–18. Transferred prosecutors were not a typical sample as the charges were mainly for grand larceny. However, poorer prosecutors did not confine themselves to grand larceny indictments. In 1774, for example, two labouring prosecutors brought housebreaking indictments. Hay, 'Crime Authority', pp. 79, 154. About 19 per cent of victims at the Staffordshire assizes and quarter sessions were labouring men.

[46] Pole, 'Crime', p. 140; Hay 'Crime, Authority', pp. 395–7; Emsley, *Crime*, p. 166; Beattie, *Crime*, p. 193; all figures calculated after excluding prosecutors whose occupations are unknown or given as widow, spinster, or parish official. A broadly similar pattern is seen in R. Williams, 'Crime and the Rural Community in Eighteenth-Century Berkshire 1740–1789' (Ph.D. Reading, 1985), p. 302.

in use, or exposed for sale as part of their business. Moreover as Britain's commercial wealth grew in the eighteenth century the goods owned by these groups became increasingly numerous and luxurious, offering ever more tempting targets to employees and burglars alike. Farmers were particularly vulnerable because their animals, crops, and equipment were widely spread and difficult to protect. So too were innkeepers and victuallers, whose houses and goods were in constant and often unsupervised use by the public, which helps to explain why victuallers alone brought more prosecutions than the gentry and clergy together.[47]

It is less easy to explain the substantial prosecuting role played by the labouring poor. Given the expense and trouble that a prosecution involved, it is remarkable that at least a quarter of recognizances in property crime cases and an even higher percentage in assault-related prosecutions indicate that the victim was a member of the labouring poor. As will be seen in the next section, the poor's fairly high profile among those under recognizance to prosecute may be partly explained by their different perceptions of what constituted a prosecution. Some poorer prosecutors were certainly encouraged by the financial help they received from the courts and elsewhere (Chapter 3). However, no expenses were paid in assault cases and labourers were still extensively involved in instigating these prosecutions. More important perhaps, prospective prosecutors experienced few significant technical barriers in bringing a property crime indictment. Prosecutors certainly did not need to be literate. One-third of all Essex quarter sessions' prosecutors could not sign their names, and only 17 per cent of labouring prosecutors did so.[48]

It is easy to underestimate the vulnerability of labouring families not only to the fraudulent practices of the powerful or to thefts when away from home, as Mayett, Saxby, and Hutton's autobiographies illustrate, but also to more everyday thefts from their homes and gardens. Tools left unguarded in fields and clothes hung out to dry on wayside hedges were easy targets. Labourers' dwellings and outhouses were frequently unprotected and frail. The rhetoric of the Essex assize judges, who stressed the need to safeguard the dwellings of the poor from housebreakers because they 'are obliged to leave them under no protection', was for once matched in reality by the depositions of Essex labourers such as James Chapman, whose house was broken into in 1748 'while he was gone to harvest work' and his wife and children were gleaning.[49] It should not be assumed that most labouring families had insufficient household goods to be worth robbing. Even the poorest elements within those

[47] L. Wetherill, 'Consumer Behaviour and Social Status in England 1660–1750', *Continuity and Change*, I (1986), 191–216; N. McKendrick, J. Brewer, and J. Plumb, *The Birth of a Consumer Society. The Commercialisation of Eighteenth-Century England* (London, 1982).

[48] Mark or signature is only a signpost to relative levels of literacy but 32.7 per cent of prosecutors lacked such skills. King, 'Crime, Law', p. 189.

[49] *Che.C.*, 8 Aug. 1800; E.R.O. Q/SBb 182/20.

labelled as labourers contained many families with substantial collections of household goods. Essex pauper inventories indicate that between a quarter and a half owned looking glasses, tea utensils, candlesticks, and chests of drawers, for example, while most possessed feather beds, sheets, bellows, and warming pans. Meagre though their resources were compared to the burgeoning wealth of the middling sort and the luxurious excesses of the gentry élite, the poorer elements of the community knew each other's houses, possessions, and habits well and it was often easier for the poor to prey on each other than to steal from the houses of the better off. Faced by the apparently minor nature of the goods involved, it is important to remember that the loss of a goose from the common, a hoe from the garden, or a skip of bees from the yard (to quote three 1790s examples) might seriously upset the delicately balanced makeshift economies of some labouring families.[50] They may therefore have been more likely to act against petty thieves because the loss was of much greater significance to them than it would have been to their richer neighbours. The theft of clothes, tools, food, fowls, or household goods from such families certainly lay behind about a fifth of Essex quarter sessions prosecutions.

Without systematic victim surveys it is impossible to be sure whether labouring victims had roughly the same propensity to prosecute as the middling sort or the gentry, but it remains possible that labourers and wage-earning artisans were about as well represented among prosecutors as they were among victims. Even if they were not it is evident that by this period the labouring poor did not meet the law only as criminal sanction. They made extensive use of the courts as prosecutors and they were able to exercise the vast discretionary powers available to victims in property crime cases. All social groups could not use the law with equal freedom and the middling sort used it in a greater range of circumstances than other groups, but within certain constraints the law in relation to property crime was a resource available to and used by almost every group in eighteenth-century society. Historians have sometimes been tempted to move from this type of evidence towards broader conclusions about the extent to which the labouring poor accepted 'the legitimacy of the criminal law'. However, the complex ways that the different groups in eighteenth-century society experienced and thought about the law cannot be discussed on the basis of prosecutors' occupations alone (see Chapter 11). The prosecution process meant different things to different groups and was used by them in different ways, as an examination of victims' decisions between the committal proceedings and the trial indicates.

4. Prosecutors' Discretion between Committal and Trial

The victim's choices were not exhausted when he took the offender before a JP. The discretionary nature of magistrates' pre-committal hearings offered

---

[50] P. King, 'Pauper Inventories', pp. 162–5; E.R.O. Q/SBb 349/54, 347/55–8, 354/56.

further possibilities for negotiation (Chapter 4). Moreover, those hearings did not commit the offender to a particular charge. Few recognizances specified the exact nature of the offence and, as Cottu noted, prosecutors were often involved in modifying the severity of the law by 'diminishing the value ... of the thing stolen and ... omitting the mention of any aggravating circumstances, such as committing the crime in the night, or making forcible entry'. Several Essex quarter sessions depositions describe housebreakings that were eventually indicted only as petty larceny, and if the offender was young, assize prosecutors often chose to indict simply for housebreaking rather than for burglary (Chapter 6). Prosecutors were not always motivated by humanity in downgrading the charge. Victims from boroughs such as Colchester showed a predilection for petty larceny charges because those indictments could be tried at the local borough court, thus saving them a long and expensive sojourn in Chelmsford. Whatever their motives, however, Essex prosecutors seem to have experienced few constraints in choosing the offence named in the indictment and therefore the range of sanctions imposed if a conviction was obtained.[51]

In other ways, once the offender had been committed to gaol awaiting trial, the prosecutor's position appeared to change. Coercion was now applied and the victim would usually be bound by recognizance to appear and prosecute on pain of forfeiting a large sum if he or she failed to do so. Langbein has therefore suggested that the recognizance transformed the prosecutor's role 'from option to obligation' and that the fear of being fined terrorized many poor prosecutors, thus limiting their discretion. However, in practice the assize judges and quarter sessions bench, who decided whether or not prosecutors should be punished for failing to turn up, usually took a lenient view, thus giving the victim considerable leeway. In twelve sample years from the period 1765–87, twenty-eight of the 227 prosecutors bound by recognizance to appear at the Essex quarter sessions never brought an indictment.[52] Two of these were prevented from doing so by the death of the accused, but of the remaining twenty-six only two were disciplined by having their recognizances estreated. Between 1755 and 1786 the Estreat Books record only five property crime prosecutors and one witness suffering a similar fate, although more than 700 theft prosecutions were brought to the quarter sessions in that period. Thus, while about 10 per cent of prosecutors failed to bring indictments, less than 1 per cent were estreated. At the assizes 8 per cent of the prisoners in the gaol

<hr/>

[51] Cottu, 'The Administration', p. 17; E.R.O. Q/SBb 224/24, 182/16 and 20; D. Hay, 'Controlling the English Prosecutor', *Osgoode Hall Law Journal*, 21 (1983); P. King 'Urban Crime Rates and Borough Courts in Eighteenth-Century Essex', *Essex Journal. A Review of Archaeology and Local History*, 22 (1987), 39–42.

[52] J. Langbein, *Prosecuting Crime in the Renaissance. England, Germany, France* (Cambridge, Mass., 1974), p. 35; Langbein, 'Albion's Fatal Flaws', p. 104; E.R.O. Q/SMg 19–24 Oct. 1764 to July 1774, Oct. 1786, and Oct. 1788. Recognizances to prosecute were checked against indictments. Not found indictments usually survive but if a few did not the number of delinquent prosecutors would be reduced.

calendars were eventually discharged by proclamation 'because no prosecutor had appeared'.[53]

Why did nearly a tenth of Essex prosecutors and a similar proportion of Surrey ones fail to fulfil the conditions of their recognizances? The death or illness of the prosecutor, a key witness, or the accused may account for some of these cases, as may genuine failures of memory, but in most the victim seems to have avoided bringing the prosecution either by not turning up and deliberately risking having his recognizances estreated or by persuading the magistrates to let him drop the case. The courts allowed a large number of assault and misdemeanour cases to be settled without indictments being brought and in a small but significant number of felony proceedings they seem to have shown a similar flexibility.[54] They did so because they found themselves in a quandary. In property crime cases the accused was rarely bailed and usually endured many weeks in prison, an outcome that was manifestly unjust if they were never brought to trial. However, if the recognizances were estreated the prosecutor became liable to a fine of £10, £20, or even £40, and unless he was fairly wealthy he could find himself confined in a debtors' prison for a long period. Strict enforcement might therefore discourage other victims from initiating committal proceedings and thus undermine the authorities' expensive attempts to persuade more victims to prosecute. By 1764, during a period of increased anxiety about crime following the end of the Seven Years War, Parliament was so concerned about the imprisonment of 'ignorant people' in these circumstances that it passed an act under which a victim estreated and liable to imprisonment for no other crime than a failure to prosecute at the quarter sessions or assizes could henceforward petition for a discharge at a nominal cost. The next year the Essex bench changed its procedure in the prosecutor's favour, passing an order 'that no recognizances be estreated but what have been particularly directed so to be'.[55] Since such particular directions were only issued against property crime prosecutors once or twice a decade in this period many victims remained in the driving seat between committal and trial, although the journey was becoming increasingly risky for those who wanted to keep their options open.

In Essex it was the poor who were most likely to take such risks. When the quarter sessions recognizances are compared with the indictments that were eventually brought to the grand jury, a clear pattern emerges. Virtually no gentry, clergy, or professionals failed to bring an indictment once bound over to do so and only 2 per cent of farmers defaulted, but more than 10 per cent of

[53] Q/SPe 2/2–3, 'Estreat Books'. For the assize figures see P.R.O. Assi 31/10, 15–18 based on a sample of twenty sessions 1772–1800 in which the reasons for the prisoner being discharged by proclamation are given.

[54] J. Beattie, 'Crime and the Courts in Surrey 1736–1753', in J. Cockburn (ed.), *Crime in England 1550–1800* (London, 1977), p. 162; for pleas of illness E.R.O. Q/SBb 227/3, 340/29.

[55] Burn, *The Justice* (1776), 4, pp. 61–2; E.R.O. Q/SMg 20; for fears that victims' concerns about their recognizances might discourage prosecutions, Shoemaker, *Prosecution*, p. 115.

tradesmen and artisans and nearly a quarter of labourers and husbandmen disappear from the records between the taking of their recognizance and the grand jury hearing. It appears that poorer victims very often abandoned their prosecutions whereas richer ones did not.[56] Why? Poorer prosecutors may have found it more difficult to build a watertight case and have therefore been more easily persuaded to abandon the prosecution. The poor would rarely have been able to spare time or money to gather evidence, and many of the perishable items stolen from them were not distinctive enough to be positively identified. When the Essex labourer George Crab accused Mary Broad of stealing a peck of flour, half a loaf of bread, and some butter from his house, she claimed she had just bought them and, although the local shopkeeper refuted her testimony, Crab appears to have abandoned the prosecution after the committal hearing, for no indictment was ever brought. Labouring prosecutors and witnesses may also have been more easily bought off or intimidated. In 1791, for example, a prospective prosecutor wrote to the Essex quarter sessions explaining that an 'indictment could not be brought before the court' because the key witness, a fellow workman of the accused, refused to give evidence. Some of these aborted proceedings may have been started purely from malice or avarice, but malicious prosecutions were not confined to the poor alone and Hay has recently argued that such prosecutions were usually brought by middling men.[57] More important perhaps the authorities' willingness to fudge the issue if the errant prosecutor was poor may have opened up another means by which the poor could mould the judicial process to their own needs.

From the prosecutor's point of view, the committal of the accused for a period of several months awaiting trial often constituted a sufficient sanction in itself. The Essex records certainly contain references to prosecutors recommending convicted offenders to the mercy of the court because they had 'suffered a long confinement' before the trial.[58] Committal followed by non-prosecution would allow a labouring family to impose a similar sanction for minor thefts of food, coal, or fowls as summary legislation already allowed farmers and gentry to inflict on game offenders and wood or vegetable thieves. Moreover, taking the offender to a local committal hearing involved the same relatively small expenditure of time and energy as a summary trial. Of course, using an aborted prosecution of this sort to punish an offender was

[56] Based on the period 1782–98, using only those cases when the victim's occupation is known from recognizances or in the case of gentry prosecutors from indictments also. E.R.O. Q/SMg 23–27, Q/SR 827–904. To quote one example, Q/SMg 26, Q/SBb 346/46, the basketweaver Richard Perry was imprisoned for over two months awaiting trial for stealing a labourer's feather bed. No indictment was ever brought and he was 'discharged'.

[57] E.R.O. Q/SBb 198/4; E.R.O. Q/SBb 347/39 and 46; Colquhoun, *Police*, p. 225; Hay, 'Prosecution and Power', p. 368.

[58] E.R.O. D/DEL L4. Prisoners awaiting trial at the assizes could wait up to seven months, those tried at quarter sessions up to three months.

much more problematic than a summary hearing. Labouring prosecutors were occasionally estreated, and the quarter sessions minute books sometimes record that others were 'written to', warned, or reprimanded. However, after 1764 the impoverished prospective prosecutor had less to lose and even those whose recognizances were estreated may have escaped with a relatively small penalty.[59] Each year the quarter sessions bench appears to have been prepared to let two or three recognizances be broken hoping, perhaps, that by reserving the ultimate sanction of estreating for a few obvious cases of abuse they could prevent too many other prosecutors from taking up this option without frightening most victims away from prosecuting altogether. Although the court's role in this process remains obscure, it appears that a small group of poorer victims approached the idea of prosecution in a rather different way to the élite, and created in the process another semi-informal means of punishing property offenders without actually indicting them.

As always with pretrial processes there is more darkness than light; more silences than explanations; more anecdotal evidence than systematic data. However, despite the patchwork of sources it has been necessary to refer to, this attempt to reconstruct the interactions of victims, offenders, and local communities during the pretrial part of the judicial process has highlighted not only the vast discretionary powers available to victims and the broad cross-section of eighteenth-century society that used those powers but also the delicate balance that the authorities had to maintain. On the one hand they wanted to reinforce the legal rulings designed to ensure both that offenders were prosecuted and that victims did not abuse the law and incarcerate untried men and women unnecessarily. On the other hand they needed to encourage victims to get involved in the judicial process, which made it difficult to punish them for compounding, lessening the charge against the accused, or breaking the terms of their recognizances. As so often in eighteenth-century society, the authorities defined the outer limits beyond which victims' discretionary choices could not go, but within those very broad boundaries there was immense room for various groups to shape pretrial negotiations and sanctions in ways that met their own needs, problems, and perspectives.

[59] E.R.O. Q/SMg 27 12 July 1796, Sarah Hurlock was bound to appear and prosecute 'on pain of imprisonment', the only reference I have found to a warning like this. Burn, *The Justice*, (1776) 4, pp. 61–2 indicates a £1 penalty to be likely.

3

Resources Available to Victims: Public Funding, Prosecution Associations, Print, and Policing

Victims of property appropriation in the eighteenth century did not have to rely solely on their own resources in order to detect, apprehend, and prosecute offenders. They were often able to use the physical, financial, and informational resources provided by public funding and statutory incentives, by prosecution associations, by the printed media, by neighbours and friends, and by public or private policing networks. Some of these resources were available whatever the victim's wealth or status; others were not. Some cost money; others provided it. To understand the decisions that were made during the pretrial stages of the accused's journey towards formal prosecution it is necessary to ask several questions about these resources. Who decided what assistance would be given, and who was responsible for giving it? How helpful were the people and material resources made available, and what effect did they have on detection and prosecution rates? Which social groups found it easiest to mobilize these resources, and to what extent did using them place restraints upon the victim's discretionary powers? The answers to these questions are complex because the support mechanisms provided for victims by local parishes, by the central state, by voluntary associations, and by entrepreneurs such as printers and thieftakers changed rapidly between 1740 and 1820.

1. Public Funding and Statutory Incentives to Prosecution

Contemporaries were well aware of the need to overcome victims' disinclinations to prosecute. 'It would tend much to the furtherance of justice', one pointed out, 'if a provision was made for destroying the expense attending the prosecution of criminals. The loss of time in this business is more than many decent people can bear.' Although Henry Fielding described potential prosecutors as absurdly fearful and delicate, infamously indolent and avaricious and erroneously tenderhearted, he also pointed out that many were too poor to afford the time and expense involved, and recommended that their costs should be defrayed from county or national funds. If prosecuting crime in the eighteenth century was not normally an easy or rewarding task, many felt that the state must try to make it so. Apart from offering immunity to offenders who impeached their accomplices, the central authorities' attempts to provide counter-incentives that would encourage victims to prosecute took three main forms. Before Fielding's time those who successfully prosecuted major offenders were offered financial rewards or lifelong exemption from having to perform onerous parish offices via a 'Tyburn Ticket'. After 1752 this was supplemented by refunding the prosecution expenses of certain categories of victims and witnesses. The reward system remained an important plank of judicial policy throughout this period. From the late seventeenth century onwards a patchwork of parliamentary rewards for major offences developed in the same *ad hoc* fashion as the capital statutes themselves. By 1750 the capital conviction of a highway robber, coin counterfeiter, or housebreaker carried a £40 reward, and that of a sheep or cattle thief was worth £10, but other capital offences, such as stealing from a dwelling house, carried no rewards. For horse theft and a small number of other capital crimes the only recompense was a Tyburn Ticket, the value of which varied according to local circumstances. The system was far from comprehensive. During the period 1750–99 only 16 per cent of Essex assize prosecutors obtained rewards and a further 4 per cent were eligible for a Tyburn Ticket. Under the judge's direction rewards were shared out between prosecutor, witnesses, and those who had helped to take the offender. In Essex most were split between three, four, or five recipients, and the prosecutor usually took at least a quarter of the reward, but in complex cases a dozen individuals were sometimes given a share.[1]

The reward system was heavily criticized in this period. Using avarice to overcome inertia created many problems. 'Blood money' scandals gave the impression that innocent men were frequently being 'sworn away' for the sake of the rewards. Law-enforcement officers and private thieftakers were accused of ignoring minor offenders until they 'weighed forty pounds'.[2] If the system encouraged some victims to prosecute, others may have deliberately avoided involvement with an aspect of the judicial system that many considered odious. The practice of allowing accomplices to gain immunity from prosecu-

---

[1] *The Times*, 15 July 1785; H. Fielding, *Enquiry into the Causes of the Late Increase of Robbers* (1751), in W. Henley (ed.), *The Complete Works of Henry Fielding* (New York, 1902), 13, pp. 109–12; Beattie, *Crime*, pp. 50–5 on the occasional rewards offered by specific proclamations; Radzinowicz, *A History*, 2, pp. 57–111; Colquhoun, *Police*, pp. 202–3; *P.P.*, 1816, V, 224–5; although each Tyburn Ticket was valued by Colquhoun at £15 to £30, in some areas its real value was much lower, R. Paley, 'Thief-Takers in London in the Age of the McDaniel Gang *c.*1745–1754', in Hay and Snyder (eds.), *Policing*, pp. 317–18. Essex Assizes 1784 to Lent 1788, 53% of rewards were shared between three and five recipients, 26% between six and nine, 11% between ten or more. P.R.O. Assi. 34/43–44. For distribution criteria, see Sir Dudley Ryder's Assize Diary, pp. 24–8. Harrowby Manuscripts, Sandon Hall (I am grateful to John Langbein for making available a typescript; page numbers are from that document).

[2] J. Langbein, 'Shaping the Eighteenth-Century Criminal Trial. A View from the Ryder Sources', *University of Chicago Law Review*, 50 (1983), 106–14; *Parliamentary History*, XXV, col. 893; *P.P.*, 1817, VII, 222–3; *P.P.*, 1816, V, 214.

tion by turning King's evidence exacerbated the problems raised by rewards. Unfortunately it was also extremely useful. Burn felt that without crown witnesses, 'it would be generally impossible to find evidence to convict the greatest offenders'. Turning King's evidence was a risky business. Several Essex offenders made detailed confessions only to find that one of their accomplices had beaten them to it and that their own confession was then used against them. Nevertheless more than 3 per cent of those awaiting trial were crown witnesses and, since many were responsible for the arrest of several accomplices, a significant proportion of the Essex accused faced evidence from their fellow offenders. However, the frequent appearance of accomplices swearing away the lives of others in order to gain a pardon, and of witnesses with very strong financial interests in a conviction did not necessarily increase the number of successful prosecutors. Juries' verdicts and judges' attitudes to the way evidence was presented probably moved in favour of the prisoner as the dangers of such practices became apparent.[3]

The reimbursement of prosecutors' costs by the courts was less counter-productive. While Tyburn Tickets and rewards were given automatically on conviction, the expenses payments made under a series of acts beginning in 1752 were discretionary. The court controlled both the amount given and the number of prosecutors to whom costs were allowed. Theoretically between 1752 and 1778 payment could only be made on conviction but these legal constraints were not adhered to (Table 3.1). A quarter of the Essex assize prosecutors receiving expenses in the early 1770s had failed to get a conviction and some had had their indictments 'not found' by the grand jury.[4] The 1778 act, which granted the courts the right to pay expenses whether the accused was found guilty or not, was therefore codifying existing practice, but this does not mean that it was without influence. A much larger proportion of unsuccessful prosecutors was granted costs in the late 1780s than had been the case fifteen years earlier (Table 3.1). The Essex courts clearly responded to statutory developments—the two main periods when the proportion of Essex prosecutors receiving expenses showed a sustained increase were 1752–67 and 1778–90 (Figure. 3.1). However, recorded crime rates were also important. The policies of the quarter sessions bench and the assize judges did not always move exactly in unison but both responded to lengthening gaol calendars after the American war by increasing the proportion of prosecutors allowed expenses. Since a further one-sixth of assize prosecutors received rewards but were, for that reason, usually excluded from receiving expenses payments, more than

---

[3] Burn, *The Justice* (1766), I, p. 477; Langbein, 'Shaping', pp. 84–105; for an Essex example '*Whole Proceedings . . . Essex . . . March 1774*', p. 5. In a sample of twenty Essex Assizes 1772–1800, 3.4% of offenders held awaiting trial were crown witnesses. In the quarter sessions gaol calendars 1765–70 and 1787–9, the figure was 3.0%. Trial reports and depositions suggest this was an underestimate (see Table 2.1); Beattie, *Crime*, pp. 366–9; Langbein, 'Shaping', p. 133.

[4] For the statutory background, Radzinowicz, *History*, 2, pp. 76–7. Surrey courts followed a similar pattern, Beattie, *Crime*, p. 44.

Fig. 3.1 Percentage of Essex Property Crime Prosecutors Receiving Expenses, 1750–1800 (3-year moving average)

Source: PRO Assi 31/1–18; ERO Q/SMg 17–28.

Table 3.1. Verdicts Gained by Essex Assize Prosecutors Receiving Expenses, 1770–3 and 1787–9

Period	Not found		Not guilty		Guilty		Total	
	No.	%	No.	%	No.	%	No.	%
1770–3	4	7.4	9	16.7	41	75.9	54	100
1787–9	22	15.8	44	31.6	73	52.5	139	99.9

Source: P.R.O. Assi 31/10, 14 and 15.

three-quarters of assize prosecutors were being given financial help by 1790.[5] When war and lower indictment rates returned in the early 1790s, however, both courts slightly reduced their willingness to make expenses payments.

The average level of costs paid to each prosecutor was higher at the assizes than the quarter sessions. Initially the difference was small but by 1790s the average amounts were £4 10s and £2, respectively.[6] Expenses were meant to cover 'reasonable' costs incurred in carrying on the prosecution, with an allowance for 'time and trouble'. By 1780–1800 most Essex payments were based on an allowance of 5 shillings per person per day for prosecutors and their witnesses and an additional sum, rarely exceeding 10 shillings, for all

[5] For separate graphs of assize and quarter sessions expenses, see P. King, 'Crime, Law', p. 174; 1787–9: only four prosecutors eligible for rewards were also given expenses at the Essex assizes. Those receiving rewards rarely got further assistance. Ryder, Assize Diary, p. 13.

[6] For a detailed breakdown of assize awards in the 1760s and 1790s, see King, 'Crime, Law', pp. 174–6.

court fees. Transport expenses and the costs or time lost in detecting the offender and taking him before a magistrate were sometimes claimed, but such payments were exceptional and may well have been confined to prosecutors who the bench felt were particularly meritorious. Most victims, even if they were fortunate enough to be considered eligible for expenses payments, did not therefore recover all their costs until a rather more generous policy was instituted in the early nineteenth century.[7]

Who received this assistance? The payment of prosecution costs was more specifically targeted than that of rewards. While the awarding of the latter was simply based on success in certain categories of indictment, the criteria used by assize judges and quarter sessions magistrates in awarding costs included the circumstances and means of the victim. By the late eighteenth century 75 per cent of the Essex labourers bound by recognizance to prosecute felons at the quarter sessions were paid expenses by the court (Table 3.2). Since most of the remainder failed to turn up, this suggests that poorer prosecutors would virtually be guaranteed to receive some recompense if they brought a property crime indictment. Although some may have received help from elsewhere, the prosecutions brought by the poor were not, therefore, usually paid for by employers, landlords, or local associations.[8] It was the courts themselves that increasingly took on the task of helping poorer prosecutors in property crime cases. Better-off victims were less well served. Dudley Ryder's Home Circuit diary suggests that in the mid-1750s assize judges usually excluded them and in the 1760s only 7 per cent of farmers and 16 per cent of tradesmen and artisans were receiving financial help at the Essex quarter sessions. As the criteria used by the bench widened in the 1780s an increasing number of prosecutors from the middling sort began to feel the benefit (Table 3.2), but throughout the eighteenth century farmers and tradesmen remained very uncertain whether they would receive any help, while those of gentry or professional status could be fairly sure they would not. In fraud and uttering cases, where tradesmen were most at risk, the statutes made no provision for assisting victims, and many middling men resented the relative paucity of assistance offered to them. In 1772 the *Chelmsford Chronicle* stressed that the expense of many prosecutions fell 'very hard on a man of middling circumstances'.[9] The farmers and better-off tradesmen of eighteenth-century Essex responded in two ways. A small minority attempted to get help from the local vestries on which they often carried so much weight, whilst a much larger number formed or joined a local prosecution association.

[7] Burn, *The Justice* (1766), 3, p. 73; E.R.O. Q/SBb 347/41 and 340/27. Ryder excluded 'the costs of pursuing the prisoner and taking him beforehand', Ryder, Assize Diary, pp. 13–16, but for more generous policies, Q/SBb 201/25. Major changes came through Bennet's Act of 1818, Radzinowicz, *History*, 2, pp. 74–81.
[8] Hay, 'Property', pp. 36–7 implies that they were.
[9] Ryder, Assize Diary, p. 7 and p. 25 considered 'that none but poor persons should have expenses'. However, some uttering prosecutions were financed by the Mint; *Che.C.*, 28 Aug. 1772.

Table 3.2. Occupations of Prosecutors Receiving Expenses, Essex Quarter Sessions, 1760s and 1780s

Occupation or social status of prosecutor	Proportion of prosecutors in each status group receiving expenses					
	1760–9			1780–9		
	Number	Total	%	Number	Total	%
1. Gentlemen and professionals	2	6	33	2	16	13
2. Farmers and yeomen	3	43	7	32	61	52
3. Husbandmen and gardeners	2	8	25	3	3	100
4. Tradesmen and artisans	6	37	16	33	70	47
5. Maritime occupations	1	5	20	3	8	38
6. Labourers	14	21	67	24	32	75
7. Widows and single women	3	9	33	2	8	25
8. Others (servants, military etc.)	0	0	0	2	9	22
Total (excluding unknown)	31	129	24	101	207	49

Notes: Group 7 consists of widows, singlewomen, and spinsters but does not include married women who have been placed in the occupational group of their husbands unless their own occupation is specified. These figures relate to felony prosecutions only. The court did not pay expenses to prosecutors in cases of assault. Payments to witnesses can also be seen, in much smaller numbers, in the sessions books.

Source: as Table 2.2.

Between 1765 and 1800 at least a dozen Essex vestries were prompted by a particularly heinous crime or series of crimes to offer individual rewards in the *Chelmsford Chronicle* for the conviction of the offenders. The East Ham Vestry took a more general approach in 1739 when it agreed to reimburse the expenses incurred by any ratepayer in prosecuting those who had committed felony or petty larceny in the parish. At least two other vestries, Steeple Bumstead in 1748 and Wethersfield in 1774, went a step further by passing resolutions covering all victims in the parish against such costs. The very patchy survival of the vestry minute books makes it impossible to establish exactly how widespread such resolutions were, but it is unlikely that a significant number of parishes followed suit. The 1752 and 1778 acts reduced the need to cover the costs of poorer prosecutors, while the better-off found it more convenient to make mutual agreements to help each other out with prosecution expenses. A handful of these agreements were simply recorded in the parish records without any public announcement but, in Essex at least, the vast majority of such initiatives resulted in the foundation of a formal prosecution association.[10]

[10] E.R.O. Halstead, D/P 96/8/3; Ardleigh D/P 263/8/I; Steeple Bumstead D/P 21/8/I; Felstead D/P 99/8/2; Wethersfield D/P 119/8/3; Woodford D/P 167/8/2, and E. J. Erith, 'Woodford Essex 1600–1850. A Study of Local Government in a Residential Parish', *Woodford and District Historical Society Proceedings and Transactions*, 10 (1950), p. 89; E. Stokes, *East Ham: from Village to County Borough* (London, 1933), pp. 54, 82–3. *Che.C.*, 26 Dec. 1766, 20 May 1774, 11 June, and 19 Nov. 1784, 16 Dec. 1785, 31 Oct. 1789, 5 Jan. 1790, 21 Jan. 1791, 8 Feb. 1793, 18 Nov. 1799; Radzinowicz, *History*, 2, pp. 106–8.

2. Prosecution Associations

The second half of the eighteenth century witnessed the growth of numerous prosecution associations in many areas of England. Recent research on general prosecution association development between 1760 and 1860, and on the eighteenth-century Essex associations, provides a detailed picture of the development, nature, and impact of these institutions. Unlike those in some other parts of England, most Essex prosecution associations made widespread use of the local newspapers and identified themselves overtly in their reward advertisements.[11] It can therefore be established that at least a hundred associations had been formed in the county by the early nineteenth century. They did not develop in a uniform way. After a period of small-scale and sporadic parish-based experimentation and of association activity by game preservers, three interrelated stages of development can be identified. The initial upsurge of prosecution associations from the later 1760s to 1775 was based mainly on horse-theft associations covering relatively wide areas of rural Essex. The concentration of these farmer-dominated organizations on horses reflected their value, their vulnerability, the lack of statutory rewards in such cases, and the particular assistance that newspapers could offer in their recovery.

From the mid-1770s the emphasis changed with the formation of the ambitious Essex Association and the emergence of other subscriptions covering large areas and aiming to assist in the prosecution of all types of major felony. Formed in a period of widespread anxiety about crime, the Essex Association was a unique and highly energetic attempt to weld together a countywide organization. The magistrates and gentry, inspired perhaps by Fielding's wider schemes, played an important role in this initiative, but with its demise in the early 1780s the emphasis changed again and their contribution waned. As gaol calendars and popular anxiety grew after the end of the American war, waves of new prosecution associations were founded. This very rapid growth between 1786 and 1791 was accompanied not only by a proportional increase in smaller subscriptions but also by a growing interest in minor thefts and summary offences such as wood, yarn, and vegetable stealing. The last fifteen years of the eighteenth century witnessed the establishment of a much broader range of local associations arising

[11] D. Philips, 'Good Men to Associate and Bad Men to Conspire. Associations for the Prosecution of Felons in England, 1760–1860', in Hay and Snyder (eds.), *Policing and Prosecution*, pp. 113–70; P. King, 'Prosecution Associations and their Impact in Eighteenth-Century Essex', pp. 171–210 in the same volume, contains the detailed Essex analysis underpinning this section. Hay, 'Crime, Authority', pp. 355–95; Hay, 'Manufacturers', pp. 16–19; Beattie, *Crime*, pp. 48–50; Pole, 'Crime', pp. 119–20; A. Shubert, 'Private Initiative in Law Enforcement. Associations for the Prosecution of Felons, 1744–1856', in V. Bailey (ed.), *Policing and Punishment in Nineteenth Century Britain* (London, 1981), pp. 25–41. For problems caused by the failure of associations to identify themselves in reward advertisements elsewhere, J. Styles, 'Print and Policing. Crime Advertising in Eighteenth-Century Provincial England', in Hay and Snyder (eds.), *Policing*, pp. 62–5.

out of the concerns of smaller groups of farmers, fishermen, manufacturers, and commercial men.[12]

The geography of association development is difficult to analyse from their advertisements, partly because Essex's only newspaper, the *Chelmsford Chronicle*, did not cover the entire county. However, the replies to the Royal Commission's questionnaire in 1836 support the evidence of the advertisements, which suggest that areas near to London had less dense association networks than did central and eastern Essex.[13] In non-metropolitan Essex associations grew up in both rural and urban areas. Rural subscriptions were dominated by farmers, particularly the larger occupiers, whilst the majority of urban members were retailers, victuallers, food processors, or manufacturers. Apart from a small minority of associations which concentrated on specific offences, such as poaching or oyster-theft, most subscriptions had fairly similar aims: to assist their members in prosecuting and apprehending a wide range of property offenders. They used a common stock, gathered by either regular or occasional subscriptions, to refund all reasonable expenses incurred by members in the detection and prosecution of offenders and to offer rewards to non-members who helped to apprehend those committing offences against subscribers. Some associations also hired a solicitor to take the burden of orchestrating prosecutions off their members' shoulders, but only one or two ever attempted to provide policing and watching facilities or offered help to non-members who became victims of crime, and those who did so soon abandoned the experiment as impractical.

Most associations had a small standing committee who referred major decisions to the main body of subscribers at general meetings. The latter were the main focus of the more convivial functions of these associations, and some subscriptions arose out of earlier market day clubs, whose members set up an association in order to formalize their previous dining arrangements. The cost of membership was not usually large but the dinners could be expensive. Carrington's diary records rich combinations of roast beef, calves' head, ham, turkey, and mock turtle with 'puddings and pyes' and 'plenty of wine and punch' at his association's dinners, which cost the equivalent of a labourer's weekly income. It is hardly surprising therefore that labourers and artisans rarely joined these associations.[14]

---

[12] King, 'Prosecution Associations'; J. Styles, 'Sir John Fielding and the Problem of Criminal Investigation in Eighteenth-Century England', *Transactions of the Royal Historical Society*, 5th ser., 33 (1983), 127–49.

[13] P.R.O. HO 73/5, 6, and 9. Only two out of seven responding Becontree hundred parishes (East and West Ham) had associations compared with half of the rural parishes in the Lexden, Witham, and Hinckford hundreds.

[14] King, 'Prosecution Associations'. Policing initiatives did begin to develop in the early nineteenth century in West Ham (*P.P.*, 1828, VI, 201), but the 1836 replies only refer to one or two policing initiatives by associations. Philips, 'Good Men', pp. 145–7; Harriott, *Struggles*, I, pp. 432–3; Branch-Johnson (ed.), *Memorandoms*, pp. 66, 78, 106, 164.

What impact did these subscriptions have on the detection and prosecution of crime? In Essex they seem to have been least active in the hundred nearest to London, which produced the highest indictment rates. Moreover, the chronology of association development in Essex suggests that their growth was usually a response to, rather than an initiator of, rises in recorded crime. Although Essex indictment levels rose rapidly between 1782 and 1784, association activity did not fully take off until 1786–91. How much prosecution activity did members engage in? Outside the county's only large borough, Colchester, 13–15 per cent of major court prosecutors in Essex were association members in 1785–1800, but because subscribers made more use of multiple indictments than other prosecutors the proportion of offenders they brought to the courts was slightly higher, at 15–17 per cent. Since a minimum of 10–14 per cent of commercial, professional, farming, and gentry households in eastern and central Essex subscribed to an association, it appears that the overall impact of the subscribers of the sixteen associations for which lists are available was not substantially greater than one might expect the same people to have had if they had not been association members. Nor were subcribers more successful than the average prosecutor in obtaining convictions, despite the substantial fees many paid to solicitors to organize their prosecutions.[15] Individual associations varied widely in their impact. Some subscriptions went for more than a decade without bringing a single indictment. Others, such as the Colchester Borough Association or the farmer-dominated Winstree Association, had a major influence on local prosecution levels for a brief period at least.[16] Why overall did Essex subscribers only produce slightly higher than average indictment rates?

The lack of substantial manufacturing interest groups in Essex, apart from those arising from the rapidly declining cloth industry, was an important factor, but the associations' failure to make a major impact in Essex was also linked to their weak administrative and financial structures. In many of the smaller associations a single assize prosecution usually necessitated the collection of a fresh subscription, and this in turn often brought the future of the organization into question. Administratively many associations were less permanent than their resolutions and newspaper announcements suggest. Initial enthusiasm quickly dissipated. Meetings soon became irregular or non-existent.[17] More important, perhaps, many prosecution associations were not primarily intended to increase prosecution levels. Members saw them as providing a forum for discussion and conviviality, as a source of assistance in the recovery of stolen goods, or as a means of gaining reimbursement if they

---

[15] Beattie, *Crime*, p. 50; King, 'Prosecution Associations', pp. 186, and 189–92.

[16] Ibid., 191–200. If summary court records survived more fully the associations' impact there could be more easily analysed. On the role of associations in funding the pursuit and prosecution of poachers and of hedgebreakers, *P.P.*, 1826–7, VI, pp. 8 and 27.

[17] Hay, 'Manufacturers', pp. 18–19; King, 'Prosecution Associations'.

had to bear the cost of a prosecution.[18] The major reason for the associations' small impact on major court indictments was almost certainly the attitudes of the members themselves. Despite the public announcements of their associations which stressed that members would prosecute all offenders with 'the utmost vigour', most subscribers continued to use their discretion, ignoring thefts if they chose to, or using informal sanctions to punish offenders. The diary of John Carrington regularly records his attendance at the annual dinners of his association but when he was robbed by two Irishmen he did not, it seems, either actively pursue the offenders or inform the association. Although a few Essex associations did pass regulations that attempted to prevent members from compounding, their organizations were generally too loose to enable them to act effectively against such practices and there is very little evidence that most subscriptions made any attempt to limit their members' actions. Thus the options available to victims were not usually constrained by their membership of an association, nor did that membership necessarily imply any opposition to the discretionary nature of the criminal justice system. Carrington campaigned for pardons for local offenders on several occasions, as did other associations and their members. The continued growth of these organizations, despite their small impact on major court prosecutions, suggests that most subscribers did not regard them primarily as a means of producing significant changes in the administration of the criminal law. Most subscriptions were designed to supplement the existing system rather than to challenge it.[19]

The extent to which these associations provided an effective supplement remains in doubt. In 1812 one Essex subscriber complained that 'it appears to me to be perfectly useless' to continue as a member. The majority of early nineteenth-century Essex observers saw associations as limited but helpful institutions that encouraged members to indict offenders by removing the inconvenience and fear of financial loss that initiating a prosecution often engendered. Others were much more critical, describing their local associations as 'ill managed', 'lately dissolved as useless', or as 'not having had the desired effect'. Although the bigger subscriptions did sometimes offer substantial rewards, the sums involved were not particularly large and association advertisements do not appear to have been any more successful in producing prosecutions than those placed by private individuals.[20] The main strategies

[18] P.R.O. HO 73/5 (Ongar), 6 part 2 (Great Oakley) suggest one other motive—that some members believed that having their names publicly advertised in an association's membership list would mean they were less likely to be robbed 'since offenders would rather steal from non-members'.

[19] Philips, 'Good Men', pp. 128–30; King, 'Prosecution Associations', pp. 202–3; R. Branch-Johnson, *The Carrington Diary 1797–1810* (London, 1956), pp. 124–5; Branch-Johnson (ed.), *Memorandoms*, pp. 27–8, 144.

[20] E.R.O. D/DEL. CI, 19 Nov. 1812; P.R.O. HO 73/5 (Epping, Dunmow), 6.2 (Witham), 9 (Braintree) for positive Essex comments in 1836. For earlier praise, *The Times*, 4 June 1784; *Northampton Mercury*, 5 July 1788. HO 73/9 (Wendons Ambo), 6.1 (Bradwell), 5 (Cranham) for negative views. In a

adopted by the associations—the provision of rewards and the reimbursement of costs—were identical to those of the statutory system. Subscribers may have found it safer and more convenient to have financial and legal help available should they decide to prosecute, but Essex victims, whether they were association members or not, were rarely willing to give up their right to choose between formal and informal sanctions. Only a handful of associations for a few short periods succeeded in combating the inertia created by the discretionary nature of the prosecution system, and most were not designed to do so.

3. Prosecutors and the Printed Word

One of the main reasons for the rise of prosecution associations was the growing availability of printing facilities and of newspapers carrying large numbers of local advertisements. The number of provincial newspapers in England rose rapidly during the eighteenth century and after 1764 the establishment of a successful Essex-based paper, the *Chelmsford Chronicle*, meant that the county no longer had to rely on newspapers printed outside its boundaries.[21] Unlike their predecessors, eighteenth-century victims could quickly disseminate information about offences and offenders by asking the local printer to produce handbills or by placing an advertisement in a widely distributed newspaper. What role did printing play in the detection and prosecution of crime in the eighteenth century? Handbills and advertisements were not, of course, the only public means of communicating information about crime. The ancient system of hue and cry was still in active use in 1680 when 'hue and cry being sent' after two Essex highwaymen who had held up the Ipswich Coach 'they were pursued and taken ere they could reach... London'. However, apart from one or two newspaper references to a successful hue and cry just over the county's borders, there are virtually no references to it in the late eighteenth-century Essex sources and, as John Styles has recently shown, it was effectively replaced by printed handbills and advertisements.[22]

As the county's transport system improved in the eighteenth century, Essex victims may also have been able to use the growing network of turnpike gates

random sample of 132 advertisements from the *Chelmsford Chronicle*, 1775–95, 8% of those carrying an association reward can be linked to a prosecution, compared with 13% of those not mentioning an association.

[21] G. Cranfield, *The Press and Society from Caxton to Northcliffe* (London, 1978), p. 179; no other paper was published in Essex 1764–1800. The *Essex Herald* began in 1800 but virtually no copies have survived. A Colchester-based paper existed under various titles 1739–51 but few copies survive. R. Wiles, *Freshest Advices: Early Provincial Newspapers in England* (Ohio, 1965).

[22] *The Full and True Relation of all the Proceedings at the Assizes holden at Chelmsford for the Countie of Essex... 29th March... 1st April 1680*, p. 2; Styles, 'Print and Policing', pp. 56 and 82–6; Radzinowicz, *History*, 2, p. 37. *Che.C.*, 11 Jan. 1782; *The Times*, 10 Jan. 1785. On print's growing importance in murder cases, M. Gaskill, 'The Displacement of Providence. Policing and Prosecution in Seventeenth- and Eighteenth-Century England', *Continuity and Change*, 11 (1996), 348–52.

and regular coach services to their advantage. In 1836 the Chelmsford magistrates stressed that 'the public means of spreading information in this division
is excellent from the number of coaches hourly passing and repassing'. As the
activities of the paid, Bow Street-based, patrols began to reach out into south-
west Essex, victims in that area also used them as channels of information
about offenders, but elsewhere in Essex the town criers remained the main
alternative to printed forms of communication. Like other representatives of
oral traditions, the criers have left few records, but between 1784 and 1800 the
Colchester Association's most frequent reaction to offences committed against
its members was to have them 'proclaimed by the crier'. This was the usual
response to minor thefts of wood, food, or clothing. Handbills were also
frequently used but newspaper advertisements were only placed in a handful
of cases and were largely reserved for more serious felonies. Although the
rewards offered via the crier alone were usually around 2 guineas, whereas
most handbills and advertisements offered more than twice that amount, all
three methods met with at least some success. Only four of the associations'
thirty-four information initiatives resulted in prosecutions between 1784 and
1801, but the use of crying alone; crying and handbills; crying, handbills and
newspaper advertisements; and newspapers alone each produced one prosecution. Non-members also used the crier to offer rewards for lost or stolen
goods, but this method was only effective in densely populated areas. In rural
Essex handbills and newspaper advertisements were the main means of dis-
seminating information about offenders by the second half of the eighteenth
century.[23]

The ephemeral nature of the handbill makes it very difficult to discuss its use
or effectiveness, but it was probably the most widely used method of communicating intelligence about offences and offenders. Handbills could be more
accurately targeted than newspapers and if blanket coverage of a limited area
was the main requirement they were clearly preferable. Handbills were also
quicker. By the early nineteenth century most Essex parishes had a printer
within a few miles' radius. At Little Braxted, for example, handbills could be
obtained from nearby Witham 'in three hours'. At Birch, 4 miles from
Colchester, printed handbills 'could be distributed over an extent of 8 or 10
miles in 14 hours'—reaction times that the weekly provincial newspapers could
not hope to match. Handbills were also cheaper. In 1789 the Frating Association paid 5 shillings for 300 handbills, but expended four times that amount on
placing four newspaper advertisements, and other association records suggest
similar differentials. Advertising was particularly expensive for victims living
near the boundaries of different newspaper territories. In north-west Essex
victims often thought it advisable to place advertisements in both the *Ipswich*

---

[23] Brown, *Essex at Work*, pp. 77–92; HO 73/5 (Chelmsford and Becontree), 6.2 (Leyton, Little Ilford,
Wanstead). Colchester Borough Association Minute Book 1783–1809 (privately held Jackson and
Powis, Colchester); Styles, 'Print and Policing', p. 109; E.R.O. P/COR 10, 29 Dec. 1782.

Journal and the *Chelmsford Chronicle*, while in southern Essex the Barnstable and Chafford Association decided to offer rewards in a London paper as well as in the Essex one. These handbill prices do not, however, include distribution costs which were sometimes as large as the printer's bills. Rural associations made use of both handbills and newspapers, but for minor thefts and immediately consumable articles handbills were usually preferred, whereas major capital offences and those involving large animals were almost always advertised in the newspapers. Contemporaries very rarely differentiated between these two complementary forms of advertisement when evaluating their usefulness. The Witham magistrates, for example, believed that offenders were frequently detected through 'Country papers and handbills'. However, historians are forced to focus on newspaper advertisements because so few handbills survive.[24]

At its inception in 1764 the *Chelmsford Chronicle* stressed that it aimed to overcome the inconveniences, delays, and 'ill consequences' that inevitably arose because 'every advert of things lost, stolen . . . etc' had to be inserted in a paper printed in another county. After some initial difficulties in getting established, which the printer partly overcame by creating a small crime wave of his own in 1765, the *Chelmsford Chronicle* soon began to fulfil this function. The number of advertisements it carried describing the property stolen and the circumstances of the offence, as well as offering a reward for information or conviction, more than tripled in the last third of the century (Table 3.3). The size of the rewards also increased. The average in 1765 was 2 guineas. Thirty years later it was 7 guineas.[25] Horse thefts dominated the newspaper advertisements in Essex as they also did in Yorkshire. Horses were expensive and their identity was difficult to disguise. More important, they could be moved rapidly in any direction. The broader geographical range of the newspapers were therefore vital and justified the extra cost. In the 1760s nearly three-quarters of the *Chelmsford Chronicle*'s advertisements related to stolen or strayed horses, and although the proportion fell steadily as victims of sheep and cattle theft also began to make widespread use of the paper, large animal thefts continued to constitute 70–80 per cent of crime advertisements throughout the century (Table 3.3).[26]

What role did reward advertisements play in Essex? Using northern assizes depositions, Styles has shown that among the small number of horse theft cases that finally came to court, newspaper advertisements and handbills were an

[24] Styles, 'Print and Policing', pp. 68–72; E.R.O., D/DB Z1; D/DEL, B4–6, C1; Colchester Borough Association Minute Book; P.R.O. HO 73/6.2 (Little Braxted), 9.2 (Birch); for other references to the short distance to local printers, 9.2 (East Mersea), 6.2 (Belchamp Otter, Little Oakley). The Witham magistrates, H.O. 73/5. For high handbill distribution costs, E.R.O. Q/SBb 323/47.
[25] *Che.C.*, 10 Aug. 1764; King, 'Newspaper Reporting'. Averages based on adverts about stolen or strayed animals or other forms of theft excluding 'lost' watches, dogs, pocket books, for 1765 and 1795.
[26] Styles, 'Print and Policing', p. 60.

Table 3.3. Property Crime Reward Advertisements, *Chelmsford Chronicle*, 1765–90

Period	Total number	% Horse	% Sheep and cattle	% Other offences
1765–70	121	72.7	8.3	19.0
1771–5	219	63.5	9.1	27.4
1776–80	318	62.9	15.4	21.7
1781–5	354	63.8	17.8	18.4
1786–90	386	58.4	21.0	20.5

Notes: The year 1767 is excluded because of inadequate survival; Otherwise almost a complete run 1765–90. 'Lost' watches, dogs, and pocket books excluded. Stolen or strayed advertisements for all other animals included. During 1788–90 the stolen articles were horses = 124, cattle = 25, sheep = 22, pigs = 4, robbery or theft = 20, burglary = 16, miscellaneous = 17.

effective and successful method of detection. These sources are not available for south-eastern England, but trial reports indicate that advertisements could play a significant role. In 1797 the *Chelmsford Chronicle* proudly reported the trial of a horse thief who had been captured the day after the victim had placed an advertisement 'describing the horse in so particular a manner as not to escape notice'. At the Kent assizes in 1774 a Suffolk victim noted the vital role played by an *Ipswich Journal* advertisement in the arrest of a horse thief. However, the absolute impact of horse theft advertisements on prosecution levels was very small. Although more than 700 victims advertised stolen or strayed horses in the *Chelmsford Chronicle* between 1768 and 1790 only 71 horse thieves were indicted. The equivalent figures for cattle theft were 102 and 5. Moreover, those that were prosecuted were rarely apprehended through newspaper advertisements. A random sample of 45 horse theft and 20 sheep or cattle theft advertisements placed between 1775 and 1795 reveals only one tenuous link with a later Essex prosecution. This does not mean that these advertisements were all unsuccessful. Some of the animals involved were probably genuine strays. More important many horse theft cases were tried outside the county where the original theft took place, while other offenders may have been apprehended via an advertisement but then tried for other offences not mentioned in the original newspaper description.[27] However, this evidence does suggest that, in the absence of parliamentary rewards for the prosecution of horse stealers, victims had little incentive to prosecute once they had regained their animal, and that the relatively small rewards offered by the courts in sheep and cattle theft cases may have had a similar effect. Indeed, many of the advertisements that used the ambivalent phrase 'stolen or strayed'

[27] Ibid., 76–87; *Che.C.*, 4 Aug. 1797; *The Whole Proceedings on the King's Commission of Oyer and Terminer and General Gaol-Delivery held for the County of Kent at Maidstone 14th to 19th March 1774* (Rochester, 1774), p. 19; and p. 20 for another example of a non-Kent horse theft victim.

may have been covert attempts by the victim to open negotiations with the thief without offending against the 1752 act which had made it illegal to offer 'no questions asked' rewards. The *Chelmsford Chronicle* certainly advertised itself in 1764 mainly as a means of finding lost horses rather than of prosecuting offenders, and in 1792 it reported the recovery at Ipswich of a Chelmsford horse advertised in its pages, whilst noting calmly about the offender that 'at present he is not taken'.[28]

Did the offering of rewards have a greater impact in felony cases that did not involve large animals? When a housebreaker was apprehended two months after its inception, the *Chelmsford Chronicle* was quick to point out that the arrest was 'in consequence of an advert inserted in this paper' and in 1773 it proudly reproduced a letter from Sir John Fielding reporting that one of its advertisements had been instrumental in the capture of a notorious murderer. Many early nineteenth-century observers were also of the opinion that 'offenders are often detected and apprehended through the country papers',[29] but did the rhetoric match the reality? The Essex evidence suggests that for once it may have done. Among a random sample of 67 Essex advertisements about burglaries, robberies, and thefts not involving large animals, published between 1775 and 1795, 22 per cent can be definitely linked to a later prosecution. This does not mean that all these advertisements played a significant role in the detection process. At least one of the sample advertisements went to press just before the victim was informed that the offender had already been apprehended. Another, in which Samuel Boultwood offered a 10-guinea reward for the apprehension of three 'strange Irishmen' who were said to have burgled his house and killed his maid, can hardly be portrayed as producing the prosecution that followed since it was Boultwood himself who was indicted for murder. More important, those who placed such advertisements tended to be wealthier than the average victim and would often have also used either their own servants or hired pursuers and thieftakers to detect the offenders. Moreover, burglary and robbery cases, which already carried statutory rewards four or five times greater than those usually offered by the victim, formed a much higher proportion of non-animal theft advertisements than they did of indictments in general.[30] However, it is difficult to avoid the conclusion that these advertisements played a significant role. Advertisements in cases not involving statutory rewards produced much the same prosecution rates as those involving

---

[28] *Che.C.*, 10 Aug. 1764 highlighted an example of a man losing a horse in stressing its usefulness to Essex readers, 6 Jan. 1792, 27 Jan. 1792. For compounding statutes Radzinowicz, *History*, 2, pp. 313–18; Burn, *Justice of the Peace and Parish Officer* (1766) 3, pp. 72–3.

[29] *Che.C.*, 19 Oct. 1764, 2 July 1773; P.R.O. HO 73/5 (South Hinckford and Witham).

[30] *Che.C.*, 24 and 31 May, 1782, 29 July 1791. Advertisements rarely identify the victims' status but among the 67 were at least 6 gentlemen, a clergyman, 7 shopkeepers, 3 millers, 6 other tradesmen and artisans, a labourer, and a husbandman; 15% of indictments 1791–1800 involved robbery, burglary, or housebreaking but over 70% of the non-animal theft advertisement sample related to these crimes. The statutory rewards were £40; 20% of victims offered ten guineas, only 12% offered more.

robbery or burglary.[31] The number and diversity of cases involved, and the likelihood that other advertising victims regained the stolen goods but chose not to prosecute, suggest that these advertisements may well have been a very useful weapon in the victim's arsenal. The gaolers of eighteenth-century Essex certainly used them to great effect. A number of escaped prisoners were recaptured in the 1780s 'in consequence of an advertisement in the Chelmsford paper and handbills published with a reward therein'. It is not surprising that these printed forms of communication largely replaced the hue and cry. In burglary, robbery, and theft cases both advertisements and handbills seem to have had a significant impact on a victim's capacity to detect and prosecute offenders, while after incidents involving large animal thefts a newspaper advertisement offered the best hope of recovering the stolen property as well as some assistance in tracing the offender.[32]

4. Parish Constables and Other Potential Assistants

Who offered physical assistance, rather than financial backing or information services, to the victims of property crime? Magistrates were rarely involved in detecting and apprehending offenders. Although a minority of Essex JPs interested themselves in gathering and sifting the evidence once the offender had been apprehended and examined, their role in the early stages of detection was usually confined to the granting of search warrants and the nearest magistrate was often difficult to contact without considerable delay.[33] Parish officers were also hard to mobilize immediately and the victim therefore had to rely mainly on those who were close to home. Instant pursuit was often vital. If the victim had kept up good relations with his neighbours they could usually be depended on for initial assistance—a type of reciprocity that was occasionally formalized in prosecution association agreements binding members to ride in pursuit if an offence was committed against one of their number.[34]

Neighbours, fellow workers, and employees also played a vital role as witnesses. If the victim had seen the offence they merely provided useful corroboration, but if he or she had not they were of pivotal importance. In the early stages of the detection process witnesses had almost unlimited

[31] Ten out of 43 burglary and housebreaking advertisements can be linked to prosecutions, 5 out of 20 are the non-capital theft figures. Large rewards also produced better results. 17% of rewards under five guineas can be linked to prosecutions, compared with 28% of those over 5 guineas.

[32] E.R.O. Q/SBb 322/8, 323/47; Styles, 'Print and Policing', p. 88.

[33] J. Styles, 'An Eighteenth-Century Magistrate as Detective. Samuel Lister of Little Horton', *Bradford Antiquary*, 48 (1983) 98–117; Langbein, 'Shaping', pp. 56–7 for a more positive view of the role of some JPs. High Constables played a mainly administrative or tax-gathering role.

[34] P.R.O. HO 73/9 (Great Tey), for a neighbour pursuing offenders 15 miles, *Whole Proceedings . . . Essex . . . 1774*, p. 8; K. Wrightson, *English Society 1580–1680* (London, 1982), pp. 51–6. The victim had little chance of coercing his neighbours into action. The legal liability of the hundred to pay the victim's damages if the offender was allowed to escape had little effect, and damages were difficult to claim. Radzinowicz, *History* i, pp. 164–7. *Che.C.*, 22 Nov. 1771.

discretion. When a Barking employee caught Mary Clarke stealing coal in 1762 she pleaded that she had 'never took any before' and begged him not to tell the owner. Witnesses as well as victims could compound with offenders and many similar offences were never even discovered by the victim, let alone prosecuted, because witnesses were intimidated, bought off, or persuaded to be merciful. Essex victims often had to satisfy witnesses for their 'trouble' before they would help in the detection of offenders, and some witnesses made similar bargains before agreeing to give evidence in court. In 1739 a Surrey witness openly refused to give his testimony until 'the prosecutor satisfied him for his trouble and the expense of attending the assizes'. These discretionary powers were exercised by a broad cross-section of the population. At the Essex quarter sessions 42 per cent of witnesses were labourers or husbandmen, and a similar proportion were tradesmen or artisans, while only 15 per cent were farmers.[35] Although the poor were nearly as well represented among witnesses as they were in the population as a whole, they almost certainly had less freedom of action than wealthier groups. Witnesses reliant on local farmers for credit, employment, charity, or poor relief would have found it difficult to refuse to co-operate if one of the parish's wealthier inhabitants was the victim. Once an employer became aware that an offence had been committed and that his employee had seen it he could threaten the reluctant witness with dismissal, although solidarities among fellow workmen often meant that employers remained unaware that their goods were being appropriated.

The wealthy also had access to another more reliable type of witness—the paid watcher. About 6 per cent of Essex quarter sessions offenders were detected by those employed specifically to watch particular fields, haystacks, barns, woods, or tradesmen's yards (Table 2.1). In the forests of south-west Essex, where wood was systematically cut for the lucrative London market, regular watchmen were employed in addition to the officials attached to the forest courts, and other informal policing and watching networks were also developed by various public bodies and commercial interests in eighteenth-century Essex.[36] Mail coaches carried armed guards who showed little reluctance to use their pistols, and as the turnpike system grew, tollgate keepers near the edge of the metropolis became increasingly useful in apprehending offenders. Essex, unlike other East Anglian counties, did not develop an inspectorate to police its spinners but another important Essex industry—oyster fishing—was increasingly protected by a network of officers and watchmen.

[35] E.R.O. Q/SBb 225/1, 354/64; *Genuine Proceedings...Home Circuit...March 1739*, p. 19. Witnesses under recognizance in felony cases (based on 1765–9, 1775–9, 1785–9, 1795–9): Gentlemen 0%; Professional 0.6%; Farmers 15.0%; Tradesmen and Artisans 39.0%; Maritime Occupations 2.9%; Husbandmen 3.2%; Labourers 39.2%; sample 313. Single women, servants and officials excluded. Each were 5 or 6%. E.R.O. Q/SMg 19–28.

[36] E.R.O. Q/SBb 311/36, 319/25, 322/48, 377/83, 378/81; *P.P.*, 1839, XIX, p. 40; In 1800 dearth and incendiarism stimulated watching activity in Black Notley *Che.C.*, 14 Nov. 1800; for other such links *Che.C..*, 6 June 1788; *P.P.*, 1828, VI, pp. 194–203.

In addition to the Water Bailiff, who had the power to board and inspect the oyster dredgers' boats and to prosecute illegal dredging in the local courts, a growing number of watchmen were employed. In 1791 the oyster-men of Leigh and Southend announced that they had 'appointed men to watch their fishery' and by the early nineteenth century between £800 and £1,000 a year was being spent on watchmen for the fishery.[37]

An even greater sum was spent on gamekeepers. At least 240 Essex men paid the gamekeepers duty in 1786–7, and although gamekeeping deputations were still used by some lords of the manor to grant hunting rights to farmers, tradesmen, and fellow gentry, a large proportion would have been part- or full-time gamekeepers by the 1780s. As game preservation became more systematic and lucrative after 1750, gamekeepers became full-time professionals who also hired assistants and part-time watchmen. Even if only two-thirds of those listed in 1786–7 were professional gamekeepers, game preservation in Essex would still have employed more men than the new county police force did in 1841, two years after its inception. With their extensive rights to search labourers' cottages for game or poaching equipment the gamekeepers represented a powerful form of private policing. Despite the hostility they experienced from labourers, farmers, and other groups who deeply resented the game laws, gamekeepers were employed in increasing numbers by the gentry because it was widely believed that they were successful in deterring and detecting offenders.[38] Most contemporaries were less optimistic about the impact of the other two main groups of law enforcement officers: the watchmen and the parish constables.

The role, nature and impact of eighteenth-century watching systems are very difficult to analyse. Recent research suggests that in many parts of London the watch was becoming an increasingly flexible and responsive instrument of policing in this period but, unlike their metropolitan counterparts, the watchmen employed by most Essex towns have left few records. Watchmen occasionally brought complaints to the Colchester petty sessions when they had been assaulted or their parish cages damaged, but apart from indicating that only a minority were literate these depositions tell us little about their activities. Several Essex towns attempted to improve their watching arrangements in the later eighteenth century. New initiatives tended to coincide with periods of heightened anxiety about crime and often included paving and lighting changes as well as the establishment of a watch. In 1788 John Crosier's diary records 'several houses in Maldon were robbed ... after this

[37] *Che.C.*, 27 Mar. 1795; *The Times*, 10 Jan. 1785; *Che.C.*, 1 Dec. 1786; King, 'Prosecution Associations', pp. 195–8; Styles, 'Embezzlement', pp. 196–8; J. Styles, 'Policing a Female Workforce. The Origins of the Worsted Acts', *Bulletin of the Society for the Study of Labour History*, 52 (1987), 39–40; E.R.O. P/CoR 12 22 Aug. 1788; *I.J.*, 15 Feb. 1766.

[38] *Che.C.*, 10 Nov. 1786 to 12 Jan. 1787; P. Munsche, 'The Gamekeeper and English Rural Society 1660–1830', *Journal of British Studies*, 20 (1981), 82–105; Munsche, *Gentlemen*, pp. 24–32; E.R.O. Q/APr 1.

three watchmen were appointed for the security of the town. The people were not taken but a fellow or two in the town were suspected.' A year later Chelmsford obtained a paving, lighting, and watching act and the Colchester Improvement Commission also responded to the growing anxieties of the 1780s by lighting and paving the borough's main streets. During an earlier crime wave in 1765 the Colchester authorities had also attempted to light 'the public part of the town' as well as raising funds 'for persons to go in pursuit' of offenders, and similar actions were taken by the Chelmsford, Halstead, Bath, and Ipswich authorities in 1800 when high prices and a wave of incendiarism raised anxieties once again. However, these initiatives were usually short-lived and even if a permanent organization, such as an improvement commission, was set up it did not guarantee greater activity in the long term.[39]

Since public watchmen were rarely employed outside a few of the larger towns, the main official to whom victims could turn in rural Essex was the parish constable. Who were the parish constables? What discretionary powers did they have and how did they use them in property crime cases? Recent work on the wide spectrum of duties that constables performed has indicated that they were not as corrupt or inefficient as the traditional police histories implied. Caught between the demands of the central authorities and the need to avoid disrupting social relationships within their own communities, constables sometimes retreated into a kind of studied negligence, but they were usually conscientious in fulfilling the specific duties required of them. However, this research has focused almost entirely on the sixteenth and early seventeenth centuries and on non-property offences.[40] In John Beattie's words, 'much remains to be discovered about eighteenth-century constables'. The quarter sessions records are of limited use in this context. The twenty constables indicted for neglecting their duties between 1749 and 1800 included four labourers, three farmers, eleven artisans and tradesmen, a schoolmaster,

[39] E. Reynolds, *Before the Bobbies. The Night Watch and Police Reform in Metropolitan London 1720–1830* (Stanford, 1998); R. Paley, '"An Imperfect, Inadequate and Wretched System"? Policing London before Peel', *Criminal Justice History*, 10 (1989), 102–5; E.R.O. P/CoR 13, 9 Dec. 1789, 29 Jan. 1790; P/CoR 15, 15 Feb. 1792; two of the four watchmen in the quarter sessions deposition sample signed their names. St Nicholas, Colchester, had an illiterate watchman in 1792. Brown, *Essex People*, p. 40; *Che.C.*, 7 Mar. 1788; 6 Mar. and 17 July 1789; Brown, 'Colchester', p. 170; for West Ham, *P.P.*, 1828, VI, p. 202. On watching and lighting initiatives in London before 1750, see J. Beattie, *The Limits of Terror. Policing, Prosecution and Punishment in London 1660–1750* (forthcoming); King, 'Newspaper Reporting', p. 429; *Che.C.*, 4 July 1800, 14 Nov. 1800, 6 Feb. 1801; P. Corfield, *The Impact of English Towns 1700–1800* (Oxford, 1982), p. 158; R. Neale, *Bath. 1680–1850. A Social History* (London, 1981), pp. 81–2.

[40] J. Kent, 'The English Village Constable 1580–1642. The Nature and Dilemmas of the Office', *The Journal of British Studies*, 20 (1981), 26–49; J. Kent, *The English Village Constable 1580–1642. A Social and Administrative Study* (Oxford, 1986); J. Sharpe, 'Policing the Parish in Early Modern England', in *Past and Present Colloquium: Police and Policing* (1983); Wrightson, 'Two Concepts of Order', pp. 21–46; J. Sharpe, 'Crime and Delinquency in an Essex Parish 1600–1640', in Cockburn (ed.), *Crime*, pp. 90–109.

and a gentlemen, but this was not a random sample. The gentlemen, for example, was indicted not for neglecting his duties but for refusing to serve at all.[41] The records of a few well-documented Essex parishes are much more informative.

Ardleigh was a large, well-cultivated parish in north-east Essex. Fifteen household heads who served as constables between 1767 and 1814 can be traced in the detailed parish census compiled in 1796. Of the fifty-eight years these men served in the office of constable, 31 per cent were performed by labourers or husbandmen and 26 per cent by tradesmen or artisans, following trades such as blacksmith, wheelwright, tailor, or innkeeper, and 43 per cent by those labelled as farmers or yeomen (Table 3.4). Since only a fifth of household heads were farmers and more than half were husbandmen or labourers, this occupational information appears to indicate that, although the constables were drawn from a wide cross-section of Ardleigh society, they were usually men of higher than average status. However, occupational labels can be deceptive and the rate books and the parish 'flour list' of 1796, which pinpoints all the families qualifying for parish subsidized flour, suggest a different picture (Table 3.5): 41 per cent of Ardleigh households qualified for subsidized food in 1796 and exactly the same proportion of serving constables came from that group. A further third of all households neither received this relief from the parish nor paid rates to it. A fifth of serving constables were in the same

Table 3.4. Social Status and Office Holding in Ardleigh, Essex

	All household heads	Constables	Overseers	Churchwardens
	%	%	%	%
Gentry and professionals	2	0	3	0
Farmers and yeoman	21	43	65	100
Tradesmen and artisans	24	26	18	0
Husbandmen, labourers	53	31	15	0
Total %	100	100	101	100
Sample size	189	58	80	37

Notes: Office holders calculated by identifying the occupations of all adult non-dependants in the 1796 Census who had held, or would later hold, one of these offices and multiplying by the years served; 15 constables, 36 overseers, and 6 churchwardens are listed by Erith; 42 individuals were involved. Robert Munson, who is described as 'constable', and Thomas Dunningham, who was labelled a 'lodger' in the Census, both qualified for parish relief and can be identified as labourers or husbandmen. Household heads based on Sokoll, *Household and Family*, pp. 118 and excluding one widower, eleven widows, and all in the 'other' category.

Source: F. H. Erith, *Ardleigh in 1796. Its Farms, Families and Local Government* (East Bergholt, 1978).

[41] Beattie, *Crime*, pp. 70–1; E.R.O. Q/SPb 10–17, eleven trades = wheelwright, miller, maltster, tailor, currier, grocer, baker, victualler, furrier, collarmaker, and carpenter.

Table 3.5. Wealth, Poverty, and Office Holding in Ardleigh, Essex

	All	Constables	Overseers	Churchwardens	Pre-1780 Constables	Post-1780 Constables
Poor 'flour list' households	41	41	8	0	30	47
Non-ratepaying households	32	21	6	8	5	29
Ratepayers 0–9	7	12	39	0	5	16
Ratepayers 10–49	10	10	15	0	15	8
Ratepayers 50–99	5	0	18	8	0	0
Ratepayers 100–149	3	14	6	16	40	0
Ratepayers 150+	1	2	9	68	5	0
Total %	99	99	101	100	100	100
Sample size	201	58	80	37	20	38

Notes: Erith, *Ardleigh*, pp. 31–106 provided the raw data from which poor families in the flour list (ibid. 17) were identified. Ratepayers were analysed from E.R.O. D/P 263/11/1 poor rates October 1796. Thomas Dunningham, who was described as a lodger in the Census and was a husbandmen paying minimal rates, also qualified for the free flour. He has been categorized here as a ratepayer. His inclusion in the poor householder category would have increased the proportion of serving constables in that category to 43% and of overseers to 13%. Office holders calculated as in Table 3.4.

position. Moreover most of the 38 per cent of constables who did pay rates did so at relatively low levels.[42]

The holders of other parish offices in Ardleigh were men of much higher social status. Three-quarters of overseers and all those who served as church-wardens were either farmers or gentry (Table 3.4). More revealingly the churchwarden's role was largely reserved for the parish's small élite of large farmers, whilst the overseers were usually small- or medium-sized landholders. Not surprisingly those who were so economically vulnerable that they were given subsidized flour in 1796 were almost entirely excluded from the offices of overseer and churchwarden, but they were as likely as any other group to be recruited into the ranks of the parish constables (Table 3.5). Substantial farm-ers did occasionally become constables before 1780 and half of those who served as constables also took a turn as overseer but despite these overlaps office holding in Ardleigh followed a clear hierarchy of wealth within which the constables occupied the bottom rung.

At Ashdon, a medium-sized agricultural parish in north-west Essex, parish listings and taxation records are less easy to link with precision but a very similar pattern emerges. No systematic occupational information is available, but among the fourteen men who served as constable during 1772–1819 at least one was a labourer, and five were artisans or innkeepers. Ashdon's constables

---

[42] Sokoll, *Household and Family*, pp. 93–184 for a detailed analysis of Ardleigh and its sources. Those described as 'farmer' in the 1796 census included men like John Wilsmore who served as constable for eleven years but was too poor to be rated in 1796.

Table 3.6. Office Holders and Ratepayers in Ashdon, Essex

Rate assessment	All ratepayers	Constables to 1806	Overseers	Surveyors	Churchwardens	Constables 1806–19
	%	%	%	%	%	%
2	17	82	2	3	0	100
3–9	15	5	0	0	0	0
10–24	21	5	10	3	0	0
25–49	21	0	18	3	0	0
50–99	9	0	12	53	22	0
100–149	11	7	31	26	46	0
150+	6	0	27	12	32	0
Total	100	99	100	100	100	100
Sample size	66	56	49	34	59	28

Note: The main rate assessment used was 1796. Office holders calculated by identifying the rates paid by each holder of an office and then multiplying by the number of years served. Churchwardens and surveyors 1772–1806; overseers 1775–1800.

Source: E.R.O. D/P 18/5/1–3, 18/21/2.

also included men from economically vulnerable households. Two of the eight constables listed as household heads in the 1801 census were also recipients of subsidized flour in that year. At least eleven of the fourteen constables were ratepayers in the 1790s but this mainly reflected the fact that a much higher proportion of Ashdon households were rated, for more than four-fifths of Ashdon's constables were assessed at the lowest possible level (Table 3.6). Ashdon's constables, like those of Ardleigh, were mainly husbandmen, small farmers, artisans, or labourers.[43] Once again the tax records suggest a polarized hierarchy among the Ashdon officials. Its churchwardens and surveyors were almost exclusively large farmers and the office of overseer was only slightly less prestigious.

This was also the pattern in the smaller central Essex parishes of Messing and Great Braxted. Only 53 per cent of the individuals serving as constables at Messing, 1776–86, can be traced in the rate books of 1779 and 1783, whereas all the churchwardens and at least 70 per cent of the overseers were ratepayers. While the average assessment of the ratepaying constables was £7, that of the overseers was £42 and that of the churchwardens £145. At Great Braxted in 1782 one of the constables was a non-ratepaying labourer, the other was an innkeeper who paid only 0.25 per cent of the parish's total rate. The overseers that year held small- to medium-sized farms and paid around 3 per cent each. The two churchwardens each farmed 4–6 per cent of the parish.[44]

[43] A. Green, *Ashdon* (Aldham, 1989); E.R.O. D/P 18/5/1–3, 18/18/2–4. About 45 % of Ashdon's households paid rates. The equivalent figure in Ardleigh was 26%.
[44] Populations 1801: Ardleigh 1,145, Ashdon 710, Messing 542, Great Braxted 502. *V.C.H. Essex*, 2, pp. 344–54; E.R.O. D/P 188/12/1; W. Gimson, *Great Braxted 1086–1957* (Little Braxted, 1958), pp. 33–6.

These four parishes, which were mainly chosen because they were particularly well documented, therefore exhibit many similarities. In the later eighteenth century the majority of constables were husbandmen, small farmers, artisans, and lesser tradesmen, but a substantial minority were often labourers. Since artisan constables appear in both the Ardleigh and Ashdon 'flour lists', many of them were little better off than labourers and in some parishes the proportion of constables paying rates was not substantially higher than that in the community as a whole. By contrast, those occupying the posts of overseer, churchwarden, or highway surveyor were not only ratepayers but were usually substantial farmers or wealthy tradesmen.

How typical were these four communities? Erith's work on Woodford suggests a similar pattern occurred in south-west Essex. In the seventeenth century the office of constable ranked alongside that of overseer, and lesser gentry frequently served in it. However, in the eighteenth century the constable's duties became more complex and onerous. The prestige of the office fell after constables were no longer allowed to collect their own rate and, as a result, gentlemen disappeared from their ranks. Smaller ratepayers, artisans, and tradesmen filled the office, the most popular occupations being builder, shopkeeper, blacksmith, shoemaker, baker, and butcher. Emmison's general introduction to the Essex parish records also concludes that wealthy ratepayers, gentlemen, and large farmers increasingly shunned the office of constable during the eighteenth century, leaving it to small craftsmen and tradesmen; while Gyford's work on central Essex provides more solid evidence of this trend. By the late 1820s four-fifths of overseers but only one-fifth of constables were farmers. By contrast half of the constables were artisans or tradesmen and nearly a fifth were labourers. The Essex magistrates' responses to the 1836 questionnaire suggest a similar spectrum of backgrounds—small tradesmen and shopkeepers being the usual occupations of urban constables, while rural parishes made wide use of labourers and small farmers as well as of 'inferior tradesmen and mechanics'.[45]

However, the replies suggest considerable regional variation and in the eighteenth century many parishes followed highly individual policies. At Cardington in Bedfordshire, for example, the main ratepayers continued to be involved in all the parish offices on a rotation system in the 1770s and 1780s. The land tax payments made by the constables, overseers, and churchwardens that can be identified in the 1782 Cardington Census followed almost identical patterns. Thirteen of the seventeen constables were farmers, three were artisans, and only one was a labourer.[46] This Cardington pattern is much

[45] Erith, *Woodford*, pp. 82–3 and 110–30; Emmison, *Guide*, pp. 16–19; J. Gyford, 'Men of Bad Character. Property Crime in Essex in the 1820's' (Essex University M.A., 1982), pp. 70–86; P.R.O. HO 73/5 (Dunmow); see also *P.P.*, 1828, VI, pp. 192–6.

[46] D. Baker (ed.), *The Inhabitants of Cardington in 1782* (Bedfordshire Historical Record Society, 1972); 54% of Cardington households paid no Land Tax in 1782, but only 6% of its constables and none of its

closer to that found in most seventeenth-century English communities. Despite the problems posed by wide local variations, recent research on this period has suggested that, although constables were drawn from a wide spectrum of society, the vast majority were ratepaying landholders, a good proportion of whom were drawn from the wealthiest men in the parish. Petty gentry, wealthy tradesmen, and substantial farmers not only served as constables before the civil war but were also members of loose parish oligarchies which performed the other duties of overseer, churchwarden, etc. Although this kind of arrangement almost certainly survived in some Essex parishes in the second half of the eighteenth century, as it did in Cardington, in most areas of Essex the situation had become much more polarized. The rich farmers, who largely dominated the Ardleigh and Ashdon vestries, served as churchwarden and sometimes as overseer but they left the office of constable to lesser men, many of whom were non-ratepayers or labourers. This increasingly polarized hierarchy of offices was beginning to emerge in the Essex parish of Terling in the late seventeenth century but a century later it was firmly entrenched in most communities. The labouring poor were excluded from the office of constable in Terling before 1700 but a century later they formed a substantial proportion of those holding the office in many Essex parishes.[47]

This growing status gap between the constables and the other holders of parish offices almost certainly reflected the more general polarization of rural social relations in this period, but that polarization was still going on in the later eighteenth and early nineteenth centuries.[48] Both the Ardleigh and the Ashdon evidence suggests that the constables' decline in status accelerated in the later eighteenth century. In Ardleigh two-thirds of pre-1780 constables were ratepayers, but after that date only a quarter had sufficient wealth to be rated (Table 3.5) In Ashdon those paying minimum rates increasingly dominated the office (Table 3.6). In both parishes this change can be linked to the increasing use of semi-permanent constables. In the 1770s one of Ashdon's two constables was a semi-permanent official while the other post was regularly rotated. After 1790 both constables were long-term appointments (Table 3.7). John Green and Jeremiah Howes, both of whom paid rates at the lowest

churchwardens or overseers avoided paying. 9% of Cardington households were assessed at over £10 but 44% of its constables, 50% of churchwardens and 33% of its overseers were in that position.

[47] Kent, *The English Village Constable*, pp. 13–20 and 80–151; Sharpe, 'Policing', p. 5; Sharpe, 'Crime and Delinquency', pp. 94–5; K. Wrightson and P. Levine, *Poverty and Piety in an English Village. Terling 1525–1700* (London, 1979), pp. 104–5; J. Kent, 'The Centre and the Localities. State Formation and Parish Government in England 1640–1740', *Historical Journal*, 38 (1995), 381–2. Although constables were sworn in by the magistracy, they were nominated and effectively chosen by the vestry or occasionally the court leet. *P.P.*, 1828, VI, p. 193; E.R.O. D/P 271/8/1; P.R.O. H.O. 73/5 (Dunmow, Ongar, Epping).

[48] K. Wrightson, 'Aspects of Social Differentiation in Rural England c.1580–1680', *Journal of Peasant Studies*, 5 (1977), 33–47; R. Wells, 'The Development of the English Rural Proletariat and Social Protest 1700–1850', *Journal of Peasant Studies*, 6 (1978), 115–39; Charlesworth, 'The Development . . . A Comment', pp. 101–11.

Table 3.7. Parish Constables, Length of Service

Years of service	Ardleigh 1796 Census	Ashdon 1772–89	Ashdon 1790–1819	Woodford 1700–99	Woodford 1800–36	Messing 1776–92
1	7	5	1	124	22	2
2	2	2	0	4	3	4
3–4	3	2	0	3	3	4
5–9	4	0	1	0	4	2
10–14	3	0	1	1	1	0
15–19	0	0	0	0	2	0
20–29	1	(1)	1	1	0	0
30+	0	0	1	0	0	0
Total	20	10	5	133	35	12

Note: Ardleigh figures include those who were children in 1796 but later became constables. At Ashdon one constable served during 1773–96 and therefore appears in both periods used here.

Sources: see notes to text.

possible level, served for twenty-three and thirty years, respectively. A similar change can be observed in Ardleigh in 1788 when Robert Munson began ten years of service after which two semi-permanent constables were appointed. At Woodford the idea of using semi-permanent constables had a longer history but their use increased dramatically at the end of the eighteenth century (Table 3.7). By the early nineteenth century all three parishes often had two constables with many years of experience behind them.[49]

These semi-permanent parish constables were not full-time police officers. A small number received annual retainers that were the equivalent of one or two months' wages for the average labourer. Robert Munson, for example, was paid £2 a year by the Ardleigh vestry. However, most parishes simply paid their constables a daily rate or a mileage rate. Fees of 3 or 4 shillings were the norm at Ashdon around 1800 for duties involving a day's journey, and by 1832 5 shillings was the standard daily fee. Over the year these fees made a significant contribution to the constable's income, supplemented as they were by other expenses, fees for serving warrants, rewards, or informal payments for services rendered to individuals. Constables with their own horses, for example, would often have received more than £3 a year in horse hire payments, which may explain why so many blacksmiths and innkeepers took the office.[50]

[49] Erith, *Ardleigh;* Erith, *Woodford*, pp. 110–30; E.R.O. D/P 18/5/1; in both rural parishes changes occurred in the late 1780s when the reformation of manners movement generated debate about constable's roles (*Che.C.*, 27 July 1787, 10 Aug. 1787, 2 Feb. 1788).
[50] The 1832 returns suggest that only about a dozen parishes gave a fixed annual payment to a police officer. Apart from the Braintree and Walthamstow forces set up under local acts 1820–32 payments were very small. £1 to £3 was the average retainer, although a voluntary Great Yeldham subscription paid more, E.R.O. Q/CR 7/1. Erith, *Ardleigh*, p. 6; E.R.O. D/P 18/5/3;. Storch, 'Policing', p. 225 on making a living from fees; P.R.O. HO 73/5 (Witham, South Hinckford) for expenses paid to eight constables; 55% went on hiring horses. For parish constables 'long-bills', *P.P.*, 1828, VI, p. 222.

However, before 1820 only a few south-west Essex constables seem to have made a full-time living from police work and almost all Essex's constables would have continued to follow other occupations. For many their work as constable was part of a much broader pattern of parish duties and commercial activities. Jeremiah Howes, for example, not only kept a public house but was also parish clerk, pinder, schoolmaster, ratecollector, and spinning organizer. At the turn of the century he received about £3 for making up various constable's returns but his income as village schoolmaster was considerably greater than that. The Ardleigh constable, Jonathan Bull, also held the paid position of assistant overseer but as a carpenter, wheelwright, and innkeeper he found other ways of establishing a lucrative relationship with the parish. As a wheelwright he was paid to rehang the church bells and wheels. As a carpenter he made alterations to the pews and gallery. As an innkeeper he hosted the vestry's annual meeting at which the accompanying dinner cost more than his annual salary as overseer. Even when he was not officially constable he made useful money as the parish troubleshooter. When smallpox broke out he was paid to supply the poor with brandy, gin, and beer. When a reluctant bridegroom needed escorting to a parish-organized wedding and when a lunatic had to be taken into custody, Bull was called in and well rewarded for his trouble. In the 1790s he was paid nearly £70 for providing the parish with three men for the navy.[51]

By the late eighteenth and early nineteenth centuries most Essex parishes did not have an annually paid police officer, but the policies of many vestries were encouraging the emergence of increasingly experienced semi-salaried part-time constables who found the role sufficiently lucrative to continue filling it for long periods. We cannot assume that long service necessarily made constables more committed or effective, and contemporary opinion was divided on the subject. Some semi-permanent constables may have outlived their usefulness. Jeremiah Howes was still serving as schoolmaster and constable at the age of 88. On the whole, however, whether they served for long periods or not, only a small minority of Essex constables were too old for active service (Table 3.8). Most of Ardleigh's constables served in their twenties or thirties. Very few were over 50. In 1832 two-thirds of Essex constables were aged between 30 and 49.[52] Nor were the constables of the eighteenth century as illiterate as some historians have suggested. The decline in the social status of constables was not accompanied by rising illiteracy. Before 1640 about half of those serving as constables were unable to sign their names, but between 1750 and 1800 virtually all Essex constables signed rather than marked their

[51] Green, *Ashdon*, pp. 93, 101, 137–8; E.R.O. D/P 18/5/3; Erith, *Ardleigh*, pp. 26–8.

[52] J. Styles, 'The Emergence of the Police. Explaining Police Reform in Eighteenth- and Nineteenth-Century England', *British Journal of Criminology*, 27 (1987), 17; Carter, *Ashdon*, p. 93; Storch, 'Policing', p. 224 on divided contemporary opinion. At Ilford appointing the same person as substitute was believed to be 'much more efficient', *P.P.*, 1828, VI, p. 193.

Table 3.8. Age Profiles of Essex Constables

Age	Ardleigh 1796	Rural Essex 1832	Becontree hundred 1832
	%	%	%
under 30	14	7	21
30–9	47	30	39
40–9	33	35	29
50–9	6	21	7
60+	0	7	4
	100	100	100
Sample of constables	58	319	28

Sources: Erith, *Ardleigh*, including younger sons in 1796. Age in each year of service calculated; E.R.O. Q/CR 7/1 Rural Essex based on selected hundreds (Barnstable, Chafford, Dunmow, Ongar, Clavering, Uttlesford, Hinckford).

depositions. When labouring men and poorer artisans were selected as constables in the later eighteenth century care was obviously taken to ensure they were literate, and some parishes made sure of this by appointing the village schoolmaster to the office.[53] Experience levels were also rising massively in parishes such as Ardleigh, Ashdon, and Woodford and, even before the introduction of semi-permanent constables, those serving the office in parishes like Messing averaged more than three years in the post (Table 3.7). The social status of the average constable may have been falling in the later eighteenth and early nineteenth centuries but it would be unwise to assume that they were less effective as a result. In most parishes constables were literate, physically active and experienced men. What role did they play in property crime cases?

Parish constables did not lack general discretionary powers in the eighteenth century. In dealing with vagrants and travellers, constables often doled out small payments to those they considered deserving, but if they chose to take punitive action they could arrest migrants under a wide variety of statutes. The law also gave them powers to arrest local men and women whom they considered to be idle and disorderly, nightwalkers, disturbers of the peace, or refusing to work. At the constable's discretion offenders of various sorts could be imprisoned in the stocks or elsewhere until the 'heat of their passion' was over or until the constable deemed it 'a proper time' to take the offender before a justice. For example, the 'female vagrant' Mary Saxby recorded that having been seen to lodge with a 'common woman' 'the constable came in the night, obliged us to leave our bed, and secured us till morning when we were taken before a justice'.[54] These powers were temporary, of course, but at this lower

[53] T. Critchley, *A History of Police in England and Wales 900–1966* (London, 1967), p. 19; Kent, *The English Village Constable*, pp. 130–9. All twenty-two constables in the deposition sample (see notes to Table 2.1) signed their names.

[54] Shoemaker, *Prosecution*, pp. 217–24; Ritson, *The Office*, pp. 36–7; Paul, *The Parish*, pp. 155–64. Ashdon constables made twenty-two payments to travellers, 1799–1800. E.R.O. D/P 18/5/3; Saxby, *Memoirs*, pp. 15–16.

level many husbandmen, labourers, and artisans were able, as constables, to move the levers of fear and mercy in line with their own attitudes and interests. 'The Constables', Cowper wrote in 1783, 'are not altogether judicious in the exercise either of their justice or their mercy. Some who seem proper objects of punishment they have released on a hopeless promise of better behaviour; and others, whose offence has been personal against themselves, though in other respects less guilty, they have set in the stocks.' In the absence of any rural petty constables' diaries for the eighteenth century, it is difficult to know how frequently they compounded offences, took bribes, or let petty thieves go on the 'promise of better behaviour', but unless they were bound by warrant to arrest the accused they had wide discretionary powers. Contemporary legal handbooks advised the constable that he could arrest on suspicion of felony or 'finding the suspicion groundless, (he) may refuse to arrest'. In most property crime cases constables almost certainly preferred to admonish or counsel rather than arrest or prosecute, but if the offender was a stranger the constable also had other options. Because legal definitions of vagrancy and theft overlapped constables had wide discretionary powers in cases of suspected theft. Some thieves were simply dealt with as vagrants, especially after 1783 when anyone found in dwellings, outhouses, gardens, etc. and deemed to be there with intent to steal could be punished under the vagrancy laws, as could anyone carrying picklocks or weapons. On other occasions suspected thieves were initially arrested as vagrants until a case could be built against them. The constable of Stratford took two men before the local JP in 1772 after they had been stopped with geese that were believed to have been stolen. Initially they were committed as vagrants but they were later charged with felony and convicted after the owner of the geese had been traced through an advertisement.[55]

It is no coincidence that this example of a constable actively involved in detecting and prosecuting a property offender took place in south-west Essex. Asked in 1836 whether constables apprehended offenders without being specifically applied to for that purpose, the parish officials of West Ham, Woodford, and Leyton replied unequivocally that they did. In rural Essex the response was very different. Only five parishes replied positively while more than thirty replied 'No', 'Never', or 'They do not'. Given that a number of parishes did try to reform their police arrangements in the 1820s and early 1830s, it is likely that even fewer parish officials would have replied positively before 1820. The Essex quarter sessions depositions certainly suggest that eighteenth-century constables, like their counterparts in seventeenth-century Sussex, were largely reactive rather than proactive. In a sample of depositions covering 270 Essex offenders less than ten indicate any definite involvement by

---

[55] Ritson, *The Office*, p. 37; S. Webb and B. Webb, *English Local Government from the Revolution to the Municipal Corporation Act. The Parish and the County* (London, 1906), p. 68; *P.P.*, 1817, VII, p. 380; S. Palmer, *Police and Protest in England and Ireland 1780–1850* (Cambridge, 1988), p. 74; Paul, *The Parish*, p. 162; E.R.O. Q/SBb 269/24; Burn, *The Justice* (1797), 4, pp. 263–4.

constables in the initial stages of detection or pursuit. Although their activities were not systematically recorded it appears that eighteenth-century constables usually responded to, rather than initiated, the apprehension of property offenders. Their main functions were to take the prisoner into safe keeping once he had been captured, and to assist in obtaining and executing a search warrant when this proved necessary.[56]

Since even the semi-permanent constables continued to follow other occupations, it is hardly surprising that the vast majority of parish constables were reluctant to get involved in the time-consuming and sometimes dangerous business of detecting and arresting offenders, unless a reward was in the offing or they were specifically requested to do so by a JP. 'A tradesmen who happens to be chosen constable . . . will never think of exerting himself, nor indeed has he time', one commentator observed in 1816. 'If he hears that one of his neighbours is robbed he won't wag out of his own shop till the magistrate sends for him.' If the constable executed a magistrate's warrant or undertook a journey at the vestry's request he was certain to be paid for his trouble. If he pursued a suspected felon he was not. Occasionally the victim, the parish, or the statutory reward system would offer him some recompense but the outcome was uncertain and remuneration was anything but guaranteed. Constables had other reasons for ignoring, or choosing to mediate in, cases involving minor appropriations. If the accused was found on enquiry to be of 'good name and fame' they were encouraged to release him. When the offender was contrite and pleaded that this was his first offence some Essex constables agreed to resolve the matter informally. More importantly perhaps many constables were employees or small tradesmen who would rather 'connive at illegal practices' than risk alienating employers, fellow workers, or potential customers. As one Essex resident noted in 1836, 'much cannot be expected from an ignorant unpaid officer who has his own business to follow, his bread to earn, a family to maintain . . . fear, interest and affection to restrain him.' In the late eighteenth and early nineteenth centuries the constables of rural Essex were semi-salaried part-time officers who were far from ignorant or illiterate. However, they were not professional policemen. Men like Jeremiah Howes and Jonathan Bull had a school, an inn, or a workshop to run and as constables they preferred to operate on a fee-for-service basis.[57] This was not the basis on which property crime investigations were usually conducted and in rural Essex most victims therefore received little help from their parish constables in the initial stages of the detection process. However, this was not necessarily the case in every part of Essex for a new pattern was emerging in the parishes near to London.

[56] P.R.O. H.O. 73/6 and 9; Herrup, *The Common Peace*, pp. 68–70.

[57] *P.P.*, 1816, V, p. 178; Storch, 'Policing', pp. 223–5; *P.P.*, 1839, XIX, p. 96; Williams, *Everyman*, p. 79; Wrightson, *English Society*, p. 157; P.R.O. H.O. 73/5 (Lexden and Winstree); 73/9.1 (Stisted); 73/6.2 (Wanstead); Styles, 'The Emergence', p. 17.

5. The Growth of Public and Private Policing in South-West Essex

The enquiries of the early 1830s indicate that policing in south-west Essex was of a different quality from that found elsewhere in the county. Not only was the Becontree hundred the only area in which the majority of constables were willing to apprehend offenders without being specifically asked to do so; it was also the area with the youngest police force (Table 3.8). The three parishes nearest to London each had an established night patrol by the 1830s and employed more full-time salaried policemen than all the other parishes in the county. This was not a new development. In the later eighteenth and early nineteenth centuries London's continued expansion spawned various policing initiatives by both central and local government, as well as encouraging the growth of private thieftaking networks. Unlike their counterparts elsewhere in Essex, parishes on the edge of London, including Woodford, Ilford, West Ham, Barking, and East Ham, all established and maintained watch-houses by the later eighteenth century. At West Ham, the county's gateway into London, the vestry first set up a watch-house in the Stratford ward during the 1660s, and by 1800 three or four watch-houses were established, at least one of which was manned by an armed watchman paid by the parish. Mirroring developments elsewhere in the metropolis West Ham put considerable energy into reforming its watch in the late eighteenth century, but these changes were not welcomed by all the population. In 1800 the West Ham watch-house was partly demolished by a hostile crowd and the local military association had to be called out to protect the watchman from further assaults. Twelve years earlier the East Ham watch-house was levelled to the ground during a similar protest.[58]

The source of this hostility is rarely clear but the watchmen of West Ham were highly active in pursuing offenders and this undoubtedly caused resentment. In 1801, for example, the *Chelmsford Chronicle* reported that 'four watchmen of Stratford who are young men' had 'armed themselves with guns and pistols' and pursued a group of Irish footpads. Such activities were highly dangerous. Several shots were fired before one of the footpads was apprehended and persuaded to turn evidence. When the watchmen then made further arrests they were attacked in the fields by a party of Irish men and women.[59] The average rural constable would not have countenanced such dangerous activity. Why did the West Ham officers take a different approach?

Despite the lack of systematic sources the answer is clear. Several of these men were professional thieftakers who made their living from police work. In a

---

[58] P.R.O. HO 73/5, 6, and 9; E.R.O. Q/CR 7/1; D. Philips, 'A New Engine of Power and Authority. The Institutionalisation of Law-Enforcement in England 1780–1830', in V. Gatrell *et al.* (eds.), *Crime and the Law* (London, 1980), pp. 155–89; J. Oxley, *Barking Vestry Minutes and Other Parish Documents* (Colchester, 1955), p. 151; Stokes, *East Ham*, pp. 76, 86–7; Erith, *Woodford*, pp. 88–9; *V.C.H... Essex*, 6, p. 99; Reynolds, *Before the Bobbies*; Paley, 'An Imperfect'; E.R.O. Q/SBb 380/77.

[59] *Che.C.*, 11 Dec. 1801.

five-year period in the mid-1780s Stephen Reynolds, constable of Stratford, was involved in well over twenty assize cases. Eleven of these ended in capital convictions which between then netted him £75 from statutory rewards alone. In many of these cases he worked with two West Ham watchmen, Thomas Reynolds and Thomas South, who between them profited by a further £90 worth of rewards. These three men were highly active. In 1789–90 14 per cent of all Essex assize prosecutions and 38 per cent of those arising from the Becontree hundred involved at least one of them as a witness. They were not simply the arresting officers in such cases. Only a third of these offences were committed in the parish of West Ham. Victims from all over the Becontree hundred and beyond benefited from their activities and their determined pursuit of offenders was widely publicized. In 1783, for example, the *Chelmsford Chronicle* reported that 'Mr Reynolds, an active person at Strat-ford' had apprehended a violent robber after following him closely for eight hours.[60] Based at Stratford, where most of the main Essex roads converged before crossing the marshes into London, this small group of thieftakers used the Stratford Turnpike Gate as a convenient place to stop and search any suspicious travellers entering or leaving London. In 1786, for example, they apprehended a gang of burglars after stopping a coach crammed full of furniture as it was re-entering London at 2 o'clock in the morning. Several lead thieves who had raided the roofs of the rich houses of the Becontree suburbs suffered the same fate as they passed through Stratford; while in 1789 a similar search by a Mr Reynolds led to the prosecution of a Chelmsford horse thief. The quarter sessions records also indicated that both wagons and foot passengers with suspicious bundles were regularly stopped by these men. A wagon search by Thomas Reynolds and Thomas South in 1800, for example, led to the transportation of a Barking servant who had pilfered his master's potatoes.[61]

These West Ham-based officers also used their powers of search and arrest in relation to vagrants to apprehend suspected felons, and they probably made a regular income out of the vagrancy trade. The 1780s witnessed a massive public campaign against vagrancy in Essex and elsewhere, and the county expended large sums on the conveyance of vagrants and on rewards for their arrest. Since more than half of the rewards paid out for the arrest of Essex vagrants in the mid-1780s went to men operating in the Becontree hundred, parish officials in that area were particularly well placed to benefit from the

[60] E.R.O. Q/SBb 379/97, 321/30; P.R.O. Assi 34/43–46; *Che.C.*, 14 Feb. 1783. See also 22 Feb. 1782. 'Mr Reynolds' was probably Stephen, who, unlike Thomas, was literate. Other kinship links were probably useful, William Reynolds, coroner, who heard the inquest in the 1783 case lived nearby at Chigwell. Another Reynolds was the gaoler at Chelmsford. *Che.C.*, 4 Apr. 1783, 12 Sept. 1783.
[61] *Che.C.*, 1 Dec. 1786; P.R.O. Ass 34/43; *Che.C.*, 20 Nov. 1789; E.R.O. Q/SBb 321/30, 379/97; Paley, 'Thief-Takers', p. 310. On police officers searching carts at the West Ham tollhouse *P.P.*, 1828, VI, pp. 202–5.

wave of anti-vagrant activity that swept through the county in 1787–8.[62] A local JP, John Staples, may well have encouraged the growth of this thieftaking group. In a later testimonial he claimed to have spent £20 a year between 1784 and 1786 on patrols for the West Ham area and he sometimes used the Stratford watch-house as a temporary lock-up. However, these three men were certainly not dependent on his support and after his departure they continued to supplement the lucrative but irregular income they obtained from rewards in capital cases via a number of other sources. These would have included not only private payments from victims and prosecution associations, parish payments for journeys on parochial matters, shares in the sales of Tyburn Tickets, and rewards for the arrests of vagrants, but also a number of less legitimate sources such as compounding, extortion, or the exploitation of the debt laws. In the last decades of the eighteenth century the Stratford watch-house seems to have been an informal centre for various entrepreneurial policing activities by these men and, since popular hostility towards thieftakers was widespread, it is not surprising that Thomas Reynolds was one of the targets of the rioters who attacked the watch-house in 1800.[63]

These West Ham men were not the only group who responded to the growing demand for detection services. Between 1783 and 1787 at least half a dozen Bow Street officers were involved in the conviction of Essex offenders. The small salaries received by these officers were little more than retainers, and although they supplemented them widely from expenses, fines, forfeitures, private hirings, vagrancy rewards, and other sources, Essex and the other Home Circuit counties were clearly an important source of income for some officers. Patrick McManus made £24 from four separate Essex rewards share-outs between 1783 and 1787 and a further £26 from three other Home Circuit cases. He also earned a share of a £40 private reward offered in one of the Essex cases and he almost certainly earned substantial sums from rewards at the Old Bailey. Both Thomas Carpmeal and Charles Zealous, with whom McManus often operated, made between £40 and £50 from Home Circuit rewards in the same period, the majority of their cases being heard in Essex.[64]

---

[62] E.R.O. Q/SBb 379/79; on vagrants Q/SBb 322/10, 324/8; 327/65–87, £185 was spent on vagrant rewards in Becontree out of a county total of £363, 1782–6. S. Webb and B. Webb, *English Poor Law History. Part One. The Old Poor Law* (London, 1929), pp. 350–91 and N. Rogers, 'Policing the Poor in Eighteenth-Century London. The Vagrancy Laws and their Administration', *Histoire Sociale— Social History*, 24 (1991), 127–47; *Che.C.*, 14 Dec. 1787–5 Dec. 1788; Radzinowicz, *History*, 2, p. 307.

[63] R. Paley, 'The Middlesex Justices Act of 1792. Its Origins and Effects' (Reading University Ph.D., 1983), p. 138; P.R.O. HO 42/20/194 and 42/5/239–40. (I am grateful to Ruth Paley for these references.) For the thieftakers' use of Staples for Essex committals E.R.O. Q/SBb 321/30; Paley, 'Thief-Takers'; E.R.O. Q/SBb 380/77/1.

[64] For Bow Street runners' sources of income, Radzionowicz, *History*, 2, pp. 195–323; P.R.O. Ass. 34/43–6; *Che.C.*, 11 June 1784; for Zealous, P. Melville, *The Life and Work of Sir John Fielding* (London, 1934), p. 244; for Carpmeal, see G. Armitage, *The History of the Bow Street Runners* (London, 1932), p. 148; John Clark, 'a clever runner', ibid., 105 arrested an Essex offender in 1775 (*Che.C.*, 17 Mar. 1775). John Sayer and Patrick McManus attended both the King and the Prince Regent. For McManus, see A. Babington, *A House in Bow Street. Crime and Magistracy in London 1740–1881* (London, 1969), p. 190.

The closely-knit group of policing entrepreneurs who used Bow Street as their headquarters in this period did not have as big an impact on Essex prosecutions as they did at the Old Bailey, but between 1783 and 1788 Bow Street men were associated with at least one or two Essex assizes convictions each year and their activities were well publicized. Between 1770 and 1790 the *Chelmsford Chronicle* reported at least ten occasions on which Bow Street men were instrumental in detecting offenders, and Fielding's attempts to set up stronger links with the Essex magistrates in the early 1770s coincided with some of his men's best publicized successes.[65]

The Bow Street officers may sometimes have acted as thiefmakers rather than thieftakers but their successful involvement in Essex cases was mainly due to their intimate knowledge of metropolitan receiving networks combined with their ability to trace offenders once incriminating evidence had been uncovered. Occasionally more specific techniques are reported, such as the use of identification parades or the tracing of offenders through lodging house receipts, turnpike tickets or a vehicle registration number.[66] To well-off victims from the rich residential areas of south-west Essex such expertise was extremely useful since offenders in the area almost invariably used the capital as a refuge. Almost all the Essex offenders arrested by Bow Street men were taken in the London area. Although exceptions were made if a large reward was in the offing or if the officer's knowledge made a quick and easy arrest possible, provincial victims often had to pay substantial hiring fees to obtain the services of Bow Street men for tasks outside the metropolis. The cost involved was therefore well beyond the means of most Essex prosecutors.[67] How useful were the policing institutions developed by central government from the mid-eighteenth century onwards to the vast majority of Essex victims?

The information service initiated by Fielding was helpful in a fairly wide range of cases, but the networks of regular foot and horse patrols co-ordinated by the Bow Street Office from the 1780s onwards do not appear to have had a major impact until the nineteenth century. The patrol's routine activities did not extend into Essex until 1805 and before that date they may even have encouraged some footpads to move their operations into south-west Essex in order to avoid surveillance. However, when the operations of the horse patrols were extended in 1805 the two main roads into Essex were covered for more

---

[65] Radzinowicz, *History*, 2, pp. 473–4; E.R.O. Q/SBb 272/56–65; *Che.C.*, 22 Nov.1771, 29 Jan. 1773, 17 Mar. 1775, 2 July 1773, 6 Jan. 1775, 4 and 11 Aug. 1775, 8 Mar. 1776; Styles, 'Sir John Fielding'.

[66] Paley, 'Thief-Takers'; Paley, 'The Middlesex Justices', pp. 84 and 166–7; *Che.C.*, 6 Jan. 1775, 17 Mar. 1775, 4 Aug. 1775, 8 Mar. 1776. This was a lucrative business, see *P.P.*, 1816, V, pp. 122 and 214.

[67] *P.P.*, 1816, V. p. 215. The limited government aid Fielding received usually enabled him to offer follow-up facilities only to Metropolitan victims (Styles, 'Sir John Fielding', p. 146). Almost all the Essex victims who used Bow Street officers were well off. 'Parties must pay' was Bow Street's usual rule Radzinowicz, *History*, 2, p. 263.

than 10 miles out of the capital and reports of highway robberies in the area declined considerably.[68]

The initial impact of the 1792 Middlesex Justices Act on Essex was also small. Five years after it had established seven metropolitan police offices employing paid magistrates and constables, Colquhoun claimed that they were offering Essex victims 'considerable advantages in the prompt detection and apprehension of offenders'. However, as one of the magistrates involved he clearly had an interest in creating such an impression and the actual contributions of these offices may well have been small. Between 1807 and 1812 only a handful of Essex offenders were committed for trial by stipendiary magistrates from either these offices or the Thames Police Establishment formed in 1800.[69] In south-west Essex the law enforcement institutions financed by local and central government did sometimes provide the victim with a more effective means of apprehending the offender than was available elsewhere in the county. However, his main hope of assistance in the eighteenth century came not from these formal policing institutions but from the growing network of thieftaking entrepreneurs that operated partly from those institutions and partly as independent providers of policing services.

The likelihood that an offender would be detected, pursued, and apprehended could therefore be determined as much by geography as by the victim's attitudes. Where proactive entrepreneurial police networks existed offenders were sometimes apprehended by men who would pressurize the victim into prosecuting from motives of profit. Outside south-west Essex, however, the victim was usually in the opposite position. He alone had to decide whom to ask for assistance, and usually it was he alone who provided the incentives. Apart from neighbours willing to help as pursuers or witnesses, most reasonably effective means of detecting offenders cost money. A reliable promise to refund expenses or provide a reward might activate the parish constable and the latter would probably attract professional thieftakers, if they were available, but the price was often high. Newspaper advertisements were less expensive, costing the equivalent of half a labourer's weekly wage, but they were unlikely to be effective unless a substantial reward was attached, and this strategy was beyond the means of most labouring families. Such advertisements were mainly placed by the literate middling sort or by the gentry. The interrelated development of local printing facilities and of prosecution associations therefore offered new opportunities for detection to these groups but

[68] Paley, 'The Middlesex Justices', pp. 181–5; Radzinowicz, *History*, 3, pp. 7–62, 136, 293; Styles, 'Sir John Fielding'. Regular payment of a Bow Street highway patrol began in the early 1780s. Babbington, *A House*, p. 169. By the late 1790s more than seventy men were employed on foot patrol duties by Bow Street, but until 1805 the patrols only went 3 or 4 miles from the centre of London. *P.P.*, 1816, V, pp. 144 and 194; *P.P.*, 1822, IV, p. 113; C. Emsley, *Policing and its Context 1750–1870* (London, 1983), p. 27.

[69] Colquhoun, *Police*, p. 220; for the Middlesex Justices Act and the failure of its policing measures, see Paley, 'The Middlesex Justices', pp. 254–7; Radzinowicz, *History*, 3, pp. 123–35. The 1807–12 figure was just over 1%. Colquhoun made one committal.

rarely helped the labouring poor. The only new resources offered to them came from the courts who increasingly reimbursed the cost of actually prosecuting rather than of detecting offenders. Costs were awarded on a means-tested basis throughout the eighteenth century and, although the threshold was changed to include growing numbers of the middling sort, this lack of state provision persuaded many of Essex's wealthier inhabitants to make private insurance-type provision for themselves through prosecution associations.

The financial resources available to potential prosecutors from the courts or from their own subscriptions undoubtedly increased some victims' willingness to prosecute by reducing the financial risks involved [70] but outside south-west Essex neither the financial nor the physical assistance available offered the average victim any substantial help in detecting and apprehending offenders. Parish constables, despite their growing experience and their wide discretionary powers over minor offenders, were rarely primary movers in the detection process. Most preferred to diffuse conflict rather than to make arrests and they rarely did anything which would have constrained the discretionary choices of Essex victims. Membership of a prosecution association might theoretically restrict the victim's room for manoeuvre once the offender had been arrested, but in practice it rarely did so. Rewards and pre-1778 cost awards, which were usually only available on conviction, affected the victim's behaviour during the trial, but in pretrial negotiations their freedom of action was impeded only by their own poverty, their neighbours' unwillingness to help, and, if they took the process to its final stage, by the attitude of the committing magistrate.

[70] Rewards were sometimes of greater help than costs to the poor because they were given favourable treatment. *P.P.*, 1816, V, p. 43, 'If the prosecutor is poor...they give him the larger proportion of the reward.'

4

Magistrates and Summary Courts

Despite the assistance he or she sometimes received from others, it was the victim who decided whether or not to move the accused on to the next stage of the judicial process by taking him before a Justice of the Peace. The magistrates themselves rarely influenced this decision. Most eighteenth-century JPs were not directly concerned with the detection of offenders. A few diligent magistrates did sometimes involve themselves in advertising and apprehending suspects but such men were exceptional. Although initiatives and proclamations encouraging the active pursuit of offenders were supported by many Essex magistrates, they were mainly concerned with responding to the cases brought before them rather than with creating business for the courts.[1]

Their failure to initiate many prosecutions does not mean that magistrates played no part in shaping the nature of the judicial process at this stage. The English magistracy was a highly independent body whose tribunals were increasing in scope and power during the early modern period as the manorial courts declined, as new responsibilities such as the supervision of the poor laws were heaped upon them, and as many matters previously dealt with at quarter sessions were passed down to them.[2] Drawn from social groups of relatively high status and independent means, rural magistrates were voluntary and unpaid officials, over whom the legal system had little financial hold. By the eighteenth century their activities were no longer closely supervised by any central authority, although in certain circumstances aggrieved individuals could, and very occasionally did, appeal to the higher courts or to the quarter sessions about their actions. Their decisions in property crime cases were very rarely scrutinized and it is therefore easy to be misled by the strict guidelines laid down by contemporary legal handbooks into underestimating their discretionary powers and the degree to which they reshaped pretrial procedures in this period.[3]

---

[1]   Beattie, *Crime*, p. 36; *Che.C.*, 15 Dec. 1769, 27 Dec. 1771, 29 Oct. 1790, 27 July 1787.
[2]   Gisborne, *An Enquiry*, p. 257; N. Landau, *The Justices of the Peace 1679–1760* (Berkeley, California, 1984), pp. 209–21; D. Eastwood, *Governing Rural England. Tradition and Transformation in Local Government 1780–1840* (Oxford, 1994), pp. 88–95.
[3]   Landau, *The Justices*, pp. 345–57; D. Howell, *Patriarchs and Parasites. The Gentry of South-West Wales in the Eighteenth Century* (Cardiff, 1986), p. 141; J. Cockburn, *Calendar of Assize Records. Home Circuit Indictments. Elizabeth and James I. Introduction* (London, 1985) p. 91; J. Baker, 'Criminal Courts and Procedure at

This chapter begins by examining the broader and largely arbitrational character of summary hearings, and the various alternatives to formal indictment in the major courts developed and used by magistrates in property crime cases. Their activities in relation to game offences, wood theft, and other minor forms of property appropriation in which they were empowered by statute to act as both judge and jury are then explored as a prelude to evaluating the courtroom interactions and underlying attitudes which influenced the outcome of all property-related summary hearings. Finally, the magistrates themselves, their availability, and declining social status will be examined.

1. The Character and Context of Summary Hearings

Although their quarter sessions meetings had to be formally recorded, magistrates were rarely required to preserve documents relating to the local summary adjudications they made without the aid of a jury. During the eighteenth century the range of summary statutes and of petty sessions activities expanded rapidly but the summary courts' administrative procedures were still largely determined by the magistrates of each locality and a bewildering variety of practices therefore arose. Moreover, petty sessions hearings gradually changed between the late seventeenth and the mid-nineteenth centuries from largely informal meetings of neighbouring justices to regularly constituted courts with established procedures and premises. The few eighteenth-century records that survive reflect the fluid, *ad hoc* nature of the summary courts as well as the fact that solitary magistrates were more limited in the types of case they could hear than those who sat in joint meetings. They range from the detailed informal justicing notebooks left by a few individual magistrates, through various types of examination or deposition books, to petty sessions minute books, which survive in much larger numbers.[4] The eighteenth-century Essex records contain neither JPs' notebooks nor substantial correspondence relating to judicial business, but the petty sessions records and the house of correction calendars are among the best in England. By combining them with notebooks from other counties the nature of this vital arena within the judicial process can be tentatively explored.

Whether sitting alone, in informally arranged joint meetings, or in more regular petty sessions, magistrates dealt with a vast range of disputes and

Common Law 1550–1800', in Cockburn (ed.), *Crime*, p. 33; Langbein, 'Albion's Fatal Flaws', p. 103; Hay, 'Prosecution', p. 380; Beattie, *Crime*, pp. 10–18; but see also Shoemaker, *Prosecution*.

[4] J. Innes, 'Statute Law and Summary Justice in Early Modern England' (unpublished paper 1986); Landau, *The Justices*, esp. pp. 173–239 for the powers of solitary justices and those sitting in joint sessions; E. Crittall (ed.), *The Justicing Notebook of William Hunt 1744–1749* (Devizes, 1982); A. Cirket (ed.), *Samuel Whitbread's Notebooks, 1810–11, 1813–14* (Bedfordshire Historical Record Society, 1971); E. Silverthorne (ed.), *Deposition Book of Richard Wyatt, J.P. 1767–1776* (Surrey Record Society, Guildford, 1978); R. Paley (ed.), *Justice in Eighteenth-Century Hackney. The Justicing Notebook of Henry Norris and the Hackney Petty Sessions book* (London Record Society, 1991).

administrative matters. Hearings involving property appropriation represented a very small proportion of the cases they dealt with. Less than 10 per
cent of the cases recorded in the Lexden and Winstree examination books of
northern Essex, 1788–92, or in Samuel Whitbread's Bedfordshire justicing
notebooks, 1810–14, involved property appropriations. The equivalent figure
at the Colchester petty sessions in the 1770s was about 6 per cent. Almost every
stratum of eighteenth-century society brought numerous other grievances and
disputes to the summary courts. Disputes about assaults, about property
ownership, about the non-payment of wages or relief, about the behaviour
of servants or of the poor, about the settlement or bastardy laws, and about
such diverse issues as alehouse regulations, friendly society procedures, turnpike laws, or the swearing of oaths flooded into these tribunals. Most of these
cases were resolved by arbitration or by the imposition of a small fine and/or
costs, and the broader social impact of the diverse adjudicational services
offered by magistrates in these courts has been explored by the author in
detail elsewhere.[5] However, the mediation-based ethos of these hearings also
affected the way property crime cases were dealt with. What were these
preliminary hearings like? Given the almost complete absence of detailed
contemporary descriptions of summary proceedings and their diverse and
changing nature, it is dangerous to generalize. However, in rural areas at
least, most eighteenth-century summary hearings were usually characterized
by their administrative informality, their semi-private nature, their relative
fluidity and flexibility, and their tendency to become forums of negotiation and
mediation rather than of formal prosecution.

Eighteenth-century magistrates followed highly diverse administrative practices. Samuel Whitbread was available almost every day of the year, conduct-
ing many of his hearings in his dressing-gown before taking breakfast. Charles
Matthews, the most active justice in north-east Essex, also offered a fairly
comprehensive service, taking examinations on several days each week. However, these men were exceptional. The rural Buckinghamshire JP Edmund
Waller only undertook judicial business on Mondays, a service that was itself
suspended for about three months a year because he was residing elsewhere,
while most JPs never established a regular pattern of availability. The growth
of monthly, fortnightly, or weekly petty sessions meetings was partly designed
to overcome the uncertainty and expense that this caused. Although some
thinly populated areas continued to follow less regular patterns, by the beginning of the nineteenth century the Chelmsford petty sessions was meeting
regularly every Friday, and by the 1810s similar Tuesday meetings were also
being scheduled.[6]

[5] E.R.O. P/LwR 6–8; P/COR 2; Cirket, *Samuel Whitbread's Notebooks*; Landau, *The Justices*, pp. 222–
5; King, 'The Summary Courts'.
[6] Cirket, *Samuel Whitbread's Notebooks*, pp. 7–8; Buckinghamshire R.O. DC 18/39/4–5; E.R.O. P/
LwR 6–8, P/CM 1–3.

How public were summary hearings? Most individual rural magistrates conducted their judicial business in their own parlours or justicing rooms—spaces which the public would not always have found it easy to gain access to. Some petty sessions met in similar semi-privacy, but as these hearings became more frequent and regular in the eighteenth century they also became more open. The Chelmsford petty sessions met at the Shire Hall by 1801 and the majority of petty sessions used local inns where substantial audiences sometimes gathered, prompting complaints that justices had to do their business amid 'the noise and ordure of a narrow room infected with drinking and a throng'. In London pretrial hearings became highly public affairs during the eighteenth century and provincial practice may have mirrored this to some extent at the petty sessions level. However, as late as 1835 magistrates continued to have the right to exclude the public from committal proceedings, although not from hearings under specific summary statutes, and Gisborne was almost certainly right when he observed in the 1790s that most of the judicial business done by rural single magistrates was 'transacted in his own house, before few spectators and those in general indigent and illiterate'.[7]

The nature of summary hearings underwent several related changes in the later eighteenth and early nineteenth centuries, not the least of which was the growing impact of attorneys both as magistrates' clerks and as representatives of either victim or accused, but for much of the period under scrutiny here many rural magistrates continued to conduct what were effectively semi-private hearings. Partly for this reason, perhaps, legal technicalities did not take pride of place in these courts. Magistrates, Gisborne believed, had a tendency to avoid consulting legal handbooks and statutes, preferring to base their judgments 'on their own unauthorised ideas of equity', and early nineteenth-century commentators were equally concerned about magistrates' ignorance of the law. In exercising the ill-defined powers they enjoyed in relation to the disorderly and itinerant poor many eighteenth-century magistrates were little concerned about the precise statutory authority on which their actions were based. The proliferation of summary statutes in the eighteenth century, which extended the magistrates' sentencing powers in a wide range of particular contexts, may, in combination with increasing pressure from defendants and their advocates and from the King's Bench judges, have encouraged magistrates to be more precise about such matters. However, many continued to commit a broad spectrum of offenders to houses of correction as vagrants, idle, and disorderly, etc.[8]

---

[7] Landau, *The Justices*, p. 231; Webb, *The Parish*, pp. 299 and 392–3; Beattie, *Crime*, pp. 279–80; W. Hulton, *A Treatise on the Law of Convictions* (London, 1835), p. 49; T. Gisborne, *An Enquiry into the Duties of Men of the Higher and Middle Classes* (London, 1794), p. 246; Sharpe, *Crime in Early Modern England*, pp. 89–90.

[8] Beattie, *Crime*, pp. 276–80; Webb, *The Parish*, pp. 347–50; Gisborne, *An Enquiry*, p. 242; Hay, 'Prosecution', p. 380; Innes, 'Statute Law'; Shoemaker, *Prosecution*, pp. 35–40.

Eighteenth-century summary hearings could be highly fluid affairs. Victims were often undecided about the precise outcome they were looking for. Many came with a complaint or accusation that had not yet crystallized into a specific charge. Only during the hearing did the interactions between magistrate, victim, witnesses, and accused determine whether a formal prosecution would result or an informal punishment or settlement be resorted to. Alternatively, some victims brought a specific charge but, finding the magistrate unwilling to pursue it, they then opted for a different and usually less severe form of proceedings. The magistrates' central role in the majority of cases— such as disputes between parishes, between masters and servants, between assailants and assaulted, between paupers and overseers—was that of arbitrator or mediator. From Lambarde to Blackstone, and well on into the nineteenth century, magistrates were constantly told that their most important function was to act 'as a peacemaker' reconciling and healing disputes, and 'preventing vexatious prosecutions'.[9]

How fundamentally did the arbitration and negotiation-based methods which dominated many summary proceedings affect both the magistrates' approach to hearings involving property offences and the victims' expectations about, and attitudes to, such hearings? Diaries suggest that victims of theft were often willing to embrace informal resolutions. Only half of the summary hearings about potential felonies recorded by the eight main diarists surveyed resulted in the accused being sent on to the major courts. When Mary Hardy's maids stole her victuals and gave them to two young men, their offence could probably have been defined as larceny, but Mary seems to have been quite content when the local magistrate simply 'threatened them severely and made them pay the expenses'. Blundell accepted a similar decision by a local magistrate in 1710 and John Skinner's diary reveals that when his servant was raped he encouraged her to take the matter before a magistrate where it was settled 'out of court', her attacker offering to pay 5 guineas. Informal settlements had many advantages from the victims' point of view. They were convenient, less disruptive to local social relations, and potentially profitable if an informal financial payment was stipulated.[10]

The magistrate's attitude to the informal resolution of a felony accusation was often more ambivalent. His inclination to act as a mediator led him in one direction; legal handbooks and the statutes on which they were based pulled him in another. If the form of appropriation involved fell clearly under a summary statute, as it did in most cases involving game offences, the embezzlement of wool, or the theft of wood, vegetables, or growing crops, the magistrate's decision was relatively straightforward. He had clear powers to

[9] Landau, *The Justices*, pp. 173–4; Gisborne, *An Enquiry*, pp. 241–4; Shoemaker, *Prosecution*, pp. 81–94.
[10] Cozens-Hardy, *Mary Hardy's Diary*, p. 84; Bagley, *The Great Diurnal*, 1, p. 242; Fiske, *The Oakes Diaries*, p. 260; H. Coombs and C. Coombs (eds.), *Journal of a Somerset Rector 1803–1834* (Oxford, 1984), pp. 22–3.

act as judge and jury in such cases. However, most other forms of direct appropriation were defined as felonies, and where a felony had clearly been committed or was charged on oath magistrates were advised by almost all the legal handbooks that they had no powers to try the offence or act as arbitrators. The only decision they had to make was whether to bail the accused or commit him to prison awaiting jury trial—the former being an option which was largely confined to minor theft accusations and was used in less than 10 per cent of cases in both Essex and Surrey.[11]

On first reading, Burn's handbook, a key text which was distributed to every petty sessions division in Essex in the late eighteenth century, is unequivocal. 'If felony is committed', wrote Burn in a passage widely quoted in other handbooks, 'and one is brought before a justice upon suspicion thereof, and the justice finds upon examination that the prisoner is not guilty; yet the justice shall not discharge him, but he must either be bailed or committed; for it is not fit that a man once arrested and charged with felony, or suspicion thereof, should be delivered upon any man's discretion, without further trial.' However, even Burn allowed magistrates some leeway: 'If a prisoner be...expressly charged with felony upon oath, the justice cannot discharge him', he wrote 'but if he be charged with suspicion only of felony, yet there be no felony at all proved to be committed, or if the fact charged as felony be in truth no felony in point of law, the justice may discharge him.'[12] Essex property appropriation cases were not infrequently dismissed because, to quote a Chelmsford petty sessions case in 1805, 'the magistrates thought the circumstances too slight for felony'. Philip Ley, for example, was released from a horse theft charge in 1789, 'all parties being examined and no felonious intent appearing'. If the property had originally been delivered or leased to the accused, Burn also indicated that the matter could be dealt with as 'a trespass' rather than a felony, which allowed the magistrate to make what was effectively a civil judgment offering compensation to the victim. Thus, even within Burn's very restricted terms of reference, magistrates could find a number of ways to justify dismissing potential felony indictments. Those who read Blackstone would have found further justification for using their discretion in his observation that 'if...the suspicion entertained of the prisoner was wholly groundless...it is lawful totally to discharge him'.[13]

---

[11] Beattie, *Crime*, pp. 281–2; Herrup, *The Common Peace*, pp. 89–90; Blackstone, *Commentaries*, 4, pp. 293–4; between 1782 and 1787 5% of Essex quarter sessions property offenders were bailed. E.R.O. Q/SMg 23–25; *Che.C.*, 24 July 1801.

[12] Burn, *The Justice* (1766), 1, pp. 484 and 337; Anon., *The Magistrate's Assistant* (Gloucester, 1784), p. 61; H. Pye, *Summary of the Duties of the Justice of the Peace out of Sessions with Some Preliminary Observations* (London, 2nd edn., 1810), p. 23.

[13] E.R.O. P/CM1 and Q/SBb 334/16; Burn, *The Justice* (1766), I, p. 337; Blackstone, *Commentaries*, 4, p. 293; Williams, *Every Man*, p. 518. For further discussion: B. Shapiro, *Beyond Reasonable Doubt and Probable Cause* (Berkeley, Calif., 1991), pp. 131–85.

Did magistrates remain within these guidelines upholding Burn's dictum that 'criminal matters, as felonies and other indictable offences, cannot be submitted to arbitration'? When the few justicing notebooks that record informal as well as formal resolutions to summary hearings are compared with the legal handbooks, it soon becomes clear that they did not. Samuel Whitbread heard well over a dozen property crime cases that could potentially have been interpreted as felonies or petty larcenies in the two and half years covered by his notebooks, but he sent only four on for jury trial. Four were dismissed because the evidence 'did not justify commitment'. Five resulted in the return of the allegedly stolen goods and/or compensation payments. In a few of these cases the victim may well have complained of a theft when in reality all that was involved was a dispute over borrowed property or a failure to pay for property willingly exchanged. On one occasion Whitbread himself threatened a purchaser who refused to pay for a valuable item with a theft prosecution in order to recover payment for the victim. Whitbread also heard several other cases involving disputes over property in which the complainant did not claim that a theft had occurred. Faced with a spectrum of appropriation cases moving from simple, and essentially civil, disputes over borrowed property to major felonies such as burglary and sheep stealing, Whitbread did not operate a clearly defined boundary between the type of case he was prepared to deal with informally and those he sent on for trial. If an aggravated larceny was clearly alleged on oath he was more likely to send the case on. If the evidence was inadequate, or if the victim appeared willing to make an informal settlement, he would tend to avoid involving the higher courts, but he clearly used his discretion in every case. The Wiltshire magistrate William Hunt showed an even greater preference for informal resolutions. Between 1744 and 1748 he heard over twenty property appropriation cases which could have been defined as felonies but he sent an average of only one case per year on to the major courts.[14]

These two magistrates were not necessarily typical. Did most Essex magistrates take an equally flexible and discretionary line? The Essex records are difficult to use in this context. Extensive series of petty sessions examinations books survive for rural north-eastern Essex, Colchester borough, and the Epping Forest region, but these very rarely record either the JP's reaction to the case or its outcome. Only after 1801, when a complete series of Chelmsford petty sessions minute books begins, is this information available more systematically. The calendars of four of the five county houses of correction are exceptionally informative, being turnover calendars recording all committals rather than just those prisoners who were present at the time of each sessions, but they exclude all cases in which the offender was not imprisoned, and their

[14] R. Burn, *A New Law Dictionary* (2 vols., London, 1792), I, p. 45; Burn, *The Justice* (1766), 1, p. 114; Cirket, *Samuel Whitbread's Notebooks*; Crittall, *The Justicing*.

survival is fitful, while the prisoner's offence is often inadequately or inconsistently described.[15] Nevertheless these sources and evidence drawn from other counties suggest that many JPs took a highly discretionary approach to hearings involving property appropriation.

2. Magistrates' Alternatives to Committal for Trial

In dealing with accusations of felony, the Essex magistrates followed at least four courses of action apart from bailing the offender or committing him for trial. First, they used summary powers relating to vagrants, unruly servants, or the idle and disorderly poor to convict and punish minor offenders. The statutory basis of these decisions is often unclear. A considerable array of relevant statutes was available by the later eighteenth century, including the wide-ranging vagrancy acts of the 1740s and the even wider powers which many legal writers believed had been given to justices of the peace in the early seventeenth century. However, the magistrates themselves rarely felt it necessary to specify which statutory powers they were acting under.[16] Those accused of property appropriations definable as felony had often simultaneously committed a summarily triable offence, and even if they had not, they were in danger of being treated as if they had by magistrates who preferred to try them themselves rather than to send them on to the major courts. Travellers who stole minor items could be dealt with as vagrants. Servants who pilfered from their masters could be punished under master–servant legislation, while the label 'idle and disorderly' could be applied to almost every poor offender.

Although most Essex gaolers wrote only very brief and generalized descriptions of those imprisoned summarily by the local magistrates, the keepers of Newport house of correction gave more detailed offence descriptions which suggest that pilfering servants and apprentices were particularly likely to be tried summarily. In the calendar covering late 1754 and early 1755, for example, three of the four property offenders in the Newport house of correction were servants or apprentices imprisoned after summary trial; two being accused of specific thefts while the third was charged with 'being a very idle and disorderly person running away from his service and supporting himself by pilfering and begging'. Similar instances can be found in the Essex records throughout the eighteenth century. In 1792 the apprentice Jonathan Cadman

---

[15] E.R.O. P/LwR 1–12; P/CoR 1–22; P/CM and P/CF. A few Tendring examinations survive P/Tpi; examination books for the Becontree area begin in 1810 P/BRI. Excluding borough houses of correction, the county contained five of these prisons at Barking, Halstead, Newport, Colchester, and Chelmsford. Only the latter's calendars were non-turnover before the standardization of calendar recording in the 1780s and 1790s. Q/SBb.

[16] Innes, 'Prisons', pp. 70–1; J. Innes, 'Statute Law and Summary Justice in Early Modern England', *Bulletin of the Society for the Study of Labour History*, 52 (1987), 34; Shoemaker, *Prosecution*, p. 37.

was imprisoned at the Lexden and Winstree petty sessions for misbehaviour and carrying away his master's beer. In 1787 William Perry was imprisoned summarily for 'divers misdemeanours, miscarriages and ill-behaviour in his master's service' and particularly for pilfering and various dishonest practices. There are several other references to pilfering in the Newport calendars but, although the more cryptic entries of the Barking keeper imply a similar procedure, it is difficult to assess how often Essex magistrates followed the early eighteenth-century London practice of convicting pilferers of all ages at a summary level, because only the Newport calendars, before they were standardized in the late 1780s, give sufficiently detailed descriptions. This form of trial was particularly appropriate when the property had been specifically delivered to the servant by the employer, because a felony indictment was sometimes problematic in these circumstances. However, this did not prevent many masters from indicting their servants (Chapter 6) and magistrates were equally willing to follow summary procedures against servants when the master was not the victim. In 1789, for example, the *Chelmsford Chronicle* reported that a domestic servant who had stolen a fellow servant's watch had been imprisoned for one month by the local JPs.[17]

Property offenders who were not local residents and could more easily be defined as vagrants were also particularly at risk of summary imprisonment. Judith Monk was imprisoned at Newport in 1767, 'being duly convicted as a rogue and vagabond, wandering, begging and stealing'. The vagrancy laws were not infrequently used as a fallback. When a charge of horse stealing could not be substantiated at the Chelmsford petty sessions in 1804 the accused was 'discharged on that account' but immediately imprisoned for vagrancy, and a similar tactic was used by the same court in 1815. The precise proportion of Essex property offenders that was dealt with using magistrates' summary powers in relation to vagrants, servants, and the disorderly poor remains unclear, but if the Newport evidence is any guide it was very substantial. In the 1750s and 1760s nearly half of the Newport prisoners accused of thefts definable as felony were not awaiting trial but had already been convicted summarily and sentenced to a short period of imprisonment.[18] Moreover, this figure almost certainly underestimates the prevalence of this practice since

[17] E.R.O. Q/SBb 200; P/LwR 8, 15 Jan. 1792; Q/SBb 330/26. E.R.O. Q/SBb 318/24 Barking Calendar includes two women imprisoned summarily for stealing a blanket. A new format was introduced around 1790 leaving little room for offence description. Beattie, *Crime*, pp. 269–70; Shoemaker, *Prosecution*, p. 172; J. Beattie, 'Crime and Inequality in Eighteenth-Century London', in J. Hagan and R. Peterson (eds.), *Crime and Inequality* (Stanford, 1995), pp. 124–5 suggests that a good proportion of those imprisoned by the summary courts of London and Surrey in the early eighteenth century as idle and disorderly were in fact suspected of petty theft. See also Beattie, *The Limits*; Burn, *The Justice* (1797), 4, p. 47; *Che.C.*, 17 July 1789; G. Fletcher, 'The Metamorphosis of Larceny', *Harvard Law Review*, 89 (1976), 469–530.

[18] E.R.O. Q/SBb 252, P/CMi 28 Feb. 1804; P/CM 4 12 June 1815; Newport calendars Q/SBb 192–217 (1753–9) and 244–67 (1766–70); in these sample years ten out of the twenty suspected felons listed in the surviving calendars were tried summarily.

many pilferers, especially those who were servants, apprentices, or young boys, were whipped or fined rather than imprisoned.

Impressment or coercion into the armed forces offered a second convenient alternative to committal for trial. Victims sometimes used this without reference to a magistrate (Chapter 2) but more frequently it was the summary courts themselves that substituted enlistment for indictment. The practice was widely discussed by the 1819 Parliamentary Committee and Radzinowicz has suggested that in wartime property offences were daily compounded by magistrates on condition that the thief enlisted. In 1803, for example, the Essex offender John Langley 'having been committed for felony' at the Chelmsford petty sessions was 'permitted to enter into the army' and thus avoided being put on trial. The Essex sources offer no systematic indication of the frequency of pretrial enlistment but in every war the gaol calendars contain references to property offenders avoiding trial by being 'sent on board His Majesty's tender' or 'discharged by entering on board one of His Majesty's ships of war'. These entries sometimes imply that the accused maintained an element of choice but most physically able male offenders would have found the pressure to enlist virtually impossible to resist, given the magistrates' wide discretionary powers. After 1744, if the JP could find a way of labelling the offender as a vagrant, the latter could be imprisoned until the next quarter sessions when, to quote Burn, 'if such person, being a male, is above 12 years of age, the Court may, before he is discharged from the house of correction, send him to be employed in His Majesty's service by sea or land'.[19]

Enlistment was a particularly convenient way of punishing suspects when the evidence was inconclusive. The Ely petty sessions minute books record that when Daniel Ward was brought before them on suspicion of felony in 1805 'there did not appear sufficient evidence to put the defendant on his trial but he was upon being released turned over to a party of marines to enlist'. Given the extreme pressures magistrates were often under to find recruits, and the wide discretionary powers they were given in wartime to impress the idle, vagrant, and disreputable poor, it is not surprising that they found this an attractive option. There were restrictions of course. Female offenders could not be enlisted, and although Britain was at war for more than half the period 1740–1815 this option was less likely to be used in peacetime. Pretrial enlistment was not, however, confined to wartime years. Some suspected Essex felons were 'discharged by going into the India Company' in peacetime, and in 1788, when fears of renewed hostilities produced a brief resurgence of the

[19] *P.P.*, 1819, VIII, p. 108, 116; Radzinowicz, *History*, 4, pp. 96–7; E.R.O. P/CM 1, 23 Sept. 1803; S. Conway, 'The Recruitment of Criminals into the British Army, 1775–81', *Bulletin of the Institute of Historical Research*, 108 (1985), 54; E.R.O. Q/SBb 294/18 other examples 218/5, 287/7, and 361/32; Burn, *The Justice* (1797), 4, pp. 260–9; for more detailed discussion, P. King, ' "Press Gangs are Better Magistrates than the Middlesex Justices". Young Offenders, Press Gangs and Prosecution Strategies in Eighteenth and Early Nineteenth-Century England', in N. Landau (ed.), *Law, Crime and English Society 1660–1840* (Cambridge, forthcoming).

demand for recruits, at least five of the 67 male prisoners listed in the Essex sessions book calendars were 'discharged on now enlisting'. Overall, the proportion of young male offenders subjected to pretrial enlistment was almost certainly substantial. The post-committal enlistments discussed here may be only the tip of the iceberg, for many property offenders were probably sent straight into the armed forces by the summary courts without being subjected to forms of confinement which would have left any traces in the prison calendars.[20]

The magistrates' third option was to encourage the victim and the accused to make an informal settlement. While legal handbooks continued to assert that public crimes 'can never be the subject of arbitration', magistrates clearly took on a negotiative, quasi-arbitrational role in many such cases. Whitbread resolved theft accusations by using various forms of settlement. In two cases he threatened to grant a warrant if the accused did not satisfy the victim. In a third he established that the thief would pay the victim 2 shillings a week for nearly half a year—a form of compensation also used by other magistrates when the accused was too poor to make immediate payment. Many of the cases heard by the Wiltshire JP William Hunt were also resolved by the delicate use of a spectrum of informal outcomes from positive compensation, through the simple payment of expenses, to a reconciliation involving no monetary payment; 'I persuaded an agreement between them' and 'I let them agree it' being among the entries he made in property crime cases.[21]

The eighteenth-century Essex records are less forthcoming about such cases. House of correction calendars, for example, are by their very nature unlikely to include cases resolved by informal settlement, although in 1764 two men committed to Barking for stealing tools were later 'discharged by giving satisfaction'. The survival of the Chelmsford petty sessions minute books from 1801 onwards enables us to observe that Essex JPs frequently acted as mediators or arbitrators in property crime cases. In the summer of 1813, for example, three property appropriation cases were 'compromised' by order of the magistrates and in one instance it was overtly stated that the 'Defendant agreed to pay costs to avoid prosecution for felony'. The return of the stolen goods was usually a condition if this was still possible. In 1805 the minutes record that one complainant 'agreed to accept his watch and discontinue the prosecution which was allowed'. A public apology was another frequent outcome. In 1803 two pilfering servants were pardoned by their master 'on condition of

---

[20] Cambridge R.O., Isle of Ely Minute Order Book, vol. 3, 18 Aug. 1803; Radzinowicz, *History*, 4, pp. 87–94; female co-offenders were often left for trial. See William Rule and Sarah Medcalf. E.R.O. Q/SBb 223/12. Three of the five were committed for theft. E.R.O. Q/SMg 23 and Q/SBb 340, Barking Calendar for India Service enlistment. See also King, 'Press Gangs'.

[21] Williams, *Every Man*, p. 220; Cirket (ed.), *Samuel Whitbread's Notebooks*, pp. 47, 50, 129; Crittall (ed.), *The Justicing*, pp. 38–41; Shoemaker, *Prosecution*, pp. 81–94; poor defendants were sometimes required to do work for the victim as an alternative, G. Leveson-Gower, 'Notebook of a Surrey Justice', *Surrey Archaeological Collections*, 9 (1888), 174.

acknowledging their offence in the papers'. The frequency with which phrases such as 'compromised on paying costs' or 'discharged on paying expenses' occurred in property crime cases in the Chelmsford petty sessions records suggests that the arbitration and mediation-based techniques which dominated magistrates' proceedings in misdemeanour and assault cases were also applied in a significant proportion of property crime hearings. If the victim preferred an informal resolution and the magistrate considered the case a suitable one, the latter would attempt to resolve the dispute and might even bind a suspected thief over to good behaviour, or at least threaten to do so, in order to encourage an informal resolution of the case.[22]

While the creation of an informal settlement required the consent of both the victim and the accused, the magistrates' fourth option needed no such agreement—the accused could simply be discharged for lack of evidence, either immediately or after a brief period of imprisonment 'for further examination'. Whitbread 'dismissed the complaint' in several property crime cases as did many other rural JPs including Wyatt in Surrey, Waller in Buckinghamshire, D'Aronda in Kent, and Hunt in Wiltshire. Metropolitan justices such as Norris in the 1730s, Fielding in the 1750s, and the Whitechapel rotation office justices in the 1780s also dismissed felony accusations for lack of evidence. The frequency with which such dismissals were used in property crime cases varied widely between individuals. Waller and Norris used this option more carefully and less frequently than most. Hunt, by contrast, used language that indicated he had great confidence in his right to dismiss felony accusations. In two property crime cases, for example, he recorded that he had acquitted or 'excused' the accused because he found 'nothing material to prove the fact'. In another case which he did send on to the quarter sessions, he described the accused as 'convicted before me'. The JPs of the Whitechapel rotation office also made extensive use of similar practices. In 1783 only half the accused felons brought to that office were sent on for jury trial. More than a quarter were 'discharged for want of evidence' while the remainder were summarily convicted as vagrants or persons of ill fame.[23]

The Chelmsford petty sessions records include similar references to property offenders discharged immediately for lack of evidence but it was equally common for the court to hold the accused for 'further examination' before

[22] E.R.O. Q/SBb 236/10; P/CM 2A 20 July 1813; P/CMi 21 Jan. and 8 Nov. 1805; Shoemaker, *Prosecution*, pp. 23–35 and 95–126; Blackstone, *Commentaries*, 4, p. 253 indicates recognizances for good behaviour could be used as a lesser sanction against 'pilferers or robbers'. On binding over, S. Hindle, 'The Keeping of the Public Peace', in P. Griffiths, A. Fox, and S. Hindle, *The Experience of Authority in Early Modern England* (London, 1996), pp. 213–46.

[23] Cirket (ed.), *Samuel Whitbread's Notebooks*, pp. 45–6, 58–9, 117; Beattie, *Crime*, pp. 274–6; Buckinghamshire R.O. DC 18/39/4; Landau, *The Justices*, p. 178; Crittall (ed.), *The Justicing*, pp. 34–42; Shoemaker, *Prosecution*, p. 89; P.R.O. HO/42/2/99 'Return of the J.Ps Acting at the Rotation Office in Whitechapel'. 13 Jan. 1783–24 Feb. 1783, out of 28 accusations of felony, 14 were committed for trial, 8 were discharged for want of evidence, 6 were punished either informally or under summary powers.

releasing him. The eighteenth-century Essex house of correction calendars provide extensive evidence of this practice. At Halstead and Newport in the 1750s and 1760s nearly a third of those imprisoned following an accusation of felony were released after a brief period 'for want of evidence' and of the twenty nine accused felons listed in the Halstead calendars, 1753–9, only twelve were tried at the quarter sessions or assizes. Thirteen were discharged without trial and the remainder seem to have escaped indictment because their prosecutor never appeared or because they were allowed to turn evidence. The magistrates of south-west Essex used this procedure extensively. In the summer of 1757, for example, the Barking house of correction briefly harboured four suspected petty thieves but they were all later discharged without facing jury trial. The calendars of the 1760s contain many similar cases such as that of John Jay and John Gray committed on 'suspicion of sheep stealing and other crimes' but then 'discharged for want of stronger proof' by the magistrates. By the late 1780s the Barking and Colchester calendars indicate that more than a quarter of their accused felons were discharged after further examination, although the relative lack of such cases in the Halstead and Newport calendars of that decade casts some doubt on the assumption that this practice was followed in every part of Essex.[24]

The legal grounds on which magistrates assumed the right to imprison those accused of property crimes pending 'further examination' were not always clear, but the procedure was well established in London by the mid-eighteenth century. After recommending in 1751 that 'the justice be entrusted with a power of detaining any suspicious person who could produce no known housekeeper, or one of credit, to his character, for three days, within which time he might by means of an advertisement, be viewed by numbers who have been lately robbed', Fielding went on to observe that 'some such have been, I know, confined upon an old statute as persons of ill fame, with great emolument to the public'. Within a year of the publication of Fielding's recommendation a statute had been passed that placed this practice on a more secure legal footing. In the context of the magistrates' responsibilities to initiate privy searches for vagrants or disorderly persons the act gave them powers in relation to 'any person apprehended upon ... suspicion of felony (although no direct proof be then made thereof)' to 'examine such person ... and if such person shall not show that he has a lawful way of getting his livelihood, or shall not procure some responsible housekeeper to his character and to give security ... for his future appearance ... the justices may commit him to some prison

---

[24] E.R.O. P/CM 1–4; Q/SBb 192–217 (1753–9) and 244–64 (1766–70); Halstead and Newport calendars. For Barking see Q/SBb 210 and 258.1. The Barking midsummer calendar 1785, Q/SBb 320/13 contains five property offenders sent on for trial and four discharged for want of proof after a brief spell of imprisonment. By contrast the 1780s Halstead and Newport calendars record very few cases of temporary imprisonment followed by discharge for lack of evidence. This may reflect not a change of practice but a decision by the gaolers in these areas to cease recording such cases.

or house of correction, for any time not exceeding six days; and in the meantime . . . advertise in some public paper, a description of his person and anything that shall be found on him . . . which he shall be suspected not to have
come honestly by'.[25]

The Essex magistrates usually ignored the suggestion that newspaper advertisements should accompany detention for further examination. Outside
London newspapers were only published once a week and advertising in this
way would often have been impossible within the time allowed. Whether they
justified the practice by reference to 'an old statute', to the new legislation of
the 1750s or to even vaguer notions about their general powers, both provincial
and metropolitan magistrates made widespread use of this option. *The Times*
reported indignantly in 1785 that although Lord Loughborough had recently
declared the practice of postponing the examination of accused parties and
keeping them in gaol in the meantime to be 'contrary to the law and the
constitution', 'the practice is continued by the justices of the rotation offices'.
Thirty-five years later Cottu observed that the postponement of committal
proceedings and the imprisonment of some of the accused in the interim
period was normal practice in London, and in 1816–17 nearly a thousand
property offenders were committed to Coldbath-fields house of correction
alone for this reason. The earliest surviving petty sessions minute books in
both Essex and Cambridgeshire indicate that Lord Loughborough's pronouncement also had very little impact on provincial magistrates. In September 1796, for example, John Sutton was committed for further examination on
a felony charge at the Ely petty sessions and the following Monday after 'an
examination of numerous witnesses' the same magistrates 'honourably dismissed' the case against him. Two years later the same court held another
accused thief 'for further examination till Monday—when he was again
examined and discharged' after the magistrates had reviewed the motives
and character of the accused.[26]

The practice of imprisoning accused felons for a few days for further
examination had several possible advantages from the magistrates' point of
view. Committal for trial in an overcrowded and insanitary eighteenth-century
gaol was a drastic punishment in itself, lasting as it often did for several
months. A week or so in prison pending further examination was a much
less drastic curtailment of the freedom of the accused, and allowed time for
evidence to be gathered about the offence, the offender, and the victim which
frequently prevented the innocent from undergoing lengthy pretrial committal. Temporary confinement for further examination could also be used to

[25] Fielding, *Enquiry*, p. 95. Burn, *The Justice* (1776), 4, pp. 318–19; Paul, *The Parish*, pp. 164–5. 25; Geo.
2.C.36.
[26] *The Times*, 10 Dec. 1785; Cottu, *The Administration*, p. 21; Cambridge R.O., Isle of Ely Minute
Order Book, 17 Sept. 1796, 28 July 1798. Cottu's view was confirmed by other observers *P.P.*, 1818, VIII,
pp. 67 and 82; *P.P.*, 1828, VI, pp. 148–9, 195.

persuade the accused to turn King's evidence or to accept lesser sanctions, such as binding over to keep the peace or enlistment, in order to avoid committal for jury trial. In many cases a brief period in gaol would have been seen by the magistrates as a useful punishment in itself. In 1802 the Chelmsford petty sessions had to discharge three lodgers accused of stealing from their landlady 'there being no evidence of the theft ... although circumstances seemed much against them', but they did at least have the satisfaction of having subjected them to imprisonment for several days. When the theft was a minor one many magistrates may have considered a few days' imprisonment to be a sufficient punishment. The London magistrates certainly used it as a means of frightening very young petty thieves without sending them on for trial.[27] In parallel cases such as minor wood and vegetable thefts, rural magistrates often sentenced the offender to one or two weeks in the house of correction under the summary statutes. By imprisoning petty felons for about the same period awaiting further examination the magistrates therefore extended both their investigative and their sentencing powers.

The most important function of these further examination procedures, whether the accused was bound over to appear at a later summary hearing or imprisoned until that hearing, was that they enabled individual justices to transform their relationship with the increasingly formal and regularized petty sessions proceedings in their divisions. By the later eighteenth century many JPs were routinely referring property crime cases on to their local petty sessions. Thus, although many of the suspects held 'for further examination' were subsequently released by the magistrate or magistrates who had originally committed them, there is evidence that a three-tier system was used in an increasing number of property crime cases. The local petty sessions was becoming the first point of referral for many JPs, particularly if the case might prove controversial or legally problematic. The Barking calendars of the 1750s contain entries such as 'Geo Whitby and Susan his wife committed by H. Fanshaw on suspicion of stealing ... discharged at petty sessions', as well as other explicit references to offenders initially committed by a single magistrate and later discharged after a divisional hearing. Mary Green was described in 1759 as 'committed by M. Bateman Esq. for felony and tried at the petty sessions', but this second hearing did not put an end to her imprisonment since she was then 'sent to Chelmsford' and later convicted at the quarter sessions. In some areas this was becoming standard practice. The majority of the accused felons appearing before the Chelmsford petty sessions, 1801–6, had been committed by a single magistrate a short time earlier. At the end of the eighteenth century many of the felony suspects appearing at the regular weekly meetings of the Ely petty sessions had been sent there by individual magistrates

---

[27] E.R.O. P/CM 1/1 27 Aug. 1802; *P.P.*, 1817, VII, 495; *P.P.* 1828, VI, p. 149 on the use of brief periods of 'remand' to terrify children.

after earlier hearings. In 1800, for example, the minute book records 'Francis Harrison, on suspicion of felony—information taken in the week by Mr Ward and summons issued—matter heard and dismissed.'[28] Some justices continued to make their own decisions without referring cases to petty sessions hearings. Local practice depended on whether or not a regular and effective petty sessions meeting was held nearby and on the individual magistrates' perceptions of the advantages and disadvantages of referring cases to it. However, the gradual movement towards the use of two pretrial hearings and the justices' growing tendency to substitute warrants to appear at petty sessions for recognizances requiring appearance at quarter sessions were almost certainly linked to another set of changes.[29]

The eighteenth century witnessed a gradual growth in concern about the rights of the accused at preliminary hearings and about the lack of legal backing for some of the magistrates' procedures and decisions. This concern was linked to, and perhaps caused by, the fact that lawyers began to appear at some summary hearings in this period. Attorneys and hedge lawyers were available in many areas and their involvement in even a small minority of committal proceedings would probably have encouraged most individual magistrates to play it safe by referring felony accusations to the local petty sessions, where a better quality of legal advice was usually available. By the second hearing the accused would have had a chance to get legal assistance. When Cottu described the further examination process he assumed that attorneys made their main impact at the second hearing.[30] The possibility that lawyers were appearing in increasing numbers at their hearings may explain why the Chelmsford petty sessions magistrates had become very cagey about sending certain kinds of property offenders on for jury trial by the early nineteenth century. Their records in the 1810s contain a number of occasions on which property offenders were, to quote one example, 'discharged, there not being sufficient proof in the opinion of the bench to ensure a conviction although they expressed their belief of the guilt of the defendants'. The precise

[28] E.R.O. Q/SBb 210 and 204, case of Christopher Darby. Assize judges were aware of this further examination procedure, *Whole Proceedings ... Essex ... March 1774*, p. 11. E.R.O. Q/SBb 218 and Q/SPb 13 18 July 1759; for Chelmsford P/CM 1 e.g. 27 Aug. 1802; Cambridge R.O. Isle of Ely Minute Order Book 6 Sept. 1800.
[29] This practice was occasionally followed in the seventeenth century. J. Sharpe (ed.), *William Holcroft His Booke. Local Office-Holding in Late Stuart Essex* (Essex Historical Documents: 2, 1986), p. 70; Leverson-Gower, 'Notebook', p. 199.
[30] J. Innes, 'Statute Law and Summary Justice'; Beattie, *Crime*, p. 277. Hay, 'Prosecution', p. 385; for Whitbread's problems with local lawyers Cirket (ed.), *Samuel Whitbread's Notebooks*, p. 9; E.R.O. P/CM 2A 10 Sept. 1813 for a defendant's solicitor in the Chelmsford petty sessions. On magistrates' problems with 'the low and hungry solicitors', J. Fielding, *An Account of the Origins and Effects of a Police* (London, 1758), p. 36; P. Aylett, 'A Profession in the Marketplace. The Distribution of Attorneys in England and Wales 1730–1800', *Law and History Review*, 5 (1987), 1–30; Cottu, *The Administration*, p. 21; P. Corfield, *Power and the Professions in Britain 1700–1850* (London, 1995), pp. 70–101. J. Langbein, 'The Prosecutorial Origins of Defence Counsel in the Eighteenth Century. The Appearance of Solicitors', *Cambridge Law Journal*, 58 (1999), 314–65.

timing of these changes in summary court proceedings and attitudes has yet to be worked out, but they almost certainly altered the context and form of the discretionary powers exercised by magistrates. Those changes did not, however, prevent the summary courts from developing as primary adjudicators in felony cases. By 1820 Cottu assumed that in almost every case the magistrates made a choice between freeing the prisoner completely, letting him go on condition of giving security, or sending him to prison to await trial; and six years later Chitty saw magistrates as 'clearly bound' to exercise their 'sound discretion' in similar ways.[31] The lawyers' impact on this process was many-sided but by focusing on the injustice that could result if the summary courts did not sieve out ungrounded accusations, they may well have helped to persuade those courts to develop their role as primary adjudicators.

Overall, therefore, in the eighteenth and early nineteenth centuries magistrates acted as very powerful filters, and often as dual filters, in cases involving accusations of property appropriation. As the century progressed a growing proportion of them probably came to see their role less and less as simply processing cases for the higher courts. Their hearings were designed to evaluate the evidence and then decide between a number of options. One of these was committal for trial, but in a high proportion of cases they either dismissed the accused for lack of evidence, imprisoned, or impressed him using their powers in relation to vagrants etc., or acted as mediators negotiating an informal settlement between victim and accused. If the evidence provided by the records of Hunt, Whitbread, and the Whitechapel rotation office, as well as by some of the Essex house of correction calendars, is any guide, only a minority of property crime accusations which could have resulted in felony indictments were actually sent on for jury trial by the summary courts. This would not have been true for all magistrates or all areas, and would have changed over time, but in wartime in particular the summary courts acted as massive filters of felony accusations. In focusing on the formal legal frameworks, as Burn, Dalton, and other handbook writers described them, some accounts have given too little weight to the alternative procedures magistrates used to terminate felony accusations. By stressing the effects of nineteenth-century summary legislation, which transferred to the magistrates the formal power to try minor larcenies and juvenile offenders, historians have often underestimated the extent of the summary courts' previous informal jurisdictions. The legislation of the nineteenth century confirmed the already established role of the summary courts as major decision-makers in all types of property crime cases.[32] Before analysing the courtroom interactions and

[31]   E.R.O. P/CM 2A 27 Aug. 1813 and P/CP 4 5 Sept. 1815; Cottu, *The Administration*, p. 21; Beattie, *Crime*, p. 276; *P.P.*, 1819, VIII, p. 84.

[32]   Langbein, *Prosecuting Crime*, p. 7: Baker, 'Criminal Courts', pp. 32–3. Radzinowicz, *History*, 5, pp. 618–21; Philips, *Crime and Authority*, pp. 43, 133; T. Sweeney, 'The Extension and Practice of Summary Jurisdiction in England 1790–1860' (Cambridge Ph.D, 1985), pp. 4–5, 85.

underlying criteria that determined how the summary courts used their discretionary powers in individual cases, one other category of summary proceedings needs to be looked at—those property crime cases in which the magistrates' powers were more closely defined by statute.

3. Summary Trial under Specific Property Crime Statutes

In dealing with the appropriation of certain particular kinds of property, the statutory law specifically sanctioned the magistrates either singly or jointly to be both judge and jury. Although the range of appropriations covered by these provisions gradually increased during the eighteenth century, summary legislation continued to be focused mainly on game, wood, and vegetable theft, and on offences related to the embezzlement of textile materials. Historical accounts of summary justice have concentrated primarily on the first of these categories.[33] Since the game laws dispensed with the much-emphasized principle of equality before the law—exemption from prosecution being only available to those with large landed estates—they are clearly important, but the paucity of historical work on other types of summary theft may well have distorted our perceptions of both the functions of the summary courts and the attitudes of the magistracy. Although eighteenth-century writers also focused primarily on the game laws, this preoccupation had little to do with the numerical significance of game offences among the accusations brought to the summary courts. Rather, it was the symbolic importance of game to the gentry, the higher profits and heavier punishments involved, and the willingness of both the middling sort and the labouring poor to make the game laws a site of contest that caused so much attention to be focused on game.[34]

Does the Essex evidence justify Hay's contention that 'game offences . . . occupied most of the time of many country magistrates' and were 'the most common of criminal offences in many parishes'? Between 1785 and 1801 the Lexden and Winstree petty sessions of rural north-eastern Essex heard very few game offences. Wood and vegetable theft predominated and only eight of the sixty-five summary theft examinations involved game offences (Table 4.1) despite the fact that the area was far from devoid of game.[35] The relative lack of resident gentry and the campaigns against wood stealing initiated by local

[33] Hay, 'Poaching'; Munsche, *Gentlemen*; P. Munsche, 'The Game Laws in Wiltshire 1750–1800', in Cockburn (ed.), *Crime*, pp. 210–28; D. Jones, 'The Poacher. A Study in Victorian Crime and Protest', in D. Jones, *Crime, Protest, Community and Police in Nineteenth-Century Britain* (London, 1982), pp. 62–84; Freedman, 'Plebs or Predators'; J. Broad, 'Whigs and Deerstealers in Other Guises. A Return to the Origins of the Black Act', *Past and Present*, 119 (1988), 56–72.

[34] Burn, *The Justice* (1766), 2, pp. 220–2; overviews from J. Hammond and B. Hammond, *The Village Labourer 1760–1832* (1911), pp. 184–96, to Horn, *The Rural World*, pp. 172–82 assess the treatment of game offenders in depth while wood and vegetable thefts receive hardly a mention. Bushaway, 'From Custom' and Styles, 'Embezzlement' have begun to redress the balance. For the symbolic importance of game Munsche, *Gentlemen*, p. 166; Hay, 'Poaching' pp. 245–6.

[35] Hay, 'Poaching', pp. 192, 251; Brown, *Essex People*, p. 91.

Table 4.1. Essex Petty Sessions Examinations Books, Summary Property Offences, 1770–1800

Type of crime	Petty sessions division		
	Lexden and Winstree 1785–1800	Colchester Borough 1771–1800	Epping 1779–88
Wood stealing and hedge breaking	27	29	6
Vegetable and fruit theft	27	23	0
Game theft and possession of snares, etc.	8	1	9
Yarn and textile material-related offences	2	16	0
Others	1	0	0
Total	65	69	15
Felons sent to higher courts	26	31	—

Sources: E.R.O. P/LwR (Lex and Win) 2, 3, 5–12 (Jan. 1786–June '88, June '97–March '99 missing); P/COR (Colchester) 2–22 (Oct. '75–March '77, April '83–May '85, June '86–May '88 missing). Accession 6133 (Epping).

Table 4.2 Property Offenders in Halstead and Newport Houses of Correction, 1753–70

Summary theft	No. of prisoners	%
Wood theft	49	35
Vegetable and fruit theft	4	3
Yarn offences	21	15
Game offences	8	6
Total	82	59
Indictable theft		
Felony: committed for trial and tried	24	17
Felony: committed for trial and not tried	6	5
Felony: punished under summary laws	10	8
Felony: imprisoned and discharged without trial	17	12
Total	57	42
Grand Total	139	101

prosecution associations in the 1780s may well have influenced these figures, but the Newport and Halstead house of correction calendars suggest that the Lexden and Winstree area was typical of much of Essex. In the third quarter of the eighteenth century wood stealers outnumbered game offenders by more than six to one (Table 4.2) and, despite growing concern about game thefts towards the end of the century, a similar pattern can be seen in the 1790s.[36]

---

[36] The Halstead, Newport, and Barking Calendars 1789–91 list 10 wood, 11 vegetable, 2 yarn, and 3 game offenders (Q/SBb 337–344—Barking includes also 333–4).

Since the ratios of accusations to convictions, and convictions to sentences of imprisonment, are impossible to calculate outside a few cases, and tended to change as new legislation enacted fresh penalties for each type of offence, house of correction prisoners remain a very inadequate guide to the numbers of wood or game cases heard in the summary courts. However, the dearth of game offenders in the Essex houses of correction is particularly significant because the fines imposed on them were much higher and their chances of ending up in prison were usually greater. While only one of the seventeen wood and vegetable stealers brought before the Lexden and Winstree petty sessions, 1788–90, was imprisoned, all the three game offenders were gaoled.[37]

The mixture of cases was somewhat different in Colchester and in the Epping area (Table 4.1). In Colchester textile material offences made a greater impact while in the royal forests of south-western Essex, the very limited Epping petty sessions evidence suggests that the majority of cases involved game (Table 4.1). Epping Forest was an exceptional area however. It contained the only extensive woodlands in the county and accounted for a large proportion of the game conviction certificates returned to the quarter sessions (chapter 5). In the vast majority of Essex hundreds, as in William Hunt's part of Wiltshire, wood and vegetable stealing cases far outnumbered those involving game. The ratio may have changed in some areas towards the end of the century when both game preservation and poaching grew in intensity, but between 1801 and 1806 the Chelmsford petty sessions still tried three times as many wood and vegetable thieves as it did game offences.[38]

The treatment received by summarily tried property offenders, and particularly by poachers has been characterized as falling little short of automatic conviction unless an influential prosecutor chose to make a show of mercy, but the Essex evidence suggests a broader range of outcomes. Nearly a fifth of the Chelmsford petty sessions summary trials for wood, vegetable, or game theft did not result in a formal conviction, and about a quarter of Whitbread's summary hearings ended with the case against the accused being dismissed, many of those dismissals coming in game-related cases. This was roughly similar to the acquittal rate in petty larceny cases at the quarter sessions but it did not necessarily mean that the accused got off scot-free. Whitbread dismissed some game cases because the evidence was ' not sufficient to convict' or because the accuser failed to turn up. Others were dismissed on 'paying expenses', on 'promise of amendment', or on condition that they allowed their

[37] Summary conviction certificates returned to quarter sessions also give a false impression. Because penalties were higher a larger proportion of those involving game seem to have been returned. E.R.O. P/LwR 6–7 and Q/SBb 333–9.

[38] Crittall (ed.), *The Justicing*. Hunt tried ten times as many wood stealing cases as he did game. Cirket (ed.), *Samuel Whitbread's Notebooks* indicates just over half his summary cases were game-related; E.R.O. P/CM 1–2; Munsche, *Gentlemen*, pp. 100–1.

dogs to be shot, a stipulation also imposed by the Chelmsford petty sessions in 1803.[39]

Since several statutes relating to wood and fruit theft laid down that, once convicted, first offenders could avoid formal punishment by giving the victim 'recompense and satisfaction for damages', it is hardly surprising that the Chelmsford petty sessions informally resolved a number of such cases on payment of costs and damages, just as Hunt had done sixty years earlier. The fines imposed on wood or vegetable thieves ranged from 6 pence to 40 shillings, but the vast majority were between 5 and 10 shillings, a range also favoured by Whitbread, who reserved the other main sanction, whipping, almost exclusively for young hedgebreakers and fruit stealers. Fines in game cases were of a different order, 5 pounds or multiples of that amount for conviction on several counts being the norm.[40] Although some poaching gangs kept protection funds and a larger proportion of game offenders were middling men or artisans with some reserves to fall back on, this huge difference meant that a larger proportion of summarily convicted game offenders ended up suffering periods of imprisonment because they could not pay. Wood and vegetable thieves were sometimes imprisoned. Whitbread imposed sentences of between one and four weeks on about a seventh of these offenders. However, about a quarter of the game cases he resolved resulted in the offender spending three months in prison, a similar percentage to that found by Munsche in Wiltshire before the early nineteenth-century escalation of the war against poaching. Essex poachers also suffered longer periods of imprisonment than other summary offenders in the late eighteenth century. Despite the wide discretionary powers available to magistrates under a growing variety of statutes, the vast majority of game offenders were imprisoned for three months in the 1790s, while wood and vegetable thieves rarely remained in gaol for more than a third of that time, the usual statutory maximum being one month. Game offenders were not only more likely to be incarcerated but also more likely to be impressed. In the 1757 recruiting drive the only poacher in the Halstead house of correction was immediately put into the army but the wood thieves imprisoned with him were not.[41]

The house of correction calendars and petty sessions minute books do not record the whole gamut of punishments imposed on these types of offenders. Game offenders in particular might be subjected to civil or King's Bench proceedings or to the confiscation of guns, nets, snares, dogs, etc.—a common

[39] Hay, 'Poaching', pp. 241–50; E.R.O. P/CM 1, 1 Apr. 1803; Cirket (ed.), *Samuel Whitbread's Notebooks*, esp. p. 70.

[40] Burn, *The Justice* (1797), 4, pp. 307–8; E.R.O. P/CM 1–3; Crittall (ed.), *The Justicing;* Cirket (ed.), *Samuel Whitbread's Notebooks*.

[41] Munsche, *Gentlemen*, pp. 99–103. Chapter 6 for game offenders occupations; Cirket (ed.), *Samuel Whitbread's Notebooks*; E.R.O. (Q/SBb 337–344). All the wood thieves in this sample received between 21 days and a month. Turnip stealers range = 1 week to 3 months (average 1 month). Q/SBb 209 for 1757; Munsche, *Gentlemen*, pp. 88–9.

practice in the Essex forest courts in the early eighteenth century. If they were not resident in the parish where they had a legal settlement they could be subjected to a removal order or redefined as vagrants and punished or impressed accordingly.[42] Although their sentencing powers in such cases were constrained by various statutory parameters, magistrates therefore used much the same range of formal and informal sanctions in cases involving game, wood, yarn, or vegetable theft as they did in other property crime hearings. The outcomes of property appropriation cases were deeply affected by the magistrates' discretionary practices. What criteria were their decisions based on? How much were those decisions affected by the interactions between magistrate, victim, and accused inside the courtroom or by the influence of those who acted outside the formal hearing?

4. Influences on the Outcomes of Magistrates' Hearings

Unfortunately magistrates very rarely recorded their reasons for choosing a specific way of resolving a property crime case. In particular, information about the quality of the evidence or about the informal pressures put on the magistrate by interested parties either before or during the hearing is rarely available. However, a skeletal analysis of the forces which determined the outcomes of these cases can be put together. The seriousness of the offence and the depth and straightforwardness of the evidence were always important. A violent robbery or burglary attested by reliable witnesses left little room for negotiation, while a dubious minor theft accusation with little corroboration was unlikely to result in anything but a negotiated settlement. Equally, the legal frameworks within which certain kinds of property crime accusations were made could be very influential. Statutory changes pushed wood thieves onto the defensive in this period by confirming that anyone found with certain types of wood in his possession was guilty unless he could 'give a satisfactory account how he came by the same'. Magistrates probably made a similar reversal of the principle that the accused was innocent until proved guilty, when they decided the fate of suspected felons remanded for further examination. Many entries in the Halstead house of correction calendars include phrases such as 'and not clearing himself of the said charge' to explain a felony committal after a second summary hearing.[43]

More advantageously from the accused's point of view, the magistrates not infrequently refused to act against certain types of property appropriation because they did not see a legal justification for doing so. In 1806 the Chelms-

[42] Radzinowicz, *History*, 4, p. 21; Munsche, *Gentlemen*, pp. 89–91, 102–3.

[43] Burn, *The Justice* (1797), 4, pp. 309–11; Q/SBb 200–12. Elizabeth Chapman, for example, was sent on to the sessions in 1756 after 'on her examination saying nothing to clear herself'. In 1774 receivers of stolen wool were subjected to a similar reversal—A. Randall, 'Peculiar Perquisites and Pernicious Practices. Embezzlement in the West of England Woollen Industry', *International Review of Social History*, 35 (1990), 208.

ford petty sessions dismissed the case against four boys accused of taking chestnuts from Sir William Hilley's park because the offence was 'not within the statute of robbing orchards'. Seven years later they took a similar attitude when a local farmer accused several female gleaners of 'feloniously' carrying away his wheat. The case was dismissed 'being considered a trespass only', an attitude also taken by both the Lexden and Winstree magistrates and the Colchester petty sessions whenever local farmers tried to escalate their on-going conflicts with the gleaners by attempting to redefine gleaning as theft.[44]

In relatively informal tribunals such as these the character of both accuser and accused was often as important as the strength of the evidence or the legal framework within which the accusation was made. If the magistrates had doubts about the prosecutor's honesty or character they would usually settle the matter informally, as Hunt did in 1745 when a robbery charge was brought by 'a man of little credit'. In extreme cases they might be forced to discharge the prisoner even if they believed him guilty, a course reluctantly followed by the Chelmsford petty sessions in 1803 after the prosecutor twice appeared drunk at their hearings. If the prosecutor was of sound mind and character, his attitude towards an informal resolution of the case very often decided its outcome. The Chelmsford petty sessions fairly regularly allowed victims who had gained informal satisfaction to discontinue their prosecutions. By the 1830s the Bristol magistrates 'invariably' asked victims 'whether they will prosecute or not' and a third of those accused of felony were 'discharged from the parties refusing to prosecute' at that point.[45]

Not all prosecutors obtained the outcome they wanted. The inhabitants of the Braintree division complained about the expenses they sometimes in-curred in apprehending offenders whom the magistrates did not then send on for trial, because they did not consider there was sufficient evidence against them. However, the prosecutor's range of options did not necessarily become smaller when he entered a summary court. Eighteenth-century magistrates rarely insisted that a victim go on with a prosecution if he did not wish to, and victims often used summary hearings to achieve the informal sanction or settlement they preferred. Quite frequently the victim only had to get a warrant from the magistrate in order to obtain the required response. Hunt records at least eight occasions between 1744 and 1749 when he granted a warrant or summons for those accused of property appropriation to appear before him only to find that 'the parties agreed it without a hearing'.[46]

The accused's character and reputation was crucial at this stage, as it also was during pretrial negotiations and at major court hearings. The sympathy of

<hr/>

[44] E.R.O. P/CM 1/2 24 Oct. 1806; P/CP2 30 Aug. 1813 and P/CM 1/2A 31 Aug. 1813; King, 'Gleaners', pp. 126–7.
[45] Crittall (ed.), *The Justicing*, p. 41; E.R.O. P/CM 1/1–2, 8 July 1803, 8 Nov. 1805, 5 Dec. 1806; Gloucestershire R.O., D/1283/2 20 Sept. 1816; *P.P.*, 1839 XIX, p. 98.
[46] P.R.O. H.O. 73/9; Crittall, *The Justicing*, pp. 38–57.

both the victim and the magistrates could often be aroused by genuine claims of youth, previous good character, or poverty. Almost every summary tribunal for which records survive seems to have dealt with young offenders more leniently or informally, often because victims would not prosecute 'those of tender age'. Hunt allowed several boys who had stolen wood or fruit to escape punishment, providing they had made 'the required submission' to the victim, and the future Essex JP John Harriott was offered similar clemency as a boy following his raids on the local orchards. This policy was not confined to young hedgebreakers and fruit thieves. In 1805 the Chelmsford petty sessions, after finding the facts fully proved against a group of poachers, recorded that 'the defendants being young were forgiven on paying for expenses'. Victims, influenced perhaps by pressures from the local community, were often the main instigators of these lenient policies. In the late eighteenth century the Philanthropic Society argued that 'Children ... carried before a magistrate for theft ... have been discharged not in consequence of any doubt respecting their guilt, but ... through the unwillingness of the injured party to bring them to trial.' That unwillingness encouraged the magistrates to resort to physical punishment. Sometimes this was done informally. In 1783 the Whitechapel petty sessions ordered that one property offender be 'discharged' and 'corrected at school'. More frequently a semi-formal summary whipping was ordered. Faced by a boy of 13 who confessed to stealing his master's bacon, Witts 'adopted this mode, being unwilling to prosecute for felony, ordered the boy a whipping'. Whitbread used the same sanction against the three ringleaders among a larger group of boys found hedgebreaking while forcing the others simply to 'beg pardon'. He also ensured in other cases that 'the little ones' received less stripes than 'the bigger ones'.[47]

For older offenders a 'good character' was crucial. In 1811, for example, the Duke of Bedford was inclined to be much more lenient to a poacher who had been 'a good servant and ... very zealous in the discharge of his duty'. Evidence of previous offences had severe consequences. Blundell's refusal to drop Richard Ainsworth's prosecution sprang from this cause. The punishments imposed after a property offender had been summarily convicted were also related to his or her previous record. Statutory law laid down that wood thieves offending for a second or third time were to receive heavier punishments, and Hunt clearly followed these guidelines. In 1734 a Kent petty sessions bench followed a similar principle when it fined 'a notorious poacher' £1 while letting his inexperienced accomplices off with a quarter of that amount. By the 1770s new statutes laying down heavier penalties for

---

[47] Crittall, *The Justicing*, pp. 47–50; Harriott, *Struggles*, I, pp. 8–12; E.R.O. P/CM I 22 Feb. 1805; Anon., *An Account of the Nature and Present State of the Philanthropic Society instituted in 1788* (London, 1804), p. 8; P.R.O. H.O. 42/2/99, 27 Jan .1783; Gloucestershire R.O.D/1283/2 9 Oct. 1817; Cirket (ed.), *Samuel Whitbread's Notebooks*, pp. 22 and 68; whipping continued to be seen as appropriate for boys, Radzinowicz, *History*, 5, pp. 711–19.

second and third offences against various game-related laws were in place, and in 1807 an Essex JP went to considerable trouble to trace the previous convictions of two deer stealers because they were 'bad fellows' deserving heavier punishment.[48]

It is easy to underestimate the impact that the defendant's poverty might have on the outcome of a summary hearing. In 1746 Hunt pardoned nine wood stealers 'out of regard to their great poverty' and even when he convicted impoverished petty thieves, game offenders, and hedgebreakers, he related the fine imposed to the means of the offender, sometimes returning part of the resulting fines to the offender's family or encouraging the victim to do so. In 1747, for example, he fined a local labourer 5 shillings for carrying and discharging a gun without being legally qualified to do so, but then recorded, 'I returned to him as a pauper two shillings.' Two years earlier he imposed the statutory fine of £5 on a man convicted of shooting pigeons, but 'considering him as a poor man' he managed to get all but 15 shillings of it returned to the offender. Hunt may have been a particularly humane man, but many Essex magistrates took similar approaches. In 1804 Henry Maynard refused even to hear a wood-stealing case because the accused had a 'wife ... ready to lie in, without money, without clothing, without fuel but with a large family ... craving for sustenance'. John Staples's sympathy for a group of unemployed potato-stealing foreigners stranded in London at the close of the American war led him both to help them out of his own pocket and to write to the Home Office pleading their case.[49]

The magistrates' lenient attitudes towards petty thieves caused considerable resentment among farmers. After discussing the fact that low wages put many labouring families 'under the necessity of procuring a considerable part of their household necessaries by theft and plunder', Arthur Young noted that many a farmer was 'under the necessity of turning his back when he sees himself being robbed, rather than apprehend the offender and have him brought to justice, where he knows little or no redress is to be had ... the magistrate, from his known poverty, will order a small fine to be paid; the pauper will tell him he has nothing to pay it: here the matter ends'. The farmers themselves were often highly ambivalent fearing an increased burden on the rates if petty offenders were imprisoned because they could not pay their fines. Indeed the parish vestry might intervene to obtain mercy for some property offenders. In 1745, for example, a suspected watch thief was 'excused' by Hunt 'at the request of the heads of the parish'.[50]

[48] Cirket (ed.), *Samuel Whitbread's Notebooks*, p. 79; Burn, *The Justice* (1797), 4, p. 309; Bagley, *The Great Diurnal*, I, pp. 174–5; Munsche, *Gentlemen*, pp. 25–6; Kent Archives Office V.951.04; E.R.O. Q/SBb 406/45.

[49] Crittall (ed.), *The Justicing*, pp. 14–15, 48–50, 80–2; E.R.O. D/DMg C2, 13 Mar. 1804. P.R.O. H.O. 42/5/239–40.

[50] A. Young, *General View of the Agriculture of the County of Oxford* (London, 1813), pp. 336–7; Crittall (ed.), *The Justicing*, p. 42.

Although these criteria were important, the outcome of a summary hearing was not dependent solely on whether the accused could plead youth, poverty, or previous good character in his defence. Unfortunately, magistrates' inter-actions with prosecutors and with those who backed them were very rarely recorded in petty theft cases, but the social status of the prosecutor and his ability to mobilize influential connections were often important. The survival of large quantities of gentry correspondence, but of very few private letters written by other social groups, has meant that one highly untypical subgroup of prosecutors—wealthy game preservers (backed very often by well-financed game associations)—are virtually the only victims whose attempts to influence magistrates are accessible to the historian. In areas like Cannock Chase, where game was a very important element in local social and economic relations, magistrates' decisions were deeply affected by the direct requests or long-stated policies of their aristocratic neighbours, as Hay's work has shown. Moreover, in some parts of Essex the presence of several active magistrates on the subscription lists of the county's game associations suggests that local game preservers would rarely have had much difficulty in finding a reasonably sympathetic JP.

However, as Munsche has pointed out in his detailed study, the fact that many JPs were passionately devoted to field sports did not necessarily mean that their enthusiasm was translated into vindictive enforcement of the game laws. Like the magistrates of the Cannock Chase area, Whitbread entered into correspondence with local aristocratic landowners before giving judgment in a number of game cases, but although his decisions were often in line with their wishes, he not infrequently produced a different outcome from the one they had requested. In 1811 he dismissed three accusations brought by Lady Lucas's woodward and found the evidence insufficient in another game case, despite a letter from Lord Ongley alluding to the 'alarming' heights poaching had reached and the need for heavy sentences.[51] Munsche quotes a game case in which several Essex magistrates wrote to the prosecutor pleading that the accusation be dropped, and examples of acquittals and of lenient sentences in game cases can be found not only in Whitbread's records but also in those of the Epping petty sessions and of Hunt, Witts, and other individual JPs. Men like Hunt, who arbitrated or discharged for lack of evidence the majority of the game cases brought before him, support Munsche's suggestion that 'consid-erations of propriety, justice and even mercy' also entered into magistrates' judgments in such cases.[52] The intensification of interest in, and conflict over, game in the later eighteenth century may conceivably have increased the number of magistrates who wished to ignore such principles. However, since

[51] Hay, 'Poaching'; Munsche, *Gentlemen*, pp. 77; Cirket (ed.), *Samuel Whitbread's Notebooks*, pp. 60–1, 106; King, 'Prosecution Associations'; *Che.C.*, 17 Aug. 1787.

[52] E.R.O. Epping Petty Sessions book 16 Dec. 1785; P/CM 1, 22 Feb. 1805; Munsche, *Gentlemen*, pp. 95–6; Cirket (ed.), *Samuel Whitbread's Notebooks*, pp. 95, 106; Gloucestershire R.O. D/1283/2, p. 3.

lawyers were also becoming more prevalent in summary hearings during that period, fears about the civil actions or quarter sessions appeals that might be initiated against them probably made the magistracy increasingly scrupulous in cases involving farmers or well-organized poaching groups, who had sufficient funds to obtain legal help. Both the Chelmsford magistrates and Whitbread found themselves being challenged by lawyers on technical matters by the 1810s and the Essex farmer Joseph Page made sure he was advised by an attorney when he was summoned for a game offence in 1802.[53]

Most members of the labouring poor continued to face game-related accusations without the aid of a lawyer, as the Hertfordshire gardener Joseph Ansell did in 1791 after a local gamekeeper arrested him on a trumped-up charge. However, the traffic was not all one way. The paradoxical nature of the game laws meant that the poor could also mobilize those laws to their advantage. The Essex summary court records indicate that servants and labourers were not slow to accuse farmers and unqualified gentlemen of game offences. The Epping petty sessions records contain several such cases in the mid-1780s. A decade earlier the *Chelmsford Chronicle* bemoaned the fact that although 'no gentleman would think of prosecuting any farmer or creditable person, though unqualified, for openly and fairly in the daytime taking a few hours diversion', the lack of any time limit for the laying of informations in such cases made farmers vulnerable to prosecution by untrustworthy servants. Nor were the lesser gentry immune. In 1776 Henry Sperling, squire of Great Maplestead, and High Sheriff of Essex the following year, was fined £5 for an offence against the game laws at the instigation of a local hay dealer. Two decades later Gordon Kelly, esquire, of Ardleigh, suffered a similar fate although he was later able to get the decision reversed by the Tendring petty sessions. Half the fine went to the informer in such cases, but not all the game prosecutions brought by the poor were begun for financial reasons. They may have been designed to protect the accuser himself against a threatened prosecution, or have been motivated by malice or a desire for revenge. Whatever the motives involved, it is ironic that the game laws with their flagrant class bias should have made wealthy farmers so vulnerable to prosecution by those much less well-off than themselves, or by rival members of the middling sort. Although the local gentry had no objection to Joseph Page's frequent shooting expeditions, a local brewer was able to haul him and his friends before the local petty sessions for violating the game laws, a trip which cost them a guinea and an attorney's fee before the matter was settled informally.[54]

[53] Munsche, *Gentlemen*, pp. 101–4; E.R.O. P/CM 1/2A 31 Aug. 1813; Cirket (ed.), *Samuel Whitbread's Notebooks*, p. 9; Brown, *Essex People*, p. 102; Innes, 'Statute Law', pp. 34–5.

[54] W. Le Hardy, *Calendar to the Sessions Books, Sessions Minute Books and other Sessions Records 1752–1799* (Hertford, 1935), 8, pp. 169–71; E.R.O. Epping Division Petty Sessions Book, 21 Feb. 1786, 17 Sept. 1785, 17 Oct. 1783; Q/SR 803; *Che.C.*, 31 Aug. 1770; G. Mingay (ed.), *Mrs Hurst Dancing* (London, 1981), p. xii; E.R.O. P/TP1 15 Sept. 1794; Hay, 'Prosecution', pp. 355–6; Brown, *Essex People*, p. 102.

While the intervention of those with wealth and social influence could sway the outcome of a summary hearing, the magistrates did not automatically protect the rich or respond to their requests, nor were the poor devoid of potential points of leverage. Many magistrates wanted to be seen as fair and neutral adjudicators or as men of humanity and generosity, and they were loath to do anything that might give them a reputation as oppressors of the poor. They also had more practical reasons for avoiding making enemies among the local inhabitants. Public ridicule, expensive counter-suits, or physical damage to their property could result. When the Essex JP the Reverend Bate-Dudley refused Elizabeth Serjeant's husband an alehouse licence, forced him to take back an illegally discharged apprentice, and convicted him of poaching, she responded by digging up a decade-old charge of adultery and involving him in an expensive trial. The unpopularity of one Essex JP, Zachariah Button, led to him being portrayed in a printer's windows fixed into a pillory under the title 'Button Holes', while another, who was described by a local surgeon as an 'imperious troublesome and overbearing man' was lampooned in a printed song as 'the wicked vicar of Essex'. Overt opposition could be very costly. Insulting a justice in open court might result in a short sentence of imprisonment during the eighteenth century but there were less direct ways in which magistrates could be intimidated. In the late 1780s one Essex JP was hastened to his death by arson attacks on his barns and stables which the local miller attributed to the fact that 'this gentleman was a justice, and a man who subjected himself to great passions and abuse, and was by no means admired . . . for filling his office properly'.[55]

Given the deeply discretionary nature of most summary hearings, the character of the JP involved was crucial. Although the Essex landowner Charles Gray was probably correct in asserting that 'mean, low trading justices are not much heard of in the country', examples of corruption can easily be found. In 1804 Henry Maynard accused his fellow JPs of pocketing the fines they extracted, while the trial of the Harlow magistrate James Altham for adultery is revealing not only about his sexual misdemeanours and his periods in a private madhouse, but also about his attempts to obtain sexual favours from the wife of an imprisoned man by offering to obtain his release and by threatening to send him 'for a soldier'. Contemporary writers were well aware that magistrates varied widely in their motives, honesty, and ability. Gisborne not only warned potential magistrates against becoming improperly benevolent;

---

[55] D. Defoe, *The Great Law of Subordination Considered* (1724), pp. 105–10, which suggests 'gentlemen . . . bear with a thousand indignities . . . because they would not be marked for severity or for hard treatment of the poor'; Anon., *Adultery. Trial in the Court of Kings Bench . . . between Edward Dodwell Esq. Plaintiff and the Reverend Henry Bate-Dudley* (1789); *Che.C.*, 3 Feb. 1792; Anon., *The Trial of the Reverend James Altham of Harlow in the County of Essex for Adultery, Defamation and Obscenity* (1785), 2, p. 6. Large fines were imposed in 1755 and 1758 on two individuals for 'insulting the justices', E.R.O. Q/SPe 2/2. The parish cage was also used—*Che.C.*, 16 June 1779; Brown, *Essex People*, pp. 38–9; Q/SBb 174/12 for a servant imprisoned for being saucy to a JP.

he also pointed out that their position made them liable to become dictatorial, domineering, and arbitrary in their decisions. Romilly noted in 1786 that 'though there certainly are in the commission some of the most respectable gentlemen in the Kingdom...there are in it many men who are grossly ignorant'. In Essex as elsewhere the full range of judicial characters and stereotypes can be found. At one end lay corrupt or oppressive JPs like Altham or Bate-Dudley and men such as John Bull of Inworth, who was described in 1783 as 'an arbitrary and headstrong man' after colluding against and imprisoning a local victualler without allowing him to present his case, and then announcing that 'he would fine the person who said he did wrong'. At the other end of the spectrum there were some scrupulous, energetic members of the bench such as John Tindal, who cajoled his fellow magistrates into improving prison conditions in the 1760s; and Hugh Smith, who devoted nearly half his working week to providing free medical attention for the poor.[56] Such men were exceptional, of course. Most magistrates were neither dedicated nor openly dictatorial, and despite the problems caused by these wide individual variations, the evidence suggests that the general character and social status of the magistracy was changing in this period. So were two more easily quantifiable factors—the activity rates of magistrates and their availability in different areas. Since all these three factors could influence victims' reactions and the way property offenders were dealt with, they are worth analysing in detail.

5. The Availability and Activity Rates of Magistrates

In Essex as in almost every other county in England and Wales the Commission of the Peace expanded quite rapidly during the eighteenth century. The numbers involved rose from 117 in 1702 to around 200 during 1748–52 and over 320 by 1807–13, an increase which roughly paralleled the county's rise in population. In Essex the number of 'acting' magistrates, that is those who indicated at least a theoretical willingness to do judicial work by taking out the Dedimus, grew at a slightly lower rate during 1747–1807 (Table 4.3), and by the early nineteenth century about two-fifths of those who enjoyed the prestige of being on the commission were qualified to act.[57] However, qualifying entailed no firm commitment to be active. How can the actual workloads of eighteenth-century magistrates be measured?

---

[56] Webb, The Parish, p. 343 and pp. 321–73 for stereotypes drawn from contemporary fiction; E.R.O. D/DMg 2.15 Feb. 1804 and Anon. The Trial of the Reverend Mr James Altham, 1, pp. 55–60; Gisborne, An Enquiry, pp. 242–7; S. Romilly, Observations on a late Publication Entitled Thoughts on Executive Justice (1786), pp. 109–16; E.R.O. D/DO B24/54 for Bull; Webb, The Parish, p. 355; DNB, 53, pp. 20–1.

[57] Howell, Patriarchs, pp. 141–3; Landau, The Justices, pp. 365–72; Beattie, Crime, p. 60; P. Jenkins, The Making of a Ruling Class. The Glamorgan Gentry 1640–1790 (Cambridge, 1983), pp. 84–8; Essex figures are based on commissions of 1747, 1752, 1807, and 1812 P.R.O. Assi 35/187, 192, 247, 252. Figures exclude dignitaries included for formal reasons. L. Glassey and N. Landau, 'The Commission of the Peace in the Eighteenth Century: a New Source', Bulletin of the Institute of Historical Research, 45 (1972).

Table 4.3. Acting JPs, Essex Lists, 1739–1807

Date	Ranked above esquire		Esquire		Clergy		Total	Population per JP
	No.	%	No.	%	No.	%		
1739	10	11.4	71	80.7	7	8.0	88	1,640
1743	11	12.4	67	75.3	11	12.4	89	1,620
1747	6	7.8	58	75.3	13	16.9	77	1,920
1750	4	4.5	71	79.8	14	15.7	89	1,680
1754	5	4.8	75	72.8	23	22.3	103	1,500
1785	7	6.8	67	65.0	29	28.2	103	1,830
1807	12	9.3	85	65.9	32	24.8	129	1,840

Note: Esquires include professional men, 'Doctors in physick', etc.

Sources: E.R.O. Q/SMg 14–18 for 1739–54; Q/SBb 320 (1785) and P.R.O. Assi 35/247.

Quarter sessions attendance might be one indication, but the Essex quarter sessions always met at Chelmsford and this obviously discouraged those who lived in outlying areas. More than 40 per cent of the JPs whose names appear on a detailed list compiled in 1782 failed to turn up to a single quarter sessions gathering between 1778 and 1783, while a small minority, all of whom lived near to the county town, could be found at almost every meeting. Attendance levels began to improve when political anxieties and attention to law and order issues increased in the 1780s and 1790s (Figure 4.1) but they were never an accurate guide to any particular magistrate's general activity levels. William Palmer, the busiest committing magistrate, 1778–83, attended only twice in those years, discouraged no doubt by the fact that he lived in the far south-western corner of Essex.[58]

What proportion of technically 'acting' justices took a significant part in the day-to-day work of the summary courts? In Essex, as in other recently studied counties, the proportion was remarkably small. More than a third of the acting magistrates described as resident in Essex in the 1782 list did not commit a single property offender for trial between 1778 and 1783. Although this type of committal formed only a small part of a magistrate's workload and some of the men who appear inactive by this criterion may have heard many cases involving non-indictable offences or poor law disputes, a small group of diligent and regularly available JPs clearly dominated committals, taking cases

[58] For similar percentages never attending, Landau, *The Justices*, p. 262; E. Moir, *Local Government in Gloucestershire 1775–1800. A Study of the Justices of the Peace* (Bristol, 1969). Although brief rises in Essex attendance levels were sometimes caused by local issues, such as the rebuilding of the County Gaol, 1769–72, the long-term increase after 1784 was linked partly to population growth and transport improvements but mainly to swelling anxiety about law and order issues. The peak in the early 1790s came at a time of political turmoil, when many Essex magistrates placed advertisements 'reaffirming their loyalty to the King' and their desire 'to suppress levelling principles', *Che.C.*, 14 Dec. 1792. Glassey and Landau, 'The Commission', pp. 262–3; P. King, 'Crime, Law', pp. 240–2; Eastwood, *Governing Rural England*, p. 77.

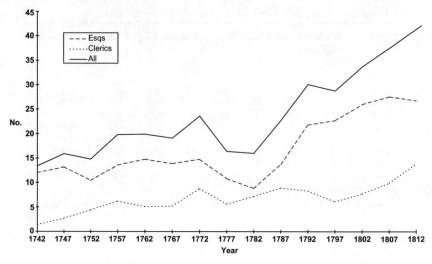

Fig. 4.1 Attendance, Essex Quarter Sessions, Clerical and Non-clerical JPs, 1740–1815
Source: ERO Q/S Mg 14–32.

from extensive geographical areas. In 1747–52 the five most active magistrates undertook more than 40 per cent of the work and it was not until the late eighteenth and early nineteenth centuries that this load was spread a little wider (Table 4.4). House of correction and petty sessions records often reveal a similar pattern at a local level. Matthew Thompson signed more than 75 per cent of the Tendring petty sessions examinations of the mid-1790s and although ten magistrates used the Halstead house of correction in 1753–4, Robert Tweed was responsible for nearly two-thirds of the committals. In Essex, as in Surrey, Kent, and Oxfordshire, only a minority of the Commission of the Peace took out the Dedimus and among those that did only a small subgroup were truly active.[59]

Contemporaries were well aware of this problem. In 1784 the author of *The Magistrate's Assistant* wrote of the difficulties of persuading gentlemen 'to dedicate some portion of their leisure hours to the preservation of the peace . . . among their neighbours', and three years later *The Times* reported that 'the very great inattention paid to the issuing of a dedimus has been justly complained of for many years'. This was partly a problem of location. Whether the entire 1782 list is used or only those who made at least one committal between 1778 and 1783 are deemed to have been 'active' magistrates, their distribution is extremely uneven. While the ratio of magistrates to population was about 1 : 1,500 in south-western and central Essex, the equivalent ratio in some of the

[59] E.R.O. Q/SBb 306/16. Only the 1782 list gives place of abode; P/TP1 and Q/SBb 192–199. Eastwood, *Governing*, p. 45; Beattie, *Crime*, p. 62; Landau, *The Justices*, pp. 138–40 and 320–3.

Table 4.4. The Distribution of JP Workloads, Essex,
1747–1812

No. of committals by each JP	1747–52 No. of JPs	%	1778–83 No. of JPs	%	1807–12 No. of JPs	%
1–4	42	66	43	60	64	57
5–9	12	19	14	19	20	18
10–14	3	5	8	11	13	12
15–19	2	3	2	3	4	4
20–29	2	3	2	3	9	8
30–39	2	3	2	3	2	2
40+	1	1	1	1	0	0
Total	64	100	72	100	112	101

The contribution of the active core of magistrates

% of all committals made by	1747–52 %	1778–83 %	1807–12 %
Single most active JP	10.9	8.6	5.1
Top 5 most active JPs	40.8	31.2	20.2
Top 10 most active JPs	59.4	48.0	35.6

Notes: Committal count based on Assize Gaol Calendar (P.R.O. Assi
35)—all types of offender (mainly property crime) and recognizances to
prosecute; E.R.O. Q/SMg—property crime and assault only. (Some
minor omissions due to non-recording of recognizances in the minute
books.)

eastern coastal hundreds was more than 1 : 5,000, and in 1782 the Winstree and
Freshwell hundreds had no resident acting magistrates at all. As the number of
acting magistrates gradually increased in the early nineteenth century (Table
4.3) the problem may have eased slightly, but the geographical distribution of
active magistrates changed little between 1740 and 1820 (Table 4.5) and in 1836
residents in outlying areas, such as the Tendring hundred, were still complain-
ing that the nearest magistrate lived a long distance away.[60]

    In other counties areas of heathland, upland, and forest, or of growing
industrial townships, often encountered difficulties in obtaining active JPs, but
in Essex this problem was most acute in the eastern hundreds. These low-lying
coastal areas were reputed to be very unhealthy and were virtually devoid of
resident gentry or substantial clergy. As one local newspaper commented in
1767, 'it is scarcely to be conceived the hardship of the people of the Dengie
hundred for want of an active magistrate in that division, they being overrun
with beggars and thieves'. One JP reported in 1788 that at Foulness a round
journey of 28 miles was necessary to reach the home of the nearest magistrate

    [60] Anon., *The Magistrate's Assistant*, p. vi; *The Times*, 22 Aug. 1787; P.R.O. HO. 73/5 part 1. For the
precise density of JP provision, King, 'Crime, Law', p. 248.

Table 4.5. The Geographical Distribution of Acting JPs, Essex, 1740–1834

Divisions (as in 1754)	Hundreds in each division	1740–9 No.	%	1750–9 No.	%	1785 No.	%	1817–34 No.	%
Brentwood	Ba, Cha	11	7	14	7	10	10	32	9
Chelmsford	Che, De	23	14	28	15	10	10	49	14
Colchester	Lex, Win, Te	16	10	27	14	13	13	44	12
Dunmow	Du	7	4	5	3	4	4	10	3
Epping	Wa, Harl, Ong	25	16	30	16	17	16	67	19
Freshwell	Fr	4	3	3	2	0	0	6	2
Hinckford	Hi	23	14	25	13	13	13	41	12
Ilford	Bec, Hav	25	16	28	15	17	16	46	13
Kelvedon	Wi, Th, Lex	9	6	10	5	9	9	28	8
Rochford	Ro	4	3	5	3	4	4	11	3
Walden	Utt, Cla	13	8	17	9	6	6	21	6
Totals		160		192		103		355	

Note: The absolute numbers are not comparable because 1740–9 is based on two listings (E.R.O. Q/SMg 15–16), 1750–9 likewise (Q/SMg 16–17). 1785 on one listing (Q/SBb 320) and 1817–34 on all magistrates who served during that period from Q/JL8. Divisional boundaries changed over the century as new smaller divisions were formed. There were 11 in 1734, 15 in 1817. The 1754 position has been used here and later numbers amalgamated as appropriate.

Key: Ba = Barstable, Bec = Becontree, Cha = Chafford, Che = Chelmsford, Cla = Clavering, De = Dengie, Du = Dunmow, Fr = Freshwell, Harl = Harlow, Hav = Havering, Hi = Hinckford, Lex = Lexden, Ong = Ongar, Ro = Rochford, Te = Tendring, Th = Thurstable, Utt = Uttlesford, Wa = Waltham, Win = Winstree, Wi = Witham. The large hundred of Lexden was split between two petty sessions divisions.

and that those who undertook it were frequently disappointed because the magistrate was not at home. Similar problems were experienced by residents in parts of northern and south-eastern Essex. 'Magistrates in this quarter we have not', wrote a correspondent from Castle Hedingham in 1787,[61] although from the 1780s listings the Hinckford hundred appears to be fairly well provided with justices. Such lists create an extremely over-optimistic picture of JP availability. Many of those listed were totally inactive in reality, and a high proportion of the remainder were only sporadically resident at their country seats.

Many of the substantial gentry spent relatively little time on their estates in the eighteenth century. The non-resident landlord who deserted his parish responsibilities was much criticized by contemporaries. Echoing similar comments by Jonas Hanway, David Davies complained in the 1790s that 'Formerly... the gentry resided constantly on their estates... but of late, by the

---

[61] Styles, 'An Eighteenth-Century Magistrate', p. 99. Jenkins, 'The Making', pp. 87–8; using Chapman and Andre's Essex Map of 1777 indicates that gentry presence was weakest in the Dengie, Rochford, Thurstable, and Freshwell hundreds. *I.J.* 19 Dec. 1767 (quoted in E.R.O. T/2 36/66); *Che.C.*, 24 Aug. 1787, Q/SBb 334/33.

non-residence of the rich the poor have lost the valuable support which they used to receive'. The gentry, he observed expended their income 'in winter upon the amusements . . . in vogue in the capital', and in summer 'at bathing and water-drinking places'. Even those country gentlemen who could not stretch to the expense of the London season or of a house at Bath found themselves increasingly drawn to the smaller spas or to the growing cultural vibrance of the many provincial towns touched by the urban renaissance during this period. Langhorne may have idealized the past when he wrote that 'fashions boundless sway has born the guardian magistrate away' but he touched a raw nerve.[62]

Many Essex magistrates were drawn away by public duties. The 1754 and 1782 JP lists include at least twelve Members of Parliament. As Parliament began to keep regular annual sittings from November to April this not only increased the attractions of the London season but also forced men like Jacob Houblon to spend a growing part of each year in the capital in order to fulfil their parliamentary duties. A number of politicians and placemen were listed as acting and resident Essex magistrates in 1782, but once again they were rarely available for judicial work. Sir James Marriott, as MP for Sudbury, Vice Chancellor of Cambridge University, and Judge of the Admiralty Court, was thoroughly occupied elsewhere, while the Irish peer Earl Nugent remained actively involved in politics despite his reputation as 'the most uninformed man of his rank in England'. Several magistrates such as Isaac Rebow and Charles Rainsford held senior posts in the militia that required them to be away from home for long periods. The absence of others was not necessarily voluntary. In 1782 at least one had fled abroad to escape his creditors and another, the ubiquitous Henry Bate-Dudley, was undergoing a year's imprisonment in the King's Bench for libelling the Duke of Richmond.[63]

Even if they were technically resident in Essex, many JPs were rarely available. In south-west Essex most maintained business or professional interests in the capital and spent much of their time there. In the 1830s Wanstead's residents complained that although five or six magistrates resided within a mile 'they are men of business and you may go to all of them in succession and not find one at home'. In rural Essex the diaries of resident JPs such as John Hanson indicate that many of them spent a lot of time away from their own houses hunting, travelling, visiting, organizing their estates, or making use of local urban facilities. The unpredictability this caused brought great problems for rural parish officials and potential prosecutors. When the nearest active JP

[62] D. Davies, *The Case of Labourers in Husbandry* (1795), p. 57; Emsley, *Crime*, pp. 51–2; Langford, *A Polite*, p. 104; Borsay, 'English'; Anon., *The Country Justice. A Poem* (attributed to Langhorne 1775), 2, p. 19; P. Langford, *Public Life and Propertied Englishmen 1689–1789* (Oxford, 1991), pp. 367–9, 377–84.

[63] A. Houblon, *The Houblon Family* (2 vols., 1907), 2, pp. 42–9, 309. Essex had seventeen resident MPs in the 1780s. P. Langford, 'Property and Virtual Representation in Eighteenth-century England', *Historical Journal*, 31 (1988), 94; *DNB*, 37, p. 198; 41, p. 270; 47, p. 183; Brown, *Essex People*, pp. 64–9; A. Barnes, *Essex Eccentrics* (Ipswich, 1975), p. 23.

Table 4.6. Age Distribution of Non-clerical Magistrates, Essex, 1739–81

Age range	No.	%
Under 30	9	8.3
30–9	21	19.3
40–9	40	36.7
50–9	25	22.9
60–9	13	11.9
70	1	0.9
Total of sample	109	100.0

Note: Based on a comparison of the freeholders' books of 1734, 1759, and 1781 with the nearest JP listing making allowance for intervening years E.R.O. Q/RJ 1/1, 2, 10, the ages appear to be reasonably accurate; F. Emmison (ed.), *Essex Freeholders Books 1734* (Chelmsford, 1982), p. ix, but clergy being ineligible for jury service, clerical magistrates are excluded.

lived some distance away it was often difficult to obtain information about his availability. On two occasions in June 1780 the overseers of Great Bromley hired horses and carts and took a group of offenders halfway round the Tendring hundred only to be frustrated because 'the magistrates were not at home'.[64]

Of the magistrates continually resident in Essex a considerable number were unwilling or physically unable to undertake judicial work. Most appear to have remained on the list of acting JPs until their death and, although the age structure of non-clerical magistrates in Table 4.6 underestimates the number of elderly men (the ages being taken from the freeholder books which exclude anyone over 70), more than a third were aged between 50 and 70. While the majority of Essex JPs were in their forties or fifties, a substantial minority had almost certainly ceased to be active well before their names were removed from the lists. When the Rochford magistrate John Harriott first qualified to act in the 1780s, the area appeared to be well endowed with magistrates, but he recorded that at first it was 'all uphill work with but little assistance; the two old magistrates in the neighbourhood being seldom able to attend'.[65]

Given the gentry's general reluctance to serve as magistrates and the many factors which reduced the availability of the minority who were prepared to act, any magistrate who could be relied upon to be in residence would have cases brought to him from a large area. Indeed, it was in response to this need, and to the requirement that two justices be present for certain types of hearing, that petty sessions meetings began to be regularized in the eighteenth and early

[64] P.R.O. H.O. 73/6.2; Brown, *Essex People*, pp. 56–63; S. Davies, 'Poor Law Administration and Rural Change in the Tendring Hundred of Essex' (B.A. Diss. Cambridge, 1981), p. 37.
[65] Harriott, *Struggles*, 2, p. 48.

nineteenth centuries. With over 400 parishes and probably no more than thirty or forty justices actually available at any particular moment, the great majority of Essex inhabitants were clearly not receiving their justice from the local squire. They very often had to travel considerable distances to find a JP, and neither victim nor accused were likely to be personally known to the magistrate before whom their case was heard.

6. The Character and Social Background of the Magistracy

Since the minimum legal qualification required to become a JP—an annual income from land of £100—fell far short of the level needed to become a substantial gentleman by the later eighteenth century, the magistracy could be recruited from a fairly broad spectrum of the landowning classes. The flexibilities this introduced became increasingly useful in the second half of the eighteenth century because a growing proportion of the substantial, long-established gentry refused to act as justices. Landau's detailed work on Kent suggests that it therefore became necessary to lower standards and elevate an increasing number of minor gentry, clergy, and professional men to the bench, despite the fact that the political persuasion of potential magistrates was no longer an issue. Jenkins found a similar change occurring in Glamorgan, where the section of the community from which JPs were drawn was widened in the later eighteenth century to include not only lawyers and stewards but also some new industrialists, a group that were still excluded from many other county benches half a century later.[66]

In both areas, as in early nineteenth-century Northamptonshire, it appears that JPs from lesser gentry families, from clerical backgrounds, or from groups striving to establish their gentry status tended to be more active, partly because they were relatively free from the counter-attractions of the London season or of Parliament. Indeed, Lawrence Stone has recently argued that in all counties in the eighteenth century the élite increasingly tended to leave the office of JP to the parish gentry and the clergy in order to allow themselves leisure to hunt, travel, and make lengthy visits to London. The eighteenth-century Essex evidence offers considerable support for this view. Clerical justices increased rapidly to form 28 per cent of active magistrates in Essex by 1785 (Table 4.3)— a figure similar to that found in Hertfordshire, Surrey, and Oxfordshire. Meanwhile the proportion drawn from those above the rank of esquire was halved between 1747 and 1785, by which time the impact of the aristocracy on the Essex quarter sessions and on judicial work in the county was minimal. Among the small minority of magistrates who carried the main burden of work in Essex, clerical men played a very prominent part. Although only 28 per cent

[66] Landau, *The Justices*, esp. pp. 132–40, 160–2; Jenkins, *The Making*, p. 87; F. M. L. Thompson, *English Landed Society in the Nineteenth Century* (London, 1963), p. 111; Howell, *Patriarchs*, p. 142; D. Foster, 'Class and County Government in Early Nineteenth-Century Lancashire', *Northern History*, 9 (1974), 48–9.

Table 4.7. JP Activity Rates by Social Background, Essex, 1782

Status	No. of JPs	Average no. of committals per JP, 1778–83	Average no. of attendances per JP, 1778–83
Above esquire	6	0.3	1.2
Esquire	57	3.6	3.0
Clerical	34	5.8	4.4
Total (resident)	97		
Out of county	17	0.1	1.5

Sources: E.R.O. Q/SBb 306/16. 'Out of County' = all those with addresses outside Essex in the 1782 list. Attendances Q/SMg 23–24. Committals as for Table 6.2.

of qualified magistrates in the 1780s were clerics, their ranks included five of the seven most active committing magistrates, and on average they dealt with 60 per cent more offenders and attended many more sessions than their non-clerical equivalents (Table 4.7). In Essex as elsewhere the influence of the clerical magistrates grew steadily until the end of the eighteenth century (Table 4.3), reflecting their increasing wealth, their growing links with the gentry,[67] and, most important perhaps, the fact that many non-clerical magistrates were often absent from the county or unavailable for judicial duty.

In counties like Essex, where the turnover of gentry families was more rapid than elsewhere, it is particularly difficult to establish the social backgrounds of some magistrates, while the chronology of change is also hard to unravel because no equivalent Essex studies are available for the late seventeenth and early eighteenth centuries. However, by the second half of the eighteenth century the non-clerical magistrates appointed to the Essex bench included not only members of the substantial gentry and of long-established lesser gentry families but also a large and growing number of recent arrivals in the county who were at best of marginal gentry status. Many, indeed, would hardly have merited the title 'gentleman' at all if the definition of that term had not begun to widen in the later eighteenth century losing its older connotations of 'gentle' birth and idle living.[68]

The Essex gentry of the late eighteenth century was a remarkably fluid group, an ever-changing combination of new wealth and traditional squirarchy in which the former tended to predominate. In surveying the contempor-

[67] Jenkins, *The Making*, pp. 89–90; Landau, *The Justices*, p. 143; R. Shorthouse, 'Justices of the Peace in Northamptonshire. Part II. The Work of the County Magistrates', *Northamptonshire Past and Present*, 5 (1975), 245; Stone, *An Open Elite*, p. 176; Beattie, *Crime*, p. 63; Langford, *Public Life and Propertied Englishmen*, pp. 410–20; D. McClatchey, *Oxfordshire Clergy 1777–1869* (Oxford, 1960), p. 179; some counties had higher proportions of clerical JPs—E. Moir, *The Justices of the Peace* (Harmondsworth, 1969), p. 107; E. Evans, 'Some Reasons for the Growth of Rural Anti-Clericalism 1750–1850', *Past and Present*, 66, (1975), 103–4, others lower—Howell, *Patriarchs*, p. 145; Beckett, *Aristocracy*, p. 386; G. Mingay, *The Gentry. The Rise and Fall of a Ruling Class* (London, 1976), p. 127.
[68] Corfield, 'Class by Name', p. 43.

ary chroniclers of the Essex gentry—Morant, Muilman, and Wright—the reader is immediately struck by the rapid turnover of many estates. 'The transitions of property are over rapid and too many family seats have changed their owners', one contemporary complained, and detailed research has confirmed that only a handful of the gentry families established in Essex prior to 1700 remained by the end of the 1770s.[69] The eighteenth-century English aristocracy may not have been an open élite, but the landowning gentry of Essex most certainly was. Large estates were not usually accumulated near to London and by the 1780s the nobility had dwindled to a small group in Essex, their influence being much less extensive than elsewhere. The substantial landowners and parish gentry of eighteenth-century Essex were not so much an open élite as a revolving door. As Stone has pointed out, the Essex and Hertfordshire gentries were exceptionally affected by the pull of London in this period. These counties were particularly favoured by nabobs, commercial men, professionals, and office holders as places in which to build a new country house, the estate around which was often kept relatively small in order to ensure that most of the owner's capital remained in more profitable ventures. These men usually remained active in their callings and had no plans to settle permanently into local gentry society, but many were willing to serve as Sheriffs and JPs during their residence in the county. It is not therefore surprising to find that the late eighteenth-century Essex bench contained a much smaller proportion of families established in the sixteenth and seventeenth centuries than those of non-metropolitan counties such as Gloucestershire. Only about 10 per cent of the men on the 1782 list can be directly linked to pre-1700 Essex gentry families. A much larger proportion was recently established smaller gentry, a considerable number of whom were at most only one generation away from the success as London officeholders, merchants, or professionals that had enabled their estates to be purchased. The close proximity of London and the 'Stockbroker belt' function of the south-western hundreds made Essex a favourite area not only among those who wanted to establish themselves as semi-permanent resident gentry but also among those who sought a retirement home, a rural residence near to their place of business, or a conveniently placed landed investment.[70] When country estates in south-west Essex came on the market they were often subdivided to meet this demand. Of the 100

---

[69] P. Morant, *The History and Antiquities of the County of Essex* (2 vols., 1768); P. Muilman, *A New and Complete History of Essex ... by a Gentleman*, (6 vols., Chelmsford, 1770); T. Wright, *The History and Topography of the County of Essex* (2 vols., 1831–6); Shrimpton, *Landed Society*, pp. 49–52; Beckett, *Aristocracy*, p. 63.

[70] J. Cannon, *Aristocratic Century. The Peerage of Eighteenth-Century England* (Cambridge, 1984), pp. 1–33; Stone, *An Open Elite*; esp. pp. 30, 100–1, 180; Beckett, *Aristocracy*, p. 53; Brown, *Essex at Work*, pp. 161–2; Landau, *The Justices*, p. 152; only a handful of the surnames on the early seventeenth-century Essex magistrates' list—J. Gleason, *The Justices of the Peace in England 1558 to 1640. A Later Eirenarcha* (Oxford, 1969), p. 250—recur in the 1782 list. E.R.O. Q SB/b 306/16. For Gloucestershire, Moir, *Local Government*, p. 46; Shrimpton, *Landed Society*, pp. 93–153.

acting Essex magistrates whose backgrounds I have been able to trace, well over a quarter were men whose wealth was not based on inherited land, and about half were first-generation property owners in the county. At least six had East India Company connections and many more were London merchants or financiers, a number of whom, like Samuel Bosanquet, Governor of the Bank of England in 1792, remained actively involved in commercial undertakings.[71]

A handful of industrial men—a shipbuilder, a brewer, a cooper, and two millers—can also be found among the active magistrates, a period as an alderman or as Lord Mayor of London often forming the bridge that brought them into the Essex gentry. Although clothiers sometimes maintained a significant presence on the benches of other cloth-manufacturing counties and contributed some personnel to the Colchester borough magistracy, their impact on the Essex county bench was minimal. A few were placed on the Commission of the Peace in the 1780s but the industry was in the final stages of decline by that time and none of them appear to have become acting magistrates in the county.[72] Outside the boroughs, food processors and manufacturers formed a relatively small group within the magistracy, and members of such families usually entered the commission only after much of their wealth had been invested in land. Professional men were better represented. The 1782 list contained four 'Doctors in Physic', the joint auditor of His Majesty's revenue, and a number of lawyers. Although formal legal training was not widespread, the extensive overlap between the metropolitan and Essex magistracy brought many men with wider judicial experience onto the bench. Apart from those whose prominent positions in city government had involved them in magisterial work, the 1782 list included at least fifteen men whose names can be found on Middlesex Commissions of the Peace. A handful of these were rotation office justices included for the sake of convenience, but most were listed as resident in Essex and spent at least a small part of their time in the county.[73]

The social background and quality of the magistracy varied widely between different areas of the county. In central Essex families like the Bramstons and the Bullocks provided magistrates with large estates and long-established gentry backgrounds, but in other areas the picture was very different. In the Becontree hundred pseudo-gentry with commercial interests in the capital

---

[71] Beckett, *Aristocracy*, pp. 71–2; the main sources used to trace magistrates' backgrounds were Morant, *The History*; Muilman, *A New*; Wright, *The History*; Shrimpton, *Landed Society*; *V.C.H* . . . . *Essex*, IV–VII; *D.N.B*; W. Addison, *Essex Worthies. A Biographical Companion to the County* (1973); Brown, *Essex People*.

[72] Addison, *Essex Worthies*, p. 82; D.N.B., 21, p. 47; although Josias and Thomas Nottidge, members of a Bocking clothing family, and Isaac and James Boggis of Colchester, were inserted in the Commission of the Peace in 1782, none of them appears in the 1785 list, (E.R.O. Q/SBb 306/15); members of the cloth-manufacturing Boggis family were active on the Colchester Bench (E.R.O. P/CoR 9). Moir, *Local Government*, pp. 50–1, Moir, *The Justice*, pp. 167–81 and Brown 'Colchester', p. 152.

[73] I am indebted to Ruth Paley for these references. R. Paley, 'The Middlesex Justices'.

dominated the magistracy, but truly active men were in such short supply that in the mid-1780s John Staples, who had extensive experience on the Middlesex bench, was paid by a local gentleman to hold weekly sittings at Stratford. Most counties had blackspots which forced their Lord Lieutenants to recruit from social groups that were normally considered unsuitable. In the Blackheath division of Kent brewers and ironsmiths were put on the bench. In Glamorgan industrialists were recruited in the Merthyr area.[74] In the unhealthy eastern Essex hundreds, which lacked both resident clergy and gentry, the Lord Lieutenant really had to scrape the barrel. Although Henry Bate-Dudley was refused entry onto the Middlesex bench in 1775— perhaps because of the series of well-orchestrated, publicity-seeking punch-ups that had earned him the title of 'the Reverend Bruiser'—when he settled in the Dengie hundred in 1783 he immediately became one of the county's main committing magistrates. John Harriott, a seafaring adventurer turned farmer, found it almost impossible to avoid the office of JP in eastern Essex. When his house was burnt down and his land was inundated by the sea, Harriott's debts far outweighed his assets, but as soon as he had settled with his creditors, the local inhabitants enlisted the support of the Lord Lieutenant in order to overcome his reluctance to rejoin the bench.[75]

Beneath these geographical variations broader changes were taking place in the character of the magistracy. Although Stone's conclusion that the eighteenth century witnessed the virtual abdication of responsibility for local government by the élite has to be treated with caution because his study excludes the lesser gentry and is based on only three counties, it fits well with the Essex evidence. So does his suggestion that in the nineteenth century growing anxieties about social order and other ideological changes encouraged the more substantial landowners to move back onto the bench in increasing numbers.[76] This countervailing movement was only just beginning in the period before 1820, but in Essex quarter sessions attendance rose quite rapidly in the early nineteenth century (Figure 4.1) and the role of clerical magistrates began to decline (Table 4.3) while an increasing number of substantial gentry returned to active service on the bench.

A more subtle model of the ways that both the character of the magistracy and the nature of summary court hearings were changing in the eighteenth century has recently been put forward by Norma Landau. Building on E. P. Thompson's discussion of the withdrawal of the eighteenth-century gentry from face-to-face contact with the poor, she argues that this period witnessed a

[74] Addison, *Essex Worthies*, p. 29; Wright, *The History*, I, p. 181; Shrimpton, *Landed Society*, p. 64. Staples was invited by Bamber Gascoyne, a JP in the Ilford division P.R.O. H.O. 42/20/194. Landau, *The Justices*, p. 316; Jenkins, *The Making*, p. 88;
[75] L. Werkmeister, *The London Daily Press 1772–92* (Lincoln, 1963), pp. 19–44; Paley, 'An Imperfect', p. 105; Harriott, *Struggles*, 2, pp. 43, 99.
[76] Stone, *An Open Elite*, pp. 176–9; Beckett, *Aristocracy*, p. 391.

transition from patriarchal rule, in which the justice's authority rested on his prestige, power, and influence as a private individual within his locality, to a patrician rule in which the justice's power was expressed in a more distanced and disinterested fashion. In the patriarchal model expressed in the justices' manuals of the sixteenth and seventeenth centuries the magistrate was the natural leader and paternal ruler of the local community. In the patrician model, which influenced Burn's eighteenth-century handbooks, the justice was primarily a neutral administrator, a disinterested and altruistic component of the legal system.

This was not a sudden or complete transformation, of course. The two models overlapped and the change in judicial styles did not occur by the simple displacement of one model by another.[77] However, given the very small number of substantial gentry willing to become active justices in the eighteenth century and the concentration of judicial business in the hands of a small group of JPs the vast majority of whom were clergy, lesser gentry, or men from commercial or professional backgrounds, Essex does appear to have experienced a movement towards what Landau terms a patrician style of justice. In the Lexden and Winstree hundreds, where detailed petty sessions examination books survive, one or two rural JPs from established local gentry families did hear some cases, but the almost continuous justicing service offered to residents of these hundreds by individual magistrates or petty sessions hearings at Colchester persuaded most of them to travel considerable distances to obtain justice there. Charles Matthews, the JP whose signature dominates the Lexden and Winstree examination books, certainly fits Landau's definition of a patrician magistrate. Matthews was a Londoner with property in Finchley and Hanover Square who had several years' experience as a Middlesex magistrate before coming to Colchester in the early 1780s. He had begun acting as a magistrate almost as soon as he took up residence, but his personal contacts with the people of the Lexden and Winstree hundreds appear to have been minimal. He owned little or no land in the area, and since he was not empowered to act in cases from Colchester borough itself, he avoided hearing the disputes of his urban neighbours.[78] In the early 1790s most complainants in this large area of north-east Essex had their cases heard by a magistrate who had virtually no involvement with their communities.

In conclusion, therefore, the types of summary hearings available to property crime victims were gradually changing in the eighteenth century. In Essex, as in Kent and Glamorgan, a much greater number of minor gentry, lesser clergymen, and other marginal members of the county élite were being

[77] E. P. Thompson, 'Patrician Society, Plebeian Culture', *Journal of Social History*, 7 (1974), 382–485; Landau, *The Justices*, esp. pp. 3–5, 328–62. On declining face-to-face contact—Langford, *Public Life and Propertied Englishmen*, p. 383.
[78] E.R.O. P/LwR 6–8. Two-thirds of all examinations 1788–92 are signed by Charles Matthews alone. A further 20% are signed by him jointly with another magistrate.

appointed to, and becoming active on, the bench by the second half of the eighteenth century. Not only would very few parishes have contained a wealthy gentleman willing to act regularly as a JP, but even in parishes that did have a resident magistrate there was no guarantee that the individual concerned had enough wealth or status to wield natural authority within that community. As the business of single justices was increasingly transferred to joint petty sessions meetings, the relationship between the magistrates and those they governed also changed. For the justice as the familiar patriarch of his neighbourhood, the petty sessions substituted the justice as one of a group of disinterested governors. The unity of the late eighteenth-century magistracy should not be overstressed. In Essex social rivalries and political disagreements were sometimes intense. Contested elections produced major local political differences, as did the controversy over the proposed Chelmer Navigation, and the decision to rebuild the Chelmsford Gaol in the 1770s. The battle over Peregrine Bertie's appointment as steward of the Waltham Forest Court of Attachments paralysed the court for fifteen years. Petty differences were often endemic. In 1804, for example, the magistrates of the Dunmow petty sessions were labelled 'the squad' by a local JP, angered by their 'closeted' exclusiveness and their tendency to override his decisions.[79] However, despite the fact that magistrates in every division often disagreed on certain issues, and that some long-established patriarchal gentry magistrates can still be found in later eighteenth-century Essex, a more distanced semi-collective patrician style of justice had almost certainly become predominant in many areas.

In these circumstances, and for a number of other reasons historians have yet to fully analyse, the controls on magisterial discretion imposed by the Marian statutes in felony cases seem to have grown weaker in this period. The preliminary hearings of property crime accusations that came before magistrates such as Charles Matthews were increasingly turned into real adjudications rather than mere ciphers for the major courts. Encouraged perhaps by the growing impact of lawyerly arguments that it was unfair to send the accused on for jury trial unless a very solid case had been presented against him,[80] magistrates overcame the legal barriers erected to limit their discretion by developing various alternatives to committal for trial. Enlistment, punishment under statutes relating to the regulation of the idle or mobile poor, informal negotiations and settlements, or simple dismissal for lack of evidence

[79] Epping Forest Commission, *The Rolls*, 2, p. 116; Fisher, *Forest*, p. 101; on political divisions, A. Pickersgill, 'Parliamentary Elections in Essex 1759–1774' (M.A. Manchester, 1953); R. Sedgwick, *The History of Parliament. The House of Commons 1715–1754* (London, 2 vols., 1970), 1, pp. 241–3; L. Namier and J. Brook, *The History of Parliament. The House of Commons 1754–1790* (London, 2 vols., 1985), 1, pp. 274–81; 2, pp. 488–9; R. Thorne, *The History of Parliament. The House of Commons 1790–1820* (London, 2 vols., 1986) 1, pp. 155–64. For controversy about the new gaol. *House of Commons Journals*, 33 (Nov. 1770– Nov. 1772), pp. 124–5, 368. E.R.O. D/DMg C2, 5 Feb. 1804 and 13 Mar. 1804.

[80] Beattie, *Crime*, pp. 271–80.

accounted for a substantial proportion, and perhaps for the majority, of potential felony accusations by the late eighteenth century.

The dynamics of summary hearings are difficult to analyse in detail. Evidence is rarely available about important aspects such as the level of lawyerly involvement, the degree of public access, the role of the magistrate's clerks, and the extent to which evidence was taken on oath.[81] More centrally the main actors virtually never recorded their interactions or underlying attitudes. While it is clear that both victims and magistrates approached most property appropriation hearings knowing that they had wide discretionary powers, the precise balance of forces between them is difficult to determine. In the small minority of cases that directly affected their interests or those of influential local game preservers, magistrates may have been strongly committed to imposing particular outcomes whatever the merits of the case. Faced by a major property crime accusation based on strong evidence, they would usually attempt to close off the victim's potential options by insisting that the accused be committed for trial in the major courts. However, despite their prestigious position, their higher status, their wider experience, their access to legal knowledge and advice, and the legal weapons (such as binding the victim under recognizance) available to them, magistrates could not necessarily impose their will on the proceedings. Without the victim's continued support a prosecution would almost certainly flounder, and even if they were bound by recognizance victims frequently found ways of avoiding bringing an indictment. Equally, victims may sometimes have undermined the justices' attempts to avoid formally prosecuting the accused by refusing to drop a well-founded felony accusation or by taking his accusation to another magistrate.[82]

However, once the bench had decided that the accused had committed an appropriation, there are a number of reasons for believing that magistrates and victims were usually in broad agreement about which sanctions should be imposed. The more distanced mode of justice that developed in the eighteenth century meant that magistrates rarely had a personal interest in the cases coming before them. The majority wished to see themselves principally as neutral servants of the law, as arbitrators or mediators as much as adjudicators, as providers of judicial services to those in the local area who demanded them. Until guilt had been established they would not necessarily see things the victim's way. Hunt actually forced two alleged victims to pay compensation and costs to the accused in 1744 when their theft accusation turned out to be false. However, once the magistrates were satisfied that the defendant was guilty, they had a predisposition towards resolving each case in a way that would be acceptable to the victim unless the latter demanded an unduly severe

---

[81] Whitbread is exceptional in recording that some witnesses gave sworn testimony, Cirket (ed.), *Samuel Whitbread's Notebooks*, e.g. pp. 38–9, 57–8, 77.

[82] E.R.O. D/DMg C2 13 Mar. 1804 for an example of a prosecutor simply taking a case to another summary court.

or inappropriate outcome. When Hunt allowed the fine imposed on a wood thief to be distributed among the local poor 'at the discretion of the complainant' he was expressing his sense that both victim and magistrate should be involved in the sanctioning process.[83] The wide variety of criteria used by the summary courts to determine the level and type of sanction to be imposed, which include the strength of the evidence, the character of both victim and accused, and the youth, poverty, and previous conduct of the latter, were not used by these courts alone. Almost exactly the same factors influenced victims in their earlier negotiations with the accused, as well as the decisions of jurors and trial judges further on up the line. Despite wide variations in attitude between individuals, decision-makers at various points in the judicial process shared the same broad assumptions about the types of offender that should be sent on for trial or given heavy summary sentences, and about those who should be treated leniently whenever possible.

Pretrial procedures from the initial contact between victim and accused right up to the grand jury hearing in one of the major courts consisted of layer upon layer of negotiation opportunities and discretionary choices. Magistrates' hearings need to be seen as part of that broader process: more formal and more subject, in theory at least, to legal regulation and control, but still an interconnected stage in the deeply discretionary and negotiative process that resolved the vast majority of disputes about property appropriation, leaving only a small residue to be dealt with by the judges and jurors of the major courts.

[83] Crittall (ed.), *The Justicing*, pp. 28 and 81.

Part 2

Offences and Offenders

5

Patterns of Crime and Patterns of Deprivation

In view of the highly personal, selective, and discretionary nature of the prosecution process, and of the varied and widely used escape routes that enabled the vast majority of those accused of property theft to avoid formal indictment in the major courts, it could be argued that the number of offenders who finally reached those courts has little value as an indicator of changing levels of appropriation. However, most contemporaries used them in precisely that way and to some extent historians have done the same. The length of the assizes gaol calendar was frequently, although not consistently, reported by most eighteenth-century provincial newspapers. In the mid-1770s the *Chelmsford Chronicle* noted that 'so great a number of felons is not remembered to have been in our gaol at any one time for upwards of fifty years past', while at the beginning of the French wars it remarked on 'the smallest number ever remembered upon the calendar'. The length of the assize calendar was clearly seen as a guide to changes in the number of crimes actually being committed. In the 1780s Madan assumed that lengthening calendars 'plainly testify' to the growth of crime. In 1801 the Chelmsford assize judge, after referring to the unprecedented size of the calendar, went on to inform the court that offences 'are doubling and trebling upon us'. He then announced that his approach to sentencing would therefore be less lenient.[1] Sentencing decisions, jury verdicts, and pardoning processes were all affected by changes in the number of offenders reaching the courts (Chapters 7 and 8). Both victims and officials were not only aware of the approximate numbers being indicted; they also allowed their sense of the prevalence of crime to affect their attitudes and policies. Pretrial processes were also affected. When it was thought that crime was increasing, the courts became more willing to grant legal aid to prosecutors, and victims became more willing to join or form prosecution associations.

If historians had simply wished to measure the impact of changing perceptions of the prevalence of crime on those involved in the criminal justice system, their best guide would probably have been these newspaper reports about the length of the assize calendar, which were the closest thing contem-

[1] *Che.C.*, 10 Mar. 1776, 8 Aug. 1794; Madan, *Thoughts*, p. 87; *Che.C.*, 24 and 31 July 1801. See also 1 Aug. 1800. For a critique of this practice, see *P.P.*, 1839, XIX, pp. 2–3.

poraries had to a public index of reported crime. However, those reports were not published consistently enough to provide a regular series. Moreover, they did not include quarter sessions prosecutions and they failed to differentiate between property offences and other types of felony. They have therefore been largely ignored in favour of a less simple process, the counting of indictments.[2]

The formal charge against any property offender tried at either the quarter sessions or the assizes was recorded briefly on an indictment. As the key official records of the trial process, indictments were kept assiduously by the court clerks. Although some of the information in them is inaccurate these deficiencies do not prevent their use as a measure of the number of persons charged with property offences at succeeding intervals, or as a starting-point for more detailed analysis of offences and offenders.[3] As they tackled the dusty, long-ignored parchment rolls in which indictments were stored, rolls which recoil when unravelled as if unwilling to give up their secrets, historians soon moved beyond simply counting the indictments. Patterns of crime across different areas and types of offence have now been studied. Indictments have been used in conjunction with depositions, process books, and other sources to reconstruct the background and character of those indicted (Chapter 6). Finally, in an attempt to understand the circumstances and motivations behind the bald details found in indictments, detailed comparisons have been made between short-term changes in indictment levels and parallel changes in living standards, armed forces recruitment, and other social and economic indicators.[4]

Given their brief and rather formulaic nature, it may seem surprising that much of the initial work on crime in early modern England relied so heavily upon indictments, but their eminent suitability for quantification was not the only reason why historians were drawn by the lure of the indictment. The number of offenders tried or convicted before the summary courts is unrecoverable. Formal records were not preserved by magistrates' clerks, and the summary conviction certificates that survive in the quarter sessions rolls are a small and unrepresentative remnant. Equally, with a few important exceptions, the English assize records lack the detailed investigative documents

---

[2] Assize calendar reports and indictment counts normally move in the same direction. In 1781–3 the Essex calendars were reported to include 69, 50, and 87 offenders. (*Che.C.*) the indictment count was 89, 62, 125.

[3] J. Cockburn, 'Early Modern Assize Records as Historical Evidence', *Journal of the Society of Archivists*, 5 (1975), pp. 221–31; J. Beattie, 'Towards a Study of Crime in Eighteenth-century England. A Note on Indictments', in P. Fritz and D. Williams (eds.), *The Triumph of Culture: Eighteenth-Century Perspectives* (Toronto, 1972), pp. 301–21; Sharpe, *Crime in Early Modern England*, pp. 36–7; Innes and Styles, 'Crime Wave', pp. 208–11.

[4] J. Beattie, 'The Pattern of Crime in England 1660–1800', *Past and Present*, 62 (1974), pp. 47–95; J. Beattie, 'The Criminality of Women in Eighteenth-Century England', *Journal of Social History*, 7 (1975), 80–116; J. Beattie, *Crime*, pp. 155–86; Hay 'War'; Hay, 'Crime, Authority'; Pole, 'Crime'; Sharpe, *Crime in Early*, pp. 41–63; For pre-1700, see, J. Sharpe, *Crime in Seventeenth-Century England. A County Study* (Cambridge, 1983); Wrightson, 'Two Concepts of Order'; P. Lawson, 'Property Crime and Hard Times in England, 1559–1624', *Law and History Review*, 4 (1986), 96–127. R. Shoemaker, *Prosecution*.

created by judicial procedures on the continent. The English records' great strength is quantity not quality, and the historiography reflects this. Moreover, some historians have argued that the eighteenth century is the ideal period to undertake quantitative work. Although indictments were created further away from the actual act of appropriation than modern indices such as 'crimes reported to the police', they are less tainted by hidden agendas. Changes in policing or public prosecution policy can severely distort more modern statistics, as can the police's desire to attract resources by manipulating crime rates and detection rates, as Howard Taylor's work has recently shown. The clerks who made out eighteenth-century indictments were unaffected by such practices, or by the need to justify their own existence. Nor were individual victims and magistrates usually subjected to systematic bureaucratic or organizational pressures. The 'accidental' nature of these indictment series may therefore make them a more useful source than the more elaborately constructed modern crime statistics.[5] Finally, it has to be admitted that nowhere are the indictments more alluring to the potential researcher than in eighteenth-century Essex. Apart from the loss of a small minority of 'not-found' indictments, a complete series is available for all the major courts of Essex including the five borough and liberty sessions with minor property crime jurisdiction— Colchester, Saffron Walden, Harwich, Maldon, and Havering. In addition, the existence of quantitative studies of indictments in sixteenth- and seventeenth-century Essex makes this virtually the only county for which long-term comparisons can be made.[6]

Any attempt to exploit this rich vein is, of course, fraught with difficulties. Almost as soon as they began wrestling with the court rolls historians became aware that the significance of indictment levels could only be explored by constant reference to the relationship between patterns of lawbreaking and the diverse reactions and interactions of victims, law-enforcement agencies, and judicial authorities. Given the vast range of unreported or summarily dealt with offences, indictment levels are clearly no guide to the absolute number of lawbreaking acts committed. Nor, in view of the array of discretionary processes involved, can it be assumed that the relationship between indictments and actual levels of appropriation remained constant. The depth of prosecutorial and magisterial discretion inevitably varies across space and time, as well as according to the type of offence or offender involved. In response to their

[5] Depositions do survive for a few areas but not for the Home Circuit. Hay, 'War', pp. 150–2; Box, *Deviance*, pp. 157–202; H. Taylor, 'Rationing Crime. The Political Economy of Criminal Statistics since the 1850s', *Economic History Review*, 51 (1998), 569–90; H. Taylor, 'The Politics of the Rising Crime Statistics of England and Wales 1914–1960', *Crime, Histoire et Sociétés / Crime, History and Societies*, 2 (1998), 5–28.

[6] Borough courts heard 9 per cent of Essex property crime indictments, 1760–1800. Other studies have had virtually to ignore borough jurisdictions: Beattie, *Crime*, p. 17; Hay, 'Crime, Authority', pp. 594–602; Sharpe, *Crime in Seventeenth Century England*; J. Samaha, *Law and Order in Historical Perspective. The Case of Elizabethan Essex* (New York, 1974); King, 'Crime, Law', p. 33.

growing awareness of these problems, many historians switched their attention from offences to judicial processes, but the leading writers in this field have continued both to analyse the internal patterns of indictments and to maintain, in the short term at least, that indictment series could be used as more than just a guide to contemporaries' perceptions about changing levels of crime. Beattie has argued that fluctuations in the level of indictments 'derive ultimately from changes in real offences'. Hay, after skilfully comparing short-term changes in the relevant indicators, suggested that 'changes in the level of indictments for theft are congruent . . . with what we know of the incidence of dearth and the timing and nature of demobilization. These seem strong reasons for suggesting that indictment levels in the courts do reflect changes in the amount of illegal appropriation.' Both these writers have assessed the alternative possibility that even short-term changes in indictment levels may be more affected by the changing anxiety levels and opinions of victims, magistrates, and others who influenced the prosecution process than by changes in real levels of appropriation, but John Beattie in particular has argued that ultimately it was indictments that shaped opinion rather than vice versa.[7]

This chapter aims to evaluate this work in two ways. By comparing the evidence of the Essex indictments—the types of offence indicted, the geography of indictments, the relationship between changing indictment levels and other indices—with that found in other counties, and by using the analysis of pretrial processes already developed (Chapters 2–4) to raise further questions about the meaning of the data extracted from the indictments. First, however, proper attention must be given to the relationship between the two figures that will dominate these discussions: the tiny but brightly illuminated figure representing the indicted (dressed in a fine array of clothes created by extensive academic research); and the huge looming presence of 'the dark figure of unrecorded crime', a mere silhouette, whose immense size is occasionally discernible from diaries and other exceptional documents. The extreme sensitivity of indictment levels to the reactions of prosecutors and magistrates implied in contemporary estimates that only one in ten, one in fifty, or one in a hundred felonies were ever indicted (Chapter 1) is easily passed over with a brief genuflection in the direction of the dark figure. If *The Times* was right that 'nine-tenths of the breaches against the laws escape detection from the trouble and charges consequent on prosecution' a 10 per cent rise in the proportion of prosecutors willing to indict would produce the same effect as a doubling of real appropriations.[8] Moreover, there are many indirect indications that this was an underestimate of the size of the dark figure.

Absolute levels of indicted crime were incredibly low in the eighteenth century. In Essex between 1740 and 1779 four indictments per 10,000

---

[7] Hay, 'War', esp. p. 145; Beattie, *Crime*, pp. 199–237, esp p. 202; Beattie, 'Crime and Inequality', p. 120. For an extreme alternative, J. Ditton, *Contrology. Beyond the New Criminology* (1979), pp. 20–1.

[8] *The Times*, 5 Dec. 1785; for other contemporary estimates see Chapter 1.

Table 5.1. Property Crime Indictment Rates, Essex, 1740–1820

Decade	Essex population[a]	Indictments[b] per annum	Indictment rates per 10,000	Period
1740–9	146,250	58.3	3.91	1740–59
1750–9	155,110	59.4		
1760–9	163,000	56.6	4.03	1760–79
1770–9	174,190	79.4		
1780–9	188,370	116.0	5.91	1780–99
1790–9	211,430	120.3		
1800–9	233,390	143.9	7.18	1800–19
1810–19	268,310	216.3		

Notes: [a] Brown's Essex population estimates for 1700, 1723, 1768, 1778 always form between 2.5 and 2.6 per cent of the English population totals reconstructed by Wrigley and Schofield. The population of Essex has therefore been estimated for each decade by taking the average percentage for these four years and for 1801 (Essex population = 2.58% of English) out of the mid-decade English total in Wrigley and Schofield, *The Population of England*, pp. 533–4. Brown, *Essex at Work*, 1700–1815, p. 95.
[b] Based on all Essex indicted property offenders.

Sources: Assize rolls' indictments and agenda books, P.R.O. Assi 35/180–244 and 31/2–20. Quarter Sessions rolls' indictments and process books, E.R.O. Q/SR 658–917 and Q/SPb 9–17; for 1776–81 there is no process book and the rolls for five sessions (Jan. 77, Apr. 77, July 79, July 80, and Oct. 80) are slightly damaged. Minute books, prison calendars, and order books were reconstructed to fill this gap, but in these five sessions one or two offenders may be missed out. Borough courts—a unique series—Colchester Record office, borough sessions files and books; Saffron Walden order books and minute books, Maldon sessions books, Havering Liberty sessions books (all in the E.R.O. TA/419, D/B/3/1/25–8, Q/Hm 1); Harwich Minute book (Harwich Record Office). For 1805–20, P.R.O. H.O. 27/1–19 include all these jurisdictions. Not found bills appear to have been fairly systematically kept but this cannot be consistently relied upon, particularly in the minor jurisdictions. The count is based on 'court years' not calendar years and includes all offenders committed for trial from August the previous year to July of the year named. See Hay, 'War', p. 123 for detailed explanation.

inhabitants was the yearly average (Table 5.1) or about one every 500 households. In northern and central Essex the figure was even lower, as it was in some other counties. At this rate, if only one offender in ten was indicted, the average household would only fall victim to a property crime once every half century. Since the diaries suggest that two or three times per decade might be a better estimate, at least for those sections of the population that kept such records (Chapter 2), Colquhoun's pessimistic figure of one in a hundred may be nearer the truth for the mid-eighteenth century. Indictment rates did rise after 1780 (Table 5.1), but even if the prevailing rate between 1801 and 1820 is used as the basis for calculation the average Essex household would only have produced about three property crime indictments every thousand years. Many parishes went for whole decades without creating a single indictment. Some substantial market towns fared little better. Despite the general rise in indictment levels in the last quarter of the eighteenth century, the rapidly growing market town of Witham, with a population of 2,186 in 1801, produced no property crime indictments, 1793–5. In the entire decade 1791–1800, which included two periods of extreme dearth, only five offenders were indicted for property crimes committed in the town. Although it is possible to paint too pessimistic a picture of lawbreaking activity in the smaller towns of early modern England, it seems unlikely that the innkeepers, shopkeepers, and other commercial people of Witham, not to mention the numerous well-off visitors to its spa and the town's many labourers and artisans, suffered between them only five appropriations per year,[9] let alone five per decade. Unprosecuted crime must surely have been much more than ten times greater than indicted crime. Even if this is balanced by the fact that among the tiny group of victims who were committed enough to advertise major thefts in the newspapers about one in five ended up indicting the offender, indictments still cut a pitiful figure when compared to the huge number of indictable but unprosecuted acts of appropriation which such communities experienced. The statistical analysis of indictments can sometimes produce some remarkable patterns, but if prosecution was as abnormal as these figures suggest, explaining the meaning of these patterns may prove to be extremely complex.

1. Long-Term Changes and Types of Crime

Pretrial processes changed in a number of contradictory ways during the early modern period and the effects of those changes are rarely quantifiable. The growth of expenses payments to prosecutors and of private and public policing initiatives, for example, almost certainly increased the proportion of property offenders indicted. The growing disillusionment with the capital sanction, and the summary courts' increasing willingness to deal with indictable offenders informally had the opposite effect. It is therefore impossible to determine whether the late eighteenth-century rise in indictment levels seen in Essex and in other counties such as Sussex and Somerset was caused by a rise in the proportion of property offenders being indicted or by an increase in actual lawbreaking activity.[10] The same problem undermines the analysis of more long-term changes. In Essex and, it appears, on the Home Circuit in general, indictment rates per head of population reached a high point in the late sixteenth and early seventeenth centuries. A rapid decline then ensued which was followed, in every non-metropolitan area so far studied, by a century or so

---

[9] In Surrey indictment rates were higher than Essex, in Sussex they were lower: Beattie, 'The Pattern of Crime', pp. 74–8; P. Laslett and R. Wall (eds.), *Household and Family in Past Time* (Cambridge, 1972), pp. 125–204; Brown, *Essex at Work*, pp. 105, 140. Beattie, *Crime*, p. 185 suggests a similar paucity of indictment activity in many parishes.

[10] Hay, 'War', pp. 122–5; Innes and Styles, 'Crime Wave', pp. 210–11; Beattie, 'The Pattern of Crime', pp. 74–8; Pole, 'Crime', pp. 135–6; for the changing regional distribution of Essex indictments, King, 'Crime, Law', p. 35.

Table 5.2. Property Crime Indictment Rates, in Essex, 1569–1800

Period	Annual average indictments (charges)	Estimated population	Indictment rate per 10,000
1569–73	42.8	64,000	6.7
1584–93	94.9	75,000	12.7
1625–9	88.6	104,000	8.5
1650–4	72.2	120,000	6.0
1660–9	45.1	123,000	3.7
1750–9	66.7	155,100	4.3
1770–9	83.7	168,600	5.0
1790–9	128.2	211,430	6.1

Sources and problems:

Record survival: the best periods were selected from Samaha's work on 1559–1603, using Cockburn's survey of years in which assize records are complete, and from Sharpe's work on 1620–80, using his graphs of record survivals. Samaha, *Law and Order in Historical Perspective*, p. 19, J. Cockburn, 'The Nature and Incidence of Crime in England 1559–1625. A Preliminary Survey', in Cockburn (ed.), *Crime*, p. 68; Sharpe, *Crime in Seventeenth Century England*, pp. 182 and 199; two assize and two quarter session files are missing (1625–9) and 1660–9 suffers from roughly the same deficiency. Quarter sessions survival 1569–73 and 1584–93 is not noted by Samaha. In terms of the relationship between the post-1750 rise and that of the earlier period this would tend to underestimate the height of the latter.

Counting. Since counting methods in earlier periods excluded borough court indictments and used offences rather than offenders as a basis, similar procedures have been used here for 1750–99 (hence the difference between these figures and those in Table 5.1).

Not found bills. These do not appear to have been included in the 1569–73, 1584–93, and 1625–29 figures but are in the later ones (ibid., 188). This will have the same effect as the differences in record survival, reducing by between 10 and 20 per cent the late sixteenth- and early seventeenth-century peak.

Very approximate population estimates were reached by the method used in Table 5.1. Since the estimated population of Essex was 1.95 per cent of English totals in 1550, 1.99 per cent in 1600, and 2.40 per cent in 1670 (Samaha, *Law and Order in Historical Perspective*, p. 33; Brown, *Essex at Work 1700–1815*, p. 95). For 1569–73 and 1584–93, 1.95 was used; 1625–9, 2.20; 1650–4, 2.30; 1660–9, 2.40.

of stagnation or decline until a new upsurge in the later eighteenth century (Table 5.2) which continued until the 1840s.[11] This puts the sustained increase in indictments in the later eighteenth century into a wider perspective. Essex indictment rates in the 1790s were still less than half the level reached at the end of the sixteenth century.

This pattern also links changes in indictment rates to broader social, economic, and demographic movements. Both the late sixteenth and early seventeenth centuries and the late eighteenth and early nineteenth centuries were periods of rapid population growth and of increasing pressure on the

[11] J. Cockburn, *A History of English Assizes 1558–1714* (Cambridge, 1971), p. 102; *P.P.*, 1819, VIII, pp. 164–74. The Palatinate of Chester 1580–1719 followed the same pattern. Sharpe, *Crime in Early Modern England*, pp. 57–60; Beattie, *Crime*, pp. 202–3; Emsley, *Crime*, pp. 27–30.

employment prospects and living standards of the poor. Equally they were both periods in which crime became the repository for broader fears about rapid social change as anxieties grew about methods of relieving the poor, about vagrancy, and about law and order issues in general. Whether the material deprivation, and increased mobility and vulnerability, of the poor created higher levels of lawbreaking or whether the heightened reactions of the authorities caused most of the increase in property crime indictments remains unclear.[12] However, these figures highlight the fact that the period studied here witnessed a major transition from an age of relatively relaxed and stable social relations and of low recorded crime rates to one of rising indictment rates and heightened awareness of the threat potentially posed by the poor.

By contrast, the types of crime indicted in the Essex courts changed very little in the period studied here (Table 5.3). The main non-capital offences—grand and petty larceny—represented about two-thirds of indictments in the 1790s, a slight increase over the mid-century figure. About a sixth of indictments were for burglary, housebreaking, or robbery and a further tenth were for large animal thefts—figures which are very similar to those found in Surrey and Sussex 1660–1800. There are many problems with these figures. Since certain types of lawbreaking and lawbreakers are by their nature more visible and/or more appealing to law enforcers as candidates for prosecution, indictments are not a random sample of lawbreaking activity and therefore offer little indication of the prevalence of different forms of illegal appropriation. Moreover, people were not necessarily indicted for the type of crime they had actually committed. The deliberate manipulation of offence definition by prosecutors makes the slight increase in non-capital indictments, 1748–1800, (Table 5.3) particularly difficult to assess. The quarter sessions depositions show that a considerable number of victims were bringing petty larceny indictments against offenders clearly guilty of housebreaking or other capital larcenies, such as stealing from the person. In 1793, for example, a gang of young pickpockets from London were committed to gaol after their large-scale operations at the Harlow Fair were discovered, but when they came to court the indictments were for petty larceny only.[13] Did prosecutors become more willing to downgrade offences as discontent with the capital sanction grew, or was the increase in minor theft indictments linked to other factors such as the growth of expenses payments to prosecutors which might have increased the range of minor offenders they were willing to take to court?

[12] Sharpe, *Crime in Early Modern England*, pp. 183–7; V. Gatrell, 'Crime, Authority and the Policeman State', in F. M. L. Thompson (ed.), *The Cambridge Social History of Britain 1750–1950. Social Agencies and Social Institutions* (Cambridge, 1990), 3, pp. 244–5. For an interesting analysis of the relationship between changing levels of inequality and both prosecution and punishment levels—D. Hay, 'Time, Inequality and Law's Violence', in A. Sarat and T. Kearns (eds.), *Law's Violence* (Ann Arbor, 1992), pp. 145–51.

[13] Beattie, *Crime*, p. 147. For a comparison of seventeenth- and eighteenth-century types of crime in Essex, King, 'Crime, Law', pp. 39–42. E.R.O. Q/SBb 182/16 and 20 for two cases clearly involving breaking-in as well as theft. Q/SBb 352/51 (1793 case).

Table 5.3. Types of Property Crime Indictments: Essex Quarter Sessions and Assizes, 1748–1800

	1748–67 %	1791–1800 %
Highway robbery	6.4	5.5
Burglary and house breaking	10.6	9.8
Sheep stealing	4.9	4.9
Horse stealing	5.0	2.5
Cattle stealing	0.4	1.2
Game offences	0.5	0.1
Grand and petty larceny	61.8	66.4
Capital larceny	3.0	2.6
Receiving	3.5	3.2
Coining and uttering	0.1	1.1
Other indirect approp. (fraud, forgery, embezzlement, extortion)	3.8	2.9
Total	100	100.2

Note: The count is based on charges (i.e. when two individuals are charged in relation to one offence the count is 2 rather than 1).

Sources: As for Table 5.1.

Some distortions were also caused by the transfer of cases between the major courts and the summary courts. In particular, more than 4 per cent of seventeenth-century indictments related to game offences. By the 1790s the figure was 0.1 per cent, but this reflected the removal of these prosecutions into the lower courts rather than a decline in poaching. Movements in the four main types of summarily triable property offences—wood, vegetable, textile material, and game theft—are even more difficult to gauge. The surviving summary conviction certificates are a very small and untypical sample. Magistrates rarely bothered to return them to the quarter sessions before the early nineteenth century, and some appear to have been selective in their recording policy, taking much greater care in game and particularly in deer stealing cases, where larger fines were involved. The disappearance of certificates relating to textile material offences after the 1790s clearly reflected the demise of the cloth industry, but the rise in game and wood convictions at the end of the eighteenth century mainly reflected changing attitudes towards the return of certificates, although it may also be an indication that the prosecution associations and other initiatives recently set up by farmers and game preservers were having an impact.[14] Given these problems, however, the relative importance of various types of summary offence is better evaluated through the more

[14] Vegetable thefts appear regularly in petty sessions examinations but are virtually absent from the conviction certificates. The transfer of game cases to the lower courts also occurred elsewhere. Munsche, *Gentleman*, pp. 77–8; King, 'Crime, Law' p. 40. Essex conviction certificates 1740–99 = 146 game, 129 wood, 42 textile, 12 vegetable; 1800–19: 272, 310, 0, 8.

detailed information found in gaol calendars and petty sessions records (Chapter 4).

2. The Geography of Crime

In the later eighteenth century, Essex indictment rates were lower than those found in Surrey and considerably higher than those of Sussex, Staffordshire, and Somerset, but the precise significance of these differences remains obscure. When nationwide comparisons become possible in the early nineteenth century, it is difficult to find any regular pattern between counties or any systematic relationship between indictments and economic variables such as the level of urbanization or the proportion of the inhabitants employed in manufacturing. However, in the eighteenth century London did have a systematic impact. In Kent, Surrey, and Essex, parishes in the immediate proximity of the capital had much the highest indictment rates and in Essex they varied fairly systematically according to the distance between a particular area and the metropolis (Map 5.1 and Table 5.4). Between 1791 and 1800 major court prosecution rates in the Becontree hundred were more than four times greater than those found in the remote rural areas of the north-west and north-east, and about three times higher than those of the cloth manufacturing hundreds, which in their prime had made a large contribution to Essex indictments. They were also more than double those of central Essex, where access to the Chelmsford courts was much easier. The area nearest to London had the highest rates for every type of crime except sheep theft which was most prevalent in the sheep pasturing hundreds of the south-east.[15]

Table 5.4. Assize Property Crime Indictments, 1782–7, Home Circuit

% of each type of crime	All 5 %	Sussex %	Herts %	Essex %	Surrey %	Kent %
Petty and grand larceny	36.1	28.8	31.9	39.0	35.7	37.4
Aggravated larceny	10.7	1.7	3.7	7.3	12.0	15.6
Burglary	20.1	32.2	23.9	19.9	18.4	18.0
Highway robbery	19.3	12.7	10.1	18.5	23.1	20.7
Horse stealing	6.2	14.4	13.3	7.3	4.4	3.2
Sheep stealing	3.9	6.8	9.0	4.1	2.0	3.0
Indirect appropriations	3.7	3.4	8.0	3.8	4.2	2.0
	100	100	99.9	99.9	99.8	99.9
Indictments per 1,000 population (all crime)	2.1	0.9	2.1	1.6	2.5	2.7

Sources: P.R.O. Assi 31/13–15.

[15] Hay, 'War', p. 126; Beattie, 'The Pattern of Crime', p. 81; Pole, 'Crime', pp. 135–6; V. Gatrell and T. Hadden, 'Criminal Statistics and their Interpretation', in E. Wrigley (ed.), *Nineteenth-Century Society. Essays in the Use of Quantitative Methods for the Study of Social Data* (Cambridge, 1972), p. 359. Beattie, *Crime*,

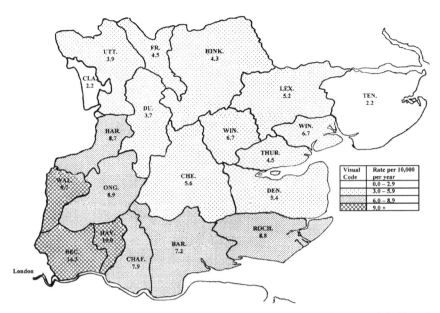

Map 5.1 Property Crime Indicment Rates by Hundred, Essex, 1791–1800 (per 10,000 inhabitants)

Although it is difficult to use assize indictments without reference to the varying jurisdictions of each county's quarter sessions, the geography of recorded crime on the Home Circuit suggests a similar pattern (Table 5.4). In the years 1782–7 assize property crime indictment rates appear to have been related to the level of metropolitan involvement, being highest in Surrey and Kent, which had the largest urban areas contiguous to the capital, and lowest in Sussex.[16] The geography of different kinds of indictments also followed a fairly systematic pattern on the Home Circuit. Although burglary rates were higher in absolute terms nearer to London, as a proportion of each county's indictments burglary was highest in the most rural areas, falling to its smallest percentage in counties nearest to London. Horse and sheep stealing followed a similar pattern, while highway robbery and aggravated larcenies such as pickpocketing, shoplifting, and stealing from warehouses or docks showed the opposite tendency.

It is not difficult to relate some of these geographical patterns to the availability and vulnerability of particular types of target. Among Essex

p. 215; Landau, *The Justices*, pp. 180–3; Map 5.1 is based on the 1801 Census. Indictments recorded where the crime was committed not where the accused lived.

[16] 1782–7 grand larceny cases were heard at the quarter sessions in Surrey but not in Essex, which could have affected assize indictment rates. This pattern fits in well with the high London rates observable in *P.P.*, 1819, VIII, p. 129; 1805 indictment rates per 1,000 inhabitants in 1801 were 1.4 in Middlesex, 0.6 in Essex. (Rates in Table 5.4 = for 1782–7 as a whole.)

indictments, for example, cattle stealing was particularly important in the dairying region around Epping and in the southern coastal hundreds favoured by the London butchers. Highway robbery was largely confined to the hundreds traversed by major roads. Although the geographical distribution of summary conviction certificates partly reflects the places of residence of the few diligent JPs who bothered to send them in, they reveal similar links. Wood theft certificates were most heavily concentrated in the Epping Forest region and in central and north-west Essex, where coal prices were highest. Game certificates were more evenly spread, as were the county's game preservers, but deer stealing convictions came almost entirely from the forests of south-west Essex. Conviction certificates for vegetable stealing were heavily concentrated in the intensive potato-growing area of the Becontree hundred. Textile manufacture-related offences—primarily false reeling or the embezzlement of materials—were almost entirely confined to the northern weaving area and to north-west Essex, a major source of spinning labour.[17] Although London's dominance over the geography of indictments is partly related to the fact that the summary statutes focused primarily on rural offences such as wood and game theft, this does not in itself explain why indictment rates were so systematically affected by the proximity of the metropolis.

The simplest and most tempting explanation is that the higher indictment rates nearer to London were a reflection of higher levels of actual lawbreaking. The economic and social structure of south-west Essex suggests several reasons why property appropriation levels there may have been particularly high. The occupational structure of London in the late eighteenth century was dominated by unskilled and semi-skilled workers and the area nearest to Essex, the East End, was one of the poorest parts of the metropolis. Both Fielding and Colquhoun commented on the extreme 'misery and wretchedness' of the London poor, and although Colquhoun's calculations that the capital contained 2,000 thieves, robbers, burglars and pickpockets, 8,000 part-time thieves, 4,000 receivers, and thousands of minor offenders were pure speculation, there is little doubt that the capital nurtured, or gave temporary shelter to, a number of well-organized networks of lawbreakers.[18] The south-western hundreds with their numerous large residences, intensive market gardening areas, specialized industrial enterprises, and increasingly busy roads presented

[17] For the geography of different indictable and summarily triable Essex offences, King, 'Crime, Law', pp. 47–59. Burglary may have formed a higher proportion of rural indictments because isolated houses were easier targets. Young, *General View... Essex*, 1, p. 382; Brown, *Essex People*, p. 80.

[18] L. Schwarz, 'Income Distribution and Social Structure in London in the Late Eighteenth Century', *Economic History Review*, 32 (1979), pp. 256–9; H. Fielding, *A Proposal for Making an Effectual Provision for the Poor* (London, 1753), 8, p. 141 noted London's outskirts contained numerous 'families in want of every necessary of life ... They starve, and freeze and rot among themselves but they beg, and steal and rob among their neighbours.' Colquhoun, *Police*, pp. vii–ix and 33; M. McIntosh, 'Changes in the Organization of Thieving', in S. Cohen, *Images of Deviance* (Harmondsworth, 1971), pp. 98–131; McMullan, 'Crime', pp. 266–7; J. McMullan, *The Canting Crew. London's Criminal Underworld 1550–1700* (New Bronswick, New Jersey, 1984).

a particularly tempting and diverse collection of targets, and their proximity to a city of unparalleled size containing such large numbers of unskilled labouring poor made them highly vulnerable. The life stories of London-based highway robbers frequently describe offences committed in south-west Essex, and the presence of the county's largest forest adjacent to two of its most important roads into London produced a particularly heavy concentration of highway robbery. Some of the burglaries and lead roofing thefts so prevalent in the south-west can also be directly linked through life stories and trial reports to the deliberate forays of metropolitan offenders.[19]

However, most of those indicted for property crimes in the Becontree hundred were probably local residents. Outside West Ham the majority of respondents to the 1836 Policing questionnaire suggested this was the case. Some contemporaries did blame many of the county's crimes on its close connection with 'the grand scene of vice'. In 1810 an Essex assize judge suggested that 'a considerable proportion (of the cases in the calendar) should be considered . . . as arising not from the state of morals in this county but from the vicinity of the county to a vicious metropolis. Many strangers, it is reasonable to suppose . . . will be found to perpetrate crimes amongst you.'[20] However, assize judges only saw the offenders brought to them by those involved in pretrial processes. Did the areas nearer to London experience more indictable crime, or did they merely send a higher proportion of their property offenders on to the major courts?

Because of its large population of wealthy pseudo-gentry, south-west Essex had a relatively high density of active JPs until the early nineteenth century. By contrast, isolated hundreds such as Freshwell, Tendring, and Winstree had both low indictment rates and very low densities of active JPs. Although many Becontree magistrates had business interests in the City which lowered their day-to-day availability, the prospect of a much longer and often fruitless journey in search of a magistrate undoubtedly discouraged a higher proportion of victims from prosecuting offenders in remote rural areas. The stronger social networks and communal loyalties operating in many rural parishes probably meant that victims were more willing to use informal sanctions than residents of the Becontree area, whose rapidly growing communities had fewer traditions of informal conflict resolution and whose wealth made them more able to afford a prosecution. Although it could be argued that detection would be

[19] The extensive calico bleaching grounds of West Ham (*V.C.H. Essex*, 6, p. 76) produced five indictments a decade. Its turpentine factory was also a target: *Che.C.*, 7 Nov. 1783. 1765–1800 the *Chelmsford Chronicle* reported more than 100 robberies in Epping Forest—Jenkins, 'The Hazards of Highway Travel in Epping Forest 1764–1814' (paper held in ERO), pp. 131–7. For life stories, *Che.C.*, 10 Aug. 1798, and 'Narrative of the Lives of John Toon and Edward Blastock', in Saffron Walden Museum, Crime Drawer. *Che.C.* 1 Apr. 1785, 1 Dec. 1786. *Whole Proceedings . . . Essex . . . March 1774.* In 1788–9 alone, twelve Becontree lead thieves were prosecuted.

[20] P.R.O H.O. 73/6, typical responses were 'generally neighbours', 'principally people living in the union', and 'partly inhabitants, partly outsiders'. *Che.C.*, 17 Mar. 1809; 16 Mar. 1810.

easier in smaller rural communities where outsiders were quickly recognized,[21] this may have been more than counterbalanced by the growth of new semi-professional policing networks in and around the metropolis.

The contribution of the London police offices set up in the 1790s and of the Bow Street horse patrols may not have been large before 1805, but in other ways policing networks in south-west Essex were much more intense (Chapter 3). The constables of the Becontree hundred were younger and much more proactive. A significant number made a living as thieftakers operating from the watch-houses which were only available in parishes on the edge of London. Unlike rural constables and the majority of victims, the West Ham-based thieftakers and the group of Bow Street runners who operated extensively in Essex were committed to indicting and convicting as many offenders as possible. Their impact should not be underestimated. In 1789–1790 three West Ham thieftakers were witnesses in at least 14 per cent of all Essex assize hearings and in 38 per cent of those from the Becontree hundred. Between 1784 and 1787, when records about those receiving rewards are available, these men and five Bow Street runners were involved in at least 60 per cent of the burglary and highway robbery convictions in the Becontree hundred and about a third of those in the other south-western hundreds, but received no rewards for any convictions from elsewhere in Essex. It is unlikely that these were the only thieftakers and proactive reward-seeking constables or watchmen operating in south-west Essex and some of these men were probably thief-makers as well as takers.[22] It is surely no coincidence that south-west Essex, where a growing number of law enforcement agents appear to have made their living partly from rewards, had much the highest proportion of capital indictments—cases which offered the greatest prospects of material gain for those involved in detection. The impact of the few thieftakers whose activities can be monitored in the records suggest that 'the vicious metropolis' influenced indictment rates in ways that the assize judges had failed to consider. The entrepreneurial policing networks established in and around the metropolis during the eighteenth century probably created more capital indictments in Essex than the London-based thieves. Some men came out of London to take material goods. Others came out of London to take thieves. It was the interaction between the two which produced the exceptionally high capital indictment rates of the Becontree hundred. Here, as nowhere else in Essex, a victim committed to pursuing and prosecuting offenders knew where to go to find active detection networks which would help him to orchestrate the prosecution of as many thieves as could possibly be implicated. Given the tiny proportion of offenders prosecuted in rural areas, differences in policing may well have been the key variable in the complex forces which shaped the geography of indictments.

[21] Beattie, *Crime*, p. 184; Shoemaker, *Prosecution*, pp. 91–2.
[22] P.R.O Assi 31/13–15; 35/224–30; 34/43–6; Paley, 'Thief-Takers', pp. 326–7.

The distance of any given area from the assizes and quarter sessions town of Chelmsford was also important. The two northern hundreds furthest from Chelmsford—Clavering and Tendring—had the lowest indictment rates in Essex (Map 5.1) and a Tendring JP pleaded for the major courts to alternate between Chelmsford and Colchester because 'this hundred is above 40 miles in places from Chelmsford...witnesses are therefore unwilling as well as prosecutors to travel that distance'.[23] Indictment rates in the small urban centres of Essex were also affected by the availability of a local court. Although on aggregate the twelve towns surveyed in Table 5.5 had a 35 per cent higher indictment rate in 1791–1800 than the rural parishes that surrounded them, much of this difference was due to the three borough towns where the equivalent figure was 60 per cent. The availability of local borough courts with petty larceny jurisdiction and of easily accessible magistrates undoubtedly attracted prosecutions. In Essex as a whole, 1771–1800, only a third of property crime indictments were heard at the quarter sessions. In Colchester, where the borough court had the same jurisdiction as the county sessions, the figure was three-quarters; in Saffron Walden it was 90 per cent. The existence of a local borough court did not always have an impact, as the Harwich figures indicate (Table 5.5), but in Colchester and Saffron Walden it persuaded many prosecutors to downgrade the charge in order to avoid indicting the offender at the Chelmsford assizes and it increased overall property crime indictment rates considerably. Colchester's indictment rate was higher than that of the surrounding parishes, whereas the average rate of the four cloth-manufacturing towns without a borough court was not. Apart from Saffron Walden and Epping, which contained an extensive forest area on a major road out of London, the six market towns sampled made no significant impact on the level of major court prosecutions.[24] There may have been significant differences between the law enforcement strategies and lawbreaking activities observable in rural areas and those found in the small towns of Essex, but the indictments offer few indications that there were. Apart from the impact of borough court availability, only one urban variable can be identified. By 1800 the proximity of London had the same deep effect on indictment levels as it had on the economic and social life of south-west Essex.

The low indictment rates found in Halstead, Coggeshall, and Bocking (Table 5.5) are particularly remarkable because the cloth-making industries of all these three towns were in terminal crisis in the 1790s. In 1793 nearly half of Bocking's household heads worked in the cloth industry. By 1807 the industry was on its knees, poor rates had increased fourfold, and the population was declining. Neighbouring Braintree, where indictment rates were much higher, experienced similar industrial decline but its population was

[23] H.O. 73/6.2 Little Oakley.
[24] For discussion of the impact of the temporary closure of the Colchester Borough Court 1742–64, King, 'Urban Crime Rates', pp. 39–42. For Bridgwater parallels, Pole, 'Crime', pp. 267–329.

Table 5.5. Urban Crime Rates, Essex, 1791–1800

No. of recorded crimes	Town	Town crime rate	Surrounding area crime rate
5 market towns			
5	Witham	2.3	4.5
13	Dunmow	6.2	3.3
17	Chelmsford	4.5	5.6
12	Harlow	7.9	8.3
32	Epping	17.7	9.9
Total 79	Average	6.9	5.5
4 cloth industrial centres			
22	Braintree	7.8	4.3
13	Bocking	4.9	4.3
8	Halstead	2.4	4.3
12	Coggeshall	4.9	5.2
Total 55	Average	4.8	4.5
3 borough court towns			
83	Colchester	7.2	5.2
24	Saffron Walden	7.5	3.7
7	Harwich	2.5	2.4
Total 114	Average	6.5	4.0
Overall average	All 12 towns	6.2	4.6
Overall average	9 non-borough	5.9	4.8

Note: In 1801 two of these towns had only 1,500–2,000 inhabitants, 6 had 2,000–3,000, 3 had 3,000–5,000, and Colchester had 11,000. The extent to which some of these can be described as 'urban' is debatable, particularly in view of the large rural area within the parish boundaries of Epping (1,812 population in 1801). Table 5.5 is based on the 1801 Census; indictment sources as for Table 5.1 'Surrounding area' means the hundred in which the town was situated.

rising by the 1790s because, unlike Bocking, it was developing as a market and social centre. Ironically, therefore, the three most impoverished cloth industrial towns had much lower property crime indictment rates than the two towns, Colchester and Braintree, that were diversifying economically and experiencing growing prosperity as recreational, commercial, and social centres. Taken at face value, the geography of indictments in late eighteenth-century Essex would suggest a negative correlation between poverty and recorded crime. Levels of poverty, as measured by the admittedly inadequate index of poor rates per head in 1803, bore little relationship to indictment rates. These were highest in the Becontree hundred, which was the least poverty-stricken area in Essex (Table 5.6). Wage rates followed a similar pattern. Almost every hundred in the low-wage area of the north and in the declining cloth manufacturing region had below average indictment rates. As wage levels increased nearer the metropolis so did property crime indictment rates.[25]

[25] Brown, *Essex at Work*, pp. 111–15. Although the 1803 figures excluded county rates, etc., relief per head is a very inadequate index. High rates may mean more generous payments rather than more paupers, and returns were sometimes defective. On wages, Young, *General View...Essex*, 2, p. 387.

Table 5.6. Property Crime Indictments and Poor Relief Levels per Head: Subregions of Essex, 1791–1800

	(1) Population in 1801	(2) Reported crimes per year	(3) Reported crime rate per 10,000	(4) Poor relief expenditure per head
Subregion (group of hundreds)				
A Becontree hundred	20.9	29.9	14.3	0.54
B Other south-western hundreds (Cha, Hav, Wal, Ong)	28.7	25.9	9.0	0.80
C Other hundreds part of which was under 20 miles from London (Har, Che, Bar)	35.1	23.1	6.6	0.90
D Hundreds, no part of which was within 20 miles of London	140.8	64.5	4.6	0.84

Sources: Population = 1801 Census, E.R.O. Q/CR 2/5/1. Reported crimes are charges not persons accused. Poor relief expenditure, from *P.P.*, 1803–4, XIII, pp. 150–67, was divided by 1801 population.

If systematic evidence about summary convictions were available it might indicate a more positive spatial relationship between economic distress and property crime prosecutions, but in their attempts to link these variables historians have, not surprisingly, largely ignored the geography of indictments and relied instead on the relationship between short-term changes in indictment levels and fluctuations in other indicators of economic deprivation such as the price of food.

3. Crime and Dearth

In the absence of any systematic evidence on unemployment levels, historians of the eighteenth century have concentrated mainly on dearth, and more specifically on wheat prices, in their attempts to assess the short-term relationship between property crime and economic hardship. In Essex, as in many other southern counties, the diet of the labouring poor was heavily reliant on wheaten bread, and, given the relative stability of wages in the short term, wheat prices inevitably form the basis of any attempt to measure rapid changes in levels of destitution. In the eighteenth century almost every county for which information is available experienced significant increases in indictments in at least a few years of extremely high wheat prices. However, despite Frank McLynn's recent suggestion that 'it is a commonplace that crime showed a constant correlation with periods of dearth and high prices', the influence of dearth on indictment rates was far from consistent or constant. Although wheat prices rose rapidly in 1756–7 and in 1795, and there were widespread

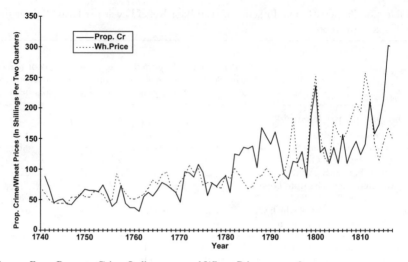

Fig. 5.1 Essex Property Crime Indictments and Wheat Prices, 1740–1817

Sources: For indictments see note to Table 5.1; wheat Prices, 1771–1820, monthly Essex wheat prices in *Gentleman's Magazine*; pre-1771 London wheat prices in *Worcester Post Boy, Cambridge Journal, Cambridge Chronicle, Ipswich Journal.*

food riots, indictment levels in many counties, including Essex, did not respond (Figure 5.1)[26]

By calculating correlation coefficients for detrended series of indictments and for either wheat prices or cost of living series, historians have attempted to bring greater precision to this subject. Have they succeeded? The Essex coefficient for the period 1742–1802 (positive 0.19) is almost identical to that for Staffordshire. Those for urban and rural Surrey (0.30) and for Sussex (0.52) between 1740 and 1802 appear more significant, but grave doubts remain about the usefulness of such figures. If coefficients are calculated for each of the seven subperiods of peace and war (Table 5.7) only two wartime periods, the 1740s and 1793–1802, have significant positive coefficients in these four counties; while in Essex, Staffordshire, and urban Surrey two peacetime periods, 1749–54 and 1783–92, have inverse correlations.[27] The results for other periods are highly problematic. In Essex, Staffordshire, and rural Surrey prices and indictments show no correlation between 1777 and 1782, but the figure for urban Surrey is 0.82 and that for Somerset is 0.70, which can be taken to mean

[26] P. Deane and W. Cole, *British Economic Growth 1688–1959. Trends and Structure* (2nd edn., Cambridge, 1967), p. 63; Beattie, 'The Pattern of Crime', pp. 87–92; Pole, 'Crime', pp. 144–9; Hay, 'War', pp. 128–32. McLynn, *Crime*, p. 305.

[27] Beattie, *Crime*, pp. 211–36; Hay, 'War', pp. 124–32—for the method used, R. Floud, *An Introduction to Quantitative Methods for Historians* (London, 1973), pp. 93–108, 135–54. (All three series have been detrended using linear trends. The figures are calculated by squaring the Pearson-product-moment coefficient of correlation.) The Essex data are based on persons accused, not on charges, and included all those indicted in the borough courts. Essex wheat prices: for sources see Figure 5.1.

Table 5.7. Coefficients of Determination,
Detrended Series, Indictments, and Wheat
Prices, Essex, 1740–1802

	Essex property crime & wheat price (detrended) R^2	
1740–8	+	.81
(1742–8)	+	.38
1749–54	Inv.	.44
1755–62	+	.18
1763–76	+	.24
1777–82	−	.00
1782–92	Inv.	.01
1793–1802	+	.63
War Years		
1742–1802	+	.50
Peace Years		
1742–1802	Inv.	.02
Overall		
1742–1802	+	.188

Sources and methods: see note 27.

that in this period of relatively minor price fluctuations between 70 and 82 per cent of variations in indictments can be predicted from the cost of living index or from wheat prices. Since in precisely the same period an inverse correlation of 0.75 existed in Sussex, figures calculated for such short periods remain extremely questionable.[28] Much depends on the precise timespan used. When 1755 is added to the period 1749–54, for example, the coefficient of determination in Essex changes from inverse 0.44 to positive 0.33.

Overall calculations for all peacetime and wartime years appear to be more useful (Table 5.7). In Essex, Staffordshire, and urban Surrey, although not in rural Surrey and Sussex, the peacetime relationship between wheat prices and indictments was negligible. However, the wartime coefficients are positive in all five areas ranging from 0.28 to 0.75, the Essex figure being about average.[29] Extreme care must be taken in interpreting these figures, however. The main difficulty is the ability of one or two years of drastic price increases to exert a disproportionate influence on the overall correlations. The exclusion of 1800–1 from the Essex coefficients reduces the overall wartime figure from 0.50 to 0.20 and lowers the Staffordshire one by a quarter. The removal of 1740–1 from the first Essex subperiod (Table 5.7) more than halves the coefficient. In moving from these coefficients to the more general conclusion that in various circumstances and subperiods 30, 50, or even 75 per cent of variations in indictments

[28] Pole, 'Crime', p. 145 uses wheat prices while Beattie, *Crime*, p. 235 uses the Schumpeter–Gilboy index as does Hay, 'War', p. 132.
[29] Beattie, *Crime*, p. 212; Hay, 'War', pp. 126–8.

can be predicted from the cost of living index or from wheat prices; historians may not have taken sufficient notice of the statisticians' warnings that in series like this 'the effect of one or two extreme values is to produce a moderately high correlation where none exists among the remaining cases'.[30] Given the problems of establishing a more extensive relationship between indictment levels and prices it may be more helpful to concentrate on exploring the extent and nature of the relationship between these two variables in the small subgroup of years when prices rose very substantially.

Elite commentators were not given to over-generous analyses of the behaviour of the poor in the eighteenth century, but few doubted that labouring families suffered real hardships in years of severe dearth, and many were prepared to admit that it was deprivation that pushed the poor into illegal activity. In 1801 the *Chelmsford Chronicle* commented on 'the deplorable situation of the lower orders of the community in consequence of the extravagant price of provisions' and reported that 'many a tear has dropped from the eye of pity upon that melancholy picture of depravity instigated by necessity so lately exhibited in the calendar of our county prison'. A few years earlier *The Times* reported that 'The poorer classes of people . . . by the high prices of provisions were compelled to acts of petty pilfering for the purpose of procuring a temporary subsistence.'[31] What proportion of the population was in this vulnerable position? Hay's destitution index indicates that in some years of harvest failure between 20 and 25 per cent of the population would have been unable to buy enough bread even if they had spent all their income on that commodity. In 1800–1 the figure was 45 per cent. However, recent work has suggested that the poor were not necessarily as sensitive to harvest failure as this model implies. John Walter's important article on the social economy of dearth suggests that the threat of famine has been exaggerated and the labourers' defences against that threat underestimated. Grain could often be bought from local farmers or employers at reduced prices, as it was from John Carrington in 1800. Credit could be obtained from the better-off members of the community. Charitable relief was widely distributed in times of dearth. Gleaning provided an important source of grain for most labouring families in arable areas even when the harvest was poor. Moreover, the role of mutual aid and neighbourliness can easily be underestimated. Neighbourhood exchange systems protected many from the tyranny of the open market, as did the widespread survival of peasant-style family-based production. The growth of formal relief in years of high food prices, exemplified by the famous Speenhamland system, has received more attention from historians because it is better recorded. However, informal systems of credit, reciprocal borrowing, pawning, and the exploitation of smallholdings and of various customary

---

[30] Beattie, *Crime*, p. 212; Hay, 'War', pp. 126–32; H. Blalock, *Social Statistics* (New York, 1960), p. 290.
[31] *Che.C.*, 27 Mar. 1801; *The Times*, 2 Nov. 1786.

rights, which many continued to enjoy despite the enclosure process, may well have been more important.[32] Our knowledge is very limited but, given the various other strategies the poor could use to defend themselves against dearth, it seems likely that only very large rises in levels of destitution would have driven substantial numbers of men and women to theft. This in turn may explain why correlations between indictment levels and prices are so low outside a few years of extreme hardship.

This line of argument cannot, however, be applied to years of extreme harvest crisis and dearth. In 1794–6 and 1800–1 wheat prices more than doubled. So did the poor rates. If the labouring budgets collected by Eden and Davies are anywhere near accurate, even the elaborate network of defence mechanisms just described would not have protected the poor. The economy of makeshifts, which kept many labouring families above water when prices rose less rapidly, could rarely survive without help in these rare but shattering years of extremity. In 1795–6 many Essex parishes found it necessary to offer relief or subsidized grain to a very sizeable proportion of the community. In Ardleigh, for example, 41 per cent of households were given subsidies.[33] The ratepayers and vestries of late eighteenth-century England did not give such extensive relief unless they absolutely had to. Their actions confirm the desperate realities behind the peaks in Hay's destitution index, realities which the meagre levels of relief they offered did little to alleviate.

Did these years of extreme destitution always coincide with higher indictment levels? Between 1740 and 1810 Essex experienced three years or groups of years when wheat prices were between 70 and 115 per cent higher than the average for the preceding decade, and three others when prices rose by over 25 per cent but less than 45 per cent (Table 5.8). These six periods between them included almost all the occasions when bread riots occurred in or around the county.[34] One of the three periods of intense dearth, 1800–1, witnessed a

[32] Hay, 'War', pp. 130–3; Branch-Johnson (ed.), *Memorandoms for*, p. 52; Walter, 'The Social Economy'; Wrightson, *English Society*, pp. 51–63; Reed, 'Gnawing it out'; D. Mills, 'The Nineteenth-Century Peasantry of Melbourn, Cambridgeshire', in R. Smith (ed.), *Land, Kinship and Lifecycle* (Cambridge, 1984), pp. 481–518; Reed, 'The Peasantry'; Brown, *Essex at Work*, pp. 132–3; M. Reed, 'Nineteenth Century Rural England. A Case for Peasant Studies?', *Journal of Peasant Studies*, 14 (1986), 78–99; King, 'Gleaners'; P. King, 'Customary Rights and Women's Earnings. The Importance of Gleaning to the Rural Labouring Poor 1750–1850', *Economic History Review*, 44 (1991) 461–76; J. Humphries, 'Enclosures, Common Rights and Women. The Proletarianisation of Families in the Late Eighteenth and Early Nineteenth Centuries', *Journal of Economic History*, 100 (1990), 17–42; R. Malcolmson, *Life and Labour in England 1700–1780* (London, 1981), pp. 24–35, 136–46; King, 'Pauper Inventories' suggests that many labouring families had pawnable household goods.

[33] Baugh, 'The Cost', pp. 54–8; Brown, *Essex at Work*, pp. 132–5; T. Sokoll, 'Early Attempts at Accounting the Unaccountable: Davies and Eden's Budgets of Agricultural Labouring Families in late Eighteenth-Century England', in T. Pierenkemper (ed.), *Zur Ökonomik des Privaten Haushalts* (Frankfurt, 1991), pp. 34–58; T. Sokoll, 'The Pauper Household Small and Simple? The Evidence from Listings of Inhabitants and Pauper Lists of Early Modern England Reassessed', *Ethnologia Europaea*, 17 (1987), 34.

[34] Since price rises and destitution were experienced by the poor not on a trend line calculated from data before and after the year in question but in terms of the immediate past, price changes and

Table 5.8. Indictments and Years of Severe Dearth, Essex

Year	% rise in wheat prices	% rise or fall in indictments
1740	28.9	?
1757	72.7	− 21.0
1765	34.2	+ 15.7
1767	35.0	+ 53.2
1768	42.4	+ 36.8
1773	36.7	+ 41.8
1795	43.8	− 38.2
1796	104.9	− 13.5
1800	91.0	+ 56.3
1801	114.3	+ 91.6

Note: All years in which prices were 25 per cent or more above the average for the previous decade are included. Indictments = number of property crime offenders indicted each court year. Rise or fall in indictments is also related to average indictment levels for the previous decade.

massive rise in indictment levels. In the other two, 1757 and 1795–6, indictments not only failed to rise but actually fell by about 20 per cent—a pattern also found in Staffordshire and Surrey to some extent. Two of the three periods that experienced price rises of between 25 per cent and 45 per cent, 1765–8 and 1773, definitely witnessed parallel increases in indictments and although no indictment data have been collected for the period before 1740, the same was probably true in that year. The pattern is therefore contradictory. Despite the fact that overall correlations between prices and indictments are negligible in peacetime and stronger in wartime, a clear link is observable in both peacetime periods of extreme dearth but in only one or two of the four wartime ones. However, a strong connection can be seen between dearth and rising indictments in 1765–8, 1772–3, 1800–1, and almost certainly in 1740–1 (Figure 5.1, Table 5.8).

What lay behind this pattern? Contemporaries may well have been correct in assuming that an increasing proportion of the poor, faced with misery in the midst of plenty, turned to illegal appropriation as a supplementary source of income or food in years of extreme dearth. The temptation to steal certainly rose, but given the fact that changes in the proportion of victims who chose to prosecute exerted ten, twenty, or even perhaps fifty times more influence on indictment levels than changes in the number of actual thefts, it cannot be assumed that it was the lawbreakers rather than the law users who were mainly responsible for rising indictment rates in these four periods of extreme dearth. How did dearth effect the various alternatives to prosecution discussed in

indictment levels are best compared with average levels over the previous decade. It should be noted that I have followed Hay's practice of using 'Court years' running from August of the previous year to July of the year in question. Hay, 'War', p. 122; Charlesworth, *Atlas*, pp. 63–71, 83–103.

Chapter 2? Its impact on the use of informal or communal sanctions is very difficult to unravel. On the one hand, some potential prosecutors may have taken a more lenient attitude to offenders whose families were clearly destitute at the time of the offence,[35] while poorer victims' willingness to prosecute may also have been eroded by their increased need to obtain compensation or restitution of the stolen goods and by their growing inability to meet the initial costs of a prosecution in times of dearth. On the other hand, extreme dearth may well have caused a significant decline in the ubiquitous practice of compounding because it made it much more difficult for the accused or his family and friends to find the resources to offer as compensation.[36] More important, in almost every period when a link between dearth and rising indictments can be found there is evidence that the farmers, traders, and commercial men who brought the majority of prosecutions became extremely anxious about law and order issues, and this may well have eroded their willingness to use informal sanctions. Although only a small proportion of these men actually became victims of food riots, the reactions of those that did were often anything but lenient. Aware that food rioters were frequently acquitted and that sentences for rioting were rarely very severe,[37] a number of Essex farmers and tradespeople indicted them for theft instead. Since indictments rarely describe the broader context in which the alleged theft occurred, the prevalence of this practice is usually obscured, but the survival of a trial report from the 1740 Essex assizes offers revealing insights. George Mallard, for example, was convicted and transported for stealing 5 bushels of wheat, despite the fact that the prosecutor's case appears to have rested almost entirely on his role as spokesman for a group of Colchester food rioters who 'came down in great droves' to prevent the victim from exporting grain. When the ensuing negotiations for a placatory handout broke down, Mallard seems to have been the natural choice for an exemplary prosecution. At the same assizes another food rioter, Abraham Denny, was also transported for breaking and entering and was saved from a capital sentence only by the leniency of the jury. In 1772 prosecutions of this sort account for at least 10 per cent of all property crime indictments. Disturbances throughout central and northern Essex resulted in thirty indictments for riot but a further nine participants were indicted for 'thefts' arising out of their attempts to seize

---

[35] Some historians have argued that since jurors tended to bring in more partial verdicts in years of dearth, it is likely that many victims would also have been more lenient during pretrial processes. However, in both Essex and Staffordshire acquittal rates were lower in times of dearth. Hay, 'War', pp. 154–6. It is possible, however, that as a greater proportion of the labouring poor became reliant on charity from the better off or on neighbourly assistance, the opportunities for victims to use the withdrawal of such help as an alternative to prosecution increased.

[36] Innes and Styles, 'Crime Wave'; p. 214.

[37] J. Bohstedt, *Riots and Community Politics in England and Wales 1790–1810* (Cambridge, Mass., 1983), p. 223. In 1795, for example, only 6 of the 17 food rioters indicted after the Saffron Walden riots were convicted. Of the 48 Essex rioters indicted at the 1772 and 1796 assizes only 3 (who had also pulled down the local mill) were eventually transported. A third were imprisoned (none for more than a year).

food and sell it for a fixed price. Difficult though it often is to identify theft indictments against rioters, they were not necessarily exceptional[38] and may account for part of the correlations observable between prices and indictments in years of extensive food riots. More importantly, indictment levels in years of extensive food riots, and in the case of 1800–1 of widespread incendiarism, were almost certainly affected by a more general moral panic among farmers, traders, and middlemen, who formed the majority of felony prosecutors, and among the gentry and magistracy, whose discretionary powers were so influential.

Did raised anxieties produce a higher propensity to prosecute in most victims which would have more than counterbalanced the humanitarian impulses of others in dearth years? The years 1800–1, which produced the largest increase in indictment levels in any period of dearth, were clearly a time of fear and increasing panic. In Essex, as elsewhere, rising prices sparked off a wave of threatening letters and incendiarism. In June 1800 several parishes received letters threatening 'to burn and destroy the corn and buildings unless provisions were lowered', threats which the *Chelmsford Chronicle* linked to broader fears of sedition by ascribing the letters to 'those who wish to stir up mischief and incite rebellion'. In the same month 'a tumultuous and dangerous insurrection', which resulted in several indictments for conspiracy to raise wages, was reported among the labourers of the Dengie hundred. In September the *Chelmsford Chronicle* reported food riots in Harwich and Ipswich and letters threatening riots in Chelmsford. By October threats had turned to arson. In one week the paper reported fires and letters threatening fires at Bocking, Braintree, Halstead, Rayne, Linsell, Haverill, Boreham, and Great Braxted. After announcing that in view of 'the present alarming state of the public mind' he had considered withholding 'that painful information which we are daily receiving of fires in the county', the printer published several pieces on the fruitlessness of incendiarism as a solution to dearth. The Sun Insurance Company was more pragmatic. After pointing out that arson was 'unjust in those who are displeased with the high price of grain' because it hit the company and not the farmer, it offered large rewards if the culprits were convicted. Rewards were also offered by other individuals and parishes, but this was not the only way the propertied reacted to the anxieties produced by these threats, riots, tumults, and fires. Nightly watches were set up in Halstead and elsewhere. The number of associations being formed increased while other older ones reactivated themselves. By 1801 the assize judge was backing

---

[38] *Proceedings at the Assizes ... Essex ... July 1740*, pp. 12, 16. For 1772 see P.R.O. Assi 35/212/2; *Che.C.*, 24 Apr. 1772. Thomas Marshall, who was eventually imprisoned for riot, was acquitted on two indictments for robbery. The indictment of eight others for stealing 300 lb of pork also arose from a riot in which a farmer refused to allow the rioters to seize and sell his wheat and meat for a fixed price. Four other indictments look suspiciously like riot dressed up as theft. If so 15 per cent of property offenders indicted that year were actually rioters. A. Charlesworth and A. Randall, 'Comment. Morals, Markets and the English Crowd in 1766', *Past and Present*, 114 (1987), 210.

his argument that mercy had failed and heavier punishment must be resorted to by leaving nine men to be hanged.[39]

Arson is a notoriously difficult crime to detect and arson indictments did not increase in 1800–1. Property crime indictments did. In March 1801 the length of the assize calendar was described as 'unprecedented'. In July it was 'the heaviest ever experienced at this season of the year'. This may partly have reflected a real increase in lawbreaking activity but 'the present alarming state of the public mind' was probably the key factor. Better watching facilities may have detected more offenders, but more importantly the proportion of victims who chose to prosecute and the proportion of cases sent on to jury trial by the summary courts would surely have increased in response to these raised anxiety levels.[40] An increase of 5 or 10 per cent in the former alone could have accounted for almost all the increase in indictments. Thus the dearth period with the largest indictment rises, 1800–1, is also the period for which there is clearest evidence of a moral panic. A study of the second and third highest price rises of the period, 1740–1810, offers little comfort to those wishing to link prices to levels of lawbreaking. In 1757 and 1795–6 prices were more than 70 per cent higher than the average for the previous decade but indictment levels were more than 20 per cent lower (Table 5.8). In these years, although obviously not in 1800–1, war had a detrimental effect on indictments. Why? These years, unlike 1800–1, were years of rapid remobilization when another pretrial option, enlistment, would have been particularly attractive to magistrates, constables, and victims, whose communities were being pressurized to produce recruits. Constables and victims might find this option particularly attractive in years of financial hardship because it was potentially lucrative. In 1779, for example, constables were offered a pound for every impressed man and the recruiting acts also offered other potential bounties.[41] The impact of recruitment was complex, however, and needs to be considered within a broader assessment of the relationship between war and indictment rates.

4. War, Peace, and Indictments

Between 1740 and 1820 every outbreak of war led to a reduction in Essex indictments while the coming of peace always increased them (Figure 5.2 and Table 5.9). On average, peacetime indictment rates were over a third higher

[39] E. P. Thompson, 'The Crime of Anonymity', in Hay *et al.* (eds.), *Albion's Fatal Tree*, pp. 258, 262–3, 274–8, describes 1800 as the *annus mirabilis* for threatening letters. For examples, pp. 297, 301–2, 330–5. S. Hussey and L. Swash, *Horrid Lights. Nineteenth-Century Incendiarism in Essex* (Chelmsford, 1994); *Che.C.*, 27 June 1800; 13 June 1800; 8 Aug. 1800; 19 Sept. 1800; 26 Sept. 1800; 24 Oct. 1800; 31 Oct. 1800, 7 Nov. 1800; 14 Nov. 1800; 28 Nov. 1800; King, 'Prosecution Associations', pp. 186–95; *Che.C.*, 31 July 1801.

[40] *Che.C.*, 6 Mar. 1801; 24 July 1801; 31 July 1801. The fact that less serious offences increased more rapidly than serious ones (Hay, 'War', p. 134) in high-price years may be related to the heavier impact social fears associated with dearth had on the relative propensity to prosecute minor theft victims.

[41] *I.J.*, 6 Mar. 1779.

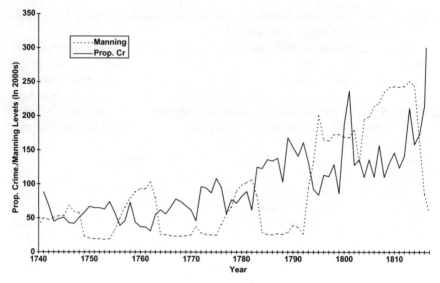

Fig. 5.2 Essex Property Crime Indicments and Armed Forces Manning Levels, 1740–1817

Sources: For indictments see footnotes to Table 5.1; annual armed forces manning levels based on numbers borne into the Navy and numbers of men voted for the Army (Excl. ordinance), *P.P.*, 1868–9, XXXV, pp. 1177–86.

than wartime ones, a pattern broken only in a few years of either peacetime recruitment (1770–1, 1787–8) or exceptionally bad wartime harvests (1740–1, 1800–1). In Essex, as elsewhere, the state of military operations was a more decisive influence than the state of the harvest. Most of the major peaks in indictments followed or accompanied demobilization rather than dearth, while almost every significant fall came during or immediately after a period of heavy recruitment (Figure 5.2). In the sixteenth and seventeenth centuries war was often accompanied by higher indictment levels. By the early eighteenth century the opposite was the case.[42] Did the eighteenth- and early nineteenth-century pattern reflect real changes in levels of lawbreaking? One possible link, the effects of post-war slumps, rarely seems to have been important and in Essex this explanation is clearly unacceptable. The county's main industry, cloth manufacturing, tended to revive at the end of every war and it contained no significant numbers of industrial employers dependent on wartime demand.[43] Overall, however, rapid demobilization and glutted

---

[42] Hay, 'War', pp. 135–45; Pole, 'Crime', pp. 138–44; Beattie, *Crime*, pp. 213–35; London gaol calendar figures 1749–69 published in *The Times* (14 Oct. 1787) tell the same story. Between 1762 and 1763 they increased by 62 per cent. For the earlier pattern, Sharpe, *Crime in Early Modern England*, pp. 62–3; Lawson, 'Property Crime', pp. 114–16.

[43] For the weavers' celebrations of trade revival in 1783, *Che.C.*, 28 Feb. 1783 and 6 June 1783. The contribution of the cloth-making hundreds to Essex indictments fell, 1783–5, but this pattern was not repeated in other trade revivals. Some London industries such as shipbuilding were affected and this could have had some effect on Essex. Hay, 'War', pp. 136–8.

Table 5.9. Essex Indictments in Peace and War, 1740–1820

	Population estimates	Average of indictments p.a.	Indictment rate (per 10,000)	Peace/war
1740–8	145,970	58.3	3.98	w
1749–54	151,410	65.3	4.31	p
1755–62	158,120	45.9	2.90	w
1763–76	168,380	74.8	4.44	p
1777–82	181,070	73.2	4.04	w
1783–92	195,340	138.3	7.08	p
1793–1814	235,370	134.8	5.72	w
1815–20	278,795	269.0	9.64	p
War years average	196,480	95.5	4.86	All years of war
Peace years average	191,440	124.0	6.48	All years of peace
All years average	194,240	108.1	5.57	All years

Notes: Population estimates based on an average of estimates for the first and last years of each period. Indictments as per Table 2.1.

peacetime labour markets did cause substantial problems in the eighteenth century. The four major demobilizations of the period 1740–1820 were extremely rapid and the largest involved more than a third of a million men. Although the authorities made various piecemeal attempts to mitigate their effects, demobilization policies continued to be based on one central principle—the minimization of expenditure by the release of the vast majority of wartime personnel at the first opportunity. It appears that the market for unskilled and semi-skilled labour had trouble in absorbing these large influxes of young adult males.[44] In the absence of any direct indices of unemployment, the precise impact of demobilization is difficult to assess, but many contemporaries were in no doubt about the link between postwar crime waves, demobilization, and rising unemployment.

In 1763 a correspondent from London pointed out that 'not a day passes without robberies, such swarms of rogues has the peace let loose upon us, which are daily increasing as the ships are paid off'. In the mid-1780s *The Times* frequently linked the increase of crime to the number of disbanded men 'now wandering about our streets for want of employment'. 'Sailors and Soldiers', it observed, 'who went abroad to fight for their country, come home to starve or be hanged.' At the end of the temporary mobilization of 1790 the same paper warned its readers, 'Take care of your pockets gentlemen for the blackguards are all to be let loose upon us again. Fasten your doors and your windows well for the occupation of our tars is no more.'[45] Many contemporaries also

[44] Hay, 'War', pp. 138–45; Beattie, *Crime*, pp. 225–35. For the authorities' mitigational policies, J. Innes, 'The Domestic Face of the Military-Fiscal State. Government and Society in Eighteenth-Century Britain', in L. Stone (ed.), *An Imperial State at War. Britain from 1689 to 1815* (London, 1994), pp. 108–17.

[45] *Maryland Gazette*, 20 June 1763. (I owe this reference to Roger Ekirch.) *The Times*, 6 Oct. 1785, 6 Jan. 1787, 6 Nov. 1790.

believed that the armed forces brutalized those who enlisted, training them only in idleness and pillage. 'After employing your people in robbing the Dutch', wrote a correspondent of Romilly's in 1785, 'is it strange that, being put out of that employ by peace, they still continue robbing and rob one another?' Military service in their formative years did little to encourage the often limited law-abiding tendencies of the younger recruits and this, combined with the general difficulties of re-establishing a settled way of life in peacetime, probably pushed some into illegal activity for the first time. For many others demobilization merely entailed a return to the marginal way of life from which the war had plucked them. The coming of peace released large numbers of experienced offenders who had either enlisted to avoid being indicted or had been convicted in wartime and then pardoned on condition that they enlist. Matthias Keys of Billericay, for example, was sentenced to death for highway robbery at Chelmsford in 1747 but obtained a conditional pardon and sailed with Admiral Boscawen to the East Indies where he lost an eye at the siege of Pondicherry. He then returned home and committed a further series of robberies before being hanged in 1751. The reopening of shipping channels at the end of each war also brought a limited influx of returning transportees. Prosecutions for returning illegally usually increased in peacetime, and those who wanted to return before their time was up would have had less trouble finding a ship or avoiding the press gangs once peace was declared.[46]

Clearly the effects of demobilization cannot be studied in isolation from recruiting policies, whether voluntary or compulsory. Historians have suggested that wartime mobilization tended to reduce the level of illegal appropriation in two ways—by mopping up pools of surplus labour in depressed regions such as north Essex, where large numbers of unemployed cloth workers joined the armed forces in the later eighteenth century; and by removing from almost every parish some of those who were thought by the principal inhabitants to be living on the margins of illegality. 'During the war many convicts and idle and disorderly persons go into the army and navy', wrote Colquhoun in 1797; 'the present war gives employment... to many of these mischievous members of the community.' Recruitment policies and impressment acts were often aimed specifically at these groups but this does not mean that the eighteenth-century armed forces were mere receptacles for vagrants, pilferers, and undesirables of various sorts. In absolute terms the contribution of these groups to recruitment may not have been particularly great. However, in Essex as elsewhere wartime recruitment offered a useful penal strategy.

[46] Romilly, *Observations*, appendix—'A letter from a Gentleman Abroad'; Jones, *Crime, Protest*, p. 186; J. Western, *The English Militia in the Eighteenth Century* (London, 1965), pp. 270–1, 286–7; Hay, 'War', pp. 142–3; *Gentleman's Magazine*, 1751, p. 423. In 1761 more than 100 convicts were pardoned from transportation on condition they enlisted—J. Reddington (ed.), *Calendar of Home Office Papers of the Reign of George III*, I, pp. 109–17; Pole, 'Crime', pp. 141–3.

Although on average less than one Essex offender a year was enlisted at the sentencing stage, 1740–1805, many more were pardoned by the King on condition that they serve in the forces, and in a few years of extensive recruitment such as 1746, 1758–60, and 1777–80 the Essex quarter sessions used enlistment to deal with about a quarter of all petty larceny convicts.[47]

Unfortunately, no simple link between real levels of lawbreaking and wartime falls or peacetime rises in indictment rates can be made because magistrates and victims also used the armed forces as an alternative to indictment in two ways. First, as the analysis in Chapters 2 and 4 has shown, a large number of male offenders were either taken straight to the recruiting authorities by the victim or persuaded to enlist by the magistrates in order to avoid formal indictment. Diaries, gaol calendars, and summary court records offer no systematic figures on the numbers involved but all suggest that in years of heavy recruitment a very high proportion of young adult male offenders probably avoided indictment in this way. Indictment levels fell very consistently in the first two years of each war. Heavy recruiting more than doubled manning levels, 1754–6, 1775–7, 1793–5, and on each of those occasions Essex indictments fell by about 45 per cent. The brief recruiting drive in 1771 raised manning by 47 per cent for one year and produced a 26 per cent fall in indictments. These consistent correlations may have been due to the general impact of mobilization in removing many of the marginal poor and improving the employment prospects of the remainder. However, the immediacy and consistency of the change and the fact that it still occurred in years of dearth, and in 1770–1 when there was insufficient time for employment levels to change significantly or for most of the marginal population to be creamed off,[48] suggest that pretrial procedures played a vital role.

Wartime also increased the likelihood that victims would artificially depress indictment levels by a second means. Those who fell victim to thefts by soldiers could avoid the expense and trouble of a prosecution by giving the accused up to military law. Many chose to do so. Four of the five privates apprehended for violently robbing two Suffolk butchers in the early 1780s 'were turned over to the military law'. The other, who had fired at the victims and killed one of their horses, was committed for trial at the assizes. Regimental courts dealt

---

[47] Western, *The English Militia*, pp. 271–2; Hay, 'War', pp. 141–2; Colquhoun, *Police*, pp. 92–3; M. D. George, *London Life in the Eighteenth Century* (Harmondsworth, 2nd edn., 1966), p. 146; Radzinowicz, *History*, 4, pp. 87–94; S. Gradish, *The Manning of the British Navy during the Seven Years War* (London, 1980), pp. 83–4; D. Baugh, *British Naval Administration in the Age of Walpole* (Princeton, 1965), pp. 159–61; J. Houlding, *Fit for Service. The Training of the British Army 1715–95* (Oxford, 1981), p. 118; M. Lewis, *A Social History of the Navy 1793–1815* (London, 1960), pp. 118 and 139; C. Emsley, *North Riding Naval Recruits. The Quota Acts and the Quota Men 1795–7* (1978), pp. 8–12; and Conway 'The Recruitment'.

[48] A brief mobilization also occurred in late 1787 (i.e. at the beginning of the court year 1788) *Che.C.*, 28 Sept. 1787; 5 Oct. 1787; *The Times*, 28 Sept. 1787; 1, 2, 5, 6, 9, 11, 12, 27, 30 Oct. 1787; 8 Nov. 1787; 14 Dec. 1787, which linked the decrease in the number to be tried to 'the influence of the press gangs'. Essex property crime indictments fell by 25 per cent between 1787 and 1788; 1788 saw fewer offenders indicted than any other peacetime year 1783–93.

with many robberies, burglaries, and thefts from civilians, and such offences were punished very heavily. In the regiment studied by Steppler such cases account for a quarter of all trials or about fifteen offences a year, 1778–84. Given the large number of troops moving through the county and the sizeable army camps at Warley, Colchester, and elsewhere, military courts held in Essex may have heard many more cases involving thefts from civilians than this specific regiment did.[49] Recruitment rarely reduced the lawbreaking activities of those involved but even when it did not remove them from the country it may still have removed them from the jurisdictions that historians have relied upon in their attempts to measure changing levels of recorded crime.

A number of soldiers and deserters can be found among those indicted in the major courts but in Essex the only period in which they made a substantial impact was 1800–1. At the Lent assizes in 1801 the judge expressed his sorrow that 'so many soldiers, . . . had dared to lift their hands against the lives and property of those they were paid to protect'. At the summer assizes that year eighteen soldiers from a regiment stationed at Colchester were indicted for housebreaking, robbery, and sheepstealing, and nine were executed. If the heightened anxieties of 1800–1 persuaded those involved to indict these offenders rather than follow the more usual practice of referring them to military tribunals, a considerable proportion of the increases in indictments in periods of wartime dearth such as 1800–1 and 1740–1 may reflect transfers between jurisdictions rather than actual increases in prosecutions.[50]

Thus in the eighteenth century pretrial enlistment and transfers to the military courts artificially depressed wartime indictment levels by decreasing the proportion of offenders brought to the major courts, and it is possible that the wartime increases in indictments observed in the sixteenth century may reflect the fact that these filters were not working as effectively in earlier periods as well as the more seasonal nature of warfare in the early modern era. Conversely peacetime conditions throughout the period 1740–1820 clearly increased the proportion of indictable property offenders eventually brought to trial. At the end of every war anxieties about crime rose rapidly. War brought a sense of security. 'The appearance of war is a present safety to the public', *The Times* announced. 'Press gangs are better magistrates than the Middlesex Justices.' In peacetime the forces no longer took away the idle, unattached young men whom contemporaries identified as the main perpetrators of property crime. Lengthening gaol calendars in the early years of

---

[49] *Che.C.*, 31 Jan 1783; Steppler, 'British', esp. pp. 867, 879, 884; the average punishment was 320 lashes. For military court alternatives elsewhere—Morgan and Rushton, *Rogues, Thieves*, p. 137, and J. Cockburn, 'Patterns of Violence in English Society: Homicide in Kent 1560–1985', *Past and Present*, 130 (1991), 88.

[50] *Che.C.*, 3 Apr 1801; 31 July 1801; *A Particular Account of the Trial and Condemnation of John Highly . . . and Thomas Bedow, in all 18 soldiers of the First Regt of Footguards . . .* (Newcastle, 1801).

peacetime reinforced the fears of the propertied that they were in danger of being washed away by a rising tide of vagrancy and crime. In peacetime periods such as 1748–54 and 1783–92 these fears combined with more specific panics about particular kinds of offender tended to coalesce into a general sense of alarm and insecurity.[51] Law and order issues became a major focus of public attention, which in turn produced various counter-initiatives by the authorities.

The early 1780s, the first major demobilization period after the establishment of the *Chelmsford Chronicle*, provides an interesting case study. Two years after demobilization began, in 1783, the Solicitor-General spoke of 'the alarming height' of 'depredations' and even the opponents of the 1785 London Police Bill had to agree that 'thieves and rogues of all denominations had increased to an almost incredible number'. In the *Chelmsford Chronicle* the images became almost apocalyptic. 'Robberies', it reported in 1785, 'are become awfully frequent and abandoned miscreants (not withstanding the ... vast numbers that have lately suffered ignominious deaths for their atrocious crimes) appear to take no warnings but, like Hercules many headed monster, while great numbers are cut off, others rise up and appear to increase in their stead.' A year later the same paper devoted nearly a fifth of one edition to Mainwaring's call 'to guard against those outrages and depredations which have, of late, so greatly annoyed and terrified the inhabitants of the Metropolis and the adjacent parts'. Another article linked the growing depredations on property to the 'loose idle persons' lurking about the country with no means of gaining their livelihood except begging and stealing and then demanded that magistrates, and indeed all citizens, check the evil by increased vigilance. Housebreakers were one focus of particular attention, but much of that vigilance was directed against the most visible target—the 'unfed, unclothed, uneducated banditti of vagrant poor' whom the magistrates were said to encourage by overlooking their early crimes.[52] In 1787 the *Chelmsford Chronicle* blamed vagrants for 'three-fourths of the burglaries committed in the county', and elsewhere the authorities took a similar line. As early as November 1782 the government requested that constables be given strict orders to search for, apprehend, and prosecute all vagrants or idle and disorderly persons, and many counties quickly responded. At the beginning of 1783, for example, the Hertfordshire quarter sessions, having taken 'into consideration the numerous robberies, felonies ... lately committed in the county' not only resolved that more constables be appointed but also ordered a crackdown on vagrants and suspicious persons. In Essex, as in other counties, similar initiatives were begun in the early 1780s and vagrancy arrests reached a new high by the middle of the decade, but after 1786 the main impetus in Essex moved from the quarter

[51] *The Times*, 3 Nov. 1790; Beattie, *Crime*, pp. 218–28; Hay, 'War', pp. 152–8.
[52] *Parliamentary History*, XXV, cols. 888–902; *Che.C.*, 1 Apr. 1785, 21 Apr. 1786, 12 Oct. 1784, 6 July 1787.

sessions to the parishes.[53] A large number of vestries advertised their deter-mination to suppress vagrancy in 1787–8, a campaign which was much praised by *The Times* and described as highly successful.[54]

Unfortunately these anti-vagrancy campaigns are one of the few instances in which the reactions of those involved in pretrial processes can be evaluated from the surviving records. In the 1780s it is possible to establish that the courts became better attended by magistrates, that they adopted harsher sentencing and pardoning policies, and that they encouraged prosecutions by increasing the proportion of property crime victims given expenses—a service offered to increasing numbers of the middling sort by the prosecution associations which mushroomed in this period. In some areas the county bench also emulated the associations by systematically supplementing the statutory rewards already available; the highest rewards being offered for the conviction of burglars whose ranks were believed to have been greatly swelled by the ending of transportation.[55] By contrast the vital points in pretrial processes relating to property crime cannot be directly monitored, but in postwar panics such as the 1780s the proportion of victims who chose to indict rather than settle inform-ally almost certainly rose significantly. Since the magistrates experienced much the same anxieties and were also being pressurized from above to act with greater vigilance, it seems equally likely that they would have increased temporarily the proportion of potential felony cases they sent on to the major courts.

In the eighteenth century the English state was not sufficiently centralized to enable the early stages of the criminal justice process to be controlled in a concerted way. Limited regulation drives were sometimes attempted by the authorities, but property crimes were rarely involved. Interest groups such as the oyster-dredgers, the yarnmasters, and the Epping Forest authorities did sometimes make co-ordinated attacks on those they believed were appropriat-ing their property, but they usually used the local courts or the summary courts.[56] Apart from one or two brief initiatives by members of the most active

---

[53] *Che.C.*, 28 Dec. 1787; *I.J.* 2 Nov. 1782; Le Hardy (ed.), *Calendar . . . 1752–1799*, 8, pp. 311–12. The Essex Quarter Sessions set up a special committee to monitor vagrancy which first reported in 1785. E.R.O. Q/SBb 322/10. See also 324/8; 327/15, 65–87; 332/30; *Che.C.*, 12 Oct. 84. If the surviving Essex vagrancy examinations are any guide arrests more than doubled between 1782 and 1784. King, 'Crime, Law', p. 67; Emmison, *Guide*, p. 38.

[54] The main parish advertising campaign against vagrants began in December 1787. *Che.C.*, 14 Dec. 1787; Webb, *English Poor Law*, pp. 375–7; *The Times*, 29 Mar. 1788; for links with the Royal Proclamation against Vice, *Che.C.*, 10 Aug. 1787 and J. Innes, 'Politics and Morals—the Reformation of Manners Movement in Later Eighteenth-Century England', in E. Hellmuth (ed.), *The Transformation of Political Culture in Late Eighteenth-Century England and Germany* (Oxford, 1990).

[55] For punishment changes, see Chapter 8. On county rewards, Beattie, *Crime*, p. 225.

[56] Wrightson, 'Two Concepts of Order'; Hay, 'War', pp. 153–4; King, 'Prosecution Associations', pp. 194–9. In the Epping Forest Court of Attachments the three short periods (1726–33, 1739–43, and 1746–55) which accounted for 85 per cent of the game-related presentments 1725–71, coincided exactly with periods in which game preservers, through Treasury-backed rewards in the 1730s and through the newly formed Game Association in the early 1750s, were particularly active. Epping Forest Commis-

prosecution associations, the key actors in the process which brought property offenders to the major courts very rarely made a concerted effort to change the proportion of offenders indicted.[57] However, by reacting with increasing vigilance to the heightened anxieties of peacetime years, victims, magistrates, and law enforcement officers tended to move along parallel paths, unconsciously creating rising indictment rates which in turn fuelled further anxieties and crackdowns on offenders. Did the cessation of pretrial enlistment and of much military court activity at the end of each war, combined with the ways that victims and officials reacted to the extended moral panics of peacetime years account for most of the 35 per cent difference between wartime and peacetime indictment rates, found in both Staffordshire and Essex, or were contemporaries correct in assuming that real increases in lawbreaking, linked to demobilization and the deprivation it brought, lay behind the peacetime rises in indictments? On balance, given the extreme sensitivity of those rates to changes in the behaviour of prosecutors, much of the responsibility surely belonged to the victims and those who assisted or influenced them. However, a scenario which neither marginalizes the role of the lawbreakers nor undermines the central part played by law users in the shaping of indictment levels can be constructed. If the acute panics of the first year or two of each peacetime period were sparked off by real increases in lawbreaking, the lawbreakers could have played an important role in kickstarting the upward spiral of indictments, even if the continued high indictment rates of the rest of each peacetime period were due almost entirely to the impact of moral panics on prosecutors, policing policies, and pretrial procedures. On closer inspection, however, there is some evidence that even this scenario may overstate the role the lawbreakers played in generating the large wave of indictments and vagrancy arrests which usually accompanied the coming of peace.

5. Moral Panics and Transitions from War to Peace

Newspaper reports suggest that postwar increases in crime were often anticipated before they actually happened. In 1748, for example, 'upon the first news of the signing of the preliminaries and the prospect of an approaching peace' a correspondent wrote in the *Norwich Gazette* of his 'apprehension of the mischief

sion, *The Rolls*, 2 and 3. At the Colchester Petty Sessions 13 of the sixteen yarn stealing prosecutions between 1772 and 1800 were brought in either 1785, following the Essex clothiers' open advertisement of their intention to prosecute these offences more severely, or in 1791–2, during or just after the Weavers' strike of June 1791. E.R.O. P/CoR 2–17; *Che.C.*, 16 June 1784; Styles, 'Embezzlement'; Randall, 'Peculiar Perquisites', p. 208 for similar patterns.

[57] King, 'Prosecution Associations', esp. pp. 184–5, 194–5; the only Essex regulation drive against an indictable theft identified was an advertisement campaign against 'the growing evil of base copper coin' in 1780–1 (*Che.C.*, 25 Feb. 1780, 3 Mar. 1780, 16 Feb. 1781, 7 Sept. 1781). At the Summer Assizes 1782, three offenders were indicted for making counterfeit copper coin. Seven uttering offences were tried 1784–6. P.R.O. Assi/35 222–6.

we are to expect from that deluge of vagabonds, used to plunder and slaughter, which the reducing of our sea and land forces must necessarily pour in upon us...the reduction of the navy and army will turn loose upon the nation 20,000 sixpence-a-day heroes with perhaps a crown in their pockets and very little inclination to starve for want of recruiting some of other people's property'. He then laid out his vision of the immediate future, a vision of every county laid 'under contribution' by these men, of remote country houses attacked by gangs of robbers, and of roads 'lined with shoals of tattermedallions either begging relief with an air intimating that they will not be denied or boldly taking it pistol or cutlass in hand'. To avert this fearful future he demanded immediate measures by the authorities and a double vigilance by magistrates 'to stem the torrent that is ready to break in upon us'. If magistrates responded to such pre-demobilization fears by increasing the proportion of offenders sent on to trial; if constables increased their vigilance against vagrants and petty thieves (as they were constantly told to do); or if the proportion of property offenders that victims prosecuted increased, these decisions, combined with the cessation of pretrial enlistment in the final months of war, could have produced a substantial increase in prosecutions even before the tars and tattermedallions arrived back in force. In 1782–3 the authorities clearly anticipated that demobilization would be accompanied by an increase in both vagrancy and crime. Many felt that property offences had begun to increase well before the early months of 1783. In May 1783 the King himself wrote that 'the increase of highway robbers has been very great even during the war and now will naturally increase from the number of idle persons that this peace will occasion'.[58]

The anxiety that arose in 1782 was partly related to the problems created by the suspension of transportation seven years earlier. Despite the large numbers imprisoned in the Thameside hulks, many county gaols were severely overcrowded with prisoners awaiting transportation. Since no alternative location was available, the prospect of a large number of new offenders entering the penal system was clearly alarming. More important, in 1782 the long-term consequences of the development of the hulks system in 1776 were beginning to cause great concern. In that year prisoners who had spent their entire transportation sentence in the hulks began to be released into the community for the first time and the newspapers were not slow to use that fact to fan the anxieties of the inhabitants of nearby counties. In April 1782 the *Chelmsford Chronicle* and the *Ipswich Journal* followed reports of the capture of a large gang of violent highway robbers, most of whom were said to be 'from the lighters', by linking various other robberies with 'convicts newly set at large'. They also demanded that the government do something to protect society from the

[58] *Norwich Gazette*, 5–12 Nov. 1748; J. Fortescue (ed.), *The Correspondence of King George the Third from 1760 to 1783* (London, 6 vols., 1927), 6, p. 387; Hay, 'War', p. 157 on other anticipations of postwar crime in 1760 and 1801.

increasing outrages arising from the discharge of 'convicts who had served their time on board the Hulks'. These 'seminaries of villainy' soon became a recurring theme in the newspaper reports. In June the *Ipswich Journal* commented that 'it is greatly suspected that the many late cruel murders and robberies have been committed by men discharged from them'. By November this view was being described as 'the general belief of the public'. The role of 'the floating academy at Woolwich' was particularly stressed by the Bow Street magistrates who declared that 'such has been the industry of the London house-breakers whilst on board the ballast lighters, in collecting from other convicts . . . the situation of gentleman's seats . . . that not a gentleman's house . . . (be it ever so remote from the metropolis) can escape unless government will immediately interfere and form a resolution of sending the banditti . . . to Africa or some other place beyond the seas'.[59]

Although a few convicts were sent to Africa, the transportation system was not overhauled until 1787 and fears about the consequences of releasing offenders hardened in these 'schools of iniquity' continued to be expressed until that time. However, by the final months of 1782 a related, but more general, sense of anxiety about the growth of violent property crime began to develop and produced significant changes in the administration of criminal justice. In August and September press gangs were sent out to apprehend and enlist 'some of those desperate villains who have so long infested the environs of the metropolis'. The focus then shifted from pretrial enlistment to post-trial punishment. Both the *Chelmsford Chronicle* and the *Ipswich Journal* announced in early September that in view of the 'many daring and desperate robberies lately committed' the King had ruled that 'no pardon or respite' would be granted to such offenders, a ruling extended a week later to burglars and housebreakers.[60] In the same month the Home Secretary was informed that crime, rather than military events, such as the siege of Gibraltar, was now the main topic of interest among the middling sort. In November a further government announcement stressed that 'His Majesty being very concerned at the frequent robberies and disorders' in London 'and parts adjacent' was now demanding increased vigilance from magistrates and constables and requiring written returns about the zeal and diligence of all officers of the peace. It also launched the first of a series of initiatives against vagrants which

---

[59] Ignatieff, *A Just Measure of Pain*, pp. 80–4; *The Times*, 14 July 1785; W. Branch-Johnson *The English Prison Hulks* (London, 1957), p. 7 describes escapes into Essex which would have particularly alerted its inhabitants; Beattie, *Crime*, pp. 573, 592–9; *I.J.*, 6 Apr. 1782, 20 Apr. 1782, 11 May 1782, 1 June 1782, 16 Nov. 1782 (the contractor's attempt to prove few ex-ballast men reoffended), 4 Jan. 1783, 25 Jan. 1783; *Che.C.*, 19 Apr. 1782, 4 Nov. 1782.

[60] Beattie, *Crime*, pp. 225, 598–9; *I.J.*, 14 Sept. 1782; in 1786 petitions were being presented and the Essex Quarter sessions received a circular from the Secretary of State demanding information about offences by those released from the hulks. E.R.O. Q/SBb 323/17; Emsley, *Crime*, p. 218; *I.J.*, 24 Aug. 1782, 7 Sept. 1782, 14 Sept. 1782; *Che.C.*, 20 Sept. 1782; P.R.O. H.O. 42/1, 23 Sept. 1782, cited in Ignatieff, *A Just Measure of Pain*, p. 87.

were taken up immediately by county benches in Hertfordshire and elsewhere. In the following months a bill increasing the punishment for receiving stolen goods from burglars and highway robbers, and another enabling magistrates to imprison those found in possession of housebreaking implements were introduced into Parliament because 'the crimes of burglary and robbery have of late become more frequent and been committed with circumstances of great violence, cruelty, and inhumanity'.[61]

The precise timing of demobilization is difficult to establish but until December 1782 hot presses were still being regularly reported on shore and on the Thames, and the process does not appear to have begun until after the announcement of a preliminary negotiated peace at the end of January 1783. In Essex, as elsewhere, full demobilization does not seem to have gathered pace until the militia was disbanded in the last two weeks of March.[62] This means that demobilization was preceded by half a year or so of growing anxiety about violent property crime to which the government responded with initiatives designed to harshen sentencing policies, increase the powers and vigilance of the magistracy and the police, and attack the most visible and vulnerable group of potential depredators, the vagrants. The situation in 1782 therefore presents some very interesting parallels with that of 1862, when, as Davis has shown, public concern about the final demise of transportation formed an important part of the background to a newspaper-led moral panic about violent property crime, which resulted in both a sudden rise in prosecutions and significant changes in policing and penal policy. Although the impact of eighteenth-century law and order news is less well studied, the influence of newspaper reporting about violent property crime in 1782–3 should not be underestimated. In the 1760s the *Chelmsford Chronicle*, locked in a life-and-death circulation war with the *Ipswich Journal*, effectively created a wave of reports about violent crime in the Colchester area which generated a brief moral panic and resulted in substantial short-term changes in penal, policing, and prosecution policies. The newspaper's role in 1782–3 is less easy to unravel, but the amount of space given to law and orders news by the *Ipswich Journal* in the first quarter of 1783 was more than double that found in the same period a year earlier. The peak came in January 1783, the last month before demobilization, when over 10 per cent of the paper and about 20 per cent of its non-advertising space was devoted to news about riots, violent crime, property crime, court hearings, punishments, prisons, and criminal justice policy.[63] Without further

[61] Beattie, *Crime*, p. 224; *I.J.*, 2 Nov. 1782; Le Hardy, *Calendar*, pp. 311–12. *I.J.*, 8 June 1782 and 3 May 1783; *Che.C.*, 4 Apr. 1783; *Parliamentary History*, 23 col. 364 (1783).

[62] *I.J.*, 6 Apr. 1782, 24 Aug. 1782, 7 Sept. 1782, 2 Nov. 1782, 7 Dec. 1782, 25 Jan. 1783, 1 Feb. 1783, 8 Mar. 1783, 15 Mar. 1783, 22 Mar. 1783. The recall of ships from the West Indies and elsewhere took a long time and demobilization continued into 1784.

[63] J. Davis, 'The London Garotting Panic of 1862. A Moral Panic and the Creation of a Criminal Class in Mid-Victorian England', in Gatrell et al. (eds.), *Crime*, pp. 190–213; King 'Newspaper Reporting'; this *Ipswich Journal* crime news survey excluded advertisements, military trials, duels, civil trials,

work on other newspapers over longer periods and on the ways those who had access to a paper read and interpreted it, it would be dangerous to assume that they were the major determinants of communal perceptions about the prevalence of crime. However, contemporaries had few other ways of gaining extensive information on crime and as peace came closer the newspapers may well have focused the general apprehensions of the propertied into more specific fears about the growing prevalence of violent crime, which in turn encouraged them to prosecute offenders more vigorously.[64]

There was certainly a rise in major court prosecutions before the militia was disembodied in late March. On 7 March the *Chelmsford Chronicle* reported 'the greatest number known in the memory of man' on the Hertfordshire assizes calendar. In Essex the number reported was more than a third higher than the average for the years 1777–82. At the Suffolk assizes property crime indictments were more than double the wartime average. Indictment levels therefore seem to have been rising before the demobilization process was properly underway, although our knowledge of that process is too fragmented to draw any firm conclusions. By the summer assizes of 1783 the full impact of both the raised anxieties of the winter of 1782–3, and the first stages of demobilization are visible. Both the Essex and Suffolk calendars were the largest since the summer of 1772, when there were widespread bread riots in both counties.[65] Once the moral panic of the early and mid-1780s was in full swing the newspapers clearly played their part in reinforcing it. Hanway's observation made at the end of the previous peacetime panic in 1775 was equally applicable ten years later. 'Our newspapers are full of accounts of robberies, examinations of robbers and executions . . . if we go on, shall we not become fearful of our own domestics, or our own children and yet more terrified at the faces of each other, when we meet in the streets or roads even under a meridian sun?' Hanway apparently assumed rising reports were related to rising crime, but were they? The *Chelmsford Chronicle*'s admission in 1786 that 'it has long been a general complaint that our public papers during the recesses of parliament, especially since the return of peace . . . have become exceedingly dull and unentertaining' suggests another factor. In the absence of any other exciting events to report crime may well have been used as a fallback. From its earliest editions in the mid-1780s *The Times*, for example, reported 'the numberless robberies and burglaries' committed in London in considerable detail and

treason, smuggling, crime outside Britain. There was only a 15 per cent increase in crime reporting between the first and second halves of 1782 but a 114 per cent rise between Jan. and Mar. 1782 and Jan.– Mar. 1783. On the 1860s see also R. Sindall, *Street Violence in the Nineteenth Century* (Leicester, 1990).

[64] For a discussion of moral panics, newpapers, etc., S. Hall, C. Critcher, T. Jefferson, J. Clarke, and B. Roberts, *Policing the Crisis. Mugging, the State and Law and Order* (London, 1978), pp. 181–4; D. Howitt, *Mass Media and Social Problems* (Oxford, 1982), pp. 121–8—see also D. Statt, 'The Case of the Mohocks: Rake Violence in Augustan London', *Social History*, 20 (1995), 183–4.

[65] *Che.C.*, 7 Mar. 1783; *I.J..*, 8 Mar. 1783; P.R.O. Assi. 33/6–7. *Che.C.*, 1 Aug. 1783 compared with the previous twelve summer assize reports.

advertised burglar alarms to combat them. It also produced an ongoing analysis of the likely impact of mobilization and demobilization on levels of crime.[66]

The role of the press in the initial upsurge of indictments at the beginning of 1783 is less clear but it remains possible that by focusing on a few convenient 'folk devils'—'the vagrant banditti' and 'the ballast men'—and by reporting that in the provinces as well as in London 'scarce a night passes but robberies are committed', the newspapers may have encouraged greater vigilance among prosecutors, magistrates, and other representatives of authority, thus helping to create the very wave of indictments that would reinforce their fears. If year-by-year figures alone are analysed, the initial rise of property crime indictments in 1783-4 is extremely persuasive. It coincided with a large scale demobilization; it occurred in many different counties; and within Essex it was most important nearest to London, where the effects of demobilization were most likely to be felt. However, since anxiety levels were rising before demobilization the criminal justice system itself may already have been generating increasing numbers of indictments before the labour market became flooded or significant numbers had been released from the armed forces. As the newspapers and the reactions of the government focused attention on law and order issues in the last months of peace, did they also kickstart a moral panic and thus initiate a feedback mechanism of increasing fear, more intense prosecution, rising indictments, and further anxiety, which could have been as important as demobilization itself in creating the large and immediate rises in indictments observable at the end of every war? In the early 1780s, at least, this remains a strong possibility.

Given the huge impact that small variations in the attitudes of prosecutors or magistrates could have on indictments, changing levels of deprivation may only have had a significant effect on movements in indictment levels in a handful of years of extreme dearth or massive demobilization. For the rest of the time short-term fluctuations in indictment levels, as well as long-term ones, may be more fruitfully explained by analysing the complex reactions of those involved in pretrial processes. Did the poor turn to crime in larger numbers in response to dearth or demobilization, or were they turned into indicted criminals by the interconnected but essentially informal responses of magistrates, central authorities, newspapers, and victims? The question remains open but the Essex evidence at least suggests a heavier emphasis may well need to be put on the latter set of forces. Moreover, it is not necessary to

---

[66] Hanway, *The Defects*, p. 61; *Che.C.*, 11 Aug. 1786; *The Times*, 8 Jan. 1785, 25 Oct. 1786; in late 1787 *The Times* spoke of the 'decrease in the prisoners to be tried' and linked it to 'the influence of the press gangs' (14 Dec. 1787; for the same theme 1 Oct. 1787, 2 Oct. 1787, 30 Oct. 1787, 8 Nov. 1787); after a brief mobilization, demobilization once again brought rising indictment levels and by 1790 it was making the familiar demands that magistrates do something to prevent the depredations 'which may be naturally expected from the discharge of so many people ... in consequence of the peace' (2 Dec. 1790).

prove that recorded crime rates rose and fell with food prices or unemployment levels in order to establish a link between poverty and crime. The
accused frequently pleaded poverty in their attempts to avoid prosecution or
heavy punishment and magistrates such as Staples, Maynard, and Hunt often
accepted these pleas as genuine and reacted accordingly.[67] A substantial
proportion of the population suffered from chronic poverty and economic
vulnerability in this period despite the various strategies that they could often
use to fend off complete destitution. The budgets and earning schedules
collected by Eden and Davies in the late eighteenth century bear eloquent
testimony to this. So do the stories left by the poor themselves. The autobiographies of labouring men and women, such as Mayett, Clare, and Saxby, and
the early lives of more successful artisans such as Hutton and Place are suffused
with the harsh colours of uncertainty and grinding poverty.[68] At the heart of
their stories is the theme of struggle—struggle to obtain a living wage and
regular employment, struggle to get relief from parish, boxclub, neighbours, or
kin in times of crisis.

The court records occasionally offer brief insights into such struggles. Faced
by possible transportation for stealing a beaver coat in the winter of 1774, Ann
Ford simply pleaded 'I was drove to the greatest distress'; but another witness
was more eloquent, informing the court that 'she was turned out of the parish
workhouse, they thought her capable of getting her living, which she was not,
but what she did was through want'. Faced by the prospect of the gallows for
highway robbery John Flint confessed 'We did it through poverty. I have a
wife; I have had three children in three years and my wife is now big with child;
my children were crying for bread.' Such insights are rare, however, and it is
impossible to calculate the proportion of property offences that arose because
a destitute man or women had simply run out of other survival strategies.
What is clear is that the vast majority of contemporary writers, including those
more sympathetic to the poor, assumed that most crime was committed by
the poorer sections of the community. 'Poverty leads to all sorts of evil consequences', Cobbett wrote in 1821; 'want, horrid want is the great parent of
crime.'[69] Since a subgroup of both the propertied and the unpropertied
showed a natural propensity to seek out and exploit various ways of appropriating the wealth of others, this assumption may well have been incorrect but
it was very convenient from the point of view of the propertied. It underpinned

---

[67] Gatrell 'Crime, Authority', pp. 304–5; Beattie, *Crime*, p. 234; Rudé, *Criminal and Victim*, pp. 81–2;
for magistrates reactions, see Chapter 4.

[68] Walter, 'The Social Economy'; Hutton, *The Life*; Robinson (ed.), *John Clare's*; J. Clare, *The Parish. A
Satire* (Harmondsworth, 1985); Kussmaul (ed.), *The Autobiography*; M. Thale (ed.), *The Autobiography of
Francis Place* (Cambridge, 1972), pp. 98–9; for pre-1834 parliamentary reports linking crime and poverty,
see *P.P.*, 1826–7, VI, p. 26; *P.P.*, 1834 XXX; T. Sokoll, 'Early Attempts'; Davies, *The Case*; W. Eden, *The
State of the Poor* (London, 3 vols., 1797).

[69] *The Whole Proceedings . . . Kent . . . March 1774*, pp. 18–19; *The Whole Proceedings . . . Herts . . . March 1774*,
p. 7; W. Cobbett, *Cottage Economy* (London, 17th edn., 1926) p. 10.

and reinforced their selection of certain kinds of appropriation as proper targets for judicial action. However, that did not mean that all groups within the labouring poor were equally likely to be subjected to prosecution in the courts. The attitudes, practices, and legal rulings on which the prosecution system was based selected certain subgroups for particular attention and those subgroups may or may not have also shown a greater propensity to actual acts of appropriation. The complex relationship between poverty and crime can therefore be analysed in a different way by pinpointing precisely which subgroups were most vulnerable to prosecution.

6

The Offenders: Property Crime and Life-Cycle Change

Who was accused of property theft in the eighteenth-century courts? The evidence available is often minimal and summary offences are particularly difficult to contextualize for that reason, but by the 1780s new recording practices in the major courts enable a dimension previously neglected by historians to be analysed. That dimension is the life-cycle. Modern criminologists implicitly assume that most offenders are juveniles or young adults and this pattern has been confirmed by self-report studies and longitudinal surveys as well as by the statistics on prosecuted offenders; but although the early nineteenth-century rise of juvenile delinquency has been studied, eighteenth-century historians have yet to examine in detail the relationship between crime and life-cycle change.[1] By focusing initially on the age structure of the accused, and by relating this evidence both to the experiences of certain key groups across the life-cycle, and to contemporary attitudes towards the regulation of different age ranges, this chapter will use that relationship as the core of a discussion of both male and female offenders. It will then assess more traditional concerns about the social status and the professional or casual nature of offenders, before drawing together all these threads in order to reassess historians' traditional emphasis on the importance of severe economic hardship as an explanation of changing patterns of recorded crime. In doing so it will also explore the ways in which the vulnerability of different subgroups to formal prosecution was the product of the interaction between two forces—the selection policies used by victims, magistrates, etc., and the differing levels of appropriation indulged in by the offenders themselves.

1. The Age Structure of the Accused

Systematic age data on offenders is almost non-existent for most of the eighteenth century. However, during the transportation crisis of the 1770s a few

---

[1] Heidensohn, *Crime*, pp. 38–9; N. Walker, *Crime and Criminology. A Critical Introduction* (Oxford, 1987), p. 121. Exceptions are Beattie, *Crime*, pp. 243–8 and for females only—P. King, 'Female Offenders. Work and Lifecycle Change in Late Eighteenth-Century London', *Continuity and Change*, 11 (1996), 61–90. For the most recent work on the history of juvenile delinquency P. King, 'The Rise of Juvenile Delinquency in England 1780–1840: Changing Patterns of Perception and Prosecution', *Past and Present*, 160 (1998), 116–66; H. Shore, *Artful Dodgers. Youth and Crime in Early Nineteenth-Century London* (London, 1999).

assize courts began to record the ages of convicts sentenced to transportation or hard labour. On the Home Circuit this practice was gradually extended and between July 1782 and July 1787 the ages of all those tried by the petty jury were recorded. After transportation was resumed the Home Circuit information became very patchy, but in another brief period in 1799 and 1800 it was once again virtually complete.[2] The age distribution of all those accused of property crimes on the Home Circuit between 1782 and 1787, seen in Figure 6.1, is based on over 1,600 individuals, 88 per cent of whom were male. There is some evidence that a minority, when asked their age in court, approximated it, did not accurately know it, or deliberately distorted it. Younger prisoners tended to avoid the age of 21, while some older ones rounded their ages or had them rounded by the court's officials. An independent check using Cobley's book on the 1787 convict fleet reveals, however, that in the great majority of cases prisoners were consistent in the statements they made to different officials about their age, thus confirming Linebaugh's conclusion that the recorded ages of convicts were generally accurate to within one or two years.[3]

In the 1780s more than two-thirds of those indicted for property offences on the Home Circuit were under 30 (Table 6.1). The peak age range was centred on the late teens and early twenties. Nearly half of the male offenders were aged between 18 and 25. This age structure was not confined to the assizes. After 1789 the Gloucestershire gaol calendars record the ages of quarter sessions as well as assizes accused, and both had very similar age structures, although the petty larceny accusations brought to the quarter sessions included slightly more juveniles and rather greater numbers of offenders in their thirties or early forties.[4] Age distributions were rarely static. Bad harvests or changes in armed forces' manning levels produced significant short-term variations, and in the long term changes in the general age structure of the population and in attitudes to, and prosecution policies towards, juveniles would have had a considerable impact. However, until the early nineteenth century the age peak between 18 and 26 remained strongly in evidence whatever the state of the harvest or of international relations, and this dominance was out of all proportion to the size of that age group in the population as a whole. Between 1782 and 1787 the two age ranges 15–29, and 40 or above each contained about a third of the population aged over 9,

---

[2] All the Home Circuit data are based on the 11 sessions (July 1782 to July 1787 inclusive. Assi 31/13–15). The ages of prisoners whose indictments were 'not found' were not recorded. Assi 31/18 for 1799–1800.

[3] K. Thomas, '*Age and Authority in Early Modern England*', Raleigh Lecture on History (1976), p. 4. Snell, *Annals*, p. 334, discusses the age of 21. J. Cobley, *The Crimes of the First Fleet Convicts* (Sydney, 1970). In three-quarters of cases ages given to the court and to the ship's surgeon match within one and a half years. Beattie, *Crime*, p. 244; P. Linebaugh, 'The Ordinary of Newgate and his Account', in Cockburn (ed.), *Crime*, p. 262. On the growth of more precise age consciousness, see Thomas, *Age*, p. 5.

[4] Gloucestershire R.O. Q/SG.2. For graph see King, 'Crime, Law', p. 85.

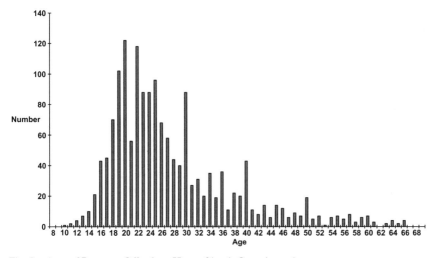

Fig. 6.1 Ages of Property Offenders, Home Circuit Counties, 1782–7

Source: P.R.O. Assi 31/14–15.

Table 6.1. The Age Distribution of Home Circuit Property Offenders and of the English Population in the 1780s

Age group	(A) % of population over 10	(B) % of Home Circuit accused	(C) % of Essex assizes accused
10–14	14.1	1.6	3.9
15–19	12.6	17.3	12.9
20–4	11.3	29.3	27.5
25–9	10.0	19.1	18.1
30–4	9.6	12.5	14.9
35–9	8.3	6.7	7.8
40–4	7.0	5.2	6.5
45–9	6.5	2.9	3.9
50–4	5.9	2.4	2.3
55–9	4.3	1.7	0.6
60+	10.2	1.4	1.6
Total	99.8	100.1	100.0

Sources: (A) is based on detailed information provided by the Cambridge Group for the History of Population and Social Structure for 1786. See also Schofield and Wrigley, *The Population History of England*, pp. 528–9; (B) P.R.O. Assi 31. 13–15, Summer assizes 1782 to Summer assizes 1787 inclusive. All accused property offenders; (C) same source as (B).

but the former group contributed two-thirds of the accused, the latter less than one-seventh.[5]

Although each of the Home Circuit counties followed the same basic pattern, there were noticeable variations. The Essex courts tried slightly higher

---

[5] Since Table 6.1 is based on national overall age data it is only an approximate guide. For the post-1815 growth of juvenile prosecutions, King, 'The Rise of Juvenile Delinquency'.

proportions of offenders that were either under 15 or over 30 (Table 6.1). The Surrey peak came at 19. The Sussex one came about five years later and the Essex peak was equidistant between them. These differences do not necessarily reflect regional variations in either lawbreaking activity or prosecutors' attitudes. The age structures of each county's general population almost certainly had a very important influence. Surrey seems to have attracted more young migrants than any other Home Circuit county between 1780 and 1800, while Sussex experienced the greatest outmigration and consequent loss of youthful population. Age structures also varied between different types of indictment. Those accused of murder, sexual crimes, and other non-property offences tended to be older—the peak age for alleged murderers being the later 20s.[6] Among property offenders, the small minority that were not accused of being directly involved in thieving were the only category that differed fundamentally from the basic pattern. Three-fifths of receivers were over 35 and one-fifth were over 55, reflecting both the general age structure of the shopkeeping class and the tendency for those involved in illegal appropriation to turn to secondary entrepreneurial activities as they grew older. Frauds, forgers, and coinage offenders were also closer to the age range of the commercial tradesmen among whom they operated. Only 15 per cent were under 25.

Among those accused of theft the small number indicted under the special statutes relating to naval stores were exceptional. Their age structure was more extended, reflecting perhaps the importance of 'chips' to workers of all ages in the government's Deptford shipyards.[7] Among other offences differences were less fundamental. Burglary or breaking and entering, in which diminutive size could be a useful asset, included a higher proportion of teenagers. Fielding's observation that housebreakers were 'chiefly young fellows ... about 18 or 19 years of age' coincides almost exactly with the most important age range for this offence. By contrast highway robbers reached a high peak in the early twenties but this physically demanding crime also attracted fewer older men. Committing highway robbery and getting caught was a young man's activity. Although the intervening period witnessed massive economic, social, and demographic changes and an extensive restructuring of the policing, penal, and judicial systems, it is interesting to note that twentieth-century studies have also shown that the age distribution of burglars peaks earlier than that of those arrested for robbery and that the highest point for murderers, frauds, and receivers comes much later.[8]

[6] King, 'Crime, Law', p. 87 for different county and types of crime graphs; Beattie, *Crime*, p. 246; Cole and Deane, *British Economic Growth*, pp. 108–9; Schofield and Wrigley, *Population History*, p. 622.

[7] Linebaugh, *The London Hanged*, pp. 371–401. R. Knight, 'Pilfering and Theft from the Dockyards at the Time of the American War of Independence', *The Mariner's Mirror*, 61 (1975), 217 spotlights labourers rather than apprentices as the 'chief offenders'.

[8] J. Fielding, *An Account*, p. 17; and *P.P.*, 1812, II, p. 128; King, 'Crime, Law', p. 89 for graphs. Comparisons of modern age distributions, Walker, *Crime*, p. 121. D. West, *The Young Offender* (Harmonds-

2. Children and Early Teenage Offenders

Only one in twenty of those accused of property crime on the Home Circuit in the 1780s was under 17 and very few of the accused would therefore have been described by contemporaries as boys, girls, or children. Despite the publicity sometimes given to very young offenders, less than 1 per cent were under 14.[9] Unless the accused had reached that age the principle of *doli incapax* made it much more difficult to establish criminal responsibility. The ages of 7, $10\frac{1}{2}$, and 14 were all regarded by the law books as potentially important turning-points. However, although it was legally possible to convict children under the age of 10, no one below that age was tried by a Home Circuit petty jury between 1782 and 1787. In 1783 the Essex quarter sessions refused to try a 12-year-old girl because she was 'an infant under the age of discretion',[10] and similar reasons almost certainly lay behind the small number of assizes accused aged between 10 and 14. Other categories of young offenders also enjoyed more limited immunities. Apprentices of any age and servants under 18 could not be prosecuted for felony if the goods they had stolen had been formally entrusted to them by their masters. Non-capital thieves under 15 years of age were also immune from indictment provided that they 'discovered' two receivers, as were apprentices under 15 accused of the capital crime of stealing goods worth more than 40 shillings from a dwelling house.[11]

However, the relative absence of offenders aged between 14 and 17 was not mainly a reflection of formal legal immunities. Those immunities were both reinforced by, and a reflection of, deeper beliefs and customs concerning the treatment of young offenders. As the analysis in Chapters 2 and 4 indicated, prosecutors and magistrates tended to favour informal sanctions in cases involving offenders under the age of 17 or 18. This was particularly true if the indictment was a capital one, as it was in the majority of Home Circuit cases. After describing the general forbearance of prosecutors, one early nineteenth-century observer reported that 'where the offender is of tender years, the chance of impunity is still greater... mankind are naturally more compassionate to youthful errors... there is scarcely anyone of common

worth, 1967), pp. 19–22; D. Greenberg, 'Delinquency and the Age Structure of Society', *Contemporary Crises*, 1 (1977), 189–223.

[9] P. Griffiths, *Youth and Authority. Formative Experiences in England 1560–1640* (Oxford, 1996), p. 25 indicates 98 per cent of those labelled 'child' were under 17, as were 93 per cent of those labelled 'boy' and all of those labelled 'girl'.

[10] Burn, *The Justice* (7th edn., 1766), 2, p. 256; Blackstone, *Commentaries*, 4, pp. 22–4; S. Margarey, 'The Invention of Juvenile Delinquency in Early Nineteenth-Century England', *Labour History*, 34 (Canberra, 1978), pp. 18–19; Radzinowicz, *History*, 1, pp. 11–14. No one under 7 could be guilty of felony. Until the accused was 14 the prosecutor had to prove the child had the capacity to discern between good and evil. E.R.O. Q/SBb 312/34.

[11] Williams, *Every Man*, p. 521; Burn, *The Justice* (1797), 4, p. 47; Radzinowicz, *History*, 2, p. 41.

humanity who would not shudder at taking away the life of a child under 16 or 17'.[12]

When prosecutors chose lesser indictments for young offenders, they revealed a parallel set of attitudes. Since burglary and housebreaking are very similar offences, it is unlikely that those involved in these two crimes were markedly different in age, but although nearly a quarter of those indicted for housebreaking were under 18, only 11 per cent of burglars came from the same age group. Prosecutors and their advisers were well aware that convicted burglars were more severely treated at the sentencing and pardoning stages and it appears that this affected their choice of indictment when the defendant was young. Examples of similar behaviour can also be found amongst magistrates. A London JP told the 1816 parliamentary committee: 'When a child has been committed for further examination, we do not tell the prosecutor himself, but we find the means of giving him a hint, that if he does not wish to prosecute he may afford us an opportunity of discharging him, being fully aware that it would be the ruin of that child.'[13]

The very small number of 1780s accused who were aged under 17 was clearly no indication of the level of criminal activity engaged in by children and those in their early teens. The contemporary comments of Firmin, Hanway, and Fielding all suggest that young offenders were by no means inactive during the seventeenth and eighteenth centuries, and Mayett, Hutton, Saxby, Clare, Somerville, and Harriott all admitted in their autobiographies that they had committed minor thefts when they were young. Institutional initiatives such as the Marine Society in the 1750s and the later Philanthropic Society were set up partly to tackle this problem.[14] The reports on 'juvenile delinquency' that began to proliferate in the second decade of the nineteenth century were not analysing a new problem, even though they gave it a new (if rather loosely defined) label. As I have discussed in detail elsewhere, those reports coincided with, and contributed to, a massive post-1815 increase both in the absolute number of juveniles reaching the courts and in the proportion of indicted offenders who were aged 17 or under—this being probably the most common contemporary definition of the word 'juvenile'.[15] In the years

[12] W. Sanders, *Juvenile Offenders for a Thousand Years. Selective Readings from Anglo-Saxon Times to 1900* (Chapel Hill, North Carolina, 1970), p. 111.

[13] Burglary was effectively housebreaking at night. D. Philips, *Crime and Authority in Victorian England* (London, 1977), p. 238. P.R.O. Assi 31/14–15 (1782–7) = 22.6 per cent of housebreakers were hanged; 43.0 per cent of burglars. *P.P.*, 1816, V., p. 57. See also *An Account . . . of the Philanthropic Society*, p. 8.

[14] Sanders, *Juvenile Offenders*, pp. 18–90; I. Pinchbeck and M. Hewitt, *Children in English Society* (2 vols., London, 1969–73) 1, pp. 91–125; 2, pp. 414–46; *An Account . . . of the Philanthropic Society*, pp. 1–23; Fielding, *An Account*; J. Taylor, *Jonas Hanway Founder of the Marine Society. Charity and Policy in Eighteenth Century Britain* (London, 1985); Kussmaul (ed.), *The Autobiography*, pp. 14–15; Harriott, *Struggles*, 1, pp. 7–12; Hutton, *The Life*, p. 34; Robinson, *John Clare's*, p. 33; Saxby, *Memoirs*, pp. 13–15; A. Somerville, *The Autobiography of a Working Man* (London, 1967), p. 45.

[15] King, 'The Rise of Juvenile Delinquency', esp. pp. 120–2; P. King and J. Noel, 'The Origins of "the Problem of Juvenile Delinquency". The Growth of Juvenile Prosecutions in London in the Later Eighteenth and Early Nineteenth Centuries', *Criminal Justice History*, 14 (1993), 17–41; *P.P.*, 1816, V; 1817,

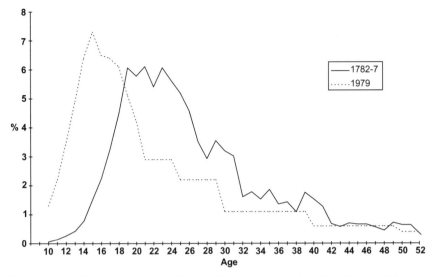

Fig. 6.2 Ages of Property Offenders, Home Circuit, 1782–7 and of all Indictable Offenders, England and Wales, 1979

Source: P.R.O. Assi 31/13–15 and Criminal Statistics, England and Wales 1979, HMSO (London, 1979).

studied here, however, juveniles remained a peripheral group among the accused and this raises a further question. Was the age structure of the accused in the 1780s merely a truncated version of a more general pattern still observable today? In a fairly representative international study Gibbens and Ahrenfeldt concluded that 'in most countries the incidence of delinquency is highest at some time during adolescence, usually between 14 and 16, and falls away rapidly after 21 or at most 25 . . . on the whole if acts of delinquency begin very early in life, they are abandoned at a relatively early stage of manhood.'[16] The stronger filters of the 1780s clearly removed a higher proportion of potential accused from the ages of about 17 or 18 downwards than would be the case today but, apart from this distortion, was the 1780s pattern substantially different from those found in most modern Western societies? Superficially it appears that it was not but a closer scrutiny reveals important variations, the most central of which concerns the age range between the late teens and mid-twenties (Figure 6.2).

VII; 1818, VIII; 1819, VIII; M. May, 'Innocence and Experience. The Evolution of the Concept of Juvenile Delinquency in the Mid-Nineteenth Century', *Victorian Studies*, 17 (1973), 15; P. Rush, 'The Government of a Generation. The Subject of Juvenile Delinquency', *Liverpool Law Review*, 14 (1992), 3–43.

[16] T. Gibbens and R. Ahrenfeldt (eds.), *Cultural Factors in Delinquency* (London, 1966); Walker, *Crime and Criminology*, p. 122; K. Christiansen, 'Industrialization and Urbanization in relation to Crime and Juvenile Delinquency', *International Review of Criminal Policy*, 16 (1960), 4. Farrington highlights some differences but confirms the general pattern. D. Farrington 'Age and Crime', *Crime and Justice. A Review of Research*, 8 (1986), 189–99.

3. Late Adolescence and Young Adulthood

Modern age distributions in Britain, the United States, Denmark, and elsewhere show a steady decline in recorded criminal activity between the ages of 19 and 25 (Figure 6.2)—the number of accused aged 19 or 20 being always at least 50 per cent higher than that of the 25-year-old group. Self-report studies suggest a similar pattern. On the Home Circuit in the 1780s there was no overall decline between the ages of 19 and 25.[17] Selective leniency by prosecutors or magistrates does not appear to have operated extensively in favour of those aged over 19. In order to explain the height and consistency of the peak between the ages of 19 and 25 it is therefore necessary to look elsewhere. The position of young adults in eighteenth-century society made them both particularly likely to commit crimes and especially vulnerable to prosecution. In wartime that vulnerability sometimes took a different form— many were enlisted rather than prosecuted—but although these war/peace changes are important, the peacetime pattern of the 1780s will be used as a starting-point here. Since men dominated the recorded crime figures, the analysis will be primarily concerned at this point with the experience of young males.

Although boys did not leave home at any one particular age in the eight-eenth century, the great majority had done so by the time they were 15 or 16. Most became servants in husbandry, the children of labourers leaving earlier and in larger numbers than those whose fathers were tradesmen or farmers. Those apprenticed to established trades usually departed from their families at around 14. Pauper apprentices left a few years earlier.[18] Since the average age at first marriage for males was about 26 in the late eighteenth century, it was usual for men to experience a period of ten years or more away from home before setting up families of their own. For most males childhood ended early; full adulthood was late to arrive.[19] Between sexual maturity and full indepen-

---

[17] A moving average based on three-year age groupings has been used in dealing with the 1780s data which largely eliminates the effects of age rounding. H.M.S.O., *Criminal Statistics, England and Wales 1979*, p. 106; West, *The Young Offender*, p. 15; D. Greenberg, 'Delinquency', p. 190; Christiansen 'Industria-lization', p. 4; Farrington, 'Delinquency'; in London 1791–3 and Surrey 1782–7 the peak at the beginning of the twenties was higher and fell more quickly by twenty-five: King and Noel, 'The Origins'.

[18] R. Schofield, 'Age-Specific Mobility in an Eighteenth-Century Rural English Parish', *Annales de Démographic Historique* (1970); Kussmaul, *Servants*, pp. 70–8; R. Wall, 'The Age at Leaving Home', *Journal of Family History*, 3 (1978), pp. 181–202; Snell, *Annals*, pp. 323–32; J. Lane, *Apprenticeship in England 1600–1914* (London, 1996), p. 14; P. Sharpe, 'Poor Children as Apprentices in Colyton 1598–1830', *Continuity and Change*, 6 (1991), 255–6; E. Thomas, 'The Yealampton Pauper Apprentices', *Devon and Cornwall Notes and Queries* (1980), pp. 192–4; H. Cunningham, 'The Employment and Unemployment of Children in England, 1680–1851', *Past and Present*, 126 (1990), 132–3.

[19] Malcolmson, *Life and Labour*, p. 63; E. Wrigley and R. Schofield, *The Population History of England 1541–1871. A Reconstruction* (London, 1981), p. 424; Kussmaul, *Servants*, p. 83; Griffiths, *Youth and Authority*, p. 121; R. Outhwaite, 'Age at Marriage in England in the Late Seventeenth to the Nineteenth Century', *Transactions of the Royal Historical Society*, 5th ser., 23 (1973), 55–61. Many servants returned home after leaving for a while.

dence at marriage they experienced an extended period of partial subordination and partial freedom, a life-cycle phase which most contemporaries called
'youth'. The regulation of this 'slippery age' and the socialization of young
people into stable and responsible adults was much discussed in the eighteenth
century. The masters of living-in servants and apprentices, under whose
authority the majority of the poor spent their youth, had much the same
disciplinary role as parents but master–servant relationships were less intimate,
less durable, more instrumental and contractual.[20] The level of subordination
and surveillance imposed by masters was of great concern to contemporary
commentators, who generally conceptualized youth as a period of vulnerability, malleability, and recklessness. To many vice was a progressive disease that
male youths were very likely to succumb to unless they were properly sub-
ordinated within a paternalistic and disciplinary household regime. 'Where
the young men are not entered as servants in farmers' families', an Essex vicar
observed in 1800, 'but are left entirely to conduct themselves in early life, they
are less likely to become sober and steady members of the community, for want
of some wholesome and regular restraints which are frequently found in
families.' Employment in either 'apprenticeship or services' was often seen
by the authorities as virtually the only means of controlling those who would
otherwise 'habituate themselves to an idle and profligate course of life and
become dangerous . . . to the public', but masters rarely lived up to these ideals.
'There is but a small number of masters, in these days', Hanway wrote, 'who
will or can keep their apprentices within doors in the evening when their shops
are shut. These boys and young men challenge it as a kind of right and . . . the
master . . . takes no thought till he finds himself robbed.'[21] However, although
the gradual spread of outdoor apprenticeship, and later of outdoor service (in
which the young person was not required to live in his master's household),
further undermined the regulatory role of these institutions, in rural areas
service in husbandry and, to a lesser extent, apprenticeship continued to be
very important as a means of social regulation. The proportion of young
people entering living-in service in south-east England was beginning to
decline by the end of the century, but as late as the 1780s the late teens and

[20] M. Mitterauer, 'Servants and Youth', *Continuity and Change*, 5 (1990), 11–29; J. Gillis, *Youth and
History. Tradition and Change in European Age Relations 1770–Present* (London, 1974), pp. 2–5; Thomas, *Age*, p.
16; P. Rawlings, *Drunks, Whores and Idle Apprentices. Criminal Biographies of the Eighteenth Century* (London,
1992), pp. 19–22. The best general discussions of youth are M. Mitterauer, *A History of Youth* (Oxford,
1992); and Griffiths, *Youth and Authority*. R. Houlbrooke, *The English Family 1450–1700* (London, 1984), p.
176; Kussmaul, *Servants*, p. 3; I. Ben-Amos 'Service and the Coming of Age of Young Men in
Seventeenth-Century England', *Continuity and Change*, 3 (1988), 41–3.

[21] Thomas, *Age*, pp. 12–30; Rawlings, *Drunks, Whores*, pp. 19–22; Anon., *A Present for Servants*, pp. 26–8;
Defoe, *The Great Law*, pp. 7–15, 81–8; Hanway, *Defects*, pp. 57–9, J. North, 'State of the Poor in the Parish
of Ashdon', *Annals of Agriculture*, 35 (1800), p. 471; Hewitt and Pinchbeck, *Children*, 1, p. 109; J. Rule, *The
Experience of Labour in Eighteenth-Century Industry* (London, 1981), pp. 99–101; Griffiths, *Youth and Authority*,
pp. 351–89.

early twenties continued to be a period of waiting and of living-in service for most of the rural poor.[22]

Although the level of control exercised by masters varied considerably and although many servants found ways of carving out time for leisure activities, servanthood undoubtedly involved the acceptance of many constraints. The position of servants was a profoundly ambivalent one. They were in the household but not of it. In a society still hostile to the early achievement of economic independence, they were full-time workers contributing much to the productivity of the master's household but they remained largely dependent on him and under his authority. Servanthood had its positive aspects. Servants may well have welcomed the opportunity to leave parental controls behind and for the duration of each hiring they were not as vulnerable to rises in the cost of living as they would otherwise have been. Moreover, their frequent moves from one position to another gave them opportunities to gain skills, accumulate savings, and meet potential marriage partners. However, many young men clearly disliked living-in. The constraints were severe and prolonged. Their period in service could last for more than a quarter of the average lifespan and there was relatively little they could do to advance the date when it would be over.[23]

Petty pilfering was widely prevalent amongst servants, who were ideally placed to effect minor appropriations of their master's goods at regular intervals. Alcohol, food, and other consumables were the main targets. Such thefts were almost a tradition among servants, who may have regarded them as an informal part of their wages. In 1792 John Bridge of Thundersley admitted that he had frequently taken his master's ale, and stated in his defence that he had been given a key to the ale cellar by the servant he had succeeded. Servants sometimes stole from one another, but the great majority appropriated their master's property by pilfering the materials entrusted to them in the household and on the cart, or by fraudulently purchasing materials in their master's name. There is extensive evidence that servants often combined forces in order to obtain alcohol or food. In 1784 a group of five servants, after drinking together at the Duke's Head in Walthamstow, obtained fresh supplies by breaking into the wine cellar of a house where one of them worked. They then retired to a field to consume the proceeds. Twenty years earlier a large gang of servants was reported to have 'made a practice of robbing gardens and outhouses, stealing corn for the horses, breaking open the cellars of the several masters they lived with and stealing the strong beer'. Their frequent thefts of

---

[22] Rule, *The Experience*, pp. 100–1; Snell, *Annals*, pp.67–103 and 228–69; George, *London Life*, pp. 268–9. London apprentices were less heavily regulated. Thale (ed.), *The Autobiography of Francis Place*, p. 73; Houlbrooke, *The English*, pp. 171–8; Kussmaul, *Servants*, pp. 120–3.

[23] Malcolmson, *Life and Labour*, p. 63; Kussmaul, *Servants*, pp. 44–5 and 145–6; Griffiths, *Youth and Authority*, p. 133; D. Souden, 'Pre-industrial English Local Migration Fields' (Cambridge Ph.D., 1981), pp. 287–9; Snell, *Annals*, pp. 67–103.

ale culminated in an invitation being sent to over twenty acquaintances 'to meet them in a neighbouring wood on a Sunday where they regaled over a tub of beer stolen for that purpose'.[24] Alehouses also acted as focal points for these activities. In 1783 Parliament was told of the need to prevent 'idle young men from meeting at night in public houses . . . for the purpose of . . . mischief' and in 1788 the *Chelmsford Chronicle* carried a number of articles about their suppression which stressed that the village alehouse was usually a harbour for thieves, poachers, and idleness. Modern studies have suggested that unemployed or poorly paid male youths steal in order to support their leisure-time, group-centred activities. Many of the crimes for which eighteenth-century servants were indicted may have been rooted in similar needs.[25]

Gangs of servants were extremely likely to be prosecuted if their activities came to light, but individual servants or apprentices who had stolen from their masters were usually dealt with in other ways. A variety of informal controls were available and diaries suggest that, despite their sense that servant thefts were also treacheries, relatively few masters used the courts (Chapter 2).[26] Nevertheless, magistrates had extensive powers to punish offences by servants, and in the second half of the eighteenth century substantial numbers were imprisoned after summary trial. In 1753–4 and in 1790 nearly 10 per cent of the prisoners listed in the Essex house of correction calendars were servants or apprentices confined for disorderly behaviour, disobeying their masters or going away without permission. In Gloucestershire between 1791 and 1807 nearly 700 servants were imprisoned for these offences[27] and, as the analysis in Chapter 4 made clear, a significant proportion of these had been caught pilfering from their masters.

Since informal controls or summary prosecution prevented many servants from reaching the major courts and since the law relating to embezzlement by servants sometimes made it a difficult offence to prosecute, this category of

[24] E.R.O. Q/SBb 348/41 (other food and drink thefts 242/21 and 249/5); Q/SBb 317/29; Beattie, 'The Criminality of Women', pp. 92–3; *Che.C.*, 17 May 1765; Kussmaul, *Servants*, p. 43. For youth culture, recreation activities, etc., Griffiths, *Youth and Authority*, pp. 110–75.

[25] K. Wrightson, 'Alehouses, Order and Reformation in Rural England 1590–1660', in E. Yeo and S. Yeo (eds.), *Popular Culture and Class Conflict 1590–1914. Explorations in the History of Labour and Leisure* (Brighton, 1981), pp. 7–11; Sharpe, 'Crime and Delinquency', pp. 102–3; R. Houston, 'Vagrants and Society in Early Modern England', *Cambridge Anthropology*, (1980), p. 20; *Parliamentary History*, 23 (1783), p. 364; Fielding, *An Account . . .*, p. x discusses gangs plotting theft in alehouses; *Che.C.*, 21 Apr. 1786, 27 July 1787, 10 Aug. 1787, 22 Feb. 1788. For broader context, J. Innes, 'Politics and Morals'; Greenberg, 'Delinquency', pp. 197–8. For the many functions of alehouses, P. Clark, *The English Alehouse. A Social History* (London, 1983).

[26] Kussmaul, *Servants*, p. 33. For an Essex master horsewhipping a thieving servant Emsley, *Crime*, p. 40. W. Fleetwood, *The Relative Duties of Parents, Husbands, Masters and Children, Wives and Servants* (London, 1705), p. 371.

[27] 1753–4 based on Halstead and Chelmsford house of correction calendars, 1790 on the two middle sessions of the year for Colchester, Barking, Newport, Halstead, and Chelmsford. Innes, 'English Houses of Correction', pp. 47–8; J. Whiting, *Prison Reform in Gloucestershire, 1776–1820* (London, 1975). Appendices C and F; Burn, *The Justice* (1797), 4, pp. 40–46. For Essex examples, see *Che.C.*, 17 July 1789; E.R.O. Q/SBb 330/26.

offender was probably underrepresented among indictments. It is therefore surprising to find such a large number of servants appearing in these courts. On the indictments themselves servants were subsumed under the general label of labourers, but depositions are a more informative, if not a definitive, guide. Among the Essex quarter sessions depositions between 1748 and 1800 about one-sixth of the male accused can be definitely identified as living-in servants and a number of others were almost certainly in the same position.[28] The assize depositions have not survived, but five of the twenty-five offenders whose trials are reported in the 1774 Essex assize proceedings can definitely be identified as servants of the victim on or around the date of the crime. In early modern England about 13 per cent of the population were servants, and this figure may have been slightly lower in late eighteenth-century Essex, but in spite of their masters' extensive use of lesser sanctions they formed a much larger group among quarter sessions offenders in both eighteenth-century Essex and seventeenth-century Wiltshire.[29]

Although servants' extensive criminal activities were partly related to opportunity, they were also a reflection of the structural position of adolescents and young unmarried adults in eighteenth-century society. Coming of age was a complex and protracted process of socialization and integration. It was not simply an undifferentiated period of subordination to masters or parents. The journey to maturity involved successive gains of independence as family ties weakened and young people learned to make decisions about how to change masters, gain skills, obtain higher wages, and reshape their relationship with their parents.[30] Each individual's capacity to negotiate that journey without falling foul of the law, or opting for the often problematic alternative of joining the armed forces, depended partly on his own personality, partly on his family background, and partly on the peer-group pressure to which he was exposed, but it was also structurally linked to the intermediate and ambivalent nature of both servanthood and apprenticeship. The fragments of autobiographical writing left by the poor suggest that their reactions to the constraints of living-in service included strategies of both appropriation and migration. Joseph Mayett, one of the few servants-in-husbandry who has left any record of his experiences, found 'the reins of government' very irksome by the time he was 18. As a result, he later admitted, 'there was hardly any mischief done in the place but I had a hand in' until, after nearly being caught robbing the local orchards with some of his fellow servants, he resolved 'to give out thieving

[28] Burn, *The Justice* (1797), 4, p. 47; Radzinowicz, *History*, 1, pp. 638–9. Almost a quarter of those whose occupations are identifiable were described as servants or carters working for the victim but the term 'servant' was sometimes applied to day labourers. Based on all available depositions in a 26-year sample.

[29] *The Whole Proceedings . . . Essex . . . March 1774*; Laslett and Wall (eds.), *Household*, p. 152. Kussmaul, *Servants*, p. 13; M. Ingram, 'Communities and Courts. Law and Disorder in Early Seventeenth-Century Wiltshire', in Cockburn (ed.), *Crime*, p. 130.

[30] Ben-Amos 'Service'; Mitterauer, 'Servants', pp. 29–30; Kussmaul, *Servants*, pp. 31–77.

for ... if I still practised it, it would ... bring me to the gallows'. John Clare also joined with local boys and with 'the young fellows' he met at a local alehouse in poaching expeditions and in 'stealing peas in church time when the owners was safe'. As the diaries of their masters indicate, many servants and apprentices pilfered their masters' goods in order to improve their diet, lubricate their social activities, or enhance their savings. Purefoy, Blundell, and Cole all had their cellars or larders raided by their servants. Mary Hardy found her maids throwing her victuals out of their garret window to the young men in the yard below. Francis Place observed that many of his fellow apprentices financed their boat club and drinking bouts by stealing from their masters.[31]

The autobiographies also indicate that a considerable proportion of young people chose to react in a very different way. They abandoned their positions as servants or apprentices and ran away from their masters either temporarily or permanently. John Clare's apprenticeship to a head gardener ended when after 'nearly a twelve month I fled him for I could not stand him no longer'. Joseph Mayett left a difficult master after only a few days as a living-in servant and managed to get through a dozen hirings by the time he was 20, while almost all of the apprentices William Hutton's uncle took ran away before their time was up.[32] Absconding from service did not necessarily launch a young person into destitution, unemployment, and crime. Some returned to their masters and were forgiven, as William Hutton eventually was in 1741. Many, like Mayett and Clare, went home to their parents if their families lived fairly close by and were willing, however grudgingly, to take them back. For others running away was a much riskier decision because they either could not or would not return home. When Samuel Hutton ran away from his master, whose occupation he described as 'repugnant to the spirit and activity of youth' he could expect no support from home. His mother was dead. His father and stepmother had no affection for him. He found himself 'frequently in absolute want of food' and was severely tempted when invited by highwaymen 'to join them and share their plunder'. Instead he concluded 'there was but one asylum before me—the army'. In 1741 Samuel's brother, William, his pride wounded by a public beating from his master, and his patience exhausted by a mean mistress and a hatred for stocking weaving, stole 2 shillings from his master and ran away. In doing so he launched himself into a

---

[31] Kussmaul (ed.), *The Autobiography*, pp. 7–15; Robinson (ed.), *John Clare's*, pp. 33–42. Mary Saxby ran away from her father and stepmother and eventually joined up with a group of gypsies who lived by stealing anything they could lay their hands on, *Memoirs*, pp. 1–14. Mitchell (ed.), *The Purefoy Letters*, pp. 138–41; Bagley (ed.), *The Great Diurnal*, 1, pp. 96–7; Stokes (ed.), *The Bletchley Diary*, p. 11; Cozens-Hardy (ed.), *Mary Hardy's Diary*, p. 84; Thale (ed.), *The Autobiography of Francis Place*, p. 77.

[32] Robinson (ed.), *John Clare's*, p. 11; Kussmaul (ed.), *The Autobiography*, pp. xi and 8; Hutton, *The Life*, pp. 28–31; R. Palmer (ed.), *The Rambling Soldier* (Gloucester, 1985), p. 15 for Samuel Hutton's comment that 'nothing is more common than for the apprentices to abscond'. For a farmer who lost or dismissed servants regularly, G. Mingay, 'The Diary of James Warne, 1758', *Agricultural History Review*, 38 (1990), 72–8.

precarious existence of homelessness and semi-destitution because potential employers, suspicious that he was a runaway apprentice, would not give him work.[33]

A servant or apprentice might lose or leave his 'place' for a variety of reasons. For many the change was a totally involuntary one. Servants who had completed one hiring sometimes found it impossible to obtain another. Apprentices whose masters went out of business were not always able to find an alternative. Others were dismissed for laziness or dishonesty, many masters using this as their main sanction (Chapter 2). In 1755 William Moore, on discovering that three of his servants had stolen carnations from a neighbour's garden and planted them in his own, committed only one of them for trial, but paid all three of them off and 'turned them out'. Some servants and apprentices, such as William Hutton, reversed this process, making a positive decision to run away and to avail themselves of their master's goods in the process. In 1774, for example, three servants of a Stanford Rivers farmer gathered together his silver and headed for London. More frequently, however, servants and apprentices were driven to leave by the neglect or harsh behaviour of their masters; by the feeling that the constraints of their position had become unbearable; or by the fear that their illegal activities were about to be discovered.[34]

Whatever the sequence of events that led them to leave, many of these young men were propelled into a highly marginal existence by that process. Those that had absconded or had been dismissed were in a particularly difficult position unless they could return to their parents. Unable, in many cases, to use the employment market of their previous locality, they were forced to move considerable distances and ran the risk of being labelled as vagrants.[35] In their search for employment they often found it necessary to commit minor property offences in order to survive and as strangers without 'character' or position they were then highly vulnerable to prosecution.

Contemporaries' comments and the life stories of criminals written under the shadow of the gallows frequently made connections between lawbreaking activity and the problems of young men either dismissed from their positions or on the run. Colquhoun's 'Dismal Catalogue of... Thieves in and about this Metropolis' stressed the importance of 'Servants... out of place' and of 'idle

[33] Hutton, *The Life*, pp. 31–50 and 384–9; Robinson (ed.), *John Clare's*, p. 11; Kussmaul (ed.), *The Autobiography*, p. 12; Palmer (ed.), *The Rambling*, pp. 16–17.

[34] Kussmaul (ed.), *The Autobiography*, p. 11: 'provisions dear and many servants out of place'; E.R.O. Q/SBb 202/27; *Whole Proceedings...Essex...March 1774*, p. 18; P. Rushton, 'The Matter in Variance. Adolescents and Domestic Conflict in the Pre-industrial Economy of Northeast England 1600–1800', *Journal of Social History*, 25 (1991), 95–100; Griffiths, *Youth and Authority*, pp. 328–30. *Che.C.*, 20 Mar. 1772 for an advert promising forgiveness to runaway servants; Lane, *Apprenticeship in England*, pp. 215–27.

[35] For some the mere act of running away from their masters turned them into thieves because their masters owned the clothes they ran away in. Eustace, 'The Tomkins Diary', p. 41; P. Colquhoun, *A Treatise on Indigence* (London, 1806), p. 11. For hiring areas, A. Kussmaul, 'The Ambiguous Mobility of Farm Servants', *Economic History Review*, 24 (1981), 227–34.

and disorderly mechanics ... who having on this account lost the confidence of their masters ... resort to thieving as a means of support'. In some life stories, dismissal is almost immediately followed by lawbreaking activity. When John Price was about 18 'a gentleman with whom he had lived in the country turned him out of his service purely on account of his excessive lying: when going towards London and robbing a market woman ... near Brentwood ... he was taken ... and committed to Chelmsford Gaol'. More commonly, running away from apprenticeship or service, joining and then deserting the armed forces, and thieving are inextricably bound together. John Morris, a 21-year-old executed at Chelmsford in 1798, claimed to have committed numerous property crimes liberally interspersed with enlistments and desertions. 'I was born in the parish of Woodford', he wrote, 'by trade a carpenter and ran away after I had served four and a half years and went to sea; then came all my trouble.'[36]

4. Mobility, Crime, and Young Adulthood

Young men on the run were not the only migrants who found themselves being indicted for property crime in the eighteenth century. Jacob Soames, for example, when asked what he had to say in his defence at the Essex assizes in 1740 replied, 'he could say nothing and as to living he shifted anywhere he could'. George Lovell, alias Gypsy George, who was hanged for highway robbery at the age of 30, was described as 'born at Rumford in Essex and followed the trade of a tinker'. Many of the accused where clearly strangers to the communities where their alleged crimes were perpetrated. In early seventeenth-century Wiltshire nearly half of quarter sessions felony prosecutions were directed against itinerants or persons operating more than 5 miles from their homes, and an intensive study of the Essex village of Kelvedon in the same period suggests a similar pattern.[37] The eighteenth-century Essex depositions are rather less informative. Over 40 per cent fail to record either the accused's place of residence or any other evidence about his previous relationship to the victim. Two-fifths of the depositions sampled indicated that the accused came from within 5 miles of the place where the crime was committed, whilst just under one-fifth definitely described the offender as a vagrant or indicated that the accused was a stranger. However, among the depositions as a whole, it is unlikely that known offenders outnumbered strangers by as much as two to one because the depositions that give no description of the

[36] Colquhoun, *Police*, p. 89; G. Crook and J. Rayner, *The Complete Newgate Calendar* (5 vols., London, 1926), 4, p. 266; *Che.C.*, 10 Aug. 1798.
[37] *Proceedings at the Assizes for ... Essex July 1740*, p. 26; *The Ordinary of Newgate's Account*, 14 October 1772, p. 4. For gypsy crime, see P.R.O. H.O./11 7 Apr. 1790. A highway robbery committed on the Essex border. Ingram 'Communities and Courts', pp. 130–2; Sharpe, 'Crime and Delinquency', p. 101; Sharpe, 'Enforcing', pp. 118–19.

accused almost certainly contain a much higher proportion of outsiders. Thus, although there may have been some decline since the years of exceptional anxiety over vagrancy at the beginning of the seventeenth century, over a third of indicted property offences in the eighteenth and early nineteenth centuries were committed by the more mobile elements in the population.[38]

The relationship between mobility and recorded crime is difficult to unravel from the limited sources available. In the eighteenth century the population of the Home Counties was highly mobile. Migration levels were generally greater in eastern England than in the west and the counties around London were particularly affected by the capital's role as a migrant entrepôt. How did migration patterns influence the type of person indicted and the age structure of offenders? Mobility levels as well as indictment rates were much higher among those in their later teens and twenties than they were in other age groups. The settlement laws may have restricted the mobility of those with families to support, but young adults were much less constrained by them. In 1788 the vicar of Dunmow observed, 'how seldom do the young and healthy, while single, find any difficulty in changing their residence, and fixing where they please'.[39]

However, some types of mobility were more dangerous than others. The majority of migrants were apprentices or servants moving within fairly well-established networks. In the case of service a series of moves was the norm, but this mobility did not necessarily expose servants to journeys that would have made them vulnerable to prosecution for theft. Few servants moved outside the hiring area in which they were 'known' and, like the great majority of all migration patterns, their mobility was short-distance and short-term in character.[40] To understand the impact that patterns of mobility could have on indictment levels, it is necessary to focus on the smaller categories of migrants that travelled longer distances under less protective circumstances.

Systematic analysis of these marginal groups is extremely difficult. Those in authority tended to attach the label of vagrant to any migrant whose

[38] Depositions sample: E.R.O. Q/SBb 1748–9, 1754–65, 1771–4, 1783–6, 1792–4, 1800. Those designated as strangers included all offenders described as vagabonds, strollers, travellers, etc.; all those with abodes more than 5 miles away and those whose names were not known by the victim (although this is not systematically recorded). Robson concludes that a third of the convicts reaching Australia did not come from the county in which they were tried: L. Robson, *The Convict Settlers of Australia* (Melbourne, 1965); and given the great mobility described in the life stories of many highwaymen and horse thieves, the assizes accused probably included more strangers than those indicted at the quarter sessions.

[39] P. Clark, 'Migration in England during the Late Seventeenth and Early Eighteenth Centuries', *Past and Present*, 83 (1979), 57–90; Souden, 'Pre-industrial', pp. 72–5, 97–130, 220, 313; John Howlett quoted in J. Poynter, *Society and Pauperism English Ideas on Poor Relief 1795–1834* (London, 1969), p. 5; J. Taylor, 'The Impact of Pauper Settlement 1691–1834', *Past and Present*, 73 (1976), 55; P. Styles, 'The Evolution of the Law of Settlement', *University of Birmingham Historical Journal*, 9 (1963), 62; E. Hampson, 'Settlement and Removal in Cambridgeshire 1662–1834', *Cambridge Historical Journal*, 11 (1928), p. 286.

[40] Souden, 'Pre-industrial', pp. 287–98; Kussmaul, 'The Ambiguous Mobility'.

activities could not be clearly identified as legitimate. Vagrants were stereo-typed as evil rogues and a sharp distinction was often drawn between the honest poor and the threatening, idle, pilfering beggar. However, this distinc-tion appears to have had little basis in reality. Although some of those labelled as vagrants may have been professional strollers, beggars, or thieves, most were moving in response to unemployment or other specific economic and social crises. Most of the subgroups in danger of being treated as vagrants, such as servants and apprentices out of 'place', deserters, seasonal workers, journey-men, artisans on tramp, and demobilized soldiers or sailors, were very close in background, occupation, and life experience to the majority of the labouring poor.[41]

This did not prevent contemporaries from regarding many of them as 'vagrant banditti'. At the beginning of a widespread parish campaign against vagrants in 1787, for example, the *Chelmsford Chronicle* suggested that most of the crimes committed in the county are 'through the medium of these vagrants', who, it observed, 'are generally drove out from London and its environs for petty theft...they then disperse themselves in the country within 60 or 70 miles of the metropolis'. The widespread assumption that vagrants must, of necessity, be thieves was enshrined in both the statutory law and the hand-books which guided the law's administrators. Dalton suggested that 'if a man liveth idly or vagrant...it is a good course to arrest him upon suspicion', and Burn put forward a similar principle. While theft frequently led to summary trial and punishment under the vagrancy laws (Chapter 4), being labelled as a vagrant might equally lead to arrest on suspicion of felony and subsequent indictment. Local communities were often extremely hostile towards stran-gers. Parson Woodforde, for example, investigated the backgrounds of 'strange suspicious men' appearing in the parish and automatically assumed that 'a strange man' found in an outhouse 'was upon no good there'. If apprehended near the scene of a crime, those labelled as strangers or vagrants were highly vulnerable to suspicion and prosecution.[42]

Who were the vulnerable mobile poor? By their nature they left few records and unfortunately the main sources created by the surveillance of the author-ities, vagrancy examinations, are extremely problematic. Young fit men ar-rested for vagrancy tended to be either impressed or moved on informally to avoid the expense of an examination. Physically vulnerable groups, particu-larly those who were sick or elderly, were more likely to be examined so that

---

[41] R. Houston, 'Vagrants and Society', pp. 18–29; P. Slack, 'Vagrants and Vagrancy in England 1598–1664', *Economic History Review*, 27 (1974), pp. 360–80; A. Beier, 'Vagrants and the Social Order in Elizabethan England', *Past and Present*, 64 (1974), 3–29; N. Rogers, 'Policing the Poor', pp. 132–7.

[42] *Che.C.*, 12 Nov. 1784, 28 Dec. 1787. Chapter 5 for 1780s context. Many arrested vagrants did come from London—up to a quarter in the seventeenth century: A. Beier, *Masterless Men, the Vagrancy Problem in England 1560–1640* (London, 1985), p. 45. W. Chamliss, 'A Sociological Analysis of the Law of Vagrancy', *Social Problems*, 12 (1964), 66–77; Burn, *The Justice* (1766), 1, p. 91; Beresford, *Diary of a Country Parson*, 1, p. 94; 2, p. 213.

Table 6.2. Runaways Advertised in the Essex Newspapers, 1760–91

	Apprentices		Servants		Deserters		Parish	
	No.	%	No.	%	No.	%	No.	%
Under 15	7	6.6	1	1.9	—	—	—	—
15–17	19	18.1	7	13.0	3	2.8	—	—
18–20	71	67.6	20	37.0	30	28.3	4	4.0
21–3	8	7.6	12	22.2	27	25.5	4	4.0
24–6	—	—	8	14.8	19	17.9	18	18.2
27–9	—	—	1	1.9	13	12.3	7	7.1
30–4	—	—	3	5.5	7	6.6	19	19.2
35–9	—	—	1	1.9	5	4.7	13	13.1
40–4	—	—	1	1.9	1	0.9	20	20.2
45–9	—	—	—	—	1	0.9	4	4.0
50+	—	—	—	—	—	—	10	10.1
Total	105	99.9	54	100.1	106	99.9	99	99.9

Sources: a complete survey of the *Ipswich Journal*, 1760–4 and the *Chelmsford Chronicle*, 1765–91. The only substantial gap in the surviving copies is 1767, of which two-thirds are missing.

they could be passed on to their parish of settlement.[43] The proportion of those arrested for vagrancy who were adolescents or young adults cannot therefore be calculated, but their importance among the various subgroups who had run away from their previous locality or employment position can be confirmed from the advertisements describing the age and appearance of runaways placed in the Essex newspapers by masters or other interested parties attempting to trace them (Table 6.2). These are not necessarily a typical sample of those who ran away. Only the more valuable males were usually advertised and the usefulness of a servant, apprentice, or recruit varied with age, skills, and the state of the labour market or of international relations. However, some indication of the age structure of runaways can be gained in this way. Within the three main groups the late teens and early twenties were undoubtedly dominant. Among apprentices 19 was the peak and servants' ages, equally predictably, were clustered in the early twenties. Servants in husbandry were relatively rarely advertised but among those summarily tried for servant offences in Gloucestershire a similar age pattern emerges. Finally, nearly three-quarters of advertised deserters came from the age range between 18

---

[43] Before 1700 youths were well represented among examined vagrants: Slack, 'Vagrants and Vagrancy', p. 335; Houston, 'Vagrants and Society', p. 22; Beier, 'Vagrants', p. 10; Beier, *Masterless Men*, pp. 54–6, but arrested vagrants in eighteenth-century London were predominantly women or older men. Less than 20 per cent of males were in their twenties. N. Rogers, 'Policing the Poor'. The Essex vagrancy examinations 1779–90 do not record ages consistently but only 10 per cent were males aged between 18 and 26 and nearly half were women (E.R.O. Q/RSW 1/1, 2, 7, 8, 12, 14–18, 20).

and 26, confirming Burroughs's findings that army deserters were mainly recent recruits under 25 years' old.[44]

Apart from deserters and runaway servants or apprentices, three other specific groups made up predominantly of young adults were also involved in patterns of long-distance migration that were often accompanied by greater vulnerability to prosecution. Many of those released from the armed forces at the beginning of each peacetime period experienced great difficulties in getting back home, finding employment, and re-establishing a settled place in the community. Although their precise age structure varied according to the specific type of personnel involved, armed forces recruits were mainly adolescents or young adults. On average, sailors were probably slightly older than soldiers and some militia recruits were family men, but most armed forces personnel were young and unmarried. The peak age of the Quota men recruited in the mid-1790s for example was 18–20, while three-quarters of ordinary seamen, two-thirds of midshipmen, and more than half of able seamen were aged between 16 and 25.[45]

The movement of these young adults in and out of the forces not only affected the level of indictments in various ways (Chapter 5); it also had a substantial impact on the age structure of those who were prosecuted. In Bedfordshire, for example, during the wartime period 1801–12 only 38 per cent of indicted offenders were aged between 18 and 29 (Table 6.3). By 1818–22 the figure was 62 per cent—a change observable at both the quarter sessions and assizes. Work on Lancashire, Gloucestershire, and Bristol has revealed similar changes and the Home Circuit age distribution was also affected by war. Comparisons between 1782–7 and 1799–1800 are complicated by the severe dearth of 1800, but in the wartime period the proportion of the accused aged 30 or below was considerably lower (Figure 6.3). The burdens created by the rapid war/peace transitions of the eighteenth century were mainly shouldered by young unmarried males. In wartime they were more vulnerable to enlistment either before or after they had committed an offence. In peacetime labour markets were glutted, preference was often given to family men, and anxieties about crime tended to focus on mobile unemployed males, increasing the likelihood that they would be prosecuted if they committed a crime. The problems of those wanting to be hired as servants were particularly acute. Masters had less incentive to hire men by the year when a sufficient supply of

---

[44] Littledean house of correction registers in the 1790s and 1800s, recorded servants' ages as follows: 11–15 = 7; 16–20 = 10; 21–5 = 7; 26–30 = 2; 30 and above = 2. Gloucestershire R.O. Q/Gli 16/1. P. Burroughs, 'Crime and Punishment in the British Army 1815–1870', *English Historical Review*', 100 (1985), 554.

[45] Hutton, *The Life*, pp. 387–8; Kussmaul (ed.), *The Autobiography*, p. 61. Western, *The English Militia*, p. 269 suggests 'regular soldiers as a class were unmarried'. Emsley, *North Riding*, pp. 7–11 for discussion, and p. 18 for age structures in a variety of counties. N. Rodger, *The Wooden World* (London, 1986), pp. 360–3. The age structure of deep-sea sailors also peaked massively between 20 and 29—M. Rediker, *Between the Devil and the Deep Blue Sea* (Cambridge, 1987), p. 299.

Table 6.3. The Age Distribution of Bedfordshire Indicted Offenders, 1801–12 and 1818–22

| Court | Period | % in age groups | | Over 30 | Total |
		0–17	18–29		
Quarter sessions	1801–12	6.8	37.7	55.5	100
	1818–22	6.8	58.7	34.5	100
Assizes	1801–12	9.9	37.3	52.8	100
	1818–22	6.3	67.6	26.1	100
Both courts	1801–12	7.9	37.6	54.5	100
	1818–22	6.6	61.7	31.7	100

Note: Sample sizes: quarter sessions 236 and 412, assizes 142 and 207.

Source: Bedfordshire Record Office QSS 4.

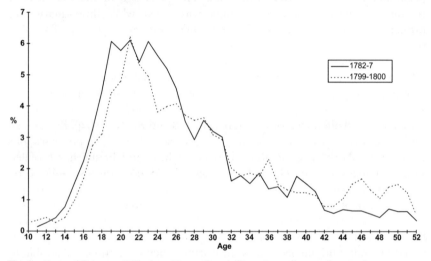

Fig. 6.3 Ages of Property Offenders, Home Circuit Counties, 1782–7 and 1799–1800
Source: P.R.O. Assi 31/13–15 and Assi 31/18–19.

short-term labour was available whenever they needed it.[46] Without regular employment a significant number of young men failed to make the difficult adjustment to civilian life, and their resultant mobility and marginal lifestyle made them highly vulnerable and visible targets when the authorities responded to postwar panics about crime by cracking down on those labelled as 'vagrant banditti'.

The second very specific set of migrant groups dominated largely by young unmarried males were the tramping artisans. The period immediately following the completion of an apprenticeship was often one of great insecurity for

[46] For a detailed analysis of the impact of war on offenders' age profiles, King, 'Press Gangs'; Kussmaul, *Servants*, pp. 97–134.

those whose trades were already burdened with a surplus of skilled manpower. In 1785 the journeymen shoemakers of Essex complained bitterly that 'many hundreds of workers who have served a legal apprenticeship . . . are destitute of employment'. In the late eighteenth century these problems stimulated the growth of the tramping system. Designed specifically for single men and particularly for the period immediately following apprenticeship, the system took men in their early twenties away from family and friends and often exposed them to a long series of journeys into areas where they were neither known nor recognized.[47]

The vulnerability of tramping journeymen to hunger and to the need to resort to petty theft was at least reduced by the fact that they were usually able to obtain accommodation and limited supplies of food and drink from their brother artisans. However, the third group exhibiting exceptional mobility, the seasonal migrants, very rarely received such help. Seasonal migration increased rapidly in the eighteenth and early nineteenth centuries. The extension of tillage stimulated the demand for labour in the peak summer months, and the expansion of corn and root crop cultivation in the south-eastern counties made them a particularly strong magnet for seasonal migrants in search of harvest work. Much of this migration was long-distance in character. By the mid-eighteenth century the south-east attracted large numbers of Irish and Scottish harvest workers as well as shorter-distance migrants from London and from the pastoral areas of England. The amount of labour that would be required and the particular weeks it would be needed were difficult to predict, and when bad weather disturbed seasonal employment patterns harvest workers were put in a very vulnerable position. In July 1766 the *Chelmsford Chronicle* followed a report about the failure of the local hay crop by observing that 'many poor persons whose sole employ at this season is the making of hay, through want of some means of employ whereby to gain a subsistence, are drove on the public roads to rob, or left to the sad necessity of returning home (perhaps many miles) without a farthing to support them on the road'.[48]

Arthur Young clearly had his doubts about harvest workers. 'They are seldom the best and most industrious, who make these annual excursions', he wrote. They were certainly ideally placed for the more opportunistic forms of theft. In 1774 two travelling harvesters broke into a labourer's house at

[47] E. Hobsbawm, *Labouring Men* (London, 1964), pp. 34–63; R. Leeson, *Travelling Brothers* (London, 1979), pp. 79–99; H. Southall, 'The Tramping Artisan Revisits: Labour Mobility and Economic Distress in Early Victorian England', *Economic History Review*, 44 (1991), 279–81 confirms that young men travelled more frequently and longer distances, being unrestricted by families; *Che.C.*, 17 June 1785 and 10 Aug. 1785. Autobiographies suggest that apprenticeship was almost always followed by a period on tramp. D. Vincent, *Bread, Knowledge and Freedom* (London, 1980), p. 68.

[48] Clark, 'Migration in England', pp. 88–9; E. Collins, 'Migrant Labour in British Agriculture in the Nineteenth Century', *Economic History Review*, 29 (1976), pp. 41–52; D. Morgan, *Harvesters and Harvesting 1840–1900* (London, 1982); Young, *General View . . . Essex*, 1, p. 305; D. Morgan, 'The Place of Harvesters in Nineteenth-Century Village Life', in R. Samuel (ed.), *Village Life and Labour* (London, 1975), p. 35; *Che.C.*, 4 July 1766.

Eastwood while the victim was working in the fields. They were eventually apprehended because they had bargained with a local farmer about harvest wages just before committing the crime. Seasonal workers travelling long distances could be subjected to resentment, prejudice, and poorly grounded prosecutions. In 1787 John Bayne, 'a native of North Briton' who had 'been accustomed for some few years past to come into England to do harvest work', was accused of highway robbery after asking a local woman for a halfpenny fare for the Humber ferry. The Home Office was sufficiently convinced of his innocence to give him a free pardon. Harvest workers were drawn from a broader range of ages and occupations than most other migrant groups, but those seasonal workers who undertook longer journeys were predominantly young, able-bodied, and single.[49] Among harvesters the relationship between mobility, recorded crime, and young adulthood may not have been as strong as it was among other groups, but it was still important. In the 1780s the high proportion of indicted offenders aged between 18 and 25 was linked to the various challenges faced by this age group and in particular to the frustrations and temptations of living-in service, and to the greater mobility and consequent vulnerability to prosecution of the young.

These were not static phenomena, however, and it is therefore important to be very specific about the period under study here. By the early nineteenth century the institutions governing the working lives of young males were entering a period of crisis and transformation. Living-in service collapsed in rural southern England after 1815 and apprenticeship also continued to decline, leaving most young men reliant on the casual labour market and tying them increasingly to their father's parish by removing the main means through which they could establish a settlement elsewhere. By the mid-nineteenth century youthful 'roving' was discouraged and mobility was more transient. When contemporaries began to talk about a rural 'juvenile vagrancy problem' in the 1840s the situation was very different from that found in the 1780s, and youthful crime in the first half of the nineteenth century therefore requires separate study.[50] However, almost all these changes had not developed sufficient momentum by the 1780s to affect the 1782–7 data that have formed the cornerstone of the analysis presented here.

The dominant role played by late adolescents and young adults among the eighteenth-century accused reflected the interaction between the ways young people reacted to their various situations by committing crimes and the ways their victims reacted to those crimes. The importance of the latter is easily underestimated. The main reason why this age group was so dominant among

---

[49] Young, 'General View ... Essex', 1, p. 304; Whole Proceedings ... Essex ... March 1774, p. 7; E.R.O. Q/SBb 345/41; P.R.O. H.O. 47/6; Collins, 'Migrant Labour', p. 54.

[50] Kussmaul, Servants, p. 121; Snell, Annals, pp. 71–84, 259–61, 322, and 334–50; A. Armstrong, Farmworkers. A Social and Economic History 1770–1980 (London, 1988), pp. 60–2; King, 'The Rise of Juvenile Delinquency'.

the accused may have been less related to what they did than to what they failed to do. Unlike the indictment of younger children or of those who were married, the prospect of prosecuting a young adult aroused little fear or sympathy among victims or parish authorities. If a married man or woman was imprisoned, transported, or hanged the community would have to watch his wife and children suffer too, while the local ratepayers would effectively serve their own sentence because they would have to offer the offender's family material support. If a young unmarried person was subjected to one of those penalties the community would only suffer if there was a severe labour shortage, which was not the case in south-east England by the late eighteenth century. The mobility and rootlessness of the young, their physical strength, and the sense that they were liable to commit rash, uncontrollable acts may have created greater anxiety and therefore motivated a higher proportion of victims to prosecute them. However, the main problem faced by young adults in their attempts to avoid prosecution for theft was the lack of any compelling argument in favour of treating them leniently. This was certainly not the case, by contrast, once the offender was married and had children to support.

5. *Family Poverty, Old Age, and Property Crime*

'A farmer's servant in this neighbourhood', Arthur Young recorded in his 1807 volume on Essex agriculture, 'continued in service till he was seven or eight and twenty years old . . . Having by this time accumulated about 40 pounds, he married a young woman, careful and industrious like himself . . . He had now no longer the plentiful and strengthening food of his master's table. His laborious efforts, however, instead of being remitted were . . . increased . . . With . . . persevering abstinence and industry, he maintained a family consisting of his wife and four or five children, without the smallest parochial assistance. These children, each successively at the age of fourteen or fifteen, went to service . . . He is now sixty years of age . . . Dry bread and small beer will no longer do, but it becomes necessary, occasionally, to add a little comfortable strengthening ale, to recruit his declining powers.' Young used this idealized life story as an example of the 'extraordinary' rise of a poor servant to the status of small farmer through 'frugality and active labour' but the overall life-cycle pattern it reveals was not untypical. Richard Smith uses a similar grouping (married at 27 and having four children) in his calculations about the changing fortunes of the average pre-industrial family across the life-cycle. Those calculations and parallel work on poor relief recipients indicate that, after a period of relative affluence prior to and immediately following marriage (i.e. in their twenties and early thirties), most couples entered a period of extreme poverty and vulnerability from their mid-thirties to their mid-forties as their families grew larger. If they were both still alive by their fifties they might then experience a period of relative affluence as their children left home and sometimes became net contributors to the family income. By their sixties, however, old age, declining earning powers, and the likely death of their spouse, combined with the fact that their children increasingly had families of their own to support, pushed most of the propertyless poor back into destitution or dependence on parish relief.[51]

Thus, most individuals were especially vulnerable to poverty at three stages in their lives—in childhood, when they were largely protected from prosecution for theft by legal immunities; in old age, when they were often too decrepit to commit most forms of direct theft; and in their child-rearing years. Given the tendency for childbearing to continue into the wife's later thirties, most couples faced the greatest risk of destitution in their later thirties and early forties.[52] This was also the peak age for parish runaways. Among the fathers (and occasionally mothers) who were advertised by their parishes in the Essex newspapers after deserting their families, 20 per cent were aged between 40 and 44 and more than half between 30 and 44 (Table 6.2). By contrast only 5 per cent of the property crime accused were aged between 40 and 44 and only 19 per cent were in their thirties (Table 6.1). While those in their late twenties were nearly twice as important among the accused as they were among the population in general, those in their forties were nearly twice as important within the general population as they were within the accused. The later thirties age range, when vulnerability to poverty was rising most rapidly, witnessed the greatest decline in vulnerability to prosecution for theft. Although a disproportionate number of offences may have been committed by those who had married early and were therefore burdened with children much sooner than most of their contemporaries, on the whole married men and women in the most vulnerable period of the family life-cycle were clearly prosecuted very much less frequently than single young adults and those in the less poverty-prone years immediately after their marriage.

Why? Lacking self-report studies, it is difficult to assess whether this decline in vulnerability to indictment mainly reflected a decline in lawbreaking activity by those in their thirties and forties or a change in the policies pursued by victims and magistrates. The attitudes of potential offenders may have changed over the life-cycle. Modern research has highlighted the connections between youthful crime and the need for excitement and peer approval, and has suggested that adults tend to desist from crime as concerns about employ-

---

[51] Young, *General View...Essex*, I, pp. 53–7. R. Smith, 'Some Issues Concerning Families and their Property in Rural England 1250–1800', and T. Wales, 'Poverty, Poor-Relief and the Life-Cycle. Some Evidence from Seventeenth-Century Norfolk' both are in R. Smith (ed.), *Land, Kinship and Lifecycle* (Cambridge, 1984), pp. 68–85, 351–88. A Beier, 'Poverty and Progress in Early Modern England', in A. Beier, D. Cannadine, and J. Rosenheim (eds.), *The First Modern Society* (Cambridge, 1989), pp. 212–13; Sokoll, *Household and Family*, pp. 165–7, 264–7. For a critical discussion, see B. Stapleton, 'Inherited Poverty and Life-Cycle Poverty: Odiham, Hampshire, 1650–1850', *Social History*, 18 (1993), pp. 339–55.

[52] Anderson, 'The Emergence', p. 73; Cunningham, 'The Employment', pp. 126–7 stresses that lack of suitable employment meant that children were often a burden until their early teens.

ment, income, spouse, and children become more central. A similar rhythm of changing preoccupations can be observed in the eighteenth-century autobio-graphies of Harriott, Mayett, Saxby, and William Hutton.[53] Although it is unclear how many potential offenders made conscious decisions along these lines, the personal costs of conviction were obviously much less severe for single young adults than for married men or women. Transportation, the central plank of major court penal policies and the maximum punishment for the petty larcenist, would wrench married men and women away from their families, usually forever. Contemporaries were much less certain that single unemployed young males would view this 'easy migration to a happier and better climate' in such a negative light.[54] However, given the central import-ance of the pretrial decisions of victims and magistrates, it was the tendency of both these groups to be particularly lenient towards offenders with children to support (Chapters 2 and 4) that was probably the key factor. The much lower indictment rates of those in their thirties or forties seen in Figures 6.1 and 6.3 were not merely a reflection of an inherent tendency for marriage, middle age, and geographical immobility to reduce lawbreaking activity. When the offence committed could only be tried in the major courts, victims had every reason to be highly selective. The more children a married offender had to support the greater the incentive to avoid bringing a formal prosecution against him or her.

This does not mean that poverty, economic vulnerability, or family destitu-tion did not play a part in a substantial proportion of property crime prosecu-tions. The accused not infrequently pleaded poverty and there is little reason to doubt that their pleas were genuine. Thomas Budder, accused of stealing oats at the Essex quarter sessions, confessed, 'it was his great poverty drove him to do it'. In 1785 William Fear stole some wool because he had 'a wife and five small children now reduced to great distress'. Two years later David Lewis stole two geese and a turkey. At the age of 44 he had ten children; the youngest was 1, the oldest 18. A glance at the precarious nature of the labourers' budgets collected by Eden and Davies is sufficient to explain his crime. As Table 6.1 indicates, prosecutions for felony were not, of course, reserved for young single adults alone. Nearly a third of the Home Circuit accused in the 1780s were over 29 and about 40 per cent were on or above the mean age at marriage. Since only a tiny fraction of the population as a whole managed to reach their early forties without marrying, a substantial minority of those accused of property crime were clearly married.[55] The court records do not usually

[53] Farrington, 'Age and Crime', pp. 231–2; Hutton, *The Life;* Kussmaul (ed.), *The Autobiography;* Harriott, *Struggles;* Saxby, *Memoirs*, pp. 13–14.

[54] For an interesting modern analysis of the ways the external costs of delinquency increase with age, Greenberg, 'Delinquency'; Radzinowicz, *History*, 1, pp. 31–2.

[55] E.R.O. Q/SBb 232/24; P.R.O. HO 47/6; Sokoll, 'Early Attempts'. For other pleas of destitution, Emsley, *Crime*, p. 33; E. A. Wrigley, 'Marriage, Fertility and Population Growth in Eighteenth-Century

record the marital state of male offenders, but more than a third of female assizes accused were either wives or widows. The life stories of male Essex-based criminals, despite their untypicality (highway robbers with long careers made the best copy), suggest a similar figure for men. At least twelve of the twenty-nine offenders described in these accounts had been married, or were still married when they were arrested. All those aged under 27 appear to have been single, but at least two-thirds of those in their thirties or forties were married and half of these had children.[56]

Since even those members of the labouring poor who were not burdened with families could sometimes be brought near to destitution by illness, unemployment, a severe winter, or an acute harvest failure, it would be unwise to conclude that severe deprivation did not form the background to a very significant proportion of property crime prosecutions. The seasonal distribution of food and fuel indictments focused mainly on the winter months, and Essex indictment rates for all property crimes were also slightly higher in winter than in summer—a pattern usually associated with the greater unemployment and material deprivation experienced by the poor in these months and with the opportunities provided by longer winter nights.[57] However, the seasonal distribution of property crime indictments in Essex did not display a uniform pattern of low rates over the whole summer period. The early summer months witnessed the lowest prosecution rates, but indictment levels in the second half of the summer were as high as those of January and February (Figure 6.4). Seasonal migration may well have been as important in shaping the seasonality of indictments as the deprivations and high unemployment levels of winter. The second half of the summer not only saw the largest influx of migrant workers; it was also the peak period for advertisements involving deserters and runaway apprentices, as well as being the time of year when artisans made most use of the tramping system.[58] In predominantly pastoral counties like Somerset indictment rates were uniformly low throughout the summer months but in expanding arable areas such as Essex, which required large influxes of workers for the grain harvest, indictment rates

England', in R. Outhwaite (ed.), *Marriage and Society. Studies in the Social History of Marriage* (London, 1981), pp. 149–51.

[56] Female marital status based on all Essex assize offenders for whom marital status and age are recorded, 1776–1799. P.R.O. Assi 31/12–19. I have so far traced only 21 Essex life stories giving the offender's age; 11 were under 30, 7 were in their thirties. Most are from the *Chelmsford Chronicle* or the Saffron Walden Museum crime drawer. Other sources: *Ipswich Journal; The Ordinary of Newgate's Account; The Genuine and Particular Narrative.*

[57] Seasonal distributions rely on the dates in indictments. Cockburn doubts their reliability in earlier assize records because peaks sometimes occur just before each assizes, but no such pattern is observable for the Essex Lent assizes or for any of the four quarter sessions sittings 1786–95. Cockburn, 'Early Modern Assize Records', pp. 225–6; King, 'Crime, Law', pp. 115–20

[58] Rule, *The Experience*, p. 51; Snell, *Annals*, p. 20, for high winter unemployment. Nearly a quarter of adverts about deserters appeared in August and September and 22 per cent of adverts for runaway apprentices were placed in August alone. Southall, 'The Tramping', p. 280.

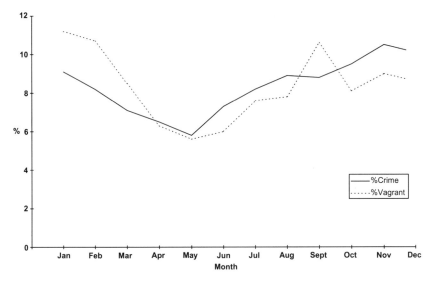

Fig. 6.4 Seasonal Distribution, Essex Property Crime Indictments, 1785–95, and Vagrancy Arrests, 1779–91

Source: E.R.O. Q/RSV 1/2, 8, 12, 18, 20, 27, 31 and Q/SR 839–83, P.R.O. Assi 35/225–36.

and vagrancy arrest rates were much higher around harvest time than they were in spring (Figure 6.4).[59]

The dominance of young adults among those indicted for property crime and the tendency for indictment rates to decline rapidly at precisely the point in the life-cycle where vulnerability to family destitution was highest indicate that prosecution patterns were not primarily linked to the deprivations suffered by those who were indicted. However, the limited information available about summary prosecutions, which entailed less drastic punishments and did not therefore leave a married offender's family permanently chargeable to the parish, suggests that the age structure of summarily convicted offenders contained slightly higher proportions of older men and women.[60] If systematic

[59] For Somerset, see Pole, 'Crime', pp. 148–9; King, 'Crime, Law', pp. 115–20. In Essex, July and October (when harvest workers were either moving between hay-making and corn-harvesting, or returning to their previous localities) witnessed particularly high levels of indictments. Since some harvest workers who had outstayed their welcome were labelled as vagrants. (Collins, 'Migrant Labour', p. 54; D. Jones, 'The Vagrant and Crime in Victorian Britain. Problems of Definition and Attitude', in Jones, *Crime*, p. 183), it is interesting to note that vagrancy in Essex followed a similar seasonal pattern. Fig. 6.4 does not show these peaks because it is based on a three-month moving average.

[60] The Gloucestershire gaol calendars and Littledean house of correction registers reveal the following: 0–14 = 0, 15–19 = 2, 20–4 = 5, 25–9 = 10, 30–4 = 5, 35–9 = 4, 40–9 = 3, 50–9 = 2. Gloucestershire RO. Q/GLi 16/1, Q/SG2. These are almost all wood and game convictions. In Essex the seasonal distribution of summary convictions for these two offences was heavily weighted towards the winter months. Two-thirds of Essex wood stealing convictions and half of game ones were recorded between December and March. Game theft was also related to opportunity, nearly one-third of the

information about the ages of offenders in the lower courts became available, it might well enable somewhat closer links to be made between family poverty and property crime prosecutions.

6. Female Offenders

In the eighteenth century the sex of the potential accused was a crucial variable in predicting their vulnerability to prosecution. Although in cities such as London and Newcastle women sometimes had a major impact, in non-metropolitan areas such as Sussex and rural Surrey females accounted for only a small proportion of property crime indictments and relatively few women were accused of capital offences or violent forms of theft.[61] This pattern is fully confirmed by the Essex evidence. Only 13 per cent of those indicted for property crime between 1740 and 1804 were female and only a handful of highway robbery, horse, or sheep theft accusations were directed against women (Table 6.4). In the late eighteenth century females constituted 9 per cent of the accused at the Essex assizes but more than twice that figure at the quarter sessions which dealt only with minor thefts. Among summary offenders they formed about one-ninth of wood and vegetable thieves, but were very rarely prosecuted for taking game. The main targets of female thieves were fuel, clothing, and shop goods. In the eighteenth century, as in the twentieth, simple larceny, receiving, and shoplifting were the main types of reported property crime that attracted above average proportions of females[62] (Table 6.4).

Table 6.4. Female Property Offenders, Essex, 1740–1804

	Females	Total	% Female
Petty larceny	332	1,709	19.4
Grand larceny	243	1,996	12.2
Burglary and housebreaking	84	669	12.6
Horse stealing	1	222	0.5
Sheep stealing	2	264	0.8
Highway robbery	6	379	1.6
Indirect appropriation	77	411	18.7
All property crimes	745	5,650	13.2

Sources: Offenders, not charges. Assizes, quarter sessions, and all borough courts, 1740–1805.

convictions being brought in October or November, when game was particularly plentiful: King, 'Crime, Law', p. 117.

[61] Beattie, *Crime*, pp. 237–43; Beattie, 'The Criminality of Women', pp. 80–116; see also Rudé, *Criminal and Victim*, pp. 40–62; on London and Newcastle—Beattie, 'Crime and Inequality', pp. 135–6; Morgan and Rushton, *Rogues, Thieves*, p. 68.

[62] F. Heidensohn, *Women and Crime*, pp. 5–10; C. Smart, *Women, Crime and Criminology. A Feminist Critique* (London, 1976), pp. 10–11. On the Home Circuit, 1782–7, 62 per cent of shoplifters and 42 per cent of receivers were women: Pole, 'Crime', p. 139. There seems to have been very little change in

Women's crimes were almost certainly less well reported than men's. In their attempts to explain why twentieth-century crime figures also contain relatively few women, criminologists have used self-report studies to show that gender differences in offence rates are rather less marked than the official statistics suggest. However, the differences are still there. Self-report and victim surveys, Heidensohn has recently concluded, 'broadly... confirm the picture of crime as a largely male activity'.[63] Such a conclusion, in relation to property crimes at least, would not have surprised early Victorian writers. While some stressed that women's lack of physical strength prevented them from committing violent robberies and other property thefts, most had little difficulty in accepting low female crime rates because they expected women to be morally superior to men; to be innately less acquisitive or competitive and therefore less likely to steal or defraud. While Jonas Hanway, writing in the late eighteenth century, embraced some of these notions he also introduced other themes. 'I believe the lives of women are comparatively more free from atrocious guilt', he wrote, 'and that from a habit of obedience they live more submissively to the decrees of heaven; perhaps being less deeply engaged in views of avarice and ambition, and not subject to such a variety of temptations.'[64]

Was the socialization process women were subject to so deeply patriarchal that it created habits of obedience and passivity that made them much less likely to commit property crimes? More centrally perhaps, were their spheres of operation so much more constrained than men's and their behaviour and movements subjected to so much more surveillance that they inevitably experienced fewer opportunities to commit thefts? Mitterauer has argued that young women had considerably less freedom to pursue postwork leisure activities and there is clear evidence that the exclusion of women from the majority of work roles outside the household reduced the likelihood that they would be accused of property crimes. The absence of women among those indicted for stealing stores from naval shipyards, coal from delivery carts, or grain from threshing floors is hardly surprising since they rarely had any involvement in these forms of work. By contrast, summary convictions for the theft of textile materials indicate how deeply the opportunities provided by work affected sexual differences in recorded crime rates. Most of these offences

---

Essex between the mid-seventeenth century, when 14.4 per cent of quarter sessions and assizes accused were women, and 1740–1804, when 13.2 per cent were. For a different view based on Old Bailey evidence, M. Feeley and D. Little, 'The Vanishing Female. The Decline of Women in the Criminal Process 1687–1912', *Law and Society Review*, 25 (1991), 719–57; Sharpe, *Crime in Seventeenth-Century England*, p. 95; G. Walker, 'Women, Theft and the World of Stolen Goods', in J. Kermode and G. Walker (eds.), *Women, Crime and the Courts in Early Modern England* (London, 1994).

[63] Heidensohn, *Crime*, p. 87; A. Morris, *Women, Crime and Criminal Justice* (Oxford, 1987), pp. 24–5. About a fifth of the suspects named by the rural diarists sampled in Chapter 2 were women, a higher proportion than that found among indictments in rural areas.

[64] L. Zedner, *Women, Crime and Custody in Victorian England* (Oxford, 1991), pp. 23–4; J. Hanway, *Advice from Farmer Trueman to his Daughter* (2nd edn., Pontefract, 1805), pp. 67–71.

were committed during the female-dominated spinning process and two-thirds of the accused were women.[65]

The tendency for urban women to form a higher proportion of the accused than their rural counterparts may also be linked to differences in work opportunities and levels of personal freedom. In south-east England women clearly appeared more frequently among the accused the nearer the area was to London. While 24 per cent of property crime offenders at the Surrey quarter sessions and assizes were women, the equivalent figure for Sussex was 13 per cent. The percentages at the assizes were generally lower because only major crimes were involved, but the differentials remained the same. In Surrey the figure was 15 per cent; in Sussex 7 per cent (Table 6.5). At the Old Bailey around a quarter of offenders were women in the early 1790s—a differential that was too large to be caused only by the fact that women may have formed a higher proportion of the London population.[66] John Beattie has argued that these differences reflected the much closer controls placed on women's working lives and social contacts in rural communities, and the tendency for the London labour market to become over-stocked because it was such a magnet for young rural women. Employment was more irregular in the capital and anxieties about the independence women enjoyed were greater. In addition, many young female migrants, lacking strong support networks, could quickly become destitute if they lost their 'place' and might then be forced to earn their living illegally as part of London's exceptionally well-developed receiving networks, rookeries, and prostitution trade.[67] Arguments applicable to the metropolis may, however, have little relevance to most provincial towns. London was a colossus. A magnet for luxury goods, leisure activities, and entertainment which offered unique opportunities and temptations. Although the provincial towns attracted many young female migrants and had a distinctly female-biased sex structure as a result, it cannot be assumed that they also produced a higher percentage of female indictments. In the six Essex towns without borough courts sampled between 1781 and 1800 the proportion of female accused was lower than the county average. Where a major court was available within the town, however, the picture was very different. In the county town of Chelmsford the proportion of females was 75 per cent higher and in the three boroughs with active quarter sessions

---

[65] Mitterauer, A History, p. 44. On false reeling—Styles, 'Policing a Female Workforce'; P. Lane, 'Work on the Margins. Poor Women and the Informal Economy of Eighteenth and Early Nineteenth-Century Leicestershire', Midland History, 22 (1997), 98–9.

[66] Beattie, Crime, pp. 239–40: urban Surrey 28.5 per cent, rural 14.3; King, 'Female Offenders', p. 67; Rudé, Criminal and Victim, pp. 40–62; P.R.O. H.O 26/1–2; B. Hill 'The Marriage Age of Women and the Demographers', History Workshop Journal, 28 (1989), 134.

[67] Beattie, 'The Criminality of Women'; Beattie, 'Crime and Inequality', pp. 134–6; McMullan, The Canting Crew; Corfield, The Impact, pp. 66–81; King, 'Female Offenders'; George, London Life; pp. 119–20; T. Henderson, Disorderly Women in Eighteenth-Century London. Prostitution and its Control in the Metropolis 1730–1830 (London, 1999).

Table 6.5. Female Offenders in the Five Home
Circuit Counties, 1782–7 and 1799–1800

County	Female	Total	% Female
Surrey	98	667	14.7
Kent	83	713	11.6
Essex	42	467	9.0
Herts	18	230	7.8
Sussex	10	146	6.8
Total	251	2223	11.3

Sources: Assi 31/13–15 and 18–19.

jurisdictions it was more than twice the county average. This pattern is also observable in Surrey where nearly 40 per cent of those indicted at the South-wark Borough sessions were female.[68]

Since the economic profiles of the borough and non-borough towns in the Essex sample were very similar, the contrasts in female involvement levels almost certainly reflect differences in the behaviour of magistrates and victims. Borough magistrates were usually more readily available and were drawn from commercially minded town élites, who may well have been more willing to commit women for trial than their rural counterparts. Moreover, in minor larceny cases the pleas of female offenders for lenience were much less likely to fall on deaf ears when the victim was faced with a costly and time-consuming journey, while the lighter punishments usually given by borough courts may also have eroded their inhabitants' reluctance to prosecute in cases involving women. Rural communities seem to have had strong traditions about the importance of using informal sanctions when the suspect was female. So, it appears, did small towns some distance from a quarter sessions or borough court. The number of women prosecuted in many of these towns was extremely small. In 1793 Bocking contained a thousand women aged 15 or above, yet the town produced only one female indictment per decade between 1781 and 1800. Halstead and Dunmow could manage only one female indictment between them in these twenty years although they contained nearly 2,000 adult women. Informal sanctions, negotiated settlements, and summary prosecutions were clearly the dominant responses of such communities to female crime.[69]

[68] P. Borsay (ed.), *The Eighteenth-Century Town. A Reader in English Urban History 1688–1820* (London, 1990), pp. 8–9; P. Clark (ed.), *The Transformation of English Provincial Towns* (London, 1984), p. 18; Beattie, *Crime*, p. 241. Between 1781 and 1800 in six non-borough towns (Bocking, Braintree, Halstead, Waltham Abbey, Epping, Dunmow) 18 of the 194 property offenders indicted at the assizes or quarter sessions were female (9 per cent). The Halstead figures were 0 out of 17, Dunmow's were 1 out of 21. In Chelmsford, the assizes town, 23 per cent were female. In the three borough towns the figures were Colchester 31 per cent, Saffron Walden 27 per cent, Harwich 31 per cent. The average for the whole county was 13 per cent.

[69] P. King, 'Urban Crime Rates' discusses the general impact of borough court availability. C. Rowntree, *Saffron Walden Then and Now* (Chelmsford, 1951). *V.C.H. Essex*, 2, pp. 346–9.

The fragments of information available suggest that women had the advantage at virtually every stage of the pretrial process. If, as seems likely, it was widely assumed that women were less criminally inclined than men and less physically capable of committing certain crimes, they would be in less danger of becoming suspects. Moreover, the types of indirect appropriation that women were perceived as most likely to commit were among the most difficult property offences to prosecute successfully. Women's deep involvement in the retail trades and in buying provisions meant that they were much better represented among the small number of offenders indicted for receiving stolen goods or for uttering false coin than they were among indictments in general, but charges involving these indirect appropriations were very difficult to bring, because it was rarely possible to prove that the accused had knowingly committed the offence. Women certainly seem to have fared better in post-arrest negotiations just as they do today in cautioning processes. All the nine female offenders who were suspected of stealing from the diarists sampled in Chapter 2 avoided prosecution.[70] In the late eighteenth century a male victim of the Essex thief Fanny Davis refused to indict her despite having her committed for trial because he 'did not like to prosecute a poor weak woman lest he should meet the contempt of the crowd and the laugh of the lawyers'. Finally, in the summary courts, as Shoemaker has shown, magistrates tended to refer a smaller proportion of cases involving women on for further action or indictment. This may have been partly because women committed relatively minor thefts or because they were perceived to be less persistent or troublesome offenders, rather than simply because they were female,[71] but gender stereotypes played a significant part in the process by which many women avoided detection and prosecution.

There can be no doubt that the relentless logic of patriarchy protected many married women who committed property offences in the presence of their husbands. 'Neither a son or a servant are excused...of any crime...by the command or coercion of the parent or master', wrote Blackstone. However 'if a woman commit theft...by the coercion of her husband; or merely by his command; ...she is not guilty of any crime: being considered as acting by compulsion and not of her own will'. This dictum was widely quoted by justices' handbooks and by judges. In 1785 the Recorder of London announced that 'wives committing any crime except treason or murder in the presence of their husbands were by law exempt from bearing any share in the punishment due to the offence because they were supposed to be acting under

---

[70] Zedner, *Women*, p. 27; Beattie, *Crime*, pp. 189–92; Mitchell (ed.), *The Purefoy Letters*, pp. 137–40; Bagley (ed.), *The Great Diurnal*, 2, pp. 112–14; Beresford (ed.), *Diary of A Country Parson*, 2, pp. 225–6; 5, p. 297; Cozens-Hardy (ed.), *Mary Hardy's Diary*, p. 84; Stokes (ed.), *The Bletcheley Diary*, p. 11; Ayers (ed.), *Paupers and Pig-killers*, pp. 25–9. On modern cautioning ratios by sex, Walker, *Crime and Criminology*, p. 124; Morris, *Women*, pp. 80–1.

[71] Shoemaker, *Prosecution*, pp. 212–13; *Authentic Account...Fanny Davies*, p. 31.

the influence of their husbands, whose orders the law did not suppose them daring enough to resist'. This was not mere rhetoric. Between 1776 and 1800 almost every Essex codefendant wife whose husband was found guilty was acquitted. Moreover, only a dozen or so wives in this situation were indicted at all, which suggests that many victims were discouraged from prosecuting wives in these circumstances. The Chelmsford petty sessions used pretrial imprisonment as an alternative sanction in such cases. In 1804 Stephen Harvey was 'fully committed' and tried for burglary but his wife was 'committed but not intended to be indicted'. The protection offered to wives was even extended to some unmarried women who had cohabited with their male codefendants. In 1785 the Recorder argued that 'in criminal courts it was not the practice ... to insist on the production of a marriage certificate, or any other proofs of matrimony than that the parties had lived together as man and wife'. Although the resulting acquittal was hotly contested in *The Times* because it encouraged 'immoral living', a similar defence saved Elizabeth Jacobs when she was prosecuted with William Reed in 1792. After three witnesses had proved that they had lived together as man and wife and had 'always passed so', she was acquitted and he was transported.[72] Since patriarchal assumptions were therefore institutionalized within both formal legal rulings and pretrial practices, the relative paucity of women among indicted property offenders probably had less to do with the ways different socialization processes, physical capacities, and levels of social surveillance limited women's lawbreaking activities than with the ways social definitions of gender roles not only limited women's access to public employment but also affected the decisions of victims, parish officials, and magistrates.

Did female indictment rates follow roughly the same life-cycle patterns as male ones? Despite the fact that only 11 per cent of Home Circuit property crime indictments involved women, the patterns are very similar. Both male and female age structures peaked massively between the ages of 16 and 26 (Figure 6.5). Those aged 16 to 26 represented 56 per cent of all the accused and 52 per cent of the female accused. For both genders the highly mobile period between the usual age of leaving home and the average age of marriage was the key period of vulnerability to prosecution for major offences.[73] Around this central core, however, a number of significant differences between genders can be observed. Female age structures rose earlier and to a slightly more pronounced peak around 20 and 21. They then fell more rapidly so that the percentage of female accused in their mid-twenties was considerably smaller

---

[72] Blackstone, *Commentaries*, 4, p. 28; *The Times*, 15 and 27 Jan. and 1 Feb. 1785; *OBSP*, January 1792. Williams, *Every Man*, p. 421; Burn, *The Justice* (1797), 4, pp. 351–6. For a more cautious view, Beattie, 'The Criminality of Women', pp. 95–6. E.R.O. P/CM 1, 6 July 1804. For a more detailed discussion of this principle of 'femme covert', see Chapter 8.

[73] Women married between one and two years earlier than men on average. Schofield and Wrigley, *Population History*, p. 255; they left home slightly later: Snell, *Annals*, pp. 323–6. For parallel London evidence, King, 'Female Offenders'.

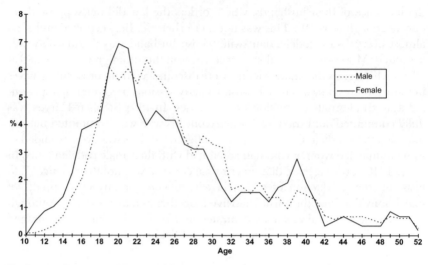

Fig. 6.5 Age Structure of Male and Female Property Offenders, Home Circuit Counties, 1782–7
Source: P.R.O. Assi 31/13–15.

than that of males. In the late thirties the impact of females on the accused rose briefly by about a third. Women also formed a slightly larger proportion of elderly offenders, reflecting their relative longevity and, perhaps, the problems of widowhood.

Given that assizes indictments were biased towards major offences in which women's involvement was less extensive, these data must be interpreted with care. However, the age structures of females at the Gloucestershire assizes and quarter sessions were fairly similar, and although the quarter sessions accused may have included slightly higher proportions of young girls and of women over 35, the Home Circuit pattern would probably not have been very different if the more minor offenders tried at the quarter sessions could be included.[74] The female age structure at the assizes certainly fits in well with the limited information available on other dimensions of the lives of female offenders—their marital status, migration patterns, work roles, and vulnerability to poverty and unemployment.

The eighteenth-century criminal records, unlike their counterparts in earlier centuries, appear to have recorded female offenders' marital status fairly accurately. The differing vulnerabilities to prosecution of single women, wives, and widows can therefore be examined. Marriage was a key turning-point for many women. As the percentage of the female population that were married

---

[74] Gloucestershire R.O. Q/SG2. Calendars of prisoners in the county gaol, which survive sporadically and include only a sample of assizes prisoners. 7 per cent of females indicted at the Gloucestershire quarter sessions 1789–1815 were below 16. At the assizes the figure was 4 per cent; 26 per cent and 19 per cent were the figures for those over 35. Sample sizes: 154 quarter sessions, 108 assizes.

increased rapidly from the early or mid-twenties to the early thirties, the likelihood of prosecution for theft declined with equal rapidity. A women in her twentieth or twenty-first year was four times as likely to be indicted for property crime as her equivalent who was a dozen years older. Less than 2 per cent of women were married when they reached 20, but well over 70 per cent of those aged 30–4 years were either wives or widows.[75] The average age at marriage for females was just over 24 years in the late eighteenth century. Averages can be misleading, however. Many women married much earlier or later than the mean, widowhood and remarriage were common, and between 4 and 7 per cent never married at all. It is possible, for example, that those marrying earlier were more likely to commit offences because their larger families made them particularly vulnerable to extreme poverty or destitution.[76]

Did married women form a larger or smaller percentage of the accused than they did of the population as a whole? Around 12 per cent of the female population over 9 were widows, the remainder being fairly evenly divided between single women and wives (Table 6.6). Among female offenders, whether they were indicted at the Essex assizes or at the quarter sessions, single women were much more dominant. Three-fifths of offenders were single. Only 25–30 per cent were married. The rapid decline in the age structure of female offenders around the average age at marriage was not coincidental. Married women were less vulnerable and single women considerably more vulnerable to prosecution. Widows formed about the same proportion of the accused as they did of the general population. Their greater

Table 6.6. Marital Status of all Females and Female Offenders in the Late Eighteenth Century

	Essex assizes 1776–1804	Essex quarter/sessions 1750–75	All females over 9 in 1801	Essex assizes, 1776–99 Marital status by age group		
				0–19	20–29	Over 30
% Single	61.5	60.7	44–5	100	76	31
% Married	29.6	25.0	43–4	0	21	46
% Widowed	8.9	14.3	12	0	3	23
Total	100	100	99–101	100	100	100
n =	135	84	—			

Sources: Third column based on Laslett and Wall, Household, p. 145 adjusted by removing those aged under 10 using the 1801 figures for female age structures in Wrigley and Schofield, Population, p. 121. E.R.O. Q/SPb 10–15; P.R.O. Assi 35/216–44.

[75] Cockburn, 'Early Modern Assize Records', p. 223; P. Laslett, Family Life and Illicit Love in Earlier Generations (Cambridge, 1977), p. 27.

[76] Schofield and Wrigley, Population History, p. 424; P. Earle, 'The Female Labour Market in London in the Late Seventeenth and Eighteenth Centuries', Economic History Review, 42 (1989), 345; Wrigley, 'Marriage, Fertility', pp. 149–51. Women marrying in their early twenties had considerably larger families; Laslett and Wall, Household, p. 145.

prevalence at the quarter sessions (Table 6.6) suggests either that they were more involved in minor offences or that they benefited from prosecutor leniency when it came to the choice of court.

The proportions of spinsters, married women, and widows within each age group among Essex offenders (Table 6.6) reveal that all female offenders under 20 were single—a similar pattern to that in the population as a whole; while three-quarters of offenders in their twenties were also single.[77] By the 30–45-year-old age group married women and widows formed a majority among offenders for the first time but nearly a third were still single—a much higher proportion than that found among this age group in the general population. Thus, single women were much more vulnerable to prosecution than wives or widows, but this does not mean that married women committed fewer crimes. Co-defendant immunity, wives' genuine pleas of destitution, and ratepayers' anxieties about future burdens almost certainly meant that a smaller propor-tion of married female thieves were prosecuted. Equally prosecutors and magistrates may have been particularly keen to prosecute property offences by single women in their teens and early twenties for two other reasons. First, young girls were thought by many to be in particular need of protection or regulation. Contemporaries often commented on the frequency with which unsupervised female servants became pregnant or took to prostitution, and the few statistics available to them appeared to confirm this: 70 per cent of the unmarried mothers admitted to the Foundling Hospital were servants, the peak age for such pregnancies being the early twenties.[78] Second, young women in their mid-to-late teens or early twenties were much more mobile than at other points in the life-cycle. The age structure of the female vagrants examined by Essex magistrates, which was not distorted by enlistment as the male equivalent was, reached a sharp peak between 18 and 21. In the period 1779–91 56 per cent of Essex female vagrants were aged between 16 and 26.[79] The complex relationship between mobility, living-in service, and vulnerabil-ity to prosecution outlined earlier in this chapter seems to have worked in much the same way for both sexes. However, in the late eighteenth century both service in husbandry and (Snell has argued) women's employment opportunities in agriculture were beginning to decline, as were spinning employment and the range of trades to which they could gain access. Con-versely, the feminization of domestic service was gathering momentum.

[77] Some of these were single parents. When an Essex constable was asked in relation to two spinsters accused of shoplifting 'what manner of livelihood do they follow?' he replied 'they lodge in one room, ... they have both ... got bastards', *Proceedings ... Essex. March 1774*, p. 2.

[78] Anon., *A Present*, pp. 44–5; Hanway, *Advice*, p. 114; Although the absolute numbers are small, the fact that a quarter of the accused aged under 16 were women may indicate that anxieties about the need to regulate young girls as they matured sexually eroded victims' reluctance to prosecute minor acts of appropriation by females. For a modern analysis of the tendency to 'sexualize' normal female delinquency, Heidensohn, *Women*, p. 48.

[79] E.R.O. Q/R.S.V. 1/1, 2, 7, 8, 12, 14–18, 20.

London had long been a powerful magnet for young women. Some were seasonal migrants who came to work for the summer in the market gardening areas around London, but the majority had longer-term plans. As Arthur Young commented in 1771, 'Young men and women in the country fix their eye on London as the last stage of their hope; they enter into service in the country for little else but to raise enough money to go to London...the number of young women that fly thither is almost incredible.' In the eighteenth century most female migrants came relatively late to London. They left home slightly later, on average, than males and would usually gain considerable experience of work before they came to the capital. To quote Peter Earle: 'A common experience was for a girl to leave home in her late teens or very early twenties, work for a year or two ... with a country family or in the nearby market town and then make the move to London.' Only about a quarter of the migrants whose detailed movements he was able to reconstruct were less than 20 on arrival in London, while nearly half were aged 20–5.[80] If the female migrants on average moved rather later to London but in greater numbers, this outmigration from the Home Counties may partly explain why the involvement of women among the Home Circuit accused declined more rapidly than that of men between the ages of 20 and 25.

What was the relationship between women's work patterns and their vulnerability to prosecution at different points in the life-cycle? Outside the limited areas where lacemaking or other specialized women's work enabled them to continue in full-time employment after marriage, female labour participation ratios followed the same pattern as female vulnerability to prosecution, rising rapidly to a peak in the early twenties and then falling away steeply following marriage. More specific links are, however, difficult to make because the status labels used in indictments and other court records only record women's relationships to men. However, fifteen of the thirty-one trials involving female accused described in the few printed trial reports that survive for the Home Circuit do give indirect information about the occupation of the accused.[81] Nine of the fifteen were living-in servants or ex-servants, thus confirming the contemporary observation that 'our sessions papers of late are crowded with instances of servant maids robbing their places'. The prevalence of female servant crime is not particularly surprising. As Fielding

---

[80] Snell, *Annals*, pp. 15–103 and 270–319; Sharpe, *Adapting to Capitalism*, pp. 75–7 finds Snell unconvincing; Kussmaul, *Servants*, pp. 115–25; B. Hill, *Women, Work and Sexual Politics in Eighteenth-Century England* (Oxford, 1989), p. 128; George, *London Life*, pp. 145, 157; Earle, 'The Female Labour', pp. 344–5; P. Earle, *A City Full of People. Men and Women of London 1650–1750* (London, 1994), pp. 123–30; Mitterauer, *A History*, p. 127.

[81] O. Saito, 'Who Worked When: Life-Time Profiles of Labour Force Participation in Cardington and Corfe Castle in the Late Eighteenth and Mid-Nineteenth Centuries', *Local Population Studies*, 22 (1979), 14–29; King, 'Female Offenders'; *Genuine Proceedings...Home Circuit...March 1739; Proceedings at the Assizes...Surrey and Essex...July 1740; Whole Proceedings...March 1774* (all counties) on the Home Circuit reports that survive in full. To this were added *Proceedings...Surrey March 1759; Whole Genuine Proceedings...Kent...March 1766* and a case in *Che.C.*, 17 Mar. 1786.

pointed out in 1758, 'The infinite variety of professions, trades and manufactures joined to the army, navy and services, leave few men idle except from choice; whilst women have but few trades and fewer manufactures to employ them. Hence it is, that the general recourse of young women is to go to service.'[82]

Pilfering was clearly as much a tradition among female servants as among their male counterparts. The wages of female servants were low and the temptations were great. Advice books listed the many forms of petty appropriation maid servants could use to improve their living standards. 'The most pernicious', Defoe noted in a pamphlet on the 'private abuses... of our women servants', 'are those who beggar you inch-meal. If a maid is a downright thief she strips you at once and you know your loss, but these retail pilferers waste you insensibly ... What harm is there, say they in cribbing a little matter for a junket, a merry bout or so.' In his 'Country Housewife's Family Companion' the Hertfordshire farmer William Ellis suggested that this was also a familiar pattern in the Home Counties when he described a local maid servant 'who was both a drunkard and a thief... insomuch that she would carry out bread, cheese and other provisions and give them away to a neighbouring gin-seller, where she now and then got intoxicated'.[83]

Although most of the female servants appearing in the trial reports had committed thefts while still in residence, others took their employer's goods after being dismissed or deciding to run away. Mary Mann, for example, after leaving her position with an Essex farming family in 1774, soon found herself without 'a farthing in the world'. She therefore returned to her old mistress saying that 'if she did not get a place in a few days she would go down to the waterside and sell herself'. Her old employers having offered her temporary shelter, she quickly changed her plans, stole £10 from their cupboard, and eventually found herself bound for America by order of the Essex assizes. Because many young women who had lost or abandoned their place found it very difficult to make ends meet in the eighteenth century, the fluid seasonal and insecure world of female service often overlapped with the world of prostitution. Defoe, for example, believed that female servants 'if they are out of place ... must prostitute their bodies or starve; so that from chopping and changing, they generally proceed to whoring and thieving'.[84] It is less easy

---

[82] A. Moreton (D. Defoe), *Everybody's Business is Nobody's Business* (1725) p. 8; Laslett, *Family Life*, p. 34; D. Kent, 'Ubiquitous but Invisible. Female Domestic Servants in Mid-Eighteenth Century London', *History Workshop Journal*, 28 (1989), 111–27. Hill, *Women*, p. 128.

[83] Anon., *A Present*, lists many forms of dishonesty; Sharpe, *Adapting to Capitalism*, p. 115; V. Bell, *To Meet Mr Ellis. Little Gaddesden in the Eighteenth Century*, p. 72; King, 'Female Offenders', pp. 75–7; Defoe, *Everybody's*, pp. 9–11; Hill, *Women, Work*, pp. 140–1. For London, see P. Humfrey, 'Female Servants and Women's Criminality in Early Eighteenth-Century London', in G. Smith, A. May, and S. Deveraux (eds.), *Criminal Justice in the Old World and the New* (Toronto, 1998), pp. 58–84.

[84] *Whole Proceedings ... Essex March 1774*, p. 5; Defoe, *Everybody's*, p. 8; George, *London Life*, p. 119 for a similar Fielding quote. After running away from home Mary Saxby was sorely tempted by hunger to steal or to become a prostitute—Saxby, *Memoirs*, pp. 7–8. Henderson, *Disorderly Women*, pp. 14–16.

to link property offences with prostitutes in the provinces than it is to do so in London, where prostitution was a vast, and highly visible, trade. However, at least three of the female offenders described in the trial reports were following this calling at the time of their offences. Usually the theft took place during or after the promised sexual transaction, but occasionally the offence arose from a dispute within the trade. In 1774 two Essex prostitutes insisted that a third, who was probably straying onto their territory, should pay what they called 'footing'. When she refused they cut off the front of her gown, took her money, and stabbed her in the groin.[85]

The only other female offenders whose occupations are indicated in the Home Circuit trial reports were an 'old clothes' dealer indicted for receiving and a Deptford broker accused of paying too low a price for some furniture. Two others were clearly destitute and presumably unemployed. Ann Ford was 'drove to the greatest distress' after being thrown out of the Deptford work-house in the middle of winter. She stole a beaver great coat. Rose Pluckrose, an Essex defendant accused of stealing 5 shillings simply pleaded, 'I have a bad husband and three children ready to starve with hunger.' Rose's testimony suggests that the slightly larger proportion of those indicted in their late thirties that were female (Figure 6.5) was probably linked to women's particular vulnerability to destitution in these peak child-rearing years—years when many had tempting access to the households of the wealthy in their roles as daily chars, nurses, or washerwomen.[86] However, the dominance of young single women among the Home Circuit accused suggests that family poverty played a very minor role in shaping patterns of recorded crime. Women were most vulnerable to prosecution for property crime in the period of high mobility and intermittent spells of living-in service they experienced between leaving home for the first time in their mid-teens and their marriage in the early or mid twenties—a period which also coincided with the peak point of official anxieties about the need to regulate young women's behaviour.

7. The Social and Occupational Status of the Accused

The reactions of victims, magistrates, and those involved in detection affected not only the age and sex structure of those indicted for property offences, but also the occupations and social status of the accused. The likelihood that an offence would be detected or prosecuted varied according to the social position

[85] *Proceedings ... Surrey ... July 1740*, p. 10; *Proceedings ... Essex ... March 1774*, p. 26. Fanny Davis was a prostitute but her thieving activities were not confined to that context: *Authentic Account ... Fanny Davis*, pp. 35–47; Sharpe, *Adapting to Capitalism*, pp. 132–3; Sharpe, *Crime in Early Modern England*, pp.110–15; King 'Female Offenders', pp. 77–80; McMullan, *The Canting Crew*, pp. 117–42; Henderson, *Disorderly Women*, pp. 27–74.
[86] *Genuine Proceedings ... Home Circuit March 1739*, p. 15; *Proceedings ... Surrey ... March 1759*, p. 4; *Whole Proceedings ... Kent ... March 1774*, p. 19; *Proceedings ... Essex ... July 1740*, p. 15. On older women's vulner-ability to prosecution in London—King, 'Female Offenders', pp. 80–2.

of the offender. A skilled artisan accused of pilfering from his master, or a shopkeeper confronted with a neighbour who had discovered his son illegally removing property, had many more options open to him than a labourer. Masters needed skilled workers. Shopkeepers could offer a substantial package of material rewards to encourage the victim to compound. Should these prove ineffective, more subtle social pressures and influences might be brought to bear if a section of the local community was reluctant to allow a useful member to be committed for trial. The likelihood of detection also varied significantly. The embezzlement or fraudulent practices of commercial men rarely received the same attention as burglary, robbery, or horse theft, and if they did, civil remedies were as likely to be used as criminal ones. When property had disappeared, families or individuals with a reputation for idleness were much more likely to be suspected than those perceived to be of good character and honest occupation. In the twentieth century the effects of these selection mechanisms are easier to uncover. Although recorded crime is predominantly a lower-class phenomenon, the majority of self-report studies have failed to produce any substantial evidence that lower-class adolescents commit more crime per head than their middle-class contemporaries. Prosecution and detection practices clearly have specific class biases. Although the historical evidence is less systematic, the occupational structure of recorded offenders cannot be taken as an accurate guide to differentials within the lawbreaking population as a whole. The dominance of those labelled as labourers among the eighteenth-century accused may be more a reflection of victims' behaviour than an indication that theft was predominantly an activity of the poor.[87]

Summary conviction certificates, quarter sessions and borough court indictments, and assize agenda books all contain information about the occupation of the accused (Table 6.7 *a* and *b*), but the quality of this evidence and the number of years for which it is available are severely limited. The quarter sessions and borough court indictments are the most reliable source. After the mid-1780s they begin to move towards the long-established and stereotyped practice used at the assizes, but before that time they offer much more consistent information and include a wide spectrum of occupational descriptions. The size of the main occupational groups is similar to that found in other counties. At the Essex quarter sessions less than 2 per cent of the accused were gentlemen, professionals, or farmers; two-thirds are described as labourers; a quarter as tradesmen or artisans.[88] Of the latter, a considerable number were

---

[87] Sharpe, 'Enforcing', pp. 107–19; shopkeepers indicted for false weights and measures received minimal fines and were not usually seen as criminals. For a gentleman negotiating to avoid being prosecuted for hunting deer, Mitchell (ed.), *The Purefoy Letters*, pp. 160–4. Box, *Deviance*, pp. 56–84; West, *The Young Offender*, pp. 56–60.

[88] The proportion of labourers among quarter sessions male accused was 64.7 per cent 1750–9; 65.0 per cent 1760–9; 61.0 per cent 1770–4; but 80.0 per cent 1786–8, and 94.6 per cent by 1798–1800. If occupations in indictments and depositions are compared before the 1780s the labels are very similar. After 1785 those described as labourers in indictments began to include men who were clearly artisans.

in a very similar position to those labelled as labourers. 3 per cent were weavers; others were building workers of varying levels of skill; and an unknown proportion were apprentices rather than trained workers or masters. Those accused at the Colchester sessions contained a slightly smaller proportion of labourers and many more cloth workers, thus reflecting the general occupational structure of the borough. The brief burst of occupational recording at the Essex assizes, 1786–8, suggests a broadly similar pattern to the quarter sessions but a slightly smaller proportion of tradesmen and artisans

Table 6.7a Occupation, Status, and Gender of Indicted Property Offenders, Essex, 1750–88

	Essex quarter sessions petty larceny, 1750–75		Colchester borough sessions petty larceny, 1764–82		Essex assizes all property offences 1786–8	
	No.	%	No.	%	No.	%
Male	346	78.8	51	67.1	189	92.2
Female	93	21.2	25	32.9	16	7.8
Total	439		76		205	
Male occupation known	336		50		186	
Male occupation unknown	10		1		3	
Total	346		51		189	
Occupation or Social Status of Males						
1. Gentleman	0		0		0	
2. Professional	2	0.6	0		1	0.5
3. Yeomen or farmer	4	1.2	0		0	
4. Husbandmen	21	6.3	2	4.0	4	2.2
5. Sea and water trades	11	3.3	1	2.0	9	4.8
6. Tradesmen and artisans	85	25.3	19	38.0	32	17.2
7. Labourers	213	63.4	28	56.0	140	75.3
Total	336	100.1	50	100.0	186	100.0
Subdivisions of Tradesmen and Artisans						
a. Innkeepers and victuallers	5	1.5	3	6.0	0	
b. Food processors	9	2.7	0		6	3.2
c. Shopkeepers and traders	5	1.5	0		1	0.5
d. Building workers	21	6.3	4	8.0	5	2.7
e. Metal workers	13	3.9	2	4.0	5	2.7
f. Clothing and leather trades	14	4.2	3	6.0	7	3.8
g. Cloth manufacturing trades	12	3.6	7	14.0	3	1.6
h. Other trades	6	1.8	0		5	2.7

Sources: E.R.O. Q/SR 698–865; Q.SPb 10–15; Q/RSc 1/1; Colchester sessions files, 1764–82, P.R.O. Assi 31/14–15.

E.R.O. Q/SBb 377/78 related to a carpenter; 345/9 to a weaver. Both are labourers in the indictments. For comparable analyses, Hay, 'Crime, Authority', pp. 395–7; Pole, 'Crime', p. 139; Beattie, *Crime*, pp. 248–52; R. Shoemaker, 'Using Quarter Sessions Records as Evidence for the Study of Crime and Criminal Justice', *Archives*, 20 (1993), pp. 150–1.

Table 6.7*b* Occupation, Status, and Gender of Summarily Convicted Property Offenders, Essex, 1748–1804

	(a) Game theft		(b) Wood and vegetable theft		(c) Yarn theft	
	No.	%	No.	%	No.	%
Male	187	99.5	173	89.6	13	38.2
Female	1	0.5	20	10.4	21	61.8
Total	188		193		34	
Male occupation known	168		110		11	
Male occupation unknown	19		63		2	
Total	187		173		13	
Occupation or Social Status of Males						
1. Gentleman	9	5.4	1	0.9	0	
2. Professional	2	1.2	1	0.9	0	
3. Yeomen or farmer	26	15.5	1	0.9	0	
4. Husbandmen	2	1.2	3	2.7	0	
5. Sea and water trades	0		1	0.9	0	
6. Tradesmen and artisans	30	17.8	8	7.3	11	100.0
7. Labourers	99	58.9	95	86.4	0	
Total	168	100.0	110	100.0	11	100.0
Subdivisions of Tradesmen and Artisans						
a. Innkeepers and victuallers	2	1.2	1	0.9	0	
b. Food processors	7	4.2	1	0.9	0	
c. Shopkeepers and traders	1	0.6	0		0	
d. Building workers	8	4.8	0		0	
e. Metal workers	4	2.4	3	2.7	0	
f. Clothing and leather trades	4	2.4	1	0.9	2	18.2
g. Cloth manufacturing trades	2	1.2	0		9	81.8
h. Other trades	2	1.2	2	1.8	0	

Sources: E.R.O. Q/SR 698–865; Q/SPb 10–15; Q/RSc 1/1.

among the accused, which may well reflect different recording practices rather than real differences in the offenders' backgrounds.[89]

Although summary convictions do not always contain occupational information, those that have survived offer some interesting insights. Convicted yarn offenders reflected the make-up of the industry's workforce. Female spinners or males with cloth-manufacturing occupations predominated. The great majority of wood and vegetable thieves were described as labourers,[90] but game offenders were a much less socially specific group. Gentlemen were

[89] Harwich borough accused also reflected the general occupational structure of the town. A third were mariners or fishermen. At least three of the eleven artisans indicted between 1740 and 1800 were apprentices. Harwich Borough Court Minute Books 98/16–18. Beattie, *Crime*, p. 250 shows that Sussex had similar assizes occupational patterns to Essex, while Surrey had more artisans.

[90] Styles, 'Embezzlement', pp. 179–80; 80 per cent of wood stealers appearing before the Lexden and Winstree Petty Sessions, 1785–1800, were also described as either labourers or husbandmen: E.R.O. P/LwR 1–11.

well represented and farmers, in Essex as elsewhere, formed a larger proportion than they did in the population as a whole. Although more than half of the
accused were labourers, the prosecution of game-related offences was not just
a reflection of the poor's desire for game and the gentry's desire to stop them
taking it. It also mirrored the complex conflicts and negotiations that surrounded the hunting of these animals by the middling sort and the lesser
gentry.[91]

The category of 'labourer' is a very misleading one. Between a third and a
half of those given this title in the quarter sessions indictments appear from the
depositions to have been servants, paupers, or itinerants. Servants in husbandry, carters, buyers of old iron, workhouse inmates, demolition workers, and
temporary harvest workers all became labourers in indictments. The depositions also have their drawbacks. They do not survive for all indicted offences
and the occupational categories used by victim and accused did not always
agree. William Cranfield described himself as a labourer, for example, but his
prosecutor was less complimentary, calling him 'an idle and disorderly fellow
at present residing at Vange'.[92] In the period 1748–1800, 43 per cent of the
male accused whose occupations are identified in depositions are described as
labourers, 15 per cent as travellers or vagrants, 23 per cent as servants or
carters, and 15 per cent as artisans or tradesmen. These figures are not directly
comparable with the indictment information, but depositions do reveal important influences not visible elsewhere. A large number of quarter sessions
offences were committed while the accused was at work. Living-in servants
were not the only group that were prosecuted for pilfering their master's
goods. Transport workers, journeymen, building workers, and day labourers
all had similar traditions. Although solidarities were not easily broken and
evidence was sometimes difficult to obtain, several Essex depositions record
the regular off-loading of small quantities of hay, corn, peas, or coal by those
employed to transport them. In 1783 a 'servant in husbandry', Robert Cunningham, was sent to Colchester with his master's wagon to deliver rye and
pick up two cauldrons of coals. On his way home he decided to 'make a dead
man or two'. His claim that he had only made illegal deliveries of coal to two
'poor people' to whom he returned part of the price did not gain him lenient
treatment. The authorities wanted to crack down on this type of crime and five

[91] Hay, 'Poaching', pp. 200–1; Munsche, *Gentlemen*, pp. 28–9; In Epping and Waltham forests
landowners, forest officers, freeholders, farmers, and labouring poor each had their own claims, rights,
and traditions of appropriation. There were clashes over wood, grazing rights, turfs, and lesser game,
but deer were a particularly important focus of conflict. The local farmers were angry at 'the losses they
constantly sustain from the deer breaking down their fences, trespassing upon their fields and destroying their crops' and both the summary convictions certificates and the Epping petty sessions records
show that they responded by hunting both deer and smaller game. Fisher, *Forest*; Young, *General
View... Essex*, 2, p. 153; Epping Petty Sessions Book E.R.O. Accession 6133, 20 Dec. 1782 and 17 Oct.
1783; *Che.C.*, 16 Oct. 1801.
[92] This comparison between indictments and depositions is based on 1750–75 E.R.O. Q/SR and Q/
SBb 180–5, 196–242, 263–77. For William Cranfield, see Q/SBb 197/19.

years later the chairman of the quarter sessions publicly condemned 'the too prevalent custom' of employees 'robbing their masters wagons of the coals'.[93] Petty pilfering by building workers was also seen almost as a traditional right and journeymen in other trades often took the same approach, stealing a wide variety of work materials from their masters: blacksmiths lost their nails; bricklayers lost their trowels; perukemakers lost their hair. Among rural workers the largest group of workplace offences were committed by threshers, a group that farmers were often advised to watch very closely. The authorities had considerable difficulty in persuading working people that these forms of appropriation were not legitimate. In 1804 the *Chelmsford Chronicle* published an account of the conviction of one such offender in the hope that it would 'be the means of putting a stop, in some degree, to that system of plunder on the property of employers so often practised by servants, under the fraudulent opinion that they have a right to convert certain articles belonging to their masters . . . to their own use or advantage'.[94]

The majority of quarter sessions depositions did not, however, describe workplace crimes. A large proportion involved casual opportunistic thefts. The goods stolen were the most readily available and most vulnerably placed commodities of domestic and working life; 50 per cent of thefts involved clothing, fowls, or victuals. In a further 25 per cent, crops or tools were the main targets.[95] Apart from the minority of cases where the offence was made possible by the special access given to servants and employees, the depositions often remain silent about whether the accused was a stranger or a local man, but despite the problems this causes it appears that the majority of the property crimes indicted in this court were not committed by marginal, mobile groups living outside normal patterns of social relationships. Men and women from outside the community where the crime was committed did constitute an important subgroup of the indicted, but most quarter sessions depositions relate to crimes located firmly in the lives of the local labouring poor—in workplace relationships, in living-in service, or in the everyday transactions of economic and social life.

The backgrounds of those accused of major crimes at the Essex assizes are more difficult to trace because depositions do not usually survive for the Home Circuit. Printed trial reports, newspapers, and Home Office reports suggest

[93] Cunningham was sentenced to be twice whipped and to undergo a period of hard labour. E.R.O. Q/SBb 312/13 and 347/46 for the dropping of dead men phrase from another servant carter; *Che.C.*, 10 Oct. 1788. For an Essex farmer's extensive comments on thefts by carters and farm servants, *P.P.*, 1839, XIX, pp. 39–40.

[94] E.R.O. Q/SBb 348/58; Q/SBb 197/24, 208/26 and 274/30; for threshers Q/SBb 201/38, 215/12, 232/24, 273/31, 380/79; *Che.C.*, 10 Oct. 1788 for a theft of 700 lb of lead by bricklayers; *Che.C.*, 23 Mar. 1804;

[95] For detailed tables analysing stolen goods and the environments where the offences were committed, King 'Crime, Law', p. 133. The latter were fairly predictable. Domestic buildings 16 per cent; barns, outhouses, and storage buildings 25 per cent; yards or drying grounds 17 per cent; fields, woods, or roads 19 per cent; shops or industrial premises 10 per cent.

that many assize indictments were also related to workplace offences or to crimes committed within the established social networks of the locality,[96] but although the majority of the accused are very difficult to contextualize, it is important to assess whether a significant proportion of assizes offenders were more professional, more organized, or more mobile than those indicted at the quarter sessions.

The small-scale nature of most of the thefts indicted at both the quarter sessions and the assizes combined with the age structure of the accused and the broad spectrum of working trades from which they were drawn suggest that most indicted crimes were not committed by 'professionals'. The great majority seem to have been opportunistic acts limited by the small range of possibilities available to the labouring poor in their everyday lives. However, a small minority chose, in varying degrees, to change their way of life in order to expand that range of possibilities. For some the nature of their offences may have begun to shape their lifestyle rather than being shaped by it, and the widespread contemporary view that most major offenders quickly became committed to full-time lawbreaking may not therefore have been entirely incorrect. In reality there was no sharp distinction between the full-time criminal and the casual thief. The surviving records suggest a spectrum of different types of offender and offence involving various levels of activity, of organization, and of geographical mobility. Near to London a higher proportion of offenders may have been connected to the criminal organizations, subcultures, and receiving networks of the capital, although metropolitan historians by no means agree about the importance or extent of London's 'criminal underworld'.[97] Elsewhere the degree to which offenders were committed to lawbreaking as a full-time activity often depended on the type of crime they were involved in. Poaching, for example, was largely a casual, occasional, or part-time form of appropriation but in the forests of south-west Essex some deer stealers may have gained the greater part of their livelihood in this way. In the 1860s an ageing verderer claimed that in his time the forest had still supported a number of very desperate characters who lived 'entirely by deer stealing'.[98]

Sheep thieves were involved in a similar spectrum of activities, from individual one-off thefts often motivated by poverty, through the periodic taking of a single sheep, to the systematic rustling of whole flocks. In Essex, as in the areas studied in more detail by Wells, Rule, and Beattie, the severe dearths of 1740 and 1800–1 witnessed considerable increases in indictments and reports

---

[96] P.R.O. H.O. 47/11. 15 Jan. 1790, and 20 Mar. 1790 for two typical examples.

[97] Beattie, *Crime*, pp. 251–62; McMullan, 'Crime', pp. 265–6; J. Davis, 'Law-Breaking and Law-Enforcement. The Creation of a Criminal Class in Mid-Victorian England' (Ph.D. Boston, 1984); Sharpe, *Crime in Early Modern England*, pp. 111–17; Linebaugh, *The London Hanged*.

[98] Fisher, *The Forest*, p. 212; Thompson, *Whigs*, p. 234; D. Barlow, *Dick Turpin and the Gregory Gang* (Chichester, 1973), pp. 12–14; Munsche, *Gentlemen*, pp. 64–72, 138–43.

relating to sheep theft, indicating that some animals were stolen to supplement the family diet or income. The Essex newspapers also confirm that other motivations were important. Organized gangs linked to local butchers were reported to have taken small flocks from southern and central Essex and occasional sheep thefts by settled men over an extended period were not uncommon.[99] Since horse theft usually involved longer-distance movement and required well-spread-out receiving networks, horse thieves were less frequently local inhabitants. Some runaway servants stole their masters' horses and local men were sometimes caught joy-riding on a neighbour's animal, but many horse thieves had a longer-term commitment. In 1740 Thomas Whiting confessed that with two companions he 'used to make a practice of stealing horses about the country' and in 1777 members of 'a large gang of horse stealers' who had 'committed great depredations on the farmers of different counties all round London' were tried at the Essex assizes. In the 1780s Madan commented on the ease with which stolen horses were being sold to horse boilers in the City, and from Poulter's accounts it is clear that 'prad priggers' in other parts of the country had also developed well-organized methods of selling stolen animals, although London remained a favoured outlet.[100]

Some burglars and housebreakers were also highly organized. The burglaries of the violent and highly active 'Gregory gang' were mainly committed in Essex and from the 1770s onwards several gangs of London-based burglars were reported to be making journeys into Essex aided, contemporaries believed, by that 'great set of villains infesting London and its environs ... hackney coachmen'. In general, however, breaking and entering was closer in context and type of offender to simple larceny. The value of the stolen goods was usually relatively small and burglaries accounted for a larger proportion of recorded crimes in remote rural areas than they did near London.[101] Contemporary accounts give the impression that those who committed highway robbery usually became partly or wholly reliant on crime for their livelihoods. Newspaper reports and pamphlets suggest that these offenders operated over a wide area, the heathlands and forests of the various counties around London being their favourite environment. 'Those persons who rob upon the highway

[99] Beattie, *Crime*, pp. 170–2; Rule, 'The Manifold Causes'; R. Wells, 'Sheep-Rustling in Yorkshire in the Age of the Industrial and Agricultural Revolutions', *Northern History*, 20 (1984), 127–45; Hay, 'Crime, Authority', pp. 67–80. *Che.C.*, 17 Nov. 1786 and 10 Jan. 1800 for gang involvement and 1 Jan. 1790 for a local man's extended sheep stealing activities; 31 July 1801, *I.J.*, 9 Feb. 1760, 8 Jan. 1762; and *Che.C.*, 11 Oct. 1765.

[100] Beattie, *Crime*, pp. 167–70; P. Edwards, *The Horse Trade in Tudor and Stuart England* (Cambridge, 1988), pp. 105–39. *Che.C.*, 26 Nov. 1784, 14 Apr. 1780. For full-time thieves—*Cambridge Chronicle*, 14 June 1788; *Proceedings at the Assizes ... Essex ... July 1740*, p. 16; and *Che.C.*, 25 July 1777; Madan, *Thoughts*, pp. 40–2; P.R.O. H.O. 47/1 Henry Snook; J. Poulter, *The Discoveries of John Poulter alias Baxter* (Sherborne, 1761).

[101] Beattie, *Crime*, pp. 161–7; *Che.C.*, 2 Aug. 1775 for hackney carriagemen; *Che.C.*, 12 Jan. 1781 for other London-based burglars; Barlow, *Dick Turpin and the Gregory Gang*. The modal value of stolen goods in burglary cases was £1 to £2.

within twenty miles of London', wrote John Fielding 'set out from thence for that purpose... they retire thither for shelter.' Dick Turpin was not the only Essex highwayman whose activities were reported extensively, if sometimes unrealistically, in the eighteenth-century newspapers. In the 1760s the *Ipswich Journal* reported that 'the Flying Highwayman now engrosses the conversation of most of the towns within twenty miles of London' by visiting 'almost all the public roads round the metropolis'. This shadowy figure, whose reputation was based mainly on the jumping of countless turnpike gates, was one of a long line of highway robbers and other violent or particularly threatening groups of offenders who were given extensive coverage in the Essex press from the 1760s onwards.[102] 'The Thaxted gang', 'The Hertford gang', the 'Colchester robbers', and gangs variously described as notorious, violent, or desperate were reported at various times to be 'infesting' different parts of the county. Many were said to be exclusively involved in highway robbery, but others specialized in horse stealing, fowl theft, potato stealing, or poaching. According to the *Chelmsford Chronicle* some of these groups were highly organized. The Epping Forest gang uncovered in 1784 appear to have come from Oxfordshire. They leased a small farm, kept their own horses and stables, and set up facilities that enabled them to be self-sufficient in all the major necessities. Under this cover their members carried on a good trade as highwaymen around the forest for an extended period.[103]

Although the violence used by a minority of highway robbers and burglars should not be ignored, there can be little doubt that many newspaper reports were unreliable, inaccurate, and highly selective, favouring the violent and the sensational rather than the typical. Reports of 'gangs infesting' a particular neighbourhood may have been grounded more in the local community's fears and stereotypes or in newspapers' needs to increase their circulation than in observed reality.[104] The activities of less threatening groups such as petty thieves or single robbers were much less likely to be reported. Unfortunately, the other major sources available, the printed life stories of condemned offenders, pose equal problems. The multiple functions of these documents make them difficult to interpret. They were designed not only to sell and to amuse but also to sermonize, to mythologize, to legitimize the gallows and even, if Faller is correct, deliberately to confuse and anaesthetize the reader.[105]

[102] J. Fielding, *A Plan for Preventing Robberies within 20 miles of London* (London, 1755), p. 9; *I.J.*, 26 Dec. 1761; 2 Jan. 1762, 16 Jan. 1762, 23 Jan. 1762.

[103] *I.J.*, 15 Mar. 1760, 1 May 1762; *Che.C.*, 30 Jan. 1783, 15 June 1787; for gangs not involved in robbery, Edwards, *The Horse Trade*, p. 120; *Che.C.*, 29 Nov. 1765; Munsche, *Gentleman*, p. 71. The Epping Forest Case. *Che.C.*, 5 Mar. 1784.

[104] For a discussion of the limited levels of violence involved in highway robbery and burglary, King, 'Crime, Law', pp. 138–40. 'Gangs' like their modern equivalents, 'Criminal subcultures'; are easier to label than actually to locate. Thompson, *Whigs*, pp. 194–5; King, 'Newspaper Reporting'.

[105] L. Faller, *Turned to Account. The Forms and Functions of Criminal Biography in Late Seventeenth and Early Eighteenth-Century England* (Cambridge, 1987). It is possible that the confusion and plotlessness of many of the accounts was not constructed, as Fuller suggests, in order to desensitize the reader, but rather

Although the life stories describe the lives of highwaymen in a variety of ways, they are usually represented as following a typical 'career' pattern, in which idleness or profligacy led to loss of 'place', failure in business, or a decision to join the armed forces. Once the first step into crime had been taken, the accounts often became mere listings of offences, desertions, and bizarre incidents. The impression is therefore given that once launched into a life of crime an individual was inextricably caught in a downwardly spiralling criminal career. The selective nature of the accounts thus reinforced the contemporary rhetoric that small vices left unchecked led inevitably to the gallows. The individual exploits of the offenders are seldom placed within the support networks they used, and after their initial apprenticeship has been described the legitimate employments they may still have pursued are very rarely considered worthy of mention. Some of those eventually indicted for highway robbery may have become isolated and brutalized as the Gregory gang seems to have been, but it would be wrong to label even the offenders whose life stories have survived as full-time criminals on this evidence alone. The proximity of London almost certainly increased the proportion of Essex offenders that were permanently attached to a criminal lifestyle, but the great majority of the Essex accused came from a very different type of background. Only a small minority were highly organized operators or experienced, mobile full-time thieves.[106] Occasional opportunistic small-scale pilfering of the goods of masters, near neighbours, or wayside inhabitants were the most characteristic forms of theft, while a significant subgroup of offenders operated between these two extremes moving in and out of crime, just as they moved in and out of the armed forces, of employment, or of any given region according to the particular circumstances they found themselves in.

Conclusion

By looking in detail at life-cycle and gender-related issues, it is therefore possible to develop new perspectives on the paradoxical relationship between poverty and crime in this period. In one sense poverty defined crime in the eighteenth century. Indictable crime was designed to focus primarily on the appropriational strategies of the poor, and the vast majority of indicted property offenders were therefore unpropertied men and women. This said, however, detailed investigation into the background of those accused of property crimes suggests that within the labouring poor those most likely to

reflected the uncertain alliances, ever-changing survival strategies, and makeshift economies of the offenders themselves. For the publishing history, M. Harris, 'Trials and Criminal Biographies. A Case Study in Distribution', in R. Myers and M. Harris (eds.), *Sale and Distribution of Books from 1700* (Oxford, 1982), pp. 15–27.

[106] McIntosh 'Changes', p. 110; Barlow, *Dick Turpin and the Gregory Gang*; McMullan, *The Canting Crew*; *P.P.*, 1816, V, pp. 176 and 222.

be prosecuted were not necessarily those who were experiencing the most acute poverty or distress. The sex most vulnerable to economic exploitation and below subsistence wages—women— contributed only a small proportion of recorded offenders. The age groups most vulnerable to extreme poverty— the very young, those with large families to support, and the old—were also drastically underrepresented among the indicted. Committing crime and getting prosecuted for it was as much about masculinity, mobility, and opportunity as it was about poverty. Most crucially it was about the ability of young adult males to excite extreme anxiety among those with property to protect. Deprivation and possible destitution were never far from the door of many labouring households in the eighteenth century and this was probably the main reason why those with large families to support turned to crime. However, between committing a theft and getting prosecuted for it the accused went through several highly selective filters. Thus, while poverty provides the foundations for an analysis of the relative vulnerability of different groups to indictment for theft, the core explanation for many prosecutions probably lay elsewhere, most centrally perhaps in the changing reactions of victims and magistrates to the group most affected by war, recruitment, and demobilization— unattached, unskilled, mobile young men. In this light it becomes much less surprising that the fluctuating indictment levels explored in Chapter 5 showed only a rather distant relationship to changes in levels of deprivation among the poor outside a handful of crisis years, or that the areas of Essex where indictment rates were highest were also those where wage rates were highest and poor rates lower than average.

Part 3

From Trial to Punishment

7

Trials, Verdicts, and Courtroom Interactions

Having analysed pretrial processes and assessed the impact of their deeply discretionary nature on recorded crime rates and on the vulnerability of different groups to prosecution, Part 3 now focuses on the final stages of the accused's journey through the judicial process. Chapter 7 deals with trials and verdicts, Chapters 8 and 9 with sentences and pardoning, and Chapter 10 with rituals of punishment.

Although trials and verdicts were better documented than pretrial hearings and decisions, severe evidential problems remain. The first stage of the trial process, the grand jurors' private deliberations, remained shrouded in mystery and even the public trials held before petty juries were rarely systematically recorded because they were primarily intended to be oral confrontations between victim and accused. Newspapers, judges' reports, private correspondence, and formal court records all provide some insights into the trial process, but the most important source was created by the London printers who published detailed reports of every Old Bailey sessions. The survival of these sessions papers has enabled several historians[1] to study metropolitan trials in detail but provincial trials are more problematic. Surrey, with its substantial metropolitan core, did produce a considerable number of assizes trial pamphlets and Beattie's excellent chapter on trial proceedings is therefore based on that county, but elsewhere the potential market for these pamphlets was usually too small to make the enterprise worth while. Fortunately, Essex is better served than most rural counties. Complete privately printed proceed-

---

[1] J. Langbein, 'The Criminal Trial before the Lawyers', *University of Chicago Law Review*, 45 (1978), 265–316; J. Langbein, 'Shaping the Eighteenth-Century Criminal Trial. A View from the Ryder Sources', *University of Chicago Law Review*, 50 (1983), 1–136; J. Langbein, 'The English Criminal Trial Jury on the Eve of the French Revolution', in A. Schioppa (ed.), *The Trial Jury in England, France, Germany* (Berlin, 1987), pp. 13–39; J. Langbein, 'The Prosecutorial Origins of Defence Counsel in the Eighteenth Century. The Appearance of Solicitors', *Cambridge Law Journal*, 58 (1999), 314–65; S. Landsmen, 'The Rise of the Contentious Spirit. Adversary Procedure in Eighteenth-Century England', *Cornell Law Review*, 75 (1990), 497–609; J. Beattie, 'Scales of Justice. Defence Counsel and the English Criminal Trial in the Eighteenth and Nineteenth Centuries', *Law and History Review*, 9 (1991), 221–67; J. Beattie, 'London Juries in the 1690s', in Cockburn and Green (eds.), *Twelve Good Men*; S. Deveraux, 'The City and the Sessions Paper: "Public Justice" in London 1770–1800', *Journal of British Studies*, 35 (1996), 466–503.

ings are available for one assize session in 1680, 1739, 1740, and 1774 and lengthy trial summaries can occasionally be found in the *Chelmsford Chronicle* after that date. Moreover in 1739 and 1774 two printers unsuccessfully tested the provincial market by publishing assizes proceedings for all the Home Circuit counties.[2] These collections, combined with more occasional sources, provide provincial material that can extend and refine the existing London-based research.

1. The Changing Nature of Trial Proceedings

Jurors, judges, and specific aspects of trial procedure all had their critics in the eighteenth century, but the broad principle of trial by jury was widely accepted and seen by most commentators as the 'grand bulwark' of every Englishman's liberties. Its political, social, and legal functions were widely lauded and even Burn's manual, which rarely displayed such enthusiasm, called it 'that happy way of trial' and saw it as 'one of the pillars' on which the state was founded. The poor were more ambivalent. Bamford's view that 'trial by peers . . . is to a poor working man, a mockery', was not shared by all working men, but when seen from below, the jury system rarely lived up to the *Chelmsford Chronicle's* description of it as 'the union of wisdom with integrity, impartiality with humanity'.[3] The deeper historians have delved into the history of the criminal trial in the eighteenth century, the more it has become clear that the trial process would have been regarded as anything but happy by many of those who were forced to defend themselves before these tribunals.

Property crime trials followed the same basic pattern at assizes, quarter sessions, and borough sessions, although unfortunately only the assize proceedings were usually considered worth reporting. The indictment was scrutinized twice but the accused had no opportunity to put his case at the initial grand jury hearing, which was held in private and was confined to an examination of the prosecution evidence. If the grand jury deemed it insufficient the indictment was labelled 'not found' and the accused was discharged without a public trial, but in most cases the majority of the grand

---

[2] Beattie, *Crime*, pp. 314–78; the main Essex pamphlets are *Proceedings at the Assizes . . . Chelmsford . . . March 1680*, *Proceedings at the Assizes . . . Essex. March 1739*, *Proceedings at the Assizes . . . Essex . . . July 1740*, *Whole Proceedings . . . Essex . . . March 1774*. The latter was part of an attempt by Joseph Gurney to expand a lucrative trade based on the Old Bailey. He also published *The Whole Proceedings . . . Hertford, Surrey, Kent . . . March 1774*. In 1739 the equivalent was published as one pamphlet by J. Standen, *The Genuine Proceedings at the Assizes on the Home Circuit* (London, 1739), pp. 1–24. Joseph Gurney also published *The Whole Genuine Proceedings at the Assizes . . . Kent . . . March 1766* (London, 1766). Harris 'Trials', pp. 1–36; *Che.C.*, 17 Mar. 1775, 25 July 1777, 14 Mar. 1800.

[3] Blackstone, *Commentaries*, 4, pp. 342–3; Williams, *Every Man*, p. 171; for discussion of contemporaries' views, Green, *Verdict According to Conscience*. D. Hay, 'The Class Composition of the Palladium of Liberty. Trial Jurors in the Eighteenth Century', in Cockburn and Green (eds.), *Twelve Good Men*, pp. 305–9; Burn, *The Justice*, 2, p. 462. S. Bamford, *Passages in the Life of a Radical* (Oxford, 1967), p. 495; *Che.C.*, 24 Dec. 1784.

jurors found it a 'true bill' and the accused was then publicly indicted before the petty jury.[4]

Trial before the petty jury was the principal public moment in the long chain of decision-making processes that determined the fate of the accused, but it was often a very brief moment. Some trials lasted only a few minutes and on average the court got through the whole process from arraignment to the conclusion of the juries' brief huddled deliberations in little over half an hour.[5] Until the nature of the criminal trial began to change towards the end of our period, the victim usually put his case quickly and simply, both he and his witnesses being kept to the point by the judge. Extensive cross-examination of the prosecution case by either the prisoner or his representatives was exceptional. The accused was then given an opportunity to call witnesses and tell his own story. His defence was rarely lengthy or technical and very often it consisted of little more than a flat unsubstantiated denial. Only the more fortunate were able to produce counter-evidence or character witnesses.[6] In essence, the trial was a brief contest of stories in which the prisoner was often on the defensive. There was no positive presumption of innocence in the early eighteenth century. If the prosecutor produced a coherent account, the prisoner was expected either to say something of substance that would under-mine it or to produce a viable alternative. Undernourished and often under-prepared after their confinement awaiting trial, or overawed perhaps by the large audience pressing in about them, many eighteenth-century prisoners found it difficult to do either. The gradual lawyerization of the trial meant that by the nineteenth century the defendant often had the assistance of a professional advocate, but until the late eighteenth century this remained rare and the prisoner's only possible source of assistance was the judge himself.[7]

In the early and mid-eighteenth century the judges undoubtedly played an important role. They were often highly proactive examiners who pointedly questioned witnesses and directed the hectic flow of evidence in order to ensure that, despite occasional interruptions from defendants, jurors, and others,[8] the central issues at stake were rapidly brought into focus. Throughout the

---

[4] For a more detailed description of trial procedure, Baker, 'Criminal Courts'; Langbein, 'The Criminal Trial'; Langbein, 'Shaping'; Beattie, *Crime*, pp. 314–77.

[5] Beattie, *Crime*, pp. 376–8; Langbein, 'Shaping', pp. 115–20 suggests eleven in less than a day at the Chelmsford assizes 1754.

[6] Trial reports were heavily edited and therefore give a false impression of the brevity of the proceedings, but the 1774 account, aided by Joseph Gurney's much-publicized shorthand technique, covered twenty-seven large pages and was the most comprehensive. Less than a quarter of the cases record cross-examination of the prosecutor or his witnesses. In the twenty-three thoroughly reported cases only four prisoners produced character witnesses. Only three produced alibis or corroborating evidence to support their defence. *Whole Proceedings . . . Essex . . . March 1774.*

[7] Green, *Verdict According to Conscience*, pp. 134–5 and 270–1; Beattie, *Crime*, pp. 341–9; Cockburn, *Calendar of Assize Records . . . Introduction*, pp. 106–9.

[8] *Genuine Proceedings . . . Home Circuit . . . March 1739*, p. 9 for an example of jurors asking direct questions; Beattie, *Crime*, pp. 342–3; Langbein, 'The Criminal Trial'.

eighteenth century many commentators argued that the judge acted as counsel for the prisoner. In 1795 the vicar of Ardleigh stressed in the Chelmsford assize sermon, 'that when the process of law brought a man before the tribunal of this country he found that his innocence was not his only protection—his very judge was his advocate'. Reality and rhetoric seldom coincided however. Judges might take a neutral stance but they were rarely protective. Their approaches varied widely. There were occasions when two men tried by different judges for a joint offence received widely disparate sentences.[9] If the prisoner struck an unsympathetic chord in the judge's mind, or was accused of a crime that he considered it important to suppress, the bench's neutrality might soon evaporate. The judge's individual character and attitudes were also important. Some, such as Judge Carter, who sat at the Essex Lent assizes in 1739, made extremely sarcastic responses to the accused's fumbling attempts to erect a defence. Other judges were much more even-handed. Since the two Home Circuit judges rarely recorded the way they divided the civil and criminal business between themselves, the policies of individual judges are difficult to assess, but Lord Mansfield, who regularly travelled the circuit, provides an exception. His activities on the criminal side at Chelmsford during 1757–83 can be traced in his private papers. Mansfield took a tough attitude to reprieves. In this period his fellow assize judges sent only 30 per cent of capital convicts to the Essex gallows but when Mansfield was involved this increased to over 40 per cent.[10] Only one female property offender was hanged in Essex, 1740–1805: it was Mansfield who sent her to the gallows. Acquittal rates were also nearly 5 per cent lower when Mansfield was on the bench and although the sample is rather a small one, this lends further weight to his reputation among eighteenth-century radicals as 'a judge who confounds, controls, and browbeats a jury'. Mansfield was an exceptional man, however. As Lord Chief Justice he was partly responsible for enlarging the scope of the Black Acts and he used his political muscle to silence Judge Foster's more lenient views.[11] The trial reports suggest that in most cases the judge took no particular line towards the prosecutor or the accused, but simply drew out the details of the offence, the degree of positive identification, and the evidence about the accused's

[9] McGowen, 'The Image', pp. 118–20; Beattie, *Crime*, p. 345; *Che.C.*, 13 Mar. 1795; P.R.O. H.O. 42/4. 19 Jan. 1784 for a judge's report on co-offenders—one capitally convicted, one receiving a partial verdict. One offender was captured and tried earlier than the other and they therefore appeared before different judges. Radzinowicz, *History*, 1, p. 327.

[10] *Genuine Proceedings...Home Circuit...March 1739*, p. 10; P.R.O. Assi 31 records the two judges' names but not which one began on the civil or criminal side. E. Heward, *Lord Mansfield* (Chichester, 1979) pinpoints sixteen assizes at which he took the crown side, 1757–83. In these 33 of the 82 capitally convicted property offenders were hanged. In the rest of the period 1757–83, 64 out of 220 went to the Essex gallows. Analysis of the Old Bailey material also suggests Mansfield was an unsympathetic judge—J. Oldham (ed.), *The Mansfield Manuscripts and the Growth of English Law in the Eighteenth Century* (2 vols., Chapel Hill, 1992), 1, pp. 116–17.

[11] J. Brewer, 'The Wilkites and the Law, 1763–74', in Brewer and Styles (eds.), *An Ungovernable People*, p. 158—the *North Briton* on Mansfield; Thompson, *Whigs*, pp. 251–4.

character or actions. Most judges almost certainly did not lean heavily against the prisoner and some may have leaned towards him or her, but the early eighteenth-century form of trial, with its lack of strong evidentiary rules and its direct confrontation between accused and accuser, inevitably tended to put the prisoner on the defensive.

This was not, however, a static pattern. During the eighteenth century the criminal trial underwent several interrelated changes and by the mid-nineteenth century trial proceedings were fundamentally different from those of a century earlier. A network of evidentiary rules developed, skilled counsel became increasingly involved, trial judges gradually withdrew from their role as active examiners, and the assumption that the accused was innocent until proved guilty took shape, eventually becoming axiomatic.[12] Hearsay was one of the first categories of evidence to come under scrutiny. Until the early eighteenth century the courts not infrequently allowed words written or spoken on a previous occasion by someone unavailable for cross-examination to be admitted as evidence. By the 1760s Burn was stating flatly that 'it is a general rule that hearsay is no evidence'. As early as 1739 the Essex prosecutor Jonas Greygoose failed to gain a conviction, despite obtaining a confession at the committal hearing and producing a witness who had bought the stolen goods from the prisoner, because vital evidence about the crime was based on hearsay. In 1774 the Chelmsford assize judge prevented the prosecution from introducing hearsay evidence about the accused's purchase of expensive items but later admitted a letter from a former employer of the prisoner after ascertaining that it would be helpful to the defence.[13]

Confessions were also gradually coming under more careful scrutiny. By the 1730s judges were beginning to enquire increasingly closely whether any threats, promises, or force had been used to induce the prisoner to confess. The confession of a Kent offender was only allowed in 1774 after prosecution witnesses had been subjected to a battery of questions—Did he make it freely?... Were there any threats or promises?... Was the confession read over to him before he signed it? Was the prisoner sworn? Although these investigations did not necessarily lead to the rejection of the confession or the acquittal of the accused,[14] a number of Home Circuit prisoners did gain advantage from them. In 1774, for example, one was acquitted because his confession

---

[12] Landsman, 'The Rise'; Langbein, 'Shaping'; Beattie, 'Scales of Justice'; Beattie, *Crime*, p. 341; T. Gallanis, 'The Rise of Modern Evidence Law', *Iowa Law Review*, 84 (1999), 499–560.

[13] Baker, 'Criminal Courts', p. 39; Burn, *The Justice*, 1, p. 478; Landsmen, 'The Rise', pp. 564–72; Langbein, 'The Criminal Trial', pp. 301–2; Shapiro, *Beyond Resonable Doubt*, p. 199; *Genuine Proceeding... Home Circuit... March 1739*, p. 9; *Whole Proceeding... Essex... March 1774*, p. 11; Gallanis, 'The Rise' pp. 530–7.

[14] Beattie, *Crime*, pp. 364–5; *Whole Proceedings... Kent... March 1774*, pp. 2–3; and *Whole Proceeding... Essex... March 1774*, pp. 4–5 for examples of heavy questioning. In 1740 two Essex offenders whose confessions were investigated 'proved to be made voluntarily and without compulsion' and they were sentenced to death. *Proceedings at the Assizes... Essex... July 1740*, pp. 14–15.

'appeared to have been extorted from him under a promise of not being prosecuted', and another because he confessed after being ordered to be whipped by the committing magistrate for vagrancy. Although voluntary admissions of guilt continued to be seen as highly incriminating in some cases, after the middle of the eighteenth century Essex magistrates became less enthusiastic about extracting signed confessions at the committal stage as confessional evidence in general became more circumscribed. In the late 1790s one Essex assize judge made it clear when dismissing evidence of a partial confession that 'it was a maxim in law... that no man shall convict himself', thus giving weight perhaps to Langbein's suggestion that a more general privilege against self-incrimination was developing by that time.[15]

The evidence given by accomplices in order to avoid prosecution was increasingly regarded as problematic. Turning 'King's evidence' was extremely common. Two or more co-offenders not infrequently tried to outbid one another to achieve this privileged status and the losers in this race to the death could find themselves condemned from their own mouths, as the Essex offender Charles Davis was in 1774. However, from the early eighteenth century onwards the uncorroborated testimony of an accomplice was looked upon as extremely suspect. In 1774 two consecutive cases at the Kent assizes collapsed for this reason, the judge announcing that 'I cannot examine the accomplice as there is no other evidence to confirm his testimony.'[16] Similar cases can be found throughout the final two-thirds of the eighteenth century but the courts did not exclude all uncorroborated accomplices' testimony in this period. The judicial authorities remained ambivalent. Fielding believed that the capture of hardened street robbers would be very difficult without accomplices' evidence and argued that the rules requiring 'corroboration' might 'perhaps be opened a little wider... without either mischief or inconvenience'. Many judges agreed. When the admissibility of uncorroborated accomplice's testimony was formally tested in 1788 the assembled judges ruled that 'a conviction supported by such testimony alone is perfectly legal'.[17] Where a suspicion existed that professional thieftakers were involved there was little hope that this type of evidence would be allowed to stand, but in

---

[15] Whole Proceedings... Herts... March 1774, p. 18; Whole Proceedings... Surrey... March 1774, p. 8. In 1740 a Surrey housebreaker was acquitted 'the court not being satisfied' that his confession 'was made voluntarily', as was a female servant who confessed to taking her master's money but proved he had agreed to make it up for £5. Proceedings at the Assizes... Surrey... July 1740, p. 10; 40 per cent of Essex quarter sessions depositions 1748–65 had a confession attached. By the 1780s this was much less common. Che.C., 18 Mar. 1796; J. Langbein, 'The Historical Origins of the Privilege against Self-Incrimination at Common Law', Michigan Law Review, 92 (1994), 1047–85 and on the party-witness rule—J. Oldham, 'Truth-Telling in the Eighteenth-Century Courtroom', Law and History Review, 12 (1994), 95–121.

[16] Whole Proceedings... Kent... March 1774, pp. 4–5; Whole Proceedings... Essex... March 1774, p. 4; Beattie, Crime, pp. 366–9. For the problems of the crown witness system and its influence on the development of evidentiary rules—Langbein, 'Shaping', pp. 96–105.

[17] Fielding, Enquiry, pp. 113–16; Beattie, Crime, p. 372; Langbein, 'Shaping', pp. 96–103.

other late eighteenth- and early nineteenth-century cases the circumstances of the crime were crucial. In 1801, for example, Lord Kenyon, faced by an apparent crime wave (which he believed was 'enough to alarm everybody') and determined to put the law into 'rigorous execution', succeeded in getting two groups of three offenders sentenced to death on the basis of accomplices' evidence and little else. In both cases he began by announcing that juries should not 'proceed to convict on the evidence of an accomplice only', but in his summing up he then went on to make the most of chance remarks by the accused and scraps of other testimony to argue for corroboration where little or none existed. The rule that accomplices' evidence needed corroboration would usually apply, especially if the prisoner was perceived as deserving or the prosecution as particularly dubious, but in years like 1801, when the gaol calendar was the longest ever recorded, it seems that other priorities necessitated a certain flexibility. Another Essex case reported two years later illustrates the discretionary way in which these evidential rules were applied. James Fitch and 'a number of others were committed for stealing casks, malt etc. . . . but the evidence resting upon an accomplice only, it was thought fit to convict but one upon it'.[18]

Other exclusionary rules were also developing in this period. The logic of patriarchy had always constrained the circumstances under which wives could testify against their husbands. Similar questions were raised in the eighteenth century about the testimony of children, of deaf and dumb witnesses, and of those with a pecuniary interest not related to rewards.[19] The development of evidentiary rules, and the growth by the early nineteenth century of a considerable body of legal literature on the laws of evidence, arose from a number of sources. These included the growth of suspicious thieftaking activity stimulated by the rewards system, as well as broader social, political, and intellectual changes such as the gradual replacement of absolute certainty as the standard of truth by notions of probability.[20] However, a formative role in the growth of evidential rules and of adversarial procedure was clearly played by the growing influence of solicitors and of counsel for both defence and prosecution. Lawyers first began to appear in the London courts in the first third of the eighteenth century, prosecution counsel narrowly preceding those for the defence. Defence counsel were not normally allowed to sum up on the prisoner's behalf or make statements about the facts until 1836, but just over a century earlier

---

[18] *Che.C.*, 24 and 31 July 1801; for jurors acquitting after being warned to have 'the strictest caution in determining upon the evidence of witnesses who are entitled to rewards in case of conviction': *The Times*, 29 Apr. 1786; *Che.C.*, 18 Mar. 1803.

[19] Cockburn, *Calendar of Assize Records . . . Introduction*, p. 106; children's testimony was especially problematic in cases of infant rape—*Che.C.*, 29 July 1802; Beattie, *Crime*, p. 374; *The Trial of John Taylor for Forgery* (Chelmsford, 1800).

[20] Beattie, 'Scales of Justice', pp. 222–36; Landsman, 'The Rise', pp. 572–602; B. Shapiro, *Probability and Certainty in Seventeenth-Century England. A Study of the Relationship between Natural Science, Religion, History, Law and Literature* (Princeton, 1983) and Shapiro, *Beyond Resonable Doubt*.

judges began to waive their previous restrictive rulings, enabling defence counsel to argue points of law, seek the enforcement of evidentiary rules, and interrogate witnesses. Cross-examination in particular developed as the century wore on into a means of commenting on the evidence, refuting or discrediting the prosecution case, and aggressively battling for the accused.[21]

The London sessions papers frequently omit to mention the presence of counsel but between the 1730s and the early 1780s defence counsel were involved in a minimum of around 10 per cent of London cases. After 1780 this rose rapidly so that by 1800 between a quarter and a third of London prisoners had counsel, as did about a fifth of prosecutors. Provincial practice is more difficult to evaluate, but a similar change was taking place. The 1739 and 1740 Home Circuit pamphlets indicate that at least 4 per cent of defendants and 3 per cent of prosecutors had counsel. In 1774 the equivalent figures are 6 per cent and 4 per cent. All these figures are considerable underestimates since counsel's presence was only noted if they made decisive interventions.[22] After 1774 no reports covering all the trials at an assizes survive, but the *Chelmsford Chronicle* did publish brief accounts of the trials of about fifty offenders between 1770 and 1810. These indicate that at least a quarter of defendants and 15 per cent of prosecutors were represented by counsel. Since many of these trials were sketchily reported, and since Cottu believed that defence counsel were more common outside London than at the Old Bailey, the real figure may have been higher. However, the *Chelmsford Chronicle* trial reports are an untypical sample. With its predominantly commercial and farming readership in mind, the Essex paper tended to report either sensational cases or those in which propertied men were accused of offences such as fraud or forgery. Typicality is even more of a problem in analysing the handful of detailed pamphlets on individual cases produced in these years but in almost every case counsel played a substantial role. In 1800 the Essex forgery trial of John Taylor involved three defence counsel (including the famous William Garrow), two prosecution counsel, and several attorneys.[23]

Garrow's successes and the involvement of other prominent counsel in both civil and criminal trials were extensively reported in the Essex newspapers.

---

[21] Landsman, 'The Rise', pp. 533–64, 607; Beattie, 'Scales of Justice', pp. 224–6; Langbein, 'The Criminal Trial', pp. 307–12; Beattie, *Crime*, pp. 352–62; Langbein, 'The Prosecutorial Origins'.
[22] Landsman, 'The Rise', pp. 539–64; Beattie, 'Scales of Justice', pp. 227–9; *Proceedings at the Assizes... Surrey, Essex. July 1740*; *Genuine Proceedings... on the Home Circuit... March 1739*, *Whole Proceedings... Kent, Surrey, Essex, Herts, March 1774*.
[23] A. May, 'The Old Bailey Bar, 1783–1834' (Toronto Ph.D., 1997) also suggests around a quarter of defendants and between 1 in 10 and 1 in 5 prosecutors definitely had counsel at the Old Bailey, 1805–30. The sample of fifty-three cases includes some non-property offences and a few quarter sessions cases. *Che.C.*, 17 Mar. 1775, 8 Mar. 1776, 25 July 1777, 17 Mar. 1786, 19 Mar. 1790. 7 Oct. 1791, 19 Mar. 1793, 7–14 Mar. 1800, 31 July 1801, 29 July 1802, 23 Mar. 1804, 27 July 1804, 9 Aug. 1805, 12 Aug. 1808; *The Trial of John Taylor*, *The Genuine Trial of John Motherill for a Rape... Assizes East Grinstead... March 1786* (London, 1786); *The Trial of Miss Broderick for the Wilful Murder of George Errington... Chelmsford 1794* (Edinburgh, 1794); Cottu, *The Administration*, p. 48; Gisbourne, *An Enquiry*, pp. 226–7.

FROM TRIAL TO PUNISHMENT 229

Ten years before his victory in Taylor's trial, for example, Garrow was instrumental in obtaining acquittals for two Essex farmers indicted for forgery, and in 1793 his success on the civil side in extracting £200 in damages for a labouring family was also much remarked upon. Although counsel were still involved in only a minority of criminal cases by the turn of the century, they were clearly beginning to transform the nature of the trial and the judges' role in it. In 1795 Gisborne welcomed them as 'watchmen appointed to superintend the judges' and felt every judge would be more cautious because he was 'acting in the presence of men scrupulously observant of every step which he takes'. The Essex material amply illustrates Garrow's particular impact. At John Taylor's trial in 1800 Garrow challenged every witness, prevented prosecution witnesses from answering key questions by introducing points of law, and arrogantly told the court that 'where the law of England does bear me out, I am not afraid of giving offence to any judge'. He also argued that defence counsel's right to cross-examine was effectively a right to address the court on all matters. 'I had a right', he maintained, 'if I could, indirectly to convey observations to the fact; and whatever other people may say, I shall certainly take the liberty of doing it; for what the law of England will not permit me to do directly, I will do indirectly, where I can.' Garrow was not always popular—the jury in the Taylor trial harangued him for wasting their time—but his aggressive advocacy, his knowledge of complex evidential rulings and his systematic scrutiny of the prosecution case could be very influential.[24]

Garrow's success and wealth were, of course, untypical. 'Damn the Home Circuit' exclaimed the writer of a soliloquy in 1788. 'This business will never do . . . better far better to drop the profession at once than to be trudging through the different counties of England with our wigs and gowns upon our backs.' The number of counsel on the Home Circuit more than doubled between 1785 and 1820, and although the civil and administrative business of both the quarter sessions and assizes provided a considerable income to the lawyers in attendance, their numbers were often greater than this work required. Many therefore may have been keen to take on criminal work. By 1820 many quarter sessions defendants were also receiving professional assistance. Cottu observed that at these courts 'the bar is filled with lawyers who are either occupied with pleading against, or defending, the accused or are employed by parish officers to conduct . . . disputes . . . so that these assemblages present the same appearance as the . . . assizes themselves'.[25]

[24] *Che.C.* 19 Mar. 1790, 8 Mar. 1793; Gisborne, *An Enquiry*, pp. 226–7; J. Beattie, 'Garrow for the Defence', *History Today*, Feb. 1991, pp. 49–53; Beattie, 'Scales of Justice', pp. 236–47. *The Trial of John Taylor*, esp. pp. 14–15.
[25] *The Times*, 21 Apr. 1788; D. Duman, 'The English Bar in the Georgian Period', in W. Prest (ed.), *Lawyers in Early Modern Europe and America* (London, 1981), p. 97; D. Duman, *The Judicial Bench in England 1727–1875. The Reshaping of a Professional Elite* (London, 1982), pp. 22–7; Cottu, *The Administration*, p. 18.

As counsel grew increasingly important, as evidentiary rules proliferated, as cross-examination became more crucial, and careful case production by prosecution and defence developed the late eighteenth and early nineteenth centuries witnessed the springtime of a more adversarial, less judge-dominated form of trial. However, these changes came relatively late in the period under study here and important though they were, they should not be allowed to obscure the grave disadvantages many of the accused laboured under in the eighteenth century. Most prisoners did not have the benefit of counsel and if, as they occasionally did, they faced prosecution counsel without a professional advocate of their own they had to rely on the judge to counterbalance counsel's impact. Moreover, although the presence of counsel undoubtedly had a long-term effect on the nature of the trial and the attitude of the judge, from the individual prisoner's point of view they offered no guarantee of success. In 1775 the *Chelmsford Chronicle* reported that at the trial of three burglars

> There were 23 evidences... all of whom were ordered out of court by desire of the prisoners, to prevent their hearing what each other said, and connecting what they might have to say. As counsel was employed in behalf of the prisoners they apprehended some benefit would accrue from this manoeuvre, which however did not answer their expectations.[26]

Throughout the eighteenth century most of those accused of property offences continued to face severe difficulties when they came to trial. While prosecution witnesses were bound over by the magistrate to appear and give evidence, the prisoner had no such powers of coercion and was reliant on the kindness of those who might be able to offer evidence of his innocence or good character. The courts were offering increasing financial help to prosecutors and their witnesses but those appearing for the defence were ineligible and the prisoner was rarely rich enough to compensate them in full. If the accused was a stranger in the area his chances of obtaining character witnesses were small. While the prosecutor was free to gather his witnesses and marshal his arguments, the prisoner was hampered by his imprisonment and in most cases by his lack of literacy. Nor does he seem to have had an established right to prior knowledge of the evidence that would be used against him, although in an exceptional case in 1777 when the prisoner claimed 'he knew nothing at all of that prosecution', the judge was reported to have 'looked narrowly into it as counsel for the accused and reprobated in strong terms the conduct of the prosecutor in bringing forward a trial... where no notice had been given'.[27]

---

[26] Landsman, 'The Rise', pp. 591–603; Beattie, *Crime*, p. 375; Beattie, 'Scales of Justice', pp. 226–7; *Che.C.*, 17 Mar. 1775; see also *Proceedings... Assizes...Essex...March 1739*, pp. 8–9—William Rogers, facing the possibility of a death sentence under the Black Acts, obtained counsel who pleaded eloquently that the offence was outside the scope of the acts but the judge was hostile. Rogers was sentenced to death.

[27] P.R.O. S.P. 37/1/54. Thomas Godfrey's petition claimed he was 120 miles from home and unable to send for friends to appear on his behalf at the Essex assizes. When a Kent accused claimed that vital

The judge's role may have been gradually changing in ways that were usually helpful to the prisoner and by the early nineteenth century Landsman has suggested that 'the days of unfettered judicial examination were drawing to a close'. However, Kenyon's manipulation of certain trials in 1800–1 warns us against any assumption that the judges had become neutral bystanders. Throughout the eighteenth century and well into the nineteenth century many of the accused found it difficult to construct an effective defence. A significant number presented virtually no defence at all.[28] It is therefore somewhat surprising to find that at the end of almost every assizes or quarter sessions in the eighteenth century the majority of the accused obtained either a not found, a not guilty, or a partial verdict.

2. Verdicts

In contrast to the early seventeenth century when courtroom confessions and plea bargaining played an important role in the trial process, very few offenders pleaded guilty to property crime indictments by the second half of the eighteenth century. In Essex only about three per cent did so in the 1790s, a figure very similar to that found in Surrey. By contrast, between 1740 and 1805 at least one-seventh of the indictments brought before the grand jurors of Essex were dismissed as not found.[29] The petty jury then acquitted almost a third of the remainder and brought in partial verdicts, reducing the charge and effectively lessening the sentence, in a further 10 per cent (Table 7.1). The Staffordshire and Surrey courts followed much the same pattern although both acquittal and partial verdict rates were slightly higher in Essex.[30] In the 1780s the pattern of not guilty verdicts was very similar in all the Home Circuit counties, Essex jurors bringing in only 1 per cent less acquittals than the circuit average (Table 7.2).

The disparity in partial verdict rates amongst the Home Circuit counties (Table 7.2a) may partly reflect differences in jurors' attitudes, but partial

witnesses were unavailable the judge encouraged him to get them to make affidavits and when these cast doubt on the prosecution case the judge reprieved him. *Whole Proceedings . . . Kent . . . March 1774*, p. 17; *Che.C.*, 25 July 1777.

[28] Landsman, 'The Rise', p. 524; three examples from *Proceedings at the Assizes . . . Essex . . . July 1740* are—'The prisoner said nothing in his defence', 'he made no defence', 'he had no person to speak for him nor said anything in his defence'.

[29] Cockburn, *Calendar of Assize Records . . . Introduction*, p. 66, 21 per cent of Essex assize accused pleaded guilty, 1591–1617; Beattie, *Crime*, p. 336. Essex guilty pleas based on quarter sessions and assizes for the first two-thirds of the 1790s. Since these not found bills have not always survived systematically for the quarter sessions, one-seventh is a minimum figure, but only a small number of not found bills are untraceable.

[30] Beattie, *Crime*, pp. 411–15; Green, *Verdict According to Conscience*, pp. 278–88; Hay, 'Crime, Authority', p. 476; *P.P.*, 1819, VIII, pp. 128–31 gives national rates for the first time. For 1810–12 (property crimes only). Not found percentage = 17.1 nationally and 20.4 Essex; not guilty = 25.9 and 27.4, respectively. Essex source P.R.O. H.O. 27/6–8.

Table 7.1. Essex Verdicts, Various Types of Property Crime, 1740–1804

	A Total	B Not found	C Found	D Not guilty	E Partial verdict	% Not found (B/A)	% Not guilty (D/C)	% Partial verdict (E/C)
Petty larceny	1,710	286	1,424	363	4	16.7	25.4	0.3
Horse theft	223	25	198	57	3	11.2	28.8	1.5
Sheep theft	265	39	226	111	6	14.7	49.1	2.7
Grand larceny	2,020	295	1,725	540	241	14.6	31.3	14.0
Housebreaking	670	40	630	129	212	6.0	20.5	33.7
Highway robbery	381	35	346	98	5	9.2	28.3	1.4
Other (receiving, etc.)	412	58	354	146	—	14.1	41.2	0
All property offences	5,681	778	4,903	1,444	471	13.7	29.5	9.6

Sources: As for Table 2.1. Grand larceny includes aggravated larcenies.

Table 7.2. Property Crime Verdicts, Home Circuit, 1782–7

a By County

	Surrey No. %		Kent No. %		Essex No. %		Herts No. %		Sussex No. %		Total No. %	
Not guilty	178	36.3	184	32.5	106	32.7	63	34.6	39	35.1	570	34.1
Partial verdicts	65	13.3	84	14.8	35	10.8	17	9.3	5	4.5	206	12.3
Total found indictments	490		567		324		182		111		1,674	

b By Type of Crime

	Grand larceny %	Aggravated larceny (Capital) %	House breaking %	Highway robbery %	Horse stealing %	Sheep stealing %	Receiving and misc. %	Total %
Not guilty	33.6	36.1	28.7	32.8	34.5	45.5	52.2	34.1
Partial verdicts	5.5	34.8	31.3	3.4	0	0	0	12.3
Total found indictments	604	158	341	317	110	77	67	1,674

Sources: P.R.O. Assi 31/13–15. Summer 1782–Summer 1787.

verdicts were largely confined to certain types of offence (Table 7.2*b*) and legal definitions of predominantly rural crimes such as sheep or cattle theft left little room for the jury to develop this kind of discretionary power.[31] By contrast, in Surrey and Kent indictments for privately stealing from the person, shoplifting, and stealing from the dwelling house were much more important than

---

[31] Essex juries very occasionally tried to bring in partial verdicts in sheep and horse stealing cases. P.R.O. Assi 35/183/1 indictment of John Smith.

elsewhere, and it was these aggravated larcenies, most of which had only recently been made capital offences, that attracted the largest proportion of partial verdicts (Table 7.2b). Acquittal levels also varied between offences. Indictments for receiving were much more likely to result in a not guilty verdict. Sheep stealers found it much easier to gain an acquittal than those charged with horse theft (Table 7.1). Evidentiary and detection problems partly explain these differences. By rapid flight, horse thieves could greatly increase their chances of avoiding detection but horses had more distinctive and less easily removable markings than sheep and once they had been traced and apprehended horse thieves may have found it much more difficult to challenge the victim's evidence. Similarly, the very real possibility that a shopkeeper could have inadvertently bought stolen goods made it particularly difficult to obtain positive proof against receivers, while indictments of this sort were also very open to abuse by malicious prosecutors. Traditions about levels of proof almost certainly differed between offences. Jurors appear to have required a higher level of positive proof if the offence gave them no opportunity to bring in a partial verdict, particularly if it was a capital crime such as forgery, for which pardons were rarely allowed.[32]

The pattern of jury verdicts also changed over time. Both acquittal rates and to a lesser extent not found rates began a nationwide decline after 1800 and the Essex courts followed the same pattern. Equally in the late eighteenth century the use of partial verdicts to reduce grand larceny charges to petty larceny declined rapidly in Essex, as sentences for these two offences became less distinct and the quarter sessions began to take on both types of case. However, the most important function of partial verdicts—to prevent capital sentences in burglary, housebreaking, and aggravated larceny cases—continued to be extensively used.[33] These movements were not, of course, caused by changes in trial procedure and jury attitudes alone. Trial verdicts were also sensitive to pre- and post-trial activity. The early nineteenth-century decline in acquittal rates, for example, may have been largely a result of magistrates' growing willingness to filter out prosecutions supported by insufficient evidence at the pretrial stage. Indeed, that decline is difficult to explain without looking out-side the trial itself since it occurred at a time when the stricter application of rules of evidence and the increasing availability of defence counsel were almost certainly swinging the balance of petty jury trial in the prisoner's favour, and

---

[32] *P.P.*, 1819, VIII, pp. 118–21, national acquittal levels 1810–12 = receiving 52.1%, forgery 39.8%, sheep stealing 34.5%, horse stealing 19.6%. Hay, 'Prosecution', pp. 368–9. *P.P.*, 1819 VIII, p. 50 on reluctance to convict in forgery cases. R. McGowen, 'The Punishment of Forgery in Eighteenth-Century England', *International Association for the History of Crime and Criminal Justice Bulletin*, 17 (1992–3), 30.

[33] *P.P.*, 1819, VIII, pp. 26–7. National acquittal rates (all crimes) fell from 29.7% 1806 to 23% 1817–18, not founds from 15.8% to 15.2%. Essex acquittal rates reached a peak of 35.1% 1790–99 and then fell steadily to 24.8% by 1815–19—not founds fell from 22 to 18% 1805–18. Partial verdict levels in housebreaking cases were 50% 1740–59 but then fell before rising to average about a third 1790–1804—King, 'Crime, Law', p. 305.

when many commentators were arguing that changing sensibilities were making juries less willing to convict in property crime cases.[34]

Despite these fluctuations and the complex changes at various levels of the judicial system which lay behind them, the fundamental pattern of verdicts remained the same throughout the period 1740–1820. At least a third and often nearly half of the accused both in Essex and elsewhere were discharged by either the grand or the petty jury, while a further 10 per cent gained partial verdicts. This is difficult to equate with the prisoners' disadvantaged position at the trial and their widespread inability to put up an adequate defence, which led Langbein to conclude that 'only a small fraction of eighteenth-century criminal trials were genuinely contested enquiries into guilt or innocence. In most cases the accused…possessed no credible defence.'[35] How can this contrast be explained? Partial verdicts in particular were affected by the importance jurors attached to the reputation of the accused. Character evidence was a vital theme in many eighteenth-century trials and the prisoner's defence was not infrequently confined to the calling of one or two character witnesses. Despite the apparent rigidity of the capital statutes, the courts operated an elaborate system of mitigations and their punishment policies were highly individualized. Character evidence was therefore mainly introduced in order to persuade both jury and judge to lessen the sanction. The reputation of the accused among his neighbours clearly affected partial verdicts, sentences, and pardoning decisions (Chapters 8 and 9), but did it also influence his chances of full acquittal?

If the case against the accused was subjected to challenge, character information might occasionally be decisive. Carrington's diary records that at the Hertfordshire assizes three young men who claimed they had only borrowed a publican's silver were 'all…given good characters so they was acquitted'. By contrast in 1739 a young horse thief who said he was only joyriding 'had nobody to speak for his character, so the jury found him guilty'. The character of the prosecutor and his witnesses could also influence the verdict. For example, at the Essex quarter sessions in 1773 William Ruffle was found not guilty of petty larceny after a witness had given him a 'good character and Fitch (the main prosecution witness) a bad one'.[36] There is little evidence, however, that the occupation or social status of the victim alone had a major impact on the verdict. Despite the inadequacies of the data, which are

---

[34] The reformers' arguments, that jurors were increasingly reluctant to convict because they disliked the use of the capital sanction in property crime cases, cannot be accepted uncritically, however. The 1819 committee ignored its own statistics. Between 1810 and 1818 nationwide acquittal rates in property crime cases fell substantially: *P.P.*, 1819, VIII, pp. 128–32; Radzinowitz, *A History*, I, pp. 399–601; M. Rustigan, 'A Reinterpretation of Criminal Law Reform in Nineteenth-Century England', in D. Greenberg (ed.), *Crime and Capitalism* (Palo Alto, 1980), pp. 256–65; McGowen, 'The Image', p. 112.

[35] Langbein, 'Shaping', p. 41.

[36] Branch-Johnson, *'Memoradoms'*, p. 161; *Genuine Proceedings…Home Circuit…March 1739*, p. 16; E.R.O. Q/SBb 274/14.

Table 7.3. Verdicts and Victims' Social Status, Essex Quarter Sessions, 1782–98

Social status	No. not found	All indictments	% not found	No. not guilty	All found indictments	% not guilty	Not found + not guilty % of all indictments
Gentry/professionals	11	66	16.7	18	55	32.7	43.9
Farmer	35	176	19.9	38	141	27.0	41.5
Labourer/husbandman	16	72	22.2	14	56	25.0	41.7
Tradesman/craftsman	23	152	15.1	29	129	22.5	34.2
Total/Average	85	466	18.2	99	381	26.0	39.5

Source: E.R.O. Q/Smg 23–28. Recognizances to prosecute status categories as for Table 6.8. Maritime occupation classified as craftsmen: officials, female prosecutors, servants, military men excluded. Direct prosecution without previously being bound under recognizance occurred occasionally but no record of the status of these prosecutors survives.

available only for the quarter sessions and which do not provide a large enough sample for definitive conclusions, the three main groups in rural society all achieved similar results as prosecutors (Table 7.3). Grand jury hearings produced below average not found rates when gentlemen or tradesmen were prosecuting and above average ones when the victim was a labourer, but Essex petty juries counterbalanced this by convicting a rather smaller percentage of those prosecuted by farmers or gentlemen. Only tradesmen and artisans achieved better than average results from both juries. Just over two-fifths of those accused by gentlemen, farmers, or labourers avoided punishment by either a not found or not guilty verdict. For tradesmen and artisans just over a third achieved the same outcome. Since the only two groups of petty jurors so far studied—those of early seventeenth-century Sussex and late eighteenth-century Essex—both tended to convict a rather higher proportion of those indicted by labourers and husbandmen than of those indicted by farmers or gentlemen, there is no evidence as yet to suggest that higher social status was an advantage to the prosecutor at this stage.[37]

To what extent did the gender of the accused affect their chances of obtaining a favourable verdict? In Essex women were much more likely to attract partial verdicts—a pattern seen particularly strongly in robbery and housebreaking cases (Table 7.4a). Female property offenders were 40 per cent more likely to attract a partial verdict than their male equivalents. Female housebreakers were more than 60 per cent more likely to do so. However, if assizes, quarter sessions, and borough court cases are analysed together, as they are in Table 7.4a, not found and not guilty decisions only marginally favour females. Essex women did achieve higher acquittal rates in every category of offence, but because a much higher proportion of females were

[37] Herrup, *The Common Peace*, p. 154. Lacking information on Essex assizes prosecutors, this conclusion remains tentative.

accused of petty larceny (which had relatively low acquittal rates) overall female acquittal rates were less than 1 per cent higher than male ones. Not found rates also favoured women but again the difference was small—just over 1 per cent more women escaped conviction by this route. Beattie found differences of 2–5 per cent for an earlier range of years in Surrey, but this may partly be because his sample excluded the borough courts. In Essex these courts convicted 3 per cent more women than men and also marginally favoured men at the grand jury stage. Although this is difficult to explain, it was partly linked to the fact that only minor thefts were tried in the borough courts. It appears that in the borough and quarter sessions courts, where the stakes were much lower because the capital sanction was not available and transportation was relatively rarely used, jurors had little inclination to favour women. However, this was not the case at the assizes (Table 7.4b). On the Home Circuit in the 1780s women were 40 per cent more likely to be acquitted and more than 70 per cent more likely to attract a partial verdict—a pattern which recent work suggests was also found in London and several other counties throughout the period 1780–1830 although not, it appears, in Durham or in the borough of Newcastle.[38]

Table 7.4a. Essex Property Crime Verdicts, Male and Female Accused, 1740–1805

	Sex	A Total	B Not found	C Found	D Not guilty	E Partial verdict	% Not found (B/A)	% Not guilty (D/C)	% Partial verdict (E/C)
Petty larceny	M	1,379	238	1,141	290	4	17.3	25.4	0.4
	F	331	48	283	73	—	14.5	25.8	—
Horse theft	M	222	24	198	57	3	10.8	28.8	1.5
	F	1	1	—	—	—	—	—	—
Sheep theft	M	263	38	225	111	6	14.4	49.3	2.7
	F	2	1	1	0	—	—	—	—
Grand larceny	M	1,769	255	1,514	471	200	14.4	31.1	13.2
	F	251	40	211	69	41	15.9	32.7	19.4
Housebreaking	M	587	36	551	110	171	6.1	20.0	31.0
	F	83	4	79	19	41	4.8	24.1	51.9
Highway robbery	M	375	33	342	95	4	8.8	27.8	1.2
	F	6	2	4	2	1	33.3	50.0	25.0
Other (receiving, etc.)	M	335	44	291	118	—	13.1	40.5	—
	F	77	14	63	28	—	18.2	44.4	—
All property	M	4,930	668	4,262	1,252	388	13.5	29.4	9.1
Offences	F	751	110	641	191	83	14.6	29.8	12.9

Source: As for Table 5.1.

[38] Beattie, Crime, 404, 414, and 437; Herrup, The Common Peace, p. 150; Cockburn, The Calendar of Assize Records ... Introduction, pp. 189–97; in the five Essex borough courts. Not found = Male 12.2%, female 11.7%. Not guilty = male 28.6%, female 25.5%. For a detailed national study of the impact of gender on verdicts and punishments, P. King, 'Gender, Crime and Justice in Late Eighteenth and Early

Table 7.4*b*. Home Circuit, Verdicts by Gender,
Property Offenders, 1782–7

	Male %	Female %
0 – Failed to reach court	0.13	0.47
1 – Discharged before public trial	0.69	0.47
2 – Not guilty	31.19	44.13
3 – Guilty	52.27	35.21
4 – Partial verdict	11.43	19.72
5 – Unknown verdict	4.29	0.00
Sample size	1,584	213

Source: As for Table 7.2.

Table 7.5. Essex Verdicts and Wheat Price Changes, 1740–1804

	Not found No.	%	Not guilty No.	%	Partial verdict No.	%	Total
High wheat price years	178	13.4	315	27.5	127	11.1	1,325
All years	778	13.7	1,444	29.5	471	9.6	5,681
Low wheat price years	134	14.6	237	30.3	75	9.6	915

Sources: As for Table 3.1. High wheat price years = 1740–1, 1757, 1766–8, 1772, 1789, 1795–6, 1800–1. Low price years = 1745–6, 1755–6, 1760, 1769–70, 1779–80, 1787, 1798, 1803.

Any attempt to link a significant proportion of acquittals to the character of the accused must, however, account for the fact that while partial verdicts and sentences varied widely with age, favouring both adolescents and those with families to support (Chapter 8), not guilty verdicts did not. Acquittal rates remained the same for every age group except those under 15, who gained limited protection from legal rulings concerning the age of discretion. The insensitivity of acquittal rates to changes in economic conditions also suggests that the character of the accused was relatively unimportant in these decisions. The Essex material supports Hay's conclusions that 'juries did not acquit more men and women outright during periods of high prices . . . but they did alter the number of convictions on reduced charges'. Although the proportion of the accused with reasonably good character backgrounds almost certainly rose in times of dearth, Essex acquittal levels did not (Table 7.5), while partial verdicts did.[39] Here as elsewhere the character of the accused might affect

Nineteenth-Century England', in M. Arnot and C. Usborne (eds.), *Gender and Crime in Modern Europe* (London, 1999), pp. 44–74; Morgan and Rushton, *Rogues, Thieves*, p. 70.

[39] Hay, 'War', p. 155. Essex verdicts did not respond in any systematic way to changing recorded crime rates. In ten selected high crime years, 38.2% of indictments were either not found or returned

both jury mitigation practices and punishment policies but it was largely peripheral when it came to decisions about outright acquittal.

Why then were acquittal rates so high? Some contemporaries believed that grand juries were to blame. In 1785 *The Times* expressed its surprise that 'grand juries... find bills of indictment which are not afterwards sustained before petit juries by a shadow of evidence', while in 1812 Williams argued that grand jurors 'serve no purpose whatsoever'. However, other contemporaries defended the grand jury and its functions, and while high acquittal rates may partly reflect grand jurors' tendencies to give the prosecution the benefit of the doubt, over a sixth of indictments were still not found between 1810 and 1819. The main focus of explanation must therefore be the petty jury trial itself. By the end of the eighteenth century the repugnance of juries at the possibility that relatively minor property offenders might be sentenced to death, often on the evidence of professional thieftakers, was certainly felt by many both inside and outside the reform camp to be escalating the extent of both acquittals and partial verdicts. Colquhoun, for example, attacked the 'false mercy of juries', and even the system's great apologist, William Paley, launched a diatribe against injudicious acquittals, blaming 'the over strained scrupulousness, or weak timidity, of juries... which holds it the part of a safe conscience not to condemn any man whilst there exists the minutest possibility of his innocence'. In capital cases the role played by the long-standing tradition of jury nullification (i.e. to quote Green's definition, the exercise of jury discretion in favour of a defendant whom the jury none the less believes to have committed the act with which he is charged) should not be underestimated.[40]

Acquittal levels were probably less affected by this tradition than were partial verdicts. The development of a viable alternative punishment, transportation, in the early eighteenth century left juries increasingly free to respond to capital indictments by committing what contemporaries called 'pious perjury', changing the nature of the offence or the value of the stolen goods so that the crime fell outside the scope of the capital statutes.[41] However, high acquittal rates were not confined to capital cases alone. More than a quarter of petty larceny offenders were also found not guilty. Repugnance at the multiplication of the capital statutes and a growing reluctance to see offenders hanged for theft were therefore not the only reasons for low conviction rates. That repugnance did, however, feed into the more general framework of ideas that underpinned the high level of proof which jurors and judges

not guilty. In ten low-crime years, the figure was 38.5%. In Essex during the four years of most extreme dearth (1740–1, 1772, 1800) acquittals were slightly below average.

[40] *The Times*, 15 Jan. 1785; Williams, *Every Man*, p. 172; Langbein, 'The English Criminal Trial', p. 22; Blackstone, *Commentaries*, 4, pp. 300–1; on grand juries' problematic evidentiary standards, Shapiro, *Beyond Resonable Doubt*, pp. 43–113; Green, *Verdict According to Conscience*, pp. 267–317; Beattie, *Crime*, pp. 411–12; Colquhoun, *Police*, p. 3; W. Paley, *The Principles of Moral and Political Philosophy* (1785), in E. Paley, *The Works of W. Paley... and a Corrected Account of the Author* (7 vols., London, 1825), 4, p. 446.

[41] Green, *Verdict According to Conscience*, pp. xiii, 275–7; Beattie, *Crime*, pp. 424–30.

felt to be necessary before guilt could be established. Most acquittals in the eighteenth century occurred in cases where either there was no direct and reliable eye-witness identification of the accused or where strong circumstantial evidence, such as possession or pawning of the stolen goods, could not be established.[42] As a more adversarial form of trial developed in the late eighteenth century, the difficulties of establishing an adequate prosecution case may have increased, but the failure of grand jurors and committing magistrates to filter out cases which lacked either of these forms of evidence remained one of the main reasons for high acquittal rates. A number of other factors were, however, also very important.

Although the dynamics of jury decision-making and the role of foremen in that process are difficult to assess, the requirement that the petty jury should be unanimous in their decisions may well have increased acquittals. Paley, for example, believed that this rule operated 'considerably in favour of the prisoner, for if a juror find it necessary to surrender to the obstinacy of others, he will much more readily resign his opinion on the side of mercy than of condemnation'. Despite the unanimity rule juries reached almost all their verdicts after a very brief huddled discussion in open court. This reflected both the straightforward nature of the evidence in many routine cases and the jurors' determination to resolve disagreements swiftly—a determination inspired in part by the uncomfortable and potentially lengthy confinement they would suffer if they failed to do so.[43] In this context it would usually have been easier to override a minority in favour of a full guilty verdict than to browbeat a subgroup of jurors holding out for an acquittal or partial verdict. Indeed Adam Smith believed it had become customary to resolve disagreements by taking the more merciful option. In 'criminal cases', he argued, 'the favourable side is always to be taken, and this is generally looked on as a rule of quasi-justice, and though the party that desires to acquit the criminal be the fewest, yet the others, when they see that there are men of integrity who think him innocent, they will readily agree to think him so'.[44]

Many eighteenth- and early nineteenth-century writers also believed that the courts' scrupulousness over technical matters such as the wording of the indictment contributed substantially to acquittals. Colquhoun complained for example that 'every trifling inaccuracy in the indictment is allowed to become a fatal obstacle to conviction'. A number of such cases were reported in the

[42] T. Green, 'A Retrospective on the Criminal Trial Jury 1200–1800', in Cockburn and Green (eds.), *Twelve Good Men*, pp. 394–5; Beattie, *Crime*, p. 415.

[43] Paley, *Works*, 4, pp. 422–3; King, '"Illiterate Plebeians, Easily Misled". Jury Composition, Experience and Behaviour in Essex 1735–1815', in Cockburn and Green (eds.), *Twelve Good Men*, pp. 294–9 for a more detailed discussion of foremen. In 1795 an Essex jury, having failed to reach agreement by 10 p.m., 'were then impanelled in the room during the whole night without fire or any nourishment . . . at 4 o'clock their candle went out when they remained in the dark' until 7 o'clock when the judge reappeared. *Che.C.*, 20 Mar. 1795.

[44] R. Meek, D. Raphael, and P. Stein (eds.), *Adam Smith Lectures in Jurisprudence* (Oxford, 1978), p. 285.

press. At the Chelmsford assizes in 1793 Henry James appeared to be facing almost certain conviction on a capital charge until a bystander brought the judge's attention to an error in the description of the stolen goods. The judge promptly 'directed the jury to acquit the prisoner which they accordingly did'. In 1800 a Harlow corn merchant narrowly escaped receiving sentence of death for forgery through a similar discovery of a misspelt Christian name, while another prisoner was acquitted because the brass locks he had stolen were described as brass cocks in the indictment. Thus, while Hale's earlier suggestion that 'more offenders escape by the over-easy ear given to exceptions in indictments, than by their own innocence' exaggerates the impact of technical acquittals in this period, the increasingly formalistic rules surrounding indictments clearly saved some prisoners from conviction, particularly in the late eighteenth century when the involvement of counsel was growing.[45] Unfortunately the trial reports give little indication of how many prosecutions were involved, because such cases often collapsed early on and were not therefore reported.

The reports do, however, suggest that what might be called prosecutor nullification also played a substantial role in boosting acquittals. Many prosecutors achieved this by simply failing to turn up and many poorer victims in particular did precisely that without apparently having their recognizances estreated (Chapter 2). Some non-appearing prosecutors and witnesses were fined, however, and a safer line of action was to appear but then to deliberately throw the case away. It was widely known in the early nineteenth century that a prosecutor or witness, wishing to avoid both forfeiting his recognizances and being held responsible for an offender being hanged, would often go through 'the form of [his] part in the prosecution taking care to shape [his] evidence in favour of the accused'. Sometimes the lack of a strong prosecution case arose from the fact that the indictment was a deliberately malicious act. If so the bench would, of course, encourage an acquittal and in some cases the court would even use the term 'honourable acquittal', as the *Chelmsford Chronicle* did in 1770, to indicate that the prosecutor was more culpable than the accused. Occasionally, out of sympathy for the defendant, the judges even colluded with legitimate prosecutors in the misrepresentation of the evidence. A Somerset shopkeeper told the 1819 committee that when he indicted two girls, aged 11 and 14, for shoplifting the bench advised him not to adduce evidence against them and they were therefore acquitted.[46] The trial reports suggest, however, that judges not infrequently faced forms of prosecutor nullification with which they were very definitely not in agreement. At the Essex assizes in 1804 the

[45] Colquhoun, *Police*, pp. 232–3; Radzinowitz, *The History*, 1, pp. 97–100; *Che.C.*, 12 July 1793; 14 Mar. 1800; *Whole Proceedings... Surrey... March 1774*, p. 16.

[46] Green, *Verdict According to Conscience*, p. 362. There was no formal legal concept of honourable acquittal—Hay, 'Prosecution', p. 343; but it was a phrase used quite widely *Che.C.*, 6 Apr. 1770; *P.P.*, 1819, VIII, p. 104.

prosecutor in a highway robbery case gave such sympathetic evidence, min-imalizing the degree to which he had been put in fear by the accused before parting with his money, that the judge commented sarcastically 'why I think you seem to have got very good friends', to which the victim replied, 'why my Lord I think so too'. The judge had immediately to instruct the jury to acquit the prisoner. At the Essex assizes sixty-five years earlier Judge Carter angrily asked one prevaricating prosecutor, 'if you have nothing to allege against him why was he brought here?' At the same assizes Carter was involved in the following altercation in another case that ended in acquittal.

Court: Are these your goods?
Prosecutor: They are like mine; but I can't be positive.
Court: How do you know your house was broke open?
Prosecutor: My wife told me so.
Court: Where is your wife?
Prosecutor: At home.
Court: And so might you too, for the good you have done here.[47]

While the judge's anger and impotence in such cases is clear, the motives of prosecutors and witnesses are rarely spelled out. The weakness of the pro-secutor's presentation may often have arisen simply from naivety or lack of assiduousness. Sometimes the absence of key witnesses was due to organiza-tional problems. Several contemporaries commented on the difficulty of keeping witnesses hanging around for several days and on the likelihood that when they were finally called they might be out of earshot or ensconced in a local inn. The costs a prosecution entailed were also highly detrimental to the strength of the case eventually presented. 'The expense of attending the sessions 3 or 4 days together', *The Times* argued, 'is ... more than numbers will submit to; whereby many notorious offenders are too often acquitted for want of proper evidence'. The number of prosecutors and witnesses who deliberately chose to ensure that the accused got off should not be under-estimated. There were many reasons why such motives may have governed prosecutors' and witnesses' behaviour. Some considered the time the accused had spent in gaol awaiting trial as sufficient punishment. Many witnesses, Colquhoun agreed, were 'cajoled, threatened or bribed either to mutilate their evidence or to speak doubtfully on the trial although they swore positively before the committing magistrate'. Likewise prosecutors 'either intimidated by the expense or softened down by appeals to their humanity' did not 'take the necessary steps to bring forward evidence' with the result that the indictment was either returned ignoramus or ended in acquittal because of 'deficient evidence'.[48] The motives behind prosecutor and witness nullification were mixed. A genuine humanity was balanced against a desire to avoid reprisal or

---

[47] *Che.C.*, 27 July 1804; *Genuine Proceedings ... Home Circuit ... March 1739*, pp. 10–11.
[48] *P.P.*, 1816, V, p. 241; *The Times*, 15 July 1785; Colquhoun, *Police*, pp. 11–23.

community censure. The need to avoid expense and trouble was paramount in some cases, but so too was the desire to get compensation and restitution. Many prosecutors may well have been willing to 'give faint evidence' if they were promised that the stolen goods would then be returned. A high proportion of assault and misdemeanour indictments resulted in private agreements and monetary payments to the victim[49] and although compounding a felony was illegal many contemporaries believed the practice was widespread. A considerable number of property crime prosecutors or witnesses almost certainly failed to appear or deliberately weakened their evidence for this reason.

Jury nullification is easier to study than the equivalent activity among prosecutors or witnesses. Partial verdicts and acquittals were decided in open court and systematically recorded. Partial verdicts in particular became a légitimate and vital part of the range of mitigation opportunities many considered necessary to counterbalance the severity of the capital code. Prosecutor mitigation via a deliberate reduction of the charge or via selective presentation of the evidence in court was, by contrast, a private, unrecorded decision,[50] although occasionally the prosecutor, having established the prisoner's guilt, would then openly plead for a partial verdict. In 1739, for example, an Essex victim obtained a partial verdict in a capital case after informing the court, 'I believe it is the first fact he ever committed and I hope the court will be favourable to him.' Prosecutors' and witnesses' attempts to obtain outright acquittals rather than partial verdicts have also left little evidence for historians. Prosecutor nullification went unrecorded both because it was often an illegal act arising from an agreement to compound and because the grand jury hearings, where prosecutors could most quickly and efficiently get their recognizances discharged by a perfunctory performance, were held in secret and no record of the proceedings permitted. However, a considerable proportion of the petty jury trials for which records do survive suggest that prosecutor and witness nullification remained a distinct possibility at this stage also. For example the printer summarized Margaret Southouse's trial in 1739 as follows: 'no evidence appearing she was acquitted'. Likewise in 1803 the non-appearance of an Essex coachman, who had witnessed the transfer of some stolen goods, meant that the judge 'stopped the prosecution and directed the jury to find the prisoner not guilty'. It may never be possible to produce a history of prosecutor or witness nullification to parallel the detailed work on the history of jury nullification Green has done, but if the influence of victims and witnesses is ignored there is a danger that the role of judges and juries, vital though it was, may be overemphasized.[51]

---

[49] Gatrell, *The Hanging Tree*, p. 407; Shoemaker, *Prosecution*, pp. 127–65.

[50] Occasionally evidence about prosecutor mitigation comes to light when the charge made at the committal proceedings is different from that in the indictment: Beattie, *Crime*, p. 333.

[51] *Genuine Proceedings . . . Home Circuit . . . March 1739*, pp. 11 and 16; *Che.C.*, 18 Mar. 1803; Green, *Verdict According to Conscience*.

3. Courtroom Decision-Makers and their Interactions

Acquittal and partial verdict rates, and indeed the whole experience of the accused during the trial, were influenced not only by the decisions of prosecutors, witnesses, jurors, and judges but also by the backgrounds from which the main decision-makers came, by the interactions between them, and by the role of the crowds that gathered in and around the courtroom. The social backgrounds of prosecutors have already been analysed (Chapter 2). Roughly two-thirds were middling men, a quarter were members of the labouring poor, the remainder were gentry or professionals. More than two-fifths of witnesses at the quarter sessions were labourers or husbandmen, two-fifths were craftsmen or tradesmen, virtually none were gentry, and 15 per cent were farmers.[52] The extent to which plebeian witnesses found it necessary to represent or safeguard their employers' interests rather than their own when giving testimony remains difficult to gauge, but witnesses as well as prosecutors could often shape the roles they played during the trial in line with their own interests or sense of justice, and many of these roles were played by those with little or no property. Many of the character witnesses, whose testimonies could be so important in obtaining a partial verdict or a lesser sentence, came from a similar section of society. Some were employers, landlords, or parish worthies, but many were simply neighbours, relatives, fellow workers, or keepers of lodging houses.[53] With a few exceptions, however, prosecutors and witnesses rarely had extensive experience of major criminal trials and this probably meant that they used their discretionary powers less systematically or effectively than judges or jurors. Judge–jury relationships remained at the heart of the trial and both might bring considerable expertise to the process. Their social status and patterns of service are therefore worth discussing more fully.

Eighteenth-century jurors in London, Surrey, Essex, and Staffordshire have been the subject of extensive published research and a brief review is therefore all that is necessary here.[54] Apart from the grand jury at the assizes, which was drawn exclusively from the gentry élite throughout this period, the Essex juries—the assizes petty jury, the grand and petty juries at quarter sessions—were dominated by farmers, artisans, and tradesmen, who represented 90–7 per cent of acting jurors. The participation of the established gentry was very small, that of the landless poor was non-existent. A few men described as

---

[52] Essex witnesses under recognizance to appear in felony cases at quarter sessions (based on 1765–9, 1775–9, 1785–9, 1795–9): Gentlemen 0%; Professionals 0.6%; Farmers 15%; Tradesmen and artisans (including maritime occupations) 42%; Husbandmen 3%; Labourers 39%; sample size 313. Single women, servants, and officials excluded (each = 5 or 6%).

[53] All these categories appear in the 1774 trial reports, *Whole Proceedings ... Essex, Surrey, Kent, Herts ... March 1774*.

[54] Much of what follows is based on P. King, ' "Illiterate Plebeians, Easily Misled". Jury Composition, Experience and Behaviour in Essex, 1735–1815', and for comparison on Hay, 'The Class Composition' and J. Beattie, 'London Juries', all in Cockburn and Green (eds.), *Twelve Good Men and True*; Beattie, *Crime*, pp. 318–33, 378–95.

labourers, who owned small pieces of land sufficient to meet the minimum £10 freehold requirement, did serve on late eighteenth-century Essex juries, but essentially the bottom half of the population was excluded from jury service by the property qualification. For the average property offender trial by jury was clearly not trial by 'his equals or neighbours indifferently chosen' to quote Blackstone's phrase. 'What peership, what equality', Bamford rightly demanded, 'can be said to exist between the class of working men—whose only property is their labour—and the class from which even common jurors are at present taken— ... because they have that which the working class has not ... a certain amount of visible property.'[55] Locating the jurors within the wealthier half of the population is much more difficult, however. Although only 8–10 per cent of Essex male household heads were listed as eligible for service in the freeholders' books, this certainly did not mean that jurors were drawn exclusively from the richest tenth of the population. Qualification for jury service was not based on total wealth but on the possession of certain categories of land. Various wealthy non-landowning groups, such as large tenant farmers and commercial men whose main assets were in stock, were therefore excluded, while many small farmers with very limited capital or income served on juries. Work on individual parishes suggests that in many areas a substantial number of small owner-occupiers well outside the top quarter of the local income structure qualified as jurors. Although the estate valuations in the uniquely informative Essex freeholders' books need to be treated with care, they suggest that two-thirds of quarter sessions petty jurors and two-fifths of assizes petty jurors were in the lowest eligible landowning category; moreover, those who actually served as petty jurors contained a larger proportion of these smaller landowners than the freeholders' book in general. Thus in Essex, outside the assizes grand jury, a fairly broad range of middling men dominated the decision-making process.[56]

Broadly similar results have emerged from research on other areas, although every county and borough had slightly different selection procedures. John Beattie describes Surrey petty jurors as men in the middling ranks, men of moderate wealth and social status. Douglas Hay has located the jurors marginally higher in the top quarter of the scale of income but the difference is relatively small. The Essex material places most jurors in much the same range of middling wealth but indicates that a significant, if by no means dominant, subgroup of poorer smallholders also served. Since few non-qualified talismen were used in the eighteenth and early nineteenth centuries, and since the trial administrators were reasonably efficient in ensuring that only qualified jurors were called, the statutes that deliberately excluded the poorer half of the

---

[55] King, 'Illiterate Plebeians', esp. pp. 263–7. The property qualification was complex but in Essex the £10 freehold was central; Burn, *The Justice*, 2, pp. 463–6; Hay, 'The Class Composition', pp. 311–13; Blackstone, *Commentaries*, 4, p. 343; Bamford, *Early Days*, pp. 48–9.

[56] King, 'Illiterate Plebeians', pp. 266–74.

population from juries succeeded in making the trial an expression as well as a reflection of the studied inequality which can be seen at every level of office holding in this period. Equally, however, the gentry also largely avoided service on petty juries. In late eighteenth- and early nineteenth-century Essex 11 per cent of qualifying jurors were labelled as gentlemen but only 0.3 per cent of quarter sessions petty jurors and 2.7 per cent of those at the assizes were gentry. Petty jury trial was trial by middle-aged or later middle-aged middling men. Despite élite commentators' tendency to label them as ignorant or illiterate, almost all the Essex jurors were literate and most had considerable decision-making experience, having served several times in various parish offices.[57] Moreover, by the end of the eighteenth century most would also have already gained considerable experience in the courtroom itself. In the 1770s and 1780s only about 10 per cent of Essex jurors had previous experience of sitting on a jury. However, in 1784 a policy of recalling most of those who had been empanelled three years earlier was instituted. The introduction of this triennial system meant that henceforward most jurors had both previous experience of jury work and a previous acquaintance with their fellow jurors. By 1800 most jurors had brought in dozens of verdicts, some had brought in hundreds. Although experience levels were not as high in Surrey or Stafford-shire, virtually every jury would have contained some men who had served before.[58] Thus many late eighteenth- and early nineteenth-century juries brought considerable expertise into the courtroom, which would have in-creased the confidence with which they dealt with the trial process, the lawyers, and, most important, the judges.

The judges were men of high social and economic status. At the quarter sessions the bench was chaired by wealthy and long-established magistrates such as Charles Gray or Thomas Berney Bramston.[59] At the assizes the trial was controlled by judges drawn from the élite of eighteenth-century society, most of whom were judges of the superior courts in London. The rituals that surrounded the judges' arrival at Chelmsford may have further enhanced their status in the eyes of the inhabitants, but many of them were already men of considerable wealth and reputation in their own right. The eighteenth-century bar was something of a lottery, but for those who were successful it was extremely lucrative. Judges were not usually appointed until they were in their forties and many had already been practising barristers for two decades. With the large salaries, fees, and other income sources available to them the judges

[57] Beattie, *Crime*, pp. 378–95; Hay, 'The Class Composition'; King, 'Illiterate Plebeians'.

[58] King, 'Illiterate Plebeians', pp. 284–9; Hay, 'The Class Composition', pp. 344–7; Beattie, *Crime*, p. 385.

[59] *Che.C.*, 10 Oct. 1788, 18 July 1800, 26 July 1805; ERO D/DR F61 11 Jan. 1825; although some counties appointed permanent quarter sessions chairmen, the Essex chair operated on a semi-rotational basis well into the nineteenth century. Landau, *The Justices*, p. 253; Webbs, *English Local Government. The Parish*, p. 353; ERO Q/SBb 303/33; 304/7; Addison, *Essex Worthies*, p. 88; Eastwood, *Governing Rural England*, p. 55.

were wealthy men. More than half were MPs at some time during their career and several were given peerages. Influential titled judges such as Mansfield and Kenyon showed a particular liking for the Home Circuit, returning to it every year, but of the forty-five judges who presided at the Essex assizes, 1750–1800, only six came to Chelmsford more than ten times. The majority came only once or twice in the entire period,[60] their judicial work being undertaken mainly on other circuits or in London. However, despite their parallel obligation to hear civil cases most of the judges who sat at the Chelmsford assizes had wide experience of handling criminal evidence and crown juries. How did the relationship between these members of the élite and the middling jurors of eighteenth-century England shape the criminal trial?

4. Judge–Jury Relationships

Contemporaries often found the complex nature of the relationship between judge and jury hard to unravel. The juries were obviously deeply embedded at the heart of the mitigation and selection processes which played such an important part in many trials, but it was difficult to ascertain whether the judges were pulling the strings or whether the jury was acting independently. Historians have had the same problem. It is relatively easy to show, as Green, Beattie, and Langbein have done, that in the great majority of routine property crime cases judge and jury worked in harmony, or at the very least without any sign of open conflict. Moreover, the rapidity of most trials certainly suggests a substantial degree of practical co-operation. Both groups had a vested interest in ensuring that the proceedings were not drawn out. The circuit judges had an increasingly tight schedule to follow.[61] The jurors were performing an unpaid duty which took them away from their homes and businesses. It appears that both sides were willing to make compromises in order to prevent the proceedings from slowing down. What is less easy to assess is the extent to which, in order to create and preserve those compromises, each side was willing to accept outcomes they would not have accepted if they alone had been deciding the case.

At first sight the relationship between judge and jury appears to have been a very one-sided affair, at least until the coming of more adversarial forms of trial in the late eighteenth century. The vast difference in social status between the two groups, the assize judges' expert knowledge of the law, and their role as

---

[60] D. Duman, *The Judicial Bench*. The median for judges' personal estates was £ 25,000. For the judges' gravitation to a few prestigious university colleges, D. Duman, *The English and Colonial Bars in the Nineteenth Century* (London, 1983), p. 24. In the 1820s the judges' average age was 65—Gatrell, *The Hanging Tree*, p. 506. P.R.O. Assi 31/2–18.

[61] Beattie, *Crime*, p. 408; Green, *Verdict According to Conscience*, pp. 267–79; Green, 'The English Criminal Trial Jury and the Law-Finding Traditions on the Eve of the French Revolution', in Schioppa (ed.), *The Trial Jury*, pp. 50–1; Langbein, 'The English Criminal Trial', p. 34; Langbein, 'Shaping', p. 122.

orchestrators of the trial proceedings suggest that juries may have played only a subsidiary part in shaping final verdicts. In the first half of the eighteenth century, as Langbein has shown, the judges could use a wide variety of methods to influence the juries' decisions, including commenting on the evidence, terminating the case before the verdict (thus effectively directing an acquittal), and sending the jury back to deliberate again if they had brought in a verdict with which the bench disagreed.[62] However, most of these techniques were rarely used and even when they were they were not necessarily successful. The almost complete absence of any records written by the jurors themselves has forced historians to be dangerously reliant on the judges' views of the proceedings and they may therefore have underestimated the influence that jurors could have on trial proceedings and on acquittal rates by the later eighteenth century.

The independence of petty juries is most easily observable in cases not involving routine property offences. The inability of the judges to control jury verdicts in cases of a political nature was well exemplified in the treason trials and sedition cases of the later eighteenth century. Jury independence may have been reinforced in some areas by the Wilkites' campaigns to protect jury powers, increase jurors' sense of their own authority, and limit judicial discretion,[63] but it was not a new phenomenon. Throughout the eighteenth century provincial and metropolitan juries had often refused to convict certain types of offender. Paley was clearly upset by this. 'Trial by jury is sometimes found inadequate', he wrote. 'This imperfection takes place chiefly in disputes in which some popular passion or prejudice intervenes; as ... where an order of men are obnoxious by their profession, as are officers of the revenue ... or where one of the parties has an interest in common with the general interest of jurors, and that of the other is opposed to it, as in contests between landlords and tenants.' Paley had his own prejudices but juries undoubtedly favoured those whose interests were adjacent to their own. Styles has suggested that the acquittal of some coinage offenders may have been linked to the hostility felt by farmers, tradesmen, and manufacturers to the Mint Monopoly, and where the middling sort were widely involved in activities which were against the law, but which they considered to be legitimate, jury 'prejudice' was virtually complete. In Essex, for example, both excise and game offenders were very rarely indicted before a criminal trial jury by the late eighteenth century.[64]

---

[62] Langbein, 'The Criminal Trial', pp. 284–300; Langbein 'The English Criminal Trial', pp. 36–7.

[63] E. P. Thompson, *The Making of the English Working Class* (Harmondsworth, 2nd edn., 1968), pp. 87, 148–9; J. Brewer, 'The Wilkites and the Law 1763–74', in Brewer and Styles (eds.), *An Ungovernable People*; Langbein, 'Albion's Fatal Flaws', p. 109; T. Green, *Verdict According to Conscience*, pp. 318–55; C. Emsley, 'An Aspect of Pitt's Terror: Prosecutions for Sedition during the 1790s', *Social History*, 6 (1981), pp. 162–72; *Che. C.*, 24 Dec. 1784; Green, 'The English Criminal Trial Jury', pp. 52–70.

[64] Paley, *The Works*, 4, pp. 412–13; Styles 'Our Traitorous Money Makers', pp. 181–2; King, 'Crime, Law', pp. 323–4. Smuggling was very common in Essex (*Che. C.*, 20 Feb. 1784) but although relevant cases are occasionally found in the petty sessions courts (E.R.O. P/CM, 26 Mar. 1803; P/TP 1 22 Feb.

Game preservers and their associations faced by the crown juries' over-riding tendency to acquit may have made increasing use of the civil courts, where the damage they could inflict on a poacher was potentially greater, but civil assize juries were not necessarily any more compliant. In 1754, just after indictments against three labourers for poaching a gentleman's fish had been thrown out by the grand jury at the Essex quarter sessions, the Game Association brought a civil action against three game poachers at the Chelmsford assizes. However, this newly formed national association was very unpopular with the Essex farmers and the jury brought in verdicts for the defendants.[65] Over the eighteenth century as a whole, civil prosecutions against game offenders appear to have been relatively rare. Juries continued to exercise their own very independent judgment and only the large landowners and the financially secure associations could safely risk the high costs that might be incurred if a civil case was lost. Lesser gentry rarely had the resources to use this method of prosecution and although the threat of civil proceedings remained a potent weapon, the majority of game preservers were largely reliant on informal coercion or summary proceedings. Thus here, as else-where, the discretionary power of the middling group shaped the administra-tion of the law and limited the ways that it could be used by wealthier groups. By removing the judicial process to their own parlours, the gentry avoided the expense and possible humiliation of a jury trial and made the prosecution of game offenders more convenient, but the price they had to pay was consider-able since the summary conviction laws usually allowed only the relatively minor punishments of a fine or imprisonment.[66]

Jurors' tendencies to follow their own inclinations rather than those of the judge can also be observed in riot prosecutions. In 1794, for example, eighteen rioters were tried for attacking a northern Essex Wesleyan congregation. When only three were convicted the *Chelmsford Chronicle* commented that 'if the jury had followed the opinion and directions of the learned judge', the number would have been four times as great.[67] Jury independence is therefore easy to exemplify in certain exceptional types of case, but what was the nature of judge–jury relationships in run-of-the-mill property crime trials? The re-ports the judges wrote in response to petitions for pardon suggest wide differences of approach but many judges appear to have distanced themselves from verdicts, leaving the jury to evaluate 'the credit of the evidence' and

1794 and 31 Mar. 1794) and in the Westminster Central Courts (*Che.C.*, 3 Dec. 1779) successful prosecutions before a jury were rare.

[65] Munsche, *Gentlemen*, pp. 22–4, 89–90; for an article showing concern that jurors often followed their own inclinations and gave 'a verdict to the weaker side without regard to truth or justice', *Che.C.*, 15 July 1791; E.R.O. Q/SR 717; *Norwich Mercury*, 24 Aug. 1754.

[66] Munsche, *Gentlemen*, pp. 90–3; for one steward's complaint that 'there is no answering for a common jury . . . as they have in general a strong bias . . . in favour of poachers', Hay, 'Poaching', p. 211; *Che. C.*, 2 Aug. 1799 for an Essex poacher facing 'an action at law'.

[67] *Che.C.*, 21 Mar. 1794.

avoiding direct involvement or instruction unless they felt that a specific case required their intervention or needed to be used as an example. Their reports often contain phrases such as 'the jury chose' or 'the jury thought fit' and when asked to assess the reasoning behind jury verdicts they were often uncertain. A Recorder's report in 1786 commented that the accused 'was convicted of stealing the things but the jury thought fit (probably in compassion to his youth) to acquit him of the violence'. In 1819 a retired judge admitted: 'In what instances . . . convictions may have been evaded, it is impossible for anyone to say, but it is a very strong symptom . . . of preventing convictions to see the extreme avidity with which juries will look to . . . favour the prisoner.'[68] It is not difficult to find cases in which juries took their lead from the bench, particularly if a merciful partial verdict was being suggested. Judge Hotham, reporting on a 1790 case, noted: 'I recommended it to the jury to acquit him of the capital charge as he appeared to be very young.' Thirteen years later a letter written by a 17-year-old servant to his master pleading for mercy in another capital case so 'excited the feelings' of the same judge that he 'directed the jury to find the prisoner guilty of stealing, but not in the dwelling house'.[69] In both cases the jury returned a partial verdict.

Many eighteenth-century commentators stressed that judges should remain as neutral as possible when addressing jurors, and should, to quote Gisbourne, 'State . . . the evidence on each side of the question in perspicuous order, and with perfect impartiality'. In 1788 *The Times* argued that 'the office of the judge empowers him . . . to explain the law, examine the witnesses, sum up the evidence, and give it in a clear distinct manner to the jury, without any comment which may lead to a discovery of what his opinion on the merits may be'. It did not authorize him 'to tell a jury they ought to acquit or condemn'. In voicing the fear that the jury might become the 'puppets' of the bench *The Times* implied that some judges may not have been following these guidelines, but the majority appear to have done so by the early nineteenth century, confining themselves, in Cottu's words, 'to exhibiting the substance (of the evidence) to the jury in its simple nudity'. A number of late eighteenth-century judges' reports suggest a relatively passive attitude even when the outcome was not what the bench had expected. Judge Grose, for example, reported after a partial verdict that 'I thought it a very bad offence, it seemed to me that the jury might have found him guilty of the capital part' and after another case that the accused had been 'acquitted by the jury although I had no doubt of his guilt'. While this evidence broadly supports Green's recent conclusion that while 'juries were frequently influenced by the bench and usually resolved cases in a way the bench approved . . . in many cases they were

[68] P.R.O. H.O. 47/5 letter from the Recorder of London 31 Dec. 1786; *P. P.*, 1819, VIII, p. 46.
[69] P.R.O. H.O. 47/11 Thomas Brown; *Che.C.*, 18 Mar. 1803; for a similar Hotham case where a partial verdict recommendation was acted on P.R.O. H.O. 47/6, 18 Apr. 1787. However, although he recommended that one of the accused be acquitted, the jury refused to go that far.

left by the bench to determine the matter on their own',[70] it also raises a further question. How often did the judges follow Grose's approach, quietly recording verdicts that they did not agree with? When an Old Bailey clerk was asked in 1819, 'do the juries often resort to the expedient of finding prisoners guilty of a lesser offence in a manner not suggested by the judge?', his unequivocal reply was ,'They do.' However, the 1819 witnesses are not necessarily representative and since acquittals were never followed by petitions for pardon, judges' reports can only be used in the small minority of cases where the bench took the prisoner's side against the jury. In the 1780s several juries of Welsh farmers, whose dislike of sheep stealers led to stubborn refusals to reverse convictions, certainly gave substance to Dagge's observation that 'the jury frequently persevere in their first determination, however erroneous, without regard to the information or advice of the judge'. In 1787, for example, Justice Williams reported on the conviction of Thomas Jones for sheep stealing: 'I, being much dissatisfied with their verdict refused to receive it and recommended it to the jury to reconsider the evidence . . . felony having not been proved they ought to find the prisoner not guilty.' When the jury refused to be brow-beaten the judge 'a second time recommended it to the jury to reconsider the evidence . . . the jury . . . obstinately persisting in the verdict . . . I was forced at last to receive their verdict'. In this situation the bench could have the last word by organizing a pardon or in non-capital larceny cases by passing a minimal sentence, such as that of 5 minutes' imprisonment ordered by the Essex quarter sessions in 1796.[71] However, in the vast majority of cases the jury exerted themselves on the side of mercy and when this happened the judges' options were less clear-cut.

Twentieth-century studies have suggested that judges disagree with a substantial proportion of the jury verdicts they record. Overwhelmingly, it is with acquittals rather than convictions that they take issue. The balance of forces and the severity of punishments was very different in the eighteenth-century courts but the contrast in attitudes may well have been similar. Contemporaries frequently referred to the jurors' lenient tendencies. Fielding attacked them for acquitting 'against clear and positive evidence' and his fellow magistrate Richard Wyatt was clearly unhappy when a man he had committed for trial was 'acquitted by an ignorant jury at Kingston assizes, not one circumstance appearing in his favour'. However, few suggested that this type of verdict was directly encouraged by the judges. Even Madan, who criticized the bench for their passivity on these occasions and their tendency to 'take little

[70] Gisbourne, *An Enquiry*, p. 230; *The Times*, 18 Sept. 1788; Cottu, *The Administration*, p. 49; Gatrell, *The Hanging Tree*, p. 524, on vexed judges frequently blaming juries for delivering verdicts against their advice; P.R.O. H.O. 47/11 Joseph Ellis and John Pankhurst; Green, *Verdict According to Conscience*, p. 370.
[71] *P.P.*, 1819, VIII, p. 24; H. Dagge, *Considerations on Criminal Law* (London, 1774), I, p. 155; P.R.O. H.O. 47/6 6 Feb. 1787 and for a similar case 25 Apr. 1787. Judges were only asked to report on a case when a reprieve or pardon was being requested. If the jury acquitted, this stage was never reached. ERO Q/SPb 17 Jan. 1796 indictment 20.

further notice of the matter' beyond telling the prisoner 'that he has had a very merciful jury', saved his main invective for the jurymen who took it 'upon themselves to acquit the prisoner against all fact and truth'. Asked in 1819 whether there was 'any leaning on the part of the court, the jury and the prosecutor not to convict', a court clerk replied, 'on the part of the jurors there certainly is; the court attend very much to see that the circumstances... be proved; but there is no other leaning on their parts'.[72]

If the judge wanted to oppose the lenient approach of the jury, he was not in a particularly strong position once a not guilty verdict had been returned. Since he could no longer fine the jury for returning a verdict contrary to his instructions, his main weapon was his right to demand that they reconsider their decision. Trial reports did not record these negotiations systematically but they contain little indication that judges made much use of this tactic. If the jury stuck to their original verdict the judge was forced to accept and record it, and in most cases he was probably keen to avoid such a public defeat. In the 1760s Burn implied that the technique was falling into disuse. 'If the jury acquit... against manifest evidence, the court may... order them to go out again and reconsider the matter; but this by many is thought hard, and seems not of late years to have been so frequently practiced as formerly.' By 1789 this procedure was being openly challenged at the Old Bailey. Surprised by an acquittal when he thought 'the charge sufficiently proved,' Justice Heath heavily criticized the jury, pointing out that if other juries took the same approach 'they would let go all the thieves in London'. He then called another witness, summed up the evidence and told the jury to reconsider. The jury, however, not only stuck to their not guilty verdict but also took a public stand against the bench's right to demand that they reconsider by announcing that 'they thought it not only inconsistent with equity and good conscience, but altogether contrary to the law of Trials by Jury in as much as they (the jurors) had once declared the prisoner not guilty'.[73]

A report in the *Chelmsford Chronicle* six years later implied that the judge's right to bring in a directed verdict of not guilty due to insufficient evidence, which was occasionally used by the bench to terminate a trial before the jury had a chance to deliberate, was also being challenged. During the trial of a father for receiving goods stolen by his daughter, the judge 'stopped the evidence in favour of the prisoner and observed that it was needless to take up the time of the court as he was well satisfied of the innocence of the father and directed the jury to bring in their verdict accordingly'. However, 'on the jury saying that there remained a doubt on that head, the evidence was

---

[72] W. Cornish, *The Jury* (London, 1968); Fielding, *A Proposal*, 13, p. 180; Silverthorne, *Deposition Book*, p. 3; Madan, *Thoughts*, pp. 137–8; Romilly, *Observations*, pp. 88–91, a positive view of jury leniency; *P.P.*, 1817, VII, p. 420.

[73] Bushell's case in 1670 established that jurors could not be fined for verdicts contrary to judges' instructions. Burn, *The Justice* (1766), 2, p. 487; *The Times*, 30 Oct. 1789 and 13 Nov. 1789.

continued' and after long debate the father was eventually found guilty.[74] Cases involving directed verdicts or judicial demands that jurors reconsider were, of course, relatively rare and the evidence available about every aspect of judge–jury relationships is very fragmentary, but overall this evidence broadly supports Green's recent conclusion that while 'in many cases ... the jury took its lead from the bench ... the jury's willingness to do so must be understood in the light of the fact that when the jury wanted to go its own way it had the power to do so'. Until the criminal law reforms of the second quarter of the nineteenth century undermined the foundations of the jury-based mitigation system, the relationship between judge and jury remained one of compromise, of mutual dependence, or, at the very least, of mutual acceptance.[75] As a result the judicial authorities may have had to accept that the jurors' standards and attitudes, including their more merciful approach to capital cases involving theft without violence, would have had a considerable influence on verdict patterns and (via partial verdicts) on the punishments convicted offenders received. The delicate balance of judge–jury relations not only helped to legitimize the judicial system and make it work more effectively; it also gave the jury a role in shaping the criteria on which judgments were made. In the process it contributed to the high acquittal rates and partial verdict rates that were such a marked feature of the eighteenth-century courts.

5. The Criminal Trial in its Social and Spatial Context

Finally, the physical context within which trials took place and the role played by the crowds that gathered in and around the courtroom also influenced verdict patterns substantially. Fragmentary though the sources are, they suggest that these courtrooms were not always easy to stage-manage. Cynthia Herrup concluded that 'the early modern trial ... resembled a multi-ringed extravaganza more than a distinct, solemn ritual' and little seems to have changed by the eighteenth century. On first reading Madan's description of the problems assize judges had in controlling the noisy, rude, curious, 'hardly restrainable', 'low rabble', who were often found 'forcing themselves into and about the court', seems an exaggeration, but was it? Many of the buildings used for the county assizes in the eighteenth century were small and decrepit, yet in and around them milled a large concourse of participants and spectators. The audience was rarely a select one. 'Tis one of the advantages of trials in this country that our courts of justice are open to all persons', an eminent lawyer pointed out at the Essex assizes in 1800. Most trials took place in the presence of a large and often disorderly crowd drawn from all levels of society. Prosecutors whose indictments were deemed malicious were hissed and

[74] On directed verdicts, see Langbein, 'The English Criminal Trial', pp. 36–7 which gives less room for jury discretion than is being suggested here; *Che.C.*, 20 Mar. 1795.
[75] Green, *Verdict According to Conscience*, p. 358.

shouted down, verdicts were questioned by heckling spectators, missiles were thrown across the courtroom, and constables sometimes had to be called in to restore order and protect jurors from threatening behaviour.[76] The crowds were not kept at a distance. 'The judge', Cottu observed, 'suffers the space allotted to him to be intruded upon by the crowd of spectators' and especially by the prettiest relatives of the county élite. The less favoured simply barged in. When, as a 20-year-old student, Woodforde 'could not get a tolerable place' at the Oxford assizes, he records that he 'jumped from two men's shoulders and leaped upon the heads of several men and then scrambled into the prisoner's place where the judge said I must not stay, so one of the counsellors desired me not to make a noise, and he would let me have his place, which was immediately under the prisoners and opposite the judge'.[77]

The Essex assizes had similar crowd management problems in the eighteenth century. When the prisoners were 'brought upon a chain through the heart of the town' at assize time, one Chelmsford observer noted that 'country people flock to see them, and attend them from the gaol to the court-house'. The Essex Crown Court was reported to be 'a very old building, very much out of repair', 'incommodiously situated, too small', and 'very inconvenient'. There was frequently not enough room for those who had to attend on court business, let alone for 'the improper company that is admitted'. Until the last decade of the eighteenth century the Essex sessions house was an old, timber-framed building and since it was right next to the principal thoroughfare through the centre of Chelmsford, which was only 11 feet wide at that point, the noise of the carriages regularly interrupted the proceedings. Described by the judges who presided in it as more like a vault than a county court, the wretched state of the Shire Hall was notorious. There was no grand jury room, and the eminent gentlemen who performed this role at the assizes complained of 'the very indecent and inconvenient practice of their being obliged to resort to a public house for the purpose of finding their bills'. Here they were 'crammed into a room that would scarcely contain their number' and then 'had frequently to penetrate through a crowd' to present the resulting indictments. The overlap between the world of the drinking house and the sessions house, seen in Madan's complaints about the noisy drunken state of spectators, jurors, and witnesses, and in other contemporary observations about 'the disorderly crew' who attended Old Bailey trials, is equally well evidenced in

[76] Herrup, *The Common Peace*, p. 141; Madan, *Thoughts*, pp. 145–6. *Che.C.*, 14 Mar. 1800; on the 'very crowded court', *Che.C.*, 25 July 1777, 10 Oct. 1788, 7 Mar. 1800, 25 July 1800, and on the 'improper company admitted' 7 Mar. 1788, 27 July 1798; on the crowd's mixed social composition, Linebaugh, *The London Hanged*, p. 87; Hay, 'Property', p. 27; Harris, 'Trials', p. 3; on specific crowd reactions, Hay, 'Prosecution', p. 343; Beattie,*Crime*, p. 399; *Genuine Proceedings...Home Circuit...March 1739*, p. 21; Gatrell, *The Hanging Tree*, p. 95.

[77] Cottu, *The Administration*, p. 56; Beresford, *Diary of a Country Parson*, 1, p. 16; when they wanted to leave, friends in the crowd shouted across to each other and barged out again: Gatrell, *The Hanging Tree*, p. 95.

Chelmsford. 'The witnesses who were...to give evidence on...criminal prosecutions' also had to seek shelter in different alehouses 'having no other places to resort to', a leading magistrate observed, 'where...having liquor at hand and in sight, frequently rendered those of the best intention, and most deserved credit, unfit for the testimony they had to give'.[78]

Many counties rebuilt their courthouses in the eighteenth century and Essex was no exception. Rebuilding was completed in 1791 after a false start in the early 1770s. The new building had an impressive façade, a somewhat larger pair of courtrooms, and separate rooms for grand and petty jurors, etc. but at the first assizes held there the court was immediately described as 'very crowded' and the character of the trial does not appear to have been greatly affected by the rebuilding. Despite the announcement in 1798 that 'some new regulations' had been adopted aimed at 'preserving the court from the usual influx of disorderly spectators', little had changed by 1800. In March 'the crowd was so immense immediately on the opening of the doors, that it was very difficult to obtain a situation within hearing'. At the summer assizes 'the crowding and noise to gain admittance several times prevented their Lordships from proceeding'. One trial in March 1800 'having been interrupted several times' and 'there being considerable noise in the court', counsel for the prosecution complained, 'it is a most distressing thing...that persons who come here from idle curiosity...almost deprive the prisoner...of a fair trial'. After discovering that several of the character witnesses he called could not even get into the building, the prisoner's counsel observed: 'If anyone stepped into court they would have thought they were at Bartholomew Fair.'[79]

The courts tried various tactics to gain a greater measure of control. Later in 1800 'several alterations' were made 'to secure the entrance to The Shire Hall' but there is no record of whether these innovations were any more successful than those introduced two years earlier, and the circuit judges continued to complain that the courts were noisy and ill-suited to the solemnity of the proceedings well into the nineteenth century. Individuals were occasionally disciplined by the bench. The Surrey trial reports of 1739 record that 'the court ordered a man into custody for saying, when the jury had brought in their verdict, that Brookes (the convicted man) was as honest a man as any in court, but on his submission he was discharged'. However, hecklers were hard to identify in crowded courtrooms and galleries, and hisses, boos, or other forms

---

[78] *Che.C.*, 7 Mar. 1788; N Rowley (ed.), *Law and Order in Essex* (undated Essex Record Office Seax Series Illustrations 7 and 30); N. Briggs, *John Johnson 1732–1814. Georgian Architect and County Surveyor of Essex* (Chelmsford, 1991); *House of Commons Journals*, xxxiii (Nov. 1770–1), pp. 124–5, 368; *Che.C.*, 17 Oct. 1788; Madan, *Thoughts*, pp. 142–6; Linebaugh, *The London Hanged*, pp. 86–8; Gatrell, *The Hanging Tree*, p. 533.

[79] *Che.C.*, 5 Aug. 1791, 27 July 1798, 7 Mar. 1800, 25 July 1800. At the Old Bailey admittance money was sometimes charged. When Wilkes put an end to this the crowds then admitted proved so rowdy trials could not proceed uninterrupted (Deveraux, 'The City', p. 486). However, when the door-keepers tried to extort money from those attending in Essex they were severely fined by the assize judge and Essex assize crowds are usually described in terms that suggest a heavy plebeian presence (*I.J.*, 17 Mar. 1783). *The Trial of John Taylor*, esp. p. 4; *Che.C.*, 14 Mar. 1800.

of crowd disapproval could not be dealt with in this way. In March 1800 the Essex assize judge Baron Hotham threatened that unless a proper and becoming silence was maintained he would 'order the court to be cleared of everybody except counsel, attorneys and the witnesses', but whether he could actually have done so remains unclear. Later in the same trial the court was not even able to ensure that all the character witnesses could gain entry and prosecution counsel remained doubtful that this threat would be effective in preventing further interruptions.[80]

This evidence suggests it would be incorrect to portray all assizes trials as dramas staged solely by the authorities or as processes which always communicated the solemnity and majesty of the law. Many assize proceedings may perhaps be more fruitfully seen as 'participatory theatre', reflecting the broader structures of gentry–crowd reciprocity which Thompson has argued were so central to eighteenth-century social relations. The crowd had to, and did, accept the courts. The courts needed the crowd. Paley listed as an important prerequisite of any court of justice 'that its proceedings be carried on in public ... before a promiscuous concourse of by-standers'. The openness of jury trial was one of the foundations of the law's legitimacy and if the courts' proceedings were to affect potential offenders, the labouring poor as well as the propertied had to be admitted. The result, as Peter Linebaugh has recently pointed out, was that the theatre of the bench was balanced by what he calls the counter-theatre of the crowd.[81] Ultimately the court could, of course, prevent the trial audience from going beyond certain outer limits of acceptable behaviour but the vigorous and vibrant nature of non-élite culture did not necessarily disappear when its members gathered in the crowded open courtrooms of eighteenth-century England. The existing records offer only rare glimpses of the voices and expressions of the crowd, but they suggest that theatre and counter-theatre were indeed played out on occasions and that in the process the crowd sometimes moderated the behaviour of both the bench and the jury.

The judges rarely admitted this in public but their confidential reports indicate that it could and did happen. After capitally convicting a young boy at the Chelmsford assizes in 1800 Judge Hotham was put under considerable popular pressure. 'The scene was dreadful on passing sentence', he recorded, 'and to pacify the feelings of a most crowded court, who all expressed their horror ... by their looks and manners, after stating the necessity of the prosecution ... I hinted something slightly of its still being ... open to clemency.'[82]

[80] Che.C., 25 July 1800; Eastwood, 'Governing', p. 318; Genuine Proceedings ... Home Circuit March 1739, p. 21; The Trial of John Taylor, p. 4.
[81] Thompson, 'Patrician Society', p. 395; E. P. Thompson, 'Eighteenth Century English Society: Class Struggle without Class', Social History, 3 (1978), 145–54; Thompson, Customs in Common, pp. 56–96; Paley, The Works, 4, p. 404; Linebaugh, The London Hanged, pp. 87–8.
[82] Radzinowicz, History, 1, p. 13.

The boy was eventually pardoned, and by vividly expressing the popular belief that young offenders should not be hanged for property offences the crowd had clearly affected the outcome. The crowd's potential influence on jurors and prosecutors was even greater. The judges were partly protected from such pressures because reprieves were announced later and in private. Prosecutors gave their evidence and jurors usually made their decisions in open court,[83] often only a few feet from the audience. Many contemporaries observed that apart from a few types of case, such as child rape—when the crowd demanded the harshest punishment and then helped to execute it if the accused was put in the pillory—trial audiences tended overwhelmingly to favour mercy. In capital property crime cases in particular, unless extreme violence had been used, the dynamics of crowd–court interaction and the body language of the crowd pushed all involved towards more merciful outcomes. 'Those whose duty it is to conduct the evidence', Sir John Hawkins observed, 'fearing the censure that others have incurred by a contrary treatment of prisoners, are restrained from enforcing it; and as it is an exercise of compassion that costs nothing and is sure to gain the applause of vulgar hearers, everyone interests himself on the side of the prisoner'. Cottu also believed that 'persons labouring under accusation meet on all sides with nothing but looks of encouragement . . . it seems as if the spectators, in a league against the rigour of those laws which society requires, against even justice itself, were all eagerly endeavouring to rescue a victim from its decrees'.[84]

Given the way the unanimity rule affected jury interaction, if the crowd persuaded even a minority of the jury to go for a merciful verdict, they could have a major impact on the outcome of the trial. The attitudes of jurors and court audiences may often have overlapped and in this situation the crowds' presence would have reinforced already existing jury mitigation and nullification traditions. 'When a man suffers death for so trivial an offence as stealing a few shillings', Hanway wrote, 'it is not reasonable to think that pity will be the prevailing emotion in the breast of the spectator and that he will acquit the malefactor of his crime.' The applause 'vulgar hearers' gave to the merciful, and the open censure incurred by those who failed to favour the prisoner should not be underestimated as a potential semi-plebeian influence on acquittal and partial verdict rates and on the nature of the trial itself. In the absence of any detailed evidence about the composition of trial audiences, firm conclusions are impossible. However, the Essex evidence supports John Beattie's suggestion that 'we have perhaps been in some danger of exaggerating the dignity and order of the eighteenth century courts and perhaps of overem-

---

[83] Petty jurors rarely retired to discuss their verdicts. Unless the case was complex or controversial, and often even when it was, the outcome was determined during a brief huddled hearing in open court. Beattie, *Crime*, p. 396; Cottu, *The Administration*, p. 54. For exceptional jury withdrawals in Essex, *Che.C.*, 22 July 1803; *Norwich Mercury*, 21 Mar. 1752.

[84] Radzinowicz, *History*, i, p. 27; Hay, 'Property', p. 32; Cottu, *The Administration*, pp. 50–1.

phasizing their success as theatre—taking the robes, full bottom wigs and black caps as guarantees...that the solemnity and hushed seriousness the judges would have wanted was in fact always achieved'.[85] This theme will be taken up again when the impact of the rituals of the death sentence is discussed in Chapter 10, but in explaining the high acquittal and partial verdict rates of the eighteenth century it is important to remember that the courtroom was not simply a glorified prosecution association meeting. Its doors were open to people whose attitudes may, as Green has pointed out, have induced jurors to see their roles in a more representative fashion. The crowd, whether by murmur and audible comment or by its looks and manners, was a force for mercy in most property crime trials and its influence should not be overlooked.

Conclusion

Many questions about the complex and evolving nature of property crime trials in the eighteenth and nineteenth centuries remain unanswered, but while legal historians have produced a growing body of work on the lawyerization of the trial, and on the growth of evidentiary rules and adversarial procedures, a more holistic picture of the social interactions that took place in these court-rooms has proved difficult to construct. The key decision-makers who shaped the trial process came from right across the social spectrum—from judges, barristers, and assize grand jurors, who represented the social and legal élite; through various elements of 'the middling sort', who dominated the other trial juries and provided most of the prosecutors; to the labouring men and women, who made contributions as prosecutors, witnesses, and members of the court-room audience. The precise balance of power between these decision-making groups and the impact of each on trial processes and outcomes remains extremely difficult to evaluate. The best-documented element—the roles played by the élite—should not be underestimated. The trial judges' status as legal experts, their control over the trial process, and the more limited powers they had to discipline jurors, prosecutors, witnesses, and audience mark them out as central actors in the courtroom drama. Moreover, their willingness to follow increasingly strict procedural rules and to acquit on technicalities almost certainly strengthened the myth of equality before the law that underpinned the rule of the landowning élite. However, despite the broad agreement about ends and means which characterized many trials, jurors, prosecutors, witnesses, and courtroom audiences also possessed the capacity to act as separate and often allied forces pressurizing for their own outcomes. While both jury and prosecutor nullification could at times be

[85] J. Hanway, *Distributive Justice and Mercy* (London, 1781), p. 148; Beattie, *Crime*, p. 399. On trial audiences, Hay, 'Property', suggests an audience across the social scale, and diaries broadly confirm this. For examples of diarists or their spouses attending—Cozens-Hardy, *Mary Hardy's Diary*, pp. 120, 125; Branch-Johnson, *Memorandoms*, pp. 41, 102.

responses to instructions given from the bench, the frequency of these practices almost certainly reflected the extent to which other participants in the
trial process themselves exercised a degree of independence from the judges.
The high acquittal and partial verdict rates of this period reflected not only the
acceptance or acquiescence of the judges combined with more fundamental
social attitudes towards what constituted sufficient evidence, but also the
capacity of jurors, prosecutors, and other non-élite courtroom actors to take
their own line and represent their own ideas, interests, and inclinations
towards mercy.

The vital role played by the judge and the relatively small number of trials
that have left evidence of judge–jury conflict or of any overt opposition to the
bench should not automatically be taken to imply élite dominance. It may
rather suggest that the judicial authorities came to a compromise adapting to
and adopting the more merciful inclinations of jurors, prosecutors, and crowd
in most types of case. The élite may ultimately have found it very useful to
develop a large sheaf of capital statutes but then to mitigate or nullify their
effects in many cases through the establishment of apparently merciful and just
court procedures. However, it is difficult to disagree with Green's conclusion
that since literal enforcement of the capital felony laws was beyond the power
of the authorities, enforcing the law through the courts inevitably involved an
accommodation in which many parties played a role.[86] The criteria on which
verdicts were reached were not decided by the élite and the judges alone but
rather by the interaction between their values and interests, and those of
jurors, prosecutors, witnesses, and court audiences.

'The English common law', E. P. Thompson has observed, 'rests upon a
bargain between the law and the people. The jury box is where the people
come into the court: the judge watches them and the jury watches back. A jury
is the place where the bargain is struck. The jury attends in judgement not only
upon the accused, but also upon the justice and humanity of the Law.'[87] If the
role of the crowd and the ability of prosecutors and witnesses to mitigate the
harshness of the capital code are also included; if the very real, but more
limited, sense in which they too sat in judgment on the criminal law and the
ways it was administrated in property crime cases was also given due weight—
this statement would come close to crystallizing the nature of the sometimes
fragile but enduring alliance between the judicial authorities, the jurors, and
the more plebeian elements in the courtroom which allowed the courts to
operate relatively smoothly while simultaneously underpinning the high partial verdict and acquittal rates of the century that proceeded the early nineteenth-century reform of the criminal law.

---

[86] Green, *Verdict According to Conscience*, p. 312.
[87] E. P. Thompson, *Writing by Candlelight* (London, 1980), p. 108.

8

Sentencing Policy and the Impact of Gender and Age

> Hail venerable shade, to whom,
> villains for crimes of merit come...
> When whips and pillories prove vain,
> and men their native wickedness maintain,
> just where the devil and those engines leave them,
> your pious arches gratefully receive them.
>
> D. Defoe, *A Hymn to Tyburn*.[1]

Any accused person who failed to avoid being convicted of an indictable property crime by finding an appropriate escape route during pretrial negotiations, committal proceedings, grand jury hearings, or petty jury trial faced a bleak set of prospects in the eighteenth century. Fines or nominal periods in gaol were very occasionally employed but the range of punishments used against the vast majority of convicted property offenders was stark and uncompromising. By 1740 there were no widely used sentences equivalent to modern non-custodial and non-corporal sanctions, such as community service orders, conditional discharges, or probation orders.[2] Convicted property offenders faced humiliation, pain, incarceration, deprivation, separation, death. The specific combination of these sensations experienced by any particular individual depended on the sanction selected for him or her. For a few fraudsters a public, painful, and occasionally health-threatening spell in the pillory would be the final destination.[3] For the rest the horrors of hanging (so well described in Gatrell's recent book); the uncertainties, partings, incarcerations, and exploitation associated with a transportation sentence; the humiliations and physical agonies of whippings; the pains of intention or the

---

[1] D. Defoe, *A Hymn to Tyburn*, a four-page poem, is undated.

[2] Most late twentieth-century offenders receive non-custodial sentences. A. Bottomley and K. Pease, *Crime and Punishment: Interpreting the Data* (Milton Keynes, 1986), p. 83. Branding for first offenders who, if convicted a second time, would be hanged could be broadly interpreted as the equivalent of a suspended sentence.

[3] Fraud was virtually the only type of property offender against whom the Essex courts used the pillory, Apr. 1790 E.R.O. Q/SPb 16; *Che.C.*, 27 Jan. 1786. Occasionally it was also used against those found guilty of false balances—*Che.C.*, 18 Jan. 1765. On the horrors of the pillory, *Che.C.*, 29 Jan. 1790; Gatrell, *The Hanging Tree*, pp. 69–70.

pains of neglect suffered by prisoners in the gaols or prison hulks of eighteenth- and early nineteenth-century England marked the end of their journey through the criminal justice system.[4]

Despite Defoe's depiction of the punishment process as a graded correctional ladder in which only those who failed to be reformed by lesser sanctions went on up to the gallows, there was no equivalent of today's finely tuned 'tariff' system in the eighteenth century. An ill-advised act of appropriation and an unsympathetic prosecutor, jury, and/or judge could catapult the accused into lifetime separation from his or her home country or into the 'venerable' shade of the gallows. In analysing sentencing and pardoning policies, it is easy to anaesthetize ourselves from the shock and terror the prospect of these punishments would often have produced—even in the eighteenth century when pain, physical punishment, and death were much closer to everyday experience than they are to the modern Western reader. There was nothing 'pious' about the 'arches' of the gallows. They were not arches at all. They were crudely formed bits of wood with a crude and terrible set of tasks to perform, and the 'hulks' and the transport ships fitted that description equally well.[5] This said, however, it was in the process of selecting which of the accused should be subjected to these harsh punishments that the criminal justice system created the most detailed records about the nature of judicial discretion—about what kind of justice was given by and to whom, on what basis, ·and with what purposes in mind. The last two groups of interconnected rooms through which the offenders passed on their journey through the judicial system—those in which sentencing and pardoning decisions were made— are therefore worthy of very careful study.

The next chapter will focus on the pardoning process and the revealing archive it created, approaching it primarily through a qualitative analysis of the language, assumptions, social status, and impact of those who involved themselves in post-sentencing negotiations. The bulk of this chapter will concentrate on the two main dimensions of sentencing and pardoning policy that can be subjected to quantitative study, that is on the impact of the age and gender of the accused. However, the background against which these discretionary decisions about sentencing and pardoning were made was also changing. Although recent work has cast doubt on chronologies which put too much emphasis on the late eighteenth and early nineteenth centuries as the key period of change in sentencing and punishment policies, there can be no doubt that important changes were occurring between 1740 and 1820. Indeed, the causes and significance of those changes has been the subject of widespread and long-standing historical debate.[6] Although sentencing alternatives con-

---

[4] Gatrell, *The Hanging Tree*; R. Hughes, *The Fatal Shore* (London, 1987).

[5] Branch-Johnson, *The English Prison Hulks*; Hughes, *The Fatal Shore*, pp. 138–42.

[6] Beattie, *Crime*; P. Jenkins, 'From Gallows to Prison? The Execution Rate in Early Modern England', *Criminal Justice History*, 7 (1986), 51–71; Innes and Styles, 'Crime Wave', pp. 229–50; J. Innes,

tinued to be severely limited by law throughout the eighteenth and early nineteenth centuries, the courts' discretionary powers were wide and punishment policies were therefore fundamentally affected by their changing sense of the appropriateness and usefulness of the various sanctions available. The first section of this chapter therefore begins by exploring how the forms of penalty favoured by the courts in various types of property crime cases varied between 1740 and 1820.

1. Continuity and Change in Punishment Policies, 1740–1820

The form and depth of judicial discretion differed widely between capital and non-capital offences (Table 8.1). If the crime had been excluded from benefit of clergy, the judge had no choice but to record a sentence of death unless the jury had brought in a partial verdict or the prosecutor had chosen to indict the offender for an attempted, rather than for a full, capital theft. This did not prevent the bench from selecting certain capital convicts and certain types of capital offence for more lenient treatment, since they were able to use their power to reprieve as an extension of sentencing policy in such cases. However, it did shape the initial punishment recorded in court, particularly when highway robbery or large animal theft was involved. The legal definitions of these offences, unlike those of housebreaking and aggravated larcenies, rarely provided grounds for a partial verdict, and sentence of death was usually the automatic consequence of conviction (Table 8.1).[7]

About 20 per cent of Essex guilty verdicts resulted in a capital sentence between 1740 and 1805, but more than three-quarters of these involved full convictions for horse stealing, highway robbery, and housebreaking—three offences made capital long before the period being studied here. In Essex, as elsewhere, few of the capital statutes passed after 1740 made much impact on the courts. The main exception was the 1741 act against sheep stealing, which the Essex farmers had specifically petitioned for in order to counter growing night-time raids on their flocks. About an eighth of the county's capital convictions between 1740 and 1804 involved sheep stealing. A further 3 per cent involved cattle thefts or thefts from bleaching grounds, both of which were also made capital offences in the early 1740s, but only a tiny fraction of

'Periodising the History of the Prison—Reflections Arising Especially from a Study of the English Case' (unpublished paper). For an introduction to this complex debate, see Ignatieff, *A Just Measure of Pain*, and Ignatieff, 'State, Civil Society', pp.183–211; M. DeLacy, *Prison Reform in Lancashire, 1700–1850. A Study in Local Administration* (Stanford, Calif., 1986).

[7] For benefit of clergy, see Blackstone, *Commentaries*, 4, pp. 358–67; Ignatieff, *A Just Measure of Pain*, p. 18. Juries did occasionally acquit robbers of 'putting in fear' or convict horse thieves of stealing the saddle but not the horse! John Pluckrose, P.R.O. Assi 35/181/2. The figures in Table 8.1 include attempted thefts which, with occasional partial verdicts, accounts for the few cases where convicted highway robbers and horse thieves were not sentenced to death. The years 1740–2 account for almost all the non-capital sentences in sheep stealing cases.

Table 8.1. Sentences for Property Crime, Essex, 1740–1805

	% Sentence unknown	% Fine	% Burnt in hand	% Whipped	% Imprisoned	% Armed forces	% Thames	% Transported	% Hanged reprieved	% Hanged	Total guilty
Petty larceny	5.5	0.3	—	31.2	46.2	4.2	0.4	12.2	—	—	1,061
Horse stealing	3.5	—	—	—	—	0.7	0.7	2.1	72.3	20.6	141
Sheep stealing	2.6	0.9	0.9	1.7	1.7	—	—	7.8	76.5	7.8	115
Grand and aggravated larceny	4.9	1.6	3.9	11.8	35.4	2.0	2.4	32.3	4.5	1.3	1,185
Housebreaking and burglary	6.4	—	0.4	2.4	10.4	0.2	1.0	30.1	28.1	21.0	501
Highway robbery	3.6	0.4	0.4	—	0.8	—	1.6	8.9	39.1	45.2	248
Other	30.3	9.1	—	6.7	33.7	2.4	2.4	13.9	0.5	1.0	208
All crimes	6.6	1.2	1.5	14.4	30.2	2.2	1.4	21.0	13.9	7.9	3,459

Sources: as for Table 5.1. The majority of the 68 aggravated larceny capital convictions were for stealing from the dwelling house. Nearly a quarter were for cattle stealing. The remainder were for privately stealing from the person, from a shop or a warehouse, stealing from a bleaching ground, or letter theft by Post Office employees. Most of the offenders actually hanged had stolen from a dwelling house.

Essex offenders were sentenced to death under other post-1740 statutes. Historians continue to debate the significance of the growth of the 'bloody code' in the eighteenth century. Some see it as an outstanding feature of that particular century, while others have argued cogently that there is little to support the view that eighteenth-century legislators were more inclined to create capital statutes than their predecessors.[8] However, what is clear from all existing studies and from the Essex evidence is that the vast majority of property crime victims avoided indicting offenders for any crimes made capital after the early 1740s.

The proportion of Essex property offenders sentenced to death changed very little in the long term between 1740 and 1820, but nearly 80 per cent of the prisoners sentenced by the courts had either been indicted for a non-capital crime or had had their offence reduced to this level by the jury, and in these cases the judges' sentencing options were much wider. The relatively limited alternatives available before 1700 had been greatly augmented by the Statutes of 1707 and 1718 which had confirmed the courts' right to use direct sentences of imprisonment and transportation in addition to the existing non-capital punishments of branding and whipping. The new secondary punishment-based sentencing regime set up by these two acts, which was reinforced by the 1776 and 1779 acts passed during the transportation crisis engendered by the American War,[9] continued to be the foundation on which punishment policies were based throughout the period from 1740 to 1820. However, that period also witnessed major changes in the ways that existing options were used. Since Beattie has provided a detailed analysis and chronology of penal change in this period, the Essex sentencing patterns (Figure 8.1 *a* and *b*) will be outlined fairly briefly here with an eye to regional variations or similarities.

The most obvious change in sentencing policy was the decline of physical and often publicly inflicted punishments such as whipping and branding, and the rise of imprisonment (Figure 8.1 *a* and *b*), but this was more than a simple movement from 'an art of unbearable sensations' to 'an economy of suspended rights'. Each of the available sanctions underwent subtle and sometimes complex changes, and imprisonment did not necessarily gain its initial ascendancy because it offered a better-regulated, potentially more reformatory, form of punishment. It could be argued that attitudes to transportation were the main motive forces behind changes in penal policy after 1750. The sudden collapse of transportation at the beginning of the American War has tended to obscure the fact that the courts had already begun to cut back its use

---

[8] Radzinowicz, *History*, I, p. 633; J. Rule, 'The Manifold Causes of Rural Crime: Sheep-Stealing in England, 1740–1840', in Rule (ed.), *Outside the Law*, p. 107. For the debate—Hay, 'Property', pp. 18–22; Langbein, 'Albion's Fatal Flaws', pp. 115–19; Innes and Styles, 'Crime Wave', pp. 240–50.

[9] Essex non-capital sentences were confined to these two punishments, 1620–80, apart from some remands for transportation. Sharpe, *Crime in Seventeenth-Century England*, pp. 94–107, 148. For the acts— A. Smith, *Colonists in Bondage. White Servitude and Convict Labour in America, 1607–1776* (Chapel Hill, NC, 1947), p. 111; and Radzinowicz, *History*, I, p. 633; Beattie, *Crime*, pp. 498–513 and on 1776–9, pp. 565–76.

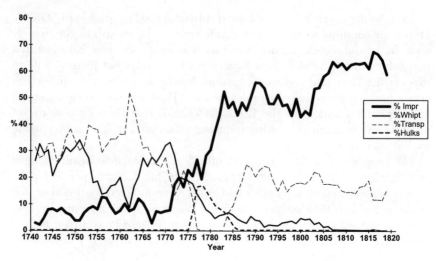

Fig. 8.1a Sentences for Property Offenders, Essex, 1740–1820 (3-year moving average)
Source: As for Table 5.1, note (b).

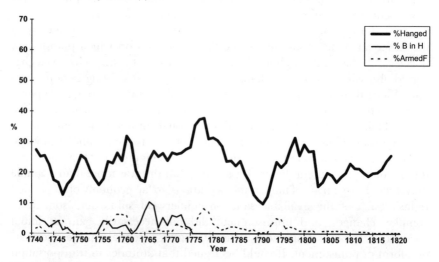

Fig. 8.1b Sentences for Property Offenders, Essex, 1740–1820 (3-year moving average)
Source: See Fig. 8.1a.

more than a decade earlier.[10] An analysis of the sentences imposed on property offenders as a whole (Figure 8.1) gives a broad indication of this change but it is most clearly seen in the punishments handed out for petty larceny and grand

[10] Foucault, *Discipline and Punish*, p. 11. A. Shaw, *Convicts and the Colonies* (London, 1966), p. 25 and Ignatieff, *A Just Measure of Pain*, pp. 80–1 did not notice the pre-1775 change. Beattie, *Crime*, p. 546 does spotlight the early 1770s as the crucial point.

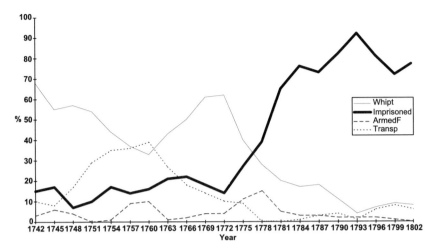

Fig. 8.2 Sentences, Petty Larceny, Essex, 1740–1805 (6-year moving average)
Source: See Fig. 8.1*a*.

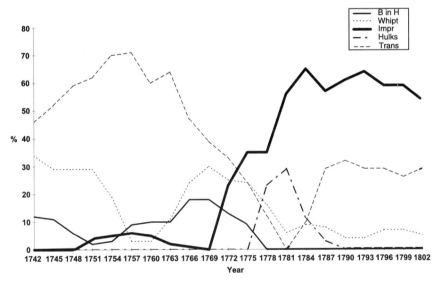

Fig. 8.3 Sentences, Grand Larceny, Essex, 1740–1805 (6-year moving average)
Source: See Fig. 8.1*a*.

larceny (Figures 8.2–8.3). These sentencing profiles were unaffected by changes in the types of indictment brought before the courts and in each a decisive decline in transportation can be seen in the early 1760s.

In the mid-eighteenth century nearly half of the property offenders convicted in the Essex courts were either sentenced directly to transportation or forced to accept it as a condition of being spared from the gallows.[11] The reasons for its subsequent decline are complex. Contemporaries were divided about its usefulness. Sir John Fielding stressed that it 'removes the evil' while 'answering the great ends of punishment viz example, humanity and reformation'. Eden, Paley, and others were much more critical, emphasizing that conditions for transportees were too pleasant to deter crime, that notorious offenders found it all too easy to return, and that it drained the manpower resources of the home country.[12] Since the decline of transportation accelerated after 1763, when English labour markets were almost certainly glutted by demobilization, it seems unlikely that this punishment was being abandoned because of a short-term increase in the demand for labour at home. The initiative came partly from the colonists themselves. In 1770 the *Chelmsford Chronicle* reported complaints from the people of Maryland that they were 'overstocked with transported felons', but the general deterioration of Anglo-American relations during the 1760s also exercised minds on the other side of the Atlantic. In 1770 an Essex magistrate, in proposing that the government begin transporting felons to Asia and Africa, stressed the implications of events in North America. 'As from appearances an insurrection in the Northern provinces may be justly apprehended', he wrote, 'it would be highly impolitic to furnish the malcontents with succours of the worst kind.'[13]

Whatever their reasons for reducing the use of transportation, this decision caused substantial problems for the Essex courts. Initially both assizes and quarter sessions increased their use of whipping (Figures 8.1–8.3) and in grand larceny cases clergyable discharge after burning in the hand—a punishment usually considered to be wholly inadequate[14]—also underwent a short revival in the 1760s (Figure 8.3). The assizes did not immediately turn to the imprisonment option. Although it was used by the Essex quarter sessions (Figure 8.2), in the higher court imprisonment remained extremely rare in property crime cases between 1740 and 1771. In Essex it was Lord Mansfield who ended more than a decade of temporary expedients and wider penal debate by sentencing every prisoner convicted of grand larceny at the 1772 Summer assizes to two years' imprisonment. The Surrey assizes followed suit early

[11] The vast majority of pardoned captial convicts were sentenced to fourteen years' transportation. Radzinowicz, *History*, 1, pp. 113–19 for the 1761–5 figures. The proportion transported fell in wartime however, offenders being pardoned on condition they enlist. Redington (ed.), *Calendar*, I, pp. 382–5.

[12] For a fuller discussion of transportation debates—Beattie, *Crime*, pp. 540–4; Ekirch, *Bound for America*, pp. 225–30; Radzinowitz and Hood, *History*, 5, pp. 465–79; R. Roberts (ed.), *Calendar of Home Office Papers of the Reign of George III* (1899), 4, document number 39; W. Eden, *Principles of Penal Law* (London, 1771), p. 33; Paley, *Works of W. Paley*, 4, p. 440; S. Deveraux, 'In Place of Death. Transportation, Penal Practices and the English State, 1770–1830', in C. Strange (ed.), *Qualities of Mercy. Justice, Punishment and Discretion* (Vancouver, 1996), pp. 52–76.

[13] *Che.C.*, 11 May 1770. On India's need for troops, H. Bowen, 'The East India Company and Military Recruitment in Britain 1763–71', *Historical Research*, 59 (1986), pp. 78–90.

[14] In 1769 branding or whipping were described as 'no punishment at all, or next to none'. Blackstone, *Commentaries*, 4, p. 363. Ryder made a special note of one offender that he 'had actually burnt in the hand', and of another who 'should be really whipped', Dudley, Ryder, Assize Diary, pp. 5, 28.

in 1773.[15] This change was certainly not unprecedented. In the decade before the 1718 act some assize circuits had made considerable use of imprisonment[16] and in 1757 and 1764 one or two similar sentences had been handed out at the Essex assizes. However, 1772 was an important turning-point. The use of imprisonment increased rapidly in the early 1770s, gathering further momentum after the American colonies were finally closed to transportees in 1776. The dominant position it gained in these years was not lost for over a century. Faced by the rapidly increasing indictment levels and overcrowded gaols of the mid- and later 1780s the courts welcomed the chance to renew their use of transportation, but it never regained its mid-century ascendancy. After 1787 banishment was rarely used in petty larceny cases (Figure 8.2) and the proportion of grand larceny convicts that were transported never reached more than half the pre-1760 level. The newly founded Australian settlements could only absorb a limited percentage of the growing numbers sentenced by the courts and the hulks had to be kept in service in order to deal with the surplus of offenders under sentence of transportation. Since the other potential, and possibly less expensive, destinations suggested—Russia, Algiers, East Florida, the East Indies, the West Indies, Honduras, Canada or Nova Scotia, Tristan da Cunha, Madagascar, the Coast East of Cape Town, the Falkland Islands, Gibraltar, Greenland—were never successfully developed, banishment began to be increasingly reserved for more serious offenders and imprisonment grew in importance partly as a result.[17]

By the later 1770s the claims of men such as Howard and Hanway that hygienic and highly regulated prison regimes, preferably with some element of solitary confinement, might offer a way of reforming and deterring offenders were being widely publicized.[18] What influence did these ideas have on prison building and prison regimes in Essex? A full study of the Essex prisons in this period would require a separate volume. However, in a less well publicized and less thoroughgoing way than counties such as Gloucestershire,[19] Essex

---

[15] P.R.O. Assi 31/10; Beattie, *Crime*, pp. 560–2; Ekirch, *Bound for America*, p. 228.

[16] Beattie, *Crime*, pp. 492–500.

[17] Among the more bizarre suggestions made in *The Times* were making the Empress of Russia an annual present of transported felons to help populate inhospitable regions (28 Sept. 1785) and exchanging cargoes of criminals for 'unfortunate Christian slaves' held in Algiers, Tripoli, and elsewhere (19 Oct. 1985). For East Florida and the East Indies—K. Morgan, 'English and American Attitudes Towards Convict Transportation, 1718–1775', *History*, 72 (1987), 423; the West Coast of Africa was the original front runner—*The Times*, 17 and 18 Jan. 1785, 6 Apr. 1785, and as late as Jan. 1787 proposals to use convicts to extract African gold were still being made (P.R.O. H.O. 42/11/64 for a 'plan for erecting a Colony in the river Gambia'); Beattie, *Crime*, pp. 594–9; Hughes, *The Fatal Shore*, pp. 64–5; Shaw, *Convicts and the Colonies*, pp. 44–7 and 150; Robson, *The Convict*, pp. 7–10. Only a third of those sentenced to transportation, 1811–17, were actually sent to Australia. Those selected were usually the greatest offenders.

[18] Ignatieff, *A Just Measure of Pain*, pp. 47–79; separation and solitude are an ever-recurring theme in Hanway, *The Defects*, pp. xii, 31, 59, 64, 79, 213.

[19] Ignatieff, *A Just Measure of Pain*, pp. 96–109; S. Webb and B. Webb, *English Prisons under Local Government* (London, 1922), pp. 54–7; R. McGowen, 'The Well-Ordered Prison. England, 1780–1865', in

seems to have gone through a fairly familiar cycle of rebuilding, reform, and relapse in the late eighteenth and early nineteenth centuries. The degree of change varied widely between the county gaol, the five Essex houses of correction and the tiny borough prisons,[20] being often centred on the former. The Essex quarter sessions, spurred into action partly by an outbreak of gaol distemper, began to discuss the rebuilding of the county gaol in the late 1760s. After protracted wrangling the new Chelmsford gaol was finally completed in 1777, the year that Howard published *The State of the Prisons*. Although it was an improvement on the old prison, which was described by Howard as 'close and frequently infected with the gaol distemper',[21] neither the new gaol nor the small Newport house of correction, rebuilt in 1775, show any signs of having been built with a penitentiary-style regime in mind. When they were originally opened neither prison contained either cells designed for solitary confinement or any particular indication that stricter work regimes were to be introduced. A decade later, however, attitudes were changing and solitary confinement was being much more widely discussed. Once it was realized that the penitentiary planned for the Home Counties in the 1779 Act was unlikely to materialize, the Essex authorities, like those of many other counties, began to introduce their own penal experiments.[22]

In 1786, at the height of the transportation crisis and the postwar rise in recorded crime, the Essex quarter sessions decided to alter their principal gaol, and by 1789 eight solitary cells had been introduced at Chelmsford. Several provincial newspapers responded by commending the Essex magistrates for their intention to deny virtually 'all human intercourse' to the prisoners incarcerated in this new section of the county gaol, and by announcing that thirty-two more solitary cells would soon be constructed. However, this attempt to impose what Hanway called 'the humane rigour of solitary confinement'[23] remained limited in scope. Four solitary cells were built in the

N. Morris and D. Rothman (eds.), *The Oxford History of the Prison* (Oxford, 1995), pp. 89–92; R. Evans, *The Fabrication of Virtue. English Prison Architecture 1750–1840* (Cambridge, 1982), pp. 132–42. For individual studies—De Lacy, *Prison Reform*; Whiting, *Prison Reform*.

[20] J. Neild, *State of the Prisons* (London, 1812) includes information on the very small Essex borough prisons, pp. 139–40, 261–6, 511; so does *P.P.*, 1819, XVII, pp. 383–4.

[21] 'Gaol distemper' brought from Newgate caused the death of nineteen Essex prisoners, 1767–8, *House of Commons Journals*, XXXIII, pp. 368–98. In Lancashire fear of fever also encouraged decisions to rebuild—De Lacy, *Prison Reform*, p. 81. Evans, *The Fabric of Virtue*, pp. 111–12; *Che.C.*, 19 July 1771, 17 July 1772, 6 Aug. 1773. J. Howard, *The State of the Prisons* (Warrington, 3rd edn., 1784), p. 259. Howard's first visit was in 1775, this later edition recording his earlier view.

[22] Howard, *The State of the Prisons* (Warrington, 2nd edn., 1780), pp. 219–22; (3rd edn., 1784), pp. 259–62. Howard commended the 'stately fabrick' of the new gaol but was less impressed by 1784, noting that the felons were too crowded at night and that the gaol had not been whitewashed since it was first occupied. *The Times* was also advocating solitary imprisonment a few months before the Essex initiative (*The Times*, 23 Feb. 1786). Evans, *The Fabric of Virtue*, pp. 135–9; S. Devereaux, 'The Making of the Penitentiary Act, 1775–1779', *Historical Journal*, 42 (1999), 405–33.

[23] Briggs, *John Johnson*, links the decision to recommendations made by the Chief Justice of Common Pleas. See also A. Baker 'Prison Reform in Essex 1770–1820' (Middlesex Polytechnic undergraduate

Halstead house of correction at the end of the 1780s and a similar number may have been provided in the Barking house of correction when it was rebuilt in the early 1790s, but no major rebuilding programme involving solitary cells was ever undertaken, and by the 1820s overcrowding and 'the want of separate cells' were among the reasons given for the complete rebuilding of the county gaol.[24]

Although the quarter sessions bench made some use of the newly built cells between 1788 and 1793, sentencing an average of three property offenders and three non-property offenders a year specifically to periods of solitary confinement of between one and twelve months, after 1793 no further such sentences were passed. This experiment with solitary confinement, opposed as oppressive from the outset by an article in the *Cambridge Chronicle*, therefore seems to have foundered even more quickly than those introduced in other counties.[25] Attempts to introduce harsher work regimes were equally unsuccessful. The amount of work done by the prisoners does not seem to have increased significantly between 1780 and 1820. Many Essex sentences stipulated that the offender be 'kept to hard labour', but although there is evidence that some eighteenth-century prisoners were put to work in spinning and other tasks related to the cloth industry, and although some early nineteenth-century prisoners were recorded as doing a limited amount of oakum picking and shoemaking, major changes were not introduced until treadmills were installed in the mid-1820s.[26] Some very gradual, and by no means unilinear, progress may have been made in providing more adequate payment systems

dissertation, 1987). Positive comments, *Cambridge Chronicle*, 19 July 1788; the *Northampton Mercury*, 19 July 1788; *Chelmsford Chronicle*, 25 July 1788; which reported the sentencing of an Essex petty larcenist to imprisonment in the newly built cells; Hanway, *The Defects*, p. xii.

[24] Briggs, *John Johnson*, pp. 114–20; E.R.O. T/2 13/65. Plans to build further solitary cells were drawn up in the early 1790s (Briggs, *John Johnson*, p. 115) but observers in the 1810s noted only eight solitary cells for felons in Chelmsford gaol and none elsewhere. Neild, *The State of the Prisons*, pp. 26, 117–24, 139–42, 261–2, 430, 511; Anon., *Report of the Committee of London Aldermen Appointed to Visit Several Gaols in England* (London, 1816), pp. 52–5. On 1820s overcrowding, J. White 'Chelmsford Gaol in the Nineteenth Century'; *Essex Journal*, 11 (1976/7), pp. 83–94.

[25] E.R.O. Q/SPb 16–17 reveal twenty-nine offenders who were given sentences involving solitary cells. The first was in July 1788, the last in Jan. 1796. Fifteen were property offenders. *Cambridge Chronicle*, 9 Aug. 1788; Ignatieff, *A Just Measure of Pain*, pp. 103–7, 115–28; Evans, *The Fabrication of Virtue*, p. 194; C. Harding et al. (eds.), *Imprisonment in England and Wales. A Concise History* (London, 1985), p. 136. In Essex one contributory factor was an attack in 1789 by the Lord Chief Justice who, following another bout of gaol fever at Chelmsford, laid a fine on the county for not providing proper sick rooms, forcing the justices to use the solitary cells as a male sick ward. Briggs, *John Johnson*, p. 115; *The Times*, 27 July 1789.

[26] Howard, *The State of the Prisons* (2nd edn., 1780), pp. 219–23; (3rd edn., 1784), pp. 259–63; J. Howard, *An Account of the Principal Lazarettos in Europe* (London, 2nd edn., 1791), pp. 143–44; Neild, *State of the Prisons*, pp. 26, 117–24, 139–42, 261, 430, 511; Anon., *The Report of the Committee of London Aldermen*, P.P., 1819, XVII. By 1821, however *The Third Report of the Committee of the Society for the Improvement of Prison Discipline* (London, 1821) described shoemaking work and training in coarse weaving at Chelmsford at least—Appendix, pp. 19–20; *The Fourth Report* (London, 1822) described a winch mill by which the prisoners ground corn, Appendix, p. 15; by *The Sixth Report* (London, 1824) the county gaol and Halstead house of correction had a treadmill—Appendix, pp. 30–2.

for prison staff and in improving the sanitation and the general quality of the county's prison buildings. The 'wooden and very ancient' Barking house of correction, for example, was rebuilt in the 1790s, and after Neild attacked 'the loathsome old Bridewell' at Chelmsford and the 'despicable gaol' at Colchester in the *Gentleman's Magazine*, improvements were made and the former was rebuilt. However, it was not until the 1820s that systematic attempts were made to introduce a more regulatory regime. Before 1820, prison reform was piecemeal, patchy, and often short-lived[27] with prisoners continuing to enjoy a measure of free association. It therefore seems unlikely that the Essex courts' growing use of imprisonment between 1770 and 1820 was based mainly on the belief that new 'reformatory' qualities were being introduced into the county's prisons. Although the key decisions at the assizes in 1772 coincided with the first stirrings of thinking about prison reform, elsewhere the greater use of imprisonment came much earlier. Between the 1720s and the 1750s the proportion of Newcastle thieves sentenced to imprisonment rose from 10 per cent to 60 per cent, and by the mid-1760s half of Northumberland petty larceny convicts and over 20 per cent of Essex ones received similar sentences.[28] Moreover, even after the reform movement gathered momentum in the 1780s its impact on prison practice was limited. The Essex evidence clearly supports Ignatieff's conclusion that by the mid-1790s the reforming impetus that gave birth to the penitentiary had largely spent itself. In Essex, as elsewhere, it was not until a second generation of reformers emerged in the early nineteenth century that more long-lasting changes in the nature of imprisonment began to be introduced.[29]

It would be wrong to suggest, however, that prison sentences gained favour merely because the courts were no longer willing to whip minor offenders and were no longer able to transport them. Imprisonment offered much greater flexibility in attuning the level of the sanction to the nature of both offence and offender, and all the Essex courts, like their Surrey counterparts, made use of a wide range of prison terms (Tables 8.2 and 8.3). The average length of the sentence varied according to the seriousness of the offence. Most petty larceny sentences were counted in weeks rather than months and few were substantially longer than the period the offender had already spent in gaol awaiting trial (Table 8.2). The assize judges, after a brief experiment with longer grand larceny sentences in the 1770s, quickly established a norm of between six months and a year (Table 8.3). Both these patterns remained relatively stable

---

[27] Briggs, *John Johnson*, pp. 113–20; *P.P.*, 1819, XVII, pp. 12–15. For increasing salaries, compare Howard, *The State of the Prisons* (2nd edn., 1780), pp. 219–23 with Neild, *State of the Prisons*, pp. 26, 117–22, 261, 430, and 140–2 for his attack on Colchester gaol. For the problems experienced in trying to create a strict regime in the new county gaol after 1828, see White, 'Chelmsford Gaol', pp. 90–1.

[28] Morgan and Rushton, *Rogues, Thieves*, pp. 74–5.

[29] Ignatieff, *A Just Measure of Pain*, pp. 114, 142.

Table 8.2. Range of Imprisonment Sentences, Essex Quarter Sessions, 1740–1804

	% Petty larceny	% Petty larceny	% Petty larceny	% Grand larceny
Imprisonment	1740–75	1776–85	1786–1804	1786–1804
Length unknown	11.0	2.0	1.1	5.0
1 week or less	13.0	13.3	17.7	16.0
1.1 week–1 month	25.0	35.7	33.2	23.5
1.1 month–3 months	35.0	32.7	32.9	28.6
3.1 months–6 months	11.0	9.2	11.9	16.0
6.1 months or more	5.0	7.1	3.2	10.9
Total %	100.0	100.0	100.0	100.0
Sample size	100	98	277	119
% Imprisonment with solitary confinement	—	—	1.4	5.9
% Whipped as well as imprisoned	42.0	36.7	18.4	27.7

Source: E.R.O. Q/SPb 5–17.

Table 8.3. Range of Imprisonment Sentences, Grand
Larceny Convictions, Essex Assizes, 1770–1804

	% 1770–9	% 1780–9	% 1790–1804
Imprisonment			
1 week or less	2.0	—	—
1.1 week–1 month	17.6	7.4	9.4
1.1 month–3 months	19.6	14.7	12.6
3.1 months–6 months	11.8	35.3	50.9
6.1 month–1 year	11.8	22.1	22.6
1.1 year–2 years	23.5	5.1	4.4
2.1 years or more	3.9	—	—
Thames			
0 year–1 year	—	2.2	—
1.1 year–2 years	2.0	6.6	—
2.1 years–3 years	5.9	6.6	—
3.1 years–5 years	2.0	—	—
5.1 years or more	—	—	—
Total %	100.1	100.0	99.9
Sample size	51	136	159

Note: Includes burglary and aggravated larceny charges reduced by the
jury to grand larceny convictions. These formed a fairly constant proportion at around 20 per cent 1770–1804. Excludes 1799 and 1800.

Source: P.R.O. Assi 31/9–20.

until the early nineteenth century, although the average length of quarter sessions' sentences rose slightly when the lower court began taking grand larceny cases in the 1780s.[30]

The decline of physical, publicly inflicted, punishments was not a uniform process in Essex between 1740 and 1820. Branding underwent a considerable revival only a few years before its final abolition in 1779[31] and the courts' use of hanging and whipping also fluctuated extensively (Figures 8.1a and b). However, significant long-term changes did occur. Since the pillory was rarely employed against property offenders whipping was by far the most important physical punishment in non-capital cases. Although public whipping declined rapidly as a separate sanction after the mid-1770s (Table 8.4 and Figure 8.1), its use as an adjunct to imprisonment sentences actually increased in the late eighteenth century. When the Essex quarter sessions began to imprison a large number of offenders after 1775, the court continued its established practice of sentencing around a quarter of male petty larceny prisoners to the additional punishment of a public whipping (Table 8.4). Far from abandoning ritualistic corporal punishment the courts took great care in these years to stipulate the exact time and place of its infliction, and increased its impact by staging the event either in the market-place on market day or near the scene of the crime.[32] By favouring its use as an additional punishment for grand larceny after 1788, the quarter sessions further increased the proportion of sentences that included a whipping, and although the assizes employed this sanction slightly less frequently than the lower court, nearly a quarter of male grand larceny prisoners received a public whipping between 1790 and 1797.[33] Around the turn of the century however, the practice was suddenly dropped. The quarter sessions continued to sentence a small minority of those they imprisoned to a private whipping (Table 8.4), as they had regularly done since 1760, but for reasons that are not entirely clear both the major courts ceased to pass sentences involving public corporal punishment. In these years of dearth and widespread incendiarism the magistrates may have thought that such punishments would arouse unnecessary popular hostility. However, reformers had long argued that the public humiliation of the offender eroded his chances

[30] Beattie, *Crime*, p. 580. The assizes ceased to use sentences of hard labour on the Thames when transportation was resumed in the late 1780s, hence the change in Table 8.3. For the lighter range of sentences used by the borough courts of Essex: King, 'Crime, Law', pp. 346–8.

[31] Beattie, *Crime*, pp. 560–1.

[32] William Hicks, for example, was sentenced to be whipped at the cart's tail on market day from Braintree market-place to the end of the town of Bocking—a long journey through a heavily populated area. E.R.O. Q/SPb. 15 (July 1773).

[33] 1788–97 the quarter sessions added a whipping to 39 per cent of grand larceny sentences, 22 per cent of petty larceny. The assizes first used a public whipping with imprisonment in 1781. In Lent 1782 a brief experiment resulted in all imprisoned males being publicly whipped and all the females being privately whipped. Thereafter the policy became more discriminating: 18 per cent was the figure for 1776–89 and 1790–7. Beattie, *Crime*, pp. 461–2, 561 indicates that in Surrey also whipping was more widely used at the quarter sessions.

Table 8.4. Sentences of Public and Private Whipping, Essex Quarter Sessions, 1760–1804

	1760–75	1776–89	1790–7	1798–1804
Imprisoned and whipped	%	%	%	%
Imprisoned without whipping	55	72	64	92
Imprisoned with public whipping	37	22	28	1
Imprisoned with private whipping	8	6	8	7
Total %	100	100	100	100
Total number imprisoned =	52	170	166	147
Whipping as a complete sentence				
Public whipping	44	23	0	0
Private whipping	56	77	100	0
Total %	100	100	100	0
Total no. whipped as a complete sentence	85	22	4	0

Source: See table 8.2.

of obtaining gainful employment, thus driving him back into crime,[34] and the complex development of more general 'humanitarian' sensibilities about the depraving effects of these rituals may have been adding further weight to this view by the early nineteenth century.[35]

The courts' use of the ultimate physical punishment, death by hanging, also underwent a fundamental change at the beginning of the nineteenth century but this was not reflected in the immediate sentences pronounced in court. The proportion of Essex convicted offenders sentenced to death did not decline during the period being studied here (Figure 8.1*b*). It averaged 21 per cent in the 1740s and about 22 per cent between 1810 and 1819. This stability was not necessarily a reflection of the judges' attitudes. Apart from the indirect influences they were able to exert over jury verdicts, they had few opportunities to affect the number of capital sentences they passed, and short-term changes in capital convictions were therefore mainly related to variations in the types of indictment brought to the courts. The judges expressed their sentencing priorities and their attitudes to different offences

[34] Ignatieff, *A Just Measure of Pain*, p. 90; Eden, *Principles of Penal Law*, pp. 56–63; for contemporary comments on the shame of public whipping—G. Smith, 'Civilised People Don't Want to See That Kind of Thing. The Decline of Public Physical Punishment in London 1760–1840', in Strange (ed.), *Qualities of Mercy*, pp. 31–7.

[35] The precise role of such changing sensibilities is difficult to unravel. Change was many-layered. The campaign against public flogging in the army was still in its infancy in 1800—P. Burroughs, 'Crime', p. 561; E. Steiner, 'Separating the Soldier from the Citizen. Ideology and Criticism of Corporal Punishment in the British Armies, 1790–1815', *Social History*, 8 (1983), 19–35; J. Dinwiddy, 'The Early Nineteenth-Century Campaign against Flogging in the Army', *English Historical Review*, 97 (1982), 308–31. Attitudes to the whipping of women were affected first (Gatrell, *The Hanging Tree*, pp. 336–8), but in relation to males the flogging culture ran deep (ibid., 507 and 578) and remained entrenched—Radzinowicz and Hood, *History*, 5, pp. 689–719, J. Cockburn, 'Punishment and Brutalization in the English Enlightenment', *Law and History Review*, 12 (1994), 177.

Table 8.5. Home Circuit Pardoning Policy, Various Property Crimes, 1755–1815

	No. capitally convicted	No. hanged	% hanged
Forgery	41	28	68.3
Coining	20	13	65.0
Robbery	34	17	50.0
Highway robbery	877	344	39.2
Burglary	699	233	33.3
Post Office, mail robbery	10	3	30.0
Naval stores	17	5	29.4
Miscellaneous offences	15	4	26.7
Bleaching ground, larceny from	4	1	25.0
Cattle stealing	42	7	16.7
Navigable river, larceny on	40	6	15.0
Horse stealing	549	73	13.3
Housebreaking	326	35	10.7
Sheep stealing	381	35	9.2
Larceny in dwelling house	264	22	8.3
Shops, warehouses, privately stealing	60	2	3.3
Larceny from the person	12	0	0

Source: *P.P.*, 1819, VIII, pp. 168–175. The figures for Essex alone are rarely large enough to compare offences but Essex does not seem to have been untypical among the Home Circuit counties (see Table 8.1).

primarily through pardoning policies. In Essex, as in Surrey and elsewhere, murderers and sexual offenders were very likely to be left to hang. Among property offenders execution rates were highest in highway robbery, burglary, and forgery cases and lowest where no violence to persons or property was involved (Table 8.5). In horse, sheep, or cattle stealing cases, where the court could not express their desire for a lenient sentence by using a partial verdict, about 90 per cent of convicted offenders escaped the gallows. Where the offence had only recently been made capital or involved privately stealing from a shop, a warehouse, or a pocket all but a handful of convicted offenders were spared.[36]

The judges' policies also varied according to the length of the gaol calendars. In Essex the large rises in indictment levels that followed the demobilizations of 1748 and 1782–3 were accompanied by a distinct toughening of pardoning policies (Figure 8.4) and similar patterns can be seen on other circuits[37] (Figure 8.5). During these two periods of growing disquiet about crime and the administration of the criminal law the central authorities sometimes attempted to put pressure on the judges. In the early 1750s Dudley Ryder referred to 'the King's late injunction' against pardons for highway robbery

[36] Emsley, *Crime* (2nd edn.), pp. 256–62; Beattie, *Crime*, pp. 433–4, 515.

[37] Figures 8.4 and 8.5 may be slightly inaccurate because a few late pardons were probably not recorded. The circuit figures include all capital convicts. Non-property crimes were relatively unimportant (8.2 per cent Home Circuit, 1755–1814) but their presence may have slightly reduced short-term variations in hanging rates. The Essex figures are for property crimes only.

Fig. 8.4 Percentage of Capital Convicts Hanged, Essex and Home Circuit, 1740–1818 (6-year moving average)

Sources: Home Circuit, *P.P.*, 1819, VIII, pp. 168–174; and Essex P.R.O. Assi 31/1–23.

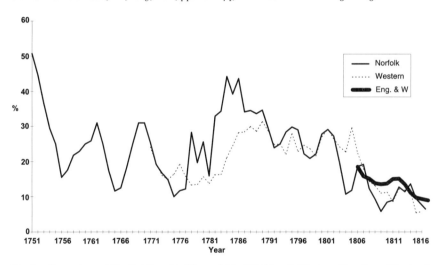

Fig. 8.5 Percentage of Capital Convicts Hanged, Norfolk Circuit, Western Circuit, and England and Wales, 1750–1818 (3-year moving average)

Sources: *P.P.*, 1819, VIII, pp. 126–7, 176–183, and 194–223; J. Howard, *An Account of the Principal Lazarettos in Europe* (1791), p. 252.

and in 1782 the Essex newspapers made it clear on several occasions that the judges had been notified of the need for a more vigorous execution of the criminal laws. Daring robbers, servants who had betrayed a trust, burglars and housebreakers, and anyone 'whose crimes had any particular marks of barbarity', were all warned not to expect any abatement of their sentence from

Table 8.6. Pardoning Policy, 1778–94, Various Assize Circuits

| | Home Circuit, housebreaking only | | Home, Western and Norfolk Circuits, all capital crimes | |
	Number capitally convicted	% Hanged	Number capitally convicted	% Hanged
1778–82	55	42	546	24
1783	20	65	271	29
1784	23	61	224	28
1785	26	69	238	47
1786	33	58	216	35
1787	25	28	236	36
1788	10	30	145	25
1789–94	66	29	809	28

Sources: P.P., 1819, VIII, pp. 168–83, 194–223.

His Majesty.[38] Although these injunctions undoubtedly had an effect on the judges' decisions, that effect was limited and relatively short-lived (Table 8.6). On the Home Circuit the proportion of fully convicted housebreakers that were hanged rose from 42 per cent before the injunction to a peak of 69 per cent in 1785, but by 1787 it had fallen again to below the 1782 level and from then onwards nearly three-quarters of these offenders were reprieved (Table 8.6). Pardoning policies towards capital offenders as a whole followed a similar pattern. On the three best-documented provincial circuits 22.3 per cent were hanged in the 1770s compared with just under a third in 1782–7, but even at the peak of harsher policies in 1785 the majority of capital convicts were still reprieved (Table 8.6).

It may be no coincidence that the peak was reached in the year that Madan published his famous attack on lenient pardoning policies. During the heated debate that ensued the judges were clearly not in agreement among themselves. Although Judge Perryn immediately defended reprieves and Romilly quickly published a persuasive counter-attack, for a brief period Madan's views do seem to have influenced some of the judges. On the Home Circuit in July 1785 Judge Eyre warned the grand jurors to 'be careful what bills you find . . . for if the parties are convicted for a capital offence, I have made up my mind as I go through the circuit, to execute everyone'. Eyre kept his word. At the Chelmsford assizes all the ten capitally convicted offenders were hanged despite applications by 'the first interest of the county' for the reprieve of the 18-year-old sailor John Moore.[39] However, the summer of 1785 was a pecu-

---

[38] Rogers, 'Confronting the Crime Wave', pp. 77–98; Beattie, Crime, pp. 521–31; Dudley Ryder, Assize Diary, pp. 16–17 shows the influence of these instructions. Parliamentary History, XXV, col. 904; P.P., 1816, V, p. 143. For reports and proclamations concerning the new severity in pardoning policy, Che.C., 20 Sept. 1782, 22 Nov. 1782; I.J., 14 Aug. 1782; 23 Nov. 1782 and Ignatieff, A Just Measure of Pain, pp. 86–7.
[39] Madan, Thoughts; Radzinowicz, History, I, pp. 231–67. For Madan's parliamentary supporters, Parliamentary History, XXV, cols. 901–7, and his opponents, Gentleman's Magazine, 1785, p. 533. Romilly,

liarly sensitive time and Eyre's 100 per cent hanging policy was never seen again at the Chelmsford assizes. An extensive press campaign calling on the government 'to restore mercy to the judgement seat' went on throughout that year, and despite the London Aldermen's petition in March 1786 demanding that all sentences 'be fully executed' pardoning decisions were quickly returned to their usual discretionary basis. It was widely believed that neither jurors nor prosecutors would tolerate executions on this scale for very long and the authorities very quickly dropped their much-criticized policy of 'sanguinary sacrifice'. As early as the Lent assizes of 1786 more than half the Essex property offenders sentenced to death were later reprieved and during the final third of the 1780s hanging rates declined in Essex, Sussex, and on every provincial assizes circuit for which information is available (Figures 8.4 and 8.5).[40] Similar short-term variations can be observed in 1800-2. Lord Kenyon, faced by the longest gaol calender he had ever seen at Chelmsford announced in 1801 that

For a series of years the judges of this country have tried what mercy would do and whether humanity, almost unbounded humanity would reform the world... That mercy and that humanity have had no effect. The tables must now be turned and it must be seen what a rigorous execution of the laws can do.

Kenyon's definition of 'rigorous' was more flexible than Eyre's. Only twelve of the thirty-one men he sentenced to death were eventually hanged.[41] Although sentencing policy continued to be influenced by judicial perceptions of the prevalence of crime, Kenyon's brief retreat into terror marked the end of an era; 1801 was the last year that as many as a dozen offenders died on the Essex gallows and during the following decade pardoning policy in capital cases underwent a final and fundamental shift.

Although Radzinowicz suggested that the second half of the eighteenth century witnessed a progressive decline in the proportion of capital convicts that were hanged, the evidence he used was highly selective and mainly London-based,[42] and his conclusions do not fit the evidence available for the

Observations; *P.P.*, 1816, V, p. 145, Eyre travelled the Home Circuit that summer: P.R.O. Assi. 31/14; *Che.C.*, 29 July 1785.

[40] *The Times*, 13 May 1785, 17 May 1785, 5 Oct. 1785, 20 Oct. 1785; Gatrell, *The Hanging Tree*, p. 327. *The Times*, 25 and 27 Mar. 1786; and *Parliamentary History*, XXV, cols. 902–4. In Lent 1786 less than half the capital convicts were hanged although they were all convicted of offences usually treated with severity—forgery, highway robbery, and burglary. At the Essex Lent assizes in 1788 no property offenders were hanged. For public reaction, Romilly *Observations*, pp. 88–91. *The Times*, 13 May 1785; Ignatieff, *A Just Measure of Pain*, p. 87. For Sussex, Beattie, *Crime*, pp. 588–9.

[41] *Che.C.*, 31 July 1801; P.R.O. *Assi* 31/19. Many of those hanged were soldiers who had committed a large number of crimes. *A Particular Account of the Trial and Condemnation of John Highly*. Kenyon was also fighting very different battles, at this time—D. Hay, 'The State and the Market in 1800: Lord Kenyon and Mr Waddington', *Past and Present*, 162, (1999), 101–61.

[42] Radzinowicz, *History*, I, p. 151. Hay, 'Crime, Authority', pp. 482–526 discusses this in more detail. Radzinowicz's comparison of 1749–58 and 1790–9 produces a false sense of decline because execution rates were particularly high in the postwar period after 1748. On London evidence source problems, Emsley, *Crime* (2nd edn.), pp. 256–7.

provincial circuits. Pardoning policies did become more lenient in the century before 1740, encouraged perhaps by the increasing availability of the intermediate punishment of transportation, and the period 1630–1740 has rightly been pinpointed by recent historians as one in which execution rates fell very significantly.[43] However, the pattern was very different after 1740. Between 1740 and 1800 reprieve rates in Essex and on the Home, Norfolk, and Western Circuits (Figures 8.4 and 8.5) remained virtually static in the long term. The vital change in Essex came between 1805 and 1818 (Figure 8.4) and this timing is confirmed by the national figures in which the proportion of capital convicts actually hanged declined from 19 to 8 per cent. The decade-long campaign against capital punishment which finally resulted in the setting up of the 1819 Parliamentary Committee coincided with a major change in judicial attitudes. The reformers achieved little statutory change until the second quarter of the century but they may have influenced the most important decision-makers— the judges. Although many judges strongly opposed the parliamentary repeal of the capital statutes, which would have greatly reduced their discretionary powers, they pardoned an increasing proportion of offenders as the nineteenth century wore on—influenced no doubt by the fact that if they had not done so the absolute numbers reaching the gallows would have risen alarmingly.[44] By changing their attitudes in this way they decisively, if rather belatedly, altered the balance of pardoning policy in the prisoner's favour.

In the half century after 1820 the repeal of almost all the capital statutes, the declining availability and final demise of transportation, the increasing public disquiet about the use of flogging, and the relative lack of armed engagement (which made the armed forces less useful as an alternative sanction) brought an end to the penal pluralism of the eighteenth and early nineteenth centuries.[45] However, between 1740 and 1820 the range of sentencing options available was extremely wide and this highlights the need to study another central aspect of the eighteenth-century penal process, the ways that the sanction was adjusted to the nature of the individual offender.

2. Gender and Punishment

Both the gender and age of the accused affected eighteenth-century sentencing policies in a number of ways. The gendered nature of those decisions is seen clearly in Table 8.7 which is based on data taken from all five Home Circuit counties for 1782–7 and 1799–1800.[46] Taking property offenders as a whole,

[43] The proportion of Home Circuit offenders actually hanged was 54% 1689–1718, 24% 1754–84, 35% 1785–94, *P.P.*, 1819, VIII, pp. 167–72. Jenkins, 'From Gallows to Prison'; Sharpe, *Crime in Early Modern England*, pp. 64–5.

[44] *P.P.*, 1819, VIII, pp. 126–7; Radzinowicz, *History*, 1, pp. 541–607; Gatrell, *The Hanging Tree*, pp. 7–21.

[45] Innes and Styles, 'Crime Wave', p. 234.

[46] These years were selected for reasons unrelated to gender—they are the only periods when the age of the accused is recorded—but work done on the 1820s suggests the same pattern, as does parallel work on London, 1791–3—King, 'Gender, Crime and Justice', pp. 44–74.

Table 8.7. Home Circuit Property Offenders, Sentences Analysed by Gender, 1782–1800

Sentence	All property offenders		Simple/grand larceny		Stealing in dwelling house		Housebreaking and burglary	
	%	%	%	%	%	%	%	%
	M	F	M	F	M	F	M	F
Fined	1.6	1.9	3.1	4.7	0	0	0.3	0
Whipped	2.1	5.8	4.5	12.5	0	0	0.7	0
Imprisoned	33.1	63.6	59.2	73.4	36.4	75.0	19.6	46.0
Transported	17.7	8.4	24.1	7.8	42.4	8.3	19.9	18.9
Death/ reprieved	19.1	15.6	0.7	1.6	15.2	16.7	20.6	29.7
Hanged	20.5	3.9	0.9	0	6.1	0	34.7	5.4
Punishment unknown	5.9	0.7	7.4	0	0	0	4.1	0
Total	100.0	99.9	99.9	100.0	100.1	100.0	99.9	100.0
Sample size	1,337	154	552	64	33	12	291	37

Note: Sample years = Summer assizes 1782–Summer 1787 and Summer 1799 to Summer 1800

Source: P.R.O. Assi 31/13–15, 18.

females were more than twice as likely to receive one of the two lightest punishments—whipping or fining. They also suffered the two heaviest sanctions much less frequently. Men were more than twice as likely to be sentenced to death, and more than twice as likely to be given a direct sentence of transportation (Table 8.7). Moreover, whilst more than half of capitally convicted males actually went to the gallows, only 20 per cent of females suffered the same fate. By contrast nearly two-thirds of female property crime convicts were sentenced to the relatively light punishment of imprisonment compared to only one-third of males.[47]

Did this more lenient treatment simply reflect the fact that women were usually charged with less serious offences and were therefore underrepresented among those indicted for crimes such as highway robbery, burglary, and horse stealing which attracted the heaviest sentences? The data available on individual offences (final columns of Table 8.7) suggest not. Females accused of simple, non-aggravated larceny were much more likely to be fined or whipped and were three times less likely to receive the most severe sentence usually available— transportation.[48] Male housebreakers were six times more likely to go to the gallows, while the least severe sentence—imprisonment—was more than twice as likely to be handed out to female housebreakers than to male

---

[47] The length of prison sentences favoured women only marginally. 27% of women were sentenced to less than 6 months compared with 21% of men. In Surrey 1660–1800, 60% of male capitally convicted property offenders were hanged compared with 20% of females, Beattie, *Crime*, p. 438.

[48] Since those accused of simple non-aggravated larceny could not be sentenced to death, the handful of cases where sentence of death was recorded almost certainly reflect the misdescription of the offence by the court clerk in the agenda books.

ones—a pattern also repeated in cases involving stealing from the dwelling house.

The Essex data for the much longer period 1740–1805 (Table 8.8) broadly confirms the Home Circuit findings. Overall Essex female property offenders were more likely to be branded, fined, whipped, or imprisoned. They were equally likely to be transported and much less likely to be sentenced to death. Once again when housebreakers and grand larceny convicts are analysed separately the pattern of relative leniency remains. Nearly four-fifths of Essex female housebreakers, for example, avoided being sentenced to death compared with less than half of their male counterparts; and among those that were capitally convicted, 104 of the 223 males but only one of the thirteen females were actually hanged—a pattern also broadly replicated in Surrey.[49] In grand and aggravated larceny cases the Essex evidence, which is based on quarter sessions as well as assizes cases, is less polarized. However, once again women were less likely to be sent abroad than men and much more likely to receive the less severe punishments of a fine, a branding or a whipping (Table 8.8). The data on petty larceny—an offence which was usually tried at the quarter sessions—suggest that when the stakes were smaller sentencing policies were much less gendered (Table 8.8). Although the borough courts tended to slightly favour women,[50] at the county quarter sessions female petty larceny convicts received only marginally more favourable treatment—in Essex as a whole 81 per cent were fined, branded, whipped, or imprisoned compared with 77 per cent of males. Indeed, females were marginally more likely to be transported, mainly because the Essex quarter sessions made quite extensive use of the armed forces as a wartime option for males only.[51]

The relationship between gender and sentencing policy was therefore complex and the relative leniency shown to women seems to have increased with the seriousness of the offence, but by the second half of the eighteenth century the courts were clearly very reluctant to send women to the gallows. Even allowing for the fact that women were usually charged with less serious offences, it is remarkable that only one female property offender was hanged in Essex between 1740 and 1804, a period in which 271 males died on the gallows for this range of crimes (Table 8.8). That one offender—the 22-year-old Elizabeth Holmstead—failed to get a reprieve partly because her offence was considered a particularly heinous one. She had betrayed her master's

---

[49] Beattie, *Crime*, pp. 536–7; 74 males housebreakers and 1 female one were hanged in Surrey 1749–1802.

[50] The Colchester borough sessions 1740–1804 transported only two female petty larceny convicts (6%) compared with ten males (16%).

[51] An additional reason was the introduction in 1776 of the exclusively male sentence of hard labour on the Thames, which was occasionally used against petty thieves as a direct substitute for transportation: Beattie, *Crime*, p. 566.

Table 8.8. Sentences for Property Crime, Male and Female, Essex, 1740–1805

		% Sentence unknown	% Fine	% Burnt in hand	% Whipped	% Imprisoned	% Armed forces	% Thames	% Transported	% Hanged reprieved	% Hanged	Total guilty
Petty larceny	M	5.5	0.2	0.1	31.0	45.7	5.3	0.5	11.8	—	—	851
	F	5.8	0.5	—	31.9	48.1	—	—	13.8	—	—	210
Grand and aggravated larceny	M	5.1	1.2	3.4	10.8	35.5	2.3	2.7	33.0	4.6	1.4	1,043
	F	2.8	4.2	7.7	19.1	35.2	—	—	27.5	3.5	—	142
Housebreaking	M	6.7	—	0.5	1.4	8.2	0.2	1.1	29.3	29.3	23.6	441
	F	5.1	—	—	10.0	26.7	—	—	36.7	20.0	1.7	60
Other	M	31.3	9.8	—	7.5	31.2	2.9	2.9	12.7	0.6	1.2	173
	F	25.7	5.7	—	2.9	45.7	—	—	20.0	—	—	35
All crimes	M	6.6	1.1	1.3	13.2	28.3	2.5	1.6	20.9	15.4	9.0	3,009
	F	6.2	2.0	2.4	22.4	40.9	—	—	21.8	4.0	0.2	450

Note: Horse and sheep theft and highway robbery excluded. Only 3 female offenders were convicted of these offences; 2 were transported, 1 was imprisoned. The offences are included in the 'all crimes' totals.

Sources: As for Table 5.1.

trust by helping her lover to rob the house where she lived as a servant.[52] However, her main problem was her appalling timing. In September 1782 a rising tide of anxiety about burglary led the King to announce that since 'humanity to such criminals would be cruelty to the rest of the community' his pardon would henceforth be denied them. Unfortunately for Elizabeth her case came up for review two months after the King's pronouncement. When the Essex assize judge sentenced her to death in July she was pregnant and had therefore been able to 'plead her belly'—a plea which her friends rightly assumed would usually 'secure her from execution as well after as before her delivery'. However, for this brief period neither her sex nor her newborn infant could save her. She was hanged in November that year.[53]

Although pleading the belly was a declining practice by the second half of the eighteenth century, some of the other Essex females sentenced to death after 1740 may have escaped the gallows in this way.[54] However, such pleas were only relevant in a minority of capital cases and although contemporaries rarely referred to this issue in public, it is clear that more complex reasons lay behind the relatively lenient treatment received by women in this period. This is difficult territory. The surviving records occasionally contain brief statements such as reprieved 'in compassion for the frailty of her sex' or 'spared on account of her sex', and at least one assize judge, in leaving a condemned woman to hang, made specific reference to the fact that her crime was too great to allow the normal immunity of women from hanging to apply in this case,[55] but the fragmentary sources available very rarely reveal the ideas on which such attitudes were based. Late twentieth-century studies indicate the importance of analysing whether female offenders were treated differently simply because they were women, or because they were more likely than men to exhibit other attributes (fewer previous convictions, less violence, a more compliant attitude in court) which encouraged the courts to look at them more favourably.[56] Unfortunately, however, eighteenth-century historians cannot interview magistrates and judges in the way that modern criminologists have been able to do. Hypotheses are therefore much more difficult to test, but a number of potential explanations of the gendered nature of sentencing policies can be put forward despite the poverty of the eighteenth-century sources.

[52] P.R.O. Assi 31/13 and 35/222/2; *Che.C.*, 22 Nov. 1782. The gender of Clare Mountford hanged for burglary in 1790 is difficult to verify but was probably male. One other female was hanged, 1767–1820—Elizabeth Langham for murder in 1804: ERO D/DTu 235.

[53] *Che.C.*, 20 Sept. 1782; 4 Oct. 1782; 29 Nov. 1782; Beattie, *Crime*, p. 431.

[54] J. Oldham, 'On Pleading the Belly. A History of the Jury of Matrons', *Criminal Justice History*, 6 (1985), 1–64.

[55] Cockburn, *Calendar of Assize Records ... Introduction*, p. 128; Gatrell, *The Hanging Tree*, p. 548; Anon., *An Authentic Narrative of the Celebrated Miss Fanny Davis*.

[56] D. Farrington and A. Morris, 'Sex, Sentencing and Reconviction', *British Journal of Criminology*, 23 (1983), 245–6; C. Hedderman and L. Gelsthorpe (eds.), *Understanding the Sentencing of Women* (London, 1997).

First, female offenders may have been seen as less of a threat, and therefore as less deserving of heavy punishment, both because relatively few of them reached the courts and because those that did so were rarely accused of the more violent or threatening types of crime. Moreover, when they were involved in such crimes females often took a less violent role in the offence, acting as lookouts, decoys, or receivers. Within broad categories of crime such as housebreaking, pickpocketing, or forgery female offenders may have committed forms of appropriation that were either smaller in scale or were perceived as less serious, less premeditated, more 'trivial'.[57] Females involved in highway robbery also benefited from doubts about their ability to offer an effective physical threat to the victim. Juries were often willing to acquit females of 'putting in fear' but these partial verdicts were rare when a male offender was involved. On the Home Circuit 44 per cent of the small number of females found guilty on highway robbery charges gained from such rulings, compared with just 5 per cent of males.[58] Whether female robbers were really less capable of violence remains open to question, but many contemporaries clearly believed they were and these attitudes formed part of a broader frame of reference that benefited the female accused. As John Beattie has pointed out, female offenders attracted higher proportions of partial verdicts, pardons, and lesser sentences in part at least because they were felt to pose 'a less serious threat to lives, property and order'.[59]

Other forces were also at work, however. If female offenders almost certainly benefited from being perceived as less 'troublesome' than males, they may equally have gained from being seen as more 'troubled'—as more vulnerable and more motivated by economic difficulties not of their own making. Pleas of poverty, unemployment, and economic vulnerability made by females may have received a more sympathetic hearing because women were highly marginalized in the eighteenth-century labour market, being forced into lower-paid, low-status, and less secure types of employment.[60] Judges and jurors may therefore have been willing to treat economic hardship as a real mitigating factor in cases involving women, particularly if they were mothers with young children who depended wholly or mainly upon them. Hanging or transporting women with young children not only punished the

[57] Beattie, 'The Criminality of Women', p. 90. I am grateful to Deirdre Palk's current doctoral research on 'Gender and Discretion in the English Criminal Justice System, 1780–1850' for its illuminating analysis of the different types of appropriation by women and men which can fall within the same broad legal categories and of the impact this can have on gendered sentencing patterns.

[58] Based on 1782–7, 1799–1800 (sources—Table 8.7), 4 out of 9 females, 11 out of 213 males.

[59] Beattie, *Crime*, p. 439; Shoemaker, *Prosecution*, pp. 212–13. Walker, 'Women, Theft', p. 90 rightly points out that patterns of female theft should not be interpreted as indicating women lacked bravado or initiative.

[60] On 'troubled' and 'troublesome', see Hedderman and Gelsthorpe, *Understanding*, pp. 26–30. On female offenders' work backgrounds, King, 'Female Offenders'; L. MacKay, 'Why They Stole: Woman in the Old Bailey, 1779–1789', *Journal of Social History*, 32 (1999), 627.

children as well as the offender, but was also likely to produce a costly break-down in family life which would substantially increase the burden on the rates. The Essex quarter sessions evidence, which includes reasonably accurate information on the marital status of female offenders (although not on the size of the offender's family) implies strongly that those subgroups of women who were most likely to have young dependent children were more favourably treated. Between 1750 and 1775 'spinsters' and 'single-women' convicted of petty larceny were more than twice as likely to be transported as married women. The Essex assize petty jury's treatment of Rose Pluckrose in 1740 suggests that the assize courts may have taken an equally sympathetic ap-proach. Rose was indicted for stealing 5 shillings and 6 pence and 'the prosecutor fully proved the fact'. The jury returned a partial verdict, however, reducing the value of the stolen money to 10 pence. Rose's defence was 'I have a bad husband and three children ready to starve with hunger.' The court responded by selecting a sentence which allowed her to return to her family immediately.[61]

Women who were still suckling their infant children might also receive considerable popular support in their attempts to obtain mitigation. The *Chelmsford Chronicle*, for example, recorded its relief when 'a decent looking woman with a child 6 weeks old at the breast' was recommended for mercy by the judge. Having young children to support did not, of course, automatically produce a more lenient sentence. Assize judges could come down hard on mothers whom they considered to be a bad influence on their children. In 1787 Mary Bond, who had abandoned her two infants at the time of her crime, received no support from the judge when she tried to avoid transportation. However, the eighteenth-century courts, like their twentieth-century counter-parts, were usually reluctant permanently to remove women perceived to be 'good mothers' from their families and children.[62]

While the courts' general desire to punish the troublesome and be more lenient to the troubled is an appropriate starting-point for understanding why female offenders were treated less severely in this period, other forces were clearly influencing those decisions. Some of those forces can only very occa-sionally be glimpsed by the historian. For example, judges and jurors may well have reacted differently when the accused was an attractive young woman. Occasionally a judge's ambivalence in a case involving such a woman certainly suggests that her appearance did her no harm, but given the terse and opaque

---

[61] Three of the seventeen married women or widows convicted of petty larceny at the Essex quarter sessions, 1750–75, were transported compared with seventeen out of forty-two of the single women or spinsters. The proportion of each group that had children in the convict indents 1826–40 = 10.5% single female offenders, married women 67.0%, widows 71.9%—D. Oxley, *Convict Maids. The Forced Migration of Women to Australia* (Cambridge, 1996), p. 255; *The Proceedings at the Assizes . . . Essex . . . July 1740*, p. 15.
[62] *Che.C.*, 11 Jan. 1782; P.R.O. H.O.47/6 Mary Bond; S. Edwards, *Women on Trial* (Manchester, 1984), pp. 7–8.

nature of the surviving documents the consequences of the eighteenth-century courtroom's version of the male gaze remain unclear.[63]

The gendered attitudes of the eighteenth-century courts had deep roots. The male judges and jurors who made these decisions were steeped in a long tradition of patriarchal assumptions. Potentially powerful yet inconsistent and sometimes downright contradictory, that tradition exercised a considerable influence on sentencing policies, even though that influence was rarely fully articulated or even consciously recognized by the decision-makers themselves. Until further research uncovers judicial records in which gendered attitudes are made explicit the precise impact of such attitudes will remain unclear, but both the legal textbooks and the scattered pardoning archives relating to female offenders do provide some clues. In 1790, for example, a young Welsh woman was reprieved because she 'had evidently been the instrument of a male offender' and similar pleas were made by other young women. In the same year a woman found guilty of counterfeiting was reprieved 'in pity of her youth and inexperience' while her male codefendant, with whom she had lived 'as his wife', was hanged.[64]

As late as the 1760s legal writers like Blackstone were still referring to ancient traditions which absolved 'any woman transgressing in concert with a man' from guilt. Although Blackstone went on to make it clear that in formal law those doctrines were now only applicable to married women committing indictable property offences in the company of their husbands, it remains possible that other types of female offender, whether married, single, or widowed, may also have benefited more generally from the implied tendency to regard them as less culpable, less responsible for their crimes, and therefore less deserving of severe punishment. The doctrine that 'a femme covert shall not be punished for committing any felony in company with her husband', here quoted from the 1777 publication *The Laws Respecting Women*, remained an important point of reference for magistrates well into the nineteenth century and enabled a considerable number of Essex wives to obtain acquittals between 1750 and 1800. It is therefore possible that its implications spilled out into other types of case, expressing perhaps a deeper, long-established set of attitudes upon which many male adjudicators drew in cases involving women—a residual sense that women were less blameworthy or less depraved than men.[65] This is difficult territory and more research is clearly necessary,

[63] The account of Fanny Davis's trial would lend itself to such an analysis—*Authentic Narrative... Fanny Davis*. Deirdre Palk's work is uncovering semi-coded language in trials involving young females which suggests their appearance was not unimportant.

[64] The best attempt to discuss these attitudes is Zedner, *Women*. The pardoning archive is not as useful for female offenders because they were usually reprieved immediately, making a subsequent petition and judge's report unnecessary; 7% involved female offenders. P.R.O. H.O. 47/11 Gwenllyan John and Sophia Girton.

[65] Blackstone, *Commentaries*, 4, pp. 28–9; Anon., *The Laws Respecting Women* (London, 1777), pp. 70–1; B. Godfrey '"Policing the Factory": Appropriation and its Control in the West Riding Textile

but in one arena at least clear and highly gendered policy changes were emerging in the period 1740–1820 and those changes provide important clues about attitudes towards the sentencing of male and female offenders.

Even a cursory survey of the penal changes that occurred in the second half of the eighteenth century and the early years of the nineteenth reveals a distinctly gendered set of attitudes and policy decisions. As sensitivities towards the use of physical and public punishments increased in this period, the greater sympathy towards the accused which this involved seems to have manifested itself particularly early and particularly strongly in relation to female offenders. At the national level this was evident in a number of legislative changes. In 1790 burning at the stake, which was still being imposed on female coiners (but not on male ones) and on husband-murderers in the 1780s, was abolished. In 1792 female vagrants were exempted from the punishment of whipping. In 1817 and 1820 Parliament went on to put an end first to the public, and then to the private, whipping of women, although men continued to suffer corporal punishment well into the second half of the nineteenth century.[66] At the local level, however, change seems to have come much earlier. Although women continued to be sentenced to corporal punishment until the early nineteenth century, the public whipping of female offenders had been largely abandoned in Essex by the late 1750s.[67] By contrast, public flogging continued to be used extensively against male offenders until the early nineteenth century. A sea-change in attitudes towards the hanging of female property offenders seems to have occurred at about the same time. For example, between 1620 and 1680 at least twenty-four women were hanged by the Essex courts for housebreaking or burglary (48 per cent of those convicted). Between 1740 and 1804 one was hanged (1.7 per cent). In Surrey a woman was hanged for this offence on average once every two years, 1663–1715, and about once every six years, 1722–49, but only one female housebreaker was executed in the entire period 1749–1802.[68]

Execution rates declined rapidly for both male and female property offenders between the mid-seventeenth and the mid-eighteenth centuries, but while

Factories, 1840–1880' (Leicester Ph.D., 1996), pp 142–8; S. Grace, '"Criminal, Idiots, Women and Minors. Is the Classification Sound?" Shifting Definitions and the Nineteenth-Century Woman Offender', *Social History Society Bulletin*, 19 (Spring 1994), 16–17; P. King, 'Female Offenders', pp. 67–8; Ekirch, *Bound for America*, p. 38.

[66] A. Harvey, 'Burning Women at the Stake in Eighteenth-Century England', *Criminal Justice History*, 11 (1990), 193–5; R. Campbell, 'Sentence of Death by Burning for Women', *Journal of Legal History*, 5 (1984), 44–59; Smith, 'Civilised People', p. 39; Radzinowicz, *A History*, 1, p. 578.

[67] Half a dozen female offenders were sentenced to public flogging by the Essex quarter sessions 1740–59 but it was virtually abandoned after that. Elsewhere the process was slower. Public whippings of women were still being reported in the 1780s—*I.J.*, 13 Apr. 1782; Morgan and Rushton, *Rogues, Thieves*, p. 131.

[68] Sharpe, *Crime in Seventeenth-Century England*, p. 108 for the 1620–80 figures which are an underestimate because not all the assizes files survive; Essex 1740–1804 based on sources for Table 5.1; Surrey figures, Beattie, *Crime*, pp. 454, 501, 515, 536–7.

that decline reduced male numbers very considerably they remained in serious danger of reaching the gallows throughout the second half of the eighteenth century if convicted of major aggravated thefts such as robbery or burglary. The pattern for women was very different, despite the fact that they continued to form a fairly similar proportion of those accused of such crimes. This process was not unilinear. The movement towards harsher sentencing policies that occurred in the early and middle 1780s affected women as well as men. It is no coincidence that five of the nine Surrey female property offenders who reached the gallows 1749–1802 were hanged between 1776 and 1787, or that the only Essex woman to suffer that fate did so in 1782. Nor was the process fully completed by 1800. Female property thieves and forgers did occasionally reach the gallows after that date.[69] However, overall there can be little doubt that female offenders were rapidly disappearing from the main arenas of public punishment in the later eighteenth and early nineteenth centuries.

Apart from Zedner's work on Victorian England we have virtually no overall analysis of the ways in which the anxieties about gender roles aroused by the economic and social changes of this period affected the way female offenders were punished. Gatrell has recently suggested that the growing reluctance to execute, burn, or whip women in public was 'activated by the sense that even at their worst women were creatures to be pitied and protected from themselves and perhaps revered'. However, until detailed work has been done on the relationship between responses to female criminality and changing social values and gender roles, such suggestions are difficult to evaluate. What is clear, both from the policies adopted by the courts and from the ways cases involving wrongly accused or overheavily punished women were used to add emotional charge to the campaign for criminal law reform, is that physical punishments were losing their legitimacy as sanctions deemed appropriate for women long before any change of parallel proportions occurred in relation to men.[70] In Essex, Surrey, the north-east, and elsewhere judges and jurors had begun to move away from the public and physical punishment of women, whether on the gallows or at the whipping post, well before Parliament began to pass gendered penal legislation such as that of 1790, 1792, 1817, and 1820. The effects of these changes, whether local or national, on the punishments women received could be contradictory. The ending of whipping, for example, sometimes resulted in the substitution of harsher punishments such as sizeable terms of imprisonment, while on other occasions it encouraged the courts to make use of nominal fines or very short periods of confinement.[71]

---

[69] Beattie, *Crime*, pp. 536–7; between 1797 and 1818, for example, four females were executed in Lancashire (one for murder, two for forgery of banknotes, one for stealing in the dwelling house); 149 males were executed in the same period, *P.P.*, 1819, VIII, p. 228. No female property offenders were hanged in Essex after 1782—E.R.O. D/DTu 235.

[70] Zedner, *Women*; Gatrell, *The Hanging Tree*, pp. 334–7.

[71] King 'Gender, Crime and Justice', for discussion; Morgan and Rushton, *Rogues, Thieves*, pp. 134–5.

Overall, however, this increased repugnance towards the public and physical punishment of women probably made a considerable contribution to the more lenient sentencing patterns which both Table 8.7. and Table 8.8. suggest were experienced by females accused of major property crimes in the later eighteenth and very early nineteenth centuries.

3. Age and Sentencing Policy

The other main dimension of sentencing policy which can be explored via a quantitative analysis of the court records is the relationship between the ages of the accused and the punishments they received. The Home Circuit clerks recorded the ages of all the accused for two brief periods in the eighteenth century—1782–7 and 1799–1800.[72] For reasons that remain unclear, on both occasions they then ceased this practice as suddenly as they began it, but by combining these two periods the impact of age on a sample of nearly 1,350 sentencing and pardoning decisions can be assessed (Table 8.9). The range of sentences employed in these two periods was slightly different. Hanging was rather more frequently used between 1782 and 1787. Transportation was used much less frequently because a new destination for transportees had yet to be found following the American War. However, despite the fact that one is a peacetime period and the other a wartime one, separate analyses reveal that age-related sentencing patterns were very similar in 1782–7 and 1799–1800. Not surprisingly, therefore, Figure 8.6 and Table 8.9 confirm the age-related patterns first uncovered by the author's work on the 1780s alone, but this larger data set also enables a fuller analysis of all age groups to be developed.[73]

Table 8.9. Home Circuit Sentences and Reprieves by Age Group (Property Crimes Only), 1782–1800

Age group	Sample size	% Fined or whipped	% Imprisoned	% Transported	% Sentenced to hang	% Total	% of sentenced to death hanged
0–16	68	7.4	44.1	13.2	35.3	100.0	20.8
17–26	672	2.1	33.8	16.8	47.3	100.0	52.5
27–35	325	4.6	33.2	20.9	41.2	99.9	54.5
36–55	241	7.1	47.3	18.3	27.4	100.1	40.9
55+	40	10.0	50.0	27.5	12.5	100.0	40.0
All ages	1,346	4.1	37.0	18.2	40.6	99.9	50.1

Sources: As for Table 8.7.

[72] P.R.O. *Assi* 31/13–15 (Summer assizes 1782 to Summer 1787); *Assi* 31/18 (Summer 1799–Summer 1800).

[73] In both periods those aged under 17 or over 35 were more likely to be fined, whipped or imprisoned, less likely to be sentenced to death, or actually hanged than those in their late teens and early to mid-twenties. King, 'Decision-Makers'.

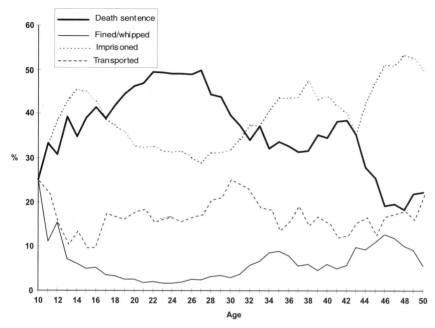

Fig. 8.6 Sentences by Age, All Property Offenders, Home Circuit, 1782–1800 (5-year moving total)

Source: P.R.O. Assi 31/13–15, 18–19.

A comparison of the two most frequently used sentences 1782–1800—hanging and imprisonment—immediately highlights the fact that those in their late teens and twenties were much more likely to receive the heaviest sentences, whilst younger and older offenders had a greater chance of being more leniently treated (Figure 8.6, top two lines). By putting the data into five broad age categories mainly selected in relation to specific life-cycle stages (Table 8.9) the general pattern visible in Figure 8.6 can be clarified and refined. Table 8.9 makes it clear that young offenders were much more likely to receive the relatively light punishments of whipping, imprisonment, and (very occasionally) a fine, while their chances of being transported or sentenced to death were well below average. Moreover, while half of all capital convicts went to the gallows only 20 per cent of the 0 to 16 age group met that fate. The exact opposite was true for the young adult age group (Table 8.9). Those in their late teens or early to mid-twenties were much less likely to be fined or whipped and considerably less likely to be imprisoned. They were much more likely to be sentenced to death and once that sentence had been passed less than half obtained a reprieve.

However, sentences did not get progressively more punitive with age. Indeed, they gradually became less harsh from about the age of 30 onwards.

The punishments imposed on those aged 27 to 35—the life-cycle stage when many got married, set up their own household, and started a family—were less harsh than those imposed on young adults and were very similar to the general figures for all age groups (Table 8.9). Those aged between 36 and 55—the period when most of the population were not only married but also had considerable numbers of dependent children—received much more lenient treatment so that their fate was fairly similar to that of those under 17. Finally, the tiny minority of offenders who were over 55 were even more leniently treated—a tenth being fined or whipped and half being imprisoned. The proportion of this age group that were sentenced to transportation was also much higher than average (Table 8.9) but this did not mean that the assize judges had a particular preference for transporting the elderly. Rather, it almost certainly reflects the court's tendency automatically to transport those found guilty of receiving—a crime more frequently committed by those in their declining years. The potentially distorting effect of the court's offence-specific sentencing policies in cases involving receiving highlights a more general problem. Since major capital offenders such as highway robbers and horse stealers, whom the courts were legally bound to sentence to death,[74] included a higher proportion of individuals aged 20 to 25 than those accused of more leniently treated offences such as grand larceny, a small part of this age-related sentencing pattern may have been due to involuntary choices forced upon the courts.[75] However, this possibility can be eliminated by separate studies of the two most common offences—grand larceny and housebreaking.

Table 8.10 indicates that sentencing in housebreaking cases favoured precisely the same groups as those indicated in Table 8.9. Those aged under 17 were nearly twice as likely to be either fined, whipped, or imprisoned as those aged 17 to 26. They were also much less likely to be transported. Moreover, less than a third of those sentenced to death before they were 17 were actually hanged while more than two-thirds of 17- to 26-year-old capitally convicted housebreakers suffered that fate. The 27–35-year-old group once again received punishments that were very similar to the averages for all age groups. Those over 35 were given more lenient treatment closely comparable to that received by those under 17, except that rather fewer older offenders were sentenced to death and rather more were transported. The contrasts between smaller age groupings could be even greater. The proportion of housebreakers sentenced to imprisonment declined from 40 per cent for those under the age of 15 to 10 per cent for those in their mid-twenties, for example, while precisely the opposite movement (a rise from 40 per cent to 70 per cent) occurred in relation to the death sentence. However, the age-sensitive nature of punishment policy is perhaps best exemplified by Figure 8.7, which uses a five-year

[74] There were exceptions but juries downgraded only 3.6% of highway robbery charges.
[75] 35% of all property offenders were aged 20 to 25; for highway robbers the figure was 46%, for horse thieves 39%.

Table 8.10. Burglary and Housebreaking, Sentences and Reprieves by Age Group, Home Circuit, 1782–1800

Age group	Sample size	% Fined or whipped	% Imprisoned	% Transported	% Sentenced to death	Total	% of sentenced to death hanged
0–16	25	4.0	32.0	12.0	52.0	100	30.8
17–26	154	0	18.8	22.1	59.1	100	68.1
27–35	75	1.3	21.3	21.3	56.0	99.9	59.5
36+	54	1.9	29.6	22.2	46.3	100	40.0
All ages	308	1.0	22.4	21.1	55.5	100	59.1

Sources: As for Table 8.7.

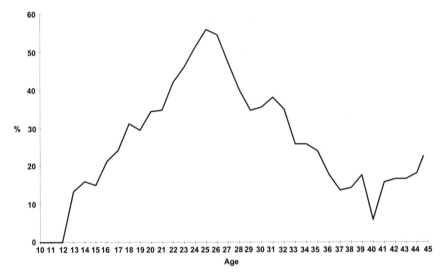

Fig. 8.7 Percentage of Housebreakers Actually Hanged, by Age, Home Circuit, 1782–1800 (5-year moving average)
Source: P.R.O. Assi 31/13–15, 18–19.

moving average to chart more clearly the proportion of convicted house-breakers that were actually hanged. The cumulative effect of the partial verdicts and reprieves which lay behind this pattern meant that while no one under 15 reached the gallows,[76] and only 15 per cent of those in their late thirties did so, 55 per cent of those in their mid-twenties were eventually hanged.

The pattern in simple larceny cases, where less was at stake because nearly three-quarters of offenders were either imprisoned, fined, or whipped, was less polarized but equally clear (Table 8.11). The middle sanction—imprison-

[76] The use of a five-year moving average makes it appear as if a 13- or 14-year-old may have been hanged (Figure 8.7) but in reality the youngest housebreaker hanged was aged 15.

ment—was used fairly consistently across all age groups, but both the young and the old were less likely to be transported and more likely to receive the least severe punishments of fining or whipping.[77] Unfortunately sample sizes are too small for comparable analyses to be worthwhile in relation to other individual offences. However, if pardoning policies in relation to all capitally convicted offenders are analysed (Figure 8.8) a very similar pattern emerges. The proportion actually hanged rises from 20 per cent for the mid-teens group to 50 per cent or 60 per cent for those in their twenties, before declining rapidly again. This graph does, however, highlight one exception to the rule that the very young and the very old received equally lenient treatment. As Tables 8.9 and 8.10 also indicate, although those over 35 were even more likely to avoid being sentenced to death, once they had been capitally convicted they were treated more harshly than the young although not as harshly as those aged between 17 and 35.[78] Until further work has been done on counties where the quarter sessions courts recorded offenders' ages (which they did not in Essex), it remains unclear whether these deeply age-related sentencing patterns had more impact on capital cases than when lesser offences were involved, but preliminary work on other assizes jurisdictions suggests that the Home Circuit was not exceptional. In the later eighteenth century, whether consciously or unconsciously, the punishment policies pursued by the courts and by those who made decisions about pardoning were extremely age-sensitive—deeply biased against young adults and in favour of younger and older offenders.

It is not easy to explore the underlying attitudes on which these policies were founded. The court records very rarely contain any explanation of the age-

Table 8.11. Simple Larceny. Sentences by Age Group, Home Circuit, 1782–1800

Age group	Sample size	% Fined or whipped	% Imprisoned	% Transported	% Other	% Total
0–16	28	14.3	64.3	17.9	3.6	100.1
17–26	238	5.9	67.2	26.1	0.8	100
27–35	130	10.0	58.5	26.2	5.4	100.1
36+	146	12.3	65.1	22.6	0.0	100
All ages	542	9.0	64.4	24.7	1.8	99.9

Sources: As for Table 8.7.

[77] The 'other' category in Table 8.11 presents a contradiction. These offenders were sentenced to death, indicating that offence definition in at least 1.8% of cases was inaccurate in the assizes agenda books, because all these larcenies must have been accompanied by some aggravating circumstance, such as pickpocketing, not recorded by the assizes clerk.

[78] Because Figure 8.8 stops at the age of 52 it suggests that older capitally convicted offenders were nearly as vulnerable as those in their twenties. The percentage is much lower, however (at 38 per cent), for the 52–80 age group.

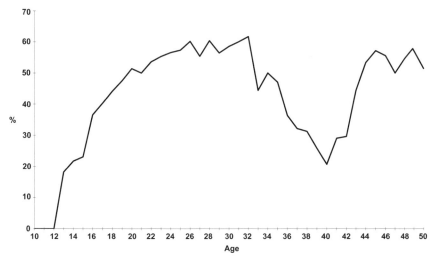

Fig. 8.8 Percentage of Capitally Convicted Property Offenders Actually Hanged, by Age, Home Circuit, 1782–1800 (5-year moving total)

Source: P.R.O. Assi 31/13–15, 18–19.

related sentencing decisions they provide evidence of, and the age of the accused was clearly only one of a number of interrelated factors that could influence the final sanction imposed. As both contemporary printed comments and the private views expressed in the pardoning archives (see Chapter 9) make clear, for a complete analysis of punishment policy information is needed about the accused's previous convictions, character, family commitments, and social status, as well as about the exact circumstances of the crime and a number of other aspects of each individual case. Unfortunately such evidence is not systematically available, but by relating the data in Tables 8.9 to 8.11 to contemporary comments and legal textbooks it is possible to gain some understanding of the ways that eighteenth-century judicial discretion was influenced by the age of the accused.

The more lenient sentences handed out to those aged under 15 were partly linked to specific legal traditions and rulings. Although children over 7 could be found guilty of felony in the eighteenth century, any victim attempting to prosecute an offender aged between 8 and 14 had to overcome the legal principle of *doli incapax* and prove that the child 'could discern between good and evil' and therefore knew that its actions were wrong. This ruling not only raised acquittal rates for those under 15; it also seems to have influenced sentencing policies. Both on the Home Circuit, 1782–1800, and at the Old Bailey during the 1790s this age group received extremely lenient treatment— a policy which seems to have enjoyed extensive popular support. In 1788, for example, *The Times* applauded the humanity of the Old Bailey Recorder when he ensured that a 10-year-old boy was not capitally convicted of shop-lifting.[79]

The more lenient sentencing policies pursued towards the young were also linked to more general notions about their gullibility and reformability. After noting in 1784 that 'young offenders deserving death by law' were 'so often' shown compassion, Hanway went on to justify this policy as follows. 'Common sense and experience teach us that many criminals are very young persons, who have been ensnared by evil companions, and the force of youthful passions, to whom great compassion is due. Many of these may be brought to a sense of their condition, and we owe it to God and our country to exercise mercy as well as justice, by affording them a fair opportunity of reforming.' The favourable treatment given to this age group also reflected a widespread popular repugnance at the thought of hanging the very young. 'The necessity of cutting off criminals of tender years is a defect of our police, which is really shocking to humanity', The Times complained in 1785, and four years later it reported that 'the extreme youth of six of the criminals...who were cast for death at the Old Bailey' produced in the observer a most 'melancholy' reflection.[80] This tendency was not new. Youth was being claimed as a mitigating circumstance in the late sixteenth century and Herrup has suggested that seventeenth-century jurors also tended to favour the young. However, its usefulness as a plea was clearly very firmly established by the late eighteenth century. Although a very small number of young property offenders continued to reach the gallows, Madan, Burke, Hanway, and others all noted with varying degrees of approval or disapproval that youth was a major source of mitigation by the 1780s.[81]

Sparse though their comments were, contemporary writers were much more forthcoming about the impact of youth on sentencing policies than they were about the ways that offenders at other life-cycle stages were regarded by the judicial authorities. However, there can be no doubt that age continued to play an important role. The harsher than average punishments received by young adult convicts partly reflected the softer treatment given to other age groups, but those in their late teens and twenties may also have been actively discriminated against. They tended on average to be less attached and less committed to a steady place in society, and included a larger number of

---

[79] Blackstone, Commentaries, 4, p. 23; Radzinowicz, History, 1, pp. 12–14; The Times, 9 May 1788; for the Old Bailey data see my forthcoming article on 'Changing Judicial Attitudes and Court Policies towards Young Offenders, 1780–1830'.

[80] J. Hanway, A New Year's Gift to the People of Great Britain (London, 1784), pp. 43–4; The Times, 20 Sept. 1785 and 11 Dec. 1789. In 1785 one was 12, another 14. For the emotional story of a young man going to the gallows—Hanway, Distributive Justice, pp. 59–63.

[81] Cockburn, Calendar of Assize Records...Introduction, p. 129; Herrup, The Common Peace, p. 158; Gatrell, The Hanging Tree, pp. 3–4; Hanway, A New Year's Gift, p. 43; Madan, Thoughts, p. 137. E. Burke. 'Some Additional Reflections on the Executions', in The Works of the Right Honourable Edmund Burke (14 vols., London, 1815–22), 9 (1818), p. 277.

migrants, vagrants, deserters, runaway servants, and particularly violent criminals towards whom the courts tended to be less sympathetic. Why did the
sentences given to offenders become progressively softer after they reached
their thirties? As has already been observed, an increasing proportion of
convicts in their thirties and forties would have had families and small children
to support. A plea of destitution by a single able-bodied man would not have
carried much weight with either judge or jury, but as an individual accumulated an increasing number of dependants the plea that poverty had driven
him, or her, to crime was more likely to be perceived as genuine. Few
contemporaries gave any indication of the precise weight they believed should
be given to pleas of extreme poverty, but Blackstone's dictum that 'theft, in
case of hunger, is far more worthy of compassion, than when committed
through avarice or to supply one in luxurious excesses' suggests that such pleas
may well have had considerable weight in certain cases. Judge Ryder's diary,
for example, indicates he was influenced by mitigating pleas describing the
destitution of the convict's wife and family at the time of the crime,[82] as does
the court's approach to the case of the destitute single mother Rose Pluckrose
quoted in the previous section of this chapter.

   More pragmatic reasons sometimes lay behind this softer treatment. The
jurors were drawn from the same middling group which formed the backbone
of the poor law system and they would not have been unaware of the cost of
keeping a family on the parish if the main breadwinner was permanently
removed. But the reprieve of a capital convict on condition of transportation
for fourteen years was unlikely to be more beneficial to his parish's finances
than allowing him to hang, and in most cases the relatively light sentences
received by convicts in their thirties and forties were probably linked to more
general sympathies for destitute convicts and their innocent families. The fact
that those over 55 received even more lenient treatment (Table 8.9) also acts as
a warning against an unduly cynical interpretation of the courts' motives in
such cases. By their mid-fifties offenders were much less likely to have dependent children but were increasingly likely to be dependent on the parish
themselves. Hanging or transporting such offenders released the parish from
a potentially large and long-term financial burden, yet 60 per cent of offenders
over 55 avoided these sentences compared with an average of 41 per cent for all
age groups. The favourable treatment given to relatively elderly offenders may
have been partly linked to the poverty that usually accompanied old age, or to
the fact that these offenders posed less of a physical threat and were more often
engaged in indirect forms of appropriation. However, since in their case it
cannot be argued that age was simply the medium through which the courts'
favourable attitude towards those who were not yet hardened offenders

---

[82] Blackstone, *Commentaries*, 4, p. 15; Langbein, 'Albion's Fatal Flaws', p. 111.

became evident,[83] it is possible that these older groups of offenders were treated more leniently primarily because of their age.

Although, as Beattie has pointed out, it is difficult to 'isolate the factor of age from several others', an offender's age was clearly significant both in itself and because each life-cycle stage brought with it a changing portfolio of potential mitigating circumstances. Single young adult males usually had much less in their portfolios than those who were younger, older, married, or female. As a result they were considerably more likely to reach the gallows. While the figures presented in this chapter (Tables 8.7 to 8.11) make it clear that when Burke highlighted 'youth' and 'sex' as key 'circumstances for mercy'[84] he was reflecting widespread contemporary practice, these were, of course, only two dimensions within a much more complex picture. In order both to develop a more holistic analysis of all the criteria that affected punishment policy, and to confirm and test the strength of the quantitative data presented here, it is therefore necessary to look at a completely different source—the petitions and reports created during the pardoning process.

[83] The more favourable treatment given to the young may have been linked to the fact that they had not yet had time to gather a reputation as hardened offenders, but the same could not be said of those aged over 55. For a critical discussion of the role of age, Beattie, *Crime*, p. 440.

[84] Beattie, *Crime*, p. 613; Burke, 'Some Additional Reflections', p. 277.

9

Pardoning Policies: The Good Mind
and the Bad

Most conditional pardons were granted by the circuit judges at the end of the assizes before they moved on to the next county, and some clues about the criteria they used can be gleaned from the ways that hanging rates differed by offence, gender, and age (Chapter 8). However, they were not required to record their reasons for making these decisions and they very rarely did so, making it difficult to assess the impact of other aspects of these cases on pardoning decisions. Fortunately some of the prisoners who were not granted immediate reprieves petitioned the King for a pardon through the Secretary of State, and whenever a petition was received the trial judge was immediately asked to send a written report of the case. The many petitions, supporting letters, and judges' reports that have survived from this process offer a rare window into the minds of the decision-makers, but even though the late eighteenth-century archive lacks the depth of documentation Gatrell found by the 1820s, these are complex documents that need to be treated with care.[1] The judges' reports were hidden transcripts, written in private between powerful people who did not expect the powerless prisoner ever to see their correspondence. The petitions, by contrast, are public transcripts written by the powerless to the powerful. Their language was therefore deferential, needful, tactical, or just plain desperate. Unlike the French, and usually murder-related, petitions recently analysed by Natalie Zemon Davis, the English petitions very rarely contained carefully crafted narratives retelling the story of the prisoner's crime in detail.[2] They focused instead on the special circumstances and personal characteristics which they wanted to stress in mitigation.

---

[1] Gatrell, *The Hanging Tree*, pp. 197–8, 613–4. The pardoning archive is mainly found in P.R.O. H.O. 47 (plus H.O. 42 and 13 for supporting material) and pre-1782 in S.P. 36, 37, and 44. For pardoning administration—R. Nelson, *The Home Office 1782–1802* (Durham N.C., 1969); S. Deveraux, 'The Criminal Branch of the Home Office 1782–1830', in G. Smith, A. May, and S. Deveraux (eds.), *Criminal Justice in the Old World and the New* (Toronto, 1998), pp. 270–308. It also includes some petitions from prisoners convicted at county or borough sessions.
[2] On hidden transcripts—J. Scott, *Domination and the Arts of Resistance. Hidden Transcripts* (New Haven, 1990); Gatrell, *The Hanging Tree*, p. 199. Some petitions were written by semi-professionals—J. Beattie, 'The Royal Pardon and Criminal Procedure in Early Modern England', *Historical Papers / Communications Historiques* (1987), p. 14. N. Zemon Davis, *Fiction in the Archives. Pardon Tales and their Tellers in Sixteenth Century France* (London, 1987).

In their attempts to appear deserving to the judges and Home Office officials they may have distorted or misrepresented those circumstances, but their pleas are, at the very least, an indication of the writer's sense of the criteria which the authorities were most likely to react favourably to.

The style and content of the petitions was far from uniform. Some were direct, unsophisticated, and sometimes semi-literate appeals by the prisoners themselves. Others were more formal—the work of attorneys or of relatively literate friends or fellow prisoners. Some were almost certainly, to quote one 1790s observer, 'those which the blood suckers of a gaol . . . prepare for prisoners when they can get money for doing it'.[3] The judges' reports also varied to some extent both across time and according to the type of case and the individual judge involved. However, most contained both a fairly detailed report of the evidence given at the trial and a brief final summary, which indicated why they favoured the petition, opposed it, or took a neutral attitude towards it.[4] These often cryptic conclusions, on which the prisoner's life so frequently depended, were sometimes defensive in tone. More often they simply responded curtly to the main points in the petition or reiterated the reasons for the judge's original sentence and for his consequent decision not to place the prisoner's name among those selected for immediate reprieve.

1. A Quantitative Approach and its Problems

The complex and uneven nature of the pardoning archives poses major methodological problems for historians and most have therefore taken a rather impressionistic approach, plucking out illustrative quotes without sampling the source in a systematic way. The author's own first attempt to work on this archive involved a different and more quantitative approach, using a factor mentions system.[5] Having selected two sample volumes from the core pardoning archive which between them covered most of the cases for 1787 and 1790, I looked at every judge's report and its accompanying petition (and/or letter) and counted each occasion on which any factor was mentioned either in favour of, or against, the prisoner.[6] The results (Table 9.1) indicate that a

---

[3] Beattie, 'The Royal Pardon', pp. 14–15; P.R.O., H.O. 47/16, Case of John Howard.

[4] The judges' recommendations varied from outright rejection—'I see no reason to think that the law ought not to take its course' (P.R.O. H.O. 47/1 John Carney), to positive support—'I take the liberty . . . to recommend him . . . as a fit object of pardon' (H.O. 47/20 Thomas Whittey). Some were either entirely neutral in tone, or rather more tentative in indicating a preference.

[5] Radzinowicz, *History*, 1, pp. 114–18; Hay, 'Property', pp. 42–50; Ekirch, *Bound for America*, pp. 33–45; P. King, 'Decision-Makers and Decision-Making in the English Criminal Law 1750–1800', *Historical Journal*, 27 (1984), 42–51.

[6] P.R.O. H.O. 47/6 and 11. In a conference paper in 1981 I used 1784 and 1787, but 1790 has been preferred to the former year here because the transportation crisis was over by then. This change and the development of a more quantitative categorization system account for the differences between the figures quoted from my work by Langbein in 'Albion's Fatal Flaws', p. 133, and those found in this study. Most of the cases were heard at the provincial assizes.

Table 9.1. Factors Affecting Judicial Decision-Making, 1787 and 1790

	Number of cases in which factor is mentioned in:		
	Judges' reports	Petitions	Either reports or petitions or both
Factors favourable to the accused			
Previous good character	40	40	66
Youth	28	25	40
No previous convictions (or evidence of multiple offences)	16	23	37
Post-crime destitution (including family size etc.)	5	29	31
Possibility of innocence or malicious prosecution	16	13	26
Drawn into crime by other (bad company or husband)	10	8	17
Previous military service	10	9	15
Prisoner or his parents respectable	5	10	15
Old employer/master gave good character reference	5	10	13
Employment offer available	8	7	12
Pre-crime destitution (and family size)	1	9	10
Crime not violent or no aggravating circumstances	9	1	10
Insane (or drunk at time)	3	7	7
Old age	2	6	6
Physical illness	5	2	6
Reformability, signs of	3	2	5
Mentally handicapped	2	2	3
Others (positive)	12	16	26
Total	180	219	345
Factors unfavourable to the accused			
Need for example against this kind of crime	20	—	
Previous character bad	19	—	
Crime involved violence or aggravating circumstances	12	—	
Crime involved betrayal of trust	12	—	
Previous convictions or evidence this not the only offence	11	—	
Part of a dangerous gang or seduced others into crime	9	—	
Crime premeditated	7	—	
Wealthy and therefore cannot claim distress	3	—	
Others negative	7	—	
Total	100		
Total Number of cases 1787 and 1790	136	97	136

Source: P.R.O. H.O. 47/6 and 11.

very broad range of criteria were frequently both pleaded by petitioners and considered by judges during the pardoning process.

Dividing the criteria favourable to the accused into seven broad categories reveals that good character or previous conduct was mentioned 131 times; sympathy for the young, the old, or the weak 56; destitution or family poverty 41; the nature of the crime 27; inadequate evidence or the possibility of innocence 26; future prospects of employment or reformation 17; and respectability or higher social status 15 times. (The three categories that also yielded factors unfavourable to the accused were: the nature of the crime 60 times; bad character or previous convictions 30, and higher social standing or wealth 3 times.) Taken at face value these findings do not accord well with previous analyses of the pardoning process which have either stressed that 'the excuse of respectability was pleaded in extenso' while poverty and distress were not, or have focused almost entirely on three elements—character, example, and respectable patronage—thus marginalizing many of the factors such as youth, old age, family poverty, infirmity, and possible innocence which Table 9.1 suggests were important. However, while this quantitative approach is helpful in evaluating the typicality of the individual quotations used by previous writers, it is by no means free of methodological problems of its own.[7]

The system used involved difficult and subjective categorization, for example, making the figures in Table 9.1 at best only rough indicators of the number of times a particular factor was mentioned. Moreover, some of the categories such as previous good character and lack of previous offences inevitably overlapped at times. More important, the mentions system makes no allowance for the relative impact of each factor. This can be partly measured by looking at how successful each group of factors was in attracting a favourable response, and the results are encouraging for those who wish to argue that character, example, and respectability were not the only significant factors. The judges showed definite signs of leaning towards the prisoner in 60 per cent of their reports, but in cases where mention was made of either the convict's future prospects of employment or reform, his youth, or his mental or physical illness, more than 80 per cent of judges' recommendations were positive. (Post-crime destitution had the lowest success rate at 45 per cent, and the remaining factors ranged between 50 per cent and 80 per cent.) However, since most cases involved not one factor but a number of interrelated elements, such figures are of only limited value. For example, if a judge made passing reference to one element of a case but then stressed the importance of another this could not be effectively identified either in Table 9.1 or in the success rates just quoted.

Equally Table 9.1 does not identify which combinations of factors were most effective and which worked less well together. It also needs to be remembered that while some factors, such as good character or lack of previous convictions, could (technically at least) be claimed by all age groups, others, such as youth, old age, and family poverty, could not. Thus, given that only about a quarter or a third of all petitioners were anywhere near young enough to claim 'youth' as a mitigating circumstance, this plea seems to have been mentioned in either petitions or judges' reports (and usually in both) in most of the cases in which it was conceivably possible to do so. Relatively speaking good character was

---

[7] D. Hay, 'Property', pp. 44–5 (however, for a more rounded discussion, Hay, 'Crime, Authority', pp. 496 and 474); Gatrell, *The Hanging Tree*, pp. 515, 539–42, and 613–14.

pleaded much less frequently than this, even though in absolute terms it was mentioned more often in the archive as a whole. Given the size of the sample and the opaque nature of the language sometimes used in the judges' reports, Table 9.1 provides at best only a crude map of the pardoning terrain. It is therefore necessary to complement it by looking in more detail at the language used in the pardoning documents and by linking this to broader contemporary discussions about sentencing and pardoning criteria as well as to the age-related punishment patterns already identified in the previous chapter.

2. The Language of Pardoning: Age, Infirmity, and Poverty

Since sympathy for the young was mentioned in judges' recommendations more frequently than any other factor except good character (Table 9.1), and since this factor attracted a considerably higher proportion of positive judicial recommendations (despite the fact that petitioners occasionally stretched the definition of 'youth' to its limit),[8] the evidence provided by the pardoning archive matches up extremely well with the age-related data found in Tables 8.9–8.11 and Figures 8.6–8.8. Sometimes the judges' language gave no indication whether the youth of the prisoner was the key element in a case. They simply noted as part of their summing up of the relevant factors that the offender was of 'tender age', 'a very young man', 'a lad of 14' etc.[9] On many occasions, however, their language suggests that youth was the key variable. 'On account of his youth I recommend pardon for transportation', concludes one 1787 report. 'On account of his youth ... the court were desirous to recommend him to his majesty's mercy', comments another. Similar language—'in consideration of his youth', 'because of his youth', 'in pity of her youth'—occurs in other reports and petitions.[10] Although some cases involved offenders aged 14 or under, I have yet to find a petition that directly challenged the conviction on the grounds that the offender was too young to have known right from wrong. Youth was pleaded not as a legal category but as a general mitigating circumstance.

The fact that the prisoner was young was often cited alone and of itself, but on other occasions it was clearly linked in the judges' minds to other criteria. Previous good character and conduct were among the most obvious. One prisoner was recommended because he 'appeared to be very young, and there was room to believe this was his first offence'; others because of their 'youth and former good character'. Youth also matched well with other strong arguments for leniency. Judges were more willing to give credence to claims that the offender was an unwilling dupe or had been seduced by bad company,

[8] In at least four of the forty cases involving pleas of youth the prisoner was over 20.
[9] P.R.O. H.O. 47/6. John Lewis, John Parsons, Henry Stamford.
[10] P.R.O. H.O. 47/6. Thomas Vaughan, James Stretton, William Glaves, James Bernard; H.O. 47/11 Sophia Girton.

for example, in cases involving young people.[11] Equally, petitioners' pleas about the potential reformability of the prisoner carried much more weight with the judge when the offender was young. In 1790 John Brown was granted a remission of sentence to three years' hard labour under the strict regime of Wymondham Bridewell because 'the prisoner being a young man may under such superintendence be reformed', while another 'extremely young' offender was reprieved and given a similar punishment because it was hoped that solitary confinement would reform her. In 1790 new penitentiary-style prisons were being, or had just been, built in a number of regions (including the Wymondham area) and hopes about their effectiveness were still running high. At other times and in counties where prison reform had less impact, a prison sentence was more frequently seen as likely to ruin rather than reform a young prisoner and more lenient treatment might well result from this. In 1787, for example, a 12-year-old Devon offender was ordered to be 'discharged as soon as possible . . . that he may not be corrupted by a gaol education'.[12]

The courts' willingness to find other non-carcereal alternatives to the gallows in cases involving young offenders was also frequently linked to their belief in the reformability of the young. In 1768, for example, the apprentice William Ludlow was described as 'sentenced to transportation solely with a view to his reformation', and it is likely that, as Ekrich has argued, judges were particularly willing to substitute transportation for the gallows when the prisoner was young, partly because they believed that it offered a real opportunity to rehabilitate those who were not yet hardened offenders.[13] Another alternative for prisoners in their early or mid-teens was apprenticeship. This was particularly attractive because it offered the opportunity both to reform and re-employ the prisoner. The report on William Ludlow in 1768 went on to suggest that 'if the [Foundling] Hospital will find him another master in some remote part of the kingdom, some hope may be entertained of his reformation' and the pardoning archives indicate that a considerable proportion of very young offenders gained reprieves partly because apprenticeship was regarded as a potential alternative to transportation or imprisonment—provided that the offence was not too serious and that the potential master was of good repute. The Essex offender Joseph Hall was recommended for a free pardon, for example, partly because the judge believed that apprenticeship was 'a more effectual means to reform him than transportation' and another Essex prisoner avoided transportation by a similar means in 1787. A year earlier William Smart was recommended by the judge not only because he was 'a very young boy' but also because a 'man of character' was willing to take him as apprentice.[14]

---

[11] P.R.O. H.O. 47/11 Thomas Brown; HO 47/1 Benjamin Wood. Ekirch, *Bound for America*, p. 39.
[12] P.R.O. H.O. 47/11 John Brown and Gwenllyan John; HO 47/6 Richard Baile; Ignatieff, *A Just Measure of Pain*, p. 97.
[13] Redington (ed.), *Calendar*, p. 405; Ekirch, *Bound for America*, p. 40.
[14] Ekirch, *Bound for America*, p. 42; P.R.O. H.O. 47/7 Samuel Cole, 47/5 William Smart.

Although other criteria, such as Australia's need for certain kinds of convicts, should not be ignored,[15] the judges' sense that lesser sanctions like apprentice-ship, imprisonment under a new penitentiary regime, or transportation might achieve the reformation of the young almost certainly meant a considerable number of younger offenders received less severe punishments than would otherwise have been the case.

Thus the judges' reports not only confirm the patterns of positive discrimin-ation towards the young seen in Tables 8.9–8.11 and Figures 8.6–8.8; they also reveal the various levels at which the youth of the prisoner affected sentencing and pardoning decisions. Youth was an important mitigating circumstance not only because the young were seen as more impetuous, more easily led, less hardened in character, but also because it added resonance to claims about reformability and re-employability, which were less powerful when pleaded by other types of offender. In non-capital cases such arguments might encourage the court to whip and/or immediately discharge younger offenders. In capital cases it meant that the young had a very much better chance of avoiding the gallows.[16]

The relatively lenient treatment given to elderly offenders—another theme that emerges from the quantitative data in Chapter 8—also finds some echoes in the pardoning archive. 'If he really is of the age of 66 (which was not stated to me at the trial) I should certainly entertain a hope that his majesty might . . . extend . . . a free pardon', the assize judge wrote in 1787 about a sheep stealer he had already reprieved from the gallows. Three years later a 52-year-old capitally convicted horse thief was pardoned on condition of a short prison term partly 'in consideration of his age and the state of his family' which included one child who was an 'idiot' and another who was seriously ill.[17] Serious illness and physical debility could also provide powerful arguments for avoiding transportation. In 1787 one Norfolk offender got his sentence reduced to a year's imprisonment by providing clear evidence of 'his bodily infirmity'. Evidence of mental infirmity met a more mixed response. If the prisoner clearly had severe and permanent learning difficulties a more lenient outcome might well ensue. In 1787 Joseph Swan who was generally called 'silly' and was notoriously 'deficient in intellect' avoided the gallows for this reason despite the fact that he was 'the mayhem of his fellows in gaol—swallowing live mice

[15] Young offenders may have been more in demand in the colonies but the judges' reports very rarely mention the demand side of the equation. For an exception P.R.O. H.O. 47/6 Margaret Wood. The judges' tendency to reprieve relatively small proportions of fit young adults (Chapter 8) suggests pardoning policies were relatively little affected by such criteria, although in absolute terms, of course, this group was still dominant. Robson, *The Convict*, p. 182.

[16] The military courts also favoured the young. For an example of a death sentence commuted to 300 lashes, 'on account of his youth', *I.J.*, 24 Apr. 1790.

[17] P.R.O. H.O. 47/6 John Aston; H.O. 47/11 Richard Wiltshire. In John Cable's case jury and judge conspired to ensure this 81-year-old man received a whipping and a short prison sentence when he could have been hanged, P.R.O. Assi 35/221/1 and 31/13. On the courts avoiding transporting the very old for physical reasons, Ekirch, *Bound for America*, p. 41.

for a halfpenny and then swallowing the halfpenny itself'. A year later James Ling was acquitted of assault with intent to rob at the Essex quarter sessions after the prosecutor gave evidence that 'he now believes the prisoner was an idiot and had he thought so before (he) would not have indicted . . . him'.[18]

Attitudes to mental instability and pleas of insanity in property crime cases were more ambivalent. Cases like that of Robert Walpole Chamberlayne, who was conditionally pardoned in 1787 after evidence had been produced of his previous confinement in Mr Harrison's mad house, were highly exceptional, as Walker's work has pointed out.[19] Other pleas on these lines, such as that of 42-year-old Amelia Gill, which claimed that she was 'sometimes a little flighty from a decline of life' were not so successful. However, Joel Eigen's recent work, which shows that those pleading insanity in property crime cases had a significantly higher chance of obtaining a not guilty verdict (or its equivalent), suggests that the Hertfordshire servant who obtained a partial verdict in 1739 by pleading that 'I know nothing of all this. I am almost mad' and by providing witnesses who said 'he was out of his senses at times' was not untypical.[20] Understandably perhaps, the courts remained ambivalent about those who claimed to be temporarily out of their minds when they committed their crimes, particularly if drunkenness was advanced as the reason for this, but if claims of insanity were thought to be genuine, mitigation might well be offered. Although the evidence is rather anecdotal because so few prisoners were in a position to claim old age or mental or physical disability, it seems clear that the courts frequently took a very positive attitude in such cases. The elderly, the infirm, the 'idiot', the insane, and the ill usually received relatively sympathetic treatment during the pardoning process. Indeed, the fact that both judges and prosecutors were sometimes at pains to point out that if they had known that the offender fell into one of these categories they would have treated him or her more leniently suggests that victims who were seen to have harshly treated such offenders might well experience considerable social censure in this period.

The judges could, of course, afford to be generous in such cases. These groups presented little threat to society and the numbers involved were small. By contrast, economic hardship and destitution, either before or after the crime, was pleaded in mitigation in a high proportion of cases (Table 9.1). The petitions put particular stress on the future destitution of the prisoner's family,

---

[18] P.R.O. H.O. 47/6 Hervey Howling and Joseph Swan; E.R.O. Q/SBb 330/9. For another case in which claims that the prisoner was 'next to an idiot' led to a reprieve, Morgan and Rushton, *Rogues, Thieves*, p. 55.

[19] P.R.O. H.O. 47/6; N. Walker, *Crime and Insanity in England. Volume 1. The Historical Perspective* (Edinburgh, 1968), pp. 200 and 194–203 for a general discussion.

[20] J. Eigen, *Witnessing Insanity. Madness and Mad-Doctors in the English Court* (New Haven, 1995), pp. 22–3. P.R.O. H.O. 47/6 Amelia Gill; *Genuine Proceedings . . . Home Circuit . . . March 1739*, p. 5. For a successful insanity plea in an Essex murder case, *The Trial of Miss Broderick for the Wilful Murder of George Errington Esq.* (Edinburgh, 1794).

listing his or her dependants and describing their great distress in phrases that recur all too frequently—'he has a very aged mother, a wife and several children all of whom must be left destitute', 'his wife and four children must be reduced to the greatest distress', 'for the sake of his poor wife and 10 children'.[21] On some occasions such pleas almost certainly influenced the judges. The offender with a 'poor wife and 10 children', who had only stolen two geese and a turkey, was pardoned from transportation, for example. However, judges remained very sceptical about such claims and they were well aware that highly pragmatic considerations sometimes prompted this kind of special pleading. The report on Henry Moyce's case, for example, suggested that 'the persons who have signed his petition are chiefly parish officers and persons contributing to the rates . . . the desire of getting rid of the burden of the prisoner's family may have some share in the application'.[22] For these reasons, perhaps, pleas about post-crime destitution were less likely to be linked to positive judges' recommendations than almost any other factor. However, the same was not true of pre-crime destitution.

The distress of the prisoner at the time the crime was committed was also among the ten most frequently mentioned factors found in petitions. In 1790, for example, a journeyman pleaded that 'business being very slack your petitioner was unable to procure sufficient employment for his livelihood and in a moment of distress and want fell into the commission of the crime'. Other petitions either spoke simply of 'penury and necessity', 'extreme poverty', 'excruciating distress', 'extreme necessity', etc. or built up a more composite picture of unemployment, weak health, a severe winter, extreme want, and the need 'to satisfy the cry of a tender and distressed family'.[23] In referring to their families' extreme distress just prior to their crimes, petitioners were calling on a broad tradition of sympathy for such cases:

> Still mark if vice or nature prompts the deed;
> Still mark the strong temptation and the need;
> on pressing want, on famine's powerful call,
> at least more lenient let they justice fall,

a Somerset justice wrote in the 1770s. Blackstone made similar comments in the same decade and in 1785 *The Times* argued strongly that 'a poor thief pinched by want, or pressed by necessity should not suffer equally with notorious offenders and cruel murderers'.[24]

[21] H.O. 42/12/98–100 Thomas Morris; H.O. 47/6 Joseph Moreland and David Lewis. Other cases in 1787 include 'having a wife and 5 children now reduced to great distress' (William Fear); 'a wife and nine infant children . . . depend on prisoner' (Joseph Pedley).

[22] P.R.O. H.O. 47/6 Henry Moyce and for another example 47/11 John Foster.

[23] P.R.O. H.O. 47/11 William Thompson, William Earps, William Green; H.O. 47/6 John Smith, Henry Moyce, and Rose Elliott.

[24] Anon., *The Country Justice. A Poem. Part the First by One of His Majesty's Justices of the Peace for Somerset* (London, 1774), pp. 16–17; Blackstone, *Commentaries*, 4, p. 15; *The Times*, 9 May 1785. For Lord Eldon giving similar weight to a starving family as mitigation, Hay, 'Crime, Authority', p. 71.

Provided that they were well documented and proved that the prisoner had a large family in great want, petitions stressing pre-crime poverty not infrequently gained a sympathetic response from the judge. Rose Elliott, for example, was given a free pardon in 1787 after a widely supported petition had shown that 'he was at the time out of imploy' and driven to crime through 'extreme poverty and want'. The judge supported Elliott's petition but in doing so he did not specifically mention his poverty in his report. The judges did sometimes cite pre-crime destitution directly as a major mitigating factor. Judge Ryder's diary includes such references and the 1780s judges' reports include such phrases as 'it appeared to be done from the pressure of great distress', 'impelled by distress', and 'poverty...tempted her to the offence'. More often the judges remained silent on this issue but the fact that direct references to pre-crime poverty were rare does not necessarily mean that the judges felt that such pleas were irrelevant. 'Necessity, aggravated by tender feelings for an helpless family, may tempt a man of no very bad disposition', Shaw argued in 1800,[25] and the judges' tendency to be more lenient towards offenders in age ranges during which the accused was most likely to have a dependent family (Tables 8.9 to 8.11) suggests that they frequently agreed with him.

Most judges almost certainly assumed that many crimes were committed, in part at least, out of necessity, for when they discovered offenders who could not plead pre-crime poverty they often came down particularly hard on them. The report on William Rose in 1784, for example, indicates that his better economic position (Rose was a farmer leasing 100 acres) was the main reason he was left to hang, and in 1764 the judge refused to recommend Thomas Heathwood for mercy because 'he having no extenuating plea of necessity. It was of more consequence...that one man in good circumstances should suffer than twenty miserable wretches.' A 1790 judge's report concluded 'it was a great aggravation of the offence that he was in a situation in life that should have placed him above the temptation of committing such a felony. I consider him a proper person to be punished with exemplary severity', while that on a Middle Temple barrister declared that his offence was 'greatly aggravated by his education, his fortune and...profession'.[26] Gisbourne observed in the 1790s that a conscientious judge 'will discard all improper reference to rank or fortune; and will rather teach those in the upper classes of society to expect their crimes to be chastised with more than usual strictness' and it is not difficult to find prisoners, such as the transportees worth many thousands of pounds that Ekirch discusses, who fell foul of the judges' conscientiousness in

[25] P.R.O. H.O. 47/6 Rose Elliott; P.R.O. H.O. 47/5 Peter Ogler; in the same volume the recorder of London uses the term 'impelled by distress' several times, 47/11 Jane Jones. R. Shaw, *Observations on a Late Publication Intitled a Treatise on the Police of the Metropolis* (London, 1800), p. 76.

[26] P.R.O. H.O. 47/1 William Rose; Redington (ed.), *Calendar*, 1, p. 486; P.R.O. H.O. 47/11 John Massey; Ekirch, *Bound for America*, p. 52.

such circumstances.[27] Property offenders from major landowning families would almost always have been able to buy, bully, or bluster their way out of trouble before matters reached the courts, as the future Essex magistrate Thomas Fanshawe did in 1712 after being accused of involvement in a violent Mohock riot, but the small number of reasonably wealthy middling men who failed to do so were very vulnerable. Although 'rolling in affluence', the Devon farmer Henry Penson was hanged in 1801 for stealing his neighbour's sheep, his crime being seen as 'aggravated by the circumstances of his wealth', while following a similar offence in 1787 the judge 'noted the difference between a poor wretch in distress committing such a crime and a man of seeming reputation', the latter being 'much more culpable than the poor man who commits such acts from real want'.[28]

Middling men of various levels of wealth also constituted the main bulk of forgery convicts and, given the authorities' great reluctance to grant pardons in such cases, Dr Dodd, the Perreaus, and William Ryland were by no means the only reasonably wealthy offenders who reached the gallows by this route.[29] Forgery was a special case. Most forms of forgery required both literacy and a certain familiarity with the wealthy whilst at the same time engendering a particularly acute sense of anxiety among the moneyed classes. However, the fact that the subgroup of capital convicts who were most likely to come from respectable backgrounds was also the group least likely to avoid the gallows,[30] along with the fact that in the non-forgery cases quoted above the prisoner's wealth was represented as a reason for harsher treatment, clearly raises important questions about the role of respectability in the pardoning process.

3. The Language of Pardoning: Character and Respectability

Much has been made of the role of respectability as a mitigating plea. Hay, for example, suggests that the magic words that pleaded or implied a respectable background recur again and again. Such claims may not have had much purchase in forgery cases, 'ministers being', Romilly suggested, 'afraid to pardon such offenders on account of the clamours of trading people', but how important were they in other types of property crime case? Positive references to the fact that the prisoner or the prisoner's family were respectable,

---

[27] Gisbourne, *An Enquiry*, p. 231; Ekirch, *Bound for America*, p. 52.

[28] Statt, 'The Case of the Mohocks', pp. 185–9; Rule, 'The Manifold Causes', p. 125; Hay, 'Property', p. 44 quoting Judge Hotham who also noted that a prosperous sheep stealer was more culpable because 'under the mask of a fair and upright character, [he] was enabled to make depredations on his neighbours and the public without being suspected'. For another sheep stealing farmer who failed to get the judge's support, H.O. 47/6 Thomas Smith.

[29] Radzinowicz, *A History*, I, pp. 155–6, 450–72; not all forgery convicts were wealthy. Those prosecuted by the Bank of England included many from labouring backgrounds.

[30] McGowen, 'The Punishment of Forgery'; and his 'From Pillory to Gallows. The Punishment of Forgery in the Age of the Financial Revolution', *Past and Present* (forthcoming). Table 8.5.

reputable, or of relatively high social standing occur in less than 5 per cent of judges' reports and in only 10 per cent of petitions in the volumes sampled for 1787 and 1790. On a few occasions the links were specific. In one the father was the secretary of the Foundling Hospital; in another the prisoner was a distant relative of a petitioning gentleman. The report on John Gill's case in 1790, for example, referred to 'his unfortunate relations, who . . . are persons of worth and credit' before suggesting that had it not been for the frequency of the offence he might have been reprieved.[31] However, in at least two-thirds of the fifteen cases counted in Table 9.1 as mentioning the respectable background of the prisoner or his family, the only indication of their claim to higher status is the use of either the label 'respectable' or the label 'reputable'.

The label 'respectable', like the title of 'gentleman', had a very elastic quality in the late eighteenth century. One petition describes the prisoner's father as a respectable master tailor, another's 'respectable' and afflicted parent turns out to be a salesman at Newgate market.[32] The term 'reputable', which was used as frequently as the word respectable, conveyed equally wide and problematic messages. Both Johnson and Sheridan defined it ambivalently as meaning either 'honourable' or 'not infamous'. In one case where the petition depicts the prisoner as having 'reputable parents' another document describes the same prisoner's father as an honest and industrious man.[33] When such prisoners' petitions were well supported by their neighbours it would be safe to assume that their families were indeed honest and were 'not infamous', but it would clearly be unwise to regard these industrious tailors and market salesmen as members of the wealthy élite or even of the prosperous middling sort. A family could be labelled as 'respectable' or 'reputable' without possessing either commercial or landed wealth and sometimes, it seems, without having much more than an honest and steady trade as its financial base. These terms were, of course, also used to describe extremely well-off petitioners or connections, and the value of having such assistance will be discussed in section 6. However, in some pardoning documents terms like respectable and reputable seem to have undergone a considerable degree of downward mobility, particularly when they were being used to describe prisoners' families. Otherwise, given the very low social status of the vast majority of prisoners, these terms would almost certainly have been used in an even smaller percentage of cases.

For most of the small group of prisoners who attempted to do so, proving that they had reputable parents was probably less important in itself than as an adjunct to a broader and more vital project—that of establishing their own

---

[31] Hay, 'Property', pp. 44 and 45 for P.R.O. H.O. 47/6 John Jones alias Collingwood, H.O. 47/11 Thomas Brown and John Gill; Romilly, *Observations*, p. 71.

[32] P.R.O. H.O. 47/6 Henry Stamford; 47/16 William Hill. In Bailey's 1782 dictionary to be respectable was 'to be respected or reverenced' (Bailey, *An Universal*) but respect had many meanings including 'partial regard'—S. Johnson, *A Dictionary of the English Language* (8th edn., London, 1792).

[33] Johnson, *A Dictionary*; T. Sheridan, *A Complete Dictionary of the English Language* (London, 1789); P.R.O. H.O. 47/11 John Didsbury.

good character. In contrast to claims about respectability, which were mentioned more than twice as frequently in petitions as they were in judges' reports and which were only relevant in just over 10 per cent of cases, both judges and petitioners made equal mention of the previous good character of the accused and did so in more than half of the cases for which adequate documentation survives.[34] The language of good character did not focus primarily on the social status of the accused but on the individual's capacity to prove that they had lived in a neighbourly, honest, and orderly manner, supporting themselves by their own labour. Prisoners whose established neighbours were willing to say that previous to the offence they had regarded them as honest, steady, trustworthy, or of good credit were well on the way to building a good case for mitigation, particularly if they were also described as sober, quiet, or inoffensive—that is as having never been a threat to the good order of the community. These adjectives established their claim to be good neighbours—another phrase which occurs not infrequently in such cases.[35] The other recurring theme—the prisoner's attitude to work—is seen in such phrases as 'always laborious and industrious according to his neighbours', has 'maintained his family in a decent manner by his own industry', 'willing and industrious', 'bore the character of an industrious man'.[36] Prisoners who could show that their previous employers would take them back, or that local people would offer them permanent work were particularly well placed. A young man was pardoned in 1787 after the judge noted his 'industrious disposition' and the fact that 'people of undoubted credit' were willing to employ him if he was discharged.[37]

Previous employers, apprentices' masters, or military officers (whose recommendations were vital if loyal military service was to be successfully pleaded) were an important subgroup among character witnesses, and JPs and other men of relatively high social standing also gave character references on occasions. However, the great majority of character witnesses appear to have been neighbours or personal contacts of the accused and were therefore, by definition, largely drawn from the middling sort or from the poorer but respectable sections of the local community. The judges rarely gave precise information on the social status of these witnesses but they quite frequently recorded the number of years each witness had known the prisoner. Character

[34] Table 9.1 indicates that in 66 out of 136 cases good character is mentioned, but since in 12 of the 136 cases virtually no reasons are given, good character effectively appears in the majority.

[35] Frequent examples occur in 1787 and 1790—P.R.O. H.O. 47/6 James Bartlett, Thomas Jones, Henry Stamford, Charles Wyatt, Fred Brown, William Fear, Rose Elliott; H.O. 47/11 James Dunning, John Nash.

[36] P.R.O. H.O. 47/6 David Lewis, Thomas Smith alias Cockle; H.O. 47/11 Elizabeth Jones, John Brown.

[37] P.R.O. H.O. 47/6 Joseph Short, John Moreby; see also H.O. 47/11 Samuel Burrows. This character-related language is also found in judges' questions to character witnesses during the trial—Beattie, *Crime*, p. 440; Gatrell, *The Hanging Tree*, pp. 540–1.

witnesses had to have at least 'some reputation and credit' (to quote Fielding) but their social status was less important than their reliability as a guide to the local community's knowledge of the prisoner. Judges were aware that prisoners might cajole acquaintances into filling the role of character witnesses and the judges' reports indicate that they quite often questioned suspect witnesses closely to ensure their reliability. Only those prisoners who had followed a sufficiently steady lifestyle to enable them to call on character witnesses or petition supporters who had known them for some time were likely to have their claims about previous good character taken seriously by the judges.[38] Since pleas that this was the prisoner's first offence were also much more credible when supported by former neighbours, character evidence, whether presented at the trial or after conviction in petitions and supporting letters, was undoubtedly a central building block in many pleas for mercy.

4. Pardoning and the Possibility of Innocence

Character evidence sometimes played a central role in another important subcategory of cases—those in which the fundamental issue of guilt or innocence was raised. John Donne, for example, who had been sentenced to transportation at the Somerset assizes in 1787, was given a free pardon when further investigation revealed that 'the prisoner had a better character than his prosecutors' and that 'the prosecution was commenced and carried on through malice'. The possibility that the prisoner was innocent and/or that the prosecution had been malicious in intent was mentioned more frequently in judges' reports than any other positive criteria except youth and previous good character or conduct (Table 9.1). In 1787, for example, at least six of the seventy-six cases in the volume sampled ended in free and unconditional pardons partly or solely because the judge expressed grave doubts about the evidence. In some cases the judge simply noted that the evidence was very poor, that the prosecution appeared to be malicious, or that the offender was 'possibly innocent'. In others he made it clear that he believed it was an 'improper conviction' or that the prisoner was 'never guilty of the crime'.[39] Sometimes the criticism of the jury's guilty verdict which these remarks implied was made explicit. Faced by a jury of Welsh sheep farmers determined to convict 'a poor man', Thomas Jones, of sheep stealing, despite evidence that he had not stolen the sheep concerned, that the prosecutor had malicious motives, and that the accused had an exemplary character over a thirty-year period given by a large posse of neighbours who turned up to give him character references, the judge first tried to browbeat the jury into changing

[38] For judges' reports meticulously noting the periods of up to thirty years witnesses had known the accused P.R.O. H.O. 47/6 Thomas Jones, HO 47/11 Richard Fosset; Fielding, *Enquiry*, p. 118.

[39] P.R.O. H.O. 47/6 Thomas Jones (Brecon), John Donne, Thomas Jones (Liverpool), John Moreby (two documents), Joseph Wright, John Bayne.

their verdict. When they obstinately persisted he, 'being greatly dissatisfied', reprieved the prisoner and ensured he got a free pardon.[40]

Given that by making such remarks and offering a complete pardon the judges were often tacitly admitting that the trials over which they had presided had produced the wrong outcome, it is interesting that a significant number of cases were resolved in this way. Although there was no official appeal court in the eighteenth century, the judges clearly used the possibility of a free pardon as an alternative in certain types of case. The judges' reasons for backing and even encouraging such appeals were mixed. Although they rarely engaged in public altercations with the jurors, when a judge was publicly defeated in such a battle pride alone might motivate him to overturn the trial verdict by using the pardoning process. More important perhaps, as one judge remarked, 'example would lose its weight as long as there was any doubt remaining'.[41] Too many convictions on poor evidence (especially if that evidence was produced by those who would then receive a reward) would not be in line with the judges' sense of how the law should work. 'I disapproved of the conviction as encouraging stale and vindictive prosecutions attended with a ten pound reward', the judge reported in another Welsh sheep stealing case in 1787, 'and the evidence though such as must be left to a jury was but slender.' The judge went on to reprieve him on condition of transportation because 'he was probably guilty'.[42]

The judge's refusal to recommend a free pardon in this case is illuminating. Free pardons constituted only one of a number of currencies the judges were prepared to deal in. While their reports sometimes suggest an informal appeal court model in which conviction on doubtful evidence would be followed by unconditional release, at other times they give off a different odour—that of privately conceived compromises primarily designed to save face rather than to save lives. When petitioners expressed grave doubts about the evidence or pleaded complete innocence, the judges' reports were often highly ambivalent. Not wishing to admit in open court that a miscarriage of justice might have occurred, judges may quite frequently have reacted to guilty verdicts they were not entirely happy with by quietly reprieving the offender on condition of a lesser sentence immediately after the assizes. However, if the offender then petitioned for a free pardon claiming complete innocence, the judge's tone was often defensive. While they were sometimes willing to put the blame on the jury and back the prisoner, in other cases they argued that the evidence, though not watertight, was sufficient to vindicate the jurors' decision to convict.

The judges' ambivalence in such cases is well illustrated by the report on Henry Abraham, who was capitally convicted at the Essex assizes in 1785. Despite the admission of additional evidence that reinforced the alibi given at

[40] P.R.O. H.O. 47/6 Thomas Jones (Brecon).
[41] P.R.O. H.O. 47/11 John Lilly and Robert Heron.
[42] P.R.O. H.O. 47/6 Richard David.

the trial and proved that two other men had confessed to the crime just before they were hanged for a different offence, the judge used complex reasoning to undermine the prisoner's case, arguing that to accept it 'would open a door to bring the rectitude of every conviction into disrepute'. However, while he claimed that he could not 'entertain the opinion' that the prisoner was innocent, the judge was happy to accept Abraham's reprieve and release on recognizance (i.e. effectively a free pardon), which strongly suggests that he had found the mountain of evidence presented against the conviction hard to dismiss.[43] Claiming innocence was a high-risk strategy from the prisoner's point of view since it might put the judge on the defensive, but it could also be a successful one. In at least half of the cases where this was mentioned as a mitigating factor a free pardon ensued, and occasionally judges even encouraged petitioners to make such pleas if they were particularly unhappy with the original verdict.

Their cryptic offhand comments, their face-saving compromises, and their far from sympathetic attitude towards some prisoners (not to mention their opposition to the repeal of the capital statutes) make it difficult for modern historians to see the assize judges of the eighteenth century in a sympathetic light. However, some of them clearly did not always act in ways which justify the conclusion that the possible innocence of convicted felons was something that the judges did not think it 'worth thinking about closely'. To poor men such as Thomas Jones, faced by a vengeful farming jury deep in sheep rearing country, Gatrell's description of the assizes judges as 'furred homicides' and 'sable bigots', based though it is on contemporary comments, might have seemed a little harsh. The judge did, after all, take the trouble not only to save Jones's life but also to save his freedom.[44]

5. Negative Criteria Discussed by the Judges

The majority of judges' reports leaned favourably towards the prisoner but just over a quarter were negative in their attitude.[45] The judges were not slow to come down hard on those offenders who did not either attract their sympathy or have a fairly strong claim to be innocent. Although nearly two-thirds of the factors mentioned in the judges' reports were positive, a considerable range of negative criteria were also put forward in these documents (Table 9.1). Two of the most important were essentially the reverse side of two of the three most frequently mentioned positive criteria—namely the failure of the prisoner to produce positive evidence relating to either character or previous lawbreaking habits. If the prisoner was unable to produce favourable character witnesses,

---

[43] P.R.O. H.O. 47/2 Henry Abraham.

[44] Gatrell, *The Hanging Tree*, pp. 497–514, esp. p. 498.

[45] Out of 136 reports 81 were positive, 38 were negative, and 17 showed no sign of leaning in either direction.

or if it became clear during the trial that he or she was a vagrant or had a reputation as idle and disorderly, trouble usually lay ahead. If the prisoner was regarded as 'an old offender' or 'a bad fellow . . . addicted to evil courses', or if the trial threw up incidental information about his or her involvement in other crimes there was likewise little hope of mercy.[46] The same was true if the offender was thought to have been a member of 'a dangerous gang' or a group who were known to have made their living by stealing, especially if the petitioner was thought to be the gang's leader. Violent property offenders such as highway robbers also had the dice severely loaded against them (Table 8.5), particularly if the judge considered that they had used excessive violence either during or after the commission of the crime.[47] Robbers who had used pistols or who had actually bludgeoned their victims with sticks could expect little mercy. Nor could those who resisted arrest. 'I never think myself warranted to recommend a prisoner to mercy who when detected commits an outrage of personal violence on the person who stops him', one judge concluded in 1796.[48]

The final major subgroup of negative factors listed in Table 9.1 involved the judges' perception of the need for an example against the particular type of crime the prisoner had committed. About half of the cases in which this criterion was mentioned involved types of appropriation, such as horse or sheep stealing, which were usually treated less harshly than many other capital offences (Table 8.5), but which were felt to require more serious treatment in this case because the specific offence concerned was thought to be especially prevalent in that area at that time. In placing emphasis on this factor the judges were often simply reacting to their own general sense that the offence was 'very prevalent in the neighbourhood' or that 'the offence prevailed much . . . on this circuit'. At other times they were acting in response to specific information offered by local interest groups, such as the Hertfordshire farmers who informed the assize judge in 1790 that they 'had suffered much by these sorts of thefts and that it was wished that an offender should suffer to prevent in future the progress of this evil'.[49] In 1790 local pressure in a number of counties brought a harsher policy towards horse stealers, and judges' reports from

[46] P.R.O. H.O. 47/11 Cooper Gadsiff, John Gill. For incidental information emerging at the trial because indictments for two crimes were preferred, P.R.O. H.O. 47/11 William Holland. Consistent evidence about previous convictions was rarely available. After 1790 attempts were made to gather this information more systematically in London—Deveraux, 'The Criminal Branch of the Home Office', pp. 284–6.

[47] P.R.O. H.O. 47/11 John Conolly, William Green, and George Moor, who was left to hang while his codefendants were reprieved both because he was 'the King leader' and because the judge believed 'whenever . . . soliders are engaged in a gang' an example was necessary. If a gang member advocated non-violence it might stand in his favour. In 1790 John Booth was reprieved because he 'opposed a violence which other prisoners were inclined to exercise'. H.O. 47/11.

[48] P.R.O. H.O. 47/6 William Rayner, H.O. 47/11 Thomas Roe, H.O. 47/20 Thomas Legg.

[49] On the importance of example, Gatrell, *The Hanging Tree*, pp. 511 and 539–40. P.R.O. H.O. 47/11 Thomas Carpenter, William Mackay, and for the farmers Stephen Bigg.

Yorkshire, Sussex, and Surrey indicate why by including such phrases as 'the crime of horse stealing being much increased of late', or 'the grand jury and justices all complained to me of the vast extent to which the crime of horse-stealing had gone'.[50] Sheep theft might provoke a similar reaction, particularly in times of dearth. In 1800, for example, the Western Circuit clearly witnessed a major crackdown on sheep thieves, and some judges at least continued to believe that such initiatives could be highly effective.[51]

However, many of the cases in which the judges mentioned the need for an example (Table 9.1) did not involve temporary policies of this kind, but rather crimes that were by their nature particularly difficult to detect or involved types of property that were especially hard to guard. In 1783, for example, two horse thieves were selected to hang 'as public examples because it appeared ... they had sold very valuable horses for the most trivial sums to people who boil and retail the flesh of them, after . . . plunging their skins in a strong lime which . . . destroys all possibility of their being sworn to', and on other occasions judges clearly felt the need to hit an unlucky offender particularly hard simply because their specific crime was 'seldom detected from the difficulty of proof'.[52] The extreme vulnerability of many employers to appropriation by their employees also made judges more inclined to make an example of such offenders, as did the betrayal of trust which such offences usually involved. In 1787 and 1790, for example, a foreman who had organized the theft of a large quantity of nails, an employee who had systematically embezzled from a Manchester brazier, two members of an 'association' who used their jobs as farm servants to pick targets for pillage, and a shoplifting shop assistant all received short shrift from the judge—the report in the latter case making it clear that the bench 'thought it necessary to inflict a severe punishment to deter offenders to whom the like situation might afford the like temptation'.[53] Thus, although the vast majority of the criteria mentioned in the pardoning documents (Table 9.1) related to the individual offender's age, character, background, and capacities, or to the violence of their crimes, the needs of particular subgroups among the propertied classes also had a say in the way punishment was individualized during the pardoning process. To what extent were powerful and propertied people also able to influence the outcome of

[50] P.R.O. H.O. 47/11 Richard Wiltshire, John Gill; see also Cooper Gadsiff for another reference to grand jury complaints about horse stealing. For a 1787 case see H.O. 47/6 James Askoe.

[51] Rule, 'The Manifold Causes of Rural Crime', p. 126. For an example against sheep theft in 1790 see H.O. 47/11 David Williams. This judge commented that 'since I ordered the execution of two sheep stealers two or three years ago the offence . . . which had filled the calendars of every circuit for several years before that example was made has not once appeared'.

[52] Che.C., 15 Aug. 1783. Judge's report on Henry Snook provides a parallel case. P.R.O. H.O. 47/1 (1784); H.O. 47/11 David Williams.

[53] P.R.O. H.O. 47/6 Robert Brown, Richard Barnes, H.O. 47/11 George Simmonds, John Saunders, and Samuel Burrows. Newspapers also indicate that crimes by servants were often labelled by judges as 'flagrant and aggravated', Che.C., 20 Jan. 1780.

individual cases simply by giving their backing to particular prisoners and petitions?

6. Petitioners for Pardon

The judges' reports are much more informative about the offenders than they are about those who petitioned on their behalf. They are very reticent about this more political aspect of the pardoning system. The approaches made by the prisoner's friends are rarely commented on and the social status of these groups is seldom indicated. The petitions are more useful, however, and from these and other sources it is clear that a very wide cast of characters was involved in the pardoning process. If, as Gatrell and others have argued, there was a limit to the number of property crime hangings the people would tolerate,[54] the unseen hand of potential crowd hostility may well have played a significant role in encouraging the King, the Home Office officials, and the judges to be merciful. More visibly and less unconsciously the pardoning process could also be affected by almost any of the actors involved in processing the case or in handling the offender. The Bow Street officer John Townsend, for example, claimed that he frequently influenced pardoning decisions by quietly informing the judge about the previous convictions (or lack of them) of the offenders he had just sentenced. Court clerks could also act as conduits of information or as a means of bringing influence to bear on the bench.[55] Turnkeys, gaolers, hedge-lawyers, and attorneys were quite frequently involved, especially in London—some acting out of genuine sympathy while others simply took money from the helpless for services that proved of no avail.[56]

The eighteenth-century sources rarely allow more than brief insights into the prisoners' attempts to mobilize support, put together petitions, or gain favourable reports from prison staff,[57] but they do offer some insights into the role that jurors and prosecutors played in the pardoning process. Once a conviction was secured the prosecutor not infrequently supported, or even initiated, a plea for mitigation of sentence—particularly if the prisoner was likely to be hanged. 'He is a very young man and . . . I for my part am heartily ready to join a petition', one victim wrote in 1739, his aim being not to pardon the offender completely but 'to have his life spared'. Prosecutors' motives were mixed. Some may have been keen to avoid the popular disapproval (and

---

[54] Gatrell, The Hanging Tree, p. 103.

[55] P.P., 1816, V, p. 144; T. Barnes, The Clerk of the Peace in Somerset (Leicester, 1961), p. 32.

[56] Thale (ed.), The Autobiography of Francis Place, pp. 133–4 for help given by Newgate turnkeys and attorneys. For a woman in Newgate who admitted that 'she had given eight guineas to a fellow who does business for the prisoners and who had promised to have her omitted from the death list', The Times, 1 July 1785.

[57] For rare but revealing prisoners' letters see Beattie, 'The Royal Pardon', p. 15; Hay, 'Property', p. 43.

sometimes violence) that could be the consequence of sending a minor property offender to the gallows. Others seem to have felt genuine sympathy for the
offender. Victims who had known the prisoner fairly intimately before the
offence were most likely to ask for mitigation, and although the breaches of
trust involved were treated very seriously by the bench, a considerable number
of masters or employers backed requests for pardon from servants or employees who had appropriated their property. Some masters even offered to re-
employ the offender.[58]

Since more than 10 per cent of petitions include evidence of prosecutorial
support, and since other victims almost certainly had a quiet, unrecorded word
with the bench in favour of leniency (or requested it in papers that no longer
survive), the prosecutor's role in the pardoning process was by no means
minimal. Their interventions could be crucial. In 1774 a Colchester grocer,
having successfully obtained a sentence of death against his former servant,
Thomas Fordham, ended the trial by recommending this 'stout lad' to 'your
Lordships mercy'. Fordham was transported instead. In 1786 another capitally
convicted Essex burglar escaped the gallows despite the King's recent crackdown on this offence after the assizes judge reported that 'I think this man's life
may be spared without any sort of mischief—the case had nothing atrocious in
it, the prosecutor is very anxious to save the offender; the public will not
conceive that either the judges or His Majesty's servants have too great a bias
to lenity from saving this man at the solicitation of his prosecutor.'[59]

Trial juries were also not infrequently involved in post-trial negotiations.
Sometimes jury and prosecutor joined together to recommend the offender for
mercy,[60] but the petty jury often acted alone. In 1751 a judge recorded that 'the
jury . . . came in a body to the bar and recommended the prisoner to mercy out
of regard to his youth'. Equally the two juries might act together. In 1799 both
the petty and the grand jury at the Sussex assizes recommended Thomas
Lucas 'on account of his youth'. As Knell has suggested, juries seem to have
been particularly likely to recommend young offenders to mercy, but they also
intervened for other reasons. In 1791 a 37-year-old London servant was
'recommended to mercy by the jury on account of her poverty', and a year
earlier a Yorkshire jury sent in their own petition for mercy because the
prosecution witnesses were 'notoriously abandoned' and because the case
was partly based on the evidence of an accomplice 'of infamous character'.[61]

[58] *Account of the Lives of Six Malefactors executed September 1739 at Newington* (London, 1739), Noah Goobee.
Gatrell, *The Hanging Tree*, pp. 102 and 170. For a prosecutor's intervention which led to imprisonment
rather than transportation—*Che.C.*, 23 Mar. 1804; P.R.O. H.O. 47/6 William Owen, H.O. 47/11
Samuel Burrows for offers of a return to employment.

[59] *Whole Proceedings . . . Essex . . . March 1774*, pp. 19–20 and P.R.O. Assi 35/204/1 and 31/11; H.O.
47/4 Christopher Theldle; Assi 35/226/2 and 31/4.

[60] *O.B.S.P.*, Feb. 1792, p. 128, a 16-year-old boy fined and released after the jury recommended him
and the prosecutor said he would take him into service, *O.B.S.P.*, Jan. 1792, p. 88.

[61] Green, *Verdict According to Conscience*, p. 282; P.R.O. Assi 31/18; B. Knell, 'Capital Punishment: its
Administration in Relation to Juvenile Offenders in the Nineteenth Century and its Possible Admin-

Which social groups got involved in petitioning for pardon and what impact did the social status of those who supported the prisoner's petition, or acted as conduits for it, have on the outcome of the case? Both the nationwide 1787 and 1790 samples and the Essex petitions, which have been surveyed for a wider group of years, indicate the involvement of a broad range of people. However, the pardoning archives are by no means easy to use in this context. In a considerable proportion of cases the judge's report is the only substantial document available[62] and many of the petitions and supporting letters that do survive contain no indication of the social status of those who wrote or signed them. Even when social status can be identified the pardoning documents rarely indicate which of the individuals involved were the initiators, or driving forces, behind the petitioning process and which were mere passengers—making it difficult to be sure which social groups had most impact. Thus, for example, when the judge received both a detailed petition from the local middling sort verifying the prisoner's previous good character etc., and a brief letter from a London-based gentleman or MP, who made it clear that he did not know the prisoner and was merely acting as a formal channel for the petition, which did the judge give most weight to? It was probably the former, but it is easy to assume that simply because someone of higher status was involved their impact and influence was invariably greater. The sources also make it much easier to identify the involvement of the élite than that of other groups. Very few of those who signed petitions recorded their occupations, but almost all of the small minority who could claim the title esquire, gentleman, JP, Bishop, Lord, etc. made sure their status was properly recorded. What is clear, however, is that although the prisoner's family and friends were often directly involved in petitioning, the labouring sort in general were underrepresented among petitioners. Although a number of the signatures found on petitions are hesitant and scrappy, suggesting that some of those who penned them were almost certainly semi-literate artisans or labourers, only the occasional petition contains a mark rather than a signature. Since the majority of the eighteenth-century labouring poor were unable to sign their names, this suggests that very few petitioners were drawn from this group. Thus, apart from those who had come into contact with the prisoner on his or her journey through the criminal justice system, the three main groups involved were the middling sort, the gentry, and the aristocracy.

Despite the problems of identifying non-élite petitioners, it is not difficult to find cases in which the middling sort successfully petitioned for mitigation of

istration in the Eighteenth', *British Journal of Criminology*, 5 (1965) 199; *The Times*, 10 Jan. 1788 for a convicted burglar 'recommended to mercy being only 16-years old'. For older prisoners—*O.B.S.P.*, Dec. 1792, p. 4; P.R.O. H.O. 47/11 case of George Moor.

[62] Only nine of the eighteen Essex cases in the twelve years sampled (1784–92, 1796–8) had full petitions as well as judges' reports (cases were only included in the sample if they involved property crimes and if a judge's report survives). P.R.O. H.O. 47/1–15 and 20–2.

sentence without the support of higher social groups. In 1787, for example, William Glaves was pardoned after nine Southwark traders—three butchers, two chandlers, a druggist, a publican, a grocer, and a ropemaker (who then took him as an apprentice) had petitioned on his behalf. Three years later another convict under sentence of death escaped with a year's imprisonment after over thirty Southwark inhabitants, including four parish officers and the prosecutor, supported his petition.[63] Equally a considerable number of petitions supported partly or wholly by the gentry can be identified. In 1787, for example, the judge clearly relied heavily on the testimony of a local gentleman in John Donne's case. 'A petition in his favour has lately been transmitted to me by Mr Luttrell of Dunster Castle', he wrote, 'by which it seems as if the prisoner had a better character than his prosecutors and Mr Luttrell says he has inquired into the business and finds that the prosecution was commenced and carried on through malice . . . all the parties live in Mr Luttrell's neighbourhood and he is likely to know the real truth of the case.' A number of successful petitioners for pardon clearly had connections in the very highest circles. When Thomas Collingwood, who had been Secretary of the Foundling Hospital for nearly thirty years, found his son under sentence of death at Chelmsford the connections his post afforded him seem to have been quickly mobilized. The case papers are marked 'pardoned on condition of transportation for life on application of Duke of Leeds'.[64]

Since the 1787 and 1790 samples contain nearly a hundred cases (Table 9.1) in which both the judge's report and either a petition or a supporting letter (or both) survive, it is possible to attempt a more quantitative assessment of the role of the three main identifiable categories of petitioner—the middling sort, the gentry, and the aristocracy. Among those that can be identified, the largest petitioning group were middling men—traders, petty jurors, town inhabitants, and poor law officials. They had an influence on over 50 per cent of pardoning cases, and had virtually the same success rate (in terms of getting a favourable judge's recommendation) as the gentry. Moreover, in more than half the cases in which there was middling-group involvement they acted, it appears, without support from anyone in a higher social group and in these cases they again had a similar success rate.[65] The small number of petitioning processes that showed signs of aristocratic connections fit in well with Hay's analysis of the usefulness of the pardoning system to the aristocracy. Although prisoners with aristocratic support were only slightly more successful in gaining a positive recommendation from the judge, they had a much greater chance of overriding him when he did not report in their favour. The judges' inclinations were followed by the King in the vast majority of cases during these years, but

[63] P.R.O. H.O. 47/6 William Glaves, HO 47/11 Richard Wiltshire.

[64] P.R.O. H.O. 47/6 John Donne. John Jones alias Collingwood; Hay, 'Property', p. 45.

[65] Success rates were all between 56 per cent and 60 per cent. The information available on the social background of petitioners is often very inadequate, however.

where they were not followed aristocratic petitioners were usually involved. Lord Hawke's petition on behalf of Richard Sheperdson was successful, for example, in spite of a hostile judge's report which suggested the prisoner wanted to be put into the Navy merely in order to effect an escape and commented cynically that 'I am afraid many petitions such as the enclosed will be framed on the like pretence.'[66]

Although only eighteen cases are involved, work recently undertaken on all the Essex pardoning cases found in twelve sample years taken from the period 1784–98 broadly confirms the nationwide pattern found in 1787 and 1790. Cases in which the county gentry were involved had almost exactly the same chances of getting a positive judge's recommendation as those that involved larger groups of middling men, local inhabitants, and parish officers. Moreover, of the four cases in which at least one Essex JP's signature can be identified on the petition, only one resulted in a positive judge's report. By contrast, the two cases in which a duke offered his support to the petition both ended in a conditional pardon, and in at least one other 1790s Essex case newspaper evidence makes it clear that a lord intervened to ensure mercy was extended.[67] Aristocratic support was not an automatic ticket to mercy. The only other member of the peerage who got involved in an Essex case during these years, Lord Kinnoul, was unsuccessful—just as he was two years later in 1800 when he was involved in the well-publicized campaign to save the Suffolk offender Sarah Lloyd from the gallows. However, in attempting to get a pardon for the twice-convicted Essex deer poacher, John Church, Kinnoul was going against the wishes of some of the largest landowners in the county who believed the prisoner to be 'a very old and notorious offender'.[68]

How typical were the years studied here? If the sample had been based only on the early and mid-1780s it could have been argued that men of higher status might have been temporarily discouraged from petitioning, and temporarily ineffective when they did so, because of the general government crackdown on the pardoning of major property offenders that occurred between 1782 and 1785. As late as July 1785 the *Chelmsford Chronicle* reported that 'several applications were made for the reprieve of...Moore, a young sailor, but Lord Sydney, the Secretary of State, convinced of the expediency of cutting off the future hopes of criminals convicted of capital offences, very judiciously refused to comply with the request though backed by the first interest of the county'. Such public rebuttals can hardly have encouraged gentry activity, but after 1785 the approach of the central authorities changed fairly rapidly. By

---

[66] Hay, 'Property', p. 46; Less than 10 per cent of cases resulted in an outcome that went broadly against the judge's wishes; for Richard Sheperdson, P.R.O. H.O. 47/11.

[67] See note 62 for years sampled. For the two Duke-related cases, P.R.O. H.O. 47/3 Matthew Hale, H.O. 47/6 John Jones alias Collingwood; *Che.C.*, 3 Aug. 1792.

[68] P.R.O. H.O. 47/22 John Church; Gatrell, *The Hanging Tree*, p. 343.

1787 the majority of petitions for pardon were successful, hanging rates were beginning to decline, and the transportation crisis had been resolved. Although some of the cases in the Essex sample came from the early to mid-1780s, which may help to explain why the proportion of judges' recommendations that were positive was rather lower in that sample,[69] overall it seems unlikely that the particular years chosen for study here have created significant distortions. In order to explain why the middling sort had much the same success rate as the gentry, it is therefore necessary to explore a number of different perspectives and to examine a few pardoners' tales in greater detail.

The judges' attitudes to those who petitioned them for pardon are difficult to unravel but the advice they were given by contemporary commentators was clear. Gisborne, for example, argued that when recommending offenders be pardoned, a good judge 'will form his determination on the solid grounds of equity and public good ... but he will feel the necessity of withstanding improper solicitations, however respectable, however potent the quarter may be from which they come'. Paley's similar insistence that the prerogative of pardon 'ought to be regarded not as a favour to be yielded to solicitation ... or ... made subservient to the conciliating or gratifying of political attachments but as a judicial act', depending on nothing but 'the quality and circumstances' of the crime[70] may have been partly written in response to cases in which aristocratic connections were known to have been influential. However, when they dealt with less exalted gentry and middling-sort petitions, many judges seem to have worked on similar principles. Judge Harding's remarks in 1790 on the case of Philip Bevan certainly had much in common with Paley's conclusion that 'the admission of extrinsic or oblique considerations, in dispensing the power of pardon is a crime'. 'The application made in his favour to me', he wrote, 'was always built on references to his reputable connections, not his own character ... it would be mischievous to make the better fortune of the culprit exempt him from the punishment which is due to the offence and inflicted upon it in others. I uniformly resisted as I now resist, the application to distinguish the mode of punishment in his favour, which application originates only in his connections and which connections afford additional ground for equal severity in his case.' Justice Heath proved equally unmovable in the same year when John Pitt Esq. petitioned on behalf of William Holland and pleaded that 'I am so respectfully and so urgently pressed that I cannot refuse and though the general rule of business will not admit relief yet I am satisfied political utility demands it.' Political utility or no political utility the prisoner received no mitigation of sentence.[71]

[69] *Che.C.*, 29 July 1785. In nine of the eighteen cases the judge's response was negative, including the four cases tried either in 1784 or in early 1785.

[70] Gisborne, *An Enquiry*, p. 234; Paley, *The Works*, 4, p. 433.

[71] P.R.O. H.O. 47/11; H.O. 13/7–8.

7. *Some Pardoners' Tales*

The four cases involving Essex JPs as petitioners that emerged from the twelve-year sample of all Essex pardoning papers also illustrate the problems that many members of the gentry had in getting a favourable response from the judges. Each of these pardoners' tales is a major study in itself and can be only briefly discussed here, but the overall picture is hardly one of overwhelming success. The petition of John Mixter, who was sentenced to transportation at the Colchester borough sessions in 1798, was transmitted to the Home Office by one of Colchester's MPs but the main force of the request came not from him but from three local Essex JPs.[72] Despite this backing, however, the report from the chairmen of the borough bench was very negative and no remission was granted. The trial judge was equally unmoved when John Conyers attempted to get a pardon for John Madell, a substantial Waltham innkeeper sentenced to transportation for receiving stolen malt in 1785. Conyers, a local JP from a well-established Essex family whose father had represented the county in Parliament during the previous decade, did not sign the petition (which had the backing of a surgeon, a curate, two parish officers, and over twenty other local inhabitants), but instead made direct representations to the authorities. However, the judge's report was very negative, and although Madell may unofficially have been permitted to transport himself, there is no indication in the Home Office's official pardoning records that any mitigation of sentence was allowed.[73]

The outcome of William Dench's petition in 1797 cannot be doubted. He was hanged despite the very public intervention of one of Essex's most prominent magistrates. Dench had also been a substantial innkeeper (in the assizes town of Chelmsford) before falling into debt and thence into crime. The prospect that a once respected member of their community would soon be on the local gallows induced over thirty inhabitants to sign a petition. That petition laid great stress on the fact that T. B. Bramston Esq., with whom Dench had lived as a servant for eight diligent, sober, and faithful years, was one of its signatories. Bramston's support was well worth having. He owned a large estate, house, and park just outside Chelmsford and in counties such as Essex, where there were few aristocratic estates, long-established families such as the Bramstons were among the leading members of the landowning élite. Like his forebears, T. B. Bramston was one of the county's two MPs and in 1797 he had held that position for nearly twenty years. He was a pillar of county society. He frequently acted as chairman of the quarter sessions, was chairman

---

[72] P.R.O. H.O. 47/22. Two were clerical magistrates, the third was Charles Matthews who had moved to the area from London in the previous decade. For the result of the case, H.O. 13/12–13.

[73] P.R.O. H.O. 47/3 case of John Madell and H.O. 13/3–5 for the lack of any record of a pardon. Although H.O. 13 appears to be a systematic record of all the pardons issued, it may not have recorded absolutely every decision. Despite the highly unfavourable judge's report Conyer's attempts to get the sentence changed to self-transportation may have been successful.

of the committee that organized the rebuilding of the Shire Hall, and laid the foundation stone of that building in 1789. His support for Dench was well publicized. The *Chelmsford Chronicle* not only reported that Dench had served him honestly for eight years but also made it clear that 'some very laudable exertions had been made ... to obtain a reprieve'. The judge was adamant, however. There were 'no merits in his case' to warrant recommending mercy. The widely reported efforts of Bramston and 'the inhabitants of the town' to keep Dench from the gallows had been defeated.[74] Nor was this Bramston's only such failure. In 1784 he had supported the petition of another highway robber, Robert Rust, who was also a Chelmsford resident but had committed his offence in Hertfordshire. Once again many Chelmsford inhabitants joined him, including a minister, three neighbouring gentlemen, five parish officers, and twenty 'tradesmen of the town', but to no avail. Rust was hanged after a brief reprieve and since the *Chelmsford Chronicle* reported both his sentencing and his execution it seems likely that the outcome of Bramston's intervention would once again have been widely known.[75]

By contrast the only Essex magistrate in the twelve-year sample who signed a petition which succeeded in gaining both a favourable judge's report and a mitigation of sentence was a clerical magistrate of relatively low social standing who may well have been only peripherally involved in the petitioning process. Samuel Cole's petition was signed by twenty-two local inhabitants including two grocers, two merchants, two mariners, a collarmaker, an innkeeper, a baker, a bricklayer, a brewer, and a fellmonger. It spoke eloquently of his 'good and honest behaviour during his residence in their neighbourhood, which was ever since he was born' and stressed his youth (he was only 13). It also included details of an agreement between the churchwardens and a local 'gentleman'—who turns out to be a mariner—to take Cole as apprentice for seven years if he was pardoned. The role played by M. Thompson, the local rector who was also one of the committing magistrates, is unknown, but the judge's report leaves little doubt that it was the apprenticeship opportunity, combined with the youth and previous good character of the offender, that swung the case in Cole's favour. Interestingly there is no evidence that the local inhabitants tried to enlist the sympathy of Richard Rigby MP, a leading figure in national politics whose estate dominated the two parishes involved. Their own efforts seem to have been enough. Cole was pardoned 'on condition he binds himself apprentice'.[76]

[74] P.R.O. H.O. 47/21 William Dench. *Che.C.*, 4, 11 and 25 Aug. 1797; E.R.O. D/Du 235; Anon., *Roxwell Revealed. An Anthology of Village History* (Roxwell, 1993), pp. 26–9; Namier and Brooke, *History ... Commons 1754–1790*, 2, p. 111; Briggs, *John Johnson*, pp. 91–6.

[75] He is not therefore in the sample of Essex cases quoted earlier. If he is included four out of the five cases in which Essex JPs were involved failed to get favourable judge's reports. P.R.O. H.O. 47/1 Robert Rust; *Che.C.*, 12 and 19 Mar. 1784.

[76] P.R.O. H.O. 47/7 Samuel Cole; occupations traced in Freeholders books E.R.O. Q/RJ 1/8 and 12 (and Edw Alston in jury lists). H.O. 13/6. On Rigby see Namier and Brooke, *History... Commons 1754–90*, 3, pp. 354–60.

Only one of the three Essex cases in which it has been possible to identify the involvement of an MP resulted in a pardon, but this may be partly because when MPs were asked to act as channels for prisoners' petitions they sometimes very deliberately took a distanced or neutral stance, as the Colchester MP did in Mixter's case. 'I have been desired by some of my constituents who have signed the enclosed to transmit it to your grace', he wrote. 'It is impossible for me to judge of the propriety of advising his Majesty to bestow his gracious pardon on the person whose case is represented.' Even when they offered some support MPs' letters were often highly ambivalent. In 1796, for example, the Hertfordshire MP William Baker made the following comment in his letter about the case of Thomas Whittey, who was due to hang three days later: 'Though he was convicted on very satisfactory evidence and his general character is not ... much in his favour, I must own the plea of a wife ... and four children of very tender years have their weight with me.'[77] Whittey escaped the gallows, but almost certainly it was not Baker's half-hearted letter that saved him, but rather the energy and intervention of a local farmer, John Carrington.

The survival of Carrington's diary gives us a completely different insight into this case from that afforded by Baker's brief letter and the judge's report— the only documents that survive in the main Home Office archive. In this period of extreme dearth Whittey's case had clearly aroused Carrington's sympathy for he described the prisoner in his diary as 'a young man ... having a wife and four children, his offence was for stealing one fat sheep ... in November last in that distressed time when corn sold at 3 pound per load'. Animal theft could still lead a man to the gallows in the 1790s. The Essex offender William Baldry was hanged a year later, despite pleading that his family were 'persons of credit' and despite the support of a considerable number of eminent gentlemen from his father's neighbourhood. Four days before Whittey was due to hang Carrington seems to have realized that the prisoner was in imminent danger and decided to act. He and a friend set off 'to London with all speed to try what we could do'. When they got there they 'made application ... for the poor fellow' to Baker and two other MPs. Although it was not until the morning of the execution that they heard that 'our request was granted for his life' their journey clearly bore fruit. The judge's positive report was written the day after their visit and although Baker, and/or one of the other men they hurriedly contacted, provided the channel, Carrington and his friend clearly created the momentum which led to the reprieve.[78]

[77] P.R.O. H.O. 47/22 John Mixter; H.O. 47/20 Thomas Whittey.

[78] Branch-Johnson (ed.), *Memorandoms*, pp. 27–8; P.R.O. H.O. 47/22 William Bawdry: five petitioners used the title esquire, five others are titled 'gent', a further five were clerics. They also included seven farmers or yeomen, two innkeepers, two attorneys, two tradesmen, a surgeon, a shopkeeper and several parish officers. H.O. 47/20 Thomas Whitley.

324 THE GOOD MIND AND THE BAD

Whittey's case illustrates both the inadequacy of the surviving pardoning archive, which completely fails to record Carrington's role, and the difficulties faced by historians in their attempts to gauge the impact made by different social groups within the pardoning process. Without compiling a collection of detailed microhistories which would require a separate volume in itself, it is not possible to draw definitive conclusions, but it seems clear that petitions came from a wide spectrum of different social groups and social alliances. Some were products of the middling sort. When there was time to do so middling men not infrequently made sure that a petition was raised. In 1807 John Carrington organized another petition on behalf of the recently convicted wife of a local innkeeper, travelling round the district persuading people to sign and then taking the petition to London himself,[79] and in the same year two Kent offenders were given free pardons following a petition signed by four innkeepers, three drapers, two victuallers, a grocer, a basketmaker, a bricklayer, a farmer, a stationer, a tanner, a druggist, an engineer, a miller, a wheelwright, a coachmaker, a butcher, a plumber, a wharfinger, a vicar, and four parish officers.[80] Where there was not time to raise a full petition middling men like Carrington had to appeal directly to London-based contacts who could communicate rapidly, if sometimes ambivalently, with the relevant authorities, but the outcome could be just as effective.

Equally some petitioning processes (although not perhaps as many as the surviving Home Office records suggest) were primarily the work of established gentlemen such as Luttrell or Pitt. However, a considerable number of pardoning processes involved both groups at least to some degree. From the judges' point of view, unless a member of the aristocracy was involved, it seems to have mattered little which subgroups of the local community were behind the petition. What they were interested in was local knowledge. If they could get it from a member of the local gentry all well and good, but as the gentry withdrew increasingly from face-to-face contact with the poor the judges were much more likely to obtain that knowledge from other, less exalted, groups of local inhabitants. As long as the judges could be sure that the petitioners were themselves established members of the local community, the bench was prepared, it seems, to give considerable weight to their testimony. If a local gentleman chose to support the petition of a prisoner he did not know in order not to appear inhumane or in order to make a paternalistic gesture, this did no harm and may have added a certain gravitas,[81] but a petition had most weight if its signatories could directly address issues of

<hr />

[79] Branch-Johnson (ed.), *Memorandoms*, pp. 144–50.

[80] P.R.O. H.O. 47/39 John Longhurst and John Lynn; H.O. 13/18.

[81] Gentlemen's letters in support of petitioners sometimes confirmed, for example, that the petitioners themselves were respected men of local good credit. This did not always help. The Colchester MP wrote of Mixter's petition: 'The names being respectable of those who have interfered on this occasion' but with no effect. P.R.O. H.O. 47/22.

character, past conduct, industriousness, and other mitigating circumstances on the basis of their everyday contact with the accused. From this perspective it no longer seems surprising that a group of merchants, mariners, and other middling men or a group of Southwark tradesmen could be more successful than leading county landowners such as Bramston—providing, of course, that the crimes and backgrounds of the prisoners they petitioned for allowed them to appeal to criteria which the judges felt were appropriate.

The judges were willing to listen to gentry pleas and would respond favourably if the right criteria were advanced, but they do not seem to have felt the need to bow to the influence of mere country gentlemen, however prestigious those gentlemen may have been in their own counties. Only to those whom the judges considered to be their social superiors—the aristocracy and the big players on the London political stage—were they likely quietly to acquiesce, and even then their decisions sometimes had to be overridden by the Secretary of State. Whether because of pride, because of a belief in the importance of not allowing influence to affect judicial decisions, or because of fears that if they did so the law's legitimacy would be increasingly questioned, judges do not seem to have been easily or frequently bent by the winds of mere gentry influence when mitigation rather than example was being requested. They may have been more amenable to gentry approaches immediately after the assizes when they selected who would be reprieved without needing to petition,[82] but these informal exchanges created virtually no records and it cannot be assumed that the gentry were any more successful at this point than they were further on down the line. T. B. Bramston was foreman of the Essex grand jury during the assizes at which William Dench was condemned and would have had ample opportunity to approach the judge informally on behalf of his former servant, but if he did he was no more successful than he was to be when he later involved himself in supporting the prisoner's petition.[83] Throughout the pardoning process most judges seem to have been more interested in the quality of the information they could obtain about the particularities of each case than in the patronage possibilities that process created for the local gentry. As Ekirch concluded on the basis of his brief analysis of the pre-1775 pardoning system, 'influence peddling on the part of rich and powerful men pervaded public life. What is surprising is that it did not exert a greater impact upon judicial recommendations to the crown.'[84]

Conclusion: The Languages of the Good Mind and the Bad

The pardoning archives are extremely complex documents and long attention is often needed before a single case reveals itself fully. However, this analysis of

[82] Madan, *Thoughts*, pp. 98–108.
[83] P.R.O. H.O. 47/21 and Assi 35/237. Bramston sat on the grand jury in nine out of the ten assizes 1796–1800 and was twice chairman—Assi 35/236–240.
[84] Ekirch, *Bound for America*, p. 36.

the criteria on which pardoning decisions were based, and of the involvement of different social groups in those decisions, suggests a number of tentative conclusions. First, it is clear that the eighteenth-century pardoning process should not be characterized as belonging to, or meeting the needs of, the aristocratic and gentry landowning élite alone. Middling men provided the momentum in a very considerable proportion of pardoning cases. The historical roots of the deep involvement of 'people of middle means', whom Gatrell found to be the majority voice in the petition archive by the 1820s, lay further back than is suggested by his conclusion that in the eighteenth century 'if great men of the locality let them pass, minor felons would hang'. More influential than upper-class intrigue, to quote Ekirch, 'was often the sheer weight of public opinion that communities marshalled to rescue condemned men'.[85] The pardoning process did favour those with connections but they had to be high connections and although the influence of a peer, as Hay has pointed out, was 'naturally greatest', the vast majority of petitions did not have such exalted backing. By the 1820s, Gatrell has shown, the judges were resisting influence from all social groups. In the later eighteenth century they may only occasionally have successfully resisted aristocratic pressure but there is little evidence that they felt the need to bow or even bend towards petitioners of mere gentry status or below. If, as Hay has suggested, 'the great majority of petitions for mercy were written by gentlemen on behalf of labourers'[86] (and although many petitions contained gentry signatures it is by no means clear that this was the case), those labourers may not have gained much more from that assistance than they would have done from that of local middling men.

The pardoning system usually enabled those at the very apex of the social hierarchy to demonstrate that they had the favour of the King or of his key ministers, and it may also have boosted the reputation of the King himself, but public failures such as those experienced by substantial country gentlemen like Bramston could hardly perform the same function. This may not have worried Bramston. The petition in Dench's case lauded him for his 'humanity' in offering his support and Hay may well be right that local gentlemen 'took no blame if the petition failed, for an unanswered plea was attributed to the determination of the King'. However, the failure of gentry support to have a discernibly greater impact than that of the middling sort does suggest that the heart of the pardoning process did not lie in the patronage games occasionally revealed in the letters that accompanied petitions. Its core lay elsewhere. If, as Beattie has recently suggested, pardoning decisions 'were not often fundamentally determined' by élite interventions, what were the guiding principles that shaped the distribution of pardons?[87]

---

[85] Gatrell, *The Hanging Tree*, pp. 418–19; Ekirch, *Bound for America*, p. 37.
[86] Hay, 'Property', pp. 45–7.
[87] Beattie, 'The Royal Pardon', p. 17. Hay, 'Property', p. 48.

Two sets of forces, two languages, were at work. The first was instrumental, pragmatic, and exemplary—a crime-invoked response. The second, and it will be suggested the most central, was potentially more humane—a reaction to the nature and personal circumstances of the offender, an attempt to use various criteria to individualize sentencing policy in line with broader ideas about the kinds of people who did or not did deserve mercy. The more instrumental elements of the system came out most clearly in the ways certain kinds of offences rather than offenders were singled out for heavier punishment—those that were particularly violent or threatening to property or commerce, for example, or those that were difficult to detect. The exemplary rather than the personalized nature of some pardoning decisions was most evident when the judge refused to pardon an offender because an example was needed against a particular crime. This might be a property crime such as burglary or horse stealing, or (much less frequently) a crime that threatened social order such as the riot against the horse tax for which Samuel Horne was imprisoned in 1787 but then discharged a year later at the commissioners' request once there was 'no probability of any further riots'.[88] In these situations certain selected offenders received no mitigation whatever their personal attributes or circumstances. They were sacrificed to the perceived needs of property and good order. But the existence of such cases should not blind us to the other core characteristic of both sentencing and pardoning decisions—their individualized nature.

As we have seen in the last two chapters the gender, age, poverty, infirmity, reformability, previous good character, possible innocence, etc. of the offender played a vital role in deciding his or her fate. This tendency to adjust the sanction to the nature of the offender maddened Madan (who railed against merciful decisions made simply because the accused 'happens to be young—it appears to be his first offence—he has before the fact which is proved against him, had a good character—he was drawn in by others ... or some other circumstance of the like kind').[89] It also highlighted a central tension that shaped both sentencing and pardoning policies. That tension can best be illustrated by analysing Henry Fielding's remarks on the inner logic of the urge to mitigate, which he found so prevalent and so repugnant in the mid-eighteenth century penal system. In his brief discussion of 'the encouragement given to robbers by frequent pardons', Fielding included a revealing dialogue between what he termed the 'good mind' and the 'bad mind'. 'To consider a human being in the dread of a sudden and violent death', he wrote,

To consider that his life or death depend on your will; to reject the arguments which a good mind will officiously advance to itself; that violent temptations, necessity, youth,

---

[88] P.R.O. H.O. 47/7. For further examples and analysis of the strategic use of pardons at times of social unrest—a subject that is outside the remit of this study—see Hay, 'Property', pp. 49–50.
[89] Madan, *Thoughts*, p. 137.

inadvertancy, have hurried him to the commission of a crime which hath been attended with no inhumanity; to resist the importunities, cries and tears of a tender wife and affectionate children, who, though innocent, are to be reduced to misery and ruin by a strict adherence to justice:–these altogether form an object which whoever can look upon without emotion must have a very bad mind.

Fielding went on to argue strongly that reason must overcome 'the good mind', that 'though mercy may appear more amiable . . . severity is a more wholesome virtue' because only severity would deter others from committing crimes.[90] However, his commentary reveals a powerful discursive framework which played a vital role in determining the final punishments received by many offenders in the eighteenth century. The arguments which the 'good mind' advanced included many of the criteria which the detailed analysis put forward in the last two chapters has shown were central to the individualization of sentencing and pardoning policies—youth, necessity at the time of the crime, the future poverty of the offender's family, lack of violence. If he had considered it necessary for his argument to do so, Fielding would probably have included the other criteria highlighted in this chapter such as infirmity, reformability, etc. He had already wrestled with the role that the character of the offender should play in his discussion of the trial, acknowledging that it could carry 'great weight', but arguing that it should only do so where the evidence was weak and the character witness trustworthy.[91]

Some judges may have managed to keep their bad minds in the ascendancy and have thought in terms of example and deterrence alone, but the majority of their reports and of the sentencing decisions they made reflected to some extent at least the power of the alternative mind set which Fielding called the 'good mind'. Judges differed widely in their style and approach, and the extent to which individual judges pursued their own particular policies still needs to be researched, but many appear to have been highly ambivalent about these issues. When faced by an offender who was clearly not violent or hardened, some judges may have genuinely and consciously embraced the discursive framework which Fielding labelled the good mind and many others were almost certainly swayed by at least some elements of that framework without being completely conscious of the fact. However, it cannot be assumed that all assize judges, or even the majority of them, had fully internalized such notions. As late as 1800 Judge Hotham was quite happy to send 'an absolute child, now only between 10 and 11' to the gallows for a property crime without any qualms. It was only when the crowded court expressed their 'horror of such a child being hanged'[92] that he was forced to acknowledge that he had made a tactical error and to offer hope of a reprieve. There were good pragmatic reasons why the judges chose to favour those offenders who appeared particularly deserving to the 'good mind'. Many of them may have imported its

[90] Fielding, *Enquiry*, p. 119.   [91] Ibid., 118.   [92] Radzinowicz, *A History*, 1, p. 13.

language because it was necessary to do so rather than because they fully embraced that language as their own.

Throughout the eighteenth and early nineteenth centuries the vast majority both of the judges and the landowning élite believed it was necessary to retain the capacity to use the death penalty even for relatively minor property crimes.[93] Popular sentiments are much more difficult to gauge but they may well have been very different. Where public anger and desire for retribution was most easily engaged—as in cases of murder and child molestation or rape for example—there was no problem. Almost everyone embraced the 'bad mind' in such cases. But when they executed offenders for relatively minor property offences 'attended with no inhumanity' or violence, the authorities came up against a very different set of attitudes. Public sentiments tended to swing towards the dangerous 'compassion, sympathy and pity' of 'the good mind'. 'Thieves and robbers alone appear to be fit objects of compassion in modern times', one commentator complained in the 1780s. 'When a man suffers death for so trivial an offence as stealing a few shillings', another observed, 'it is not reasonable to think that pity will be the prevailing emotion in the breast of the spectator.'[94]

Fielding was not the only eighteenth-century commentator who was aware of the tension between the good mind and the bad. 'The heart of a good man cannot but recoil at the thought of punishing a slight injury with death', Samuel Johnson wrote in a passage advocating the reduction of penalties 'for mere violations of property'. Adam Smith's *The Theory of Moral Sentiments* offered very similar, if more abstract, insights to Fielding's. While noting that murder excited 'the highest degree of resentment' and therefore the loudest calls for 'vengeance and punishment', Smith showed a keen awareness that when lesser offences were involved 'too violent resentment [ie. excessively heavy punishment], instead of carrying us along with it, becomes itself the object of our resentment and indignation'. 'When the guilty is about to suffer', he wrote 'with the generous and humane he begins to be an object of pity.' Like Fielding, however, he stressed the need to 'counterbalance the impulse of this weak and partial humanity' by remembering that exemplary punishment was a vital protection to the whole community. Burke was well aware of the same kinds of tension in 1780. 'The sense of justice in men is overloaded and fatigued with a long series of executions', he wrote. 'The laws thus lose . . . their reverence in the minds of the virtuous.' He was in no doubt that 'the least excess in this way excites a tenderness in the milder sort of people, which

[93] Gatrell, *The Hanging Tree*, pp. 497–558.

[94] P. Garland, *Punishment and Modern Society. A Study of Social Theory* (Oxford, 1990), p. 58; Gatrell, *The Hanging Tree*, p. 59; R. McGowen, 'A Powerful Sympathy. Terror, the Prison, and Humanitarian Reform in Early Nineteenth-Century Britain', *Journal of British Studies*, 25 (1986), 325; Faller, *Turned to Account*, p. 159 quotes a 1750 pamphlet on the 'Compassion, Sympathy and Pity' felt at the gallows. *Parliamentary History*, 25 (1785), col. 902; Hanway, *Distributive Justice*, p. 148.

330 THE GOOD MIND AND THE BAD

makes them consider government in a harsh and odious light'. By the early nineteenth century reformers like Mackintosh emphasized both the need 'to conform the laws to the opinions and dispositions of the public mind' and the 'unspeakable importance' of 'an agreement between the laws and the general feeling of those who are subject to them'. It was vital 'to make good men the anxious supporters of the criminal law', but 'excess of punishment beyond the average feelings of good men' tended, he argued, to turn 'the indignation of the calm by-stander against the culprit into pity'. Criminal laws can only be effective, therefore when 'they carefully conform to the Moral Sentiments of the age and country—when they are withheld from approaching the limits within which the disapprobation of good men would confine punishment'. Thus, throughout the period 1740–1820 the judicial authorities had to keep the powerful arguments of the good mind very much in mind when deciding on pardoning policies, and judges in particular, aware (to quote Burke) that 'a very great part of the lower and some of the middling people ... may very easily be exasperated by an injudicious severity', responded by making two compromises.[95]

First, they pardoned the majority of capitally convicted offenders in order to ensure that the numbers actually hanged were kept to reasonably low levels. Second, as the quantitative analysis in Chapter 8 and the qualitative analysis in this chapter have shown, they selected offenders for pardoning primarily because they fell into categories, such as the young, the old, those with impoverished families, those of previous good character, etc., that were most appealing to the 'good mind'. At the same time they ensured that those who were left to hang were those least likely to appeal to this way of thinking—old offenders, bad characters, gang leaders, violent thieves, young adults who could plead neither extreme youth nor a dependent family in mitigation. To a considerable extent, therefore, the individualized nature of most eighteenth-century sentencing and pardoning policies arose out of a compromise between the broadly popular sentiments of the good mind and the exemplary imperatives of the bad. By embracing the good mind and its various criteria as key elements in their systems of mitigation, the judges and the élite helped to deflect the threat which the extreme severity of the bloody code could have posed to the legitimacy of the criminal law. In doing so they preserved their right occasionally to hang offenders who had committed a wide range of relatively minor property crimes. The more frequent mitigations of sentence offered to offenders who were young, old, ill, female, etc. may have been genuine attempts to act with compassion; to bow to the good mind when this was appropriate. The judicial authorities certainly wanted to present them as

[95] D. Greene (ed.), *Samuel Johnson* (Oxford, 1984), p. 214 quoting an article in *The Rambler* in 1751; D. Raphael and A. Macfie (eds.), *Adam Smith. The Theory of Moral Sentiments* (Oxford, 1976)—published 1759, pp. 75–90; R. Mackintosh (ed.), *The Miscellaneous Works of the Right Honourable Sir James Mackintosh* (London, 1851), pp. 122 and 717–21. McGowen, 'The Image', p. 113; E. Burke, 'Some Thoughts'.

such. However, the language of pardoning used by the judges may equally have been as much a language of convenience as a language of emotional commitment.

The judges were not the only actors in the pardoning process with pragmatic and often very mixed agendas. Although the substantial landowners of many counties not infrequently used their contacts and their positions on the assizes grand jury to press for exemplary punishment, there were also occasions when minor gentry, clerical magistrates, and substantial county figures like Bramston also involved themselves in petitioning for pardon. Their signature on a petition may at times have been little more than a social gesture, but a local gentleman had little to lose by supporting a petition providing that the prisoner's personal circumstances were such that local sympathy had been aroused. To do so could only enhance his reputation as a man of humanity, and although with hindsight it appears that the gentry rarely had any greater influence than the prisoner's middling neighbours, when gentry-signed petitions were successful some local inhabitants may have believed that they did have.

Pardoning decisions were not, of course, simply choices between the good mind and the bad. A substantial number of the key criteria used in the pardoning process were tailored to the practical needs and underlying assumptions of the propertied classes. For example, the construction of good character around industriousness, honesty, and orderliness clearly met the needs of both the local gentry and the middling men who acted as employers, ratepayers, and parish officers—as well as providing the bulk of petition signatures. Middling interests were also well served, of course, by any appeal which prevented the hanging or transportation of a labouring family's breadwinner. The agendas of the middling men who involved themselves in these processes were complex. When particular kinds of property were felt to be under threat from horse thieves, sheep thieves, burglars, etc., many of the local middling sort would have been inclined to join the gentry in clamouring for 'an example against this type of crime'. The Welsh judges' battles against farmer-dominated juries intent on hanging anyone accused of sheep theft are a warning against any depiction of middling men as always and necessarily in favour of mitigation. However, there can be little doubt that many of the principal inhabitants who petitioned for pardon were not motivated by the material advantages they might hope to gain from that process. Farmer Carrington's journeys to London were not undertaken in order to keep the rates down. Neither offender appears to have had a settlement in his parish and his extensive and time-consuming efforts cannot be understood in such terms.[96] Equally when the merchants, mariners, and middling men of Manningtree organized

---

[96] Saving Thomas Whittey from death on condition of seven years' transportation would almost certainly not have saved the ratepayers any money in any case. Very few men returned once they had been transported to Australia.

an apprenticeship for young Samuel Cole, who would otherwise have been transported, they were spending ratepayers' money rather than saving it. The practical steps they took in order to gain reprieves for offenders who aroused their sympathy suggest that many middling men shared in the widespread popular repugnance at the use of very harsh penalties in property crime cases, or at the very least that they found the consequences of the bloody code hard to bear when it threatened to carry away someone they had had personal contact with. Fielding was well aware of this. In his section on 'the difficulties which attend prosecutions' he devotes considerable space to the 'tender-hearted and compassionate' disposition of many potential prosecutors—the majority of whom were middling men—whose minds he describes as 'naturally, I may say necessarily, good'.[97]

The pardoning process was therefore based on a complex interplay of attitudes and interests. In the relatively small minority of cases which involved a member of the aristocracy or a major player in the national political arena it was almost certainly true that, to quote Hay's section on pardoning, 'the claims of class saved far more men who had been left to hang by the assize judge than the claims of humanity'.[98] Elsewhere, however, the balance was more subtle and 'the claims of humanity' were less easily dismissed. The needs of all the propertied for protection from certain sorts of crime, and their periodic demands that an example be made against one particular kind of crime shaped some pardoning decisions. So too, very occasionally perhaps, did the social status of the offender's family, although wealth may often have gone against the prisoner once formal court proceeding had begun. However, the heart of the pardoning system lay elsewhere. The favourable treatment given to the young, the female, the old, the mentally and physically infirm, the potentially reformable and re-employable, those whose families were in deep distress and poverty, those whose established neighbours gave them a good character, those who had committed no violence or breach of trust, those who could cast genuine doubts on the evidence used against them, reflected a set of broadly held social ideals about how justice should work. The judges and the élite may or may not have signed up to those ideals—their willingness to respond to the discourse of the good mind depended on individual circumstances and personal predilections. However, the pardoning system had to accommodate that discourse if what Paley called 'general opinion' was to be managed with 'delicacy and circumspection'.[99] The interactions that went on during the sentencing and pardoning processes not only involved the prisoner and the various social groups (primarily middling men and gentry) who were involved in deciding the sanction or pleading for pardon. Those interactions

---

[97] Fielding, *Enquiry*, p. 109.

[98] Hay, 'Property', p. 44.

[99] W. Paley, *The Principles of Moral and Political Economy* (16th edn., London, 1806), 2, p. 131. For further use of Paley's term, Hay, 'Property', p. 49.

were also shaped by the broader identification of much of the population with the kinds of criteria that Fielding believed the good mind would naturally use in deciding levels of punishment. The result was an ever-changing accommodation,[100] a compromise in which example and deterrence played a part but which was centrally concerned with the individualization of punishment in line with the perceived nature of the offender and with the circumstances which led to the commission of the offence. Both the good mind and the bad had their place in the politics of pardoning, but the importance of the former should not be underestimated.

[100] This perspective is partly informed by Garland's discussion of the role of the outraged sentiments of onlookers in punishment decisions—Garland, *Punishment and Modern Society*, pp. 32–53. On accommodation, see Green, *Verdict According to Conscience*, p. 312.

10

Rituals of Punishment

The small minority of offenders whose journey through the judicial system ended in a capital conviction and therefore in a period in the most feared room on that journey—the condemned cell—were subjected (if they failed to negotiate a pardon) to a series of rituals which are worthy of more detailed discussion in themselves. In particular they faced both the public pronouncement of the sentence of death—the climactic emotional point of the criminal law Hay has argued[1]—and the most terrible experience the law had to offer to property offenders—the one way journey to the gallows. This chapter will look at the public rituals that accompanied these events, assessing their impact not only on the accused but also on the wider audiences which they were designed to influence.

1. The Rituals of the Assizes and the Death Sentence

The biannual visits of the assize judges were surrounded with ritual—the judges' elaborate initial welcome as they approached the assize town; the preaching of the assize sermon in the local church; the formal charge given by the bench to the grand jury; the reading of the commissions; the pronouncement of the death sentence or, more occasionally, the presentation of a pair of white gloves to mark a 'maiden' assizes; the gaol chaplain's sermon to the condemned; and finally the infliction of the public punishments handed down by the bench—the whippings, the pilloryings, and most frequently and most importantly the hangings.[2] However, while it is relatively easy to find descriptions of these events, it is much more difficult to assess what impact these more theatrical aspects of the judicial system had on the population at large. It is not always clear whether the actors successfully delivered the appropriate words or created the appropriate images. Nor is it usually possible to ascertain precisely how big, how socially diverse, or how receptive their audiences were.

The 'pomp and ceremony' of the assize judges' biannual visits was occasionally reported in the *Chelmsford Chronicle*. In 1765, for example, it described the 'splendid and elegant appearance' of the procession which accompanied the judges' arrival in the county town. In 1769 it also carried articles describing

[1] Hay, 'Property', p. 28.　　[2] Beattie, *Crime*, pp. 316–18; Cottu, *The Administration*, pp. 23–7.

the dining of the judges by local notables, and the 'brilliant' assizes ball. 'The profusion of magnificence' at the latter included elaborate decorations (pyramids of artificial flowers, triumphal arches, transparent paintings surrounded by wax lights, etc.) and a variety of dishes so great that the reporter thought that 'fancy itself must have been exhausted in their making'. What impact did these rituals of conspicuous consumption have? The shopkeeper Thomas Turner abhorred the 'luxury', 'intemperance', and 'debauchery' of the lavish entertainments put on for the Sussex assize judges by the local landowners at a time when 'hundreds of poor creatures are lamenting for want of sustenance'. Although he and his neighbours were also invited to take a limited part in the open days the Duke of Newcastle organized immediately before the assizes commenced, he recorded that he would prefer 'one hour spent in solitude' to 'a whole day in such a tumult there being nothing but vanity... in such public assemblies'.[3] Another, essentially plebeian, reaction 'What mummery is this, 'tis fit only for guisers... No mummery sir, 'tis the Stafford assizes' also suggests it would be unwise to assume that the highly theatrical progress of the assize judges to and from the court, or the well-lubricated celebrations that accompanied their visits, necessarily produced a sense of awe or a reverence for authority in most of those who witnessed them. An assize day, Gatrell has suggested, was more like a market day than a solemn moment of state.[4]

Some of the specific rituals associated with the assizes took place before a relatively limited and privileged group of spectators. Although their messages were often intended to have a wider resonance, the charges given to the grand jury and the assizes sermon were read to respectable audiences drawn mainly from the county élite.[5] Those who delivered them could therefore expect to get a supportive, or at least a reasonably passive, reaction from their hearers. Those responsible for performing the parts of the assizes' ritual that took place before a more mixed or plebeian audience could have no such expectations. The sermons preached to the condemned in the prison chapel immediately prior to their execution were often attended, to quote one highly critical Essex gaol chaplain, by many who came 'from mere motives of idle curiosity'. Such people could be very disruptive. The Ordinary of Newgate, for example, was often disturbed by spectators who swore at the turnkeys, scrambled for a view, hung from posts and beams, and pointed at, or whispered to, the prisoners. They were also disrupted by the condemned themselves. Despite their often emaciated condition, some mocked, threatened, or

[3] *Che.C.*, 15 Mar. 1765; 21 July 1769; Vaisey (ed.), *Diary of Thomas Turner*, pp. 107 and 188.
[4] Hay, 'Property', p. 27; Gatrell, *The Hanging Tree*, p. 533.
[5] On assize sermons, R. McGowen, '"He Beareth not the Sword"', pp. 192–211; R. McGowen, 'The Changing Face of God's Justice. The Debates over Divine and Human Punishment in Eighteenth-Century England', *Criminal Justice History*, 9 (1988), 64–98. For a rare printed Essex assize sermon, *Che.C.*, 17 Mar. 1769.

insulted the Ordinary. Others sang obscene songs or spat at and vandalized the pulpit.[6]

The assize judges had equally severe problems at times in controlling the crowds that entered their courtrooms (Chapter 7) but they had fewer problems in managing the prisoners. The Bishops of the Cells, as the Ordinaries were sometimes called, were often drastically outnumbered by the prisoners and could expect only minimal help from the turnkeys. The assize judges dealt with prisoners more individually and were in a position of great power over them. Since the judges did not decide who would be reprieved until after the court hearing was over, open defiance could be very costly. Did this mean that the secular equivalent of the gaol chaplain's sermon to the condemned—the assize judge's enunciation of the death sentence—was an effective and well-orchestrated piece of theatre?

The following much quoted exert from Madan's 1785 pamphlet appears to suggest that it was: 'methinks I can see him', Madan wrote,

with a countenance of solemn sorrow, adjusting the cap of judgment on his head ... He addresses in the most pathetic terms, the consciences of the trembling criminals ... He then vindicates the mercy as well as the severity of the law, ... he acquaints them with the certainty of a speedy death, and ... the necessity of speedy repentance—and on this theme he may so deliver himself, as not only to melt the wretches at the bar into contrition, but the whole auditory into deepest concern ... many of the most thoughtless among them may, for the rest of their lives, be preserved from thinking lightly of the first steps to vice, which they now see will lead them to destruction. The dreadful sentence is now pronounced—every heart shakes with terror—the almost fainting criminals are taken from the bar—the crowd retires—each ... carries the mournful story to his friends and neighbours'.[7]

However, what Madan was presenting in this passage was not the reality but his own ideal scenario. Later in the same pamphlet he strenuously attacked the judges for failing to follow either his script or his choreography. 'There is', he wrote,

a great defect in the manner of passing sentence of death on criminals. It is for the good of the public that this should be done with the utmost solemnity not only to impress the convicts with a due sense of their crimes, but also ... to impress ... the minds of the standers-by ... But instead of deferring the sentence until the end of the Assizes, when the trials are over; instead of calling to the bar all the criminals at once, and addressing them in the most pathetic manner upon their several situations, that all who hear may be apprised of what the law is and what are the consequences of offending against it—it is now too often the fashion to pass sentence on every criminal as he is convicted, and

---

[6] *Che.C.*, 4 Aug. 1815; Linebaugh, 'The Ordinary', pp. 251–3; W. Sheenan, 'Finding Solace in Eighteenth-Century Newgate', in Cockburn (ed.), *Crime*, pp. 235–7; H. Potter, *Hanging in Judgement. Religion and the Death Penalty in England* (London, 1993), pp. 23–4 for a provincial example.

[7] Hay, 'Property', pp. 17–18; Potter, *Hanging in Judgement*, pp. 17–18 quoting Madan, *Thoughts*, pp. 26–30.

this with very little preface: So that by the desultory manner in which it is done, and the frequent repetition of it, it becomes so familiar to the hearers, as to lose almost all its effect, and one grand end of the judge's office is sadly defeated.[8]

This situation had further deteriorated by the early nineteenth century when Cottu, after noting that the vast majority of capital punishments were 'subsequently commuted for transportation or confinement', observed that

the majority of the convicts, therefore, know to a moral certainty the ultimate indulgence which they will receive, according to their respective cases. Nevertheless the judge (who is obliged in every instance to pronounce the dreadful sentence of the law) covers his head with a sort of black cap, and his countenance assumes an expression of dignified and solemn regret, whilst he makes a severe and melancholy recapitulation of their offences to the prisoners, and laments the necessity which exists on account of society at large, for the absolute prevention of any repetition of their crimes. He then pronounces the fatal sentence; but the mournful ceremony, the touching address, the dreadful decree, so far from producing that terrible effect on the delinquents which might be expected, makes little or no impression on them, as they are prepared beforehand to consider it all as a mere matter of course, and seem, with a kind of insolent security, to brave the very judge himself to carry his words into effect.[9]

This quiet counter theatre of the condemned was not new. There were complaints in the early eighteenth century that some capital convicts made light of their sentence by gesture and comment even as the judge pronounced it, and later in the century the *Chelmsford Chronicle* reported similar incidents. In 1797, for example, when Edward Sewell was sentenced to death for burglary he 'did not appear the least undaunted but surveyed the court with unseeming regard to his situation, appearing rather as a spectator than a culprit'.[10] As the proportion of capitally convicted offenders who were sent to the gallows declined and it became clear that certain types of minor property offenders were never executed, contemporaries became increasingly aware that death sentence rituals, however carefully enacted, were losing their impact. The reformers made much of this. 'Nothing', Mackintosh wrote 'can...be more injurious than the frequency with which the sentence of death is at the present time pronounced from the judgement seat, with all the solemnities prescribed on such an occasion, when it is evident, even to those against whom it is denounced, that it will never be carried into effect'. However, by 1808 even some of the opponents of reform had to admit that because sentences of death were so often pronounced 'in cases where they were scarcely ever fit to be executed' this tended to very much 'diminish their effect'. By 1820 Cottu observed that, murderers, forgers, and rapists excepted, 'the punishment is

[8] Madan, *Thoughts*, pp. 82–3.
[9] Cottu, 'The Administration', p. 57.
[10] Beattie, *Crime*, p. 489; *Che.C.*, 4 Aug. 1797.

always mitigated by the judge', the death sentence being 'pronounced merely to satisfy the law'. In reality the net was still cast slightly more widely on occasions but most of the minor thieves whose arrogance during 'the mournful ceremony' Cottu found so surprising, could indeed have every confidence by the early nineteenth century that a reprieve was almost automatic.[11]

For most property offenders therefore the death sentence had lost its sting by this time. Parliament tacitly acknowledged this in 1823 when it enacted that if any capital offender was considered by the court 'to be a fit . . . subject for the Royal mercy, it shall be lawful to such court if it shall think fit so to do to abstain from pronouncing sentence of death'.[12] Even this did not prevent further displays of dissent. Judge Park, for example, was interrupted every few words by shouts of 'It is murder', 'we must be hung innocently', and 'I cannot repent of what I am not guilty' when he tried to pass sentence of death in 1834. Those convicted of non-capital crimes could be equally obstreperous, ably assisted by friends in the crowd. 'The Court was literally crammed with spectators during the passing the sentences', *The Times* reported the following year, 'and we regret to say that great confusion prevailed . . . the prisoners . . . behaved with so much levity that the learned recorder was compelled to . . . lecture them upon their indecorous and hardened behaviour . . . Some of their friends in the gallery added to the disorder by insolent exclamations toward the learned judge of the grossest kind, and others by vehement screaming and exultations. The court however, exercised great forbearance toward those who disturbed its proceedings.'[13]

Did the rhetoric of the death sentence ever have more than a fragile hold on its audience? It certainly cannot be assumed that the bustling crowds that occupied the packed provincial and metropolitan courtrooms of the eighteenth century (Chapter 7) were necessarily willing to offer a quiet, let alone a compliant and responsive, ear to the man in the black cap. Throughout the period under study here the potential impact of the death sentence was considerably weakened by the fact that it was delivered at the wrong point in the judicial process. The best time to pronounce such judgments would have been after the judge had selected which of the capitally convicted prisoners he would recommend for mercy (i.e. effectively pardon) and which he would not. By performing the solemn ceremony of the death sentence before that point the legal authorities placed the ritual and the reality in the wrong chronology, and (as Fielding acknowledged) the ritual lost much of its force as a result.[14]

[11] Mackintosh, *Miscellaneous Works*, p. 723; *Parliamentary Debates*, 11 (1808), cols. 877–8; Cottu, 'The Administration', p. 38.

[12] 4 George 4. c. 48; Gatrell, *The Hanging Tree*, p. 201.

[13] Eastwood, *Governing Rural England. Tradition and Transformation*, pp. 222–3; H. Shore, ' "An Old Offender tho' so Young in Years". The Criminal Careers of Juvenile Offenders in Middlesex in the 1830s', in Hitchcock, King, and Sharpe (eds.), *Chronicling Poverty*, p. 206.

[14] Fielding, *Enquiry*, p. 125. This practice did, however, keep the convicts themselves in fear for longer. Reprieves were occasionally withheld till the final moments on the scaffold—or beyond. The

The moment of truth, of deep emotional impact, came when the gaoler, chaplain, or other messenger informed those waiting in the condemned cells which of them had been left to hang by the bench. This occurred after the end of the assizes when the judges had left town, and was not, broadly speaking, a public moment. No elaborate ritual was involved. The damage and the darkness of imminent death came to the condemned behind closed doors. It was no less painful for that but it was rarely, if ever, a staged-managed event. Nor were there many, apart from their fellow prisoners, who directly experienced the impact of the ensuing highly emotional drama of relief or despair.[15]

Even when the drama was played out in full view, when the judge threw out dark hints as he passed sentence 'with great solemnity' that a particular offender would be on his hit list, there were those who doubted its impact on the wider audience. 'Admonitions given from an awful bench of justice are soon over and soon forgotten', Hanway observed. The terror of the death sentence for those who listened to it knowing that they were unlikely to be reprieved should not be underestimated. When the Essex assize judge made it clear in 1801 that he was going to take a tough line against the eighteen soldiers who had just been capitally convicted before him for property offences, they were greatly affected 'like men in despair' and with good reason. Half of them went to the gallows.[16] The year 1801 was an exceptional year but even at the average assizes the prospect of death, particularly the protracted and painful death to be met on the eighteenth-century gallows, gave the death sentence ritual a cutting edge which even the counter theatre of the condemned and their friends, and the hurried undramatic approach taken by many of the judges, could not entirely remove.

The paucity of relevant sources makes it very difficult to draw precise conclusions about the efficacy of these rituals. The few published death sentences that survive are hardly likely to be typical, and the demands made by writers like Gisbourne and Madan that the judges take the matter seriously can be read either way. More important, the reactions of the crowd are virtually never recorded. Hay is undoubtedly right that 'the aim was to move the court, to impress the onlookers by word and gesture, to fuse terror and argument into the amalgam of legitimate power in their minds',[17] but the extent to which the rituals of the death sentence achieved these aims in the eighteenth century remains open to doubt. By the early nineteenth century, when only a tiny proportion of capitally convicted property offenders were

reprieve for at least one Essex convict arrived twelve hours too late—E.R.O. D/DTu 235 case of Thomas Goodeve.

[15] Gatrell, *The Hanging Tree*, p. 43.
[16] Hanway, *A New Year's Gift*, p. 46; Anon., *A Particular Account of the Trial of John Highly*.
[17] 'A wise and conscientious judge will never neglect so favourable an occasion of inculcating the enormity of vice and the fatal consequences to which it leads', Gisbourne wrote (*An Enquiry*, p. 233) but it is unclear whether this was what he thought they were actually doing or what he wanted them to do. *Che.C.*, 31 July 1801; Hay, 'Property', p. 29.

actually being hanged, the slippage between the script and the action was so great that the judges could scarcely avoid looking slightly foolish.[18] Parliament therefore had to permit the judges to drop the script when it was no longer appropriate. For many types of property offender the death sentence was by then a dead letter.

2. The Gallows—Ritual and Reality

Were the rituals that surrounded the gallows any easier to manage or any more effective as didactic theatre than the death sentences that preceded them? Contemporaries were far from convinced that they were. A steady stream of criticism about hanging days and hanging crowds can be found throughout the eighteenth century, and by the early years of the nineteenth the systematic critiques of the bloody code developed by the reformers added further weight to the opinions already advanced by earlier writers such as Mandeville and Fielding.[19] Many of these writers described hangings and their attendant crowds, processions and popular customs in language which implied a spirit of carnival. Mandeville, for example, depicted hanging days as 'jubilees', 'a free mart', 'one contined fair'. Others believed that those who attended these 'hanging matches' went 'with the same ease and indifference they would go to a race'. 'The monthly shambles at Tyburn' was widely portrayed as a festival, an entertainment, a merry-making holiday at which the condemned had their 'day of glory', their triumphant procession.[20]

Hangings were not, of course, carnivals in the strictest sense. Neither the crowd nor the condemned could prevent the state expressing its sovereign power be sending chosen individuals to an agonizing and often protracted death.[21] However, while few of the condemned would have agreed with Fielding that this was their 'day of glory', most contemporaries would probably have found it hard to disagree with his observation that 'instead of making the gallows an object of terror... our executions contribute to make it an object of contempt'. 'A dirty cart... surrounded by a sordid assemblage...

---

[18] The newspaper reports tried to ignore the absurdities created by the difference between sentencing rituals and actual policies towards hanging, but with little success—'At the conclusion of the assizes', *the Chelmsford Chronicle* reported, 'Lord Ellenborough after a most impressive admonition proceeded to pass the awful sentence of death' on nine property offenders. It then recorded that he 'very humanely' reprieved them all (13 Aug. 1813).

[19] Hanway, *The Defects*, p. 243; Gatrell, *The Hanging Tree*, p. 59; Fielding, *Enquiry*, pp. 121–6; R. McGowen, 'The Body and Punishment in the Eighteenth Century', *Journal of Modern History*, 59 (1987), 667–74; McGowen, 'A Powerful Sympathy', pp. 319–20.

[20] Gatrell, *The Hanging Tree*, pp. 58–9; Beattie, *Crime*, p. 469; Gilmour, *Riot, Risings and Revolution*, pp. 158–69; R. McGowen, 'Civilizing Punishment. The End of the Public Execution in England', *Journal of British Studies*, 33 (1994), 260; Fielding, *Enquiry*, p. 122.

[21] T. Lacquer, 'Crowds, Carnival and the State in English Executions 1604–1868', in Beier et al. (eds.), *The First Modern Society*, pp. 305–55; Gatrell, *The Hanging Tree*, pp. 90–105; Thompson, *Customs in Common*, p. 48.

more inclined to ridicule than duty... a riotous mass' was how the London authorities described the processions to Tyburn in the 1780s, labelling them as 'a mockery upon the awful sentence of the law'. The Tyburn procession was eventually ended. From 1783 onwards executions took place outside Newgate, but the change of venue had little effect. The festive tradition did not die out. The crowds that gathered at Newgate were even bigger and no easier to manage, and the change of location did nothing to prevent the reformers' critique of the capital code from focusing increasing attention on the wrong messages and problematic emotions which the rituals of the gallows conveyed.[22]

Because the authorities so rarely made concerted efforts to control the reactions of the crowd, to create an elaborate architecture for the gallows, or to construct a physical site which would have enabled them to separate the crowd more effectively from the condemned, they failed to make these occasions as 'terrific and solemn to the eyes of the people', as men like Colquhoun would have liked. They also created a space characterized as much by licence as by discipline, a space within which the crowd could develop a repertoire of responses and those who were about to die could say what they wished, a space which might allow solidarities to develop between the condemned and the spectators that could challenge and sometimes completely undermine the messages the authorities intended the gallows to convey.[23]

As Gatrell's detailed analysis has shown, the complex and sometimes contradictory emotions and attitudes exhibited by the scaffold crowds—their laughter, their anguish, their voyeurism, their stoicism, their defiance, their acquiescence, their anger, their defence mechanisms—developed in this space. So too did a range of responses by the condemned themselves. Ideally those about to be hanged were supposed to behave with decency on the gallows, to show penitence and remorse, to warn others of the dangers of sliding into vice, to confess their crime, and to admit the justice of their sentence. However, despite the exertions of the prison chaplains, who worked hard on them in the days immediately before their execution (when they were assumed to be most open to religious persuasion),[24] many contemporaries complained that the condemned all too frequently broke out of this mould and rewrote the script. Instead of being a morality play the events that occurred on

[22] Fielding, *Enquiry*, p. 122; Rogers, 'Confronting the Crime Wave', p. 87; Ignatieff, *A Just Measure of Pain*, pp. 88–9; R. McGowen, 'Punishing Violence, Sentencing Crime', in N. Armstrong and L. Tennenhouse (eds.), *The Violence of Representation. Literature and the History of Violence* (London, 1989), pp. 140–56; McGowen, 'A Powerful Sympathy'. For aesthetic activism trying to reconstruct execution rituals—S. Wilf, 'Imagining Justice. Aesthetics and Public Executions in Late Eighteenth-Century England', *Yale Journal of Law and the Humanities*, 5 (1993), 51–78.

[23] Lacquer, 'Crowds, Carnival', pp. 309–23; Colquhoun, *Police*, (5th edn., 1797), p. 298; Gatrell, *The Hanging Tree*, pp. 90–9; P. Lake and M. Questier, 'Agency, Appropriation and Rhetoric under the Gallows. Puritans, Romanists and the State in Early Modern England', *Past and Present*, 153 (1996), 64–107.

[24] Gatrell, *The Hanging Tree*, pp. 56–105; Beattie, *Crime*, p. 455; Potter, *Hanging in Judgement*.

the London gallows all too frequently became a drunken farce, or an opportunity for open defiance as the condemned attempted to 'die game' or to declare the law unjust. 'There is hardly a day of execution passes without an instance of some condemned criminal ... by solemn protestations in the last moments of his life, does not endeavour to persuade the world that he dies innocent', one London commentator observed in 1721, and similar views were expressed by other Londoners throughout the following century.[25]

Were these mocking postures and claims of innocence confined mainly to the London gallows? Gatrell has suggested that they were, and that because rural crowds were smaller they gave less support to the condemned but provincial hanging rituals may not have been as different as this implies. Unfortunately the evidence available in newspapers, diaries, and broadsides can be very patchy. The *Chelmsford Chronicle*, for example, rarely recorded the reactions of the Essex hanging crowds, confining itself mainly to brief references to their size, their tears, their poignant farewells, or their willingness to allow the prisoners' friends to give them a decent burial.[26] However, the words, actions and attitudes of the Essex condemned were sometimes reported in some detail and some sense of the nature of provincial hanging rituals can be gleaned from these sources.

Almost all of the Essex hanged died at Chelmsford. Only 2 per cent of those executed in the half century after 1767 died elsewhere, although these did include the hanging in chains of two notorious murderers, both of whom were executed near the scenes of their respective crimes in the presence of 'thousands' of spectators.[27] In London the gallows crowds were sometimes considerably larger than this. By the early nineteenth century even routine hangings of property offenders might attract several thousand people while murderers and famous criminals often pulled in five-figure crowds. Since the only two Essex hangings at which the *Chelmsford Chronicle* recorded even a four-figure crowd were the executions of the two notorious murderers mentioned above,[28] it appears that the crowds that attended the routine hangings of Essex property offenders were almost certainly considerably smaller than their metropolitan equivalents. However, while the *Chelmsford Chronicle* rarely recorded the size of these crowds, on a handful of occasions involving the execution of property offenders it used phrases such as 'a vast concourse' or

---

[25] Linebaugh, *The London Hanged*, p. 18; Gatrell, *The Hanging Tree*, pp. 375–6; Anon., 'On the Penal Laws of England, with Respect to Capital Punishments', *The Philanthropist*, 1 (1811), 150–3.

[26] Gatrell, *The Hanging Tree*, p. 39; *Che.C.*, 7 Apr. 1775.

[27] Based on E.R.O. D/DTu 235/235A 'A list of the persons executed that have taken place in the County of Essex 1767–1848', and on *Che.C.*, 19 Mar. 1790, 13 Aug. 1813. Three others were hanged at Widford for violent robbery in 1781. In all around 230 offenders were hanged in Essex 1767–1817.

[28] Gatrell, *The Hanging Tree*, pp. 56–7. A late seventeenth-century pamphlet does record a crowd of 'thousands of spectators' at another famous Essex murderer's hanging—*The True Narrative of the Execution of John Marketman* (London, 1680) but he was executed on the edge of London at West Ham, which may partly explain the very large crowd. For this case, J. Sharpe, ' "Last Dying Speeches". Religion, Ideology and Public Execution in Seventeenth-Century England', *Past and Present*, 107 (1985), 144–5.

'a great number' or indicated that the crowd that attended was 'very numerous'. Although Chelmsford's population was fairly small, the vast majority of hangings (like most public whippings) took place on the town's market day when Chelmsford was crowded with people from the surrounding villages, and although the average gallows crowd would usually have been counted in hundreds rather than thousands this almost certainly ensured that a sizeable gathering was present at most Essex executions.[29]

The Chelmsford authorities certainly had problems in controlling their hanging-day crowds. Several pickpockets were reported to have operated successfully among the spectators 'notwithstanding the shocking scene' which was supposed to discourage them.[30] More important, in the early 1780s the Essex magistrates were so worried that the gallows crowds were getting out of control that they quickly followed the example of their London counterparts and put an end to the traditional carted procession to the Essex gallows by erecting a new scaffold beside the north wing of the gaol. Although this change was immediately applauded as 'highly decent and much to be commended' by the *Chelmsford Chronicle* it seems, if anything, to have increased the number of spectators and the problems of controlling them—as it did in London.[31]

Who was in the scaffold crowd? The social backgrounds of those who attended provincial hangings are even more difficult to trace than those of their metropolitan counterparts, but the fragmentary evidence available suggests that, as in London, most of those who made up the scaffold crowds were working people—labourers, servants, apprentices, and artisans—while considerable numbers of farmers and other respectable middling men and women could also be found in their ranks.[32] The majority of Essex hanging days were reported in some form in the *Chelmsford Chronicle* but many of these reports were very brief and formulaic—merely recording that the offender was 'executed according to his sentence' or using generalized and oft-repeated phrases purporting to report that the offenders 'appeared penitent' or 'behaved with

[29] *Che.C.*, 2 Aug. 1793, 29 Mar. 1799, 14 Aug. 1801. The vast majority of property offenders were executed on a Friday which was market day in Chelmsford—R. Brookes, *The General Gazetteer or Compendious Geographical Dictionary* (London, 1812); Gatrell, *The Hanging Tree*, p. 58. Beattie talks of large crowds at Surrey hangings (*Crime*, p. 453) but this was on the edge of London. In 1785 20,000 gathered at Lincoln—Davey, *Rural Crime in the Eighteenth Century*, p. 54. In 1775 Woodforde estimated 6,000 at the Oxford hanging of a murderer. Carrington estimated 10,000 at a similar event in Hertfordshire. Beresford (ed.), *The Diary of a Country Parson*, 1, p. 148; Branch Johnson (ed.), *Memorandoms*, p. 46.
[30] *Che.C.*, 2 Aug. 1793.
[31] *The Times*, 26 July 1785; *Che.C.*, 18 Mar. 1785. Other counties followed suit a little later—Eastwood, *Governing Rural England. Tradition and Transformation*, p. 221; *Che.C.*, 18 Mar. 1785, 2 Aug. 1793.
[32] The farmer John Carrington went to a hanging—Branch-Johnson, *Memorandoms*, p. 46; as did Parson Woodforde and his servants: Beresford (ed.), *Diary of a Country Parson*, 1, pp. 148 and 306–7; 3, pp. 38 and 179. For a poem said to be written by a young lady after witnessing an Essex hanging—*Che.C.*, 16 Aug. 1765; Gatrell, *The Hanging Tree*, pp. 58–68, 239–40. In March 1851 *The Times* observed that an Essex hanging crowd consisted principally of smockfrocked labourers, 'a few farmers', and 'a disgusting number of women'. N. Rowley (ed.), *Law and Order in Essex 1066–1874* (Chelmsford, Seax Series of Teaching Portfolios No.3, 1979), document 37.

decency becoming their unhappy situation'.[33] The formulaic nature of these brief entries suggests strongly that on these occasions the newspaper had received no direct information about events at the local gallows. Lacking any eyewitness accounts but hearing that a hanging had taken place, they simply put a standard sentence or two in, along with the names of the condemned, as a matter of form. Occasionally this practice caused them severe embarrassment. In April 1762, for example, the *Ipswich Journal* reported that Thomas Godfrey had died penitent on the Essex gallows. A week later the same paper had to admit that he had been reprieved and that he had never taken the journey to the gallows they had described.[34]

Fortunately, however, a considerable proportion of the hanging accounts that appeared in the provincial newspapers were much fuller than this. Between 1767 and 1807 the *Chelmsford Chronicle* included at least forty one reports of events on the Essex gallows which are sufficiently detailed to suggest that an eyewitness was almost certainly involved in their creation.[35] These reports were highly selective in tone. They made it clear that the paper approved of decent and penitent behaviour by the condemned and strongly disapproved of obstinacy or irreverence. Its printers were also very careful to take a very positive view of the legal process, sometimes pointing out, for example, when a dying man claimed to be innocent that the evidence against him at his trial had been conclusive. It is not surprising therefore that from time to time the *Chelmsford Chronicle* carried reports of dying speeches which fitted in well with the script the authorities wanted to be followed on such occasions. In 1764, for example, one of the paper's very earliest editions reported that the highway robber William Bacon 'behaved with great decency and exhorted the spectators to take warning by his untimely end. He owned the crime for which he suffered ... and several other robberies'. Twenty-four years later another highwayman, Thomas Hogg, was reported not only to have behaved properly on the gallows, 'acknowledged the justness of his sentence', 'exhorted the spectators to shun vice', and expressed the hope that 'his dreadful situation might make a proper impression on their minds' but also to have publicly confessed to many other crimes which 'he had concealed in hopes of meeting with a respite'.[36] A number of other dying speeches included salutary warnings of the dangers of 'drunkenness and

---

[33] Reports do not survive in even the most cryptic form for just under a third of the Essex hanging days 1767–1817. Sometimes this is because no copy of the edition immediately after a hanging has survived. For the shortest formula used, see *Che.C.*, 28 July 1769. For 'behaved with decency' etc. 12 Aug. 1768, 2 Aug. 1771, 25 Mar. 1785.

[34] *I.J.*, 17 and 24 Apr. 1762. P.R.O. Assi 35 202/1 confirms he was reprieved.

[35] 97 hanging days occurred 1767–1807. Some years there were more than two as some convicts were hanged within a few days (usually because they were murderers) whilst others obtained temporary but unsuccessful reprieves which meant they were hanged later than those that did not. After the Lent assizes 1784 there were five hanging days ERO D/DTu 235.

[36] *Che.C.*, 31 Aug. 1764, 25 July 1788.

fornication', or 'of keeping bad company' with 'persons of abandoned character prone to evil courses', which were equally useful from the authorities'
point of view, although what the audience made of one condemned man's
declaration that 'his ruin was occasioned by frequently driving women in post
chaises' remains unclear.[37]

What is surprising, however, is the infrequency with which reports of the
condemned's final journey to the gallows were able to deliver straightforward
didactic and deferential tales of this sort. The *Chelmsford Chronicle* itself lamen-
ted this in 1775. After reporting the 'great calmness and good manners to the
clergyman who attended him' shown by the burglar Lambert Reading, the
paper went on to contrast his behaviour with 'that daring insensibility which
many unhappy people have too frequently displayed in the like situation'.[38]
Systematic analysis of the *Chelmsford Chronicle's* own pages broadly supports this
view. 'Daring insensibility' was indeed frequently displayed by the condemned. At the majority of the forty-one hanging days reported adequately
in the *Chelmsford Chronicle*, 1764–1807, at least one, and often several, of the
condemned either openly claimed to be innocent or acted in other 'daring and
defiant' ways.

About a third of these hanging reports include at least one proclamation of
innocence from the gallows. On average five of the Essex hanged per decade
publicly challenged the fairness of the law in this way. In 1769 William
Robinson 'insisted to the last moment that he was innocent'. In 1772 Samuel
Dowsett 'declared even when the rope was around his neck that he was
innocent of the crime for which he was then going to suffer'. In 1778 four
burglars not only persisted in proclaiming their innocence and pledged 'their
eternal salvation on the truth of their assertions', but also gave their defiance
visual expression by regaling themselves with white hat bands and favours and
displaying them as 'they were carried to the place of execution in a cart'. Lewis
Arnold's declaration of innocence from the gallows five years later made an
even more powerful bid to locate God on his side:

At the fatal tree he positively denied committing the fact for which he suffered; he said
if his prosecutor had sworn to him through mistake he forgave him; and if through
malice he hoped God would forgive him, . . . if he had ever offended any of the
spectators he hoped they would now forgive him, as he freely forgave them and all
the world . . . he hoped none of them would go home with a lie in their mouths, and say
they had seen Arnold hanged for committing a robbery on the highway; hanged they
would see him—but not for committing a robbery—for he took God to witness he was
innocent of the crime with which he was charged.[39]

Since the previous week's papers had included a report indicating that the
crime for which John Bunch had been executed the previous autumn, after

[37] *I.J.*, 2 Apr. 1763; *Che.C.*, 22 Aug. 1800, 12 Apr. 1811, *I.J.*, 17 Aug. 1765.
[38] *Che.C.*, 11 Aug. 1775.
[39] *Che.C.*, 24 Mar. 1769, 17 Apr. 1772, 28 Aug. 1778, 4 Apr. 1783.

also proclaiming his innocence, had recently been confessed to by another convict, such claims of innocence could not be easily dismissed. Moreover, this pattern of dying proclamations of innocence continued unabated with either one or two of the condemned publicly denying their guilt to the assembled crowd in 1785, 1791, 1794, 1796, 1798, and 1803. In the counter theatre of the condemned claims of innocence played a far from insignificant role.[40]

The official script was also undermined by the actions and attitudes of individuals or groups of the condemned in a number of other ways, by 'behaving at the place of execution in the most daring and hardened manner, bursting with laughter when the rope was fixing around his neck'; by 'breathing a spirited revenge'; by obstinately refusing to discover his accomplices despite being 'warned of his consequent punishment hereafter'; by leaving notes with the gaoler and within their shirts 'all tending to impress an idea of their innocence'; by producing a life story including an 'incredible' number of crimes which gave 'more the appearance of a glory in his crimes than a penitential acknowledgment of his errors'; by 'a degree of boldness not strictly accordant to the calm resignation of a man whose mind was tranquilized by...a blissful futurity'; by refusing 'thoughts of a future state...notwithstanding the pains taken...by the worthy clergyman who attends on these occasions' but instead remaining 'hardened and obstinate to the last moment, declaring even then, he would not forgive his prosecutor'; by ascending the scaffold in 'good spirits' and parting with the words 'Never mind Bill we shall soon be in a better place'.[41]

Others among the condemned undermined the official script less through their courageous angry defiance than through the sympathy which their confused and defeated demeanours, their downcast and despairing final words and actions evoked in many of the spectators and newspaper readers whom their story reached. Elizabeth Holmstead was reported to have given 'attention to her infant to...her last moments, when she most affectingly requested her mother-in-law...would supply the loss of a parent and nurture it with motherly affection'. A few months after her execution she was also reported to have been innocent of the crime for which she was hanged.[42] Others among the condemned made it clear it was their first offence and that extreme poverty had driven them to crime. Thomas Brett, for example, was described as

a poor ignorant man, and had very little to say for himself, but declared it was his first offence, and that he was driven to it through necessity;...he had been so lame for a considerable time that he was unable to gain his bread; this induced him to apply to the

---

[40] *Che.C.*, 29 July 1785, 18 Mar. 1791, 19 Sept. 1794, 1 Apr. 1796, 30 Mar. 1798, 1 Apr. 1803.

[41] *Che.C.*, 29 July 1774, 20 Aug. 1802, 19 Mar. 1784, 19 Sept. 1794, 10 Aug. 1798, 20 Aug. 1802, 1 Apr. 1785, 1 Apr. 1814.

[42] Even if not all the words reported to have been spoken on the scaffold were actually spoken, reports of them reached and influenced a very wide readership via the provincial papers. *I.J.*, 30 Nov. 1782, 29 Mar. 1783; *Che.C.*, 22 and 29 Nov. 1782 for Holmstead.

parish officers for relief, which having been refused, he was driven through extreme poverty and hunger to commit the crime for which he was to die.[43]

Although the *Chelmsford Chronicle* very rarely recorded precisely how men like Brett died, the agony and terror of death on the Essex gallows can occasionally be glimpsed from other sources. The few surviving Essex execution broadsheets not only include, for example, a description of four property offenders who 'continued in a sullen humour' swearing angrily till the last moment but then 'roared out in absolute terror', one being 'almost dead before the rope was put about his neck'. They also include references to the condemned 'shaking as they mounted the gallows', so feeble they could 'scarcely ascend the steps', crying and muttering 'Lord help me' with faces in 'the agony of despair'.[44] Nor were the condemned's troubles over when they were 'launched into eternity' as the reports put it. 'He struggled much and the executioner pulled at his feet till he died' was the concluding sentence of one broadside. In 1783 the *Ipswich Journal* (but not the *Chelmsford Chronicle* which ignored this aspect of the event) reported the final moments of two Essex offenders as follows 'On the cart drawing away, from the awkwardness of the executioner, their feet touched the ground, and it is probable they would have continued a long time in misery, if the mob had not drawn the ropes round their necks till they expired'. While some relatively fortunate offenders 'appeared to die easy' others were, to use another cryptic contemporary phrase 'much convulsed'. 'After the scaffold was let down' one more detailed Essex report noted about two condemned property offenders, 'their struggles with death was extremely severe, and they appeared to suffer much—Morris in particular was two and a half minutes before he let his book fall, and four minutes and half ere he appeared to be divested of life'.[45]

Thus in attempting to draw some conclusions about the extent to which provincial hangings worked as didactic theatre it is important to recognize that these scaffold dramas were infused with the strong scent of terror. That the darkness of the gallows failed to overpower a considerable proportion of the condemned seems remarkable, but their speeches and actions as recorded in the *Chelmsford Chronicle's* hanging-day reports suggests strongly that fail it did, at least until the final moments just before the drop. Such evidence must be treated with care. We know nothing about those who reported these events or the sources the printer used. Moreover, only just over 40 per cent of the hanging days that occurred between 1764 and 1807 were reported in the *Chelmsford Chronicle* in a detailed non-formulaic way. Perhaps the paper's sparse, oft-repeated one sentence descriptions of penitent and decently

---

[43] *Che.C.*, 31 Mar. 1786 and for another claim this was a first offence 9 Aug. 1765.

[44] *A Particular Account of the Trial . . . John Highly; Che.C.*, 17 Mar. 1815; *The Last Dying Speech and Confession of George Fawcett . . . Executed at Tyburn near York April 1795; A Full and Particular Account of the Trial and Execution of John Pallet . . . at Chelmsford on Monday last December 15 1823* (Gateshead, 1823).

[45] *A Full . . . Execution of John Pallet; I.J.*, 15 Mar. 1783; *Che.C.*, 17 Mar. 1815, 10 Aug. 1798.

behaved offenders sometimes reflected the reality, despite the complete lack of authenticating detail. However, it is equally possible that the *Chelmsford Chronicle* may sometimes have declined to print accounts of hanging-day speeches or crowd reactions that its propertied readership might consider too derogatory towards the law.

Until further comparative research has been done on provincial newspapers and their hanging reports such issues remain difficult to resolve. However, the *Chelmsford Chronicle*'s accounts of events on the Essex gallows along with the overlapping but sometimes different reports printed in the *Ipswich Journal* contain enough information to suggest some tentative conclusions. If a murderer or sexual offender was to be hanged the gallows rituals usually worked well. People flocked to the hangings of murderers in very much greater numbers than they did to the executions of property offenders. Here there was no clash between the good mind and the bad. The hanging of a murderer or child rapist rarely produced significant ambivalence in the crowd. Most of the spectators at such events wholeheartedly approved of the punishment. Their hostility was obvious. In 1792, for example, the *Chelmsford Chronicle* reported that a Suffolk murderer 'was desirous of going even earlier to the place of execution ... from a fear of insult from the populace, who, indeed, appeared greatly incensed against him' and 'hooted very much' when he appeared.[46] However, when humble property offenders were sent to the gallows the authorities could not rely on the crowd's support in the same way and gallows rituals were much more likely to go awry.

This was true not only in London but also in provincial areas like Essex and Suffolk. Gatrell's assumptions that defiant display was rarer in the provinces, and that because hanging crowds were smaller they offered less support to the condemned, fit poorly with the non-metropolitan evidence presented here. The Essex scaffold crowds may have been smaller, but they were sufficiently large to offer a supportive audience if the offender aroused their sympathy. Indeed they may have been more supportive than their metropolitan counterparts precisely because they were more intimate, less hardened by large numbers of executions, more likely in some cases at least to have known the condemned over a longer period. Moreover, a more compact crowd would also have been more likely to hear what the condemned actually said on the gallows.[47] The *Chelmsford Chronicle*'s failure to record more than tiny fragments of the crowds' reactions makes it difficult to draw firm conclusions about the degree of support condemned property offenders who had not used violence received. However, the respect the crowd showed towards the bodies of the hanged[48] and the defiant counter theatre often mounted by the condemned on

[46] *Che.C.*, 13 Aug. 1813; Gatrell, *The Hanging Tree*, p. 68; *Che.C.*, 23 Mar. 1792.

[47] Harris, 'Trials', p. 22.

[48] The care taken by at least a section of the crowd to ensure a decent burial for the condemned's body was sometimes recorded. Lambert Reading's friends ensured he was buried near his mother's

the Essex gallows implies strongly that a considerable number received at least tacit support from significant elements in the crowd. In 1778, for example, the burglar John Pollard frequently spoke to those who pressed in around the cart that took him and his three accomplices to the gallows despite their claim to be innocent. ' 'Twas a shocking sight to see four healthy young men cut off in the bloom of youth and hung up like dogs in the prime of life', the *Chelmsford Chronicle* recorded him as saying but, given that commentators discussing the bloody code in several late eighteenth-century newspapers expressed similar sentiments, these remarks might equally have come from members of the crowd itself.[49] In notorious cases such as that of Sarah Lloyd, hanged for theft at Bury St Edmunds in 1800, the open solidarity of the provincial gallows crowd was well documented, as was the overt support of a local JP who denounced the Home Secretary's judicial policies from the scaffold immediately before the hanging, and the sparser Essex records indicate similar patterns of support. The crowd that watched Elizabeth Holmstead hand over her baby eighteen years earlier was no less sympathetic, but as in Sarah Lloyd's case, even the most powerful local interests could not save her.[50] In 1821 a rare insight from the Chelmsford petty sessions records indicates the depth of feeling that existed among many of the local inhabitants against the use of the gallows as a punishment for property crimes. After the hanging of four male property offenders on 30 March a great number of spectators 'betook themselves to alehouses, got intoxicated, assaulted and beat each other and insulted and obstructed persons in their business' creating 'a scene of profligacy and disorder scarcely ever witnessed before in Chelmsford'. This was no casual riot, however. Rather it was a somewhat premature celebration of the end of capital punishment for property offenders. Wrongly assuming that a parliamentary petition circulated among them which demanded the abolition of capital punishment denoted an actual change in the law itself, 'the common people' gained the mistaken impression 'that no persons would be executed in future except for murder'. They were overjoyed. 'The scene became something extraordinary' as 'many of [an] inferior walk in life' celebrated exuberantly and 'a number of constables' had to be 'employed to restore order'.[51]

grave (*Che.C.*, 18 Aug. 1775); Lewis Arnold's body was taken in a hearse and buried 'where he lately lived' (*Che.C.*, 4 Apr. 1783); the bodies of three other condemned were 'put in a hearse and carried off by their friends', *Che.C.*, 7 Apr. 1775.

[49] *Che.C.*, 28 Aug. 1778.

[50] Gatrell, *The Hanging Tree*, p. 348. Capel Lofft, the magistrate who spoke for Sarah was exceptional however. He also supported the Suffolk gleaners in their fight against local farmers—P. King, 'Legal Change, Customary Right and Social Conflict in Late Eighteenth-Century England. The Origins of the Great Gleaning Case of 1788', *Law and History Review*, 10 (1992), 6; *I.J.*, 23 Nov. 1782.

[51] Rowley, *Law and Order*, doc. 37. The people of Chelmsford were not the only Essex inhabitants to have strong feelings on this subject. The Essex village of Finchingfield, petitioned for criminal law reform two years earlier—Gatrell, *The Hanging Tree*, p. 402.

This very deep opposition to the use of capital punishment for property offenders may have been in part a product of the widespread public campaign against the bloody code being mounted in the early nineteenth century but there are plenty of indications that such opposition had a much longer history. In 1782 even the *Chelmsford Chronicle* can be found observing that 'In this kingdom the criminal who hath robbed a person of a shilling suffers the same punishment as a murderer. This seems unequal.... such frequent executions attended with so little awfulness or solemnity and so much noise and confusion rather tend to harden than to deter others'.[52] Mid-century commentators were well aware that the crowds before whom these performances took place were often disposed to support rather than to undermine the condemned's negations of the legitimacy and appropriateness of the judicial system. Faced by the sufferings of executed criminals 'the people...are affected with compassion, sympathy and pity. They rather condemn the severity of the laws, than express their horror at the crime', one observer noted in 1750. Writing in the same decade Fielding assumed (in property crime cases at least) that scaffold crowds thought little about the crime and much more about the inappropriateness of the punishment. 'No good mind', he suggested in an attempt to fathom the thinking of the scaffold crowd, 'can avoid compassionating a set of wretches who are put to death we know not why, unless, as it almost appears, to make a holiday'. 'The great business is to raise terror', he wrote, the difficulty being that 'admiration or pity or both', 'the compassion of the meek and tender-hearted', and 'the admiration... of all the bold and hardened' were the emotions most likely to be created by routine executions of property offenders.[53]

These gallows dramas, whether they were enacted in London or in the provinces, contained many elements. Terror was central. Deference and the reinforcement of the law's legitimacy was possible, but could only be relied on when murderers or sexual offenders were being executed. Despite their deepening despair those condemned for property offences not infrequently made defiance and/or potential innocence into a key issue. Their deaths before a crowd steeped in the logic of the good mind surely did little to reaffirm popular respect for the law. If their claims of innocence were believed or if their tales of poverty and previous good conduct were seen as plausible, their executions may have had the opposite affect. In Essex as in London the counter theatre of the condemned cannot be ignored. It counted for something. All too often from the authorities' point of view the gallows, like the death sentences that preceded it, spoke less of majesty than of lottery. Although enacted in the shadow of absolute terror, a considerable number of the dramas that unfolded on the scaffold were as much about defiance as about deference; as much about obstinacy as about obedience. The state's tendency to under-

---

[52] *Che.C.*, 7 Aug. 1782.   [53] Faller, *Turned to Account*, p. 159; Fielding, *Enquiry*, pp. 122–3.

state its presence, the declining purchase of religious penitence as the keynote of the drama, the authorities' acceptance of the condemned's customary right to speak without being censored, the wide range of reactions available to the crowd meant that many of the dramas enacted on the gallows were, in part at least, of the people's own making.[54] Both the London and the Essex authorities tried to rein in the crowd in the 1780s by relocating the gallows, but they continued to believe that the death of the condemned should take place in an open space accessible to the public. The scaffold therefore remained an arena in which a variety of views could be expressed, a place of contest and of dialogue in which enormous slippage sometimes occurred between the official script and a variety of alternatives.

The public infliction of other punishments created similar opportunities for the expression of popular sentiments, but, once again, the degree of support the crowd offered to the authorities depended on the type of crime involved. When an offender who had been found guilty of child sexual abuse or sodomy was publicly whipped or pilloried the crowd could be relied on to back up the court's decision. In 1809, for example, an Essex child abuser suffered 'the execrations of a large concourse of people' when he was publicly whipped in Chelmsford. Indeed, here the authorities' main problem was often the fact that the crowd went too far, as they did in 1763 when several spectators had to be arrested after a man found guilty of sodomy died in the pillory.[55] Once again, however, when petty thieves were publicly punished the crowd's attitude was often very different. Those engaged to perform public whippings were often hooted at or jostled by the crowd and in some rural areas such sentences proved very difficult to carry out as a result. 'Of all the ridiculous farces... ever... exhibited', one eye witness complained to *The Times* in 1786, 'that of a public whipping is the most so... far from having the intended effect on the culprits or the lookers on it seems to have a directly contrary one, the punishment being of itself so trifling, as to be only a matter of merriment'.[56]

Public rituals, whether they involved 'trifling' whippings, terrifying gallows dramas, or the dour delivery of death sentences, were clearly problematic moments from the authorities' point of view. These theatres of justice could all too easily become virtually unmanageable. The gap between aims and objectives on the one hand and learning outcomes on the other could be cavernous. 'The intention is to awe the populace', Hanway wrote in 1775, 'our conduct has rather a contrary effect'. From the perspective of the sources studied here,

---

[54] Lacquer, 'Crowds, Carnival'; Sharpe, 'Last Dying Speeches', p. 165; Gatrell, *The Hanging Tree*, pp. 36 and 113.

[55] *Che.C.*, 11 Aug. 1809; *I.J.* 9 Apr. 1763; Smith, 'Civilized People', pp. 21–51.

[56] Anon., *Observations on ... Corporal Punishment* (London, 1821), pp. 1–3; *The Times*, 7 June 1786; Morgan and Rushton, *Thieves, Rogues*, pp. 136–7. If the good mind was not engaged because the prisoner was 'an old offender' the crowd sometimes went the other way and gave the man performing the whipping a tip to encourage him 'to do him justice'—Beresford (ed.), *Diary of a Country Parson*, 1, p. 209.

eighteenth-century hangings seem less like a means of affording 'splendid occasions for lessons in justice and power' and more like problematic arenas in which the legitimacy of justice was contested. The scaffold far from being an uplifting combination of stage and altar all too frequently became a mockery.[57]

Why did the authorities do so little to change these rituals? They were not necessarily short of ideas. Fielding, for example, proposed to increase the solemnity of the two key moments—the death sentence and the execution— by combining them. The judges were to pronounce sentence and then immediately watch their chosen victims hang before a small selected audience —the criminals being forced to die a 'dreadful' death 'in the presence only of their enemies' because the crowd would be excluded. Perhaps, as Gatrell has suggested, the authorities had sufficient confidence in the terror of the gallows that they felt no need to change.[58] 'The mayhem at executions can be read', Gatrell has argued, 'as indicating the state's Olympian indifference to the effect achieved'. If the drama failed it mattered little, 'the King's commission, the power of the noose and the support of the great and middling... sufficed for the law to be able to afford disdain for effects if effects went awry'.[59] The problematic messages and mixed reactions which the pomp of the assizes, the rituals of the death sentence, and the dramas at the gallows engendered in Essex and elsewhere certainly suggest that these rituals could not infrequently do as much to undermine as to reinforce the legitimacy of the law and the deference of the poor towards those in authority. If 'the antics surrounding the twice-yearly visits of the high-court judges had considerable psychic force', as Hay has argued, it was mainly because 'nothing taught like death' rather than because the authorities were able to deliver well-scripted and appropriately staged rituals at regular intervals.[60]

[57] Hanway, *The Defects*, p. 243; Hay, 'Property' p. 57; Potter, *Hanging in Judgement*, p. 20.
[58] Fielding, *Enquiry*, pp. 122–6. Changes were made in relation to murderers in 1752, dissection or hanging in chains after death being added—Beattie, *Crime*, pp. 525–8; Gatrell, *The Hanging Tree*, pp. 87–8, 267–9; some Essex murderers were hanged in chains, *The Times*, 16 Mar. 1790; but few property offenders were gibbeted. For an exception, *I.J.*, 2 Aug. 1760. Radzinowicz, *A History*, I, pp. 213–20.
[59] Gatrell, *The Hanging Tree*, pp. 95–6 and 532.
[60] Hay, 'Property', p. 27; McGowen, 'He Beareth not the Sword', p. 203.

11

Conclusion: Law and Social Relations, 1740–1820

The legal institutions of the eighteenth century were complex and full of ambiguities. Although for the sake of brevity historians often use phrases such as 'the legitimacy of the law' and 'popular attitudes to the law', the law was not, of course, as monolithic as this implies. The law held different meanings for different people and its pluralistic nature meant that each individual or social group might have a range of often contradictory experiences of legal institutions.[1] There were important regional differences—between London and the provinces, for example, or between areas that had easy access to the different types of court and areas that did not.[2] More important, the administration of the law was multifaceted. The punishments it imposed and the social groups that mobilized it changed fundamentally according to the type of offence being dealt with. For example, even the limited research so far published indicates that the laws relating to assault were extensively mobilized by the labouring poor, as were the opportunities offered by the summary courts to appeal for relief, to obtain unpaid wages, or to resolve a variety of other disputes.[3] Given that a substantial number of labourers also brought theft prosecutions to the courts, it is clear that the eighteenth-century poor did not meet the law only as criminal sanction. However, it is equally apparent that in this period the criminal justice system did not process the central category of offenders focused on in this study—those who had appropriated others' property—in an impartial or neutral way.

Property crime was not confined to any particular social strata in the eighteenth century. A vast array of appropriational strategies was used by members of each social group. Rich office holders frequently raided the state, for example. The trading classes used fraud, false weights, forestalling, food adulteration, etc.[4] However, the range of tribunals and the types of prosecu-

---

[1] D. Sugarman and G. Rubin, 'Towards a New History of Law and Material Society in England 1750–1914', in D. Sugarman and G. Rubin (eds.), *Law, Economy and Society, 1750–1914. Essays in the History of English Law* (Abingdon, 1984), pp. 47–59.

[2] Hay, 'Property', pp. 54–5; Faller, *Turned to Account*, p. 155.

[3] King, 'The Summary Courts'.

[4] A. Leadley, 'Some Villains of the Eighteenth-Century Market Place', in Rule (ed.), *Outside*, pp. 21–34; D. Hay and N. Rogers, *Eighteenth-Century English Society* (Oxford, 1997), pp. 92–4, 97–113; Thompson, *Customs in Common*.

tion or dispute settlement mechanism that property appropriators were subjected to depended crucially on their wealth and social status. The fact that
relatively few men or women of substantial property ended up being labelled
as criminals did not mean they were less inclined to purloin the property of
others. Rather is was a reflection of both the more subtle (or at least less visible)
appropriation strategies they adopted and, more important, of the way that
crime was defined. As the nineteenth-century commentator Plint pointed out,
'Each distinct class has its distinct phases and forms of vice and criminality',
but the eighteenth-century authorities usually confined their definitions of
crime (to quote Godwin) to 'those offences which the wealthier part of the
community has no temptation to commit'.[5] With a few exceptions such as
forgery, the appropriations indulged in by the propertied did not result in their
being indicted for felony or summarily convicted for theft. Rather such
activities put them at risk of either civil suits or of misdemeanour indictments.
Many of the poor's theft-related strategies, by contrast, put them at great risk
of conviction under the formal criminal law as felons or summary offenders.
The eighteenth-century criminal law was not therefore a neutral garbage
collection system.[6] One person's garbage is another's evening meal, as the
thousands who daily comb the rubbish dumps of the developing world will
testify. In the eighteenth century some acts of appropriation were defined as
garbage in need of collection—that is, as felonies to be severely punished—
others were not, and the principles on which that selection was made were
predicated in part at least on the need to protect the propertied from the
predations of the poor. 'When . . . some have great wealth and others nothing,
it is necessary that the arm of authority should be continually stretched forth,
and permanent laws or regulations made which may protect the property of
the rich from the inroads of the poor', Adam Smith observed. 'Laws and
government may be considered in this and every case as a combination of the
rich to oppress the poor.'[7]

Having said this, however, having identified the fundamental inequalities
which shaped the way the legal system defined and dealt with property crime
in the eighteenth century, it is important to move on. The system may have
been designed, as Smith put it, 'to preserve . . . the inequality of goods which
would otherwise soon be destroyed by the attacks of the poor',[8] but this did not
mean that the poor could not make use of it or help to shape its outcomes. Nor
can it be assumed that the propertied were a monolithic group who usually
agreed about how the law should be used, about who should make decisions

[5] P. Jenkins, 'Into the Upperworld? Law, Crime and Punishment in English Society', *Social History*, 12
(1987), 99–102; T. Plint, *Crime in England* (London, 1851), p. 155.
[6] Langbein, 'Albion's Fatal Flaws', p. 119.
[7] A. Smith, *Lectures on Jurisprudence*, quoted in B. Davey, *Rural Crime in the Eighteenth Century*, pp. 18–19;
and Hay, 'Time, Inequality and Law's Violence'.
[8] Davey, *Rural Crime in the Eighteenth Century*, p. 19.

within it; or about the criteria on which those decisions were to be based. Equally it cannot be taken for granted that the élite's hegemony was reinforced by their involvement in the judicial process and by its public rituals. To analyse the specific role that the workings of the judicial system in relation to property offenders played in eighteenth-century social relations it is necessary to return to that much used-word 'discretion'—to assess its extent, its impact, and the degree to which it was exercised by different social groups, for different purposes, in different contexts.

Although discretionary decisions form a central strand in many criminal justice systems, and most certainly in those of early modern and Victorian England,[9] a strong case can be made for nominating the long eighteenth century as the golden age of discretionary justice—particularly if property crime is the primary focus. Jury nullification and mitigation may well have been at their peak. Until they began to decline around 1800, not found and acquittal rates allowed a very high proportion of property offenders to escape punishment, while the continued growth of the bloody code during the eighteenth century expanded the range of charges which juries could reduce using partial verdicts. Until the repeal of that code in the second quarter of the nineteenth century the pardoning system created a rich and finely tuned field of discretionary justice. The judges' right automatically to reprieve many capital convicts also extended their sentencing options. Indeed, between the 1770s and the 1820s the major courts could call upon the widest range of sentencing options they have ever enjoyed in relation to property offenders (Chapter 8). The growing use of varying lengths of imprisonment in the final quarter of the eighteenth century greatly extended the range of secondary punishments available—a range already extended immensely by the Transportation Act passed much earlier in the century. This meant that they could fine, privately whip, publicly whip, enlist, imprison, imprison and whip, or transport those accused of non-capital crimes, whilst offenders convicted of a capital crime could either be hanged or reprieved and then given anything from a free pardon to transportation for life.

Pretrial processes are much more difficult to study but the fragments of evidence available (Chapters 2 to 4) suggest that the major participants in these earlier stages exercised wide and often almost untrammelled discretion. Eighteenth-century victims of property crime were less constrained than their nineteenth-century counterparts. They could still choose whether or not to prosecute, which type of informal settlement or punishment to impose, and what type of charge they wanted to bring without the interference of professional bureaucratically organized police forces. They were also able to call on a growing range of resources—an expanding rewards system, mushrooming

---

[9] For good discussions see, for example, C. Conley, *The Unwritten Law. Criminal Justice in Victorian Kent* (Oxford, 1991); Herrup, *The Common Peace*.

networks of semi-entrepreneurial thieftakers, increasing state help with prosecution expenses, and a rapidly growing range of prosecution associations and printed media—which made it easier for them to catch and prosecute offenders without putting any substantial constraints on their discretionary powers. Magistrates also enjoyed important freedoms. Although lawyers, legal constraints, and more formal organization were beginning to intrude by the end of the period under study here, the summary courts of provincial England remained semi-private, highly discretionary bodies in the eighteenth century. Their general powers expanded greatly during that century and despite the strictures of the legal handbooks they clearly dealt with many indictable property offenders informally. Prosecutors also maintained considerable flexibility between committal proceedings and trial. Many poorer victims failed to turn up in court, contenting themselves with the fact that the accused had often spent a considerable time in gaol awaiting trial.[10] The deeply discretionary nature of these pretrial processes, and the tiny proportion of property offenders who were ever prosecuted, had important consequences for both the ways that changes in recorded crime could be interpreted and for the relative vulnerability of different groups to prosecution for theft, as Chapters 5 and 6 made clear. More centrally, however, from the point of view of historians wishing to study the nature of social relations in this period, the golden age of judicial discretion created an extensive range of decision-making opportunities for a wide range of social groups.

1. Using the Law

In following those accused of property crime along the corridor of interconnected rooms (or more accurately judicial spaces) that constituted the eighteenth-century criminal justice system, this volume has revealed a complex multidimensional set of decision-making processes. Each room from pretrial negotiations to final punishment was given a different shape by the varying levels of legal constraint and customary expectations the actors had to work within. The rooms were interconnected but they were also separate. The actors were affected both by the decisions made at previous stages and by their sense of what might happen further down the corridor, but within those contexts they acted primarily on the basis of their own interests, interactions, and ideas of justice. The key social groups involved in some rooms played very limited roles in others and the status of the most important decision-making groups tended to rise the further down the corridor the prisoner went. However, since the process was highly selective, this meant that as the decision-makers rose in social status so the number of accused affected by their decisions fell very rapidly.

---

[10] See Chapter 2.

The opportunities to exercise discretion made available to any individual within the criminal justice system were affected by a number of criteria. Age and gender were the most obvious. The young were excluded from almost every role although they could be called as witnesses. Women were also completely excluded from serving as judges, magistrates, and jurors, and were much less likely to play a role as prosecutors, character witnesses, or petitioners for pardon. Paradoxically therefore, two of the categories of property offender who were treated with the greatest leniency were those least well represented among the key decision-making groups. What impact did wealth and status have on an individual's ability to use the law? People from almost every group in eighteenth-century society took others to court. Only 5–10 per cent of major court prosecutions involved gentlemen or professionals as victims and, given the small contribution made by game cases to summary court hearings, the same may often have been true there as well. The majority of felony indictments and of the disputes about property taken to the summary courts were initiated by middling men, while about a quarter of property crime indictments were brought by labouring families. This, combined with the not inconsiderable authority given to constables (Chapter 3), put a tremendous breadth of discretionary power in the hands of non-élite groups. Record survival can sometimes mislead historians into thinking of pardoning as only happening after a sentence had been passed, but in property crime cases the vast majority of what might broadly be called pardoning decisions were made by victims. 'If the individual injured can directly, or indirectly, put an end to a criminal process', Bentham observed, 'he enjoys in effect this right of pardoning.'[11] In eighteenth-century England individual victims could, and did, end the vast majority of criminal processes well before they reached the courts and this lower, but vastly more extensive, form of pardoning was mainly in the hands of the middling sort and the labouring poor (Chapter 2).

These two groups continued to exercise power as prosecutors throughout the judicial process. The labouring poor in particular often failed to turn up and prosecute, converting the pretrial imprisonment of the accused into a species of summary imprisonment at their own discretion. The power to downgrade the charge also gave all prosecutors, including labouring ones, an equivalent to the jurors' partial verdict option. 'The law gives to a party injured, or rather, to every prosecutor, a partial power of pardon ... in giving him the choice of the kind of action he will commence', Bentham wrote disapprovingly. 'The lot of the offender depends not on the gravity of his offence but on ... the party injured ... The judge is a puppet in the hands of any prosecutor.'[12] Victims continued to exercise discretion after they had chosen the charge and turned up to prosecute. Prosecutors and witnesses could effectively nullify the trial process by deliberately weakening their

[11] J. Bentham, *The Rationale of Punishment* (London, 1830), p. 427.   [12] Ibid.

evidence (Chapter 7). The prosecutor could also request the jury to bring in a partial verdict. Moreover, both prosecutors and character witnesses played a very significant role in obtaining pardons (Chapter 9). Since almost all the most obvious decision-making roles in the criminal justice system—magistrates, jurors, judges—were confined entirely to men of property, it is easy to miss the potential significance of the long chain of discretionary choices made available to the labouring sort, as well as to those of higher status, by their roles as prosecutors. The decisions that pulled the levers of fear and mercy were not taken by propertied men alone.

The extensive roles played by members of the élite in the criminal justice process should never, of course, be downplayed. Despite the fact that they were often forced to pass death sentences on offenders they had no intention of executing, the assizes judges exercised extensive discretionary powers. After non-capital convictions their sentencing options were wide. After capital convictions they could use reprieves to shape the sanction imposed. In the small number of cases that created petitions for pardon both Home Office officials and the King himself could exercise considerable power, as could aristocratic petitioners—the only group the judges found it necessary to accede to on the basis of their social status alone. Both the assize judges and the magistrates who sat on the quarter sessions bench played a vital role in shaping the trial process, although the lawyerization of the trial, the growth of evidentiary rules, and the growing experience levels of many jurors may have reduced that role somewhat by the late eighteenth century. As grand jurors at the assizes the county élite not only played a part in various public rituals but also operated as a real filter until not found rates declined after 1800. At the summary level the few substantial gentlemen who bothered to take an active role as JPs, and the clerical magistrates and marginal gentry who did most of the work, held huge discretionary powers in property crime cases as in many other types of dispute (Chapter 4). Despite this, Brewer and Styles's broad conclusion that 'the law was not the absolute property of patricians' is clearly reinforced by the detailed study of the treatment of property offenders presented here. Through Parliament, and through the tradition that the judges should always be consulted about statutory changes, the élite may have controlled criminal legislation, but the operation of the law was a different matter. At the very least this was based on a working partnership in which most of the work was done not by members of the landowning or merchant élite,[13] but by the various overlapping groups of propertied men and women—

---

[13] Brewer and Styles (eds.), *An Ungovernable People* p. 20; Innes, 'Parliament and the Shaping', p. 79; law and order issues represented less than 3 per cent of successful bills 1760–1800 and 6 per cent of failed initiatives—Hoppitt, 'Patterns of Parliamentary Legislation', pp. 119–21. The middling sort could also influence legislative change. The Essex graziers were among the main instigators of the bill making sheep theft into a capital crime. P. Langford, *Public Life and Propertied Englishmen*, for a more general exploration; Hay 'Property', p. 61.

farmers, traders, shopkeepers, professionals, and prosperous artisans—whom contemporaries often labelled the middling sort. Although they were drawn together by credit networks, kinship, long-standing neighbourhood ties, and above all by their need as ratepayers to manage the parish in ways that suited their mutual interests, the middling sort were by no means a homogeneous group. Defined as much by the fact they were neither living off unearned income nor reliant on their labour alone, as by any commonality of experience or interest, they were more economically fragmented than either the labouring poor or the landowning élite. Often in competition with one another, often in disagreement about economic, religious, and political issues, the middling sort of any particular locality rarely avoided division or personal animosities. In Essex, for example, there were conflicts between clothiers and woolgrowers, between farmers and corn factors, between the small ratepayers and the larger ones.[14] However, although they were not always in agreement about how to use the discretionary powers it gave them, there can be little doubt that the criminal law was yet another social field, like the labour market, the poor law, and increasingly (Brooks has recently argued) the civil law[15] within which middling men were the main decision-makers, the main group that made things happen. As their diaries indicate, the farmers and commercial men of eighteenth-century England regularly dealt with property offenders using informal sanctions—substituting compensation, termination of employment, or (if the offender was young) flagellation for formal prosecution. So did other groups, of course, but focusing on the middling sort alone may help to bring the significance of this lower form of pardoning into sharper focus.

Even if the average middling household pardoned instead of indicting only one property offender per decade (and the diaries suggest this may be an underestimate), and even if our definition of the middling sort excludes master artisans and professionals and includes only farmers, shopkeepers, innkeepers, and commercial occupations, then in the 1790s an average of 800 Essex middling households per year would have used the discretionary powers available to them in this way.[16] This compares with the average of between one and two Essex petitions for pardon per year found in the Home Office papers in this decade. The detailed pardoning archive, vital though it is for any understanding of the criteria on which decisions were based, has distorted our view of who most frequently exercised discretionary power over others through the threat of punishment under the criminal law. These decisions

---

[14] J. Seed, 'From Middling Sort to Middle Class in Late Eighteenth and Early Nineteenth-Century England', in M. Bush (ed.), *Social Orders and Social Classes in Europe since 1500. Studies in Social Stratification* (London, 1992), pp. 114–35; and J. Barry (ed.), *The Middling Sort of People. Culture. Society and Politics in England, 1550–1800* (London, 1994), pp. 1–28 for discussion of definitions and conflicts within the middling sort; Brown, *Essex People*, p. 26.

[15] C. Brooks, 'Interpersonal Conflict and Social Tensions. Civil Litigation in England, 1640–1830', in A. Beier *et al.* (eds.), *The First Modern Society*, p. 399.

[16] Brown, *Essex at Work*, suggests 8,000 Essex families met this very strict definition.

were overwhelmingly made by middling households (and labouring ones too presumably, although virtually no diaries survive from this group).

The middling sort also enjoyed extensive discretionary powers at other points in the judicial process. As assize petty jurors they established a *modus operandi* with the judges that enabled them to play a major part in deciding trial outcomes and they acquitted or reduced the charges against nearly half of all indicted property offenders. At the quarter sessions jurors drawn from a wide spectrum of middling households brought either not found or not guilty verdicts in favour of nearly 40 per cent of the accused. Most character witnesses and the vast majority of the signatories to pardoning petitions were middling men. They launched, as well as responded to, petitioning initiatives and were just as successful as the local gentry, probably because they had the intimate knowledge of the local poor that the judges were looking for. There can be little doubt that the history of everyday discretionary decision-making in relation to property offenders was a history of the middling sort broadly defined. Since as employers, overseers, and vestry members the middling sort also used the summary courts and the threat of imprisonment in a house of correction extensively as a means of disciplining the errant labouring poor, it is difficult to avoid giving them a central place in any discussion of criminal justice and discretionary power in this period.

Although the extensive involvement of the labouring poor as prosecutors indicates that Brewer and Styles were too narrow in arguing that the law was 'a limited multiple-use right available to most Englishmen, apart from the labouring poor', their implicit foregrounding of the role of the middling sort therefore has much to recommend it. Moreover, since it is clear that the law in relation to property crime (and to a host of other disputes) was a resource available to, and used by, almost every layer of eighteenth-century society, it is by no means unreasonable to describe it as multi-use right.[17] However, such a description is not without its problems. The opportunities provided by legal institutions, the constraints under which the law could be used, and the extent to which it was actually mobilized differed widely between social groups, but the term 'multi-use right' takes no account of such differentials. The law was one of many social fields. In this field, as in any other, wealth and status often meant the difference between occupying the higher ground and getting caught in the marshes. Not only did the law's definitions favour the wealthy; wealth also enabled victims to hire, or pay the costs of, entrepreneurial police, lawyers, and witnesses. If a member of a rich family was accused of a minor offence he or she would often escape punishment when those of lower status would not. 'Offences of a similar kind, passed over as frolics in the sons of the rich, are treated in the children of the poor as crimes of magnitude', a

[17] Brewer and Styles (eds.), *An Ungovernable People*, p. 20. This volume also provides an interesting discussion of the court as an arena, p. 19. King, 'Decision-Makers', p. 53.

parliamentary report concluded in the 1820s. Moreover, if they were ever faced with prosecution at the hands of the poor, the wealthy could afford to use a Writ of Certiorari to remove the case to the London courts (as the Essex gleaners' great enemy Farmer Ward did in 1786) but this was something that the poor found it difficult, although not always impossible, to do.[18] The term 'multi-use right' therefore seems rather inadequate, but given the many strategic uses that the poor made of the law, it is equally unhelpful to portray it as primarily a tool of the propertied alone. In reality it was both a multi-use right and an arena of struggle, of contest, and of negotiation.

2. The Law as an Arena of Struggle and Negotiation

Conflicts took place in many different parts of the eighteenth-century criminal justice system. Its public rituals, for example, not infrequently became sites of contest. The authorities wanted to orchestrate and take control of assizes trials, sermons to the condemned, the passing of the death sentence, and events at the gallows—to use them to reinforce the legitimacy of the law in the eyes of the poor as well as to demonstrate its power. In doing so, however, they came across a vibrant plebeian culture that had its own ideas. The crowd were both the actors and the audience. The counter-theatre of the crowd and of the condemned could turn almost all these points in the judicial process into sites of contest and negotiation. The criteria on which sentencing and hanging policies were based also emerged in part at least from a struggle between plebeian and élite priorities. These ideas clearly overlapped in many areas. Prosecutors, constables, and committing magistrates (Chapters 2–4) as well as jurors and those involved in sentencing and pardoning took factors such as youth, gender, family poverty, previous offences, good character, and the nature of the offence into account in deciding whom to be lenient towards. However, in major property crime cases where a capital punishment was involved there were important differences. The individualization of sentencing policies on the basis of the character of the offender and the circumstances surrounding the crime may have been partly based on criteria all social groups were in agreement about, but it was also not infrequently the outcome of a struggle between a broadly felt desire to ensure that certain types of offender did not pay the ultimate price (seen in the sympathy that court crowds and jurors often showed towards some property offenders) and élite perceptions about the need for examples against certain kinds of crime.

Both the summary courts and the major courts were also arenas of struggle on many occasions. Sometimes those involved were from the same social group—labourers stealing from labourers, middling men assaulting or abusing

---

[18] P.P., 1828, VI, p. 12; King, 'Gleaners', pp. 123–4. On 'people of very limited means' using King's Bench—Hay and Rogers, *Eighteenth-Century English Society*, p. 145.

each other. Occasionally landowning gentlemen prosecuted middling men— usually for game-related offences. But most cases involved disputes between the propertied and the unpropertied. It should not be assumed, however, that the poor were faced by a solid alliance between gentry magistrates and the middling sort in such situations. Recent research on the vast range of cases that came to the summary courts indicates that although they were often used by the propertied to discipline the poor, the labouring sort were also able to mobilize these courts successfully in their disputes with employers over wages and hiring, and with the parish authorities about relief.[19] Country justices, as Hay and Rogers have recently pointed out, played an important mediating role, maintaining an appropriate social distance from farmers and employers and seeing themselves as arbitrators, as disinterested enforcers of the social peace.[20] As the gentry withdrew from face-to-face contact with the common people and as all but a tiny percentage of locally powerful gentry refused to take on the onerous day-to-day responsibilities of being a JP, summary justice became more and more detached. Justice was much less frequently delivered by powerful paternalists who knew the protagonists and whose interests were tied up with theirs. Instead a more distanced style of magistracy, in which the ideal justice was less the natural leader of his neighbourhood and more its disinterested administrator, became increasingly important as the eighteenth century wore on.[21] The small number of truly active JPs in most counties and the long journeys that were therefore frequently travelled to obtain a hearing often made summary justice highly impersonal. On many occasions the magistrate would have had very little knowledge of the networks of social relationships out of which the case before him arose.

In this situation a complex triangle of forces involving three broad groups— the labouring poor, the middling sort, and an increasingly distanced magistracy—frequently developed and this created a number of opportunities for the unpropertied. These opportunities can be most clearly seen in the large numbers of successful appeals for poor relief or unpaid wages found in many summary court records but they are equally evident elsewhere. Eighteenth-century industrial disputes frequently took on the character of three-sided negotiations between magistrates, employers, and workmen in which the justices sometimes took the side of the latter, and my own work on gleaning disputes has revealed similar patterns. When the farmers tried to redefine gleaning as theft in the 1780s most local magistrates steadfastly refused to allow the gleaners to be prosecuted.[22] Moreover, gleaning was not the only form of property appropriation that the summary courts were often ambivalent towards. If the accused was obviously deserving, magistrates sometimes took an

[19] King, 'The Summary Courts'.
[20] Hay and Rogers, *Eighteenth-Century English Society*, p. 32.
[21] Landau, *The Justices*, p. 3.
[22] Stevenson, *Popular Disturbances*, p. 132; King, 'Gleaners'.

equally sympathetic approach in cases involving wood stealing and other petty thefts from farmers, as Arthur Young's observations about the farmer's frustration in such cases indicates (Chapter 4). The willingness of both magistrates and assize judges to respond to the demands of the poor during bread price disturbances and to act against middlemen by using the laws against forestalling, regrating, and engrossing[23] once again points to the basically triangular nature of a considerable proportion of the struggles that occurred in eighteenth-century legal arenas. This should not, of course, be allowed to disguise the fact that when property and its attendant structures of authority were seriously threatened—when bread rioters got out of hand and destroyed property; when paupers pulled down the local workhouse (as they did in Suffolk in 1765); or when agricultural labourers attempted to form unions (as some did in Essex at the end of the eighteenth century)[24]—the middling sort and the gentry/magistracy immediately acted in concert to extinguish the threat. Such alliances were short-lived, however. On a day-to-day level there were clearly important differences of opinion between these two broad groupings.

On occasions the Essex middling sort used their discretionary powers within the judicial process to express their opposition to the gentry. In the 1750s, for example, the Essex farming community's defeat of the gentry-dominated National Game Association was reported with glee in the local newspapers. When it became known that the association was bringing an action against some local farmers' sons for game offences 'the greatest concourse of the middling landed interest and reputable farmers of the county... that was ever known' attended the trial. Not surprisingly the jury found in favour of the farmers, a verdict that was followed by 'suitable rejoicings in divers parts of Essex'. This conflict was still producing echoes in county politics a decade later, when a critique of the association was incorporated into larger accusations against 'a junto of half a dozen real gentlemen' who were said to be undermining the 'Freedom and Independence' of 'the great body of freeholders'.[25] The regular refusal of middling jurors to convict offenders against the game laws, offenders who broke the excise laws, and other groups with whom they felt themselves broadly in sympathy (such as the Richmond commoners who refused to give up their rights of access) makes it clear that the courts could also be an arena of direct conflict between the large landowners

---

[23] Hay and Rogers, *Eighteenth-Century English Society*, pp. 110–12; Hay, 'The State'; E. P. Thompson, 'The Moral Economy of the English Crowd in the Eighteenth Century', *Past and Present*, 50 (1971), 78–136; D. Williams. 'Morals, Markets and the English Crowd in 1766', *Past and Present*, 104 (1984), 69; Thompson, *Customs in Common*, pp. 259–351.

[24] For anonymous letters, threats and the destruction of a workhouse, *I.J.*, 5 Jan. 3, 10, 17, 24, Aug. 1765. For the imprisonment of three Essex labourers for combining to raise wages *Che.C.*, 8 Aug. 1800.

[25] Munsche, *Gentlemen*, p. 111; the early 1750s also witnessed two very public defeats for the Game Association in Suffolk. In one case the jury gave a verdict against them, in another the entire jury refused to turn up. *Norwich Mercury*, 11–18 Aug. 1753; *I.J.*, 19 Nov. 1763. *Che.C.*, 7 May 1773 and 31 Aug. 1787 for other detailed critiques of the Essex landowning élite written by middling men.

and the middling sort.[26] In some of these conflicts middling men and the labouring sort became temporary allies—in fighting for some forest or commoners' rights, for example; in campaigns against the Militia Acts or in many game-related disputes. On occasions therefore the poor exploited the triangular nature of local social relations in both directions, although their preferred option was usually to play on the residual paternalism of particular members of the local magistracy by exploiting the fact that they could choose which local JP to take their complaint to. Their capacity to adopt these broadly triangular strategies in any given locality depended on a number of factors such as landownership patterns, the presence or absence of permanently resident gentry, the availability and nature of local magistrates, the attitudes of the local clergy, and the economic strength and unity of the local farmers and tradesmen, as well as the poor's own traditions of resistance, and their knowledge of legal structures and of ways of making use of them. In many areas, however, as Charlesworth has pointed out, 'the labourers were not faced with the closed ranks of a like-minded alliance of squire, parson and farmers'.[27] At moments of crisis these groups acted together and used the law in a directly coercive way against the poor, but in normal times their interests did not always run in parallel. The poor not infrequently made use of the strategic space this opened up. They may not have had much mathematical knowledge, but they knew how to triangulate. 'This will never do', the Somerset parson William Holland observed. 'The overseers are harassed to death and summoned every day before a justice.... The justices attend to every complaint, right or wrong and every scoundrel in the parish crowd to make their complaints. Where will it end.... They grow insolent. Subordination is lost.'[28]

3. The Poor and the Law—Attitudes and Strategies

Holland's portrayal of the law as undermining deference by offering strategic opportunities to the poor is illuminating. Legal institutions provided labouring families with a series of arenas of struggle and of negotiation in the eighteenth century and in some of those arenas they clearly became adept at triangulating—at exploiting fissures within the ranks of the propertied. Ever present, however, in all these situations was the potential threat of penal sanction. Paupers who could be labelled as 'disorderly', employees who refused to complete their work, labourers who left their families to travel in search of work, servants who took what they regarded as customary perks might all find

---

[26] Thompson, *Customs in Common*, pp. 110–14. Some provincial gentry magistrates occasionally took the side of the poor against similar moves by the local large landowners to obstruct rights of way. Davey, *Rural Crime in the Eighteenth Century*, p. 65.

[27] On anti-Militia Act alliances—E. Stockdale, *Law and Order in Georgian Bedfordshire* (Bedfordshire Historical Record Society, 1982), 61, p. 21; Charlesworth, 'The Development...A Comment', p. 105.

[28] Ayers (ed.), *Paupers and Pig Killers*, p. 47.

themselves summarily convicted and whipped or imprisoned in the house of correction. Any labouring man or woman who committed an act of appropriation that was indictable as felony, even if their family was in dire distress at the time, risked transportation and sometimes annihilation, and even food rioters might find themselves indicted for capital crimes such as housebreaking (Chapter 5). The biases of the law were equally clear elsewhere. Despite the heated historical debates that surround them, it is difficult to believe that the language and impact of the Inclosure Acts and the various acts against workers' combinations did not leave many unpropertied people with a very strong sense that the law was being used to wage war on the poor.[29]

Thus the law appeared to the labouring sort not as one entity, but rather as a series of often contradictory opportunities and oppressions. Their attitudes were ambivalent, contingent, deeply pragmatic. The law could be a protection to their property, their persons, and even their reputations. Their widespread use of the quarter sessions to prosecute those who had stolen their food, fuel, clothing, and household goods suggests that they regarded the criminal law as an appropriate way of dealing with a fairly broad spectrum of property offenders, although that spectrum did not usually include those who appropriated game, hedgewood, or commodities which came under the broad heading of 'perks of the trade'. The labouring sort made even more extensive use of the courts in cases involving interpersonal violence. Recent research has also shown not only that the Essex poor used the summary courts to resolve large numbers of assault-related disputes throughout this period, but also that they were prepared to take such matters on to the quarter sessions if necessary.[30] This did not mean, however, that the law enjoyed widespread acceptance and legitimacy among the labouring poor. Their extensive use of both the summary courts and the major courts does imply a basic understanding of those institutions and a pragmatic acceptance of their usefulness. If the poor had not been able to use the courts in this way their attitudes to the law would almost certainly have been much more negative. However, using the law whether you were rich or poor did not necessarily imply acceptance of its legitimacy. Nor is 'the law' a very useful unit of analysis in such contexts. Like all social groups the poor used a selected subset of legal processes while ignoring or being subjected to others. Since the judicial process itself was highly fragmented at times, conveying a plurality of meanings, designed to meet a series of separate purposes, and based on a range of sometimes

[29] Snell, *Annals*, pp.138–227; J. Neeson, *Commoners. Common Right, Enclosure and Social Change in England, 1700–1820* (Cambridge, 1993), pp. 329–30; J. Neeson, 'The Opponents of Enclosure in Eighteenth-Century Northamptonshire', *Past and Present*, 105 (1984), 114–39; J. Moher, 'From Suppression to Containment. Roots of Trade Union Law to 1825', in J. Rule (ed.), *British Trade Unionism 1750–1850. The Formative Years* (London, 1988), pp. 74–9; J. Orth, 'The English Combination Laws Reconsidered', in F. Snyder and D. Hay, *Labour, Law and Crime. An Historical Perspective* (London, 1987), pp. 123–49. On the state's tendency to back the employers—Rule, 'Employment and Authority', p. 290.

[30] King, 'The Summary Courts' and 'Punishing Assault'.

conflicting and sometimes co-ordinating interests,[31] it would be surprising if any social group (least of all the poor who were particularly exposed to its ambiguities) had any one coherent 'attitude' to it.

Simply stressing the pluralistic nature of legal institutions and the consequent complexity of attitudes to them can, however, very easily lead historians to neglect an important theme that emerges from the few fragments of plebeian writing that have survived—the depth of scepticism felt towards the law by the poorer half of the population. The labouring poet John Clare, for example, was certainly not fooled by the assize sermons and élite writings that attempted to justify the capital code on religious grounds:

> Dost thou possess the dower
> Of laws to spare or kill
> Call it not heavenly power
> When but a tyrants will

he wrote in *The Midsummer Cushion*.[32] In the privacy of the unpublished parts of his poem *The Parish* he ventured a much more generalized critique:

> Why should the poor sinning starving clown
> Meet jail and hanging for a stolen crown
> While wealthy thieves with knaverys bribes endued
> Plunder their millions and are not pursued
> Nay at the foot of Tyburns noted tree
> They do deserving deeds and still go free
> Where others suffer for some pigmy cause
> They all but murder and escape the laws[33]

Clare was not alone. The smuggler Charles Bellamy, coming at the problem from a different angle expressed a similar view more succinctly. 'Rich men', he wrote, 'vilify us when there is only this difference, they rob under the cover of law, forsooth, and we plunder the rich under the protection of our own courage.' The autobiography of another labouring man, Joseph Mayett, also echoed Clare's private writings and poems in acknowledging the useful role the summary courts could play in disputes about relief or employment whilst simultaneously exuding considerable scepticism towards the law and precious little deference or respect for the individual magistrates who administered it.[34] Although the eighteenth century produced both a far from deferential anonymous letter-writing tradition, and a large popular literature marked by

---

[31] Garland, *Punishment and Modern Society*, pp. 17-21.

[32] The best discussion of the assize sermons' attempts to endow 'justice with a sacramental aura' is McGowen, 'He Beareth not the Sword'. J. Clare, *The Midsummer Cushion* (Ashington, 1990), p. 92. This was written in the 1820s but was not published in full until 1990 under the editorship of R. Thornton and A. Tibble.

[33] Clare, *The Parish*, p. 64.

[34] Gilmour, *Riot, Risings*, p. 173; Kussmaul (ed.), *The Autobiography*, pp. 92-3; Robinson (ed.), *John Clare's*, pp. 69, 122-3; Clare, *The Midsummer Cushion*, p 92.

cynicism and disrespect for the law, and although the authorities' keenness to suppress Lord Gordon's Old Testament-based critiques of the bloody code suggest that he was drawing on deep popular traditions of hostility towards the hanging of property offenders, it is difficult to assess how typical men like Mayett and Clare were.[35] It is possible that non-literate labourers (the great majority) were somewhat less inclined to be critical. It is also possible that, if writings by labouring men or women born nearer the beginning rather than towards the end of the eighteenth century could be found, a slightly different picture would emerge. In reality, no doubt, labouring men and women held a spectrum of different opinions. The radical Samuel Bamford, whose autobiography recounts very critically his own extremely negative experiences of the local magistrates and jurors in the mid-1790s, also records a conversation he overheard between three working men about English juries in which one lauded them ferociously, one thought them faulty, and one advocated majority verdicts.[36] However, Linebaugh has argued trenchantly that 'London proletarians... held the law in contempt' and amused themselves by mocking it and, if men like Clare are any guide, the rural poor and the law were also very uneasy bedfellows by the late eighteenth and early nineteenth centuries.[37] Their awareness that it could be useful to them and could protect their property as well as that of the élite cannot be taken to imply that labouring men and women had respect for, or felt any real deference towards, the law and those who administered it.

4. Justice, Authority, and Society

The criminal law gave power to the propertied élite: power to hang, transport, imprison, and whip those who appropriated their property; power to punish the disorderly poor. This was vital in a society riven by inequality, with a cavernous gap between rich and poor, an increasingly affluent middle layer and a rising proportion of landless labouring poor. But did the law produce or reinforce deference? Did it confirm the hegemony of the propertied élite in any broader sense? It would be wrong to underestimate the law's potency as a general framework of ideas. The rule of law and the powerful notions that all were equal before the law—that the freeborn Englishman was protected by habeas corpus and by the right to jury trial—may have provided potent political arguments in the face of growing radical critiques of aristocratic

[35] Hay, 'Property', p. 54; on the cynicism towards the law of *The Beggar's Opera*, see Hill, *Liberty against the Law*, pp. 9–18; Thompson, 'The Crime of Anonymity'. For examples of threatening letters occasioned by the passing of a death sentence—Gatrell, *The Hanging Tree*, pp. 220–1; D. Hay, 'The Laws of God and the Laws of Man: Lord George Gordon and the Death Penalty', in J. Rule and R. Malcolmson (eds.), *Protest and Survival. The Historical Experience. Essays for E. P. Thompson* (London, 1993), pp. 61 and 78.
[36] Bamford, *Passages*, p. 295.
[37] Linebaugh, *The London Hanged*, p. 150; Clare, *The Parish*, esp. pp. 62–7.

power and corruption.[38] However, the specific contribution of the criminal justice system and its administration to the hegemony of the landed élite, to the day-to-day domination of the ruled, is much more difficult to establish.

The early stages of the criminal justice process and in particular the private face-to-face negotiations between victim and accused, and the many types of semi-private hearings presided over by local magistrates did, of course, provide opportunities to induce fear and then offer mercy in ways that might produce or reinforce deference. However, the vast majority of potential prosecutors were middling men or labourers, and although the increasingly distanced patrician magistrates who offered limited assistance to the poor in their battles against the overseers and employers or in their disputes over property or violent behaviour, may have been accorded some respect by the poor as a result, men like Mayett and Clare were anything but deferential to them. Outcomes that might re-inforce the status of the gentry élite seem to have been even more difficult to achieve in the best-documented stage of the criminal justice system—the process of petitioning for pardon. The King and the central authorities had periodic crackdowns during which even aristocratic petitions were ignored. More important in normal times, the trial judge's approval was vital and, unless the prisoner had aristocratic backing, the judge was rarely moved by the social status of the petitioners alone. The spectacular, publicly reported failures of leading country gentlemen like T. B. Bramston to obtain reprieves may not have done their reputations any harm. But if the preliminary findings reported here are correct and the gentry did fail to achieve a higher success rate than the middling sort, it is difficult to see how this aspect of the judicial system could have acted as a major source of deference-reinforcement for the gentry.[39]

The usefulness of pardon petitioning as a 'currency of patronage' also needs to be questioned for another reason. By the second half of the eighteenth century the majority of provincial capital convicts were being reprieved. On the Home Circuit, for example (outside the 1780s), an average of two capital offenders were reprieved for every one that was hanged. By 1805 four were reprieved for every one hanged, and by 1816 ten.[40] Thus, it became increas-ingly clear that instead of choosing an occasional object of mercy the judges and state officials were choosing objects of terror. This may well have altered the meaning of pardoning. 'For mercy to evoke gratitude', Hughes has argued, 'the ruler must be seen to choose mercy so that each reprieve is a special case, to be paid for in gratitude and obedience.'[41] As it became obvious that the key

---

[38] Hay, 'Property', pp. 32–4; Rule, *Albion's People*, pp. 28 and 244–6; Ignatieff, *A Just Measure of Pain*, p. 137.

[39] Prisoners were aware that they had a better chance of success if they had the backing of character witnesses or petitioners who were responsible, settled, and preferably propertied members of the local community, but that group did not necessarily need to contain a member of the landowning gentry.

[40] Hay, 'Property', p. 45. On repreives, Chapter 8 and Gatrell, *The Hanging Tree*, p. 617.

[41] Reformers made much use of the objects of terror argument—McGowen, 'The Image', p. 100; Hughes, *The Fatal Shore*, p. 36.

choice was not whom to pardon but whom to hang, the system ran the risk of creating more resentment than it did deference. Working for the reprieve of locally known non-violent property offenders may have been seen increasingly as something that all people of humanity should do, and gentlemen who did not involve themselves, at least in a token way, in this process might provoke unfavourable comment. If only 5 per cent of offenders had been reprieved, and if those reprieved had been very clearly linked to élite petitioning, the effect might have been very different. However, by the 1740s the percentage repri-eved was ten or twelve times higher than this and the potential usefulness of the pardoning system as a mechanism for reinforcing deference may well have been seriously undermined as a result.

    Was the theatre of the law any more effective in building up the 'hegemonic charisma'[42] of the landowning élite? The rituals that accompanied the trials and punishment of property offenders frequently failed to function as the élite would have wished them to. Trial audiences were difficult to control (Chapter 7). The crowded courtrooms of eighteenth- and early nineteenth-century England were noisy places. The 'promiscuous concourse of bystanders' that gathered in them reminded some astute contemporaries of a fair. Solemn rituals require silence and a certain stillness. Neither was easily achieved in most eighteenth-century courtrooms. Even the climax of the proceedings—the death sentence—was often a desultory performance, quickly pronounced between hurried trials by assize judges aware that most of the subjects of these solemn discourses of death would soon be on the list of reprieved prisoners they had to write out before they left the county. The gallows crowds were even more difficult to control and the official script was frequently subverted by the counter-theatre of both the crowd and the condemned. The robust, vibrant plebeian culture Thompson so brilliantly described did not change its character when it entered the courtrooms of eighteenth-century England or gathered around its gallows. Here, as elsewhere, the rulers and the crowd needed each other, watched each other, performed theatre and counter-theatre to each other, and moderated each other's behaviour.[43]

    The impact of these rituals was, of course, very complex. Almost every gallows or courtroom crowd was a mixture. Some onlookers would have identified with the authorities, supported the punishment being inflicted, and had their own beliefs and sense of the law's legitimacy reinforced by the rituals involved. Others would have experienced the same rituals as coercion, as alien and illegitimate acts which reinforced their sense of injustice.[44] Many no doubt

[42] Thompson, *Customs in Common*, p. 48.
[43] Ibid., p. 57. This is not to imply that all urban crowds were oppositional or self-activating, or that all crowds can be understood in terms of Thompson's polarities—see N. Rogers, *Whigs and Cities. Popular Politics in the Age of Walpole and Pitt* (Oxford, 1989) for a more complex analysis which still stresses plebeian self-assertion embodied in the tradition of the free-born Englishman and the hearty disrespect of the plebeian crowd towards its immediate rulers, pp. 386–8.
[44] Garland, *Punishment and Modern Society*, p. 70.

had mixed reactions that were less polarized in either direction. However, when routine property offenders were sentenced to death and hanged, and especially if the offender concerned was young, old, female, or had committed the crime because his or her family were in great distress, it seems likely that the great majority of onlookers would have embraced the attitudes of the good mind, and would therefore have reacted to these judicial rituals not with solidarity but with hostility. 'It was easy', as Hay has pointed out 'to claim equal justice for murderers of all classes, where a universal moral sanction was more likely to be found, ... The trick was to extend that communal sanction to a criminal law that was nine-tenths concerned with upholding a radical division of property.' It was a trick the élite found remarkably difficult to pull off. In murder cases the common people embraced the bad mind and the exemplary hangings it demanded, but in many routine property crime cases they did not. The resultant rituals frequently failed either to stigmatize the offender or to reinforce the legitimacy of the law. The authorities had to go through with these penal ceremonies. As Thompson has suggested 'However undesirable the side effects ... the ritual of public execution was a necessary concomitant of a system of social discipline where a great deal depended on theatre', but it remains extremely debatable whether these more theatrical aspects of the law did much to reinforce the élites's overall hegemony.[45]

If neither the merciful opportunities nor the majestic spectacles afforded by the law were always as useful in creating a 'spirit of consent and submission' among the English poor as some historians have suggested,[46] how far could the 'justice' of the law persuade them. Justice had many faces in the eighteenth century and some of them could be very persuasive—the occasional hangings of rich murderers or forgers, for example, or the adherence to strict procedural rules. Moreover, in depicting the law as an arena of struggle it is easy to forget that the law was not merely a passive instrument forged by the interactions of competing interest groups. Laws, lawyers, and legal institutions had a complex history of their own. Judges, for example, sometimes pursued independent policies that were opposed to those of the government. The law was not autonomous but its procedures embodied principles and traditions that were more deeply rooted than such instrumental analogies imply. The beliefs embedded within legal rulings and administrative practices shaped and limited the choices available to the key decision-making groups involved in the criminal justice system as well as being deeply affected by those groups,[47] and sometimes those principles operated in ways which made it more likely

---

[45] Hay, 'Property', p. 35; Thompson, *Customs in Common*, p. 47.

[46] Hay, 'Property', p. 49.

[47] On the historical specificity of the relative autonomy of law, and on the problems of over-emphasizing it, see D. Sugarman, 'Law, Economy and the State in England, 1750–1914. Some Major Issues', in D. Sugarman (ed.), *Legality, Ideology and the State* (London, 1983), pp. 213–66 and esp. 250; C. Herrup, 'Crime, Law and Society. A Review Article', *Comparative Studies in Society and History*, 27 (1985), 170. On judges' independence—Hay, 'The State'.

that justice would prevail. This said, however, any serious student of the eighteenth-century legal system soon learns to mistrust justice's alluring voices. Justice was a very approximate word in the eighteenth century. Hurried trials, overawed prisoners, ambivalent judges,[48] convictions on flimsy evidence, reward-hungry entrepreneurial police, and many other more structural aspects of the judicial system, such as the gender- and property-based qualifications that had to be met by jurors and magistrates, discourage any idealization of the quality of justice in this period.

This did not mean that justice was an empty word. It was central to the rhetoric of the ruling élite and to broader ideological justifications for their rule. This meant that it was an important terrain of negotiation and compromise. Matters of justice had to be carefully balanced. The rulers were, whether willingly or unwillingly, the prisoners of their own rhetoric. For the rhetoric of the law to have any purchase, any legitimating function, it had to be seen, in part at least, to work. 'If', to quote Thompson, 'the law is evidently partial and unjust, then it will mask nothing, legitimize nothing, contribute nothing to any class's hegemony.'[49] The law's capacity to mask the real basis of élite domination is easily exaggerated, however. The tiny fragments of the poor's hidden transcripts that have come down to us do not suggest that they were easily taken in by the mummery of the assizes. 'There is no law for a poor man', wrote one prisoner's wife who had learned at first hand that the law could be deeply unjust, and when discussed around each local neighbourhood the effect of a multitude of such experiences on attitudes to the law may well have snowballed, shaping the views of the labouring poor in a way that the homilies of the rich and the tracts of Hannah Moore could rarely match.[50]

The criminal justice system was not so much about mystification as about accommodation. Accommodation with victims who wanted, and gained, flexibility in deciding whether to prosecute, compound, or forgive, in deciding what charge to bring, in deciding whether or not to turn up on the day of the trial; accommodation with the mitigating tendencies of semi-autonomous juries because as Green has pointed out, literal enforcement of the capital laws lay beyond the powers of the crown;[51] accommodation with the sentencing and pardoning priorities of the good mind. These compromises not only enabled a system that was heavily dependent on popular participation to work fairly effectively;[52] they may also have done something to prevent the law from losing its broader ideological usefulness to the propertied élite. A shallow sense

---

[48] The best evocation of the eighteenth-century trial is in Beattie, *Crime*, pp. 313–99.

[49] Thompson, *Whigs*, p. 263.

[50] Gatrell, *The Hanging Tree*, p. 219.

[51] Green, *Verdict According to Conscience*, p. 312.

[52] Herrup, *The Common Peace*, develops this theme in her conclusion on the seventeenth century—esp. pp. 195 and 205–6. The 'good mind' was not, of course, a mid- or late eighteenth-century phenomenon alone—see Mandeville's sympathy towards property offenders driven by necessity quoted in Hay, 'Property', p. 35.

of the law's legitimacy may have continued to linger around certain aspects of the law and certain legal arenas. However, since the vast bulk of the surviving evidence consists of public transcripts, of rich and poor addressing each other in public, the nature of record survival can easily beguile the historian into overstressing the role of the law in reinforcing the gentry's hegemony. As James Scott has pointed out, both the powerless and the powerful had a vested interest in keeping up hegemonic appearances in public, but this is not the full story. These postures are nothing more than a set of strategies. Surface deference is the tactical response of the poor, while the over-dramatization of their power is the tactic of the powerful. The deeply deferential postures of many petitioners for pardon, for example, can hardly be taken at face value. Deference can never be assumed to be real when it is offered by the weak to the strong in a public arena.[53]

The criminal law may have encouraged an outward conformity, an awareness of the need to be seen to play the game according to certain rules—particularly since the rules enabled the poor to achieve many limited but not unimportant concessions. However, the stuttered responses of many of the accused in court and the deferential language of the prisoners in their petitions stand in stark contrast to the fragments of private transcripts the poor have bequeathed to us. Perhaps deference was more than just double-faced defiance, more than just the deliberate masking of a deep sense of grievance. Perhaps individuals or even groups of the labouring poor had alternating identities—one accepting at least some of the rules of the legal process as legitimate, the other deeply critical of the repression that lay beneath the theatre of the assizes and the apparent paternalism of the local magistrate.[54] However, it is difficult to escape a sense that most of the time, most of the poor were deeply instrumental about the law and the range of opportunities and oppressions it presented them with. The great age of discretion was not necessarily the golden age of legitimation within the history of the English criminal law. On balance it seems that the images, rituals, discretionary opportunities, and legitimating functions of the law were of only relatively marginal use in reinforcing the cultural hegemony of the élite. The law was more useful to them as naked power, as a very visible means of marking out the limits they were willing to tolerate, enabling them, for example, to use the threat of exemplary hangings in times of disorder. It was also useful to the wider constituency of both the gentry and the middling sort as a protection to their property and as a means of shoring up their control over the disorderly poor.

It is possible to exaggerate the role of the criminal law. Phrases such as 'the hegemony of the law' or Thompson's notion that 'the controlling instruments

<hr/>

[53] Scott, *Domination and the Arts of Resistance*, p. xii; Gatrell, *The Hanging Tree*, pp. 211–21.

[54] K. Snell, 'Deferential Bitterness. The Social Outlook of the Rural Proletariat in Eighteenth- and Nineteenth-Century England and Wales', in Bush (ed.), *Social Order*, p. 165; Thompson, *Customs in Common*, pp. 10–11.

and images of hegemony are those of the law' imply that it held a more central place in eighteenth-century social relations than either a detailed study of the workings of the judicial system or a wider survey of the other institutions and potential sources of power available to the propertied (such as the poor law, landowner–tenant or employer–employee relationships, religious institutions, or the civil law) suggest.[55] However, the criminal law, and particularly the criminal law in relation to property offences, clearly played an important role in eighteenth-century social relations. Despite the problems encountered by the authorities, it would be unwise to ignore the law's potential as a system of ideas and as a creator of images, even if that potential was rarely realized on an everyday basis in the eighteenth and early nineteenth centuries. The shadow of the gallows was long, the threat of the house of correction very real, and, like their nineteenth-century equivalents—the penitentiary and the workhouse— they could affect many aspects of the lives and behaviour of the labouring poor. In the period between 1740 and 1820 the criminal laws, the plurality of legal arenas they created, and the ways those arenas were administered were full of paradoxes. Although they were very vulnerable to power they could also be very useful in curbing it. Although the criminal justice system was mainly aimed at controlling the labouring poor, the poor were able to utilize a range of legal arenas to protect their property, resolve their disputes, or appeal for wages or relief. Although the landed élite enacted the criminal law and some- times made strategic use of it to strengthen their authority, it was a very much broader grouping—the heterogeneous middling sort—who dominated its everyday workings, who most needed it to protect their property, and who therefore had most opportunity to make it their own. The criminal law was an arena not only of terror, of exploitation, and of bloody sanction but also of struggle, of negotiation, of accommodation, and almost every group in eight- eenth-century society helped to shape it, just as their behaviour was partly shaped by it.

[55] Innes and Styles, 'The Crime Wave', p. 252. For the failure of the 'supposedly hegemonic qualities' of the law to shape the views of the free miners, see Wood, 'Custom, Identity and Resistance', p. 278; Hay, 'Property', p. 55; Thompson, *Customs in Common*, p. 9. On the importance of the poor law, Hitchcock, King, and Sharpe (eds.), *Chronicling Poverty*, pp. 1–17, and on the triangular quality of many of the relationships that developed out of poor law and other disputes—P. King, 'Edward Thompson's Contribution to Eighteenth-Century Studies. The Patrician–Plebeian Model Re-examined', *Social History*, 21 (1996), 226–8.

Index

Chamberlayne, Robert 304
Chapman, James 41
character, as a factor 328
  in pretrial negotiations 33
  in sentencing and pardoning 309–10
  in summary hearings 104
  in verdicts 234
Charlesworth, Andrew 364
Chelmer Navigation 123
Chelmsford 321–2
  crowds 255
  gallows 342
  gaol 62, 123, 268, 270
  petty sessions 84–5, 90, 92–3, 96–7, 103–5, 201
  policing 65
  riots 152, 349
civil courts, boundary with criminal 8–9
Clare, John 167, 174, 181, 366–8
Clarke, Mary 63
Clavering 143
Cobbett, William 167
Cockburn, J.S. 135
Coggeshall 143
Colchester 13
  Association 28, 55, 58
  courts 10, 43, 143, 158
  crime 101, 205
  crime wave 32
  gaol 270
  Improvement Commission 65
  magistrates 120
  petty sessions 84, 88, 94
  policing 64
  riot 151
Cole, Samuel 322, 332
Colquhoun, Patrick 11, 79, 133, 140, 182, 209,
    211, 238–9, 241, 323, 341–3
compounding 23–4, 33–4, 151
community sanctions 26–7
Coney, John 29
constables, see parish constables
Cottu, M. 17, 43, 95–8, 228–9, 249, 253, 256,
    337–8
courts:
  assizes 129–333
  borough sessions 43, 131, 143
  Colchester Court of Conservancy 10
  Court of Attachments, Waltham Forest 9
  King's Bench 10
  quarter sessions 129–333
  see also judges; juries; punishments; sentencing;
    trial
Cowper, W. 74
Crab, George 45
Cranfield, William 211
crime rates 128–68
  assizes calendar length as guide to 129–30

and dearth 145–153
  in different Home circuit counties 138
  impact of court availability on 143
  impact of proximity of London on 138–142
  long-term patterns of 133–5
  low level of 132–4
  and peace/war changes 147, 153–161
  and poor rate levels 145
  urban 143–4
criminal gangs 215–6
criminal law, character of 1–2
  popular desire for reform 349–50
  role of 3–4
criminal offences:
  against property, types of 137
  assault 353
  burglary, see housebreaking
  cattle theft 137, 140, 261
  coining 137,
  forgery 172
  fraud 172
  game-related 99–103, 137, 140, 210, 213
  highway robbery 57, 137–8, 140, 172, 214–15
  horse-theft 137–8, 214
  housebreaking 137–8, 159, 172, 174, 214
  incendiarism 14,152,
  larceny, grand 137–8
  larceny, petty 137–8, 209
  receiving 137, 172
  sexual offences against children 256
  sheep-stealing 137–8, 213, 261
  textile materials embezzlement 140
  threatening letters 152
  vegetable theft 99–102, 140, 210
  wood theft 99–102, 137, 140, 210
  see also property offenders
criminal trial, see trial
Crosier, John 18, 64
crowd action against thieves 27, 29
Cunningham, Robert 211

Dagge, H. 250
Dalton, Michael 98, 185
dark figure of unrecorded crime 11–12, 132–4
Davies, David 114, 149, 167, 193
Davis, Charles 226
Davis, Fanny 21, 200
Davis, Natalie Zemon 297
death sentence, see rituals of punishment
Defoe, Daniel 27, 205, 259, 260
demobilization and crime 154–6, 162–6
Dench, William 321–6
Dengie 113, 121
Denmark 176
Denny, Abraham 151
depositions, as evidence 183–4
Deptford 170, 207